Fundamentals of Computer Graphics
Third Edition

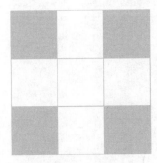

Fundamentals of Computer Graphics
Third Edition

Peter Shirley
NVIDIA Corporation

Steve Marschner
Cornell University

with

Michael Ashikhmin
Michael Gleicher
Naty Hoffman
Garrett Johnson
Tamara Munzner
Erik Reinhard
Kelvin Sung
William B. Thompson
Peter Willemsen
Brian Wyvill

A K Peters
Natick, Massachusetts

FIRST INDIAN REPRINT, 2011

A K Peters/CRC Press
Taylor & Francis Group
6000 Broken Sound Parkway NW, Suite 300
Boca Raton, FL 33487-2742

© 2010 by Taylor and Francis Group, LLC
A K Peters/CRC Press is an imprint of Taylor & Francis Group, an Informa business

No claim to original U.S. Government works

Printed and bound in India by Replika Press Pvt. Ltd.

International Standard Book Number: 978-1-56881-469-8

Visit the Taylor & Francis Web site at
http://www.taylorandfrancis.com

and the A K Peters Web site at
http://www.akpeters.com

"This book is printed on ECF card and ECF environment-friendly paper manufactured from unconventional and other raw materials sourced from sustainable and identified sources."

FOR SALE IN SOUTH ASIA ONLY.

Contents

Preface

This edition of *Fundamentals of Computer Graphics* adds four new contributed chapters and contains substantial reorganizations and improvements to the core material. The new chapters add coverage of implicit modeling and of two important graphics applications: games and information visualization. The fourth new contributed chapter is a major upgrade to the material on color science. As with the chapters added in the second edition, we have chosen the contributors both for their expertise and for their clear way of expressing ideas.

We have made a number of changes to the early chapters of the book, integrating the second author's experience teaching introductory graphics at Cornell using the first and second editions. Most of these have been revised and updated, particularly the chapters on images, viewing, ray tracing, the graphics pipeline, and the material on triangle meshes. Some of the original material from these chapters has been reorganized, sometimes with topics appearing in different chapters than in the previous editions.

Our aim in this reorganization has been to move the elementary material towards the beginning. In our thinking, Chapters 2 through 8 constitute the "core core," taking the straight and narrow path through what is absolutely required for understanding how images get onto the screen using the complementary approaches of ray tracing and rasterization. Ray tracing is covered first, since it is the simplest way to generate images of 3D scenes, followed by the mathematical machinery required for the graphics pipeline, then the pipeline itself. After that, the "outer core" covers other topics that would commonly be included in an introductory class. For example, ray tracing is split into two chapters, with the more advanced material now in Chapter 13. The material on spatial data structures (some formerly under Ray Tracing and Hidden Surfaces) is consolidated in Chapter 12 together with an expanded section on triangle meshes.

In all these revisions, we have endeavored to retain the informal, intuitive style of presentation that characterizes the earlier editions, while at the same time improving consistency, precision, and completeness. We hope the reader will find the result is a better platform for a variety of courses in computer graphics.

About the Cover

The cover image is from *Tiger in the Water* by J. W. Baker (brushed and air-brushed acrylic on canvas, 16" by 20", www.jwbart.com).

The subject of a tiger is a reference to a wonderful talk given by Alain Fournier (1943–2000) at the Cornell Workshop in 1998. His talk was an evocative verbal description of the movements of a tiger. He summarized his point:

> Even though modelling and rendering in computer graphics have been improved tremendously in the past 35 years, we are still not at the point where we can model automatically a tiger swimming in the river in all its glorious details. By automatically I mean in a way that does not need careful manual tweaking by an artist/expert.
>
> The bad news is that we have still a long way to go.
>
> The good news is that we have still a long way to go.

Online Resources

The web site for this book is http://www.cs.cornell.edu/~srm/fcg3/. We will continue to maintain a list of errata and links to courses that use the book, as well as teaching materials that match the book's style. Most of the figures in this book are in Abobe Illustrator format, and we would be happy to convert specific figures into portable formats on request. Please feel free to contact us at shirley@cs.utah.edu or srm@cs.cornell.edu.

Acknowledgments

The following people have provided helpful information, comments, or feedback about the various editions of this book: Ahmet Oğuz Akyüz, Josh Andersen, Zeferino Andrade, Adam Berger, Adeel Bhutta, Solomon Boulos, Stephen Chenney, Michael Coblenz, Greg Coombe, Frederic Cremer, Brian Curtin, Dave

Edwards, Jonathon Evans, Karen Feinauer, Amy Gooch, Eungyoung Han, Chuck Hansen, Andy Hanson, Razen Al Harbi, Dave Hart, John Hart, John "Spike" Hughes, Helen Hu, Vicki Interrante, Doug James, Henrik Wann Jensen, Shi Jin, Mark Johnson, Ray Jones, Revant Kapoor, Kristin Kerr, Erum Arif Khan, Mark Kilgard, Dylan Lacewell, Mathias Lang, Philippe Laval, Marc Levoy, Howard Lo, Joann Luu, Ron Metoyer, Keith Morley, Eric Mortensen, Koji Nakamaru, Micah Neilson, Blake Nelson, Michael Nikelsky, James O'Brien, Steve Parker, Sumanta Pattanaik, Matt Pharr, Peter Poulos, Shaun Ramsey, Rich Riesenfeld, Nate Robins, Nan Schaller, Chris Schryvers, Tom Sederberg, Richard Sharp, Sarah Shirley, Peter-Pike Sloan, Hannah Story, Tony Tahbaz, Jan-Phillip Tiesel, Bruce Walter, Alex Williams, Amy Williams, Chris Wyman, and Kate Zebrose.

Ching-Kuang Shene and David Solomon allowed us to borrow their examples. Henrik Wann Jensen, Eric Levin, Matt Pharr, and Jason Waltman generously provided images. Brandon Mansfield helped improve the discussion of hierarchical bounding volumes for ray tracing. Philip Greenspun (philip.greenspun.com) kindly allowed us to use his photographs. We are extremely thankful to J. W. Baker for helping create the cover Pete envisioned. In addition to being a talented artist, he was a great pleasure to work with personally.

Many works that were helpful in preparing this book are cited in the chapter notes. However, a few key texts that influenced the content and presentation deserve special recognition here. These include the two classic computer graphics texts from which we both learned the basics: *Computer Graphics: Principles & Practice* (Foley et al., 1990) and *Computer Graphics* (Hearn & Baker, 1986). Other texts include both of Alan Watt's influential books (Watt, 1993, 1991), Hill's *Computer Graphics Using OpenGL* (Francis S. Hill, 2000), Angel's *Interactive Computer Graphics: A Top-Down Approach Using OpenGL* (Angel, 2002), Hugues Hoppe's University of Washington dissertation (Hoppe, 1994), and Rogers' two excellent graphics texts (D. F. Rogers, 1985, 1989).

We would like to especially thank Alice and Klaus Peters for encouraging Pete to write the first edition of this book and for their great skill in bringing a book to fruition. Their patience with the authors and their dedication to making their books the best they can be has been instrumental in guiding us through three editions. This book certainly would not exist without their extraordinary efforts.

Salt Lake City, Utah
Ithaca, New York
May 2009

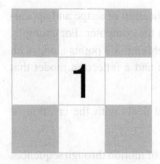

1

Introduction

The term *computer graphics* describes any use of computers to create and manipulate images. This book introduces the algorithmic and mathematical tools that can be used to create all kinds of images—realistic visual effects, informative technical illustrations, or beautiful computer animations. Graphics can be two- or three-dimensional; images can be completely synthetic or can be produced by manipulating photographs. This book is about the fundamental algorithms and mathematics, especially those used to produce synthetic images of three-dimensional objects and scenes.

Actually doing computer graphics inevitably requires knowing about specific hardware, file formats, and usually a graphics API (see Section 1.3) or two. Computer graphics is a rapidly evolving field, so the specifics of that knowledge are a moving target. Therefore, in this book we do our best to avoid depending on any specific hardware or API. Readers are encouraged to supplement the text with relevant documentation for their software and hardware environment. Fortunately, the culture of computer graphics has enough standard terminology and concepts that the discussion in this book should map nicely to most environments.

API: application program interface.

This chapter defines some basic terminology, and provides some historical background as well as information sources related to computer graphics.

1.1 Graphics Areas

Imposing categories on any field is dangerous, but most graphics practitioners would agree on the following major areas of computer graphics:

1

- **Modeling** deals with the mathematical specification of shape and appearance properties in a way that can be stored on the computer. For example, a coffee mug might be described as a set of ordered 3D points along with some interpolation rule to connect the points and a reflection model that describes how light interacts with the mug.

- **Rendering** is a term inherited from art and deals with the creation of shaded images from 3D computer models.

- **Animation** is a technique to create an illusion of motion through sequences of images. Animation uses modeling and rendering but adds the key issue of movement over time, which is not usually dealt with in basic modeling and rendering.

There are many other areas that involve computer graphics, and whether they are core graphics areas is a matter of opinion. These will all be at least touched on in the text. Such related areas include the following:

- **User interaction** deals with the interface between input devices such as mice and tablets, the application, feedback to the user in imagery, and other sensory feedback. Historically, this area is associated with graphics largely because graphics researchers had some of the earliest access to the input/output devices that are now ubiquitous.

- **Virtual reality** attempts to *immerse* the user into a 3D virtual world. This typically requires at least stereo graphics and response to head motion. For true virtual reality, sound and force feedback should be provided as well. Because this area requires advanced 3D graphics and advanced display technology, it is often closely associated with graphics.

- **Visualization** attempts to give users insight into complex information via visual display. Often there are graphic issues to be addressed in a visualization problem.

- **Image processing** deals with the manipulation of 2D images and is used in both the fields of graphics and vision.

- **3D scanning** uses range-finding technology to create measured 3D models. Such models are useful for creating rich visual imagery, and the processing of such models often requires graphics algorithms.

- **Computational photography** is the use of computer graphics, computer vision, and image processing methods to enable new ways of photographically capturing objects, scenes, and environments.

1.2 Major Applications

Almost any endeavor can make some use of computer graphics, but the major consumers of computer graphics technology include the following industries:

- **Video games** increasingly use sophisticated 3D models and rendering algorithms.

- **Cartoons** are often rendered directly from 3D models. Many traditional 2D cartoons use backgrounds rendered from 3D models, which allows a continuously moving viewpoint without huge amounts of artist time.

- **Visual effects** use almost all types of computer graphics technology. Almost every modern film uses digital compositing to superimpose backgrounds with separately filmed foregrounds. Many films also use 3D modeling and animation to create synthetic environments, objects, and even characters that most viewers will never suspect are not real.

- **Animated films** use many of the same techniques that are used for visual effects, but without necessarily aiming for images that look real.

- **CAD/CAM** stands for *computer-aided design* and *computer-aided manufacturing*. These fields use computer technology to design parts and products on the computer and then, using these virtual designs, to guide the manufacturing process. For example, many mechanical parts are designed in a 3D computer modeling package and then automatically produced on a computer-controlled milling device.

- **Simulation** can be thought of as accurate video gaming. For example, a flight simulator uses sophisticated 3D graphics to simulate the experience of flying an airplane. Such simulations can be extremely useful for initial training in safety-critical domains such as driving, and for scenario training for experienced users such as specific fire-fighting situations that are too costly or dangerous to create physically.

- **Medical imaging** creates meaningful images of scanned patient data. For example, a computed tomography (CT) dataset is composed of a large 3D rectangular array of density values. Computer graphics is used to create shaded images that help doctors extract the most salient information from such data.

- **Information visualization** creates images of data that do not necessarily have a "natural" visual depiction. For example, the temporal trend of the price of ten different stocks does not have an obvious visual depiction, but clever graphing techniques can help humans see the patterns in such data.

1.3   Graphics APIs

A key part of using graphics libraries is dealing with a *graphics API*. An *application program interface* (API) is a standard collection of functions to perform a set of related operations, and a graphics API is a set of functions that perform basic operations such as drawing images and 3D surfaces into windows on the screen.

Every graphics program needs to be able to use two related APIs: a graphics API for visual output and a user-interface API to get input from the user. There are currently two dominant paradigms for graphics and user-interface APIs. The first is the integrated approach, exemplified by Java, where the graphics and user-interface toolkits are integrated and portable *packages* that are fully standardized and supported as part of the language. The second is represented by Direct3D and OpenGL, where the drawing commands are part of a software library tied to a language such as C++, and the user-interface software is an independent entity that might vary from system to system. In this latter approach, it is problematic to write portable code, although for simple programs it may be possible to use a portable library layer to encapsulate the system specific user-interface code.

Whatever your choice of API, the basic graphics calls will be largely the same, and the concepts of this book will apply.

1.4   Graphics Pipeline

Every desktop computer today has a powerful 3D *graphics pipeline*. This is a special software/hardware subsystem that efficiently draws 3D primitives in perspective. Usually these systems are optimized for processing 3D triangles with shared vertices. The basic operations in the pipeline map the 3D vertex locations to 2D screen positions and shade the triangles so that they both look realistic and appear in proper back-to-front order.

Although drawing the triangles in valid back-to-front order was once the most important research issue in computer graphics, it is now almost always solved using the z-*buffer*, which uses a special memory buffer to solve the problem in a brute-force manner.

It turns out that the geometric manipulation used in the graphics pipeline can be accomplished almost entirely in a 4D coordinate space composed of three traditional geometric coordinates and a fourth *homogeneous* coordinate that helps with perspective viewing. These 4D coordinates are manipulated using 4×4 matrices and 4-vectors. The graphics pipeline, therefore, contains much machinery for efficiently processing and composing such matrices and vectors. This 4D coordinate system is one of the most subtle and beautiful constructs used in computer science, and it is certainly the biggest intellectual hurdle to jump when learning computer graphics. A big chunk of the first part of every graphics book deals with these coordinates.

The speed at which images can be generated depends strongly on the number of triangles being drawn. Because interactivity is more important in many applications than visual quality, it is worthwhile to minimize the number of triangles used to represent a model. In addition, if the model is viewed in the distance, fewer triangles are needed than when the model is viewed from a closer distance. This suggests that it is useful to represent a model with a varying *level of detail* (LOD).

1.5 Numerical Issues

Many graphics programs are really just 3D numerical codes. Numerical issues are often crucial in such programs. In the "old days," it was very difficult to handle such issues in a robust and portable manner because machines had different internal representations for numbers, and even worse, handled exceptions in different and incompatible ways. Fortunately, almost all modern computers conform to the *IEEE floating-point* standard (IEEE Standards Association, 1985). This allows the programmer to make many convenient assumptions about how certain numeric conditions will be handled.

Although IEEE floating-point has many features that are valuable when coding numeric algorithms, there are only a few that are crucial to know for most situations encountered in graphics. First, and most important, is to understand that there are three "special" values for real numbers in IEEE floating-point:

1. **infinity (∞).** This is a valid number that is larger than all other valid numbers.
2. **minus infinity ($-\infty$).** This is a valid number that is smaller than all other valid numbers.
3. **not a number (NaN).** This is an invalid number that arises from an operation with undefined consequences, such as zero divided by zero.

The designers of IEEE floating-point made some decisions that are extremely convenient for programmers. Many of these relate to the three special values above in handling exceptions such as division by zero. In these cases an exception is logged, but in many cases the programmer can ignore that. Specifically, for any positive real number a, the following rules involving division by infinite values hold:

IEEE floating-point has two representations for zero, one that is treated as positive and one that is treated as negative. The distinction between -0 and $+0$ only occasionally matters, but it is worth keeping in mind for those occasions when it does.

$$+a/(+\infty) = +0$$

$$-a/(+\infty) = -0$$

$$+a/(-\infty) = -0$$

$$-a/(-\infty) = +0$$

Other operations involving infinite values behave the way one would expect. Again for positive a, the behavior is:

$$\infty + \infty = +\infty$$

$$\infty - \infty = NaN$$

$$\infty \times \infty = \infty$$

$$\infty/\infty = NaN$$

$$\infty/a = \infty$$

$$\infty/0 = \infty$$

$$0/0 = NaN$$

The rules in a Boolean expression involving infinite values are as expected:

1. All finite valid numbers are less than $+\infty$.

2. All finite valid numbers are greater than $-\infty$.

3. $-\infty$ is less than $+\infty$.

The rules involving expressions that have NaN values are simple:

1. Any arithmetic expression that includes NaN results in NaN.

2. Any Boolean expression involving NaN is false.

Perhaps the most useful aspect of IEEE floating-point is how divide-by-zero is handled; for any positive real number a, the following rules involving division by zero values hold:

Some care must be taken if negative zero (-0) might arise.

$$+a/+0 = +\infty$$

$$-a/+0 = -\infty$$

There are many numeric computations that become much simpler if the programmer takes advantage of the IEEE rules. For example, consider the expression:

$$a = \frac{1}{\frac{1}{b} + \frac{1}{c}}.$$

Such expressions arise with resistors and lenses. If divide-by-zero resulted in a program crash (as was true in many systems before IEEE floating-point), then two *if* statements would be required to check for small or zero values of b or c. Instead, with IEEE floating-point, if b or c is zero, we will get a zero value for a as desired. Another common technique to avoid special checks is to take advantage of the Boolean properties of NaN. Consider the following code segment:

$a = f(x)$
if $(a > 0)$ **then**
    do something

Here, the function f may return "ugly" values such as ∞ or NaN, but the *if* condition is still well-defined: it is false for $a = $ NaN or $a = -\infty$ and true for $a = +\infty$. With care in deciding which values are returned, often the *if* can make the right choice, with no special checks needed. This makes programs smaller, more robust, and more efficient.

1.6 Efficiency

There are no magic rules for making code more efficient. Efficiency is achieved through careful tradeoffs, and these tradeoffs are different for different architectures. However, for the foreseeable future, a good heuristic is that programmers should pay more attention to memory access patterns than to operation counts. This is the opposite of the best heuristic of two decades ago. This switch has occurred because the speed of memory has not kept pace with the speed of processors. Since that trend continues, the importance of limited and coherent memory access for optimization should only increase.

A reasonable approach to making code fast is to proceed in the following order, taking only those steps which are needed:

1. Write the code in the most straightforward way possible. Compute intermediate results as needed on the fly rather than storing them.

2. Compile in optimized mode.

3. Use whatever profiling tools exist to find critical bottlenecks.

4. Examine data structures to look for ways to improve locality. If possible, make data unit sizes match the cache/page size on the target architecture.

5. If profiling reveals bottlenecks in numeric computations, examine the assembly code generated by the compiler for missed efficiencies. Rewrite source code to solve any problems you find.

The most important of these steps is the first one. Most "optimizations" make the code harder to read without speeding things up. In addition, time spent upfront optimizing code is usually better spent correcting bugs or adding features. Also, beware of suggestions from old texts; some classic tricks such as using integers instead of reals may no longer yield speed because modern CPUs can usually perform floating-point operations just as fast as they perform integer operations. In all situations, profiling is needed to be sure of the merit of any optimization for a specific machine and compiler.

1.7   Designing and Coding Graphics Programs

Certain common strategies are often useful in graphics programming. In this section we provide some advice that you may find helpful as you implement the methods you learn about in this book.

1.7.1   Class Design

A key part of any graphics program is to have good classes or routines for geometric entities such as vectors and matrices, as well as graphics entities such as RGB colors and images. These routines should be made as clean and efficient as possible. A universal design question is whether locations and displacements should be separate classes because they have different operations, e.g., a location multiplied by one-half makes no geometric sense while one-half of a displacement does (Goldman, 1985; DeRose, 1989). There is little agreement on this question, which can spur hours of heated debate among graphics practitioners, but for the sake of example let's assume we will not make the distinction.

This implies that some basic classes to be written include:

- **vector2**. A 2D vector class that stores an x- and y-component. It should store these components in a length-2 array so that an indexing operator can be well supported. You should also include operations for vector addition, vector subtraction, dot product, cross product, scalar multiplication, and scalar division.

I believe strongly in the KISS ("keep it simple, stupid") principle, and in that light the argument for two classes is not compelling enough to justify the added complexity. —P.S.

I like keeping points and vectors separate because it makes code more readable and can let the compiler catch some bugs. —S.M.

- **vector3**. A 3D vector class analogous to vector2.

- **hvector**. A homogeneous vector with four components (see Chapter 7).

- **rgb**. An RGB color that stores three components. You should also include operations for RGB addition, RGB subtraction, RGB multiplication, scalar multiplication, and scalar division.

- **transform**. A 4×4 matrix for transformations. You should include a matrix multiply and member functions to apply to locations, directions, and surface normal vectors. As shown in Chapter 6, these are all different.

- **image**. A 2D array of RGB pixels with an output operation.

In addition, you might or might not want to add classes for intervals, orthonormal bases, and coordinate frames.

You might also consider a special class for unit-length vectors, although I have found them more pain than they are worth. —P.S.

1.7.2 Float vs. Double

Modern architecture suggests that keeping memory use down and maintaining coherent memory access are the keys to efficiency. This suggests using single-precision data. However, avoiding numerical problems suggests using double-precision arithmetic. The tradeoffs depend on the program, but it is nice to have a default in your class definitions.

I suggest using doubles for geometric computation and floats for color computation. For data that occupies a lot of memory, such as triangle meshes, I suggest storing float data, but converting to double when data is accessed through member functions. —P.S.

1.7.3 Debugging Graphics Programs

If you ask around, you may find that as programmers become more experienced, they use traditional debuggers less and less. One reason for this is that using such debuggers is more awkward for complex programs than for simple programs. Another reason is that the most difficult errors are conceptual ones where the wrong thing is being implemented, and it is easy to waste large amounts of time stepping through variable values without detecting such cases. We have found several debugging strategies to be particularly useful in graphics.

I advocate doing all computations with floats until you find evidence that double precision is needed in a particular part of the code. —S.M.

The Scientific Method

In graphics programs there is an alternative to traditional debugging that is often very useful. The downside to it is that it is very similar to what computer programmers are taught not to do early in their careers, so you may feel "naughty" if you do it: we create an image and observe what is wrong with it. Then, we develop a hypothesis about what is causing the problem and test it. For example, in a ray-tracing program we might have many somewhat random looking dark pixels. This is the classic "shadow acne" problem that most people run into when they write a ray tracer. Traditional debugging is not helpful here; instead, we must realize that the shadow rays are hitting the surface being shaded. We might notice that the color of the dark spots is the ambient color, so the direct lighting is what is missing. Direct lighting can be turned off in shadow, so you might hypothesize that these points are incorrectly being tagged as in shadow when they are not. To test this hypothesis, we could turn off the shadowing check and recompile. This would indicate that these are false shadow tests, and we could continue our detective work. The key reason that this method can sometimes be good practice is that we never had to spot a false value or really determine our conceptual error. Instead, we just narrowed in on our conceptual error experimentally. Typically only a few trials are needed to track things down, and this type of debugging is enjoyable.

Images as Coded Debugging Output

In many cases, the easiest channel by which to get debugging information out of a graphics program is the output image itself. If you want to know the value of some variable for part of a computation that runs for every pixel, you can just modify your program temporarily to copy that value directly to the output image and skip the rest of the calculations that would normally be done. For instance, if you suspect a problem with surface normals is causing a problem with shading, you can copy the normal vectors directly to the image (x goes to red, y goes to green, z goes to blue), resulting in a color-coded illustration of the vectors actually being used in your computation. Or, if you suspect a particular value is sometimes out of its valid range, make your program write bright red pixels where that happens. Other common tricks include drawing the back sides of surfaces with an obvious color (when they are not supposed to be visible), coloring the image by the ID numbers of the objects, or coloring pixels by the amount of work they took to compute.

Using a Debugger

There are still cases, particularly when the scientific method seems to have led to a contradiction, when there's no substitute for observing exactly what is going on. The trouble is that graphics programs often involve many, many executions of the same code (once per pixel, for instance, or once per triangle), making it completely impractical to step through in the debugger from the start. And the most difficult bugs usually only occur for complicated inputs.

A useful approach is to "set a trap" for the bug. First, make sure your program is deterministic—run it in a single thread and make sure that all random numbers are computed from fixed seeds. Then, find out which pixel or triangle is exhibiting the bug and add a statement before the code you suspect is incorrect that will be executed only for the suspect case. For instance, if you find that pixel $(126, 247)$ exhibits the bug, then add:

> **if** $x = 126$ and $y = 247$ **then**
> print "blarg!"

A special debugging mode that uses fixed random-number seeds is useful.

If you set a breakpoint on the print statement, you can drop into the debugger just before the pixel you're interested in is computed. Some debuggers have a "conditional breakpoint" feature that can achieve the same thing without modifying the code.

In the cases where the program crashes, a traditional debugger is useful for pinpointing the site of the crash. You should then start backtracking in the program, using asserts and recompiles, to find where the program went wrong. These asserts should be left in the program for potential future bugs you will add. This again means the traditional step-though process is avoided, because that would not be adding the valuable asserts to your program.

Data Visualization for Debugging

Often it is hard to understand what your program is doing, because it computes a lot of intermediate results before it finally goes wrong. The situation is similar to a scientific experiment that measures a lot of data, and one solution is the same: make good plots and illustrations for yourself to understand what the data means. For instance, in a ray tracer you might write code to visualize ray trees so you can see what paths contributed to a pixel, or in an image resampling routine you might make plots that show all the points where samples are being taken from the input. Time spent writing code to visualize your program's internal state is also repaid in a better understanding of its behavior when it comes time to optimize it.

I like to format debugging print statements so that the output happens to be a Matlab or Gnuplot script that makes a helpful plot. —S.M.

Notes

The discussion of software engineering is influenced by the *Effective C++* series (Meyers, 1995, 1997), the *Extreme Programming* movement (Beck & Andres, 2004), and (Kernighan & Pike, 1999). The discussion of experimental debugging is based on discussions with Steve Parker.

There are a number of annual conferences related to computer graphics, including ACM SIGGRAPH and SIGGRAPH Asia, Grpahics Interface, the Game

Developers Conference (GDC), Eurographics, Pacific Graphics, High Performance Graphics, the Eurographics Symposium on Rendering, and IEEE VisWeek. These can be readily found by web searches on their names.

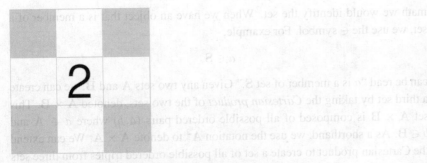

2

Miscellaneous Math

Much of graphics is just translating math directly into code. The cleaner the math, the cleaner the resulting code; so much of this book concentrates on using just the right math for the job. This chapter reviews various tools from high school and college mathematics and is designed to be used more as a reference than as a tutorial. It may appear to be a hodge-podge of topics and indeed it is; each topic is chosen because it is a bit unusual in "standard" math curricula, because it is of central importance in graphics, or because it is not typically treated from a geometric standpoint. In addition to establishing a review of the notation used in the book, the chapter also emphasizes a few points that are sometimes skipped in the standard undergraduate curricula, such as barycentric coordinates on triangles. This chapter is not intended to be a rigorous treatment of the material; instead intuition and geometric interpretation are emphasized. A discussion of linear algebra is deferred until Chapter 5 just before transformation matrices are discussed. Readers are encouraged to skim this chapter to familiarize themselves with the topics covered and to refer back to it as needed. The exercises at the end of the chapter may be useful in determining which topics need a refresher.

2.1 Sets and Mappings

Mappings, also called *functions*, are basic to mathematics and programming. Like a function in a program, a mapping in math takes an argument of one *type* and maps it to (returns) an object of a particular type. In a program we say "type;" in math we would identify the set. When we have an object that is a member of a set, we use the $\in$ symbol. For example,

$$a \in \mathbf{S},$$

can be read "a is a member of set $\mathbf{S}$." Given any two sets $\mathbf{A}$ and $\mathbf{B}$, we can create a third set by taking the *Cartesian product* of the two sets, denoted $\mathbf{A} \times \mathbf{B}$. This set $\mathbf{A} \times \mathbf{B}$ is composed of all possible ordered pairs (a, b) where $a \in \mathbf{A}$ and $b \in \mathbf{B}$. As a shorthand, we use the notation $\mathbf{A}^2$ to denote $\mathbf{A} \times \mathbf{A}$. We can extend the Cartesian product to create a set of all possible ordered triples from three sets and so on for arbitrarily long ordered tuples from arbitrarily many sets.

Common sets of interest include:

- $\mathbb{R}$—the real numbers;

- $\mathbb{R}^+$—the non-negative real numbers (includes zero);

- $\mathbb{R}^2$—the ordered pairs in the real 2D plane;

- $\mathbb{R}^n$—the points in n-dimensional Cartesian space;

- $\mathbb{Z}$—the integers;

- S^2—the set of 3D points (points in $\mathbb{R}^3$) on the unit sphere.

Note that although S^2 is composed of points embedded in three-dimensional space, they are on a surface that can be parameterized with two variables, so it can be thought of as a 2D set. Notation for mappings uses the arrow and a colon, for example:

$$f : \mathbb{R} \mapsto \mathbb{Z},$$

which you can read as "There is a function called f that takes a real number as input and maps it to an integer." Here, the set that comes before the arrow is called the *domain* of the function, and the set on the right-hand side is called the *target*. Computer programmers might be more comfortable with the following equivalent language: "There is a function called f which has one real argument and returns an integer." In other words, the set notation above is equivalent to the common programming notation:

$$\text{integer } f(\text{real}) \quad \leftarrow \text{equivalent} \rightarrow \quad f : \mathbb{R} \mapsto \mathbb{Z}.$$

So the colon-arrow notation can be thought of as a programming syntax. It's that simple.

The point $f(a)$ is called the *image* of a, and the image of a set A (a subset of the domain) is the subset of the target that contains the images of all points in A. The image of the whole domain is called the *range* of the function.

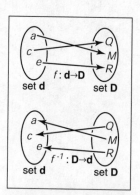

Figure 2.1. A bijection f and the inverse function f^{-1}. Note that f^{-1} is also a bijection.

2.1.1 Inverse Mappings

If we have a function $f : \mathbf{A} \mapsto \mathbf{B}$, there may exist an *inverse function* $f^{-1} : \mathbf{B} \mapsto \mathbf{A}$, which is defined by the rule $f^{-1}(b) = a$ where $b = f(a)$. This definition only works if every $b \in \mathbf{B}$ is an image of some point under f (that is, the range equals the target) and if there is only one such point (that is, there is only one a for which $f(a) = b$). Such mappings or functions are called *bijections*. A bijection maps every $a \in \mathbf{A}$ to a unique $b \in \mathbf{B}$, and for every $b \in \mathbf{B}$, there is exactly one $a \in \mathbf{A}$ such that $f(a) = b$ (Figure 2.1). A bijection between a group of riders and horses indicates that everybody rides a single horse, and every horse is ridden. The two functions would be *rider(horse)* and *horse(rider)*. These are inverse functions of each other. Functions that are not bijections have no inverse (Figure 2.2).

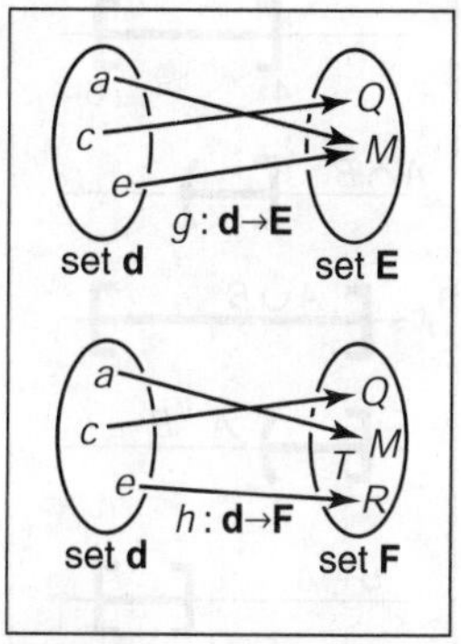

An example of a bijection is $f : \mathbb{R} \mapsto \mathbb{R}$, with $f(x) = x^3$. The inverse function is $f^{-1}(x) = \sqrt[3]{x}$. This example shows that the standard notation can be somewhat awkward because x is used as a dummy variable in both f and f^{-1}. It is sometimes more intuitive to use different dummy variables, with $y = f(x)$ and $x = f^{-1}(y)$. This yields the more intuitive $y = x^3$ and $x = \sqrt[3]{y}$. An example of a function that does not have an inverse is $sqr : \mathbb{R} \mapsto \mathbb{R}$, where $sqr(x) = x^2$. This is true for two reasons: first $x^2 = (-x)^2$, and second no members of the domain map to the negative portions of the target. Note that we can define an inverse if we restrict the domain and range to $\mathbb{R}^+$. Then $\sqrt{x}$ is a valid inverse.

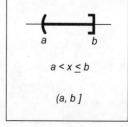

Figure 2.2. The function g does not have an inverse because two elements of **d** map to the same element of **E**. The function h has no inverse because element T of **F** has no element of **d** mapped to it.

2.1.2 Intervals

Often we would like to specify that a function deals with real numbers that are restricted in value. One such constraint is to specify an *interval*. An example of an interval is the real numbers between zero and one, not including zero or one. We denote this $(0, 1)$. Because it does not include its endpoints, this is referred to as an *open interval*. The corresponding *closed interval*, which does contain its endpoints, is denoted with square brackets: $[0, 1]$. This notation can be mixed, i.e., $[0, 1)$ includes zero but not one. When writing an interval $[a, b]$, we assume that $a \leq b$. The three common ways to represent an interval are shown in Figure 2.3. The Cartesian products of intervals are often used. For example, to indicate that a point $\mathbf{x}$ is in the unit cube in 3D, we say $\mathbf{x} \in [0, 1]^3$.

Intervals are particularly useful in conjunction with set operations: *intersection*, *union*, and *difference*. For example, the intersection of two intervals is the set of points they have in common. The symbol $\cap$ is used for intersection. For example, $[3, 5) \cap [4, 6] = [4, 5)$. For unions, the symbol $\cup$ is used to denote points in either interval. For example, $[3, 5) \cup [4, 6] = [3, 6]$. Unlike the first two operators, the difference operator produces different results depending on argument order.

Figure 2.3. Three equivalent ways to denote the interval from a to b that includes b but not a.

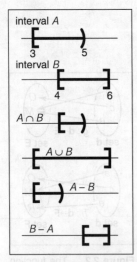

Figure 2.4. Interval operations on [3,5) and [4,6].

The minus sign is used for the difference operator, which returns the points in the left interval that are not also in the right. For example, $[3, 5) - [4, 6] = [3, 4)$ and $[4, 6] - [3, 5) = [5, 6]$. These operations are particularly easy to visualize using interval diagrams (Figure 2.4).

2.1.3 Logarithms

Although not as prevalent today as they were before calculators, *logarithms* are often useful in problems where equations with exponential terms arise. By definition, every logarithm has a *base a*. The "log base a" of x is written $\log_a x$ and is defined as "the exponent to which a must be raised to get x," i.e.,

$$y = \log_a x \iff a^y = x.$$

Note that the logarithm base a and the function that raises a to a power are inverses of each other. This basic definition has several consequences:

$$a^{\log_a(x)} = x;$$
$$\log_a(a^x) = x;$$
$$\log_a(xy) = \log_a x + \log_a y;$$
$$\log_a(x/y) = \log_a x - \log_a y;$$
$$\log_a x = \log_a b \, \log_b x.$$

When we apply calculus to logarithms, the special number $e = 2.718\ldots$ often turns up. The logarithm with base e is called the *natural logarithm*. We adopt the common shorthand ln to denote it:

$$\ln x \equiv \log_e x.$$

Note that the "$\equiv$" symbol can be read "is equivalent by definition." Like π, the special number e arises in a remarkable number of contexts. Many fields use a particular base in addition to e for manipulations and omit the base in their notation, i.e., $\log x$. For example, astronomers often use base 10 and theoretical computer scientists often use base 2. Because computer graphics borrows technology from many fields we will avoid this shorthand.

The derivatives of logarithms and exponents illuminate why the natural logarithm is "natural":

$$\frac{d}{dx} \log_a x = \frac{1}{x \ln a};$$
$$\frac{d}{dx} a^x = a^x \ln a.$$

The constant multipliers above are unity only for $a = e$.

2.2   Solving Quadratic Equations

A *quadratic equation* has the form

$$Ax^2 + Bx + C = 0,$$

where x is a real unknown, and A, B, and C are known constants. If you think of a 2D xy plot with $y = Ax^2 + Bx + C$, the solution is just whatever x values are "zero crossings" in y. Because $y = Ax^2 + Bx + C$ is a parabola, there will be zero, one, or two real solutions depending on whether the the parabola misses, grazes, or hits the x-axis (Figure 2.5).

To solve the quadratic equation analytically, we first divide by A:

$$x^2 + \frac{B}{A}x + \frac{C}{A} = 0.$$

Then we "complete the square" to group terms:

$$\left(x + \frac{B}{2A}\right)^2 - \frac{B^2}{4A^2} + \frac{C}{A} = 0.$$

Moving the constant portion to the right-hand side and taking the square root gives

$$x + \frac{B}{2A} = \pm\sqrt{\frac{B^2}{4A^2} - \frac{C}{A}}.$$

Subtracting $B/(2A)$ from both sides and grouping terms with the denominator $2A$ gives the familiar form:[1]

$$x = \frac{-B \pm \sqrt{B^2 - 4AC}}{2A}. \tag{2.1}$$

Here the "$\pm$" symbol means there are two solutions, one with a plus sign and one with a minus sign. Thus 3 ± 1 equals "two or four." Note that the term that determines the number of real solutions is

$$D \equiv B^2 - 4AC,$$

which is called the *discriminant* of the quadratic equation. If $D > 0$, there are two real solutions (also called *roots*). If $D = 0$, there is one real solution (a "double" root). If $D < 0$, there are no real solutions.

For example, the roots of $2x^2 + 6x + 4 = 0$ are $x = -1$ and $x = -2$, and the equation $x^2 + x + 1$ has no real solutions. The discriminants of these equations are $D = 4$ and $D = -3$, respectively, so we expect the number of solutions given. In programs, it is usually a good idea to evaluate D first and return "no roots" without taking the square root if D is negative.

---

[1] A robust implementation will use the equivalent expression $2C/(-B \mp \sqrt{B^2 - 4AC})$ to compute one of the roots, depending on the sign of B (Exercise 7).

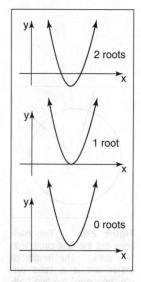

Figure 2.5. The geometric interpretation of the roots of a quadratic equation is the intersection points of a parabola with the *x*-axis.

2.3   Trigonometry

In graphics we use basic trigonometry in many contexts. Usually, it is nothing too fancy, and it often helps to remember the basic definitions.

2.3.1   Angles

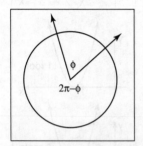

Figure 2.6. Two half-lines cut the unit circle into two arcs. The length of either arc is a valid angle "between" the two half-lines. Either we can use the convention that the smaller length is the angle, or that the two half-lines are specified in a certain order and the arc that determines angle ϕ is the one swept out counterclockwise from the first to the second half-line.

Although we take angles somewhat for granted, we should return to their definition so we can extend the idea of the angle onto the sphere. An angle is formed between two half-lines (infinite rays stemming from an origin) or directions, and some convention must be used to decide between the two possibilities for the angle created between them as shown in Figure 2.6. An *angle* is defined by the length of the arc segment it cuts out on the unit circle. A common convention is that the smaller arc length is used, and the sign of the angle is determined by the order in which the two half-lines are specified. Using that convention, all angles are in the range $[-\pi, \pi]$.

Each of these angles is *the length of the arc of the unit circle that is "cut" by the two directions.* Because the perimeter of the unit circle is 2π, the two possible angles sum to 2π. The unit of these arc lengths is *radians*. Another common unit is degrees, where the perimeter of the circle is 360 degrees. Thus, an angle that is π radians is 180 degrees, usually denoted $180°$. The conversion between degrees and radians is

$$\text{degrees} = \frac{180}{\pi} \text{ radians};$$

$$\text{radians} = \frac{\pi}{180} \text{ degrees}.$$

2.3.2   Trigonometric Functions

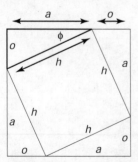

Figure 2.7. A geometric demonstration of the Pythagorean theorem.

Given a right triangle with sides of length a, o, and h, where h is the length of the longest side (which is always opposite the right angle), or *hypotenuse*, an important relation is described by the *Pythagorean theorem*:

$$a^2 + o^2 = h^2.$$

You can see that this is true from Figure 2.7, where the big square has area $(a+o)^2$, the four triangles have the combined area $2ao$, and the center square has area h^2.

Because the triangles and inner square subdivide the larger square evenly, we have $2ao + h^2 = (a + o)^2$, which is easily manipulated to the form above.

We define *sine* and *cosine* of ϕ, as well as the other ratio-based trigonometric expressions:

$$\sin \phi \equiv o/h;$$
$$\csc \phi \equiv h/o;$$
$$\cos \phi \equiv a/h;$$
$$\sec \phi \equiv h/a;$$
$$\tan \phi \equiv o/a;$$
$$\cot \phi \equiv a/o.$$

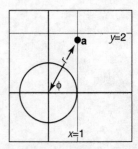

Figure 2.8. Polar coordinates for the point $(x_a, y_a) = (1, \sqrt{3})$ is $(r_a, \phi_a) = (2, \pi/3)$.

These definitions allow us to set up *polar coordinates*, where a point is coded as a distance from the origin and a signed angle relative to the positive x-axis (Figure 2.8). Note the convention that angles are in the range $\phi \in (-\pi, \pi]$, and that the positive angles are counterclockwise from the positive x-axis. This convention that counterclockwise maps to positive numbers is arbitrary, but it is used in many contexts in graphics so it is worth committing to memory.

Trigonometric functions are periodic and can take any angle as an argument. For example $\sin(A) = \sin(A + 2\pi)$. This means the functions are not invertible when considered with the domain $\mathbb{R}$. This problem is avoided by restricting the range of standard inverse functions, and this is done in a standard way in almost all modern math libraries (e.g., (Plauger, 1991)). The domains and ranges are:

$$\text{asin} : [-1, 1] \mapsto [-\pi/2, \pi/2];$$
$$\text{acos} : [-1, 1] \mapsto [0, \pi];$$
$$\text{atan} : \mathbb{R} \mapsto [-\pi/2, \pi/2];$$
$$\text{atan2} : \mathbb{R}^2 \mapsto [-\pi, \pi].$$

(2.2)

The last function, $\text{atan2}(s, c)$ is often very useful. It takes an s value proportional to $\sin A$ and a c value that scales $\cos A$ by the same factor and returns A. The factor is assumed to be positive. One way to think of this is that it returns the angle of a 2D Cartesian point (s, c) in polar coordinates (Figure 2.9).

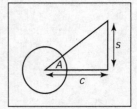

Figure 2.9. The function atan2(*s,c*) returns the angle *A* and is often very useful in graphics.

2.3.3 Useful Identities

This section lists without derivation a variety of useful trigonometric identities.

Shifting identities:

$$\sin(-A) = -\sin A$$
$$\cos(-A) = \cos A$$
$$\tan(-A) = -\tan A$$
$$\sin(\pi/2 - A) = \cos A$$
$$\cos(\pi/2 - A) = \sin A$$
$$\tan(\pi/2 - A) = \cot A$$

Pythagorean identities:
$$\sin^2 A + \cos^2 A = 1$$
$$\sec^2 A - \tan^2 A = 1$$
$$\csc^2 A - \cot^2 A = 1$$

Addition and subtraction identities:
$$\sin(A + B) = \sin A \cos B + \sin B \cos A$$
$$\sin(A - B) = \sin A \cos B - \sin B \cos A$$
$$\sin(2A) = 2 \sin A \cos A$$
$$\cos(A + B) = \cos A \cos B - \sin A \sin B$$
$$\cos(A - B) = \cos A \cos B + \sin A \sin B$$
$$\cos(2A) = \cos^2 A - \sin^2 A$$
$$\tan(A + B) = \frac{\tan A + \tan B}{1 - \tan A \tan B}$$
$$\tan(A - B) = \frac{\tan A - \tan B}{1 + \tan A \tan B}$$
$$\tan(2A) = \frac{2 \tan A}{1 - \tan^2 A}$$

Half-angle identities:
$$\sin^2(A/2) = (1 - \cos A)/2$$
$$\cos^2(A/2) = (1 + \cos A)/2$$

Product identities:
$$\sin A \sin B = -(\cos(A + B) - \cos(A - B))/2$$
$$\sin A \cos B = (\sin(A + B) + \sin(A - B))/2$$
$$\cos A \cos B = (\cos(A + B) + \cos(A - B))/2$$

The following identities are for arbitrary triangles with side lengths a, b, and c, each with an angle opposite it given by A, B, C, respectively (Figure 2.10):

$$\frac{\sin A}{a} = \frac{\sin B}{b} = \frac{\sin C}{c} \qquad \text{(Law of sines)}$$

$$c^2 = a^2 + b^2 - 2ab \cos C \qquad \text{(Law of cosines)}$$

$$\frac{a + b}{a - b} = \frac{\tan\left(\frac{A+B}{2}\right)}{\tan\left(\frac{A-B}{2}\right)} \qquad \text{(Law of tangents)}$$

The area of a triangle can also be computed in terms of these side lengths:

$$\text{triangle area} = \frac{1}{2}\sqrt{(a + b + c)(-a + b + c)(a - b + c)(a + b - c)}.$$

Figure 2.10. Geometry for triangle laws.

2.4 Vectors

A *vector* describes a length and a direction. It can be usefully represented by an arrow. Two vectors are equal if they have the same length and direction even if we think of them as being located in different places (Figure 2.11). As much as possible, you should think of a vector as an arrow and not as coordinates or numbers. At some point we will have to represent vectors as numbers in our programs, but even in code they should be manipulated as objects and only the low-level vector operations should know about their numeric representation (DeRose, 1989). Vectors will be represented as bold characters, e.g., **a**. A vector's length is denoted $\|a\|$. A *unit vector* is any vector whose length is one. The *zero vector* is the vector of zero length. The direction of the zero vector is undefined.

Vectors can be used to represent many different things. For example, they can be used to store an *offset*, also called a *displacement*. If we know "the treasure is buried two paces east and three paces north of the secret meeting place," then we know the offset, but we don't know where to start. Vectors can also be used to store a *location*, another word for *position* or *point*. Locations can be represented as a displacement from another location. Usually there is some understood *origin* location from which all other locations are stored as offsets. Note that locations are not vectors. As we shall discuss, you can add two vectors. However, it usually does not make sense to add two locations unless it is an intermediate operation when computing weighted averages of a location (Goldman, 1985). Adding two offsets does make sense, so that is one reason why offsets are vectors. But this emphasizes that a location is not a offset; it is an offset from a specific origin location. The offset by itself is not the location.

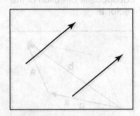

Figure 2.11. These two vectors are the same because they have the same length and direction.

2.4.1 Vector Operations

Vectors have most of the usual arithmetic operations that we associate with real numbers. Two vectors are equal if and only if they have the same length and direction. Two vectors are added according to the *parallelogram rule*. This rule states that the sum of two vectors is found by placing the tail of either vector against the head of the other (Figure 2.12). The sum vector is the vector that "completes the triangle" started by the two vectors. The parallelogram is formed by taking the sum in either order. This emphasizes that vector addition is commutative:

$$a + b = b + a.$$

Note that the parallelogram rule just formalizes our intuition about displacements. Think of walking along one vector, tail to head, and then walking along the other.

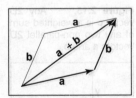

Figure 2.12. Two vectors are added by arranging them head to tail. This can be done in either order.

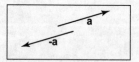

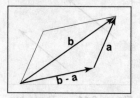

Figure 2.13. The vector −a has the same length but opposite direction of the vector **a**.

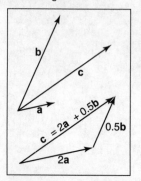

Figure 2.14. Vector subtraction is just vector addition with a reversal of the second argument.

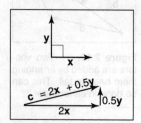

Figure 2.15. Any 2D vector **c** is a weighted sum of any two non-parallel 2D vectors **a** and **b**.

The net displacement is just the parallelogram diagonal. You can also create a *unary minus* for a vector: −**a** (Figure 2.13) is a vector with the same length as **a** but opposite direction. This allows us to also define subtraction:

$$\mathbf{b} - \mathbf{a} \equiv -\mathbf{a} + \mathbf{b}.$$

You can visualize vector subtraction with a parallelogram (Figure 2.14). We can write

$$\mathbf{a} + (\mathbf{b} - \mathbf{a}) = \mathbf{b}.$$

Vectors can also be multiplied. In fact, there are several kinds of products involving vectors. First, we can *scale* the vector by multiplying it by a real number k. This just multiplies the vector's length without changing its direction. For example, $3.5\mathbf{a}$ is a vector in the same direction as **a** but it is 3.5 times as long as **a**. We discuss two products involving two vectors, the dot product and the cross product, later in this section, and a product involving three vectors, the determinant, in Chapter 5.

2.4.2 Cartesian Coordinates of a Vector

A 2D vector can be written as a combination of any two non-zero vectors which are not parallel. This property of the two vectors is called *linear independence*. Two linearly independent vectors form a 2D *basis*, and the vectors are thus referred to as *basis vectors*. For example, a vector **c** may be expressed as a combination of two basis vectors **a** and **b** (Figure 2.15):

$$\mathbf{c} = a_c \mathbf{a} + b_c \mathbf{b}. \tag{2.3}$$

Note that the weights a_c and b_c are unique. Bases are especially useful if the two vectors are *orthogonal*, i.e., they are at right angles to each other. It is even more useful if they are also unit vectors in which case they are *orthonormal*. If we assume two such "special" vectors **x** and **y** are known to us, then we can use them to represent all other vectors in a *Cartesian* coordinate system, where each vector is represented as two real numbers. For example, a vector **a** might be represented as

$$\mathbf{a} = x_a \mathbf{x} + y_a \mathbf{y},$$

where x_a and y_a are the real Cartesian coordinates of the 2D vector **a** (Figure 2.16). Note that this is not really any different conceptually from Equation (2.3), where the basis vectors were not orthonormal. But there are several advantages to a Cartesian coordinate system. For instance, by the Pythagorean theorem, the length of **a** is

$$\|\mathbf{a}\| = \sqrt{x_a^2 + y_a^2}.$$

Figure 2.16. A 2D Cartesian basis for vectors.

It is also simple to compute dot products, cross products, and coordinates of vectors in Cartesian systems, as we'll see in the following sections.

By convention we write the coordinates of **a** either as an ordered pair (x_a, y_a) or a column matrix:

$$\mathbf{a} = \begin{bmatrix} x_a \\ y_a \end{bmatrix}.$$

The form we use will depend on typographic convenience. We will also occasionally write the vector as a row matrix, which we will indicate as $\mathbf{a}^T$:

$$\mathbf{a}^T = \begin{bmatrix} x_a & y_a \end{bmatrix}.$$

We can also represent 3D, 4D, etc., vectors in Cartesian coordinates. For the 3D case, we use a basis vector **z** that is orthogonal to both **x** and **y**.

2.4.3 Dot Product

The simplest way to multiply two vectors is the *dot* product. The dot product of **a** and **b** is denoted **a** · **b** and is often called the *scalar product* because it returns a scalar. The dot product returns a value related to its arguments' lengths and the angle ϕ between them (Figure 2.17):

$$\mathbf{a} \cdot \mathbf{b} = \|\mathbf{a}\| \, \|\mathbf{b}\| \, \cos\phi, \tag{2.4}$$

The most common use of the dot product in graphics programs is to compute the cosine of the angle between two vectors.

The dot product can also be used to find the *projection* of one vector onto another. This is the length **a**→**b** of a vector **a** that is projected at right angles onto a vector **b** (Figure 2.18):

$$\mathbf{a} \rightarrow \mathbf{b} = \|\mathbf{a}\| \, \cos\phi = \frac{\mathbf{a} \cdot \mathbf{b}}{\|\mathbf{b}\|}. \tag{2.5}$$

The dot product obeys the familiar associative and distributive properties we have in real arithmetic:

$$\mathbf{a} \cdot \mathbf{b} = \mathbf{b} \cdot \mathbf{a},$$
$$\mathbf{a} \cdot (\mathbf{b} + \mathbf{c}) = \mathbf{a} \cdot \mathbf{b} + \mathbf{a} \cdot \mathbf{c}, \tag{2.6}$$
$$(k\mathbf{a}) \cdot \mathbf{b} = \mathbf{a} \cdot (k\mathbf{b}) = k\mathbf{a} \cdot \mathbf{b}.$$

If 2D vectors **a** and **b** are expressed in Cartesian coordinates, we can take advantage of $\mathbf{x} \cdot \mathbf{x} = \mathbf{y} \cdot \mathbf{y} = 1$ and $\mathbf{x} \cdot \mathbf{y} = 0$ to derive that their dot product

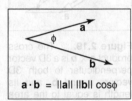

Figure 2.17. The dot product is related to length and angle and is one of the most important formulas in graphics.

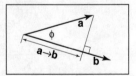

Figure 2.18. The projection of **a** onto **b** is a length found by Equation (2.5).

is

$$\mathbf{a} \cdot \mathbf{b} = (x_a \mathbf{x} + y_a \mathbf{y}) \cdot (x_b \mathbf{x} + y_b \mathbf{y})$$
$$= x_a x_b (\mathbf{x} \cdot \mathbf{x}) + x_a y_b (\mathbf{x} \cdot \mathbf{y}) + x_b y_a (\mathbf{y} \cdot \mathbf{x}) + y_a y_b (\mathbf{y} \cdot \mathbf{y})$$
$$= x_a x_b + y_a y_b.$$

Similarly in 3D we can find

$$\mathbf{a} \cdot \mathbf{b} = x_a x_b + y_a y_b + z_a z_b.$$

2.4.4 Cross Product

The cross product $\mathbf{a} \times \mathbf{b}$ is usually used only for three-dimensional vectors; generalized cross products are discussed in references given in the chapter notes. The cross product returns a 3D vector that is perpendicular to the two arguments of the cross product. The length of the resulting vector is related to $\sin \phi$:

$$\|\mathbf{a} \times \mathbf{b}\| = \|\mathbf{a}\| \, \|\mathbf{b}\| \sin \phi.$$

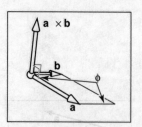

Figure 2.19. The cross product $\mathbf{a} \times \mathbf{b}$ is a 3D vector perpendicular to both 3D vectors $\mathbf{a}$ and $\mathbf{b}$, and its length is equal to the area of the parallelogram shown.

The magnitude $\|\mathbf{a} \times \mathbf{b}\|$ is equal to the area of the parallelogram formed by vectors $\mathbf{a}$ and $\mathbf{b}$. In addition, $\mathbf{a} \times \mathbf{b}$ is perpendicular to both $\mathbf{a}$ and $\mathbf{b}$ (Figure 2.19). Note that there are only two possible directions for such a vector. By definition, the vectors in the direction of the x-, y- and z-axes are given by

$$\mathbf{x} = (1, 0, 0),$$
$$\mathbf{y} = (0, 1, 0),$$
$$\mathbf{z} = (0, 0, 1),$$

and we set as a convention that $\mathbf{x} \times \mathbf{y}$ must be in the plus or minus $\mathbf{z}$ direction. The choice is somewhat arbitrary, but it is standard to assume that

$$\mathbf{z} = \mathbf{x} \times \mathbf{y}.$$

All possible permutations of the three Cartesian unit vectors are

$$\mathbf{x} \times \mathbf{y} = +\mathbf{z},$$
$$\mathbf{y} \times \mathbf{x} = -\mathbf{z},$$
$$\mathbf{y} \times \mathbf{z} = +\mathbf{x},$$
$$\mathbf{z} \times \mathbf{y} = -\mathbf{x},$$
$$\mathbf{z} \times \mathbf{x} = +\mathbf{y},$$
$$\mathbf{x} \times \mathbf{z} = -\mathbf{y}.$$

Because of the $\sin\phi$ property, we also know that a vector cross itself is the zero-vector, so $\mathbf{x} \times \mathbf{x} = 0$ and so on. Note that the cross product is *not* commutative, i.e., $\mathbf{x} \times \mathbf{y} \neq \mathbf{y} \times \mathbf{x}$. The careful observer will note that the above discussion does not allow us to draw an unambiguous picture of how the Cartesian axes relate. More specifically, if we put $\mathbf{x}$ and $\mathbf{y}$ on a sidewalk, with $\mathbf{x}$ pointing East and $\mathbf{y}$ pointing North, then does $\mathbf{z}$ point up to the sky or into the ground? The usual convention is to have $\mathbf{z}$ point to the sky. This is known as a *right-handed* coordinate system. This name comes from the memory scheme of "grabbing" $\mathbf{x}$ with your *right* palm and fingers and rotating it toward $\mathbf{y}$. The vector $\mathbf{z}$ should align with your thumb. This is illustrated in Figure 2.20.

The cross product has the nice property that

$$\mathbf{a} \times (\mathbf{b} + \mathbf{c}) = \mathbf{a} \times \mathbf{b} + \mathbf{a} \times \mathbf{c},$$

and

$$\mathbf{a} \times (k\mathbf{b}) = k(\mathbf{a} \times \mathbf{b}).$$

However, a consequence of the right-hand rule is

$$\mathbf{a} \times \mathbf{b} = -(\mathbf{b} \times \mathbf{a}).$$

In Cartesian coordinates, we can use an explicit expansion to compute the cross product:

$$
\begin{aligned}
\mathbf{a} \times \mathbf{b} &= (x_a\mathbf{x} + y_a\mathbf{y} + z_a\mathbf{z}) \times (x_b\mathbf{x} + y_b\mathbf{y} + z_b\mathbf{z}) \\
&= x_a x_b \mathbf{x} \times \mathbf{x} + x_a y_b \mathbf{x} \times \mathbf{y} + x_a z_b \mathbf{x} \times \mathbf{z} \\
&\quad + y_a x_b \mathbf{y} \times \mathbf{x} + y_a y_b \mathbf{y} \times \mathbf{y} + y_a z_b \mathbf{y} \times \mathbf{z} \\
&\quad + z_a x_b \mathbf{z} \times \mathbf{x} + z_a y_b \mathbf{z} \times \mathbf{y} + z_a z_b \mathbf{z} \times \mathbf{z} \\
&= (y_a z_b - z_a y_b)\mathbf{x} + (z_a x_b - x_a z_b)\mathbf{y} + (x_a y_b - y_a x_b)\mathbf{z}.
\end{aligned}
$$
(2.7)

So, in coordinate form,

$$\mathbf{a} \times \mathbf{b} = (y_a z_b - z_a y_b, z_a x_b - x_a z_b, x_a y_b - y_a x_b).$$
(2.8)

2.4.5 Orthonormal Bases and Coordinate Frames

Managing coordinate systems is one of the core tasks of almost any graphics program; key to this is managing *orthonormal bases*. Any set of two 2D vectors $\mathbf{u}$ and $\mathbf{v}$ form an orthonormal basis provided that they are orthogonal (at right angles) and are each of unit length. Thus,

$$\|\mathbf{u}\| = \|\mathbf{v}\| = 1,$$

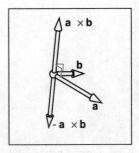

Figure 2.20. The "right-hand rule" for cross products. Imagine placing the base of your right palm where **a** and **b** join at their tails, and pushing the arrow of **a** toward **b**. Your extended right thumb should point toward **a** × **b**.

and

$$\mathbf{u} \cdot \mathbf{v} = 0.$$

In 3D, three vectors $\mathbf{u}$, $\mathbf{v}$, and $\mathbf{w}$ form an orthonormal basis if

$$\|\mathbf{u}\| = \|\mathbf{v}\| = \|\mathbf{w}\| = 1,$$

and

$$\mathbf{u} \cdot \mathbf{v} = \mathbf{v} \cdot \mathbf{w} = \mathbf{w} \cdot \mathbf{u} = 0.$$

This orthonormal basis is *right-handed* provided

$$\mathbf{w} = \mathbf{u} \times \mathbf{v},$$

and otherwise it is left-handed.

Note that the Cartesian canonical orthonormal basis is just one of infinitely many possible orthonormal bases. What makes it special is that it and its implicit origin location are used for low-level representation within a program. Thus, the vectors $\mathbf{x}$, $\mathbf{y}$, and $\mathbf{z}$ are never explicitly stored and neither is the canonical

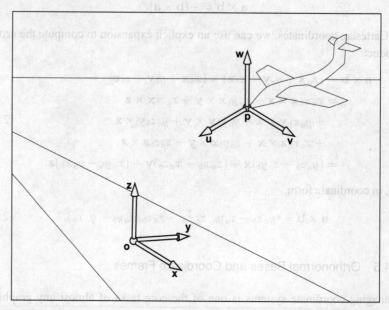

Figure 2.21. There is always a master or "canonical" coordinate system with origin $\mathbf{o}$ and orthonormal basis $\mathbf{x}$, $\mathbf{y}$, and $\mathbf{z}$. This coordinate system is usually defined to be aligned to the global model and is thus often called the "global" or "world" coordinate system. This origin and basis vectors are never stored explicitly. All other vectors and locations are stored with coordinates that relate them to the global frame. The coordinate system associated with the plane are explicitly stored in terms of global coordinates.

origin location o. The global model is typically stored in this canonical coordinate system, and it is thus often called the *global coordinate system*. However, if we want to use another coordinate system with origin p and orthonormal basis vectors **u**, **v**, and **w**, then we *do* store those vectors explicitly. Such a system is called a *frame of reference* or *coordinate frame*. For example, in a flight simulator, we might want to maintain a coordinate system with the origin at the nose of the plane, and the orthonormal basis aligned with the airplane. Simultaneously, we would have the master canonical coordinate system (Figure 2.21). The coordinate system associated with a particular object, such as the plane, is usually called a *local coordinate system*.

At a low level, the local frame is stored in canonical coordinates. For example, if **u** has coordinates (x_u, y_u, z_u),

$$\mathbf{u} = x_u\mathbf{x} + y_u\mathbf{y} + z_u\mathbf{z}.$$

A location implicitly includes an offset from the canonical origin:

$$\mathbf{p} = \mathbf{o} + x_p\mathbf{x} + y_p\mathbf{y} + z_p\mathbf{z},$$

where (x_p, y_p, z_p) are the coordinates of **p**.

Note that if we store a vector **a** with respect to the **u**-**v**-**w** frame, we store a triple (u_a, v_a, w_a) which we can interpret geometrically as

$$\mathbf{a} = u_a\mathbf{u} + v_a\mathbf{v} + w_a\mathbf{w}.$$

To get the canonical coordinates of a vector **a** stored in the **u**-**v**-**w** coordinate system, simply recall that **u**, **v**, and **w** are themselves stored in terms of Cartesian coordinates, so the expression $u_a\mathbf{u} + v_a\mathbf{v} + w_a\mathbf{w}$ is already in Cartesian coordinates if evaluated explicitly. To get the **u**-**v**-**w** coordinates of a vector **b** stored in the canonical coordinate system, we can use dot products:

$$u_b = \mathbf{u} \cdot \mathbf{b}; \quad v_b = \mathbf{v} \cdot \mathbf{b}; \quad w_b = \mathbf{w} \cdot \mathbf{b}$$

This works because we know that for *some* u_b, v_b, and w_b,

$$u_b\mathbf{u} + v_b\mathbf{v} + w_b\mathbf{w} = \mathbf{b},$$

and the dot product isolates the u_b coordinate:

$$\mathbf{u} \cdot \mathbf{b} = u_b(\mathbf{u} \cdot \mathbf{u}) + v_b(\mathbf{u} \cdot \mathbf{v}) + w_b(\mathbf{u} \cdot \mathbf{w})$$
$$= u_b$$

This works because **u**, **v**, and **w** are orthonormal.

Using matrices to manage changes of coordinate systems is discussed in Sections 6.2.1 and 6.5.

2.4.6 Constructing a Basis from a Single Vector

Often we need an orthonormal basis that is aligned with a given vector. That is, given a vector $\mathbf{a}$, we want an orthonormal $\mathbf{u}$, $\mathbf{v}$, and $\mathbf{w}$ such that $\mathbf{w}$ points in the same direction as $\mathbf{a}$ (Hughes & Möller, 1999), but we don't particularly care what $\mathbf{u}$ and $\mathbf{v}$ are. One vector isn't enough to uniquely determine the answer; we just need a robust procedure that will find any one of the possible bases.

This same procedure can, of course, be used to construct the three vectors in any order; just pay attention to the order of the cross products to ensure the basis is right handed.

This can be done using cross products as follows. First make $\mathbf{w}$ a unit vector in the direction of $\mathbf{a}$:

$$\mathbf{w} = \frac{\mathbf{a}}{\|\mathbf{a}\|}.$$

Then choose any vector $\mathbf{t}$ not collinear with $\mathbf{w}$, and use the cross product to build a unit vector $\mathbf{u}$ perpendicular to $\mathbf{w}$:

$$\mathbf{u} = \frac{\mathbf{t} \times \mathbf{w}}{\|\mathbf{t} \times \mathbf{w}\|}.$$

If $\mathbf{t}$ is collinear with $\mathbf{w}$ the denominator will vanish, and if they are nearly collinear the results will have low precision. A simple procedure to find a vector sufficiently different from $\mathbf{w}$ is to start with $\mathbf{t}$ equal to $\mathbf{w}$ and change the smallest magnitude component of $\mathbf{t}$ to 1. For example, if $\mathbf{w} = (1/\sqrt{2}, -1/\sqrt{2}, 0)$ then $\mathbf{t} = (1/\sqrt{2}, -1/\sqrt{2}, 1)$. Once $\mathbf{w}$ and $\mathbf{u}$ are in hand, completing the basis is simple:

$$\mathbf{v} = \mathbf{w} \times \mathbf{u}.$$

An example of a situation where this construction is used is surface shading, where a basis aligned to the surface normal is needed but the rotation around the normal is often unimportant.

2.4.7 Constructing a Basis from Two Vectors

The procedure in the previous section can also be used in situations where the rotation of the basis around the given vector is important. A common example is building a basis for a camera: it's important to have one vector aligned in the direction the camera is looking, but the orientation of the camera around that vector is *not* arbitrary, and it needs to be specified somehow. Once the orientation is pinned down, the basis is completely determined.

$\mathbf{u} = \mathbf{a} \times \mathbf{b}$ also produces an orthonormal basis, but it is left-handed.

A common way to fully specify a frame is by providing two vectors $\mathbf{a}$ (which specifies $\mathbf{w}$) and $\mathbf{b}$ (which specifies $\mathbf{v}$). If the two vectors are known to be perpendicular it is a simple matter to construct the third vector by $\mathbf{u} = \mathbf{b} \times \mathbf{a}$.

To be sure that the resulting basis really is orthonormal, even if the input vectors weren't quite, a procedure much like the single-vector procedure is advisable:

$$\mathbf{w} = \frac{\mathbf{a}}{\|\mathbf{a}\|},$$

$$\mathbf{u} = \frac{\mathbf{b} \times \mathbf{w}}{\|\mathbf{b} \times \mathbf{w}\|},$$

$$\mathbf{v} = \mathbf{w} \times \mathbf{u}.$$

In fact, this procedure works just fine when $\mathbf{a}$ and $\mathbf{b}$ are not perpendicular. In this case, $\mathbf{w}$ will be constructed exactly in the direction of $\mathbf{a}$, and $\mathbf{v}$ is chosen to be the closest vector to $\mathbf{b}$ among all vectors perpendicular to $\mathbf{w}$.

This procedure *won't* work if $\mathbf{a}$ and $\mathbf{b}$ are collinear. In this case $\mathbf{b}$ is of no help in choosing which of the directions perpendicular to $\mathbf{a}$ we should use: it is perpendicular to all of them.

In the example of specifying camera positions (Section 4.3), we want to construct a frame that has $\mathbf{w}$ parallel to the direction the camera is looking, and $\mathbf{v}$ should point out the top of the camera. To orient the camera upright, we build the basis around the view direction, using the straight-up direction as the reference vector to establish the camera's orientation around the view direction. Setting $\mathbf{v}$ as close as possible to straight up exactly matches the intuitive notion of "holding the camera straight."

2.4.8 Squaring Up a Basis

Occasionally you may find problems caused in your computations by a basis that is supposed to be orthonormal but where error has crept in—due to rounding error in computation, or to the basis having been stored in a file with low precision, for instance.

The procedure of the previous section can be used; simply constructing the basis anew using the existing $\mathbf{w}$ and $\mathbf{v}$ vectors will produce a new basis that is orthonormal and is close to the old one.

This approach is good for many applications, but it is not the best available. It does produce accurately orthogonal vectors, and for nearly orthogonal starting bases the result will not stray far from the starting point. However, it is asymmetric: it "favors" $\mathbf{w}$ over $\mathbf{v}$ and $\mathbf{v}$ over $\mathbf{u}$ (whose starting value is thrown away). It chooses a basis close to the starting basis but has no guarantee of choosing *the* closest orthonormal basis. When this is not good enough, the SVD (Section 5.4.1) can be used to compute an orthonormal basis that *is* guaranteed to be closest to the original basis.

If you want me to set $\mathbf{w}$ and $\mathbf{v}$ to two non-perpendicular directions, something has to give—with this scheme I'll set everything the way you want, except I'll make the smallest change to $\mathbf{v}$ so that it is in fact perpendicular to $\mathbf{w}$.

What will go wrong with the computation if $\mathbf{a}$ and $\mathbf{b}$ are parallel?

2.5 Curves and Surfaces

The geometry of curves, and especially surfaces, plays a central role in graphics, and here we review the basics of curves and surfaces in 2D and 3D space.

2.5.1 2D Implicit Curves

Intuitively, a *curve* is a set of points that can be drawn on a piece of paper without lifting the pen. A common way to describe a curve is using an *implicit equation*. An implicit equation in two dimensions has the form

$$f(x, y) = 0.$$

The function $f(x, y)$ returns a real value. Points (x, y) where this value is zero are on the curve, and points where the value is non-zero are not on the curve. For example, let's say that $f(x, y)$ is

$$f(x, y) = (x - x_c)^2 + (y - y_c)^2 - r^2, \tag{2.9}$$

where (x_c, y_c) is a 2D point and r is a non-zero real number. If we take $f(x, y) = 0$, the points where this equality holds are on the circle with center (x_c, y_c) and radius r. The reason that this is called an "implicit" equation is that the points (x, y) on the curve cannot be immediately calculated from the equation and instead must be determined by solving the equation. Thus, the points on the curve are not generated by the equation *explicitly*, but they are buried somewhere *implicitly* in the equation.

It is interesting to note that f does have values for all (x, y). We can think of f as a terrain, with sea-level at $f = 0$ (Figure 2.22). The shore is the implicit curve. The value of f is the altitude. Another thing to note is that the curve partitions space into regions where $f > 0$, $f < 0$, and $f = 0$. So you evaluate f to decide whether a point is "inside" a curve. Note that $f(x, y) = c$ is a curve for any constant c, and $c = 0$ is just used as a convention. For example if $f(x, y) = x^2 + y^2 - 1$, varying c just gives a variety of circles centered at the origin (Figure 2.23).

We can compress our notation using vectors. If we have $\mathbf{c} = (x_c, y_c)$ and $\mathbf{p} = (x, y)$, then our circle with center $\mathbf{c}$ and radius r is defined by those position vectors that satisfy

$$(\mathbf{p} - \mathbf{c}) \cdot (\mathbf{p} - \mathbf{c}) - r^2 = 0.$$

This equation, if expanded algebraically, will yield Equation (2.9), but it is easier to see that this is an equation for a circle by "reading" the equation geometrically. It reads, "points $\mathbf{p}$ on the circle have the following property: the vector from $\mathbf{c}$ to

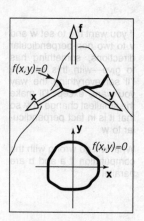

Figure 2.22. An implicit function $f(x,y) = 0$ can be thought of as a height field where f is the height (top). A path where the height is zero is the implicit curve (bottom).

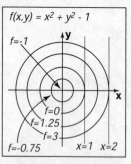

Figure 2.23. An implicit function $f(x,y) = 0$ can be thought of as a height field where f is the height (top). A path where the height is zero is the implicit curve (bottom).

p when dotted with itself has value r^2." Because a vector dotted with itself is just its own length squared, we could also read the equation as, "points **p** on the circle have the following property: the vector from **c** to **p** has squared length r^2."

Even better, is to observe that the squared length is just the squared distance from **c** to **p**, which suggests the equivalent form

$$\|\mathbf{p} - \mathbf{c}\|^2 - r^2 = 0,$$

and, of course, this suggests

$$\|\mathbf{p} - \mathbf{c}\| - r = 0.$$

The above could be read "the points **p** on the circle are those a distance r from the center point **c**," which is as good a definition of circle as any. This illustrates that the vector form of an equation often suggests more geometry and intuition than the equivalent full-blown Cartesian form with x and y. For this reason, it is usually advisable to use vector forms when possible. In addition, you can support a vector class in your code; the code is cleaner when vector forms are used. The vector-oriented equations are also less error prone in implementation: once you implement and debug vector types in your code, the cut-and-paste errors involving x, y, and z will go away. It takes a little while to get used to vectors in these equations, but once you get the hang of it, the payoff is large.

2.5.2   The 2D Gradient

If we think of the function $f(x, y)$ as a height field with height $= f(x, y)$, the *gradient* vector points in the direction of maximum upslope, i.e., straight uphill. The gradient vector $\nabla f(x, y)$ is given by

$$\nabla f(x, y) = \left(\frac{\partial f}{\partial x}, \frac{\partial f}{\partial y} \right).$$

The gradient vector evaluated at a point on the implicit curve $f(x, y) = 0$ is perpendicular to the *tangent* vector of the curve at that point. This perpendicular vector is usually called the *normal vector* to the curve. In addition, since the gradient points uphill, it indicates the direction of the $f(x, y) > 0$ region.

In the context of height fields, the geometric meaning of partial derivatives and gradients is more visible than usual. Suppose that near the point (a, b), $f(x, y)$ is a plane (Figure 2.24). There is a specific uphill and downhill direction. At right angles to this direction is a direction that is level with respect to the plane. Any intersection between the plane and the $f(x, y) = 0$ plane will be in the direction that is level. Thus the uphill/downhill directions will be perpendicular to the line of intersection $f(x, y) = 0$. To see why the partial derivative has something to do

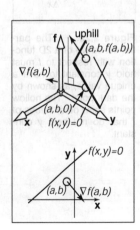

Figure 2.24. A surface height $= f(x,y)$ is locally planar near $(x,y) = (a,b)$. The gradient is a projection of the uphill direction onto the height $= 0$ plane.

with this, we need to visualize its geometric meaning. Recall that the conventional derivative of a 1D function $y = g(x)$ is

$$\frac{dy}{dx} \equiv \lim_{\Delta x \to 0} \frac{\Delta y}{\Delta x} = \lim_{\Delta x \to 0} \frac{g(x + \Delta x) - g(x)}{\Delta x}. \tag{2.10}$$

This measures the *slope* of the *tangent* line to g (Figure 2.25).

The partial derivative is a generalization of the 1D derivative. For a 2D function $f(x, y)$, we can't take the same limit for x as in Equation (2.10), because f can change in many ways for a given change in x. However, if we hold y constant, we can define an analog of the derivative, called the *partial derivative* (Figure 2.26):

$$\frac{\partial f}{\partial x} \equiv \lim_{\Delta x \to 0} \frac{f(x + \Delta x, y) - f(x, y)}{\Delta x}.$$

Why is it that the partial derivatives of x and y are the components of the gradient vector? Again, there is more obvious insight in the geometry than in the algebra. In Figure 2.27, we see the vector **a** travels along a path where **f** does not change. Note that this is again at a small enough scale that the surface height $(x, y) = f(x, y)$ can be considered locally planar. From the figure, we see that the vector $\mathbf{a} = (\Delta x, \Delta y)$.

Because the uphill direction is perpendicular to **a**, we know the dot product is equal to zero:

$$(\nabla f) \cdot \mathbf{a} \equiv (x_\nabla, y_\nabla) \cdot (x_a, y_a) = x_\nabla \Delta x + y_\nabla \Delta y = 0. \tag{2.11}$$

We also know that the change in f in the direction (x_a, y_a) equals zero:

$$\Delta f = \frac{\partial f}{\partial x} \Delta x + \frac{\partial f}{\partial y} \Delta y \equiv \frac{\partial f}{\partial x} x_a + \frac{\partial f}{\partial y} y_a = 0. \tag{2.12}$$

Given any vectors (x, y) and (x', y') that are perpendicular, we know that the angle between them is 90 degrees, and thus their dot product equals zero (recall that the dot product is proportional to the cosine of the angle between the two vectors). Thus, we have $xx' + yy' = 0$. Given (x, y), it is easy to construct valid vectors whose dot product with (x, y) equals zero, the two most obvious being $(y, -x)$ and $(-y, x)$; you can verify that these vectors give the desired zero dot product with (x, y). A generalization of this observation is that (x, y) is perpendicular to $k(y, -x)$ where k is any non-zero constant. This implies that

$$(x_a, y_a) = k \left(\frac{\partial f}{\partial y}, -\frac{\partial f}{\partial x} \right). \tag{2.13}$$

Combining Equations (2.11) and (2.13) gives

$$(x_\nabla, y_\nabla) = k' \left(\frac{\partial f}{\partial x}, \frac{\partial f}{\partial y} \right),$$

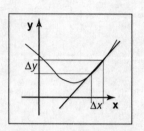

Figure 2.25. The derivative of a 1D function measures the slope of the line tangent to the curve.

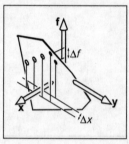

Figure 2.26. The partial derivative of a 2D function with respect to *f* must hold *y* constant to have a unique value, as shown by the dark point. The hollow points show other values of *f* that do not hold *y* constant.

where k' is any non-zero constant. By definition, "uphill" implies a positive change in f, so we would like $k' > 0$, and $k' = 1$ is a perfectly good convention.

As an example of the gradient, consider the implicit circle $x^2 + y^2 - 1 = 0$ with gradient vector $(2x, 2y)$, indicating that the outside of the circle is the positive region for the function $f(x, y) = x^2 + y^2 - 1$. Note that the length of the gradient vector can be different depending on the multiplier in the implicit equation. For example, the unit circle can be described by $Ax^2 + Ay^2 - A = 0$ for any non-zero A. The gradient for this curve is $(2Ax, 2Ay)$. This will be normal (perpendicular) to the circle, but will have a length determined by A. For $A > 0$, the normal will point outward from the circle, and for $A < 0$, it will point inward. This switch from outward to inward is as it should be, since the positive region switches inside the circle. In terms of the height-field view, $h = Ax^2 + Ay^2 - A$, and the circle is at zero altitude. For $A > 0$, the circle encloses a depression, and for $A < 0$, the circle encloses a bump. As A becomes more negative, the bump increases in height, but the $h = 0$ circle doesn't change. The direction of maximum uphill doesn't change, but the slope increases. The length of the gradient reflects this change in degree of the slope. So intuitively, you can think of the gradient's direction as pointing uphill and its magnitude as measuring how uphill the slope is.

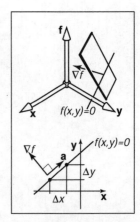

Figure 2.27. The vector **a** points in a direction where f has no change and is thus perpendicular to the gradient vector ∇f.

Implicit 2D Lines

The familiar "slope-intercept" form of the line is

$$y = mx + b. \tag{2.14}$$

This can be converted easily to implicit form (Figure 2.28):

$$y - mx - b = 0. \tag{2.15}$$

Here m is the "slope" (ratio of rise to run) and b is the y value where the line crosses the y-axis, usually called the *y-intercept*. The line also partitions the 2D plane, but here "inside" and "outside" might be more intuitively called "over" and "under."

Because we can multiply an implicit equation by any constant without changing the points where it is zero, $kf(x, y) = 0$ is the same curve for any non-zero k. This allows several implicit forms for the same line, for example,

$$2y - 2mx - 2b = 0.$$

One reason the slope-intercept form is sometimes awkward is that it can't represent some lines such as $x = 0$ because m would have to be infinite. For this

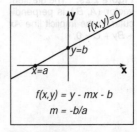

Figure 2.28. A 2D line can be described by the equation $y - mx - b = 0$.

reason, a more general form is often useful:

$$Ax + By + C = 0, \tag{2.16}$$

for real numbers A, B, C.

Suppose we know two points on the line, (x_0, y_0) and (x_1, y_1). What A, B, and C describe the line through these two points? Because these points lie on the line, they must both satisfy Equation (2.16):

$$Ax_0 + By_0 + C = 0,$$
$$Ax_1 + By_1 + C = 0.$$

Unfortunately we have two equations and *three* unknowns: A, B, and C. This problem arises because of the arbitrary multiplier we can have with an implicit equation. We could set $C = 1$ for convenience:

$$Ax + By + 1 = 0,$$

but we have a similar problem to the infinite slope case in slope-intercept form: lines through the origin would need to have $A(0) + B(0) + 1 = 0$, which is a contradiction. For example, the equation for a 45-degree line through the origin can be written $x - y = 0$, or equally well $y - x = 0$, or even $17y - 17x = 0$, but it cannot be written in the form $Ax + By + 1 = 0$.

Whenever we have such pesky algebraic problems, we try to solve the problems using geometric intuition as a guide. One tool we have, as discussed in Section 2.5.2, is the gradient. For the line $Ax + By + C = 0$, the gradient vector is (A, B). This vector is perpendicular to the line (Figure 2.29), and points to the side of the line where $Ax + By + C$ is positive. Given two points on the line (x_0, y_0) and (x_1, y_1), we know that the vector between them points in the same direction as the line. This vector is just $(x_1 - x_0, y_1 - y_0)$, and because it is parallel to the line, it must also be perpendicular to the gradient vector (A, B). Recall that there are an infinite number of (A, B, C) that describe the line because of the arbitrary scaling property of implicits. We want any one of the valid (A, B, C).

We can start with any (A, B) perpendicular to $(x_1 - x_0, y_1 - y_0)$. Such a vector is just $(A, B) = (y_0 - y_1, x_1 - x_0)$ by the same reasoning as in Section 2.5.2. This means that the equation of the line through (x_0, y_0) and (x_1, y_1) is

$$(y_0 - y_1)x + (x_1 - x_0)y + C = 0. \tag{2.17}$$

Now we just need to find C. Because (x_0, y_0) and (x_1, y_1) are on the line, they must satisfy Equation (2.17). We can plug either value in and solve for C. Doing this for (x_0, y_0) yields $C = x_0 y_1 - x_1 y_0$, and thus the full equation for the line is

$$(y_0 - y_1)x + (x_1 - x_0)y + x_0 y_1 - x_1 y_0 = 0. \tag{2.18}$$

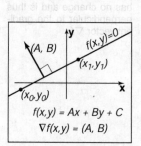

f(x,y) = Ax + By + C

$\nabla f(x,y) = (A, B)$

Figure 2.29. The gradient vector (A, B) is perpendicular to the implicit line $Ax + By + C = 0$.

Again, this is one of infinitely many valid implicit equations for the line through two points, but this form has no division operation and thus no numerically degenerate cases for points with finite Cartesian coordinates. A nice thing about Equation (2.18) is that we can always convert to the slope-intercept form (when it exists) by moving the non-y terms to the right-hand side of the equation and dividing by the multiplier of the y term:

$$y = \frac{y_1 - y_0}{x_1 - x_0}x + \frac{x_1 y_0 - x_0 y_1}{x_1 - x_0}.$$

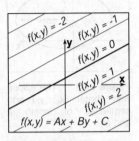

Figure 2.30. The value of the implicit function $f(x,y)$ = $Ax + By + C$ is a constant times the signed distance from $Ax + By + C = 0$.

An interesting property of the implicit line equation is that it can be used to find the signed distance from a point to the line. The value of $Ax + By + C$ is proportional to the distance from the line (Figure 2.30). As shown in Figure 2.31, the distance from a point to the line is the length of the vector $k(A, B)$, which is

$$\text{distance} = k\sqrt{A^2 + B^2}. \tag{2.19}$$

For the point $(x, y) + k(A, B)$, the value of $f(x, y) = Ax + By + C$ is

$$
\begin{aligned}
f(x + kA, y + kB) &= Ax + kA^2 + By + kB^2 + C \\
&= k(A^2 + B^2).
\end{aligned}
\tag{2.20}
$$

The simplification in that equation is a result of the fact that we know (x, y) is on the line, so $Ax + By + C = 0$. From Equations (2.19) and (2.20), we can see that the signed distance from line $Ax + By + C = 0$ to a point (a, b) is

$$\text{distance} = \frac{f(a, b)}{\sqrt{A^2 + B^2}}.$$

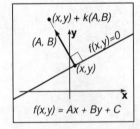

Figure 2.31. The vector $k(A,B)$ connects a point (x,y) on the line closest to a point not on the line. The distance is proportional to k.

Here "signed distance" means that its magnitude (absolute value) is the geometric distance, but on one side of the line, distances are positive and on the other they are negative. You can choose between the equally valid representations $f(x, y) = 0$ and $-f(x, y) = 0$ if your problem has some reason to prefer a particular side being positive. Note that if (A, B) is a unit vector, then $f(a, b)$ is the signed distance. We can multiply Equation (2.18) by a constant that ensures that (A, B) is a unit vector:

$$
\begin{aligned}
f(x, y) = \frac{y_0 - y_1}{\sqrt{(x_1 - x_0)^2 + (y_0 - y_1)^2}}x + \frac{x_1 - x_0}{\sqrt{(x_1 - x_0)^2 + (y_0 - y_1)^2}}y \\
+ \frac{x_0 y_1 - x_1 y_0}{\sqrt{(x_1 - x_0)^2 + (y_0 - y_1)^2}} = 0. \quad (2.21)
\end{aligned}
$$

Note that evaluating $f(x, y)$ in Equation (2.21) directly gives the signed distance, but it does require a square root to set up the equation. Implicit lines will turn out to be very useful for triangle rasterization (Section 8.1.2). Other forms for 2D lines are discussed in Chapter 14.

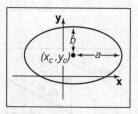

Figure 2.32. The ellipse with center $(x_c,\ y_c)$ and semi-axes of length a and b.

Try setting $a = b = r$ in the ellipse equation and compare to the circle equation.

Implicit Quadric Curves

In the previous section we saw that a linear function $f(x, y)$ gives rise to an implicit line $f(x, y) = 0$. If f is instead a quadratic function of x and y, with the general form

$$Ax^2 + Bxy + Cy^2 + Dx + Ey + F = 0,$$

the resulting implicit curve is called a quadric. Two-dimensional quadric curves include ellipses and hyperbolas, as well as the special cases of parabolas, circles, and lines.

Examples of quadric curves include the circle with center (x_c, y_c) and radius r:

$$(x - x_c)^2 + (y - y_c)^2 - r^2 = 0$$

where (x_c, y_c) is the center of the ellipse, and a and b are the minor and major semi-axes (Figure 2.32).and axis-aligned ellipses of the form

$$\frac{(x - x_c)^2}{a^2} + \frac{(y - y_c)^2}{b^2} - 1 = 0.$$

2.5.3   3D Implicit Surfaces

Just as implicit equations can be used to define curves in 2D, they can be used to define surfaces in 3D. As in 2D, implicit equations *implicitly* define a set of points that are on the surface

$$f(x, y, z) = 0.$$

Any point (x, y, z) that is on the surface results in zero when given as an argument to f. Any point not on the surface results in some number other than zero. You can check whether a point is on the surface by evaluating f, or you can check which side of the surface the point lies on by looking at the sign of f, but you cannot always explicitly construct points on the surface. Using vector notation, we will write such functions of $\mathbf{p} = (x, y, z)$ as

$$f(\mathbf{p}) = 0.$$

2.5.4   Surface Normal to an Implicit Surface

A surface normal (which is needed for lighting computations, among other things) is a vector perpendicular to the surface. Each point on the surface may have a different normal vector. In the same way that the gradient provides a normal to an implicit curve in 2D, the surface normal at a point $\mathbf{p}$ on an implicit surface is given by the gradient of the implicit function

$$\mathbf{n} = \nabla f(\mathbf{p}) = \left(\frac{\partial f(\mathbf{p})}{\partial x}, \frac{\partial f(\mathbf{p})}{\partial y}, \frac{\partial f(\mathbf{p})}{\partial z} \right).$$

The reasoning is the same as for the 2D case: the gradient points in the direction of fastest increase in f, which is perpendicular to the direction's tangent to the surface, in which f remains constant. The gradient vector points toward the side of the surface where $f(\mathbf{p}) > 0$, which we may think of as "into" the surface or "out from" the surface in a given context. If the particular form of f creates inward facing gradients and outward facing gradients are desired, the surface $-f(\mathbf{p}) = 0$ is the same as surface $f(\mathbf{p}) = 0$ but has directionally reversed gradients, i.e., $-\nabla f(\mathbf{p}) = \nabla(-f(\mathbf{p}))$.

2.5.5   Implicit Planes

As an example, consider the infinite plane through point $\mathbf{a}$ with surface normal $\mathbf{n}$. The implicit equation to describe this plane is given by

$$(\mathbf{p} - \mathbf{a}) \cdot \mathbf{n} = 0. \tag{2.22}$$

Note that $\mathbf{a}$ and $\mathbf{n}$ are known quantities. The point $\mathbf{p}$ is any unknown point that satisfies the equation. In geometric terms this equation says "the vector from $\mathbf{a}$ to $\mathbf{p}$ is perpendicular to the plane normal." If $\mathbf{p}$ were not in the plane, then $(\mathbf{p} - \mathbf{a})$ would not make a right angle with $\mathbf{n}$ (Figure 2.33).

Sometimes we want the implicit equation for a plane through points $\mathbf{a}$, $\mathbf{b}$, and $\mathbf{c}$. The normal to this plane can be found by taking the cross product of any two vectors in the plane. One such cross product is

$$\mathbf{n} = (\mathbf{b} - \mathbf{a}) \times (\mathbf{c} - \mathbf{a}).$$

This allows us to write the implicit plane equation:

$$(\mathbf{p} - \mathbf{a}) \cdot ((\mathbf{b} - \mathbf{a}) \times (\mathbf{c} - \mathbf{a})) = 0. \tag{2.23}$$

A geometric way to read this equation is that the volume of the parallelepiped defined by $\mathbf{p} - \mathbf{a}$, $\mathbf{b} - \mathbf{a}$, and $\mathbf{c} - \mathbf{a}$ is zero, i.e., they are coplanar. This can only be true if $\mathbf{p}$ is in the same plane as $\mathbf{a}$, $\mathbf{b}$, and $\mathbf{c}$. The full-blown Cartesian representation for this is given by the determinant (this is discussed in more detail in Section 5.3):

$$\begin{vmatrix} x - x_a & y - y_a & z - z_a \\ x_b - x_a & y_b - y_a & z_b - z_a \\ x_c - x_a & y_c - y_a & z_c - z_a \end{vmatrix} = 0. \tag{2.24}$$

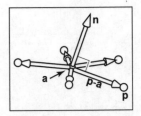

Figure 2.33.   Any of the points $\mathbf{p}$ shown are in the plane with normal vector $\mathbf{n}$ that includes point $\mathbf{a}$ if Equation (2.2) is satisfied.

The determinant can be expanded (see Section 5.3 for the mechanics of expanding determinants) to the bloated form with many terms.

Equations (2.23) and (2.24) are equivalent, and comparing them is instructive. Equation (2.23) is easy to interpret geometrically and will yield efficient code. In addition, it is relatively easy to avoid a typographic error that compiles into incorrect code if it takes advantage of debugged cross and dot product code. Equation (2.24) is also easy to interpret geometrically and will be efficient provided an efficient 3×3 determinant function is implemented. It is also easy to implement without a typo if a function $determinant(\mathbf{a}, \mathbf{b}, \mathbf{c})$ is available. It will be especially easy for others to read your code if you rename the $determinant$ function $volume$. So both Equations (2.23) and (2.24) map well into code. The full expansion of either equation into x-, y-, and z-components is likely to generate typos. Such typos are likely to compile and, thus, be especially pesky. This is an excellent example of clean math generating clean code and bloated math generating bloated code.

3D Quadric Surfaces

Just as quadratic polynomials in two variables define quadric curves in 2D, quadratic polynomials in x, y, and z define *quadric surfaces* in 3D. For instance, a sphere can be written as

$$f(\mathbf{p}) = (\mathbf{p} - \mathbf{c})^2 - r^2 = 0,$$

and an axis-aligned ellipsoid may be written as

$$f(\mathbf{p}) = \frac{(x - x_c)^2}{a^2} + \frac{(y - y_c)^2}{b^2} + \frac{(z - z_c)^2}{c^2} - 1 = 0.$$

3D Curves from Implicit Surfaces

One might hope that an implicit 3D curve could be created with the form $f(\mathbf{p}) = 0$. However, all such curves are just degenerate surfaces and are rarely useful in practice. A 3D curve can be constructed from the intersection of two simultaneous implicit equations:

$$f(\mathbf{p}) = 0,$$
$$g(\mathbf{p}) = 0.$$

For example, a 3D line can be formed from the intersection of two implicit planes. Typically, it is more convenient to use parametric curves instead; they are discussed in the following sections.

2.5.6   2D Parametric Curves

A *parametric* curve is controlled by a single *parameter* that can be considered a sort of index that moves continuously along the curve. Such curves have the form

$$\begin{bmatrix} x \\ y \end{bmatrix} = \begin{bmatrix} g(t) \\ h(t) \end{bmatrix}.$$

Here (x, y) is a point on the curve, and t is the parameter that influences the curve. For a given t, there will be some point determined by the functions g and h. For continuous g and h, a small change in t will yield a small change in x and y. Thus, as t continuously changes, points are swept out in a continuous curve. This is a nice feature because we can use the parameter t to explicitly construct points on the curve. Often we can write a parametric curve in vector form,

$$\mathbf{p} = f(t),$$

where f is a vector-valued function, $f : \mathbb{R} \mapsto \mathbb{R}^2$. Such vector functions can generate very clean code, so they should be used when possible.

We can think of the curve with a position as a function of time. The curve can go anywhere and could loop and cross itself. We can also think of the curve as having a velocity at any point. For example, the point $\mathbf{p}(t)$ is traveling slowly near $t = -2$ and quickly between $t = 2$ and $t = 3$. This type of "moving point" vocabulary is often used when discussing parametric curves even when the curve is not describing a moving point.

2D Parametric Lines

A parametric line in 2D that passes through points $\mathbf{p}_0 = (x_0, y_0)$ and $\mathbf{p}_1 = (x_1, y_1)$ can be written

$$\begin{bmatrix} x \\ y \end{bmatrix} = \begin{bmatrix} x_0 + t(x_1 - x_0) \\ y_0 + t(y_1 - y_0) \end{bmatrix}.$$

Because the formulas for x and y have such similar structure, we can use the vector form for $\mathbf{p} = (x, y)$ (Figure 2.34):

$$\mathbf{p}(t) = \mathbf{p}_0 + t(\mathbf{p}_1 - \mathbf{p}_0).$$

You can read this in geometric form as: "start at point $\mathbf{p}_0$ and go some distance toward $\mathbf{p}_1$ determined by the parameter t." A nice feature of this form is that $\mathbf{p}(0) = \mathbf{p}_0$ and $\mathbf{p}(1) = \mathbf{p}_1$. Since the point changes linearly with t, the value of t between $\mathbf{p}_0$ and $\mathbf{p}_1$ measures the fractional distance between the points. Points

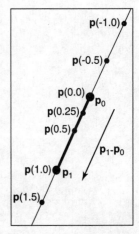

Figure 2.34.   A 2D parametric line through $\mathbf{p}_0$ and $\mathbf{p}_1$. The line segment defined by $t \in [0,1]$ is shown in bold.

with $t < 0$ are to the "far" side of $\mathbf{p}_0$, and points with $t > 1$ are to the "far" side of $\mathbf{p}_1$.

Parametric lines can also be described as just a point $\mathbf{o}$ and a vector $\mathbf{d}$:

$$\mathbf{p}(t) = \mathbf{o} + t(\mathbf{d}).$$

When the vector $\mathbf{d}$ has unit length, the line is *arc-length parameterized*. This means t is an exact measure of distance along the line. Any parametric curve can be arc-length parameterized, which is obviously a very convenient form, but not all can be converted analytically.

2D Parametric Circles

A circle with center (x_c, y_c) and radius r has a parametric form:

$$\begin{bmatrix} x \\ y \end{bmatrix} = \begin{bmatrix} x_c + r\cos\phi \\ y_c + r\sin\phi \end{bmatrix}.$$

To ensure that there is a unique parameter ϕ for every point on the curve, we can restrict its domain: $\phi \in [0, 2\pi)$ or $\phi \in (-\pi, \pi]$ or any other half open interval of length 2π.

An axis-aligned ellipse can be constructed by scaling the x and y parametric equations separately:

$$\begin{bmatrix} x \\ y \end{bmatrix} = \begin{bmatrix} x_c + a\cos\phi \\ y_c + b\sin\phi \end{bmatrix}.$$

2.5.7   3D Parametric Curves

A 3D parametric curve operates much like a 2D parametric curve:

$$x = f(t),$$
$$y = g(t),$$
$$z = h(t).$$

For example, a spiral around the z-axis is written as:

$$x = \cos t,$$
$$y = \sin t,$$
$$z = t.$$

Figure 2.34. A 2D parametric line through $\mathbf{p}_0$ and $\mathbf{p}_1$. The line segment described by $t \in [0,1]$ is shown in bold.

As with 2D curves, the functions f, g, and h are defined on a domain $D \subset \mathbb{R}$ if we want to control where the curve starts and ends. In vector form we can write

$$\begin{bmatrix} x \\ y \\ z \end{bmatrix} = \mathbf{p}(t).$$

In this chapter we only discuss 3D parametric lines in detail. General 3D parametric curves are discussed more extensively in Chapter 15.

The parametric curve is the range of $\mathbf{p}\colon \mathbb{R} \to \mathbb{R}^3$.

3D Parametric Lines

A 3D parametric line can be written as a straightforward extension of the 2D parametric line, e.g.,

$$x = 2 + 7t,$$
$$y = 1 + 2t,$$
$$z = 3 - 5t.$$

This is cumbersome and does not translate well to code variables, so we will write it in vector form:

$$\mathbf{p} = \mathbf{o} + t\mathbf{d},$$

where, for this example, $\mathbf{o}$ and $\mathbf{d}$ are given by

$$\mathbf{o} = (2, 1, \quad 3),$$
$$\mathbf{d} = (7, 2, -5).$$

Note that this is very similar to the 2D case. The way to visualize this is to imagine that the line passes though $\mathbf{o}$ and is parallel to $\mathbf{d}$. Given any value of t, you get some point $\mathbf{p}(t)$ on the line. For example, at $t = 2$, $p(t) = (2, 1, 3) + 2(7, 2, -5) = (16, 5, -7)$. This general concept is the same as for two dimensions (Figure 2.30).

As in 2D, a *line segment* can be described by a 3D parametric line and an interval $t \in [t_a, t_b]$. The line segment between two points $\mathbf{a}$ and $\mathbf{b}$ is given by $\mathbf{p}(t) = \mathbf{a} + t(\mathbf{b} - \mathbf{a})$ with $t \in [0, 1]$. Here $\mathbf{p}(0) = \mathbf{a}$, $\mathbf{p}(1) = \mathbf{b}$, and $\mathbf{p}(0.5) = (\mathbf{a} + \mathbf{b})/2$, the midpoint between $\mathbf{a}$ and $\mathbf{b}$.

A *ray*, or *half-line*, is a 3D parametric line with a half-open interval, usually $[0, \infty)$. From now on we will refer to all lines, line segments, and rays as "rays." This is sloppy, but corresponds to common usage and makes the discussion simpler.

2.5.8 3D Parametric Surfaces

The parametric approach can be used to define surfaces in 3D space in much the same way we define curves, except that there are two parameters to address the two-dimensional area of the surface. These surfaces have the form

$$x = f(u, v),$$
$$y = g(u, v),$$
$$z = h(u, v).$$

The parametric surface is the range of the function $\mathbf{p}$: $\mathbb{R}^2 \to \mathbb{R}^3$.

or, in vector form,

$$\begin{bmatrix} x \\ y \\ z \end{bmatrix} = \mathbf{p}(u, v).$$

Pretend for the sake of argument that the Earth is exactly spherical.

The θ and ϕ here may or may not seem reversed depending on your background; the use of these symbols varies across disciplines. In this book we will always assume the meaning of θ and ϕ used in Equation (2.25) and depicted in Figure 2.35.

Example. For example, a point on the surface of the Earth can be described by the two parameters longitude and latitude. If we define the origin to be at the center of the earth, and let r be the radius of the Earth, then a spherical coordinate system centered at the origin (Figure 2.35), lets us derive the parametric equations

$$x = r \cos\phi \sin\theta,$$
$$y = r \sin\phi \sin\theta, \qquad (2.25)$$
$$z = r \cos\theta.$$

Ideally, we'd like to write this in vector form, but it isn't feasible for this particular parametric form.

We would also like to be able to find the (θ, ϕ) for a given (x, y, z). If we assume that $\phi \in (-\pi, \pi]$ this is easy to do using the *atan2* function from Equation (2.2):

$$\theta = \mathrm{acos}(z/\sqrt{x^2 + y^2 + z^2}),$$
$$\phi = \mathrm{atan2}(y, x). \qquad (2.26)$$

Figure 2.35. The geometry for spherical coordinates.

With implicit surfaces, the derivative of the function f gave us the surface normal. With parametric surfaces, the derivatives of $\mathbf{p}$ also give information about the surface geometry.

Consider the function $\mathbf{q}(t) = \mathbf{p}(t, v_0)$. This function defines a parametric curve obtained by varying u while holding v fixed at the value v_0. This curve, called an *isoparametric curve* (or sometimes "isoparm" for short) lies in the surface. The derivative of $\mathbf{q}$ gives a vector tangent to the curve, and since the curve lies in the surface the vector $\mathbf{q}'$ also lies in the surface. Since it was obtained by varying one argument of $\mathbf{p}$, the vector $\mathbf{q}'$ is the partial derivative of $\mathbf{p}$ with respect to u, which we'll denote $\mathbf{p}_u$. A similar argument shows that the partial derivative $\mathbf{p}_v$ gives the tangent to the isoparametric curves for constant u, which is a second tangent vector to the surface.

The derivative of $\mathbf{p}$, then, gives two tangent vectors at any point on the surface. The normal to the surface may be found by taking the cross product of these vectors: since both are tangent to the surface, their cross product, which is perpendicular to both tangents, is normal to the surface. The right-hand rule for cross products provides a way to decide which side is the front, or outside, of the surface; we will use the convention that the vector

$$\mathbf{n} = \mathbf{p}_u \times \mathbf{p}_v$$

points toward the outside of the surface.

2.5.9 Summary of Curves and Surfaces

Implicit curves in 2D or surfaces in 3D are defined by scalar-valued functions of two or three variables, $f : \mathbb{R}^2 \to \mathbb{R}$ or $f : \mathbb{R}^3 \to \mathbb{R}$, and the surface consists of all points where the function is zero:

$$S = \{\mathbf{p}\,|\,f(\mathbf{p}) = 0\}.$$

Parametric curves in 2D or 3D are defined by vector-valued functions of one variable, $\mathbf{p} : D \subset \mathbb{R} \to \mathbb{R}^2$ or $\mathbf{p} : D \subset \mathbb{R} \to \mathbb{R}^3$, and the curve is swept out as t varies over all of D:

$$S = \{\mathbf{p}(t)\,|\,t \in D\}.$$

Parametric surfaces in 3D are defined by vector-valued functions of two variables, $\mathbf{p} : D \subset \mathbb{R}^2 \to \mathbb{R}^3$, and the surface consists of the images of all points (u, v) in the domain:

$$S = \{\mathbf{p}(t)\,|\,(u, v) \in D\}.$$

For implicit curves and surfaces, the normal vector is given by the derivative of f (the gradient), and the tangent vector (for a curve) or vectors (for a surface) can be derived from the normal by constructing a basis.

For parametric curves and surfaces, the derivative of $\mathbf{p}$ gives the tangent vector (for a curve) or vectors (for a surface), and the normal vector can be derived from the tangents by constructing a basis.

2.6   Linear Interpolation

Perhaps the most common mathematical operation in graphics is *linear interpolation*. We have already seen an example of linear interpolation of position to form line segments in 2D and 3D, where two points **a** and **b** are associated with a parameter t to form the line $\mathbf{p} = (1 - t)\mathbf{a} + t\mathbf{b}$. This is *interpolation* because **p** goes through **a** and **b** exactly at $t = 0$ and $t = 1$. It is *linear* interpolation because the weighting terms t and $1 - t$ are linear polynomials of t.

Another common linear interpolation is among a set of positions on the x-axis: $x_0, x_1, \ldots, x_n$, and for each x_i we have an associated height, y_i. We want to create a continuous function $y = f(x)$ that interpolates these positions, so that f goes through every data point, i.e., $f(x_i) = y_i$. For linear interpolation, the points (x_i, y_i) are connected by straight line segments. It is natural to use parametric line equations for these segments. The parameter t is just the fractional distance between x_i and x_{i+1}:

$$f(x) = y_i + \frac{x - x_i}{x_{i+1} - x_i}(y_{i+1} - y_i). \tag{2.27}$$

Because the weighting functions are linear polynomials of x, this is linear interpolation.

The two examples above have the common form of linear interpolation. We create a variable t that varies from 0 to 1 as we move from data item A to data item B. Intermediate values are just the function $(1 - t)A + tB$. Notice that Equation (2.27) has this form with

$$t = \frac{x - x_i}{x_{i+1} - x_i}.$$

2.7   Triangles

Triangles in both 2D and 3D are the fundamental modeling primitive in many graphics programs. Often information such as color is tagged onto triangle vertices, and this information is interpolated across the triangle. The coordinate system that makes such interpolation straightforward is called *barycentric coordinates*; we will develop these from scratch. We will also discuss 2D triangles, which must be understood before we can draw their pictures on 2D screens.

2.7.1 2D Triangles

If we have a 2D triangle defined by 2D points **a**, **b**, and **c**, we can first find its area:

$$\text{area} = \frac{1}{2} \begin{vmatrix} x_b - x_a & x_c - x_a \\ y_b - y_a & y_c - y_a \end{vmatrix} \qquad (2.28)$$

$$= \frac{1}{2} \left(x_a y_b + x_b y_c + x_c y_a - x_a y_c - x_b y_a - x_c y_b \right).$$

The derivation of this formula can be found in Section 5.3. This area will have a positive sign if the points **a**, **b**, and **c** are in counterclockwise order and a negative sign, otherwise.

Often in graphics, we wish to assign a property, such as color, at each triangle vertex and smoothly interpolate the value of that property across the triangle. There are a variety of ways to do this, but the simplest is to use *barycentric* coordinates. One way to think of barycentric coordinates is as a non-orthogonal coordinate system as was discussed briefly in Section 2.4.2. Such a coordinate system is shown in Figure 2.36, where the coordinate origin is **a** and the vectors from **a** to **b** and **c** are the basis vectors. With that origin and those basis vectors, any point **p** can be written as

$$\mathbf{p} = \mathbf{a} + \beta(\mathbf{b} - \mathbf{a}) + \gamma(\mathbf{c} - \mathbf{a}). \qquad (2.29)$$

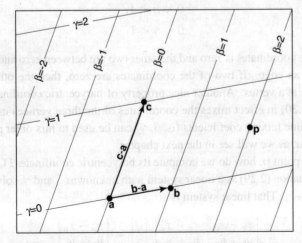

Figure 2.36. A 2D triangle with vertices **a**, **b**, **c** can be used to set up a non-orthogonal coordinate system with origin **a** and basis vectors (**b** – **a**) and (**c** – **a**). A point is then represented by an ordered pair (β, γ). For example, the point **p** = (2.0, 0.5), i.e., **p** = **a** + 2.0 (**b** – **a**) + 0.5 (**c** – **a**).

Note that we can reorder the terms in Equation (2.29) to get

$$\mathbf{p} = (1 - \beta - \gamma)\mathbf{a} + \beta\mathbf{b} + \gamma\mathbf{c}.$$

Often people define a new variable α to improve the symmetry of the equations:

$$\alpha \equiv 1 - \beta - \gamma,$$

which yields the equation

$$\mathbf{p}(\alpha, \beta, \gamma) = \alpha\mathbf{a} + \beta\mathbf{b} + \gamma\mathbf{c}, \tag{2.30}$$

with the constraint that

$$\alpha + \beta + \gamma = 1. \tag{2.31}$$

Barycentric coordinates seem like an abstract and unintuitive construct at first, but they turn out to be powerful and convenient. You may find it useful to think of how street addresses would work in a city where there are two sets of parallel streets, but where those sets are not at right angles. The natural system would essentially be barycentric coordinates, and you would quickly get used to them. Barycentric coordinates are defined for all points on the plane. A particularly nice feature of barycentric coordinates is that a point $\mathbf{p}$ is inside the triangle formed by $\mathbf{a}$, $\mathbf{b}$, and $\mathbf{c}$ if and only if

$$0 < \alpha < 1,$$
$$0 < \beta < 1,$$
$$0 < \gamma < 1.$$

If one of the coordinates is zero and the other two are between zero and one, then you are on an edge. If two of the coordinates are zero, then the other is one, and you are at a vertex. Another nice property of barycentric coordinates is that Equation (2.30) in effect mixes the coordinates of the three vertices in a smooth way. The same mixing coefficients (α, β, γ) can be used to mix other properties, such as color, as we will see in the next chapter.

Given a point $\mathbf{p}$, how do we compute its barycentric coordinates? One way is to write Equation (2.29) as a linear system with unknowns β and γ, solve, and set $\alpha = 1 - \beta - \gamma$. That linear system is

$$\begin{bmatrix} x_b - x_a & x_c - x_a \\ y_b - y_a & y_c - y_a \end{bmatrix} \begin{bmatrix} \beta \\ \gamma \end{bmatrix} = \begin{bmatrix} x_p - x_a \\ y_p - y_a \end{bmatrix}. \tag{2.32}$$

Although it is straightforward to solve Equation (2.32) algebraically, it is often fruitful to compute a direct geometric solution.

One geometric property of barycentric coordinates is that they are the signed scaled distance from the lines through the triangle sides, as is shown for β in Figure 2.37. Recall from Section 2.5.2 that evaluating the equation $f(x, y)$ for the line $f(x, y) = 0$ returns the scaled signed distance from (x, y) to the line. Also recall that if $f(x, y) = 0$ is the equation for a particular line, so is $kf(x, y) = 0$ for any non-zero k. Changing k scales the distance and controls which side of the line has positive signed distance, and which negative. We would like to choose k such that, for example, $kf(x, y) = \beta$. Since k is only one unknown, we can force this with one constraint, namely that at point $\mathbf{b}$ we know $\beta = 1$. So if the line $f_{ac}(x, y) = 0$ goes through both $\mathbf{a}$ and $\mathbf{c}$, then we can compute β for a point (x, y) as follows:

$$\beta = \frac{f_{ac}(x, y)}{f_{ac}(x_b, y_b)}, \tag{2.33}$$

and we can compute γ and α in a similar fashion. For efficiency, it is usually wise to compute only two of the barycentric coordinates directly and to compute the third using Equation (2.31).

To find this "ideal" form for the line through $\mathbf{p}_0$ and $\mathbf{p}_1$, we can first use the technique of Section 2.5.2 to find *some* valid implicit lines through the vertices. Equation (2.18) gives us

$$f_{ab}(x, y) \equiv (y_a - y_b)x + (x_b - x_a)y + x_a y_b - x_b y_a = 0.$$

Note that $f_{ab}(x_c, y_c)$ probably does not equal one, so it is probably not the ideal form we seek. By dividing through by $f_{ab}(x_c, y_c)$ we get

$$\gamma = \frac{(y_a - y_b)x + (x_b - x_a)y + x_a y_b - x_b y_a}{(y_a - y_b)x_c + (x_b - x_a)y_c + x_a y_b - x_b y_a}.$$

The presence of the division might worry us because it introduces the possibility of divide-by-zero, but this cannot occur for triangles with areas that are not near zero. There are analogous formulas for α and β, but typically only one is needed:

$$\beta = \frac{(y_a - y_c)x + (x_c - x_a)y + x_a y_c - x_c y_a}{(y_a - y_c)x_b + (x_c - x_a)y_b + x_a y_c - x_c y_a},$$

$$\alpha = 1 - \beta - \gamma.$$

Another way to compute barycentric coordinates is to compute the areas A_a, A_b, and A_c, of subtriangles as shown in Figure 2.38. Barycentric coordinates obey the rule

$$\begin{aligned} \alpha &= A_a/A, \\ \beta &= A_b/A, \\ \gamma &= A_c/A, \end{aligned} \tag{2.34}$$

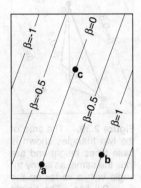

Figure 2.37. The barycentric coordinate β is the signed scaled distance from the line through **a** and **c**.

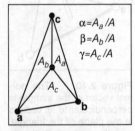

Figure 2.38. The barycentric coordinates are proportional to the areas of the three subtriangles shown.

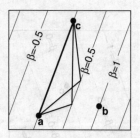

Figure 2.39. The area of the two triangles shown is base times height and are thus the same, as is any triangle with a vertex on the $\beta = 0.5$ line. The height and thus the area is proportional to β.

where A is the area of the triangle. Note that $A = A_a + A_b + A_c$, so it can be computed with two additions rather than a full area formula. This rule still holds for points outside the triangle if the areas are allowed to be signed. The reason for this is shown in Figure 2.39. Note that these are signed areas and will be computed correctly as long as the same signed area computation is used for both A and the subtriangles A_a, A_b, and A_c.

2.7.2　3D Triangles

One wonderful thing about barycentric coordinates is that they extend almost transparently to 3D. If we assume the points $\mathbf{a}$, $\mathbf{b}$, and $\mathbf{c}$ are 3D, then we can still use the representation

$$\mathbf{p} = (1 - \beta - \gamma)\mathbf{a} + \beta\mathbf{b} + \gamma\mathbf{c}.$$

Now, as we vary β and γ, we sweep out a plane.

The normal vector to a triangle can be found by taking the cross product of any two vectors in the plane of the triangle (Figure 2.40). It is easiest to use two of the three edges as these vectors, for example,

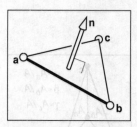

Figure 2.40. The normal vector of the triangle is perpendicular to all vectors in the plane of the triangle, and thus perpendicular to the edges of the triangle.

$$\mathbf{n} = (\mathbf{b} - \mathbf{a}) \times (\mathbf{c} - \mathbf{a}). \qquad (2.35)$$

Note that this normal vector is not necessarily of unit length, and it obeys the right-hand rule of cross products.

The area of the triangle can be found by taking the length of the cross product:

$$\text{area} = \frac{1}{2}\|(\mathbf{b} - \mathbf{a}) \times (\mathbf{c} - \mathbf{a})\|. \qquad (2.36)$$

Note that this is *not* a signed area, so it cannot be used directly to evaluate barycentric coordinates. However, we can observe that a triangle with a "clockwise" vertex order will have a normal vector that points in the opposite direction to the normal of a triangle in the same plane with a "counterclockwise" vertex order. Recall that

$$\mathbf{a} \cdot \mathbf{b} = \|\mathbf{a}\| \, \|\mathbf{b}\| \, \cos\phi,$$

where ϕ is the angle between the vectors. If $\mathbf{a}$ and $\mathbf{b}$ are parallel, then $\cos\phi = \pm 1$, and this gives a test of whether the vectors point in the same or opposite directions.

This, along with Equations (2.34), (2.35), and (2.36) suggest the formulas

$$\alpha = \frac{\mathbf{n} \cdot \mathbf{n}_a}{\|\mathbf{n}\|^2},$$

$$\beta = \frac{\mathbf{n} \cdot \mathbf{n}_b}{\|\mathbf{n}\|^2},$$

$$\gamma = \frac{\mathbf{n} \cdot \mathbf{n}_c}{\|\mathbf{n}\|^2},$$

where $\mathbf{n}$ is Equation (2.35) evaluated with vertices $\mathbf{a}$, $\mathbf{b}$, and $\mathbf{c}$; $\mathbf{n}_a$ is Equation (2.35) evaluated with vertices $\mathbf{b}$, $\mathbf{c}$, and $\mathbf{p}$, and so on, i.e.,

$$\mathbf{n}_a = (\mathbf{c} - \mathbf{b}) \times (\mathbf{p} - \mathbf{b}),$$
$$\mathbf{n}_b = (\mathbf{a} - \mathbf{c}) \times (\mathbf{p} - \mathbf{c}), \qquad (2.37)$$
$$\mathbf{n}_c = (\mathbf{b} - \mathbf{a}) \times (\mathbf{p} - \mathbf{a}).$$

Frequently Asked Questions

• Why isn't there vector division?

It turns out that there is no "nice" analogy of division for vectors. However, it is possible to motivate the quaternions by examining this questions in detail (see Hoffman's book referenced in the chapter notes).

• Is there something as clean as barycentric coordinates for polygons with more than three sides?

Unfortunately there is not. Even convex quadrilaterals are much more complicated. This is one reason triangles are such a common geometric primitive in graphics.

• Is there an implicit form for 3D lines?

No. However, the intersection of two 3D planes defines a 3D line, so a 3D line can be described by two simultaneous implicit 3D equations.

Notes

The history of vector analysis is particularly interesting. It was largely invented by Grassman in the mid-1800s but was ignored and reinvented later (Crowe, 1994). Grassman now has a following in the graphics field of researchers who are developing *Geometric Algebra* based on some of his ideas (Doran & Lasenby, 2003). Readers interested in why the particular scalar and vector products are in some sense the right ones, and why we do not have a commonly-used vector division, will find enlightenment in the concise *About Vectors* (Hoffmann, 1975). Another important geometric tool is the *quaternion* invented by Hamilton in the mid-1800s. Quaternions are useful in many situations, but especially where orientations are concerned (Hanson, 2005).

Exercises

1. The *cardinality* of a set is the number of elements it contains. Under IEEE floating point representation (Section 1.5), what is the cardinality of the *floats*?

2. Is it possible to implement a function that maps 32-bit integers to 64-bit integers that has a well-defined inverse? Do all functions from 32-bit integers to 64-bit integers have well-defined inverses?

3. Specify the unit cube (x-, y-, and z-coordinates all between 0 and 1 inclusive) in terms of the Cartesian product of three intervals.

4. If you have access to the natural log function $\ln(x)$, specify how you could use it to implement a $\log(b, x)$ function where b is the base of the log. What should the function do for negative b values? Assume an IEEE floating point implementation.

5. Solve the quadratic equation $2x^2 + 6x + 4 = 0$.

6. Implement a function that takes in coefficients A, B, and C for the quadratic equation $Ax^2 + By + C = 0$ and computes the two solutions. Have the function return the number of valid (not NaN) solutions and fill in the return arguments so the smaller of the two solutions is first.

7. Show that the two forms of the quadratic formula on page 17 are equivalent (assuming exact arithmetic) and explain how to choose one for each root in

order to avoid subtracting nearly equal floating point numbers, which leads
to loss of precision.

8. Show by counterexample that it is not always true that for 3D vectors $\mathbf{a}$, $\mathbf{b}$,
and $\mathbf{c}$, $\mathbf{a} \times (\mathbf{b} \times \mathbf{c}) = (\mathbf{a} \times \mathbf{b}) \times \mathbf{c}$.

9. Given the non-parallel 3D vectors $\mathbf{a}$ and $\mathbf{b}$, compute a right-handed orthonormal basis such that $\mathbf{u}$ is parallel to $\mathbf{a}$ and $\mathbf{v}$ is in the the plane defined
by $\mathbf{a}$ and $\mathbf{b}$.

10. What is the gradient of $f(x, y, z) = x^2 + y - 3z^3$?

11. What is a parametric form for the axis-aligned 2D ellipse?

12. What is the implicit equation of the plane through 3D points $(1, 0, 0)$,
$(0, 1, 0)$, and $(0, 0, 1)$? What is the parametric equation? What is the normal vector to this plane?

13. Given four 2D points $\mathbf{a}_0$, $\mathbf{a}_1$, $\mathbf{b}_0$, and $\mathbf{b}_1$, design a robust procedure to
determine whether the line segments $\mathbf{a}_0 \mathbf{a}_1$ and $\mathbf{b}_0 \mathbf{b}_1$ intersect.

14. Design a robust procedure to compute the barycentric coordinates of a 2D
point with respect to three 2D non-collinear points.

order to avoid subtracting nearly equal floating point numbers, which leads to loss of precision.

8. Show by counterexample that it is not always true that for 3D vectors a, b, and c, $a \times (b \times c) = (a \times b) \times c$.

9. Given the non-parallel 3D vectors a and b, compute a right-handed orthonormal basis such that u is parallel to a and v is in the the plane defined by a and b.

10. What is the gradient of $F(x, y, z) = x^2 + y^2 = 3z^2$?

11. What is a parametric form for the axis-aligned 2D ellipse?

12. What is the implicit equation of the plane through 2D points (1,0,0), (0,1,0), and (0,0,1)? What is the parametric equation? What is the normal vector to this plane?

13. Given four 2D points a_0, a_1, b_0, and b_1, design a robust procedure to determine whether the line segments $a_0 a_1$ and $b_0 b_1$ intersect.

14. Design a robust procedure to compute the barycentric coordinates of a 2D point with respect to three 2D non-collinear points.

3

Raster Images

Most computer graphics images are presented to the user on some kind of *raster display*. Raster displays show images as rectangular arrays of *pixels*. A common example is a flat-panel computer display or television, which has a rectangular array of small light-emitting pixels that can individually be set to different colors to create any desired image. Different colors are achieved by mixing varying intensities of red, green, and blue light. Most printers, such as laser printers and ink-jet printers, are also raster devices. They are based on scanning: there is no physical grid of pixels, but the image is laid down sequentially by depositing ink at selected points on a grid.

Rasters are also prevalent in input devices for images. A digital camera contains an image sensor comprising a grid of light-sensitive pixels, each of which records the color and intensity of light falling on it. A desktop scanner contains a linear array of pixels that is swept across the page being scanned, making many measurements per second to produce a grid of pixels.

Because rasters are so prevalent in devices, *raster images* are the most common way to store and process images. A raster image is simply a 2D array that stores the *pixel value* for each pixel—usually a color stored as three numbers, for red, green, and blue. A raster image stored in memory can be displayed by using each pixel in the stored image to control the color of one pixel of the display.

But we don't always want to display an image this way. We might want to change the size or orientation of the image, correct the colors, or even show the image pasted on a moving three-dimensional surface. Even in televisions, the display rarely has the same number of pixels as the image being displayed. Considerations like these break the direct link between image pixels and display pixels. It's best to think of a raster image as a *device-independent* description of the image to be displayed, and the display device as a way of approximating that ideal image.

There are other ways of describing images besides using arrays of pixels. A *vector image* is described by storing descriptions of shapes—areas of color bounded by lines or curves—with no reference to any particular pixel grid. In essence this amounts to storing the *instructions* for displaying the image rather than the pixels needed to display it. The main advantage of vector images is that they are *resolution independent* and can be displayed well on very high resolution devices. The corresponding disadvantage is that they must be *rasterized* before they can be displayed. Vector images are often used for text, diagrams, mechanical drawings, and other applications where crispness and precision are important and photographic images and complex shading aren't needed.

In this chapter, we discuss the basics of raster images and displays, paying particular attention to the nonlinearities of standard displays. The details of how pixel values relate to light intensities are important to have in mind when we discuss computing images in later chapters.

Or: you have to know what those numbers in your image actually mean.

3.1   Raster Devices

Before discussing raster images in the abstract, it is instructive to look at the basic operation of some specific devices that use these images. A few familiar raster devices can be categorized into a simple hierarchy:

- Output
  - Display
    - ∗ Transmissive: liquid crystal display (LCD)
    - ∗ Emissive: light emitting diode (LED) display
  - Hardcopy
    - ∗ Binary: ink-jet printer
    - ∗ Continuous tone: dye sublimation printer
- Input
  - 2D array sensor: digital camera
  - 1D array sensor: flatbed scanner

3.1.1 Displays

Current displays, including televisions and digital cinematic projectors as well as displays and projectors for computers, are nearly universally based on fixed arrays of pixels. They can be separated into emissive displays, which use pixels that directly emit controllable amounts of light, and transmissive displays, in which the pixels themselves don't emit light but instead vary the amount of light that they allow to pass through them. Transmissive displays require a light source to illuminate them: in a direct-viewed display this is a *backlight* behind the array; in a projector it is a lamp that emits light that is projected onto the screen after passing through the array. An emissive display is its own light source.

Light-emitting diode (LED) displays are an example of the emissive type. Each pixel is composed of one or more LEDs, which are semiconductor devices (based on inorganic or organic semiconductors) that emit light with intensity depending on the electrical current passing through them (see Figure 3.1).

The pixels in a color display are divided into three independently controlled *subpixels*—one red, one green, and one blue—each with its own LED made using different materials so that they emit light of different colors (Figure 3.2).

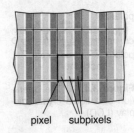

Figure 3.1. The operation of a light-emitting diode (LED) display.

Figure 3.2. The red, green, and blue subpixels within a pixel of a flat-panel display.

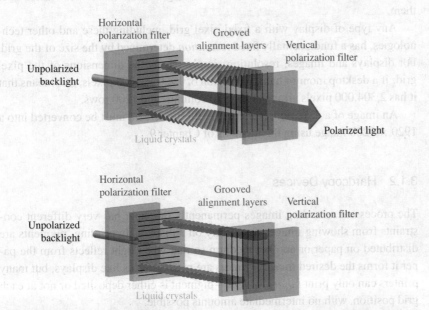

Figure 3.3. One pixel of an LCD display in the off state (bottom), in which the front polarizer blocks all the light that passes the back polarizer, and the on state (top), in which the liquid crystal cell rotates the polarization of the light so that it can pass through the front polarizer. *Figure courtesy Erik Reinhard* (Reinhard et al., 2008).

When the display is viewed from a distance, the eye can't separate the individual subpixels, and the perceived color is a mixture of red, green, and blue.

Liquid crystal displays (LCDs) are an example of the transmissive type. A liquid crystal is a material whose molecular structure enables it to rotate the polarization of light that passes through it, and the degree of rotation can be adjusted by an applied voltage. An LCD pixel (Figure 3.3) has a layer of polarizing film behind it, so that it is illuminated by polarized light—let's assume it is polarized horizontally.

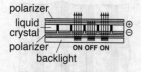

Figure 3.4. The operation of a liquid crystal display (LCD).

A second layer of polarizing film in front of the pixel is oriented to transmit only vertically polarized light. If the applied voltage is set so that the liquid crystal layer in between does not change the polarization, all light is blocked and the pixel is in the "off" (minimum intensity) state. If the voltage is set so that the liquid crystal rotates the polarization by 90 degrees, then all the light that entered through the back of the pixel will escape through the front, and the pixel is fully "on"—it has its maximum intensity. Intermediate voltages will partly rotate the polarization so that the front polarizer partly blocks the light, resulting in intensities between the minimum and maximum (Figure 3.4). Like color LED displays, color LCDs have red, green, and blue subpixels within each pixel, which are three independent pixels with red, green, and blue color filters over them.

Any type of display with a fixed pixel grid, including these and other technologies, has a fundamentally fixed *resolution* determined by the size of the grid. For displays and images, resolution simply means the dimensions of the pixel grid: if a desktop monitor has a resolution of 1920×1200 pixels, this means that it has 2,304,000 pixels arranged in 1920 columns and 1200 rows.

An image of a different resolution, to fill the screen, must be converted into a 1920×1200 image using the methods of Chapter 9.

The resolution of a display is sometimes called its "native resolution" since most displays can handle images of other resolutions, via built-in conversion.

3.1.2 Hardcopy Devices

The process of recording images permanently on paper has very different constraints from showing images transiently on a display. In printing, pigments are distributed on paper or another medium so that when light reflects from the paper it forms the desired image. Printers are raster devices like displays, but many printers can only print *binary images*—pigment is either deposited or not at each grid position, with no intermediate amounts possible.

An ink-jet printer (Figure 3.5) is an example of a device that forms a raster image by scanning. An ink-jet print head contains liquid ink carrying pigment, which can be sprayed in very small drops under electronic control. The head

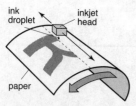

Figure 3.5. The operation of an ink-jet printer.

moves across the paper, and drops are emitted as it passes grid positions that should receive ink; no ink is emitted in areas intended to remain blank. After each sweep the paper is advanced slightly, and then the next row of the grid is laid down. Color prints are made by using several print heads, each spraying ink with a different pigment, so that each grid position can receive any combination of different colored drops. Because all drops are the same, an ink-jet printer prints binary images: at each grid point there is a drop or no drop; there are no intermediate shades.

An ink-jet printer has no physical array of pixels; the resolution is determined by how small the drops can be made and how far the paper is advanced after each sweep. Many ink-jet printers have multiple nozzles in the print head, enabling several sweeps to be made in one pass, but it is the paper advance, not the nozzle spacing, that ultimately determines the spacing of the rows.

The *thermal dye transfer* process is an example of a *continuous tone* printing process, meaning that varying amounts of dye can be deposited at each pixel—it is not all-or-nothing like an ink-jet printer (Figure 3.6). A *donor ribbon* containing colored dye is pressed between the paper, or *dye receiver*, and a *print head* containing a linear array of heating elements, one for each column of pixels in the image. As the paper and ribbon move past the head, the heating elements switch on and off to heat the ribbon in areas where dye is desired, causing the dye to diffuse from the ribbon to the paper. This process is repeated for each of several dye colors. Since higher temperatures cause more dye to be transferred, the amount of each dye deposited at each grid position can be controlled, allowing a continuous range of colors to be produced. The number of heating elements in the print head establishes a fixed resolution in the direction across the page, but the resolution along the page is determined by the rate of heating and cooling compared to the speed of the paper.

Unlike displays, the resolution of printers is described in terms of the *pixel density* instead of the total count of pixels. So a thermal dye transfer printer that has elements spaced 300 per inch across its print head has a resolution of 300 *pixels per inch* (ppi) across the page. If the resolution along the page is chosen to be the same we can simply say the printer's resolution is 300 ppi. An ink-jet printer that places dots on a grid with 1200 grid points per inch is described as having a resolution of 1200 *dots per inch* (dpi). Because the ink-jet printer is a binary device, it requires a much finer grid for at least two reasons. Because edges are abrupt black/white boundaries, very high resolution is required to avoid stairstepping, or aliasing, from appearing (see Section 8.3). When continuous-tone images are printed, the high resolution is required to simulate intermediate colors by printing varying-density dot patterns called *halftones*.

There are also continuous ink-jet printers that print in a continuous helical path on paper wrapped around a spinning drum, rather than moving the head back and forth.

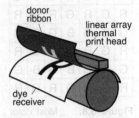

Figure 3.6. The operation of a thermal dye transfer printer.

The term "dpi" is all too often used to mean "pixels per inch," but dpi should be used in reference to binary devices and ppi in reference to continuous-tone devices.

3.1.3 Input Devices

Raster images have to come from somewhere, and any image that wasn't computed by some algorithm has to have been measured by some *raster input device*, most often a camera or scanner. Even in rendering images of 3D scenes, photographs are used constantly as texture maps (see Chapter 11). A raster input device has to make a light measurement for each pixel, and (like output devices) they are usually based on arrays of sensors.

A digital camera is an example of a 2D array input device. The image sensor in a camera is a semiconductor device with a grid of light-sensitive pixels. Two common types of arrays are known as CCDs (charge-coupled devices) and CMOS (complimentary metal–oxide–semiconductor) image sensors. The camera's lens projects an image of the scene to be photographed onto the sensor, and then each pixel measures the light energy falling on it, ultimately resulting in a number that goes into the output image (Figure 3.7). In much the same way as color displays use red, green, and blue subpixels, most color cameras work by using a *color-filter array* or *mosaic* to allow each pixel to see only red, green, or blue light, leaving the image processing software to fill in the missing values in a process known as *demosaicking* (Figure 3.8).

Other cameras use three separate arrays, or three separate layers in the array, to measure independent red, green, and blue values at each pixel, producing a usable color image without further processing. The resolution of a camera is determined by the fixed number of pixels in the array and is usually quoted using the total count of pixels: a camera with an array of 3000 columns and 2000 rows produces an image of resolution 3000×2000, which has 6 million pixels, and is called a 6 megapixel (MP) camera. It's important to remember that a mosiac sensor does not measure a complete color image, so a camera that measures the same number of pixels but with independent red, green, and blue measurements records more information about the image than one with a mosaic sensor.

A flatbed scanner also measures red, green, and blue values for each of a grid of pixels, but like a thermal dye transfer printer it uses a 1D array that sweeps across the page being scanned, making many measurements per second. The resolution across the page is fixed by the size of the array, and the resolution along the page is determined by the frequency of measurements compared to the speed at which the scan head moves. A color scanner has a $3 \times n_x$ array, where n_x is the number of pixels across the page, with the three rows covered by red, green, and blue filters. With an appropriate delay between the times at which the three colors are measured, this allows three independent color measurements at each grid point. As with continuous-tone printers, the resolution of scanners is reported in pixels per inch (ppi).

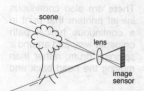

Figure 3.7. The operation of a digital camera.

G	B	G	B	G	B	G
R	G	R	G	R	G	R
G	B	G	B	G	B	G
R	G	R	G	R	G	R
G	B	G	B	G	B	G
R	G	R	G	R	G	R

Figure 3.8. Most color digital cameras use a color-filter array similar to the *Bayer mosaic* shown here. Each pixel measures either red, green, or blue light.

People who are selling cameras use "mega" to mean 10^6, not 2^{20} as with megabytes.

The resolution of a scanner is sometimes called its "optical resolution" since most scanners can produce images of other resolutions, via built-in conversion.

With this concrete information about where our images come from and where they will go, we'll now discuss images more abstractly, in the way we'll use them in graphics algorithms.

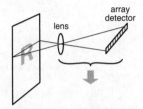

Figure 3.9. The operation of a flatbed scanner.

3.2 Images, Pixels, and Geometry

We know that a raster image is a big array of pixels, each of which stores information about the color of the image at its grid point. We've seen what various output devices do with images we send to them and how input devices derive them from images formed by light in the physical world. But for computations in the computer we need a convenient abstraction that is independent of the specifics of any device, that we can use to reason about how to produce or interpret the values stored in images.

When we measure or reproduce images, they take the form of two-dimensional distributions of light energy: the light emitted from the monitor as a function of position on the face of the display; the light falling on a camera's image sensor as a function of position across the sensor's plane; the *reflectance*, or fraction of light reflected (as opposed to absorbed) as a function of position on a piece of paper. So in the physical world, images are functions defined over two-dimensional areas—almost always rectangles. So we can abstract an image as a function

$$I(x, y) : R \rightarrow V,$$

where $R \subset \mathbb{R}^2$ is a rectangular area and V is the set of possible pixel values. The simplest case is an idealized grayscale image where each point in the rectangle has just a brightness (no color), and we can say $V = \mathbb{R}^+$ (the non-negative reals). An idealized color image, with red, green, and blue values at each pixel, has $V = (\mathbb{R}^+)^3$. We'll discuss other possibilities for V in the next section.

How does a raster image relate to this abstract notion of a continuous image? Looking to the concrete examples, a pixel from a camera or scanner is a measurement of the average color of the image over some small area around the pixel. A display pixel, with its red, green, and blue subpixels, is designed so that the average color of the image over the face of the pixel is controlled by the corresponding pixel value in the raster image. In both cases, the pixel value is a local average of the color of the image, and it is called a *point sample* of the image. In other words, when we find the value x in a pixel, it means "the value of the image in the vicinity of this grid point is x." The idea of images as sampled representations of functions is explored further in Chapter 9.

A mundane but important question is where the pixels are located in 2D space. This is only a matter of convention, but establishing a consistent convention is

"A pixel is not a little square!"
—Alvy Ray Smith (A. R. Smith, 1995)

Are there any raster devices that are not rectangular?

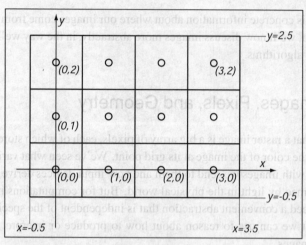

Figure 3.10. Coordinates of a four pixel × three pixel screen. Note that in some APIs the y-axis will point downwards.

important! In this book, a raster image is indexed by the pair (i, j) indicating the column (i) and row (j) of the pixel, counting from the bottom left. If an image has n_x columns and n_y rows of pixels, the bottom-left pixel is $(0, 0)$ and the top-right is pixel $(n_x - 1, n_y - 1)$. We need 2D real screen coordinates to specify pixel positions. We will place the pixels' sample points at integer coordinates, as shown by the 4×3 screen in Figure 3.10.

The rectangular domain of the image has width n_x and height n_y and is centered on this grid, meaning that it extends half a pixel beyond the last sample point on each side. So the rectangular domain of a $n_x \times n_y$ image is

$$R = [-0.5, n_x - 0.5] \times [-0.5, n_y - 0.5].$$

Some systems shift the coordinates by half a pixel to place the sample points halfway between the integers but place the edges of the image at integers.

Again, these coordinates are simply conventions, but they will be important to remember later when implementing cameras and viewing transformations.

3.2.1 Pixel Values

So far we have described the values of pixels in terms of real numbers, representing intensity (possibly separately for red, green, and blue) at a point in the image. This suggests that images should be arrays of floating-point numbers, with either one (for *grayscale*, or black and white, images) or three (for RGB color images) 32-bit floating point numbers stored per pixel. This format is sometimes used, when its precision and range of values are needed, but images have a lot of pixels and memory and bandwidth for storing and transmitting images are invariably scarce. Just one ten-megapixel photograph would consume about 115 MB of RAM in this format.

Why 115 MB and not 120 MB?

Less range is required for images that are meant to be displayed directly. While the range of possible light intensities is unbounded in principle, any given device has a decidedly finite maximum intensity, so in many contexts it is perfectly sufficient for pixels to have a bounded range, usually taken to be $[0, 1]$ for simplicity. For instance, the possible values in an 8-bit image are $0, 1/255, 2/255,$ $\ldots, 254/255, 1$. Images stored with floating-point numbers, allowing a wide range of values, are often called *high dynamic range* (HDR) images to distinguish them from fixed-range, or *low dynamic range* (LDR) images that are stored with integers. See Chapter 23 for an in-depth discussion of techniques and applications for high dynamic range images.

The denominator of 255, rather than 256, is awkward, but being able to represent 0 and 1 exactly is important.

Here are some pixel formats with typical applications:

- 1-bit grayscale—text and other images where intermediate grays are not desired (high resolution required);

- 8-bit RGB fixed-range color (24 bits total per pixel)—web and email applications, consumer photographs;

- 8- or 10-bit fixed-range RGB (24–30 bits/pixel)—digital interfaces to computer displays;

- 12- to 14-bit fixed-range RGB (36–42 bits/pixel)—raw camera images for professional photography;

- 16-bit fixed-range RGB (48 bits/pixel)—professional photography and printing; intermediate format for image processing of fixed-range images;

- 16-bit fixed-range grayscale (16 bits/pixel)—radiology and medical imaging;

- 16-bit "half-precision" floating-point RGB—HDR images; intermediate format for real-time rendering;

- 32-bit floating-point RGB—general-purpose intermediate format for software rendering and processing of HDR images.

Reducing the number of bits used to store each pixel leads to two distinctive types of *artifacts*, or artificially introduced flaws, in images. First, encoding images with fixed-range values produces *clipping* when pixels that would otherwise be brighter than the maximum value are set, or clipped, to the maximum representable value. For instance, a photograph of a sunny scene may include reflections that are much brighter than white surfaces; these will be clipped (even if they were measured by the camera) when the image is converted to a fixed range to be displayed. Second, encoding images with limited precision leads to *quantization* artifacts, or *banding*, when the need to round pixel values to the nearest representable value introduces visible jumps in intensity or color. Banding can be particularly insidious in animation and video, where the bands may not be objectionable in still images but become very visible when they move back and forth.

3.2.2 Monitor Intensities and Gamma

All modern monitors take digital input for the "value" of a pixel and convert this to an intensity level. Real monitors have some non-zero intensity when they are off because the screen reflects some light. For our purposes we can consider this "black" and the monitor fully on as "white." We assume a numeric description of pixel color that ranges from zero to one. Black is zero, white is one, and a gray halfway between black and white is 0.5. Note that here "halfway" refers to the physical amount of light coming from the pixel, rather than the appearance. The human perception of intensity is non-linear and will not be part of the present discussion; see Chapter 22 for more.

There are two key issues that must be understood to produce correct images on monitors. The first is that monitors are non-linear with respect to input. For example, if you give a monitor 0, 0.5, and 1.0 as inputs for three pixels, the intensities displayed might be 0, 0.25, and 1.0 (off, one-quarter fully on, and fully on). As an approximate characterization of this non-linearity, monitors are commonly characterized by a γ ("gamma") value. This value is the degree of freedom in the formula

$$\text{displayed intensity} = (\text{maximum intensity})a^{\gamma}, \qquad (3.1)$$

where a is the input pixel value between zero and one. For example, if a monitor has a gamma of 2.0, and we input a value of $a = 0.5$, the displayed intensity will be one fourth the maximum possible intensity because $0.5^2 = 0.25$. Note that $a = 0$ maps to zero intensity and $a = 1$ maps to the maximum intensity regardless of the value of γ. Describing a display's non-linearity using γ is only an approximation; we do not need a great deal of accuracy in estimating the γ of a device. A nice visual way to gauge the non-linearity is to find what value of a

gives an intensity halfway between black and white. This a will be

$$0.5 = a^\gamma.$$

If we can find that a, we can deduce γ by taking logarithms on both sides:

$$\gamma = \frac{\ln 0.5}{\ln a}.$$

We can find this a by a standard technique where we display a checkerboard pattern of black and white pixels next to a square of gray pixels with input a (Figure 3.11), then ask the user to adjust a (with a slider, for instance) until the two sides match in average brightness. When you look at this image from a distance (or without glasses if you are nearsighted), the two sides of the image will look about the same when a is producing an intensity halfway between black and white. This is because the blurred checkerboard is mixing even numbers of white and black pixels so the overall effect is a uniform color halfway between white and black.

Once we know γ, we can *gamma correct* our input so that a value of $a = 0.5$ is displayed with intensity halfway between black and white. This is done with the transformation

$$a' = a^{\frac{1}{\gamma}}.$$

When this formula is plugged into Equation (3.1) we get

$$\text{displayed intensity} = (a')^\gamma = \left(a^{\frac{1}{\gamma}} \right)^\gamma (\text{maximum intensity})$$

$$= a(\text{maximum intensity}).$$

Another important characteristic of real displays is that they take quantized input values. So while we can manipulate intensities in the floating point range $[0, 1]$, the detailed input to a monitor is a fixed-size integer. The most common range for this integer is 0–255 which can be held in 8 bits of storage. This means that the possible values for a are not any number in $[0, 1]$ but instead

$$\text{possible values for } a = \left\{ \frac{0}{255}, \frac{1}{255}, \frac{2}{255}, \ldots, \frac{254}{255}, \frac{255}{255} \right\}.$$

This means the possible displayed intensity values are approximately

$$\left\{ M \left(\frac{0}{255} \right)^\gamma, M \left(\frac{1}{255} \right)^\gamma, M \left(\frac{2}{255} \right)^\gamma, \ldots, M \left(\frac{254}{255} \right)^\gamma, M \left(\frac{255}{255} \right)^\gamma \right\},$$

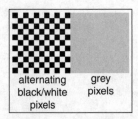

alternating   grey
black/white   pixels
pixels

Figure 3.11. Alternating black and white pixels viewed from a distance are halfway between black and white. The gamma of a monitor can be inferred by finding a gray value that appears to have the same intensity as the black and white pattern.

For monitors with analog interfaces, which have difficulty changing intensity rapidly along the horizontal direction, horizontal black and white stripes work better than a checkerboard.

where M is the maximum intensity. In applications where the exact intensities need to be controlled, we would have to actually measure the 256 possible intensities, and these intensities might be different at different points on the screen, especially for CRTs. They might also vary with viewing angle. Fortunately few applications require such accurate calibration.

3.3 RGB Color

Most computer graphics images are defined in terms of red-green-blue (RGB) color. RGB color is a simple space that allows straightforward conversion to the controls for most computer screens. In this section RGB color is discussed from a user's perspective, and operational facility is the goal. A more thorough discussion of color is given in Chapter 21, but the mechanics of RGB color space will allow us to write most graphics programs. The basic idea of RGB color space is that the color is displayed by mixing three *primary* lights: one red, one green, and one blue. The lights mix in an *additive* manner.

In RGB additive color mixing we have (Figure 3.12):

$$\text{red} + \text{green} = \text{yellow}$$
$$\text{green} + \text{blue} = \text{cyan}$$
$$\text{blue} + \text{red} = \text{magenta}$$
$$\text{red} + \text{green} + \text{blue} = \text{white}$$

The color "cyan" is a blue-green, and the color "magenta" is a purple.

If we are allowed to dim the primary lights from fully off (indicated by pixel value 0) to fully on (indicated by 1), we can create all the colors that can be

In grade school you probably learned that the primaries are red, yellow, and blue, and that, e. g., yellow + blue = green. This is *subtractive* color mixing, which is fundamentally different from the more familiar additive mixing that happens in displays.

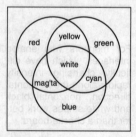

Figure 3.12. The additive mixing rules for colors red/green/blue.

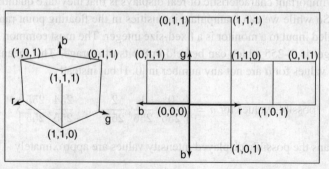

Figure 3.13. The RGB color cube in 3D and its faces unfolded. Any RGB color is a point in the cube. (See also Plate I.)

displayed on an RGB monitor. The red, green, and blue pixel values create a three-dimensional *RGB color cube* that has a red, a green, and a blue axis. Allowable coordinates for the axes range from zero to one. The color cube is shown graphically in Figure 3.13.

The colors at the corners of the cube are:

$$black = (0, 0, 0)$$
$$red = (1, 0, 0)$$
$$green = (0, 1, 0)$$
$$blue = (0, 0, 1)$$
$$yellow = (1, 1, 0)$$
$$magenta = (1, 0, 1)$$
$$cyan = (0, 1, 1)$$
$$white = (1, 1, 1).$$

Actual RGB levels are often given in quantized form, just like the grayscales discussed in Section 3.2.2. Each component is specified with an integer. The most common size for these integers is one byte each, so each of the three RGB components is an integer between 0 and 255. The three integers together take up three bytes, which is 24 bits. Thus a system that has "24-bit color" has 256 possible levels for each of the three primary colors. Issues of gamma correction discussed in Section 3.2.2 also apply to each RGB component separately.

3.4 Alpha Compositing

Often we would like to only partially overwrite the contents of a pixel. A common example of this occurs in *compositing*, where we have a background and want to insert a foreground image over it. For opaque pixels in the foreground, we just replace the background pixel. For entirely transparent foreground pixels, we do not change the background pixel. For *partially* transparent pixels, some care must be taken. Partially transparent pixels can occur when the foreground object has partially transparent regions, such as glass, but the most frequent case where foreground and background must be blended is when the foreground object only partly covers the pixel, either at the edge of the foreground object, or when there are sub-pixel holes such as between the leaves of a distant tree.

The most important piece of information needed to blend a foreground object over a background object is the *pixel coverage*, which tells the fraction of the pixel covered by the foreground layer. We can call this fraction α. If we want to composite a foreground color $\mathbf{c}_f$ over background color $\mathbf{c}_b$, and the fraction of the pixel covered by the foreground is α, then we can use the formula

$$\mathbf{c} = \alpha\mathbf{c}_f + (1-\alpha)\mathbf{c}_b. \tag{3.2}$$

Since the weights of the foreground and background layers add up to 1, the color won't change if the foreground and background layers have the same color.

For an opaque foreground layer, the interpretation is that the foreground object covers area α within the pixel's rectangle and the background object covers the remaining area, which is $(1-\alpha)$. For a transparent layer (think of an image painted on glass or on tracing paper, using translucent paint), the interpretation is that the foreground layer blocks the fraction $(1-\alpha)$ of the light coming through from the background and contributes a fraction α of its own color to replace what was removed. An example of using Equation (3.2) is shown in Figure 3.14.

The α values for all the pixels in an image might be stored in a separate grayscale image, which is then known as an *alpha mask* or *transparency mask*. Or the information can be stored as a fourth channel in an RGB image, in which case it is called the *alpha channel*, and the image can be called an RGBA image. With 8-bit images, each pixel then takes up 32 bits, which is a conveniently sized chunk in many computer architectures.

Although Equation (3.2) is what is usually used, there are a variety of situations where α is used differently (Porter & Duff, 1984).

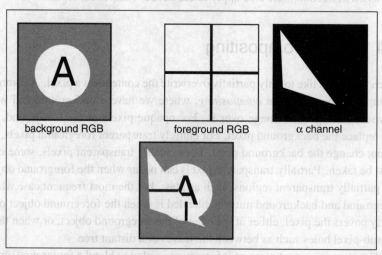

Figure 3.14. An example of compositing using Equation (3.2). The foreground image is in effect cropped by the α channel before being put on top of the background image. The resulting composite is shown on the bottom.

3.4.1 Image Storage

Most RGB image formats use eight bits for each of the red, green, and blue channels. This results in approximately three megabytes of raw information for a single million-pixel image. To reduce the storage requirement, most image formats allow for some kind of compression. At a high level, such compression is either *lossless* or *lossy*. No information is discarded in lossless compression, while some information is lost unrecoverably in a lossy system. Popular image storage formats include:

- **jpeg.** This lossy format compresses image blocks based on thresholds in the human visual system. This format works well for natural images.

- **tiff.** This format is most commonly used to hold binary images or losslessly compressed 8- or 16-bit RGB although many other options exist.

- **ppm.** This very simple lossless, uncompressed format is most often used for 8-bit RGB images although many options exist.

- **png.** This is a set of lossless formats with a good set of open source management tools.

Because of compression and variants, writing input/output routines for images can be involved. Fortunately one can usually rely on library routines to read and write standard file formats. For quick-and-dirty applications, where simplicity is valued above efficiency, a simple choice is to use raw ppm files, which can often be written simply by dumping the array that stores the image in memory to a file, prepending the appropriate header.

Frequently Asked Questions

• Why don't they just make monitors linear and avoid all this gamma business?

Ideally the 256 possible intensities of a monitor should *look* evenly spaced as opposed to being linearly spaced in energy. Because human perception of intensity is itself non-linear, a gamma between 1.5 and 3 (depending on viewing conditions) will make the intensities approximately uniform in a subjective sense. In this way gamma is a feature. Otherwise the manufacturers would make the monitors linear.

Exercises

1. Simulate an image acquired from the Bayer mosaic by taking a natural image (preferably a scanned photo rather than a digital photo where the Bayer mosaic may already have been applied) and creating a grayscale image composed of interleaved red/green/blue channels. This simulates the raw output of a digital camera. Now create a true RGB image from that output and compare with the original.

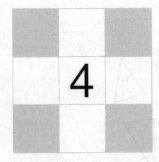

4

Ray Tracing

One of the basic tasks of computer graphics is *rendering* three-dimensional objects: taking a scene, or model, composed of many geometric objects arranged in 3D space and producing a 2D image that shows the objects as viewed from a particular viewpoint. It is the same operation that has been done for centuries by architects and engineers creating drawings to communicate their designs to others.

Fundamentally, rendering is a process that takes as its input a set of objects and produces as its output an array of pixels. One way or another, rendering involves considering how each object contributes to each pixel; it can be organized in two general ways. In *object-order rendering*, each object is considered in turn, and for each object all the pixels that it influences are found and updated. In *image-order rendering*, each pixel is considered in turn, and for each pixel all the objects that influence it are found and the pixel value is computed. You can think of the difference in terms of the nesting of loops: in image-order rendering the "for each pixel" loop is on the outside, whereas in object-order rendering the "for each object" loop is on the outside.

Image-order and object-order rendering approaches can compute exactly the same images, but they lend themselves to computing different kinds of effects and have quite different performance characteristics. We'll explore the comparative strengths of the approaches in Chapter 8 after we have discussed them both, but, broadly speaking, image-order rendering is simpler to get working and more flexible in the effects that can be produced, and usually (though not always) takes much more execution time to produce a comparable image.

If the output is a vector image rather than a raster image, rendering doesn't have to involve pixels, but we'll assume raster images in this book.

In a ray tracer it is easy to compute accurate shadows and reflections, which are awkward in the object-order framework.

69

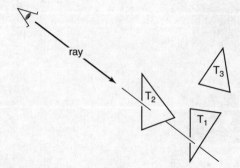

Figure 4.1. The ray is "traced" into the scene and the first object hit is the one seen through the pixel. In this case, the triangle T_2 is returned.

Ray tracing is an image-order algorithm for making renderings of 3D scenes, and we'll consider it first because it's possible to get a ray tracer working without developing any of the mathematical machinery that's used for object-order rendering.

4.1   The Basic Ray-Tracing Algorithm

A ray tracer works by computing one pixel at a time, and for each pixel the basic task is to find the object that is seen at that pixel's position in the image. Each pixel "looks" in a different direction, and any object that is seen by a pixel must intersect the *viewing ray*, a line that emanates from the viewpoint in the direction that pixel is looking. The particular object we want is the one that intersects the viewing ray nearest the camera, since it blocks the view of any other objects behind it. Once that object is found, a *shading* computation uses the intersection point, surface normal, and other information (depending on the desired type of rendering) to determine the color of the pixel. This is shown in Figure 4.1, where the ray intersects two triangles, but only the first triangle hit, T_2, is shaded.

A basic ray tracer therefore has three parts:

1. *ray generation*, which computes the origin and direction of each pixel's viewing ray based on the camera geometry;

2. *ray intersection*, which finds the closest object intersecting the viewing ray;

3. *shading*, which computes the pixel color based on the results of ray intersection.

The structure of the basic ray tracing program is:

for each pixel **do**
  compute viewing ray
  find first object hit by ray and its surface normal **n**
  set pixel color to value computed from hit point, light, and **n**

This chapter covers basic methods for ray generation, ray intersection, and shading, that are sufficient for implementing a simple demonstration ray tracer. For a really useful system, more efficient ray intersection techniques from Chapter 12 need to be added, and the real potential of a ray tracer will be seen with the more advanced shading methods from Chapter 10 and the additional rendering techniques from Chapter 13.

4.2 Perspective

The problem of representing a 3D object or scene with a 2D drawing or painting was studied by artists hundreds of years before computers. Photographs also represent 3D scenes with 2D images. While there are many unconventional ways to make images, from cubist painting to fish-eye lenses (Figure 4.2) to peripheral cameras, the standard approach for both art and photography, as well as computer graphics, is *linear perspective*, in which 3D objects are projected onto an *image plane* in such a way that straight lines in the scene become straight lines in the image.

The simplest type of projection is *parallel projection*, in which 3D points are mapped to 2D by moving them along a *projection direction* until they hit the image plane (Figures 4.3–4.4). The view that is produced is determined by the choice of projection direction and image plane. If the image plane is perpendicular

Figure 4.2. An image taken with a fisheye lens is not a linear perspective image. *Photo courtesy Philip Greenspan.*

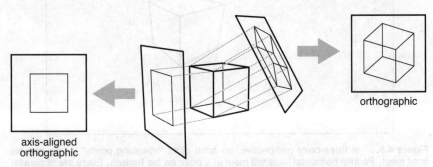

axis-aligned
orthographic

orthographic

Figure 4.3. When projection lines are parallel and perpendicular to the image plane, the resulting views are called orthographic.

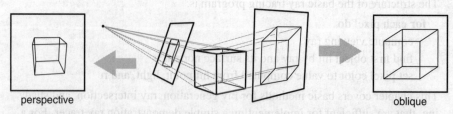

Figure 4.4. A parallel projection that has the image plane at an angle to the projection direction is called oblique (right). In perspective projection, the projection lines all pass through the viewpoint, rather than being parallel (left). The illustrated perspective view is non-oblique because a projection line drawn through the center of the image would be perpendicular to the image plane.

Some books reserve "orthographic" for projection directions that are parallel to the coordinate axes.

to the view direction, the projection is called *orthographic*; otherwise it is called *oblique*.

Parallel projections are often used for mechanical and architectural drawings because they keep parallel lines parallel and they preserve the size and shape of planar objects that are parallel to the image plane.

The advantages of parallel projection are also its limitations. In our everyday experience (and even more so in photographs) objects look smaller as they get farther away, and as a result parallel lines receding into the distance do not appear parallel. This is because eyes and cameras don't collect light from a single viewing direction; they collect light that passes through a particular viewpoint. As has been recognized by artists since the Renaissance, we can produce natural-

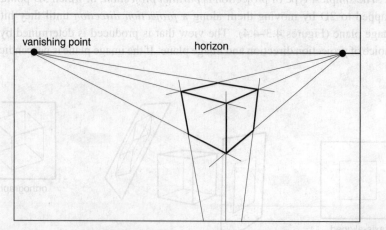

Figure 4.5.   In three-point perspective, an artist picks "vanishing points" where parallel lines meet. Parallel horizontal lines will meet at a point on the horizon. Every set of parallel lines has its own vanishing points. These rules are followed automatically if we implement perspective based on the correct geometric principles.

looking views using *perspective projection*: we simply project along lines that pass through a single point, the *viewpoint*, rather than along parallel lines (Figure 4.4). In this way objects farther from the viewpoint naturally become smaller when they are projected. A perspective view is determined by the choice of viewpoint (rather than projection direction) and image plane. As with parallel views there are oblique and non-oblique perspective views; the distinction is made based on the projection direction at the center of the image.

You may have learned about the artistic conventions of *three-point perspective*, a system for manually constructing perspective views (Figure 4.5). A surprising fact about perspective is that all the rules of perspective drawing will be followed automatically if we follow the simple mathematical rule underlying perspective: objects are projected directly toward the eye, and they are drawn where they meet a view plane in front of the eye.

4.3 Computing Viewing Rays

From the previous section, the basic tools of ray generation are the viewpoint (or view direction, for parallel views) and the image plane. There are many ways to work out the details of camera geometry; in this section we explain one based on orthonormal bases that supports normal and oblique parallel and orthographic views.

In order to generate rays, we first need a mathematical representation for a ray. A ray is really just an origin point and a propagation direction; a 3D parametric line is ideal for this. As discussed in Section 2.5.7, the 3D parametric line from the eye $\mathbf{e}$ to a point $\mathbf{s}$ on the image plane (Figure 4.6) is given by

$$\mathbf{p}(t) = \mathbf{e} + t(\mathbf{s} - \mathbf{e}).$$

This should be interpreted as, "we advance from $\mathbf{e}$ along the vector $(\mathbf{s} - \mathbf{e})$ a fractional distance t to find the point $\mathbf{p}$." So given t, we can determine a point $\mathbf{p}$. The point $\mathbf{e}$ is the ray's *origin*, and $\mathbf{s} - \mathbf{e}$ is the ray's *direction*.

Note that $\mathbf{p}(0) = \mathbf{e}$, and $\mathbf{p}(1) = \mathbf{s}$, and more generally, if $0 < t_1 < t_2$, then $\mathbf{p}(t_1)$ is closer to the eye than $\mathbf{p}(t_2)$. Also, if $t < 0$, then $\mathbf{p}(t)$ is "behind" the eye. These facts will be useful when we search for the closest object hit by the ray that is not behind the eye.

To compute a viewing ray, we need to know $\mathbf{e}$ (which is given) and $\mathbf{s}$. Finding $\mathbf{s}$ may seem difficult, but it is actually straightforward if we look at the problem in the right coordinate system.

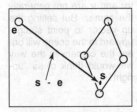

Figure 4.6. The ray from the eye to a point on the image plane.

Caution: we are overloading the variable *t*, which is the ray parameter and also the *v*-coordinate of the top edge of the image.

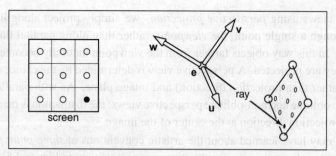

Figure 4.7. The sample points on the screen are mapped to a similar array on the 3D window. A viewing ray is sent to each of these locations.

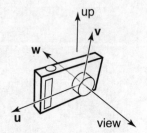

Figure 4.8. The vectors of the camera frame, together with the view direction and up direction. The **w** vector is opposite the view direction, and the **v** vector is coplanar with **w** and the up vector.

Since **v** and **w** have to be perpendicular, the up vector and **v** are not generally the same. But setting the up vector to point straight upward in the scene will orient the camera in the way we would think of as "upright."

It might seem logical that orthographic viewing rays should start from infinitely far away, but then it would not be possible to make orthographic views of an object inside a room, for instance.

Many systems assume that $l = -r$ and $b = -t$ so that a width and a height suffice.

All of our ray-generation methods start from an orthonormal coordinate frame known as the *camera frame*, which we'll denote by **e**, for the eye point, or viewpoint, and **u**, **v**, and **w** for the three basis vectors, organized with **u** pointing rightward (from the camera's view), **v** pointing upward, and **w** pointing backward, so that $\{\mathbf{u}, \mathbf{v}, \mathbf{w}\}$ forms a right-handed coordinate system. The most common way to construct the camera frame is from the viewpoint, which becomes **e**, the *view direction*, which is $-\mathbf{w}$, and the *up vector*, which is used to construct a basis that has **v** and **w** in the plane defined by the view direction and the up direction, using the process for constructing an orthonormal basis from two vectors described in Section 2.4.7.

4.3.1 Orthographic Views

For an orthographic view, all the rays will have the direction $-\mathbf{w}$. Even though a parallel view doesn't have a viewpoint per se, we can still use the origin of the camera frame to define the plane where the rays start, so that it's possible for objects to be behind the camera.

The viewing rays should start on the plane defined by the point **e** and the vectors **u** and **v**; the only remaining information required is *where* on the plane the image is supposed to be. We'll define the image dimensions with four numbers, for the four sides of the image: l and r are the positions of the left and right edges of the image, as measured from **e** along the **u** direction; and b and t are the positions of the bottom and top edges of the image, as measured from **e** along the **v** direction. Usually $l < 0 < r$ and $b < 0 < t$. (See Figure 4.9.)

In Section 3.2 we discussed pixel coordinates in an image. To fit an image with $n_x \times n_y$ pixels into a rectangle of size $(r - l) \times (t - b)$, the pixels are spaced a distance $(r - l)/n_x$ apart horizontally and $(t - b)/n_y$ apart vertically,

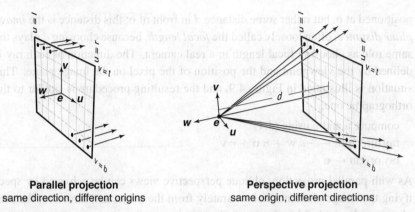

Parallel projection   **Perspective projection**
same direction, different origins   same origin, different directions

Figure 4.9. Ray generation using the camera frame. Left: In an orthographic view, the rays start at the pixels' locations on the image plane, and all share the same direction, which is equal to the view direction. Right: In a perspective view, the rays start at the viewpoint, and each ray's direction is defined by the line through the viewpoint, **e**, and the pixel's location on the image plane.

with a half-pixel space around the edge to center the pixel grid within the image rectangle. This means that the pixel at position (i, j) in the raster image has the position

$$u = l + (r - l)(i + 0.5)/n_x,$$
$$v = b + (t - b)(j + 0.5)/n_y, \tag{4.1}$$

where (u, v) are the coordinates of the pixel's position on the image plane, measured with respect to the origin **e** and the basis $\{\mathbf{u}, \mathbf{v}\}$.

In an orthographic view, we can simply use the pixel's image-plane position as the ray's starting point, and we already know the ray's direction is the view direction. The procedure for generating orthographic viewing rays is then:

compute u and v using (4.1)
ray.direction $\leftarrow -\mathbf{w}$
ray.origin $\leftarrow \mathbf{e} + u\,\mathbf{u} + v\,\mathbf{v}$

It's very simple to make an oblique parallel view: just allow the image plane normal **w** to be specified separately from the view direction **d**. The procedure is then exactly the same, but with **d** substituted for $-\mathbf{w}$. Of course **w** is still used to construct **u** and **v**.

4.3.2   Perspective Views

For a perspective view, all the rays have the same origin, at the viewpoint; it is the directions that are different for each pixel. The image plane is no longer

With l and r both specified, there is redundancy: moving the viewpoint a bit to the right and correspondingly decreasing l and r will not change the view (and similarly on the **v**-axis).

positioned at $\mathbf{e}$, but rather some distance d in front of $\mathbf{e}$; this distance is the *image plane distance*, often loosely called the *focal length*, because choosing d plays the same role as choosing focal length in a real camera. The direction of each ray is defined by the viewpoint and the position of the pixel on the image plane. This situation is illustrated in Figure 4.9, and the resulting procedure is similar to the orthographic one:

compute u and v using (4.1)
ray.direction $\leftarrow -d\,\mathbf{w} + u\,\mathbf{u} + v\,\mathbf{v}$
ray.origin $\leftarrow \mathbf{e}$

As with parallel projection, oblique perspective views can be achieved by specifying the image plane normal separately from the projection direction, then replacing $-d\,\mathbf{w}$ with $d\mathbf{d}$ in the expression for the ray direction.

4.4   Ray-Object Intersection

Once we've generated a ray $\mathbf{e} + t\mathbf{d}$, we next need to find the first intersection with any object where $t > 0$. In practice it turns out to be useful to solve a slightly more general problem: find the first intersection between the ray and a surface that occurs at a t in the interval $[t_0, t_1]$. The basic ray intersection is the case where $t_0 = 0$ and $t_1 = +\infty$. We solve this problem for both spheres and triangles. In the next section, multiple objects are discussed.

4.4.1   Ray-Sphere Intersection

Given a ray $\mathbf{p}(t) = \mathbf{e} + t\mathbf{d}$ and an implicit surface $f(\mathbf{p}) = 0$ (see Section 2.5.3), we'd like to know where they intersect. Intersection points occur when points on the ray satisfy the implicit equation, so the values of t we seek are those that solve the equation

$$f(\mathbf{p}(t)) = 0 \quad \text{or} \quad f(\mathbf{e} + t\mathbf{d}) = 0.$$

A sphere with center $\mathbf{c} = (x_c, y_c, z_c)$ and radius R can be represented by the implicit equation

$$(x - x_c)^2 + (y - y_c)^2 + (z - z_c)^2 - R^2 = 0.$$

We can write this same equation in vector form:

$$(\mathbf{p} - \mathbf{c}) \cdot (\mathbf{p} - \mathbf{c}) - R^2 = 0.$$

Any point $\mathbf{p}$ that satisfies this equation is on the sphere. If we plug points on the ray $\mathbf{p}(t) = \mathbf{e} + t\mathbf{d}$ into this equation, we get an equation in terms of t that is satisfied by the values of t that yield points on the sphere:

$$(\mathbf{e} + t\mathbf{d} - \mathbf{c}) \cdot (\mathbf{e} + t\mathbf{d} - \mathbf{c}) - R^2 = 0.$$

Rearranging terms yields

$$(\mathbf{d} \cdot \mathbf{d})t^2 + 2\mathbf{d} \cdot (\mathbf{e} - \mathbf{c})t + (\mathbf{e} - \mathbf{c}) \cdot (\mathbf{e} - \mathbf{c}) - R^2 = 0.$$

Here, everything is known except the parameter t, so this is a classic quadratic equation in t, meaning it has the form

$$At^2 + Bt + C = 0.$$

The solution to this equation is discussed in Section 2.2. The term under the square root sign in the quadratic solution, $B^2 - 4AC$, is called the *discriminant* and tells us how many real solutions there are. If the discriminant is negative, its square root is imaginary and the line and sphere do not intersect. If the discriminant is positive, there are two solutions: one solution where the ray enters the sphere and one where it leaves. If the discriminant is zero, the ray grazes the sphere, touching it at exactly one point. Plugging in the actual terms for the sphere and canceling a factor of two, we get

$$t = \frac{-\mathbf{d} \cdot (\mathbf{e} - \mathbf{c}) \pm \sqrt{(\mathbf{d} \cdot (\mathbf{e} - \mathbf{c}))^2 - (\mathbf{d} \cdot \mathbf{d})((\mathbf{e} - \mathbf{c}) \cdot (\mathbf{e} - \mathbf{c}) - R^2)}}{(\mathbf{d} \cdot \mathbf{d})}.$$

In an actual implementation, you should first check the value of the discriminant before computing other terms. If the sphere is used only as a bounding object for more complex objects, then we need only determine whether we hit it; checking the discriminant suffices.

As discussed in Section 2.5.4, the normal vector at point $\mathbf{p}$ is given by the gradient $\mathbf{n} = 2(\mathbf{p} - \mathbf{c})$. The unit normal is $(\mathbf{p} - \mathbf{c})/R$.

4.4.2 Ray-Triangle Intersection

There are many algorithms for computing ray-triangle intersections. We will present the form that uses barycentric coordinates for the parametric plane containing the triangle, because it requires no long-term storage other than the vertices of the triangle (Snyder & Barr, 1987).

To intersect a ray with a parametric surface, we set up a system of equations where the Cartesian coordinates all match:

$$\left. \begin{array}{c} x_e + tx_d = f(u, v) \\ y_e + ty_d = g(u, v) \\ z_e + tz_d = h(u, v) \end{array} \right\} \quad \text{or,} \quad \mathbf{e} + t\mathbf{d} = \mathbf{f}(u, v).$$

Here, we have three equations and three unknowns (t, u, and v), so we can solve numerically for the unknowns. If we are lucky, we can solve for them analytically.

In the case where the parametric surface is a parametric plane, the parametric equation can be written in vector form as discussed in Section 2.7.2. If the vertices of the triangle are $\mathbf{a}$, $\mathbf{b}$, and $\mathbf{c}$, then the intersection will occur when

$$\mathbf{e} + t\mathbf{d} = \mathbf{a} + \beta(\mathbf{b} - \mathbf{a}) + \gamma(\mathbf{c} - \mathbf{a}), \tag{4.2}$$

for some t, β, and γ. The intersection $\mathbf{p}$ will be at $\mathbf{e} + t\mathbf{d}$ as shown in Figure 4.10. Again, from Section 2.7.2, we know the intersection is inside the triangle if and only if $\beta > 0$, $\gamma > 0$, and $\beta + \gamma < 1$. Otherwise, the ray has hit the plane outside the triangle, so it misses the triangle. If there are no solutions, either the triangle is degenerate or the ray is parallel to the plane containing the triangle.

To solve for t, β, and γ in Equation (4.2), we expand it from its vector form into the three equations for the three coordinates:

$$x_e + tx_d = x_a + \beta(x_b - x_a) + \gamma(x_c - x_a),$$
$$y_e + ty_d = y_a + \beta(y_b - y_a) + \gamma(y_c - y_a),$$
$$z_e + tz_d = z_a + \beta(z_b - z_a) + \gamma(z_c - z_a).$$

This can be rewritten as a standard linear system:

$$\begin{bmatrix} x_a - x_b & x_a - x_c & x_d \\ y_a - y_b & y_a - y_c & y_d \\ z_a - z_b & z_a - z_c & z_d \end{bmatrix} \begin{bmatrix} \beta \\ \gamma \\ t \end{bmatrix} = \begin{bmatrix} x_a - x_e \\ y_a - y_e \\ z_a - z_e \end{bmatrix}.$$

The fastest classic method to solve this 3×3 linear system is *Cramer's rule*. This gives us the solutions

$$\beta = \frac{\begin{vmatrix} x_a - x_e & x_a - x_c & x_d \\ y_a - y_e & y_a - y_c & y_d \\ z_a - z_e & z_a - z_c & z_d \end{vmatrix}}{|\mathbf{A}|},$$

$$\gamma = \frac{\begin{vmatrix} x_a - x_b & x_a - x_e & x_d \\ y_a - y_b & y_a - y_e & y_d \\ z_a - z_b & z_a - z_e & z_d \end{vmatrix}}{|\mathbf{A}|}$$

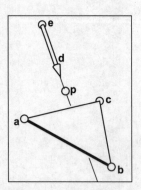

Figure 4.10. The ray hits the plane containing the triangle at point $\mathbf{p}$.

$$t = \frac{\begin{vmatrix} x_a - x_b & x_a - x_c & x_a - x_e \\ y_a - y_b & y_a - y_c & y_a - y_e \\ z_a - z_b & z_a - z_c & z_a - z_e \end{vmatrix}}{|\mathbf{A}|},$$

where the matrix $\mathbf{A}$ is

$$\mathbf{A} = \begin{bmatrix} x_a - x_b & x_a - x_c & x_d \\ y_a - y_b & y_a - y_c & y_d \\ z_a - z_b & z_a - z_c & z_d \end{bmatrix},$$

and $|\mathbf{A}|$ denotes the determinant of $\mathbf{A}$. The 3×3 determinants have common sub-terms that can be exploited. Looking at the linear systems with dummy variables

$$\begin{bmatrix} a & d & g \\ b & e & h \\ c & f & i \end{bmatrix} \begin{bmatrix} \beta \\ \gamma \\ t \end{bmatrix} = \begin{bmatrix} j \\ k \\ l \end{bmatrix},$$

Cramer's rule gives us

$$\beta = \frac{j(ei - hf) + k(gf - di) + l(dh - eg)}{M},$$

$$\gamma = \frac{i(ak - jb) + h(jc - al) + g(bl - kc)}{M},$$

$$t = -\frac{f(ak - jb) + e(jc - al) + d(bl - kc)}{M},$$

where

$$M = a(ei - hf) + b(gf - di) + c(dh - eg).$$

We can reduce the number of operations by reusing numbers such as "*ei-minus-hf.*"

The algorithm for the ray-triangle intersection for which we need the linear solution can have some conditions for early termination. Thus, the function should look something like:

boolean raytri (ray $\mathbf{r}$, vector3 $\mathbf{a}$, vector3 $\mathbf{b}$, vector3 $\mathbf{c}$, interval $[t_0, t_1]$)

    compute t

    if $(t < t_0)$ or $(t > t_1)$ **then**

        return false

    compute γ

    if $(\gamma < 0)$ or $(\gamma > 1)$ **then**

        return false

compute β
if $(\beta < 0)$ or $(\beta > 1 - \gamma)$ **then**
    return false
return true

4.4.3 Ray-Polygon Intersection

Given a planar polygon with m vertices $\mathbf{p}_1$ through $\mathbf{p}_m$ and surface normal $\mathbf{n}$, we first compute the intersection points between the ray $\mathbf{e} + t\mathbf{d}$ and the plane containing the polygon with implicit equation

$$(\mathbf{p} - \mathbf{p}_1) \cdot \mathbf{n} = 0.$$

We do this by setting $\mathbf{p} = \mathbf{e} + t\mathbf{d}$ and solving for t to get

$$t = \frac{(\mathbf{p}_1 - \mathbf{e}) \cdot \mathbf{n}}{\mathbf{d} \cdot \mathbf{n}}.$$

This allows us to compute $\mathbf{p}$. If $\mathbf{p}$ is inside the polygon, then the ray hits it, and otherwise it does not.

We can answer the question of whether $\mathbf{p}$ is inside the polygon by projecting the point and polygon vertices to the xy plane and answering it there. The easiest way to do this is to send any 2D ray out from $\mathbf{p}$ and to count the number of intersections between that ray and the boundary of the polygon (Sutherland et al., 1974; Glassner, 1989). If the number of intersections is odd, then the point is inside the polygon; otherwise it is not. This is true because a ray that goes in must go out, thus creating a pair of intersections. Only a ray that starts inside will not create such a pair. To make computation simple, the 2D ray may as well propagate along the x-axis:

$$\begin{bmatrix} x \\ y \end{bmatrix} = \begin{bmatrix} x_p \\ y_p \end{bmatrix} + s \begin{bmatrix} 1 \\ 0 \end{bmatrix}.$$

It is straightforward to compute the intersection of that ray with the edges such as (x_1, y_1, x_2, y_2) for $s \in (0, \infty)$.

A problem arises, however, for polygons whose projection into the xy plane is a line. To get around this, we can choose among the xy, yz, or zx planes for whichever is best. If we implement our points to allow an indexing operation, e.g., $\mathbf{p}(0) = x_p$ then this can be accomplished as follows:

if $(\mathrm{abs}(z_n) > \mathrm{abs}(x_n))$ and $(\mathrm{abs}(z_n) > \mathrm{abs}(y_n))$ **then**
    index0 = 0

        index1 = 1
    else if $(\mathrm{abs}(y_n) > \mathrm{abs}(x_n))$ **then**
        index0 = 0
        index1 = 2
    else
        index0 = 1
        index1 = 2

Now, all computations can use $\mathbf{p}(\mathrm{index0})$ rather than x_p, and so on.

Another approach to polygons, one that is often used in practice, is to replace them by several triangles.

4.4.4 Intersecting a Group of Objects

Of course, most interesting scenes consist of more than one object, and when we intersect a ray with the scene we must find only the closest intersection to the camera along the ray. A simple way to implement this is to think of a group of objects as itself being another type of object. To intersect a ray with a group, you simply intersect the ray with the objects in the group and return the intersection with the smallest t value. The following code tests for hits in the interval $t \in [t_0, t_1]$:

    hit = false
    for each object o in the group **do**
        if (o is hit at ray parameter t and $t \in [t_0, t_1]$) **then**
            hit = true
            hitobject = o
            $t_1 = t$
    return hit

Figure 4.11.   A simple scene rendered with only ray generation and surface intersection, but no shading; each pixel is just set to a fixed color depending on which object it hit.

4.5   Shading

Once the visible surface for a pixel is known, the pixel value is computed by evaluating a *shading model*. How this is done depends entirely on the application— methods range from very simple heuristics to elaborate numerical computations. In this chapter we describe the two most basic shading models; more advanced models are discussed in Chapter 10.

Most shading models, one way or another, are designed to capture the process of light reflection, whereby surfaces are illuminated by light sources and reflect part of the light to the camera. Simple shading models are defined in terms of illumination from a point light source. The important variables in light reflection are the light direction l, which is a unit vector pointing towards the light source; the view direction v, which is a unit vector pointing toward the eye or camera; the surface normal n, which is a unit vector perpendicular to the surface at the point where reflection is taking place; and the characteristics of the surface—color, shininess, or other properties depending on the particular model.

4.5.1 Lambertian Shading

Illumination from real point sources falls off as distance squared, but that is often more trouble than it's worth in a simple renderer.

The simplest shading model is based on an observation made by Lambert in the 18th century: the amount of energy from a light source that falls on an area of surface depends on the angle of the surface to the light. A surface facing directly towards the light receives maximum illumination; a surface tangent to the light direction (or facing away from the light) receives no illumination; and in between the illumination is proportional to the cosine of the angle θ between the surface normal and the light source (Figure 4.12). This leads to the *Lambertian shading model*:

$$L = k_d \, I \max(0, \mathbf{n} \cdot \mathbf{l})$$

Figure 4.12. Geometry for Lambertian shading.

When in doubt, make light sources neutral in color, with equal red, green, and blue intensities.

where L is the pixel color; k_d is the *diffuse coefficient*, or the surface color; and I is the intensity of the light source. Because n and l are unit vectors, we can use $\mathbf{n} \cdot \mathbf{l}$ as a convenient shorthand (both on paper and in code) for $\cos \theta$. This equation (as with the other shading equations in this section) applies separately to the three color channels, so the red component of the pixel value is the product of the red diffuse component, the red light source intensity, and the dot product; the same holds for green and blue.

The vector l is computed by subtracting the intersection point of the ray and surface from the light source position. Don't forget that v, l, and n all must be unit vectors; failing to normalize these vectors is a very common error in shading computations.

4.5.2 Blinn-Phong Shading

Lambertian shading is *view independent*: the color of a surface does not depend on the direction from which you look. Many real surfaces show some degree of shininess, producing highlights, or *specular reflections*, that appear to move around as the viewpoint changes. Lambertian shading doesn't produce any highlights and leads to a very matte, chalky appearance, and many shading models

Figure 4.13. A simple scene rendered with diffuse shading from a single light source.

Figure 4.14. A simple scene rendered with diffuse shading and shadows (Section 4.7) from three light sources.

Figure 4.15. A simple scene rendered with diffuse shading (right), Blinn-Phong shading (left), and shadows (Section 4.7) from three light sources.

add a *specular component* to Lambertian shading; the Lambertian part is then the *diffuse component*.

A very simple and widely used model for specular highlights was proposed by Phong (Phong, 1975) and later updated by Blinn (J. F. Blinn, 1976) to the form most commonly used today. The idea is to produce reflection that is at its brightest when **v** and **l** are symmetrically positioned across the surface normal, which is when mirror reflection would occur; the refelction then decreases smoothly as the vectors move away from a mirror configuration.

We can tell how close we are to a mirror configuration by comparing the half vector **h** (the bisector of the angle between **v** and **l**) to the surface normal (Figure 4.16). If the half vector is near the surface normal, the specular component should be bright; if it is far away it should be dim. This result is achieved by computing the dot product between **h** and **n** (remember they are unit vectors, so $\mathbf{n} \cdot \mathbf{h}$ reaches its maximum of 1 when the vectors are equal), then taking the result to a power $p > 1$ to make it decrease faster. The power, or *Phong exponent*, controls the apparent shininess of the surface. The half vector itself is easy to compute: since **v** and **l** are the same length, their sum is a vector that bisects the angle between them, which only needs to be normalized to produce **h**.

Putting this all together, the Blinn-Phong shading model is as follows:

$$\mathbf{h} = \frac{\mathbf{v} + \mathbf{l}}{\|\mathbf{v} + \mathbf{l}\|},$$
$$L = k_d\, I \max(0, \mathbf{n} \cdot \mathbf{l}) + k_s\, I \max(0, \mathbf{n} \cdot \mathbf{h})^p,$$

where k_s is the *specular coefficient*, or the specular color, of the surface.

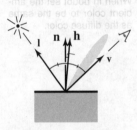

Figure 4.16. Geometry for Blinn-Phong shading.

Typical values of *p*: 10—"eggshell"; 100—mildly shiny; 1000—really glossy; 10,000—nearly mirror-like.

When in doubt, make the specular color gray, with equal red, green, and blue values.

4.5.3 Ambient Shading

Surfaces that receive no illumination at all will be rendered as completely black, which is often not desirable. A crude but useful heuristic to avoid black shadows is to add a constant component to the shading model, one whose contribution to the pixel color depends only on the object hit, with no dependence on the surface geometry at all. This is known as ambient shading—it is as if surfaces were illuminated by "ambient" light that comes equally from everywhere. For convenience in tuning the parameters, ambient shading is usually expressed as the product of a surface color with an ambient light color, so that ambient shading can be tuned for surfaces individually or for all surfaces together. Together with the rest of the Blinn-Phong model, ambient shading completes the full version of a simple and useful shading model:

$$L = k_a I_a + k_d I \max(0, \mathbf{n} \cdot \mathbf{l}) + k_s I \max(0, \mathbf{n} \cdot \mathbf{h})^n, \qquad (4.3)$$

where k_a is the surface's ambient coefficient, or "ambient color," and I_a is the ambient light intensity.

4.5.4 Multiple Point Lights

A very useful property of light is *superposition*—the effect caused by more than one light source is simply the sum of the effects of the light sources individually. For this reason, our simple shading model can easily be extended to handle N light sources:

$$L = k_a I_a + \sum_{i=1}^{N} [k_d I_i \max(0, \mathbf{n} \cdot \mathbf{l}_i) + k_s I_i \max(0, \mathbf{n} \cdot \mathbf{h}_i)^p], \qquad (4.4)$$

where I_i, $\mathbf{l}_i$, and $\mathbf{h}_i$ are the intensity, direction, and half vector of the ith light source.

4.6 A Ray-Tracing Program

We now know how to generate a viewing ray for a given pixel, how to find the closest intersection with an object, and how to shade the resulting intersection. These are all the parts required for a program that produces shaded images with hidden surfaces removed.

> **for** each pixel **do**
>   compute viewing ray
>   **if** (ray hits an object with $t \in [0, \infty)$) **then**
>   Compute **n**
>   Evaluate shading model and set pixel to that color
>   **else**
>   set pixel color to background color

Here the statement "if ray hits an object..." can be implemented using the algorithm of Section 4.4.4.

In an actual implementation, the surface intersection routine needs to somehow return either a reference to the object that is hit, or at least its normal vector and shading-relevant material properties. This is often done by passing a record/structure with such information. In an object-oriented implementation, it is a good idea to have a class called something like *surface* with derived classes *triangle, sphere, group*, etc. Anything that a ray can intersect would be under that class. The ray-tracing program would then have one reference to a "surface" for the whole model, and new types of objects and efficiency structures can be added transparently.

4.6.1 Object-Oriented Design for a Ray-Tracing Program

As mentioned earlier, the key class hierarchy in a ray tracer are the geometric objects that make up the model. These should be subclasses of some geometric object class, and they should support a *hit* function (Kirk & Arvo, 1988). To avoid confusion from use of the word "object," *surface* is the class name often used. With such a class, you can create a ray tracer that has a general interface that assumes little about modeling primitives and debug it using only spheres. An important point is that anything that can be "hit" by a ray should be part of this class hierarchy, e.g., even a collection of surfaces should be considered a subclass of the surface class. This includes efficiency structures, such as bounding volume hierarchies; they can be hit by a ray, so they are in the class.

For example, the "abstract" or "base" class would specify the hit function as well as a bounding box function that will prove useful later:

```
class surface
virtual bool hit(ray e + td, real t0, real t1, hit-record rec)
virtual box bounding-box()
```

Here (t_0, t_1) is the interval on the ray where hits will be returned, and rec is a record that is passed by reference; it contains data such as the t at the intersection when hit returns true. The type box is a 3D "bounding box," that is two points that define an axis-aligned box that encloses the surface. For example, for a sphere, the function would be implemented by

```
box sphere::bounding-box()
    vector3 min = center - vector3(radius,radius,radius)
    vector3 max = center + vector3(radius,radius,radius)
    return box(min, max)
```

Another class that is useful is material. This allows you to abstract the material behavior and later add materials transparently. A simple way to link objects and materials is to add a pointer to a material in the surface class, although more programmable behavior might be desirable. A big question is what to do with textures; are they part of the material class or do they live outside of the material class? This will be discussed more in Chapter 11.

4.7 Shadows

Once you have a basic ray tracing program, shadows can be added very easily. Recall from Section 4.5 that light comes from some direction l. If we imagine ourselves at a point $\mathbf{p}$ on a surface being shaded, the point is in shadow if we "look" in direction l and see an object. If there are no objects, then the light is not blocked.

This is shown in Figure 4.17, where the ray $\mathbf{p} + t\mathbf{l}$ does not hit any objects and is thus not in shadow. The point $\mathbf{q}$ is in shadow because the ray $\mathbf{q} + t\mathbf{l}$ does hit an object. The vector l is the same for both points because the light is "far" away. This assumption will later be relaxed. The rays that determine in or out of shadow are called *shadow rays* to distinguish them from viewing rays.

To get the algorithm for shading, we add an if statement to determine whether the point is in shadow. In a naive implementation, the shadow ray will check for $t \in [0, \infty)$, but because of numerical imprecision, this can result in an intersection with the surface on which $\mathbf{p}$ lies. Instead, the usual adjustment to avoid that problem is to test for $t \in [\epsilon, \infty)$ where ϵ is some small positive constant (Figure 4.18).

If we implement shadow rays for Phong lighting with Equation 4.3 then we have the following:

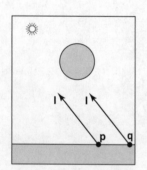

Figure 4.17. The point **p** is not in shadow while the point **q** is in shadow.

> **function** raycolor(ray $\mathbf{e} + t\mathbf{d}$, real t_0, real t_1)
> hit-record rec, srec
> **if** (scene→hit($\mathbf{e} + t\mathbf{d}$, t_0, t_1, rec)) **then**
> $\mathbf{p} = \mathbf{e} + (\text{rec}.t)\,\mathbf{d}$
>   color $c = \text{rec}.k_a\, I_a$
>   **if** (not scene→hit($\mathbf{p} + s\mathbf{l}$, ϵ, ∞, srec)) **then**
>   vector3 $\mathbf{h} = \text{normalized}(\text{normalized}(\mathbf{l}) + \text{normalized}(-\mathbf{d}))$
> $c = c + \text{rec}.k_d\, I \max(0, \text{rec}.\mathbf{n} \cdot \mathbf{l}) + (\text{rec}.k_s)\, I\, (\text{rec}.\mathbf{n} \cdot \mathbf{h})^{\text{rec}.p}$
>   **return** c
> **else**
>   **return** background-color

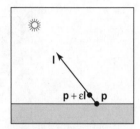

Figure 4.18. By testing in the interval starting at ϵ, we avoid numerical imprecision causing the ray to hit the surface $\mathbf{p}$ is on.

Note that the ambient color is added whether $\mathbf{p}$ is in shadow or not. If there are multiple light sources, we can send a shadow ray before evaluating the shading model for each light. The code above assumes that $\mathbf{d}$ and $\mathbf{l}$ are not necessarily unit vectors. This is crucial for $\mathbf{d}$, in particular, if we wish to cleanly add *instancing* later (see Section 13.2).

4.8 Ideal Specular Reflection

It is straightforward to add *ideal specular* reflection, or *mirror reflection*, to a raytracing program. The key observation is shown in Figure 4.19 where a viewer looking from direction $\mathbf{e}$ sees what is in direction $\mathbf{r}$ as seen from the surface. The vector $\mathbf{r}$ is found using a variant of the Phong lighting reflection Equation (10.6). There are sign changes because the vector $\mathbf{d}$ points toward the surface in this case, so,

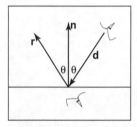

Figure 4.19. When looking into a perfect mirror, the viewer looking in direction $\mathbf{d}$ will see whatever the viewer "below" the surface would see in direction $\mathbf{r}$.

$$\mathbf{r} = \mathbf{d} - 2(\mathbf{d} \cdot \mathbf{n})\mathbf{n}, \tag{4.5}$$

In the real world, some energy is lost when the light reflects from the surface, and this loss can be different for different colors. For example, gold reflects yellow more efficiently than blue, so it shifts the colors of the objects it reflects. This can be implemented by adding a recursive call in *raycolor*:

$$\text{color } c = c + k_m \text{raycolor}(\mathbf{p} + s\mathbf{r}, \epsilon, \infty)$$

where k_m (for "mirror reflection") is the specular RGB color. We need to make sure we test for $s \in [\epsilon, \infty)$ for the same reason as we did with shadow rays; we don't want the reflection ray to hit the object that generates it.

The problem with the recursive call above is that it may never terminate. For example, if a ray starts inside a room, it will bounce forever. This can be fixed by

Figure 4.20. A simple scene rendered with diffuse and Blinn-Phong shading, shadows from three light sources, and specular reflection from the floor.

adding a maximum recursion depth. The code will be more efficient if a reflection ray is generated only if k_m is not zero (black).

4.9   Historical Notes

Ray tracing was developed early in the history of computer graphics (Appel, 1968) but was not used much until a while later when sufficient compute power was available (Kay & Greenberg, 1979; Whitted, 1980).

Ray tracing has a lower asymptotic time complexity than basic object-order rendering (Snyder & Barr, 1987; Muuss, 1995; Parker, Martin, et al., 1999; Wald et al., 2001). Although it was traditionally thought of as an offline method, real-time ray tracing implementations are becoming more and more common.

Frequently Asked Questions

- Why is there no perspective matrix in ray tracing?

The perspective matrix in a z-buffer exists so that we can turn the perspective projection into a parallel projection. This is not needed in ray tracing, because it is easy to do the perspective projection implicitly by fanning the rays out from the eye.

- Can ray tracing be made interactive?

For sufficiently small models and images, any modern PC is sufficiently powerful for ray tracing to be interactive. In practice, multiple CPUs with a shared frame buffer are required for a full-screen implementation. Computer power is increasing much faster than screen resolution, and it is just a matter of time before conventional PCs can ray trace complex scenes at screen resolution.

- Is ray tracing useful in a hardware graphics program?

Ray tracing is frequently used for *picking*. When the user clicks the mouse on a pixel in a 3D graphics program, the program needs to determine which object is visible within that pixel. Ray tracing is an ideal way to determine that.

Exercises

1. What are the ray parameters of the intersection points between ray $(1, 1, 1) + t(-1, -1, -1)$ and the sphere centered at the origin with radius 1? Note: this is a good debugging case.

2. What are the barycentric coordinates and ray parameter where the ray $(1, 1, 1) + t(-1, -1, -1)$ hits the triangle with vertices $(1, 0, 0)$, $(0, 1, 0)$, and $(0, 0, 1)$? Note: this is a good debugging case.

3. Do a back of the envelope computation of the approximate time complexity of ray tracing on "nice" (non-adversarial) models. Split your analysis into the cases of preprocessing and computing the image, so that you can predict the behavior of ray tracing multiple frames for a static model.

5

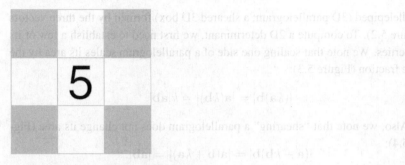

Linear Algebra

Perhaps the most universal tools of graphics programs are the matrices that change or *transform* points and vectors. In the next chapter, we will see how a vector can be represented as a matrix with a single column, and how the vector can be represented in a different basis via multiplication with a square matrix. We will also describe how we can use such multiplications to accomplish changes in the vector such as scaling, rotation, and translation. In this chapter, we review basic linear algebra from a geometric perspective, focusing on intuition and algorithms that work well in the two- and three-dimensional case.

This chapter can be skipped by readers comfortable with linear algebra. However, there may be some enlightening tidbits even for such readers, such as the development of determinants and the discussion of singular and eigenvalue decomposition.

5.1   Determinants

We usually think of determinants as arising in the solution of linear equations. However, for our purposes, we will think of determinants as another way to multiply vectors. For 2D vectors $\mathbf{a}$ and $\mathbf{b}$, the determinant $|\mathbf{ab}|$ is the area of the parallelogram formed by $\mathbf{a}$ and $\mathbf{b}$ (Figure 5.1). This is a signed area, and the sign is positive if $\mathbf{a}$ and $\mathbf{b}$ are right-handed and negative if they are left-handed. This means $|\mathbf{ab}| = -|\mathbf{ba}|$. In 2D we can interpret "right-handed" as meaning we rotate the first vector counterclockwise to close the smallest angle to the second vector. In 3D the determinant must be taken with three vectors at a time. For three 3D vectors, $\mathbf{a}$, $\mathbf{b}$, and $\mathbf{c}$, the determinant $|\mathbf{abc}|$ is the signed volume of the

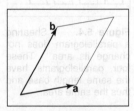

Figure 5.1. The signed area of the parallelogram is $|\mathbf{ab}|$, and in this case the area is positive.

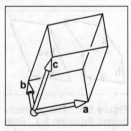

Figure 5.2. The signed volume of the parallelepiped shown is denoted by the determinant $|\mathbf{abc}|$, and in this case the volume is positive because the vectors form a right-handed basis.

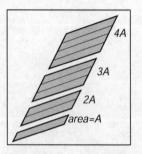

Figure 5.3. Scaling a parallelogram along one direction changes the area in the same proportion.

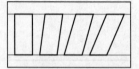

Figure 5.4. Shearing a parallelogram does not change its area. These four parallelograms have the same length base and thus the same area.

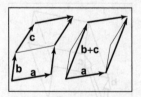

Figure 5.5. The geometry behind Equation 5.1. Both of the parallelograms on the left can be sheared to cover the single parallelogram on the right.

parallelepiped (3D parallelogram; a sheared 3D box) formed by the three vectors (Figure 5.2). To compute a 2D determinant, we first need to establish a few of its properties. We note that scaling one side of a parallelogram scales its area by the same fraction (Figure 5.3):

$$|(k\mathbf{a})\mathbf{b}| = |\mathbf{a}(k\mathbf{b})| = k|\mathbf{a}\mathbf{b}|.$$

Also, we note that "shearing" a parallelogram does not change its area (Figure 5.4):

$$|(\mathbf{a} + k\mathbf{b})\mathbf{b}| = |\mathbf{a}(\mathbf{b} + k\mathbf{a})| = |\mathbf{a}\mathbf{b}|.$$

Finally, we see that the determinant has the following property:

$$|\mathbf{a}(\mathbf{b} + \mathbf{c})| = |\mathbf{a}\mathbf{b}| + |\mathbf{a}\mathbf{c}|, \tag{5.1}$$

because as shown in Figure 5.5 we can "slide" the edge between the two parallelograms over to form a single parallelogram without changing the area of either of the two original parallelograms.

Now let's assume a Cartesian representation for **a** and **b**:

$$\begin{aligned}
|\mathbf{a}\mathbf{b}| &= |(x_a\mathbf{x} + y_a\mathbf{y})(x_b\mathbf{x} + y_b\mathbf{y})| \\
&= x_ax_b|\mathbf{x}\mathbf{x}| + x_ay_b|\mathbf{x}\mathbf{y}| + y_ax_b|\mathbf{y}\mathbf{x}| + y_ay_b|\mathbf{y}\mathbf{y}| \\
&= x_ax_b(0) + x_ay_b(+1) + y_ax_b(-1) + y_ay_b(0) \\
&= x_ay_b - y_ax_b.
\end{aligned}$$

This simplification uses the fact that $|\mathbf{v}\mathbf{v}| = 0$ for any vector **v**, because the parallelograms would all be collinear with **v** and thus without area.

In three dimensions, the determinant of three 3D vectors **a**, **b**, and **c** is denoted $|\mathbf{a}\mathbf{b}\mathbf{c}|$. With Cartesian representations for the vectors, there are analogous rules for parallelepipeds as there are for parallelograms, and we can do an analogous expansion as we did for 2D:

$$\begin{aligned}
|\mathbf{a}\mathbf{b}\mathbf{c}| &= |(x_a\mathbf{x} + y_a\mathbf{y} + z_a\mathbf{z})(x_b\mathbf{x} + y_b\mathbf{y} + z_b\mathbf{z})(x_c\mathbf{x} + y_c\mathbf{y} + z_c\mathbf{z})| \\
&= x_ay_bz_c - x_az_by_c - y_ax_bz_c + y_az_bx_c + z_ax_by_c - z_ay_bx_c.
\end{aligned}$$

As you can see, the computation of determinants in this fashion gets uglier as the dimension increases. We will discuss less error-prone ways to compute determinants in Section 5.3.

Example. Determinants arise naturally when computing the expression for one vector as a linear combination of two others—for example, if we wish to express a vector **c** as a combination of vectors **a** and **b**:

$$\mathbf{c} = a_c\mathbf{a} + b_c\mathbf{b}.$$

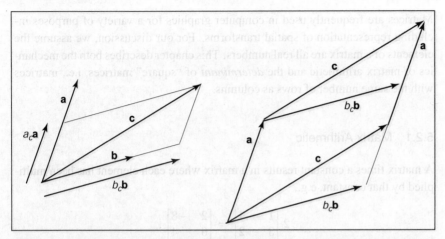

Figure 5.6. On the left, the vector **c** can be represented using two basis vectors as $a_c\mathbf{a} + b_c\mathbf{b}$. On the right, we see that the parallelogram formed by **a** and **c** is a sheared version of the parallelogram formed by $b_c\mathbf{b}$ and **a**.

We can see from Figure 5.6 that

$$|(b_c\mathbf{b})\mathbf{a}| = |\mathbf{ca}|,$$

because these parallelograms are just sheared versions of each other. Solving for b_c yields

$$b_c = \frac{|\mathbf{ca}|}{|\mathbf{ba}|}.$$

An analogous argument yields

$$a_c = \frac{|\mathbf{bc}|}{|\mathbf{ba}|}.$$

This is the two-dimensional version of *Cramer's rule* which we will revisit in Section 5.3.2.

5.2 Matrices

A matrix is an array of numeric elements that follow certain arithmetic rules. An example of a matrix with two rows and three columns is

$$\begin{bmatrix} 1.7 & -1.2 & 4.2 \\ 3.0 & 4.5 & -7.2 \end{bmatrix}.$$

Matrices are frequently used in computer graphics for a variety of purposes including representation of spatial transforms. For our discussion, we assume the elements of a matrix are all real numbers. This chapter describes both the mechanics of matrix arithmetic and the *determinant* of "square" matrices, i.e., matrices with the same number of rows as columns.

5.2.1 Matrix Arithmetic

A matrix times a constant results in a matrix where each element has been multiplied by that constant, e.g.,

$$2 \begin{bmatrix} 1 & -4 \\ 3 & 2 \end{bmatrix} = \begin{bmatrix} 2 & -8 \\ 6 & 4 \end{bmatrix}.$$

Matrices also add element by element, e.g.,

$$\begin{bmatrix} 1 & -4 \\ 3 & 2 \end{bmatrix} + \begin{bmatrix} 2 & 2 \\ 2 & 2 \end{bmatrix} = \begin{bmatrix} 3 & -2 \\ 5 & 4 \end{bmatrix}.$$

For matrix multiplication, we "multiply" rows of the first matrix with columns of the second matrix:

$$\begin{bmatrix} a_{11} & \cdots & a_{1m} \\ \vdots & & \vdots \\ a_{i1} & \cdots & a_{im} \\ \vdots & & \vdots \\ a_{r1} & \cdots & a_{rm} \end{bmatrix} \begin{bmatrix} b_{11} & \cdots & b_{1j} & \cdots & b_{1c} \\ \vdots & & \vdots & & \vdots \\ b_{m1} & \cdots & b_{mj} & \cdots & b_{mc} \end{bmatrix} = \begin{bmatrix} p_{11} & \cdots & p_{1j} & \cdots & p_{1c} \\ \vdots & & \vdots & & \vdots \\ p_{i1} & \cdots & p_{ij} & \cdots & p_{ic} \\ \vdots & & \vdots & & \vdots \\ p_{r1} & \cdots & p_{rj} & \cdots & p_{rc} \end{bmatrix}$$

So the element p_{ij} of the resulting product is

$$p_{ij} = a_{i1}b_{1j} + a_{i2}b_{2j} + \cdots + a_{im}b_{mj}. \tag{5.2}$$

Taking a product of two matrices is only possible if the number of columns of the left matrix is the same as the number of rows of the right matrix. For example,

$$\begin{bmatrix} 0 & 1 \\ 2 & 3 \\ 4 & 5 \end{bmatrix} \begin{bmatrix} 6 & 7 & 8 & 9 \\ 0 & 1 & 2 & 3 \end{bmatrix} = \begin{bmatrix} 0 & 1 & 2 & 3 \\ 12 & 17 & 22 & 27 \\ 24 & 33 & 42 & 51 \end{bmatrix}.$$

Matrix multiplication is *not* commutative in most instances:

$$\mathbf{AB} \neq \mathbf{BA}. \tag{5.3}$$

Also, if $\mathbf{AB} = \mathbf{AC}$, it does not necessarily follow that $\mathbf{B} = \mathbf{C}$. Fortunately, matrix multiplication is associative and distributive:

$$\mathbf{(AB)C} = \mathbf{A(BC)},$$
$$\mathbf{A(B+C)} = \mathbf{AB} + \mathbf{AC},$$
$$\mathbf{(A+B)C} = \mathbf{AC} + \mathbf{BC}.$$

5.2.2 Operations on Matrices

We would like a matrix analog of the inverse of a real number. We know the inverse of a real number x is $1/x$ and that the product of x and its inverse is 1. We need a matrix $\mathbf{I}$ that we can think of as a "matrix one." This exists only for square matrices and is known as the *identity matrix*; it consists of ones down the *diagonal* and zeroes elsewhere. For example, the four by four identity matrix is

$$\mathbf{I} = \begin{bmatrix} 1 & 0 & 0 & 0 \\ 0 & 1 & 0 & 0 \\ 0 & 0 & 1 & 0 \\ 0 & 0 & 0 & 1 \end{bmatrix}.$$

The *inverse matrix* $\mathbf{A}^{-1}$ of a matrix $\mathbf{A}$ is the matrix that ensures $\mathbf{AA}^{-1} = \mathbf{I}$. For example,

$$\begin{bmatrix} 1 & 2 \\ 3 & 4 \end{bmatrix}^{-1} = \begin{bmatrix} -2.0 & 1.0 \\ 1.5 & -0.5 \end{bmatrix} \quad \text{because} \quad \begin{bmatrix} 1 & 2 \\ 3 & 4 \end{bmatrix} \begin{bmatrix} -2.0 & 1.0 \\ 1.5 & -0.5 \end{bmatrix} = \begin{bmatrix} 1 & 0 \\ 0 & 1 \end{bmatrix}.$$

Note that the inverse of $\mathbf{A}^{-1}$ is $\mathbf{A}$. So $\mathbf{AA}^{-1} = \mathbf{A}^{-1}\mathbf{A} = \mathbf{I}$. The inverse of a product of two matrices is the product of the inverses, but with the order reversed:

$$\mathbf{(AB)}^{-1} = \mathbf{B}^{-1}\mathbf{A}^{-1}. \tag{5.4}$$

We will return to the question of computing inverses later in the chapter.

The *transpose* $\mathbf{A}^{\mathrm{T}}$ of a matrix $\mathbf{A}$ has the same numbers but the rows are switched with the columns. If we label the entries of $\mathbf{A}^{\mathrm{T}}$ as a'_{ij} then

$$a_{ij} = a'_{ji}.$$

For example,

$$\begin{bmatrix} 1 & 2 \\ 3 & 4 \\ 5 & 6 \end{bmatrix}^{\mathrm{T}} = \begin{bmatrix} 1 & 3 & 5 \\ 2 & 4 & 6 \end{bmatrix}.$$

The transpose of a product of two matrices obeys a rule similar to Equation (5.4):

$$(\mathbf{AB})^\mathrm{T} = \mathbf{B}^\mathrm{T}\mathbf{A}^\mathrm{T}.$$

The determinant of a square matrix is simply the determinant of the columns of the matrix, considered as a set of vectors. The determinant has several nice relationships to the matrix operations just discussed, which we list here for reference:

$$|\mathbf{AB}| = |\mathbf{A}|\,|\mathbf{B}| \tag{5.5}$$

$$|\mathbf{A}^{-1}| = \frac{1}{|\mathbf{A}|} \tag{5.6}$$

$$|\mathbf{A}^\mathrm{T}| = |\mathbf{A}| \tag{5.7}$$

5.2.3 Vector Operations in Matrix Form

In graphics, we use a square matrix to transform a vector represented as a matrix. For example if you have a 2D vector $\mathbf{a} = (x_a, y_a)$ and want to rotate it by 90 degrees about the origin to form vector $\mathbf{a}' = (-y_a, x_a)$, you can use a product of a 2×2 matrix and a 2×1 matrix, called a *column vector*. The operation in matrix form is

$$\begin{bmatrix} 0 & -1 \\ 1 & 0 \end{bmatrix} \begin{bmatrix} x_a \\ y_a \end{bmatrix} = \begin{bmatrix} -y_a \\ x_a \end{bmatrix}.$$

We can get the same result by using the transpose of this matrix and multiplying on the left ("premultiplying") with a row vector:

$$\begin{bmatrix} x_a & y_a \end{bmatrix} \begin{bmatrix} 0 & 1 \\ -1 & 0 \end{bmatrix} = \begin{bmatrix} -y_a & x_a \end{bmatrix}.$$

These days, postmultiplication using column vectors is fairly standard, but in many older books and systems you will run across row vectors and premultiplication. The only difference is that the transform matrix must be replaced with its transpose.

We can use also matrix formalism to encode operations on just vectors. If we consider the result of the dot product as a 1×1 matrix, it can be written

$$\mathbf{a} \cdot \mathbf{b} = \mathbf{a}^\mathrm{T}\mathbf{b}.$$

For example, if we take two 3D vectors we get

$$\begin{bmatrix} x_a & y_a & z_a \end{bmatrix} \begin{bmatrix} x_b \\ y_b \\ z_b \end{bmatrix} = \begin{bmatrix} x_a x_b + y_a y_b + z_a z_b \end{bmatrix}.$$

A related vector product is the *outer product* between two vectors, which can be expressed as a matrix multiplication with a column vector on the left and a row vector on the right: $\mathbf{a}\mathbf{b}^{\mathrm{T}}$. The result is a matrix consisting of products of all pairs of an entry of $\mathbf{a}$ with an entry of $\mathbf{b}$. For 3D vectors, we have

$$\begin{bmatrix} x_a \\ y_a \\ z_a \end{bmatrix} \begin{bmatrix} x_b & y_b & z_b \end{bmatrix} = \begin{bmatrix} x_a x_b & x_a y_b & x_a z_b \\ y_a x_b & y_a y_b & y_a z_b \\ z_a x_b & z_a y_b & z_a z_b \end{bmatrix}.$$

It is often useful to think of matrix multiplication in terms of vector operations. To illustrate using the three-dimensional case, we can think of a 3×3 matrix as a collection of three 3D vectors in two ways: either it is made up of three column vectors side-by-side, or it is made up of three row vectors stacked up. For instance, the result of a matrix-vector multiplication $\mathbf{y} = \mathbf{A}\mathbf{x}$ can be interpreted as a vector whose entries are the dot products of $\mathbf{x}$ with the rows of $\mathbf{A}$. Naming these row vectors $\mathbf{r}_i$, we have

$$\begin{bmatrix} | \\ \mathbf{y} \\ | \end{bmatrix} = \begin{bmatrix} - \mathbf{r_1} - \\ - \mathbf{r_2} - \\ - \mathbf{r_3} - \end{bmatrix} \begin{bmatrix} | \\ \mathbf{x} \\ | \end{bmatrix} ;$$

$$y_i = \mathbf{r}_i \cdot \mathbf{x}.$$

Alternatively, we can think of the same product as a sum of the three columns $\mathbf{c}_i$ of A, weighted by the entries of $\mathbf{x}$:

$$\begin{bmatrix} | \\ \mathbf{y} \\ | \end{bmatrix} = \begin{bmatrix} | & | & | \\ \mathbf{c_1} & \mathbf{c_2} & \mathbf{c_3} \\ | & | & | \end{bmatrix} \begin{bmatrix} x_1 \\ x_2 \\ x_3 \end{bmatrix} ;$$

$$\mathbf{y} = x_1 \mathbf{c_1} + x_2 \mathbf{c_2} + x_3 \mathbf{c_3}.$$

Using the same ideas, one can understand a matrix-matrix product $\mathbf{AB}$ as an array containing the pairwise dot products of all rows of $\mathbf{A}$ with all columns of $\mathbf{B}$ (cf. (5.2)); as a collection of products of the matrix $\mathbf{A}$ with all the column vectors of $\mathbf{B}$, arranged left to right; as a collection of products of all the row vectors of $\mathbf{A}$ with the matrix $\mathbf{B}$, stacked top to bottom; or as the sum of the pairwise outer products of all columns of $\mathbf{A}$ with all rows of $\mathbf{B}$. (See Exercise 8.)

These interpretations of matrix multiplication can often lead to valuable geometric interpretations of operations that may otherwise seem very abstract.

5.2.4 Special Types of Matrices

The identity matrix is an example of a *diagonal matrix*, where all non-zero elements occur along the diagonal. The diagonal consists of those elements whose column index equals the row index counting from the upper left.

The identity matrix also has the property that it is the same as its transpose. Such matrices are called *symmetric*.

The identity matrix is also an *orthogonal* matrix, because each of its columns considered as a vector has length 1 and the columns are orthogonal to one another. The same is true of the rows (see Exercise 2). The determinant of any orthogonal matrix is either $+1$ or -1.

A very useful property of orthogonal matrices is that they are nearly their own inverses. Multiplying an orthogonal matrix by its transpose results in the identity,

$$\mathbf{R}^{\mathrm{T}}\mathbf{R} = I = \mathbf{R}\mathbf{R}^{\mathrm{T}} \quad \text{for orthogonal } \mathbf{R}.$$

This is easy to see because the entries of $\mathbf{R}^{\mathrm{T}}\mathbf{R}$ are dot products between the columns of $\mathbf{R}$. Off-diagonal entries are dot products between orthogonal vectors, and the diagonal entries are dot products of the (unit-length) columns with themselves.

Example. The matrix

$$\begin{bmatrix} 8 & 0 & 0 \\ 0 & 2 & 0 \\ 0 & 0 & 9 \end{bmatrix}$$

is diagonal, and therefore symmetric, but not orthogonal (the columns are orthogonal but they are not unit length).

The matrix

$$\begin{bmatrix} 1 & 1 & 2 \\ 1 & 9 & 7 \\ 2 & 7 & 1 \end{bmatrix}$$

is symmetric, but not diagonal or orthogonal.

The matrix

$$\begin{bmatrix} 0 & 1 & 0 \\ 0 & 0 & 1 \\ 1 & 0 & 0 \end{bmatrix}$$

is orthogonal, but neither diagonal nor symmetric.

5.3   Computing with Matrices and Determinants

Recall from Section 5.1 that the determinant takes n n-dimensional vectors and combines them to get a signed n-dimensional volume of the n-dimensional parallelepiped defined by the vectors. For example, the determinant in 2D is the area

> The idea of an orthogonal matrix corresponds to the idea of an *orthonormal* basis, not just a set of *orthogonal* vectors—an unfortunate glitch in terminology.

of the parallelogram formed by the vectors. We can use matrices to handle the mechanics of computing determinants.

If we have 2D vectors **r** and **s**, we denote the determinant $|\mathbf{rs}|$; this value is the signed area of the parallelogram formed by the vectors. Suppose we have two 2D vectors with Cartesian coordinates (a, b) and (A, B) (Figure 5.7). The determinant can be written in terms of column vectors or as a shorthand:

$$\left| \begin{bmatrix} a \\ b \end{bmatrix} \begin{bmatrix} A \\ B \end{bmatrix} \right| \equiv \begin{vmatrix} a & A \\ b & B \end{vmatrix} = aB - Ab. \tag{5.8}$$

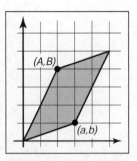

Figure 5.7. The 2D determinant in Equation 5.8 is the area of the parallelogram formed by the 2D vectors.

Note that the determinant of a matrix is the same as the determinant of its transpose:

$$\begin{vmatrix} a & A \\ b & B \end{vmatrix} = \begin{vmatrix} a & b \\ A & B \end{vmatrix} = aB - Ab.$$

This means that for any parallelogram in 2D there is a "sibling" parallelogram that has the same area but a different shape (Figure 5.8). For example the parallelogram defined by vectors $(3, 1)$ and $(2, 4)$ has area 10, as does the parallelogram defined by vectors $(3, 2)$ and $(1, 4)$.

Example. The geometric meaning of the 3D determinant is helpful in seeing why certain formulas make sense. For example, the equation of the plane through the points (x_i, y_i, z_i) for $i = 0, 1, 2$ is

$$\begin{vmatrix} x - x_0 & x - x_1 & x - x_2 \\ y - y_0 & y - y_1 & y - y_2 \\ z - z_0 & z - z_1 & z - z_2 \end{vmatrix} = 0.$$

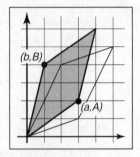

Figure 5.8. The sibling parallelogram has the same area as the parallelogram in Figure 5.7.

Each column is a vector from point (x_i, y_i, z_i) to point (x, y, z). The volume of the parallelepiped with those vectors as sides is zero only if (x, y, z) is coplanar with the three other points. Almost all equations involving determinants have similarly simple underlying geometry.

As we saw earlier, we can compute determinants by a brute force expansion where most terms are zero, and there is a great deal of bookkeeping on plus and minus signs. The standard way to manage the algebra of computing determinants is to use a form of *Laplace's expansion*. The key part of computing the determinant this way is to find *cofactors* of various matrix elements. Each element of a square matrix has a cofactor which is the determinant of a matrix with one fewer row and column possibly multiplied by minus one. The smaller matrix is obtained by eliminating the row and column that the element in question is in. For example, for a 10×10 matrix, the cofactor of a_{82} is the determinant of the 9×9 matrix with the 8th row and 2nd column eliminated. The sign of a cofactor is positive if the sum of the row and column indices is even and negative otherwise. This can be remembered by a checkerboard pattern:

$$\begin{bmatrix} + & - & + & - & \cdots \\ - & + & - & + & \cdots \\ + & - & + & - & \cdots \\ - & + & - & + & \cdots \\ \vdots & \vdots & \vdots & \vdots & \ddots \end{bmatrix}$$

So, for a 4×4 matrix,

$$\mathbf{A} = \begin{bmatrix} a_{11} & a_{12} & a_{13} & a_{14} \\ a_{21} & a_{22} & a_{23} & a_{24} \\ a_{31} & a_{32} & a_{33} & a_{34} \\ a_{41} & a_{42} & a_{43} & a_{44} \end{bmatrix}.$$

The cofactors of the first row are

$$a_{11}^c = \begin{vmatrix} a_{22} & a_{23} & a_{24} \\ a_{32} & a_{33} & a_{34} \\ a_{42} & a_{43} & a_{44} \end{vmatrix}, \quad a_{12}^c = -\begin{vmatrix} a_{21} & a_{23} & a_{24} \\ a_{31} & a_{33} & a_{34} \\ a_{41} & a_{43} & a_{44} \end{vmatrix},$$

$$a_{13}^c = \begin{vmatrix} a_{21} & a_{22} & a_{24} \\ a_{31} & a_{32} & a_{34} \\ a_{41} & a_{42} & a_{44} \end{vmatrix}, \quad a_{14}^c = -\begin{vmatrix} a_{21} & a_{22} & a_{23} \\ a_{31} & a_{32} & a_{33} \\ a_{41} & a_{42} & a_{43} \end{vmatrix}.$$

The determinant of a matrix is found by taking the sum of products of the elements of any row or column with their cofactors. For example, the determinant of the 4×4 matrix above taken about its second column is

$$|\mathbf{A}| = a_{12}a_{12}^c + a_{22}a_{22}^c + a_{32}a_{32}^c + a_{42}a_{42}^c.$$

We could do a similar expansion about any row or column and they would all yield the same result. Note the recursive nature of this expansion.

Example. A concrete example for the determinant of a particular 3×3 matrix by expanding the cofactors of the first row is

$$\begin{vmatrix} 0 & 1 & 2 \\ 3 & 4 & 5 \\ 6 & 7 & 8 \end{vmatrix} = 0\begin{vmatrix} 4 & 5 \\ 7 & 8 \end{vmatrix} - 1\begin{vmatrix} 3 & 5 \\ 6 & 8 \end{vmatrix} + 2\begin{vmatrix} 3 & 4 \\ 6 & 7 \end{vmatrix}$$

$$= 0(32 - 35) - 1(24 - 30) + 2(21 - 24)$$

$$= 0.$$

We can deduce that the volume of the parallelepiped formed by the vectors defined by the columns (or rows since the determinant of the transpose is the same) is zero. This is equivalent to saying that the columns (or rows) are not linearly independent. Note that the sum of the first and third rows is twice the second row, which implies linear dependence.

5.3.1 Computing Inverses

Determinants give us a tool to compute the inverse of a matrix. It is a very inefficient method for large matrices, but often in graphics our matrices are small. A key to developing this method is that the determinant of a matrix with two identical rows is zero. This should be clear because the volume of the n-dimensional parallelepiped is zero if two of its sides are the same. Suppose we have a 4×4 $\mathbf{A}$ and we wish to find its inverse $\mathbf{A}^{-1}$. The inverse is

$$\mathbf{A}^{-1} = \frac{1}{|\mathbf{A}|} \begin{bmatrix} a_{11}^c & a_{21}^c & a_{31}^c & a_{41}^c \\ a_{12}^c & a_{22}^c & a_{32}^c & a_{42}^c \\ a_{13}^c & a_{23}^c & a_{33}^c & a_{43}^c \\ a_{14}^c & a_{24}^c & a_{34}^c & a_{44}^c \end{bmatrix}.$$

Note that this is just the transpose of the matrix where elements of $\mathbf{A}$ are replaced by their respective cofactors multiplied by the leading constant (1 or -1). This matrix is called the *adjoint* of $\mathbf{A}$. The adjoint is the transpose of the *cofactor* matrix of $\mathbf{A}$. We can see why this is an inverse. Look at the product $\mathbf{A}\mathbf{A}^{-1}$ which we expect to be the identity. If we multiply the first row of $\mathbf{A}$ by the first column of the adjoint matrix we need to get $|\mathbf{A}|$ (remember the leading constant above divides by $|\mathbf{A}|$:

$$\begin{bmatrix} a_{11} & a_{12} & a_{13} & a_{14} \\ \cdot & \cdot & \cdot & \cdot \\ \cdot & \cdot & \cdot & \cdot \\ \cdot & \cdot & \cdot & \cdot \end{bmatrix} \begin{bmatrix} a_{11}^c & \cdot & \cdot & \cdot \\ a_{12}^c & \cdot & \cdot & \cdot \\ a_{13}^c & \cdot & \cdot & \cdot \\ a_{14}^c & \cdot & \cdot & \cdot \end{bmatrix} = \begin{bmatrix} |\mathbf{A}| & \cdot & \cdot & \cdot \\ \cdot & \cdot & \cdot & \cdot \\ \cdot & \cdot & \cdot & \cdot \\ \cdot & \cdot & \cdot & \cdot \end{bmatrix}$$

This is true because the elements in the first row of $\mathbf{A}$ are multiplied exactly by their cofactors in the first column of the adjoint matrix which is exactly the determinant. The other values along the diagonal of the resulting matrix are $|\mathbf{A}|$ for analogous reasons. The zeros follow a similar logic:

$$\begin{bmatrix} \cdot & \cdot & \cdot & \cdot \\ a_{21} & a_{22} & a_{23} & a_{24} \\ \cdot & \cdot & \cdot & \cdot \\ \cdot & \cdot & \cdot & \cdot \end{bmatrix} \begin{bmatrix} a_{11}^c & \cdot & \cdot & \cdot \\ a_{12}^c & \cdot & \cdot & \cdot \\ a_{13}^c & \cdot & \cdot & \cdot \\ a_{14}^c & \cdot & \cdot & \cdot \end{bmatrix} = \begin{bmatrix} \cdot & \cdot & \cdot & \cdot \\ 0 & \cdot & \cdot & \cdot \\ \cdot & \cdot & \cdot & \cdot \\ \cdot & \cdot & \cdot & \cdot \end{bmatrix}.$$

Note that this product is a determinant of *some* matrix:

$$a_{21}a_{11}^c + a_{22}a_{12}^c + a_{23}a_{13}^c + a_{24}a_{14}^c.$$

The matrix in fact is

$$\begin{bmatrix} a_{21} & a_{22} & a_{23} & a_{24} \\ a_{21} & a_{22} & a_{23} & a_{24} \\ a_{31} & a_{32} & a_{33} & a_{34} \\ a_{41} & a_{42} & a_{43} & a_{44} . \end{bmatrix}$$

Because the first two rows are identical, the matrix is singular, and thus, its determinant is zero.

The argument above does not apply just to four by four matrices; using that size just simplifies typography. For any matrix, the inverse is the adjoint matrix divided by the determinant of the matrix being inverted. The adjoint is the transpose of the cofactor matrix, which is just the matrix whose elements have been replaced by their cofactors.

Example. The inverse of one particular three by three matrix whose determinant is 6 is

$$\begin{bmatrix} 1 & 1 & 2 \\ 1 & 3 & 4 \\ 0 & 2 & 5 \end{bmatrix}^{-1} = \frac{1}{6} \begin{bmatrix} \begin{vmatrix} 3 & 4 \\ 2 & 5 \end{vmatrix} & -\begin{vmatrix} 1 & 2 \\ 2 & 5 \end{vmatrix} & \begin{vmatrix} 1 & 2 \\ 3 & 4 \end{vmatrix} \\ -\begin{vmatrix} 1 & 4 \\ 0 & 5 \end{vmatrix} & \begin{vmatrix} 1 & 2 \\ 0 & 5 \end{vmatrix} & -\begin{vmatrix} 1 & 2 \\ 1 & 4 \end{vmatrix} \\ \begin{vmatrix} 1 & 3 \\ 0 & 2 \end{vmatrix} & -\begin{vmatrix} 1 & 1 \\ 0 & 2 \end{vmatrix} & \begin{vmatrix} 1 & 1 \\ 1 & 3 \end{vmatrix} \end{bmatrix}$$

$$= \frac{1}{6} \begin{bmatrix} 7 & -1 & -2 \\ -5 & 5 & -2 \\ 2 & -2 & 2 \end{bmatrix}.$$

You can check this yourself by multiplying the matrices and making sure you get the identity.

5.3.2 Linear Systems

We often encounter linear systems in graphics with "n equations and n unknowns," usually for $n = 2$ or $n = 3$. For example,

$$\begin{aligned} 3x + 7y + 2z &= 4, \\ 2x - 4y - 3z &= -1, \\ 5x + 2y + z &= 1. \end{aligned}$$

Here x, y, and z are the "unknowns" for which we wish to solve. We can write this in matrix form:

$$\begin{bmatrix} 3 & 7 & 2 \\ 2 & -4 & -3 \\ 5 & 2 & 1 \end{bmatrix} \begin{bmatrix} x \\ y \\ z \end{bmatrix} = \begin{bmatrix} 4 \\ -1 \\ 1 \end{bmatrix}.$$

A common shorthand for such systems is $\mathbf{Ax} = \mathbf{b}$ where it is assumed that $\mathbf{A}$ is a square matrix with known constants, $\mathbf{x}$ is an unknown column vector (with elements x, y, and z in our example), and $\mathbf{b}$ is a column matrix of known constants.

There are many ways to solve such systems, and the appropriate method depends on the properties and dimensions of the matrix $\mathbf{A}$. Because in graphics we so frequently work with systems of size $n \leq 4$, we'll discuss here a method appropriate for these systems, known as *Cramer's rule*, which we saw earlier, from a 2D geometric viewpoint, in the example on page 92. Here, we show this algebraically. The solution to the above equation is

$$x = \frac{\begin{vmatrix} 4 & 7 & 2 \\ -1 & -4 & -3 \\ 1 & 2 & 1 \end{vmatrix}}{\begin{vmatrix} 3 & 7 & 2 \\ 2 & -4 & -3 \\ 5 & 2 & 1 \end{vmatrix}}; \quad y = \frac{\begin{vmatrix} 3 & 4 & 2 \\ 2 & -1 & -3 \\ 5 & 1 & 1 \end{vmatrix}}{\begin{vmatrix} 3 & 7 & 2 \\ 2 & -4 & -3 \\ 5 & 2 & 1 \end{vmatrix}}; \quad z = \frac{\begin{vmatrix} 3 & 7 & 4 \\ 2 & -4 & -1 \\ 5 & 2 & 1 \end{vmatrix}}{\begin{vmatrix} 3 & 7 & 2 \\ 2 & -4 & -3 \\ 5 & 2 & 1 \end{vmatrix}}.$$

The rule here is to take a ratio of determinants, where the denominator is $|\mathbf{A}|$ and the numerator is the determinant of a matrix created by replacing a column of $\mathbf{A}$ with the column vector $\mathbf{b}$. The column replaced corresponds to the position of the unknown in vector $\mathbf{x}$. For example, y is the second unknown and the second column is replaced. Note that if $|\mathbf{A}| = 0$, the division is undefined and there is no solution. This is just another version of the rule that if $\mathbf{A}$ is singular (zero determinant) then there is no unique solution to the equations.

5.4 Eigenvalues and Matrix Diagonalization

Square matrices have *eigenvalues* and *eigenvectors* associated with them. The eigenvectors are those *non-zero* vectors whose directions do not change when multiplied by the matrix. For example, suppose for a matrix $\mathbf{A}$ and vector $\mathbf{a}$, we have

$$\mathbf{Aa} = \lambda \mathbf{a}. \tag{5.9}$$

This means we have stretched or compressed $\mathbf{a}$, but its direction has not changed. The scale factor λ is called the eigenvalue associated with eigenvector $\mathbf{a}$. Knowing the eigenvalues and eigenvectors of matrices is helpful in a variety of practical applications. We will describe them to gain insight into geometric transformation matrices and as a step toward singular values and vectors described in the next section.

If we assume a matrix has at least one eigenvector, then we can do a standard manipulation to find it. First, we write both sides as the product of a square matrix with the vector a:

$$\mathbf{Aa} = \lambda \mathbf{Ia}, \tag{5.10}$$

where $\mathbf{I}$ is an identity matrix. This can be rewritten

$$\mathbf{Aa} - \lambda \mathbf{Ia} = 0. \tag{5.11}$$

Because matrix multiplication is distributive, we can group the matrices:

$$(\mathbf{A} - \lambda \mathbf{I})\,\mathbf{a} = 0. \tag{5.12}$$

This equation can only be true if the matrix $(\mathbf{A} - \lambda \mathbf{I})$ is singular, and thus its determinant is zero. The elements in this matrix are the numbers in $\mathbf{A}$ except along the diagonal. For example, for a 2×2 matrix the eigenvalues obey

$$\begin{vmatrix} a_{11} - \lambda & a_{12} \\ a_{21} & a_{22} - \lambda \end{vmatrix} = \lambda^2 - (a_{11} + a_{22})\lambda + (a_{11}a_{22} - a_{12}a_{21}) = 0. \tag{5.13}$$

Because this is a quadratic equation, we know there are exactly two solutions for λ. These solutions may or may not be unique or real. A similar manipulation for an $n \times n$ matrix will yield an nth-degree polynomial in λ. Because it is not possible, in general, to find exact explicit solutions of polynomial equations of degree greater than four, we can only compute eigenvalues of matrices 4×4 or smaller by analytic methods. For larger matrices, numerical methods are the only option.

An important special case where eigenvalues and eigenvectors are particularly simple is symmetric matrices (where $\mathbf{A} = \mathbf{A}^{\mathrm{T}}$). The eigenvalues of real symmetric matrices are always real numbers, and if they are also distinct, their eigenvectors are mutually orthogonal. Such matrices can be put into *diagonal form*:

$$\mathbf{A} = \mathbf{Q}\mathbf{D}\mathbf{Q}^{\mathrm{T}}, \tag{5.14}$$

Recall that an *orthogonal* matrix has *orthonormal* rows and *orthonormal* columns.

where $\mathbf{Q}$ is an orthogonal matrix and $\mathbf{D}$ is a diagonal matrix. The columns of $\mathbf{Q}$ are the eigenvectors of $\mathbf{A}$ and the diagonal elements of $\mathbf{D}$ are the eigenvalues of $\mathbf{A}$. Putting $\mathbf{A}$ in this form is also called the *eigenvalue decomposition*, because it decomposes $\mathbf{A}$ into a product of simpler matrices that reveal its eigenvectors and eigenvalues.

Example. Given the matrix

$$A = \begin{bmatrix} 2 & 1 \\ 1 & 1 \end{bmatrix},$$

the eigenvalues of A are the solutions to

$$\lambda^2 - 3\lambda + 1 = 0.$$

We approximate the exact values for compactness of notation:

$$\lambda = \frac{3 \pm \sqrt{5}}{2}, \approx \begin{bmatrix} 2.618 \\ 0.382 \end{bmatrix}.$$

Now we can find the associated eigenvector. The first is the nontrivial (not $x = y = 0$) solution to the homogeneous equation,

$$\begin{bmatrix} 2 - 2.618 & 1 \\ 1 & 1 - 2.618 \end{bmatrix} \begin{bmatrix} x \\ y \end{bmatrix} = \begin{bmatrix} 0 \\ 0 \end{bmatrix}.$$

This is approximately $(x, y) = (0.8507, 0.5257)$. Note that there are infinitely many solutions parallel to that 2D vector, and we just picked the one of unit length. Similarly the eigenvector associated with λ_2 is $(x, y) = (-0.5257, 0.8507)$. This means the diagonal form of A is (within some precision due to our numeric approximation):

$$\begin{bmatrix} 2 & 1 \\ 1 & 1 \end{bmatrix} = \begin{bmatrix} 0.8507 & -0.5257 \\ 0.5257 & 0.8507 \end{bmatrix} \begin{bmatrix} 2.618 & 0 \\ 0 & 0.382 \end{bmatrix} \begin{bmatrix} 0.8507 & 0.5257 \\ -0.5257 & 0.8507 \end{bmatrix}.$$

We will revisit the geometry of this matrix as a transform in the next chapter.

5.4.1 Singular Value Decomposition

We saw in the last section that any symmetric matrix can be diagonalized, or decomposed into a convenient product of orthogonal and diagonal matrices. However, most matrices we encounter in graphics are not symmetric, and the eigenvalue decomposition for non-symmetric matrices is not nearly so convenient or illuminating, and in general involves complex-valued eigenvalues and eigenvectors even for real-valued inputs.

There is another generalization of the symmetric eigenvalue decomposition to non-symmetric (and even non-square) matrices; it is the *singular value decomposition* (SVD). The main difference between the eigenvalue decomposition of a symmetric matrix and the SVD of a non-symmetric matrix is that the orthogonal matrices on the left and right sides are not required to be the same in the SVD:

$$A = USV^T.$$

We would recommend learning in this order: symmetric eigenvalues/vectors, singular values/vectors, and *then* unsymmetric eigenvalues, which are much trickier.

Here $\mathbf{U}$ and $\mathbf{V}$ are two, potentially different, orthogonal matrices, whose columns are known as the left and right *singular vectors* of $\mathbf{A}$, and $\mathbf{S}$ is a diagonal matrix whose entries are known as the *singular values* of $\mathbf{A}$. When $\mathbf{A}$ is symmetric and has all non-negative eigenvalues, the SVD and the eigenvalue decomposition are the same.

There is another relationship between singular values and eigenvalues that can be used to compute the SVD (though this is not the way an industrial-strength SVD implementation works). First we define $\mathbf{M} = \mathbf{A}\mathbf{A}^{\mathrm{T}}$. We assume that we can perform a SVD on $\mathbf{M}$:

$$\mathbf{M} = \mathbf{A}\mathbf{A}^{\mathrm{T}} = (\mathbf{U}\mathbf{S}\mathbf{V}^{\mathrm{T}})(\mathbf{U}\mathbf{S}\mathbf{V}^{\mathrm{T}})^{\mathrm{T}} = \mathbf{U}\mathbf{S}(\mathbf{V}^{\mathrm{T}}\mathbf{V})\mathbf{S}\mathbf{U}^{\mathrm{T}} = \mathbf{U}\mathbf{S}^2\mathbf{U}^{\mathrm{T}}.$$

The substitution is based on the fact that $(\mathbf{B}\mathbf{C})^{\mathrm{T}} = \mathbf{C}^{\mathrm{T}}\mathbf{B}^{\mathrm{T}}$, that the transpose of an orthogonal matrix is its inverse, and the transpose of a diagonal matrix is the matrix itself. The beauty of this new form is that $\mathbf{M}$ is symmetric and $\mathbf{U}\mathbf{S}^2\mathbf{U}^{\mathrm{T}}$ is its eigenvalue decomposition, where $\mathbf{S}^2$ contains the (all non-negative) eigenvalues. Thus, we find that the singular values of a matrix are the square roots of the eigenvalues of the product of the matrix with its transpose, and the left singular vectors are the eigenvectors of that product. A similar argument allows $\mathbf{V}$, the matrix of right singular vectors, to be computed from $\mathbf{A}^{\mathrm{T}}\mathbf{A}$.

Example. We now make this concrete with an example:

$$\mathbf{A} = \begin{bmatrix} 1 & 1 \\ 0 & 1 \end{bmatrix}; \quad \mathbf{M} = \mathbf{A}\mathbf{A}^{\mathrm{T}} = \begin{bmatrix} 2 & 1 \\ 1 & 1 \end{bmatrix}.$$

We saw the eigenvalue decomposition for this matrix in the previous section. We observe immediately

$$\begin{bmatrix} 1 & 1 \\ 0 & 1 \end{bmatrix} = \begin{bmatrix} 0.8507 & -0.5257 \\ 0.5257 & 0.8507 \end{bmatrix} \begin{bmatrix} \sqrt{2.618} & 0 \\ 0 & \sqrt{0.382} \end{bmatrix} \mathbf{V}^{\mathrm{T}}.$$

We can solve for $\mathbf{V}$ algebraically:

$$\mathbf{V} = (\mathbf{S}^{-1}\mathbf{U}^{\mathrm{T}}\mathbf{M})^{\mathrm{T}}.$$

The inverse of $\mathbf{S}$ is a diagonal matrix with the reciprocals of the diagonal elements of $\mathbf{S}$. This yields

$$\begin{bmatrix} 1 & 1 \\ 0 & 1 \end{bmatrix} = \mathbf{U} \begin{bmatrix} \sigma_1 & 0 \\ 0 & \sigma_2 \end{bmatrix} \mathbf{V}^{\mathrm{T}}$$

$$= \begin{bmatrix} 0.8507 & -0.5257 \\ 0.5257 & 0.8507 \end{bmatrix} \begin{bmatrix} 1.618 & 0 \\ 0 & 0.618 \end{bmatrix} \begin{bmatrix} 0.5257 & 0.8507 \\ -0.8507 & 0.5257 \end{bmatrix}.$$

This form used the standard symbol σ_i for the ith singular value. Again, for a symmetric matrix, the eigenvalues and the singular values are the same ($\sigma_i = \lambda_i$). We will examine the geometry of SVD further in Section 6.1.6.

Frequently Asked Questions

• Why is matrix multiplication defined the way it is rather than just element by element?

Element by element multiplication is a perfectly good way to define matrix multiplication, and indeed it has nice properties. However, in practice it is not very useful. Ultimately most matrices are used to transform column vectors, e.g., in 3D you might have

$$\mathbf{b} = \mathbf{M}\mathbf{a},$$

where $\mathbf{a}$ and $\mathbf{b}$ are vectors and $\mathbf{M}$ is a 3×3 matrix. To allow geometric operations such as rotation, combinations of all three elements of $\mathbf{a}$ must go into each element of $\mathbf{b}$. That requires us to either go row-by-row or column-by-column through $\mathbf{M}$. That choice is made based on composition of matrices having the desired property,

$$\mathbf{M}_2(\mathbf{M}_1\mathbf{a}) = (\mathbf{M}_2\mathbf{M}_1)\mathbf{a},$$

which allows us to use one composite matrix $\mathbf{C} = \mathbf{M}_2\mathbf{M}_1$ to transform our vector. This is valuable when many vectors will be transformed by the same composite matrix. So, in summary, the somewhat weird rule for matrix multiplication is engineered to have these desired properties.

• Sometimes I hear that eigenvalues and singular values are the same thing and sometimes that one is the square of the other. Which is right?

If a real matrix $\mathbf{A}$ is symmetric, and its eigenvalues are non-negative, then its eigenvalues and singular values are the same. If $\mathbf{A}$ is not symmetric, the matrix $\mathbf{M} = \mathbf{A}\mathbf{A}^T$ is symmetric and has non-negative real eignenvalues. The singular values of $\mathbf{A}$ and $\mathbf{A}^T$ are the same and are the square roots of the singular/eigenvalues of $\mathbf{M}$. Thus, when the square root statement is made, it is because two different matrices (with a very particular relationship) are being talked about: $\mathbf{M} = \mathbf{A}\mathbf{A}^T$.

Notes

The discussion of determinants as volumes is based on *A Vector Space Approach to Geometry* (Hausner, 1998). Hausner has an excellent discussion of vector analysis and the fundamentals of geometry as well. The geometric derivation of Cramer's rule in 2D is taken from *Practical Linear Algebra: A Geometry Toolbox* (Farin & Hansford, 2004). That book also has geometric interpretations of other linear algebra operations such as Gaussian elimination. The discussion of eigenvalues and singular values is based primarily on *Linear Algebra and Its Applications* (Strang, 1988). The example of SVD of the shear matrix is based on a discussion in *Computer Graphics and Geometric Modeling* (Salomon, 1999).

Exercises

1. Write an implicit equation for the 2D line through points (x_0, y_0) and (x_1, y_1) using a 2D determinant.

2. Show that if the columns of a matrix are orthonormal, then so are the rows.

3. Prove the properties of matrix determinants stated in Equations (5.5)–(5.7).

4. Show that the eigenvalues of a diagonal matrix are its diagonal elements.

5. Show that for a square matrix $\mathbf{A}$, $\mathbf{A}\mathbf{A}^{\mathrm{T}}$ is a symmetric matrix.

6. Show that for three 3D vectors $\mathbf{a}, \mathbf{b}, \mathbf{c}$, the following identity holds: $|\mathbf{abc}| = (\mathbf{a} \times \mathbf{b}) \cdot \mathbf{c}$.

7. Explain why the volume of the tetrahedron with side vectors $\mathbf{a}, \mathbf{b}, \mathbf{c}$ (see Figure 5.2) is given by $|\mathbf{abc}|/6$.

8. Demonstrate the four interpretations of matrix-matrix multiplication by taking the following matrix-matrix multiplication code, rearranging the nested loops, and interpreting the resulting code in terms of matrix and vector operations.

```
function mat-mult(in a[m][p], in b[p][n], out c[m][n]) {
    // the array c is initialized to zero
    for i = 1 to m
        for j = 1 to n
            for k = 1 to p
                c[i][j] += a[i][k] * b[k][j]
}
```

9. Prove that if $\mathbf{A}$, $\mathbf{Q}$, and $\mathbf{D}$ satisfy Equation (5.14), $\mathbf{v}$ is the ith row of $\mathbf{Q}$, and λ is the ith entry on the diagonal of $\mathbf{D}$, then $\mathbf{v}$ is an eigenvector of $\mathbf{A}$ with eigenvalue λ.

10. Prove that if $\mathbf{A}$, $\mathbf{Q}$, and $\mathbf{D}$ satisfy Equation (5.14), the eigenvalues of $\mathbf{A}$ are all distinct, and $\mathbf{v}$ is an eigenvector of $\mathbf{A}$ with eigenvalue λ, then for some i, $\mathbf{v}$ is the ith row of $\mathbf{Q}$ and λ is the ith entry on the diagonal of $\mathbf{D}$.

11. Given the (x, y) coordinates of the three vertices of a 2D triangle, explain why the area is given by

$$\frac{1}{2} \begin{vmatrix} x_0 & x_1 & x_2 \\ y_0 & y_1 & y_2 \\ 1 & 1 & 1 \end{vmatrix}.$$

6

Transformation Matrices

The machinery of linear algebra can be used to express many of the operations required to arrange objects in a 3D scene, view them with cameras, and get them onto the screen. *Geometric transformations* like rotation, translation, scaling, and projection can be accomplished with matrix multiplication, and the *transformation matrices* used to do this are the subject of this chapter.

We will show how a set of points transforms if the points are represented as offset vectors from the origin, and we will use the clock shown in Figure 6.1 as an example of a point set. So think of the clock as a bunch of points that are the ends of vectors whose tails are at the origin. We also discuss how these transforms operate differently on locations (points), displacement vectors, and surface normal vectors.

6.1 2D Linear Transformations

We can use a 2 × 2 matrix to change, or transform, a 2D vector:

$$\begin{bmatrix} a_{11} & a_{12} \\ a_{21} & a_{22} \end{bmatrix} \begin{bmatrix} x \\ y \end{bmatrix} = \begin{bmatrix} a_{11}x + a_{12}y \\ a_{21}x + a_{22}y \end{bmatrix}.$$

This kind of operation, which takes in a 2-vector and produces another 2-vector by a simple matrix multiplication, is a *linear transformation*.

By this simple formula we can achieve a variety of useful transformations, depending on what we put in the entries of the matrix, as will be discussed in

111

the following sections. For our purposes, consider moving along the x-axis a horizontal move and along the y-axis, a vertical move.

6.1.1 Scaling

The most basic transform is a *scale* along the coordinate axes. This transform can change length and possibly direction:

$$\text{scale}(s_x, s_y) = \begin{bmatrix} s_x & 0 \\ 0 & s_y \end{bmatrix}.$$

Note what this matrix does to a vector with Cartesian components (x, y):

$$\begin{bmatrix} s_x & 0 \\ 0 & s_y \end{bmatrix} \begin{bmatrix} x \\ y \end{bmatrix} = \begin{bmatrix} s_x x \\ s_y y \end{bmatrix}.$$

So just by looking at the matrix of an axis-aligned scale we can read off the two scale factors.

Example. The matrix that shrinks x and y uniformly by a factor of two is (Figure 6.1)

$$\text{scale}(0.5, 0.5) = \begin{bmatrix} 0.5 & 0 \\ 0 & 0.5 \end{bmatrix}.$$

A matrix which halves in the horizontal and increases by three-halves in the vertical is (see Figure 6.2)

$$\text{scale}(0.5, 1.5) = \begin{bmatrix} 0.5 & 0 \\ 0 & 1.5 \end{bmatrix}.$$

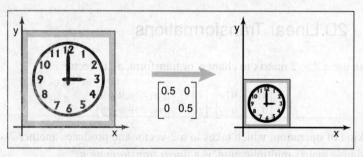

Figure 6.1. Scaling uniformly by half for each axis: The axis-aligned scale matrix has the proportion of change in each of the diagonal elements and zeroes in the off-diagonal elements.

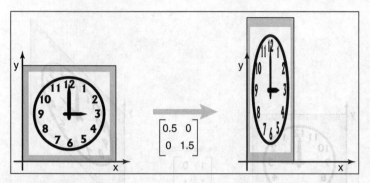

Figure 6.2. Scaling non-uniformly in *x* and *y*. The scaling matrix is diagonal with non-equal elements. Note that the square outline of the clock becomes a rectangle and the circular face becomes an ellipse.

6.1.2 Shearing

A shear is something that pushes things sideways, producing something like a deck of cards across which you push your hand; the bottom card stays put and cards move more the closer they are to the top of the deck. The horizontal and vertical shear matrices are

$$\text{shear-x}(s) = \begin{bmatrix} 1 & s \\ 0 & 1 \end{bmatrix}, \quad \text{shear-y}(s) = \begin{bmatrix} 1 & 0 \\ s & 1 \end{bmatrix}.$$

Example. The transform that shears horizontally so that vertical lines become $45°$ lines leaning towards the right is (see Figure 6.3)

$$\text{shear-x}(1) = \begin{bmatrix} 1 & 1 \\ 0 & 1 \end{bmatrix}.$$

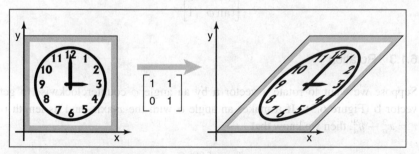

Figure 6.3. An *x*-shear matrix moves points to the right in proportion to their *y*-coordinate. Now the square outline of the clock becomes a parallelogram and, as with scaling, the circular face of the clock becomes an ellipse.

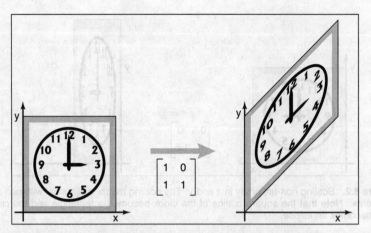

Figure 6.4. A *y*-shear matrix moves points up in proportion to their *x*-coordinate.

An analogous transform vertically is (see Figure 6.4)

$$\text{shear-y}(1) = \begin{bmatrix} 1 & 0 \\ 1 & 1 \end{bmatrix}.$$

In both cases the square outline of the sheared clock becomes a parallelogram, and the circular face of the sheared clock becomes an ellipse.

In fact, the image of a circle under any matrix transformation is an ellipse.

Another way to think of a shear is in terms of rotation of only the vertical (or horizontal) axes. The shear transform that takes a vertical axis and tilts it clockwise by an angle ϕ is

$$\begin{bmatrix} 1 & \tan \phi \\ 0 & 1 \end{bmatrix}.$$

Similarly, the shear matrix which rotates the horizontal axis counterclockwise by angle ϕ is

$$\begin{bmatrix} 1 & 0 \\ \tan \phi & 1 \end{bmatrix}.$$

6.1.3   Rotation

Suppose we want to rotate a vector **a** by an angle ϕ counterclockwise to get vector **b** (Figure 6.5). If **a** makes an angle α with the x-axis, and its length is $r = x_a^2 + y_a^2$, then we know that

$$x_a = r \cos \alpha,$$
$$y_a = r \sin \alpha.$$

Because **b** is a rotation of **a**, it also has length r. Because it is rotated an angle ϕ from **a**, **b** makes an angle $(\alpha + \phi)$ with the x-axis. Using the trigonometric addition identities (Section 2.3.3):

$$x_b = r\cos(\alpha + \phi) = r\cos\alpha\cos\phi - r\sin\alpha\sin\phi,$$
$$y_b = r\sin(\alpha + \phi) = r\sin\alpha\cos\phi + r\cos\alpha\sin\phi. \tag{6.1}$$

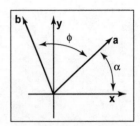

Figure 6.5. The geometry for Equation (6.1).

Substituting $x_a = r\cos\alpha$ and $y_a = r\sin\alpha$ gives

$$x_b = x_a\cos\phi - y_a\sin\phi,$$
$$y_b = y_a\cos\phi + x_a\sin\phi.$$

In matrix form, the transformation that takes **a** to **b** is then

$$\text{rotate}(\phi) = \begin{bmatrix} \cos\phi & -\sin\phi \\ \sin\phi & \cos\phi \end{bmatrix}.$$

Example. A matrix that rotates vectors by $\pi/4$ radians (45 degrees) is (see Figure 6.6)

$$\begin{bmatrix} \cos\frac{\pi}{4} & -\sin\frac{\pi}{4} \\ \sin\frac{\pi}{4} & \cos\frac{\pi}{4} \end{bmatrix} = \begin{bmatrix} 0.707 & -0.707 \\ 0.707 & 0.707 \end{bmatrix}.$$

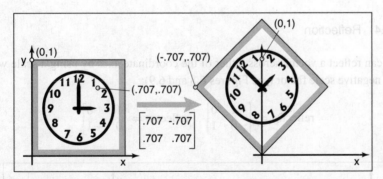

Figure 6.6. A rotation by 45 degrees. Note that the rotation is counterclockwise and that $\cos(45°) = \sin(45°) \approx .707$.

A matrix that rotates by $\pi/6$ radians (30 degrees) in the *clockwise* direction is a rotation by $-\pi/6$ radians in our framework (see Figure 6.7):

$$\begin{bmatrix} \cos\frac{-\pi}{6} & -\sin\frac{-\pi}{6} \\ \sin\frac{-\pi}{6} & \cos\frac{-\pi}{6} \end{bmatrix} = \begin{bmatrix} 0.866 & 0.5 \\ -0.5 & 0.866 \end{bmatrix}.$$

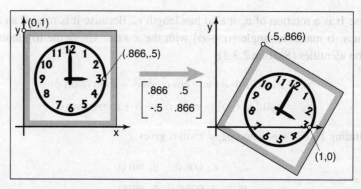

Figure 6.7. A rotation by minus thirty degrees. Note that the rotation is clockwise and that $\cos(-30°) \approx .866$ and $\sin(-30°) = -.5$.

Because the norm of each row of a rotation matrix is one ($\sin^2 \phi + \cos^2 \phi = 1$), and the rows are orthogonal ($\cos \phi(-\sin \phi) + \sin \phi \cos \phi = 0$), we see that rotation matrices are orthogonal matrices (Section 5.2.4). By looking at the matrix we can read off two pairs of orthonormal vectors: the two columns, which are the vectors to which the transformation sends the canonical basis vectors $(1, 0)$ and $(0, 1)$; and the rows, which are the vectors that the transformations sends *to* the canonical basis vectors.

Said briefly, $\mathbf{Re}_i = \mathbf{u}_i$ and $\mathbf{Rv}_i = \mathbf{u}_i$, for a rotation with columns $\mathbf{u}_i$ and rows $\mathbf{v}_i$.

6.1.4   Reflection

We can reflect a vector across either of the coordinate axes by using a scale with one negative scale factor (see Figures 6.8 and 6.9):

$$\text{reflect-y} = \begin{bmatrix} -1 & 0 \\ 0 & 1 \end{bmatrix}, \quad \text{reflect-x} = \begin{bmatrix} 1 & 0 \\ 0 & -1 \end{bmatrix}.$$

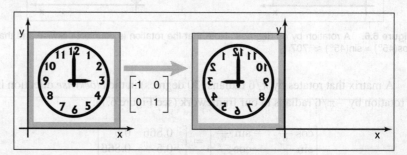

Figure 6.8. A reflection about the *y*-axis is achieved by multiplying all *x*-coordinates by -1.

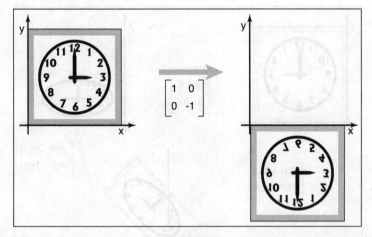

Figure 6.9. A reflection about the *x*-axis is achieved by multiplying all *y*-coordinates by -1.

While one might expect that the matrix with -1 in both elements of the diagonal is also a reflection, in fact it is just a rotation by π radians.

This rotation can also be called a "reflection through the origin."

6.1.5 Composition and Decomposition of Transformations

It is common for graphics programs to apply more than one transformation to an object. For example, we might want to first apply a scale **S**, and then a rotation **R**. This would be done in two steps on a 2D vector $\mathbf{v}_1$:

$$\text{first,} \mathbf{v}_2 = \mathbf{S}\mathbf{v}_1, \text{ then,} \mathbf{v}_3 = \mathbf{R}\mathbf{v}_2.$$

Another way to write this is

$$\mathbf{v}_3 = \mathbf{R}\left(\mathbf{S}\mathbf{v}_1\right).$$

Because matrix multiplication is associative, we can also write

$$\mathbf{v}_3 = \left(\mathbf{R}\mathbf{S}\right)\mathbf{v}_1.$$

In other words, we can represent the effects of transforming a vector by two matrices in sequence using a single matrix of the same size, which we can compute by multiplying the two matrices: $\mathbf{M} = \mathbf{RS}$ (Figure 6.10).

It is *very important* to remember that these transforms are applied from the *right side first*. So the matrix $\mathbf{M} = \mathbf{RS}$ first applies **S** and then **R**.

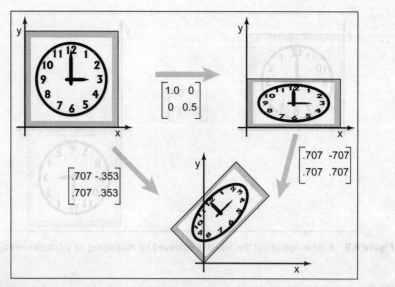

Figure 6.10. Applying the two transform matrices in sequence is the same as applying the product of those matrices once. This is a key concept that underlies most graphics hardware and software.

Example. Suppose we want to scale by one-half in the vertical direction and then rotate by $\pi/4$ radians (45 degrees). The resulting matrix is

$$\begin{bmatrix} 0.707 & -0.707 \\ 0.707 & 0.707 \end{bmatrix} \begin{bmatrix} 1 & 0 \\ 0 & 0.5 \end{bmatrix} = \begin{bmatrix} 0.707 & -0.353 \\ 0.707 & 0.353 \end{bmatrix}.$$

It is important to always remember that matrix multiplication is not commutative. So the order of transforms *does* matter. In this example, rotating first, and then scaling, results in a different matrix (see Figure 6.11):

$$\begin{bmatrix} 1 & 0 \\ 0 & 0.5 \end{bmatrix} \begin{bmatrix} 0.707 & -0.707 \\ 0.707 & 0.707 \end{bmatrix} = \begin{bmatrix} 0.707 & -0.707 \\ 0.353 & 0.353 \end{bmatrix}.$$

Example. Using the scale matrices we have presented, nonuniform scaling can only be done along the coordinate axes. If we wanted to stretch our clock by 50% along one of its diagonals, so that 8:00 through 1:00 move to the northwest and 2:00 through 7:00 move to the southeast, we can use rotation matrices in combination with an axis-aligned scaling matrix to get the result we want. The idea is to use a rotation to align the scaling axis with a coordinate axis, then scale along that axis, then rotate back. In our example, the scaling axis is the "backslash" diagonal of the square, and we can make it parallel to the x-axis with

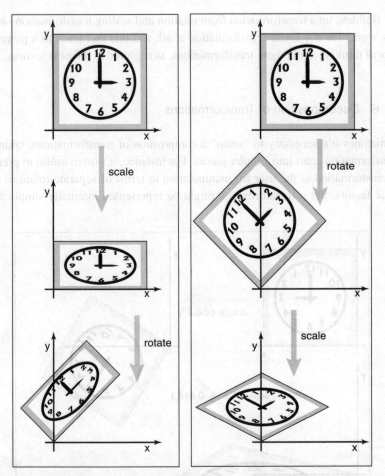

Figure 6.11. The order in which two transforms are applied is usually important. In this example, we do a scale by one-half in *y* and then rotate by 45°. Reversing the order in which these two transforms are applied yields a different result.

a rotation by +45°. Putting these operations together, the full transformation is

$$\text{rotate}(-45°)\,\text{scale}(1.5, 1)\,\text{rotate}(45°).$$

Remember to read the transformations from right to left.

In mathematical notation, this can be written $\mathbf{RSR}^{\mathrm{T}}$. The result of multiplying the three matrices together is

$$\begin{bmatrix} 1.25 & -0.25 \\ -0.25 & 1.25 \end{bmatrix}$$

It is no coincidence that this matrix is symmetric—try applying the transpose-of-product rule to the formula $\mathbf{RSR}^{\mathrm{T}}$.

Building up a transformation from rotation and scaling transformations actually works for any linear transformation at all, and this fact leads to a powerful way of thinking about these transformations, as explored in the next section.

6.1.6 Decomposition of Transformations

Sometimes it's necessary to "undo" a composition of transformations, taking a transformation apart into simpler pieces. For instance, it's often useful to present a transformation to the user for manipulation in terms of separate rotations and scale factors, but a transformation might be represented internally simply as a

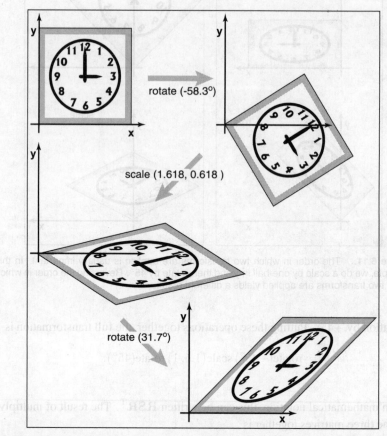

Figure 6.12. Singular Value Decomposition (SVD) for a shear matrix. Any 2D matrix can be decomposed into a product of rotation, scale, rotation. Note that the circular face of the clock must become an ellipse because it is just a rotated and scaled circle.

matrix, with the rotations and scales already mixed together. This kind of manipulation can be achieved if the matrix can be computationally disassembled into the desired pieces, the pieces adjusted, and the matrix reassembled by multiplying the pieces together again.

It turns out that this decomposition, or factorization, is possible, regardless of the entries in the matrix—and this fact provides a fruitful way of thinking about transformations and what they do to geometry that is transformed by them.

Symmetric Eigenvalue Decomposition

Let's start with symmetric matrices. Recall from Section 5.4 that a symmetric matrix can always be taken apart using the eigenvalue decomposition into a product of the form

$$\mathbf{A} = \mathbf{RSR}^{\mathrm{T}}$$

where $\mathbf{R}$ is an orthogonal matrix and $\mathbf{S}$ is a diagonal matrix; we will call the columns of $\mathbf{R}$ (the eigenvectors) by the names $\mathbf{v}_1$ and $\mathbf{v}_2$, and we'll call the diagonal entries of $\mathbf{S}$ (the eigenvalues) by the names λ_1 and λ_2.

In geometric terms we can now recognize $\mathbf{R}$ as a rotation and $\mathbf{S}$ as a scale, so this is just a multi-step geometric transformation (Figure 6.13):

1. Rotate $\mathbf{v}_1$ and $\mathbf{v}_2$ to the x- and y-axes (the transform by $\mathbf{R}^{\mathrm{T}}$).

2. Scale in x and y by (λ_1, λ_2) (the transform by $\mathbf{S}$).

3. Rotate the x- and y-axes back to $\mathbf{v}_1$ and $\mathbf{v}_2$ (the transform by $\mathbf{R}$).

Looking at the effect of these three transforms together, we can see that they have the effect of a nonuniform scale along a pair of axes. As with an axis-aligned scale, the axes are perpendicular, but they aren't the coordinate axes; instead they

If you like to count dimensions: a symmetric 2 × 2 matrix has 3 degrees of freedom, and the eigenvalue decomposition rewrites them as a rotation angle and two scale factors.

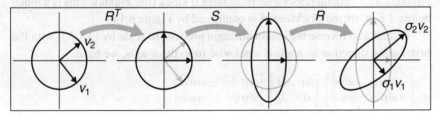

Figure 6.13. What happens when the unit circle is transformed by an arbitrary symmetric matrix **A**, also known as a non–axis-aligned, nonuniform scale. The two perpendicular vectors $\mathbf{v}_1$ and $\mathbf{v}_2$, which are the eigenvectors of **A**, remain fixed in direction but get scaled. In terms of elementary transformations, this can be seen as first rotating the eigenvectors to the canonical basis, doing an axis-aligned scale, and then rotating the canonical basis back to the eigenvectors.

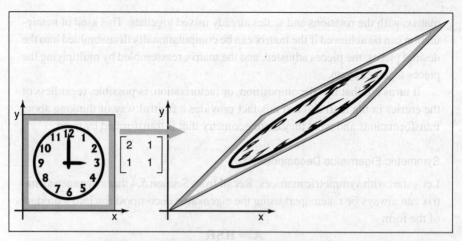

Figure 6.14. A symmetric matrix is always a scale along some axis. In this case it is along the $\phi = 31.7°$ direction which means the real eigenvector for this matrix is in that direction.

are the eigenvectors of **A**. This tells us something about what it means to be a symmetric matrix: symmetric matrices are just scaling operations—albeit potentially nonuniform and non–axis-aligned ones.

Example. Recall the example from Section 5.4:

$$\begin{bmatrix} 2 & 1 \\ 1 & 1 \end{bmatrix} = \mathbf{R} \begin{bmatrix} \lambda_1 & 0 \\ 0 & \lambda_2 \end{bmatrix} \mathbf{R}^\mathsf{T}$$

$$= \begin{bmatrix} 0.8507 & -0.5257 \\ 0.5257 & 0.8507 \end{bmatrix} \begin{bmatrix} 2.618 & 0 \\ 0 & 0.382 \end{bmatrix} \begin{bmatrix} 0.8507 & 0.5257 \\ -0.5257 & 0.8507 \end{bmatrix}$$

$$= \text{rotate } (31.7°) \text{ scale } (2.618, 0.382) \text{ rotate } (-31.7°).$$

The matrix above, then, according to its eigenvalue decomposition, scales in a direction $31.7°$ counterclockwise from three o'clock (the x-axis). This is a touch before 2 p.m. on the clockface as is confirmed by Figure 6.14.

We can also reverse the diagonalization process; to scale by (λ_1, λ_2) with the first scaling direction an angle ϕ clockwise from the x-axis, we have

$$\begin{bmatrix} \cos\phi & \sin\phi \\ -\sin\phi & \cos\phi \end{bmatrix} \begin{bmatrix} \lambda_1 & 0 \\ 0 & \lambda_2 \end{bmatrix} \begin{bmatrix} \cos\phi & -\sin\phi \\ \sin\phi & \cos\phi \end{bmatrix} =$$

$$\begin{bmatrix} \lambda_1 \cos^2\phi + \lambda_2 \sin^2\phi & (\lambda_2 - \lambda_1)\cos\phi\sin\phi \\ (\lambda_2 - \lambda_1)\cos\phi\sin\phi & \lambda_2 \cos^2\phi + \lambda_1 \sin^2\phi \end{bmatrix}.$$

We should take heart that this is a symmetric matrix as we know must be true since we constructed it from a symmetric eigenvalue decomposition.

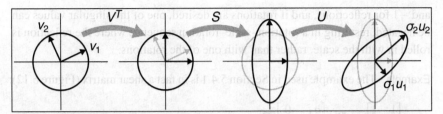

Figure 6.15. What happens when the unit circle is transformed by an arbitrary matrix **A**. The two perpendicular vectors v_1 and v_2, which are the right singular vectors of **A**, get scaled and changed in direction to match the left singular vectors, u_1 and u_2. In terms of elementary transformations, this can be seen as first rotating the right singular vectors to the canonical basis, doing an axis-aligned scale, and then rotating the canonical basis to the left singular vectors.

Singular Value Decomposition

A very similar kind of decomposition can be done with non-symmetric matrices as well: it's the Singular Value Decomposition (SVD), also discussed in Section 5.4.1. The difference is that the matrices on either side of the diagonal matrix are no longer the same:

$$\mathbf{A} = \mathbf{USV}^{\mathrm{T}}$$

The two orthogonal matrices that replace the single rotation **R** are called **U** and **V**, and their columns are called $\mathbf{u}_i$ (the *left singular vectors*) and $\mathbf{v}_i$ (the *right singular vectors*), respectively. In this context, the diagonal entries of **S** are called *singular values* rather than eigenvalues. The geometric interpretation is very similar to that of the symmetric eigenvalue decomposition (Figure 6.15):

1. Rotate $\mathbf{v}_1$ and $\mathbf{v}_2$ to the x- and y-axes (the transform by $\mathbf{V}^{\mathrm{T}}$).

2. Scale in x and y by (σ_1, σ_2) (the transform by **S**).

3. Rotate the x- and y-axes to $\mathbf{u}_1$ and $\mathbf{u}_2$ (the transform by **U**).

The principal difference is between a single rotation and two different orthogonal matrices. This difference causes another, less important, difference. Because the SVD has different singular vectors on the two sides, there is no need for negative singular values: we can always flip the sign of a singular value, reverse the direction of one of the associated singular vectors, and end up with the same transformation again. For this reason, the SVD always produces a diagonal matrix with all positive entries, but the matrices **U** and **V** are not guaranteed to be rotations—they could include reflection as well. In geometric applications like graphics this is an inconvenience, but a minor one: it is easy to differentiate rotations from reflections by checking the determinant, which is $+1$ for rotations

For dimension counters: a general 2×2 matrix has 4 degrees of freedom, and the SVD rewrites them as two rotation angles and two scale factors. One more bit is needed to keep track of reflections, but that doesn't add a dimension.

and -1 for reflections, and if rotations are desired, one of the singular values can be negated, resulting in a rotation–scale–rotation sequence where the reflection is rolled in with the scale, rather than with one of the rotations.

Example. The example used in Section 5.4.1 is in fact a shear matrix (Figure 6.12):

$$\begin{bmatrix} 1 & 1 \\ 0 & 1 \end{bmatrix} = \mathbf{R}_2 \begin{bmatrix} \sigma_1 & 0 \\ 0 & \sigma_2 \end{bmatrix} \mathbf{R}_1$$

$$= \begin{bmatrix} 0.8507 & -0.5257 \\ 0.5257 & 0.8507 \end{bmatrix} \begin{bmatrix} 1.618 & 0 \\ 0 & 0.618 \end{bmatrix} \begin{bmatrix} 0.5257 & 0.8507 \\ -0.8507 & 0.5257 \end{bmatrix}$$

$$= \text{rotate } (31.7°) \text{ scale } (1.618, 0.618) \text{ rotate } (-58.3°).$$

An immediate consequence of the existence of SVD is that all the 2D transformation matrices we have seen can be made from rotation matrices and scale matrices. Shear matrices are a convenience, but they are not required for expressing transformations.

In summary, every matrix can be decomposed via SVD into a rotation times a scale times another rotation. Only symmetric matrices can be decomposed via eigenvalue diagonalization into a rotation times a scale times the inverse-rotation, and such matrices are a simple scale in an arbitrary direction. The SVD of a symmetric matrix will yield the same triple product as eigenvalue decomposition via a slightly more complex algebraic manipulation.

Paeth Decomposition of Rotations

Another decomposition uses shears to represent non-zero rotations (Paeth, 1990). The following identity allows this:

$$\begin{bmatrix} \cos\phi & -\sin\phi \\ \sin\phi & \cos\phi \end{bmatrix} = \begin{bmatrix} 1 & \frac{\cos\phi - 1}{\sin\phi} \\ 0 & 1 \end{bmatrix} \begin{bmatrix} 1 & 0 \\ \sin\phi & 1 \end{bmatrix} \begin{bmatrix} 1 & \frac{\cos\phi - 1}{\sin\phi} \\ 0 & 1 \end{bmatrix}.$$

For example, a rotation by $\pi/4$ (45 degrees) is (see Figure 6.16)

$$\text{rotate}\left(\frac{\pi}{4}\right) = \begin{bmatrix} 1 & 1 - \sqrt{2} \\ 0 & 1 \end{bmatrix} \begin{bmatrix} 1 & 0 \\ \frac{\sqrt{2}}{2} & 1 \end{bmatrix} \begin{bmatrix} 1 & 1 - \sqrt{2} \\ 0 & 1 \end{bmatrix}. \tag{6.2}$$

This particular transform is useful for raster rotation because shearing is a very efficient raster operation for images; it introduces some jagginess, but will

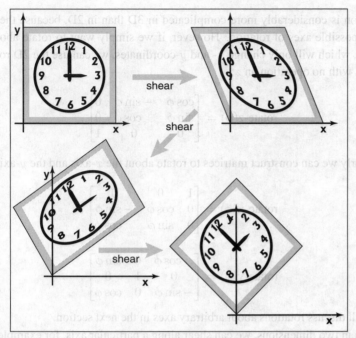

Figure 6.16. Any 2D rotation can be accomplished by three shears in sequence. In this case a rotation by 45° is decomposed as shown in Equation 6.2.

leave no holes. The key observation is that if we take a raster position (i, j) and apply a horizontal shear to it, we get

$$\begin{bmatrix} 1 & s \\ 0 & 1 \end{bmatrix} \begin{bmatrix} i \\ j \end{bmatrix} = \begin{bmatrix} i + sj \\ j \end{bmatrix}.$$

If we round sj to the nearest integer, this amounts to taking each row in the image and moving it sideways by some amount—a different amount for each row. Because it is the same displacement within a row, this allows us to rotate with no gaps in the resulting image. A similar action works for a vertical shear. Thus, we can implement a simple raster rotation easily.

6.2 3D Linear Transformations

The linear 3D transforms are an extension of the 2D transforms. For example, a scale along Cartesian axes is

$$\text{scale}(s_x, s_y, s_z) = \begin{bmatrix} s_x & 0 & 0 \\ 0 & s_y & 0 \\ 0 & 0 & s_z \end{bmatrix}. \tag{6.3}$$

Rotation is considerably more complicated in 3D than in 2D, because there are more possible axes of rotation. However, if we simply want to rotate about the z-axis, which will only change x- and y-coordinates, we can use the 2D rotation matrix with no operation on z:

$$\text{rotate-z}(\phi) = \begin{bmatrix} \cos\phi & -\sin\phi & 0 \\ \sin\phi & \cos\phi & 0 \\ 0 & 0 & 1 \end{bmatrix}.$$

Similarly we can construct matrices to rotate about the x-axis and the y-axis:

To understand why the minus sign is in the lower left for the *y*-axis rotation, think of the three axes in a circular sequence: *y* after *x*; *z* after *y*; *x* after *z*.

$$\text{rotate-x}(\phi) = \begin{bmatrix} 1 & 0 & 0 \\ 0 & \cos\phi & -\sin\phi \\ 0 & \sin\phi & \cos\phi \end{bmatrix},$$

$$\text{rotate-y}(\phi) = \begin{bmatrix} \cos\phi & 0 & \sin\phi \\ 0 & 1 & 0 \\ -\sin\phi & 0 & \cos\phi \end{bmatrix}.$$

We will discuss rotations about arbitrary axes in the next section.

As in two dimensions, we can shear along a particular axis, for example,

$$\text{shear-x}(d_y, d_z) = \begin{bmatrix} 1 & d_y & d_z \\ 0 & 1 & 0 \\ 0 & 0 & 1 \end{bmatrix}.$$

As with 2D transforms, any 3D transformation matrix can be decomposed using SVD into a rotation, scale, and another rotation. Any symmetric 3D matrix has an eigenvalue decomposition into rotation, scale, and inverse-rotation. Finally, a 3D rotation can be decomposed into a product of 3D shear matrices.

6.2.1 Arbitrary 3D Rotations

As in 2D, 3D rotations are *orthogonal* matrices. Geometrically, this means that the three rows of the matrix are the Cartesian coordinates of three mutually-orthogonal unit vectors as discussed in Section 2.4.5. The columns are three, potentially different, mutually-orthogonal unit vectors. There are an infinite number of such rotation matrices. Let's write down such a matrix:

$$\mathbf{R}_{uvw} = \begin{bmatrix} x_u & y_u & z_u \\ x_v & y_v & z_v \\ x_w & y_w & z_w \end{bmatrix}.$$

Here, $\mathbf{u} = x_u\mathbf{x} + y_u\mathbf{y} + z_u\mathbf{z}$ and so on for $\mathbf{v}$ and $\mathbf{w}$. Since the three vectors are orthonormal we know that

$$\mathbf{u} \cdot \mathbf{u} = \mathbf{v} \cdot \mathbf{v} = \mathbf{w} \cdot \mathbf{w} = 1,$$

$$\mathbf{u} \cdot \mathbf{v} = \mathbf{v} \cdot \mathbf{w} = \mathbf{w} \cdot \mathbf{u} = 0.$$

We can infer some of the behavior of the rotation matrix by applying it to the vectors $\mathbf{u}$, $\mathbf{v}$ and $\mathbf{w}$. For example,

$$\mathbf{R}_{uvw}\mathbf{u} = \begin{bmatrix} x_u & y_u & z_u \\ x_v & y_v & z_v \\ x_w & y_w & z_w \end{bmatrix} \begin{bmatrix} x_u \\ y_u \\ z_u \end{bmatrix} = \begin{bmatrix} x_u x_u + y_u y_u + z_u z_u \\ x_v x_u + y_v y_u + z_v z_u \\ x_w x_u + y_w y_u + z_w z_u \end{bmatrix}.$$

Note that those three rows of $\mathbf{R}_{uvw}\mathbf{u}$ are all dot products:

$$\mathbf{R}_{uvw}\mathbf{u} = \begin{bmatrix} \mathbf{u} \cdot \mathbf{u} \\ \mathbf{v} \cdot \mathbf{u} \\ \mathbf{w} \cdot \mathbf{u} \end{bmatrix} = \begin{bmatrix} 1 \\ 0 \\ 0 \end{bmatrix} = \mathbf{x}.$$

Similarly, $\mathbf{R}_{uvw}\mathbf{v} = \mathbf{y}$, and $\mathbf{R}_{uvw}\mathbf{w} = \mathbf{z}$. So $\mathbf{R}_{uvw}$ takes the basis $\mathbf{uvw}$ to the corresponding Cartesian axes via rotation.

If $\mathbf{R}_{uvw}$ is a rotation matrix with orthonormal rows, then $\mathbf{R}_{uvw}^{\mathrm{T}}$ is also a rotation matrix with orthonormal columns, and in fact is the inverse of $\mathbf{R}_{uvw}$ (the inverse of an orthogonal matrix is always its transpose). An important point is that for transformation matrices, the algebraic inverse is also the geometric inverse. So if $\mathbf{R}_{uvw}$ takes $\mathbf{u}$ to $\mathbf{x}$, then $\mathbf{R}_{uvw}^{\mathrm{T}}$ takes $\mathbf{x}$ to $\mathbf{u}$. The same should be true of $\mathbf{v}$ and $\mathbf{y}$ as we can confirm:

$$\mathbf{R}_{uvw}^{\mathrm{T}}\mathbf{y} = \begin{bmatrix} x_u & x_v & x_w \\ y_u & y_v & y_w \\ z_u & z_v & z_w \end{bmatrix} \begin{bmatrix} 0 \\ 1 \\ 0 \end{bmatrix} = \begin{bmatrix} x_v \\ y_v \\ z_v \end{bmatrix} = \mathbf{v}.$$

So we can always create rotation matrices from orthonormal bases.

If we wish to rotate about an arbitrary vector $\mathbf{a}$, we can form an orthonormal basis with $\mathbf{w} = \mathbf{a}$, rotate that basis to the canonical basis $\mathbf{xyz}$, rotate about the z-axis, and then rotate the canonical basis back to the $\mathbf{uvw}$ basis. In matrix form, to rotate about the w-axis by an angle ϕ:

$$\begin{bmatrix} x_u & x_v & x_w \\ y_u & y_v & y_w \\ z_u & z_v & z_w \end{bmatrix} \begin{bmatrix} \cos\phi & -\sin\phi & 0 \\ \sin\phi & \cos\phi & 0 \\ 0 & 0 & 1 \end{bmatrix} \begin{bmatrix} x_u & y_u & z_u \\ x_v & y_v & z_v \\ x_w & y_w & z_w \end{bmatrix}.$$

Here we have $\mathbf{w}$ a unit vector in the direction of $\mathbf{a}$ (i.e. $\mathbf{a}$ divided by its own length). But what are $\mathbf{u}$ and $\mathbf{v}$? A method to find reasonable $\mathbf{u}$ and $\mathbf{v}$ is given in Section 2.4.6.

If we have a rotation matrix and we wish to have the rotation in axis-angle form, we can compute the one real eigenvalue (which will be $\lambda = 1$), and the corresponding eigenvector is the axis of rotation. This is the one axis that is not changed by the rotation.

See Chapter 17 for a comparison of the few most-used ways to represent rotations, besides rotation matrices.

6.2.2 Transforming Normal Vectors

While most 3D vectors we use represent positions (offset vectors from the origin) or directions, such as where light comes from, some vectors represent *surface normals*. Surface normal vectors are perpendicular to the tangent plane of a surface. These normals do not transform the way we would like when the underlying surface is transformed. For example, if the points of a surface are transformed by a matrix $\mathbf{M}$, a vector $\mathbf{t}$ that is tangent to the surface and is multiplied by $\mathbf{M}$ will be tangent to the transformed surface. However, a surface normal vector $\mathbf{n}$ that is transformed by $\mathbf{M}$ may not be normal to the transformed surface (Figure 6.17).

We can derive a transform matrix $\mathbf{N}$ which does take $\mathbf{n}$ to a vector perpendicular to the transformed surface. One way to attack this issue is to note that a surface normal vector and a tangent vector are perpendicular, so their dot product is zero, which is expressed in matrix form as

$$\mathbf{n}^{\mathrm{T}}\mathbf{t} = \mathbf{0}. \qquad (6.4)$$

If we denote the desired transformed vectors as $\mathbf{t}_M = \mathbf{M}\mathbf{t}$ and $\mathbf{n}_N = \mathbf{N}\mathbf{n}$, our goal is to find $\mathbf{N}$ such that $\mathbf{n}_N^{\mathrm{T}}\mathbf{t}_M = 0$. We can find $\mathbf{N}$ by some algebraic

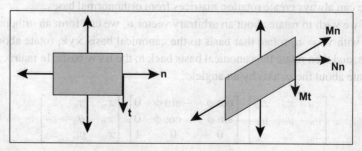

Figure 6.17. When a normal vector is transformed using the same matrix that transforms the points on an object, the resulting vector may not be perpendicular to the surface as is shown here for the sheared rectangle. The tangent vector, however, does transform to a vector tangent to the transformed surface.

tricks. First, we can sneak an identity matrix into the dot product, and then take advantage of $\mathbf{M}^{-1}\mathbf{M} = \mathbf{I}$:

$$\mathbf{n}^{\mathrm{T}}\mathbf{t} = \mathbf{n}^{\mathrm{T}}\mathbf{I}\mathbf{t} = \mathbf{n}^{\mathrm{T}}\mathbf{M}^{-1}\mathbf{M}\mathbf{t} = \mathbf{0}.$$

Although the manipulations above don't obviously get us anywhere, note that we can add parentheses that make the above expression more obviously a dot product:

$$\left(\mathbf{n}^{\mathrm{T}}\mathbf{M}^{-1}\right)(\mathbf{M}\mathbf{t}) = \left(\mathbf{n}^{\mathrm{T}}\mathbf{M}^{-1}\right)\mathbf{t}_M = \mathbf{0}.$$

This means that the row vector that is perpendicular to $\mathbf{t}_M$ is the left part of the expression above. This expression holds for any of the tangent vectors in the tangent plane. Since there is only one direction in 3D (and its opposite) that is perpendicular to all such tangent vectors, we know that the left part of the expression above must be the row vector expression for $\mathbf{n}_N$, i.e., it is $\mathbf{n}_N^{\mathrm{T}}$, so this allows us to infer $\mathbf{N}$:

$$\mathbf{n}_N^{\mathrm{T}} = \mathbf{n}^{\mathrm{T}}\mathbf{M}^{-1},$$

so we can take the transpose of that to get

$$\mathbf{n}_N = \left(\mathbf{n}^{\mathrm{T}}\mathbf{M}^{-1}\right)^{\mathrm{T}} = \left(\mathbf{M}^{-1}\right)^{\mathrm{T}}\mathbf{n}. \tag{6.5}$$

Therefore, we can see that the matrix which correctly transforms normal vectors so they remain normal is $\mathbf{N} = (\mathbf{M}^{-1})^{\mathrm{T}}$, i.e., the transpose of the inverse matrix. Since this matrix may change the length of $\mathbf{n}$, we can multiply it by an arbitrary scalar and it will still produce $\mathbf{n}_N$ with the right direction. Recall from Section 5.3 that the inverse of a matrix is the transpose of the cofactor matrix divided by the determinant. Because we don't care about the length of a normal vector, we can skip the division and find that for a 3×3 matrix,

$$\mathbf{N} = \begin{bmatrix} m_{11}^c & m_{12}^c & m_{13}^c \\ m_{21}^c & m_{22}^c & m_{23}^c \\ m_{31}^c & m_{32}^c & m_{33}^c \end{bmatrix}.$$

This assumes the element of $\mathbf{M}$ in row i and column j is m_{ij}. So the full expression for $\mathbf{N}$ is

$$\mathbf{N} = \begin{bmatrix} m_{22}m_{33} - m_{23}m_{32} & m_{23}m_{31} - m_{21}m_{33} & m_{21}m_{32} - m_{22}m_{31} \\ m_{13}m_{32} - m_{12}m_{33} & m_{11}m_{33} - m_{13}m_{31} & m_{12}m_{31} - m_{11}m_{32} \\ m_{12}m_{23} - m_{13}m_{22} & m_{13}m_{21} - m_{11}m_{23} & m_{11}m_{22} - m_{12}m_{21} \end{bmatrix}.$$

6.3   Translation and Affine Transformations

We have been looking at methods to change vectors using a matrix $\mathbf{M}$. In two dimensions, these transforms have the form,

$$x' = m_{11}x + m_{12}y,$$
$$y' = m_{21}x + m_{22}y.$$

We cannot use such transforms to *move* objects, only to scale and rotate them. In particular, the origin $(0,0)$ always remains fixed under a linear transformation. To move, or *translate*, an object by shifting all its points the same amount, we need a transform of the form,

$$x' = x + x_t,$$
$$y' = y + y_t.$$

There is just no way to do that by multiplying (x,y) by a 2×2 matrix. One possibility for adding translation to our system of linear transformations is to simply associate a separate translation vector with each transformation matrix, letting the matrix take care of scaling and rotation and the vector take care of translation. This is perfectly feasible, but the bookkeeping is awkward and the rule for composing two transformations is not as simple and clean as with linear transformations.

Instead, we can use a clever trick to get a single matrix multiplication to do both operations together. The idea is simple: represent the point (x,y) by a 3D vector $[x \; y \; 1]^{\mathrm{T}}$, and use 3×3 matrices of the form

$$\begin{bmatrix} m_{11} & m_{12} & x_t \\ m_{21} & m_{22} & y_t \\ 0 & 0 & 1 \end{bmatrix}.$$

The fixed third row serves to copy the 1 into the transformed vector, so that all vectors have a 1 in the last place, and the first two rows compute x' and y' as linear combinations of x, y, and 1:

$$\begin{bmatrix} x' \\ y' \\ 1 \end{bmatrix} = \begin{bmatrix} m_{11} & m_{12} & x_t \\ m_{21} & m_{22} & y_t \\ 0 & 0 & 1 \end{bmatrix} \begin{bmatrix} x \\ y \\ 1 \end{bmatrix} = \begin{bmatrix} m_{11}x + m_{12}y + x_t \\ m_{21}x + m_{22}y + y_t \\ 1 \end{bmatrix}.$$

The single matrix implements a linear transformation followed by a translation! This kind of transformation is called an *affine transformation*, and this way of implementing affine transformations by adding an extra dimension is called *homogeneous coordinates* (Roberts, 1965; Riesenfeld, 1981; Penna & Patterson, 1986). Homogeneous coordinates not only clean up the code for transformations, but this scheme also makes it obvious how to compose two affine transformations: simply multiply the matrices.

A problem with this new formalism arises when we need to transform vectors that are not supposed to be positions—they represent directions, or offsets between positions. Vectors that represent directions or offsets should not change when we translate an object. Fortunately, we can arrange for this by setting the third coordinate to zero:

$$\begin{bmatrix} 1 & 0 & x_t \\ 0 & 1 & y_t \\ 0 & 0 & 1 \end{bmatrix} \begin{bmatrix} x \\ y \\ 0 \end{bmatrix} = \begin{bmatrix} x \\ y \\ 0 \end{bmatrix}.$$

If there is a scaling/rotation transformation in the upper-left 2×2 entries of the matrix, it will apply to the vector, but the translation still multiplies with the zero and is ignored. Furthermore, the zero is copied into the transformed vector, so direction vectors remain direction vectors after they are transformed.

This is exactly the behavior we want for vectors, so they fit smoothly into the system: the extra (third) coordinate will be either 1 or 0 depending on whether we are encoding a position or a direction. We actually do need to store the homogeneous coordinate so we can distinguish between locations and other vectors. For example,

This gives an explanation for the name "homogeneous:" translation, rotation, and scaling of positions and directions all fit into a single system.

$$\begin{bmatrix} 3 \\ 2 \\ 1 \end{bmatrix} \text{ is a location } \quad \text{and} \quad \begin{bmatrix} 3 \\ 2 \\ 0 \end{bmatrix} \text{ is a displacement or direction.}$$

Later, when we do perspective viewing, we will see that it is useful to allow the homogeneous coordinate to take on values other than one or zero.

Homogeneous coordinates are used nearly universally to represent transformations in graphics systems. In particular, homogeneous coordinates underlie the design and operation of renderers implemented in graphics hardware. We will see in Chapter 7 that homogeneous coordinates also make it easy to draw scenes in perspective, another reason for their popularity.

Homogeneous coordinates are also ubiquitous in computer vision.

Homogeneous coordinates can be considered just a clever way to handle the bookkeeping for translation, but there is also a different, geometric interpretation. The key observation is that when we do a 3D shear based on the z-coordinate we get this transform:

$$\begin{bmatrix} 1 & 0 & x_t \\ 0 & 1 & y_t \\ 0 & 0 & 1 \end{bmatrix} \begin{bmatrix} x \\ y \\ z \end{bmatrix} = \begin{bmatrix} x + x_t z \\ y + y_t z \\ z \end{bmatrix}.$$

Note that this almost has the form we want in x and y for a 2D translation, but has a z hanging around that doesn't have a meaning in 2D. Now comes the key decision: we will add a coordinate $z = 1$ to all 2D locations. This gives us

$$\begin{bmatrix} 1 & 0 & x_t \\ 0 & 1 & y_t \\ 0 & 0 & 1 \end{bmatrix} \begin{bmatrix} x \\ y \\ 1 \end{bmatrix} = \begin{bmatrix} x + x_t \\ y + y_t \\ 1 \end{bmatrix}.$$

By associating a $(z = 1)$-coordinate with all 2D points, we now can encode translations into matrix form. For example, to first translate in 2D by (t_x, t_y) and then rotate by angle ϕ we would use the matrix

$$\mathbf{M} = \begin{bmatrix} \cos\phi & -\sin\phi & 0 \\ \sin\phi & \cos\phi & 0 \\ 0 & 0 & 1 \end{bmatrix} \begin{bmatrix} 1 & 0 & x_t \\ 0 & 1 & y_t \\ 0 & 0 & 1 \end{bmatrix}.$$

Note that the 2D rotation matrix is now 3×3 with zeros in the "translation slots." With this type of formalism, which uses shears along $z = 1$ to encode translations, we can represent any number of 2D shears, 2D rotations, and 2D translations as one composite 3D matrix. The bottom row of that matrix will always be $(0, 0, 1)$, so we don't really have to store it. We just need to remember it is there when we multiply two matrices together.

In 3D, the same technique works: we can add a fourth coordinate, a homogeneous coordinate, and then we have translations:

$$\begin{bmatrix} 1 & 0 & 0 & x_t \\ 0 & 1 & 0 & y_t \\ 0 & 0 & 1 & z_t \\ 0 & 0 & 0 & 1 \end{bmatrix} \begin{bmatrix} x \\ y \\ z \\ 1 \end{bmatrix} = \begin{bmatrix} x + x_t \\ y + y_t \\ z + z_t \\ 1 \end{bmatrix}.$$

Again, for a direction vector, the fourth coordinate is zero and the vector is thus unaffected by translations.

Example (Windowing transformations). Often in graphics we need to create a transform matrix that takes points in the rectangle $[x_l, x_h] \times [y_l, y_h]$ to the rectangle $[x'_l, x'_h] \times [y'_l, y'_h]$. This can be accomplished with a single scale and translate in sequence. However, it is more intuitive to create the transform from a sequence of three operations (Figure 6.18):

1. Move the point (x_l, y_l) to the origin.

2. Scale the rectangle to be the same size as the target rectangle.

3. Move the origin to point (x'_l, y'_l).

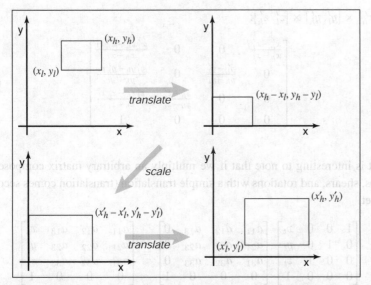

Figure 6.18. To take one rectangle (window) to the other, we first shift the lower-left corner to the origin, then scale it to the new size, and then move the origin to the lower-left corner of the target rectangle.

Remembering that the right-hand matrix is applied first, we can write

$$\text{window} \ = \ \text{translate} \ (x'_l, y'_l) \ \text{scale} \ \left(\frac{x'_h - x'_l}{x_h - x_l}, \frac{y'_h - y'_l}{y_h - y_l} \right) \ \text{translate} \ (-x_l, -y_l)$$

$$= \begin{bmatrix} 1 & 0 & x'_l \\ 0 & 1 & y'_l \\ 0 & 0 & 1 \end{bmatrix} \begin{bmatrix} \frac{x'_h - x'_l}{x_h - x_l} & 0 & 0 \\ 0 & \frac{y'_h - y'_l}{y_h - y_l} & 0 \\ 0 & 0 & 1 \end{bmatrix} \begin{bmatrix} 1 & 0 & -x_l \\ 0 & 1 & -y_l \\ 0 & 0 & 1 \end{bmatrix}$$

$$= \begin{bmatrix} \frac{x'_h - x'_l}{x_h - x_l} & 0 & \frac{x'_l x_h - x'_h x_l}{x_h - x_l} \\ 0 & \frac{y'_h - y'_l}{y_h - y_l} & \frac{y'_l y_h - y'_h y_l}{y_h - y_l} \\ 0 & 0 & 1 \end{bmatrix}. \tag{6.6}$$

It is perhaps not surprising to some readers that the resulting matrix has the form it does, but the constructive process with the three matrices leaves no doubt as to the correctness of the result.

An exactly analogous construction can be used to define a 3D windowing transformation, which maps the box $[x_l, x_h] \times [y_l, y_h] \times [z_l, z_h]$ to the box

$[x'_l, x'_h] \times [y'_l, y'_h] \times [z'_l, z'_h]$:

$$\begin{bmatrix} \frac{x'_h - x'_l}{x_h - x_l} & 0 & 0 & \frac{x'_l x_h - x'_h x_l}{x_h - x_l} \\ 0 & \frac{y'_h - y'_l}{y_h - y_l} & 0 & \frac{y'_l y_h - y'_h y_l}{y_h - y_l} \\ 0 & 0 & \frac{z'_h - z'_l}{z_h - z_l} & \frac{z'_l z_h - z'_h z_l}{z_h - z_l} \\ 0 & 0 & 0 & 1 \end{bmatrix}. \tag{6.7}$$

It is interesting to note that if we multiply an arbitrary matrix composed of scales, shears, and rotations with a simple translation (translation comes second), we get

$$\begin{bmatrix} 1 & 0 & 0 & x_t \\ 0 & 1 & 0 & y_t \\ 0 & 0 & 1 & z_t \\ 0 & 0 & 0 & 1 \end{bmatrix} \begin{bmatrix} a_{11} & a_{12} & a_{13} & 0 \\ a_{21} & a_{22} & a_{23} & 0 \\ a_{31} & a_{32} & a_{33} & 0 \\ 0 & 0 & 0 & 1 \end{bmatrix} = \begin{bmatrix} a_{11} & a_{12} & a_{13} & x_t \\ a_{21} & a_{22} & a_{23} & y_t \\ a_{31} & a_{32} & a_{33} & z_t \\ 0 & 0 & 0 & 1 \end{bmatrix}.$$

Thus, we can look at any matrix and think of it as a scaling/rotation part and a translation part because the components are nicely separated from each other.

An important class of transforms are *rigid-body* transforms. These are composed only of translations and rotations, so they have no stretching or shrinking of the objects. Such transforms will have a pure rotation for the a_{ij} above.

6.4   Inverses of Transformation Matrices

While we can always invert a matrix algebraically, we can use geometry if we know what the transform does. For example, the inverse of scale(s_x, s_y, s_z) is scale$(1/s_x, 1/s_y, 1/s_z)$. The inverse of a rotation is the same rotation with the opposite sign on the angle. The inverse of a translation is a translation in the opposite direction. If we have a series of matrices $\mathbf{M} = \mathbf{M}_1 \mathbf{M}_2 \cdots \mathbf{M}_n$ then $\mathbf{M}^{-1} = \mathbf{M}_n^{-1} \cdots \mathbf{M}_2^{-1} \mathbf{M}_1^{-1}$.

Also, certain types of transformation matrices are easy to invert. We've already mentioned scales, which are diagonal matrices; the second important example is rotations, which are orthogonal matrices. Recall (Section 5.2.4) that the inverse of an orthogonal matrix is its transpose. This makes it easy to invert rotations and rigid body transformations (see Exercise 6). Also, it's useful to know that a matrix with $[0\ 0\ 0\ 1]$ in the bottom row has an inverse that also has $[0\ 0\ 0\ 1]$ in the bottom row (see Exercise 7).

Interestingly, we can use SVD to invert a matrix as well. Since we know that any matrix can be decomposed into a rotation times a scale times a rotation, inversion is straightforward. For example in 3D we have

$$\mathbf{M} = \mathbf{R}_1 \text{scale}(\sigma_1, \sigma_2, \sigma_3) \mathbf{R}_2,$$

and from the rules above it follows easily that

$$\mathbf{M}^{-1} = \mathbf{R}_2^{\mathrm{T}} \text{scale}(1/\sigma_1, 1/\sigma_2, 1/\sigma_3) \mathbf{R}_1^{\mathrm{T}}.$$

6.5   Coordinate Transformations

All of the previous discussion has been in terms of using transformation matrices to move points around. We can also think of them as simply changing the coordinate system in which the point is represented. For example, in Figure 6.19, we see two ways to visualize a movement. In different contexts, either interpretation may be more suitable.

For example, a driving game may have a model of a city and a model of a car. If the player is presented with a view out the windshield, objects inside the car are always drawn in the same place on the screen, while the streets and buildings appear to move backward as the player drives. On each frame, we apply a transformation to these objects that moves them farther back than on the previous frame. One way to think of this operation is simply that it moves the buildings backward; another way to think of it is that the buildings are staying put but the coordinate system in which we want to draw them—which is attached to the car—is moving. In the second interpretation, the transformation is changing

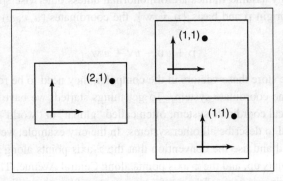

Figure 6.19. The point (2,1) has a transform "translate by (-1,0)" applied to it. On the top right is our mental image if we view this transformation as a physical movement, and on the bottom right is our mental image if we view it as a change of coordinates (a movement of the origin in this case). The artificial boundary is just an artifice, and the relative position of the axes and the point are the same in either case.

the coordinates of the city geometry, expressing them as coordinates in the car's coordinate system. Both ways will lead to exactly the same matrix that is applied to the geometry outside the car.

If the game also supports an overhead view to show where the car is in the city, the buildings and streets need to be drawn in fixed positions while the car needs to move from frame to frame. The same two interpretations apply: we can think of the changing transformation as moving the car from its canonical position to its current location in the world; or we can think of the transformation as simply changing the coordinates of the car's geometry, which is originally expressed in terms of a coordinate system attached to the car, to express them instead in a coordinate system fixed relative to the city. The change-of-coordinates interpretation makes it clear that the matrices used in these two modes (city-to-car coordinate change vs. car-to-city coordinate change) are inverses of one another.

The idea of changing coordinate systems is much like the idea of type conversions in programming. Before we can add a floating-point number to an integer, we need to convert the integer to floating point or the floating-point number to an integer, depending on our needs, so that the types match. And before we can draw the city and the car together, we need to convert the city to car coordinates or the car to city coordinates, depending on our needs, so that the coordinates match.

When managing multiple coordinate systems, it's easy to get confused and wind up with objects in the wrong coordinates, causing them to show up in unexpected places. But with systematic thinking about transformations between coordinate systems, you can reliably get the transformations right.

In 2D, of course, there are two basis vectors.

Geometrically, a coordinate system, or coordinate *frame*, consists of an origin and a basis—a set of three vectors. Orthonormal bases are so convenient that we'll normally assume frames are orthonormal unless otherwise specified. In a frame with origin $\mathbf{p}$ and basis $\{\mathbf{u}, \mathbf{v}, \mathbf{w}\}$, the coordinates (u, v, w) describe the point

$$\mathbf{p} + u\mathbf{u} + v\mathbf{v} + w\mathbf{w}.$$

When we store these vectors in the computer, they need to be represented in terms of some coordinate system. To get things started, we have to designate some canonical coordinate system, often called "global" or "world" coordinates, which is used to describe all other systems. In the city example, we might adopt the street grid and use the convention that the x-axis points along Main Street, the y-axis points up, and the z-axis points along Central Avenue. Then when we write the origin and basis of the car frame in terms of these coordinates it is clear what we mean.

In 2D, right handed means **y** is counter-clockwise from **x**.

In 2D our convention is is to use the point **o** for the origin, and **x** and **y** for the right-handed orthonormal basis vectors **x** and **y** (Figure 6.20).

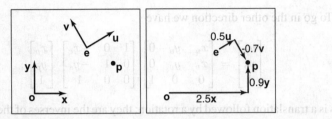

Figure 6.20. The point **p** can be represented in terms of either coordinate system.

Another coordinate system might have an origin **e** and right-handed orthonormal basis vectors **u** and **v**. Note that typically the canonical data **o**, **x**, and **y** are never stored explicitly. They are the frame-of-reference for all other coordinate systems. In that coordinate system, we often write down the location of **p** as an ordered pair, which is shorthand for a full vector expression:

$$\mathbf{p} = (x_p, y_p) \equiv \mathbf{o} + x_p\mathbf{x} + y_p\mathbf{y}.$$

For example, in Figure 6.20, $(x_p, y_p) = (2.5, 0.9)$. Note that the pair (x_p, y_p) implicitly assumes the origin **o**. Similarly, we can express **p** in terms of another equation:

$$\mathbf{p} = (u_p, v_p) \equiv \mathbf{e} + u_p\mathbf{u} + v_p\mathbf{v}.$$

In Figure 6.20, this has $(u_p, v_p) = (0.5, -0.7)$. Again, the origin **e** is left as an implicit part of the coordinate system associated with **u** and **v**.

We can express this same relationship using matrix machinery, like this:

$$\begin{bmatrix} x_p \\ y_p \\ 1 \end{bmatrix} = \begin{bmatrix} 1 & 0 & x_e \\ 0 & 1 & y_e \\ 0 & 0 & 1 \end{bmatrix} \begin{bmatrix} x_u & x_v & 0 \\ y_u & y_v & 0 \\ 0 & 0 & 1 \end{bmatrix} \begin{bmatrix} u_p \\ v_p \\ 1 \end{bmatrix} = \begin{bmatrix} x_u & x_v & x_e \\ y_u & y_v & y_e \\ 0 & 0 & 1 \end{bmatrix} \begin{bmatrix} u_p \\ v_p \\ 1 \end{bmatrix}.$$

Note that this assumes we have the point **e** and vectors **u** and **v** stored in canonical coordinates; the (x, y)-coordinate system is the first among equals. In terms of the basic types of transformations we've discussed in this chapter, this is a rotation (involving **u** and **v**) followed by a translation (involving **e**). Looking at the matrix for the rotation and translation together, you can see it's very easy to write down: we just put **u**, **v**, and **e** into the columns of a matrix, with the usual $[0\ 0\ 1]$ in the third row. To make this even clearer we can write the matrix like this:

$$\mathbf{P}_{xy} = \begin{bmatrix} \mathbf{u} & \mathbf{v} & \mathbf{e} \\ 0 & 0 & 1 \end{bmatrix} \mathbf{P}_{uv}.$$

We call this matrix the *frame-to-canonical* matrix for the (u, v) frame. It takes points expressed in the (u, v) frame and converts them to the same points expressed in the canonical frame.

The name "frame-to-canonical" is based on thinking about changing the coordinates of a vector from one system to another. Thinking in terms of moving vectors around, the frame-to-canonical matrix maps the canonical frame to the (u,v) frame.

To go in the other direction we have

$$
\begin{bmatrix} u_p \\ v_p \\ 1 \end{bmatrix} = \begin{bmatrix} x_u & y_u & 0 \\ x_v & y_v & 0 \\ 0 & 0 & 1 \end{bmatrix} \begin{bmatrix} 1 & 0 & -x_e \\ 0 & 1 & -y_e \\ 0 & 0 & 1 \end{bmatrix} \begin{bmatrix} x_p \\ y_p \\ 1 \end{bmatrix}.
$$

This is a translation followed by a rotation; they are the inverses of the rotation and translation we used to build the frame-to-canonical matrix, and when multiplied together they produce the inverse of the frame-to-canonical matrix, which is (not surprisingly) called the canonical-to-frame matrix:

$$
\mathbf{P}_{uv} = \begin{bmatrix} \mathbf{u} & \mathbf{v} & \mathbf{e} \\ 0 & 0 & 1 \end{bmatrix}^{-1} \mathbf{P}_{xy}.
$$

The canonical-to-frame matrix takes points expressed in the canonical frame and converts them to the same points expressed in the (u,v) frame. We have written this matrix as the inverse of the frame-to-canonical matrix because it can't immediately be written down using the canonical coordinates of $\mathbf{e}$, $\mathbf{u}$, and $\mathbf{v}$. But remember that all coordinate systems are equivalent; it's only our convention of storing vectors in terms of x- and y-coordinates that creates this seeming asymmetry. The canonical-to-frame matrix *can* be expressed simply in terms of the (u, v) coordinates of $\mathbf{o}$, $\mathbf{x}$, and $\mathbf{y}$:

$$
\mathbf{P}_{uv} = \begin{bmatrix} \mathbf{x}_{uv} & \mathbf{y}_{uv} & \mathbf{o}_{uv} \\ 0 & 0 & 1 \end{bmatrix} \mathbf{P}_{xy}.
$$

All these ideas work strictly analogously in 3D, where we have

$$
\begin{bmatrix} x_p \\ y_p \\ z_p \\ 1 \end{bmatrix} = \begin{bmatrix} 1 & 0 & 0 & x_e \\ 0 & 1 & 0 & y_e \\ 0 & 0 & 1 & z_e \\ 0 & 0 & 0 & 1 \end{bmatrix} \begin{bmatrix} x_u & x_v & x_w & 0 \\ y_u & y_v & y_w & 0 \\ z_u & z_v & z_w & 0 \\ 0 & 0 & 0 & 1 \end{bmatrix} \begin{bmatrix} u_p \\ v_p \\ w_p \\ 1 \end{bmatrix}
$$

$$
\mathbf{P}_{xyz} = \begin{bmatrix} \mathbf{u} & \mathbf{v} & \mathbf{w} & \mathbf{e} \\ 0 & 0 & 0 & 1 \end{bmatrix} \mathbf{P}_{uvw},
$$

(6.8)

and

$$
\begin{bmatrix} u_p \\ v_p \\ w_p \\ 1 \end{bmatrix} = \begin{bmatrix} x_u & y_u & z_u & 0 \\ x_v & y_v & z_v & 0 \\ x_w & y_w & z_w & 0 \\ 0 & 0 & 0 & 1 \end{bmatrix} \begin{bmatrix} 1 & 0 & 0 & -x_e \\ 0 & 1 & 0 & -y_e \\ 0 & 0 & 1 & -z_e \\ 0 & 0 & 0 & 1 \end{bmatrix} \begin{bmatrix} x_p \\ y_p \\ z_p \\ 1 \end{bmatrix}
$$

(6.9)

$$
\mathbf{P}_{uvw} = \begin{bmatrix} \mathbf{u} & \mathbf{v} & \mathbf{w} & \mathbf{e} \\ 0 & 0 & 0 & 1 \end{bmatrix}^{-1} \mathbf{P}_{xyz}.
$$

Frequently Asked Questions

- Can't I just hardcode transforms rather than use the matrix formalisms?

Yes, but in practice it is harder to derive, harder to debug, and not any more efficient. Also, all current graphics APIs use this matrix formalism so it must be understood even to use graphics libraries.

- The bottom row of the matrix is always (0,0,0,1). Do I have to store it?

You do not have to store it unless you include perspective transforms (Chapter 7).

Notes

The derivation of the transformation properties of normals is based on *Properties of Surface Normal Transformations* (Turkowski, 1990). In many treatments through the mid-1990s, vectors were represented as row vectors and premultiplied, e.g., $b = aM$. In our notation this would be $b^T = a^T M^T$. If you want to find a rotation matrix R that takes one vector a to a vector b of the same length: $b = Ra$ you could use two rotations constructed from orthonormal bases. A more efficient method is given in *Efficiently Building a Matrix to Rotate One Vector to Another* (Akenine-Möller et al., 2008).

Exercises

1. Write down the 4×4 3D matrix to move by (x_m, y_m, z_m).

2. Write down the 4×4 3D matrix to rotate by an angle θ about the y-axis.

3. Write down the 4×4 3D matrix to scale an object by 50% in all directions.

4. Write the 2D rotation matrix that rotates by 90 degrees clockwise.

5. Write the matrix from Exercise 4 as a product of three shear matrices.

6. Find the inverse of the rigid body transformation:

$$\begin{bmatrix} R & t \\ 0\,0\,0 & 1 \end{bmatrix}$$

where R is a 3×3 rotation matrix and t is a 3-vector.

7. Show that the inverse of the matrix for an affine transformation (one that has all zeros in the bottom row except for a one in the lower right entry) also has the same form.

8. Describe in words what this 2D transform matrix does:

$$\begin{bmatrix} 0 & -1 & 1 \\ 1 & 0 & 1 \\ 0 & 0 & 1 \end{bmatrix}.$$

9. Write down the 3×3 matrix that rotates a 2D point by angle θ about a point $\mathbf{p} = (x_p, y_p)$.

10. Write down the 4×4 rotation matrix that takes the orthonormal 3D vectors $\mathbf{u} = (x_u, y_u, z_u)$, $\mathbf{v} = (x_v, y_v, z_v)$, and $\mathbf{w} = (x_w, y_w, z_w)$, to orthonormal 3D vectors $\mathbf{a} = (x_a, y_a, z_a)$, $\mathbf{b} = (x_b, y_b, z_b)$, and $\mathbf{c} = (x_c, y_c, z_c)$, So $M\mathbf{u} = \mathbf{a}$, $M\mathbf{v} = \mathbf{b}$, and $M\mathbf{w} = \mathbf{c}$.

11. What is the inverse matrix for the answer to the previous problem?

7

Viewing

In the previous chapter we saw how to use matrix transformations as a tool for arranging geometric objects in 2D or 3D space. A second important use of geometric transformations is in moving objects between their 3D locations and their positions in a 2D view of the 3D world. This 3D to 2D mapping is called a *viewing transformation*, and it plays an important role in object-order rendering, in which we need to rapidly find the image-space location of each object in the scene.

When we studied ray tracing in Chapter 4, we covered the different types of perspective and orthographic views and how to generate viewing rays according to any given view. This chapter is about the inverse of that process. Here we explain how to use matrix transformations to express any parallel or perspective view. The transformations in this chapter project 3D points in the scene (world space) to 2D points in the image (image space), and they will project any point on a given pixel's viewing ray back to that pixel's position in image space.

If you have not looked at it recently, it is advisable to review the discussion of perspective and ray generation in Chapter 4 before reading this chapter.

By itself, the ability to project points from the world to the image is only good for producing *wireframe* renderings—renderings in which only the edges of objects are drawn, and closer surfaces do not occlude more distant surfaces (Figure 7.1). Just as a ray tracer needs to find the closest surface intersection along each viewing ray, an object-order renderer displaying solid-looking objects has to work out which of the (possibly many) surfaces drawn at any given point on the screen is closest and display only that one. In this chapter, we assume we are drawing a model consisting only of 3D line segments that are specified by

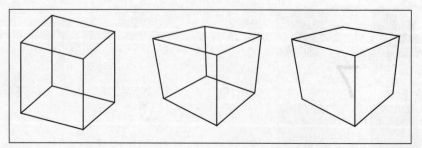

Figure 7.1.   Left: wireframe cube in orthographic projection. Middle: wireframe cube in perspective projection. Right: perspective projection with hidden lines removed.

the (x, y, z) coordinates of their two end points. Later chapters will discuss the machinery needed to produce renderings of solid surfaces.

7.1   Viewing Transformations

The viewing transformation has the job of mapping 3D locations, represented as (x, y, z) coordinates in the canonical coordinate system, to coordinates in the image, expressed in units of pixels. It is a complicated beast that depends on many different things, including the camera position and orientation, the type of projection, the field of view, and the resolution of the image. As with all complicated transformations it is best approached by breaking it up in to a product of several simpler transformations. Most graphics systems do this by using a sequence of three transformations:

Some APIs use "viewing transformation" for just the piece of our viewing transformation that we call the camera transformation.

- A *camera transformation* or *eye transformation*, which is a rigid body transformation that places the camera at the origin in a convenient orientation. It depends only on the position and orientation, or *pose*, of the camera.

- A *projection transformation*, which projects points from camera space so that all visible points fall in the range -1 to 1 in x and y. It depends only on the type of projection desired.

- A *viewport transformation* or *windowing transformation*, which maps this unit image rectangle to the desired rectangle in pixel coordinates. It depends only on the size and position of the output image.

To make it easy to describe the stages of the process (Figure 7.2), we give names to the coordinate systems that are the inputs and output of these transformations. The camera transformation converts points in canonical coordinates (or world

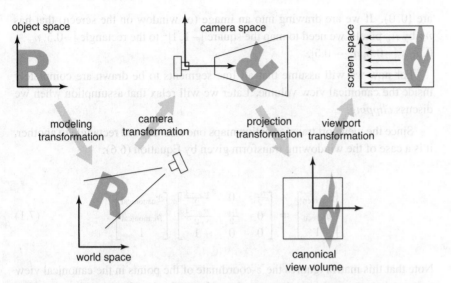

Figure 7.2. The sequence of spaces and transformations that gets objects from their original coordinates into screen space.

space) to *camera coordinates* or places them in *camera space*. The projection transformation moves points from camera space to the *canonical view volume*. Finally, the viewport transformation maps the canonical view volume to *screen space*.

Each of these transformations is individually quite simple. We'll discuss them in detail for the orthographic case beginning with the viewport transformation, then cover the changes required to support perspective projection.

7.1.1 The Viewport Transformation

We begin with a problem whose solution will be reused for any viewing condition. We assume that the geometry we want to view is in the *canonical view volume*, and we wish to view it with an orthographic camera looking in the $-z$ direction. The canonical view volume is the cube containing all 3D points whose Cartesian coordinates are between -1 and $+1$—that is, $(x, y, z) \in [-1, 1]^3$ (Figure 7.3). We project $x = -1$ to the left side of the screen, $x = +1$ to the right side of the screen, $y = -1$ to the bottom of the screen, and $y = +1$ to the top of the screen.

Recall the conventions for pixel coordinates from Chapter 3: each pixel "owns" a unit square centered at integer coordinates; the image boundaries have a half-unit overshoot from the pixel centers; and the smallest pixel center coordinates

Other names: camera space is also "eye space" and the camera transformation is sometimes the "viewing transformation;" the canonical view volume is also "clip space" or "normalized device coordinates;" screen space is also "pixel coordinates."

The word "canonical" crops up again—it means something arbitrarily chosen for convenience. For instance, the unit circle could be called the "canonical circle."

are $(0, 0)$. If we are drawing into an image (or window on the screen) that has n_x by n_y pixels, we need to map the square $[-1, 1]^2$ to the rectangle $[-0.5, n_x - 0.5] \times [-0.5, n_y - 0.5]$.

For now we will assume that all line segments to be drawn are completely inside the canonical view volume. Later we will relax that assumption when we discuss *clipping*.

Since the viewport transformation maps one axis-aligned rectangle to another, it is a case of the windowing transform given by Equation (6.6):

$$\begin{bmatrix} x_{\text{screen}} \\ y_{\text{screen}} \\ 1 \end{bmatrix} = \begin{bmatrix} \frac{n_x}{2} & 0 & \frac{n_x-1}{2} \\ 0 & \frac{n_y}{2} & \frac{n_y-1}{2} \\ 0 & 0 & 1 \end{bmatrix} \begin{bmatrix} x_{\text{canonical}} \\ y_{\text{canonical}} \\ 1 \end{bmatrix}. \tag{7.1}$$

Note that this matrix ignores the z-coordinate of the points in the canonical view volume, because a point's distance along the projection direction doesn't affect where that point projects in the image. But before we officially call this the *viewport matrix*, we add a row and column to carry along the z-coordinate without changing it. We don't need it in this chapter, but eventually we will need the z values because they can be used to make closer surfaces hide more distant surfaces (see Section 8.2.3).

$$M_{\text{vp}} = \begin{bmatrix} \frac{n_x}{2} & 0 & 0 & \frac{n_x-1}{2} \\ 0 & \frac{n_y}{2} & 0 & \frac{n_y-1}{2} \\ 0 & 0 & 1 & 0 \\ 0 & 0 & 0 & 1 \end{bmatrix}. \tag{7.2}$$

7.1.2 The Orthographic Projection Transformation

Of course, we usually want to render geometry in some region of space other than the canonical view volume. Our first step in generalizing the view will keep the view direction and orientation fixed looking along $-z$ with $+y$ up, but will allow arbitrary rectangles to be viewed. Rather than replacing the viewport matrix, we'll augment it by multiplying it with another matrix on the right.

Under these constraints, the view volume is an axis-aligned box, and we'll name the coordinates of its sides so that the view volume is $[l, r] \times [b, t] \times [f, n]$ shown in Figure 7.4. We call this box the *orthographic view volume* and refer to

Mapping a square to a potentially non-square rectangle is not a problem; *x* and *y* just end up with different scale factors going from canonical to pixel coordinates.

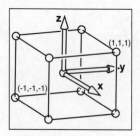

Figure 7.3. The canonical view volume is a cube with side of length two centered at the origin.

the bounding planes as follows:

$$x = l \equiv \text{left plane},$$
$$x = r \equiv \text{right plane},$$
$$y = b \equiv \text{bottom plane},$$
$$y = t \equiv \text{top plane},$$
$$z = n \equiv \text{near plane},$$
$$z = f \equiv \text{far plane}.$$

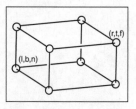

Figure 7.4. The orthographic view volume.

That vocabulary assumes a viewer who is looking along the *minus z*-axis with his head pointing in the y-direction.[1] This implies that $n > f$, which may be unintuitive, but if you assume the entire orthographic view volume has negative z values then the $z = n$ "near" plane is closer to the viewer if and only if $n > f$; here f is a smaller number than n, i.e., a negative number of larger absolute value than n.

This concept is shown in Figure 7.5. The transform from orthographic view volume to the canonical view volume is another windowing transform, so we can simply substitute the bounds of the orthographic and canonical view volumes into Equation (6.7) to obtain the matrix for this transformation:

n and f appear in what might seem like reverse order because $n - f$, rather than $f - n$, is a positive number.

$$\mathbf{M}_{\text{orth}} = \begin{bmatrix} \frac{2}{r-l} & 0 & 0 & -\frac{r+l}{r-l} \\ 0 & \frac{2}{t-b} & 0 & -\frac{t+b}{t-b} \\ 0 & 0 & \frac{2}{n-f} & -\frac{n+f}{n-f} \\ 0 & 0 & 0 & 1 \end{bmatrix}. \tag{7.3}$$

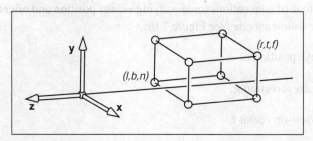

Figure 7.5. The orthographic view volume is along the negative z-axis, so f is a more negative number than n, thus $n > f$.

---

[1] Most programmers find it intuitive to have the x-axis pointing right and the y-axis pointing up. In a right-handed coordinate system, this implies that we are looking in the $-z$ direction. Some systems use a left-handed coordinate system for viewing so that the gaze direction is along $+z$. Which is best is a matter of taste, and this text assumes a right-handed coordinate system. A reference that argues for the left-handed system instead is given in the notes at the end of the chapter.

To draw 3D line segments in the orthographic view volume, we project them into screen x- and y-coordinates and ignore z-coordinates. We do this by combining Equations (7.2) and (7.3). Note that in a program we multiply the matrices together to form one matrix and then manipulate points as follows:

$$\begin{bmatrix} x_{\text{pixel}} \\ y_{\text{pixel}} \\ z_{\text{canonical}} \\ 1 \end{bmatrix} = (\mathbf{M}_{\text{vp}}\mathbf{M}_{\text{orth}}) \begin{bmatrix} x \\ y \\ z \\ 1 \end{bmatrix}.$$

The z-coordinate will now be in $[-1, 1]$. We don't take advantage of this now, but it will be useful when we examine z-buffer algorithms.

The code to draw many 3D lines with endpoints $\mathbf{a}_i$ and $\mathbf{b}_i$ thus becomes both simple and efficient:

construct $\mathbf{M}_{\text{vp}}$
construct $\mathbf{M}_{\text{orth}}$
$\mathbf{M} = \mathbf{M}_{\text{vp}}\mathbf{M}_{\text{orth}}$
for each line segment $(\mathbf{a}_i, \mathbf{b}_i)$ **do**
    $\mathbf{p} = \mathbf{M}\mathbf{a}_i$
    $\mathbf{q} = \mathbf{M}\mathbf{b}_i$
    drawline(x_p, y_p, x_q, y_q)

7.1.3   The Camera Transformation

We'd like to able to change the viewpoint in 3D and look in any direction. There are a multitude of conventions for specifying viewer position and orientation. We will use the following one (see Figure 7.6):

- the eye position $\mathbf{e}$,

- the gaze direction $\mathbf{g}$,

- the view-up vector $\mathbf{t}$.

The eye position is a location that the eye "sees from." If you think of graphics as a photographic process, it is the center of the lens. The gaze direction is any vector in the direction that the viewer is looking. The view-up vector is any vector in the plane that both bisects the viewer's head into right and left halves and points "to the sky" for a person standing on the ground. These vectors provide us with enough information to set up a coordinate system with origin $\mathbf{e}$ and a $\mathbf{uvw}$ basis,

This is a first example of how matrix transformation machinery makes graphics programs clean and efficient.

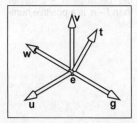

Figure 7.6. The user specifies viewing as an eye position $\mathbf{e}$, a gaze direction $\mathbf{g}$, and an up vector $\mathbf{t}$. We construct a right-handed basis with $\mathbf{w}$ pointing opposite to the gaze and $\mathbf{v}$ being in the same plane as $\mathbf{g}$ and $\mathbf{t}$.

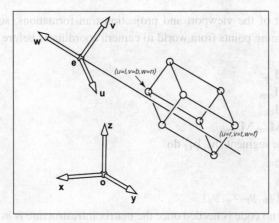

Figure 7.7. For arbitrary viewing, we need to change the points to be stored in the "appropriate" coordinate system. In this case it has origin **e** and offset coordinates in terms of **uvw**.

using the construction of Section 2.4.7:

$$\mathbf{w} = -\frac{\mathbf{g}}{\|\mathbf{g}\|},$$

$$\mathbf{u} = \frac{\mathbf{t} \times \mathbf{w}}{\|\mathbf{t} \times \mathbf{w}\|},$$

$$\mathbf{v} = \mathbf{w} \times \mathbf{u}.$$

Our job would be done if all points we wished to transform were stored in coordinates with origin **e** and basis vectors **u**, **v**, and **w**. But as shown in Figure 7.7, the coordinates of the model are stored in terms of the canonical (or world) origin **o** and the x-, y-, and z-axes. To use the machinery we have already developed, we just need to convert the coordinates of the line segment endpoints we wish to draw from xyz-coordinates into uvw-coordinates. This kind of transformation was discussed in Section 6.5, and the matrix that enacts this transformation is the canonical-to-basis matrix of the camera's coordinate frame:

$$\mathbf{M}_{\text{cam}} = \begin{bmatrix} \mathbf{u} & \mathbf{v} & \mathbf{w} & \mathbf{e} \\ 0 & 0 & 0 & 1 \end{bmatrix}^{-1} = \begin{bmatrix} x_u & y_u & z_u & 0 \\ x_v & y_v & z_v & 0 \\ x_w & y_w & z_w & 0 \\ 0 & 0 & 0 & 1 \end{bmatrix} \begin{bmatrix} 1 & 0 & 0 & -x_e \\ 0 & 1 & 0 & -y_e \\ 0 & 0 & 1 & -z_e \\ 0 & 0 & 0 & 1 \end{bmatrix}. \quad (7.4)$$

Alternatively, we can think of this same transformation as first moving **e** to the origin, then aligning **u, v, w** to **x, y, z**.

To make our previously z-axis-only viewing algorithm work for cameras with any location and orientation, we just need to add this camera transformation to the product of the viewport and projection transformations, so that it converts the incoming points from world to camera coordinates before they are projected:

construct $\mathbf{M}_{\mathrm{vp}}$
construct $\mathbf{M}_{\mathrm{orth}}$
construct $\mathbf{M}_{\mathrm{cam}}$
$\mathbf{M} = \mathbf{M}_{\mathrm{vp}}\mathbf{M}_{\mathrm{orth}}\mathbf{M}_{\mathrm{cam}}$
for each line segment $(\mathbf{a}_i, \mathbf{b}_i)$ **do**
    $\mathbf{p} = \mathbf{M}\mathbf{a}_i$
    $\mathbf{q} = \mathbf{M}\mathbf{b}_i$
    drawline(x_p, y_p, x_q, y_q)

Again, almost no code is needed once the matrix infrastructure is in place.

7.2 Projective Transformations

We have left perspective for last because it takes a little bit of cleverness to make it fit into the system of vectors and matrix transformations that has served us so well up to now. To see what we need to do, let's look at what the perspective projection transformation needs to do with points in camera space. Recall that the viewpoint is positioned at the origin and the camera is looking along the z-axis.

For the moment we will ignore the sign of z to keep the equations simpler, but it will return on page 152.

The key property of perspective is that the size of an object on the screen is proportional to $1/z$ for an eye at the origin looking up the negative z-axis. This can be expressed more precisely in an equation for the geometry in Figure 7.8:

$$y_s = \frac{d}{z}y, \tag{7.5}$$

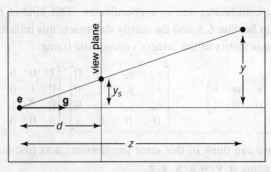

Figure 7.8. The geometry for Equation (7.5). The viewer's eye is at **e** and the gaze direction is **g** (the minus z-axis). The view plane is a distance d from the eye. A point is projected toward **e** and where it intersects the view plane is where it is drawn.

where y is the distance of the point along the y-axis, and y_s is where the point should be drawn on the screen.

We would really like to use the matrix machinery we developed for orthographic projection to draw perspective images; we could then just multiply another matrix into our composite matrix and use the algorithm we already have. However, this type of transformation, in which one of the coordinates of the input vector appears in the denominator, can't be achieved using affine transformations.

We can allow for division with a simple generalization of the mechanism of homogeneous coordinates that we have been using for affine transformations. We have agreed to represent the point (x, y, z) using the homogeneous vector $[x \ y \ z \ 1]^T$; the extra coordinate, w, is always equal to 1, and this is ensured by always using $[0 \ 0 \ 0 \ 1]^T$ as the fourth row of an affine transformation matrix.

Rather than just thinking of the 1 as an extra piece bolted on to coerce matrix multiplication to implement translation, we now define it to be the denominator of the x-, y-, and z-coordinates: the homogeneous vector $[x \ y \ z \ w]^T$ represents the point $(x/w, y/w, z/w)$. This makes no difference when $w = 1$, but it allows a broader range of transformations to be implemented if we allow any values in the bottom row of a transformation matrix, causing w to take on values other than 1.

Concretely, linear transformations allow us to compute expressions like

$$x' = ax + by + cz$$

and affine transformations extend this to

$$x' = ax + by + cz + d.$$

Treating w as the denominator further expands the possibilities, allowing us to compute functions like

$$x' = \frac{ax + by + cz + d}{ex + fy + gz + h};$$

this could be called a "linear rational function" of x, y, and z. But there is an extra constraint—the denominators are the same for all coordinates of the transformed point:

$$x' = \frac{a_1 x + b_1 y + c_1 z + d_1}{ex + fy + gz + h},$$
$$y' = \frac{a_2 x + b_2 y + c_2 z + d_2}{ex + fy + gz + h},$$
$$z' = \frac{a_3 x + b_3 y + c_3 z + d_3}{ex + fy + gz + h}.$$

Expressed as a matrix transformation,

$$
\begin{bmatrix} \tilde{x} \\ \tilde{y} \\ \tilde{z} \\ \tilde{w} \end{bmatrix} = \begin{bmatrix} a_1 & b_1 & c_1 & d_1 \\ a_2 & b_2 & c_2 & d_2 \\ a_3 & b_3 & c_3 & d_3 \\ e & f & g & h \end{bmatrix} \begin{bmatrix} x \\ y \\ z \\ 1 \end{bmatrix}
$$

and

$$
(x', y', z') = (\tilde{x}/\tilde{w}, \tilde{y}/\tilde{w}, \tilde{z}/\tilde{w}).
$$

A transformation like this is known as a *projective transformation* or a *homography*.

Example. The matrix

$$
\mathbf{M} = \begin{bmatrix} 2 & 0 & -1 \\ 0 & 3 & 0 \\ 0 & \frac{2}{3} & \frac{1}{3} \end{bmatrix}
$$

represents a 2D projective transformation that transforms the unit square ($[0,1] \times [0,1]$) to the quadrilateral shown in Figure 7.9.

For instance, the lower-right corner of the square at $(1,0)$ is represented by the homogeneous vector $[1\ 0\ 1]^{\mathrm{T}}$ and transforms as follows:

$$
\begin{bmatrix} 2 & 0 & -1 \\ 0 & 3 & 0 \\ 0 & \frac{2}{3} & \frac{1}{3} \end{bmatrix} \begin{bmatrix} 1 \\ 0 \\ 1 \end{bmatrix} = \begin{bmatrix} 1 \\ 0 \\ \frac{1}{3} \end{bmatrix},
$$

which represents the point $(1/\frac{1}{3}, 0/\frac{1}{3})$, or $(3,0)$. Note that if we use the matrix

$$
3\mathbf{M} = \begin{bmatrix} 6 & 0 & -3 \\ 0 & 9 & 0 \\ 0 & 2 & 1 \end{bmatrix}
$$

instead, the result is $[3\ 0\ 1]^{\mathrm{T}}$, which also represents $(3,0)$. In fact, any scalar multiple $c\mathbf{M}$ is equivalent: the numerator and denominator are both scaled by c, which does not change the result.

There is a more elegant way of expressing the same idea, which avoids treating the w-coordinate specially. In this view a 3D projective transformation is simply a 4D linear transformation, with the extra stipulation that all scalar multiples of a vector refer to the same point:

$$
\mathbf{x} \sim \alpha\mathbf{x} \quad \text{for all } \alpha \neq 0.
$$

The symbol $\sim$ is read as "is equivalent to" and means that the two homogeneous vectors both describe the same point in space.

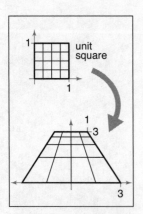

Figure 7.9. A projective transformation maps a square to a quadrilateral, preserving straight lines but not parallel lines.

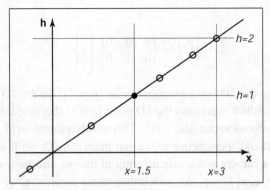

Figure 7.10. The point $x = 1.5$ is represented by any point on the line $x = 1.5h$, such as points at the hollow circles. However, before we interpret x as a conventional Cartesian coordinate, we first divide by h to get $(x,h) = (1.5,1)$ as shown by the black point.

Example. In 1D homogeneous coordinates, in which we use 2-vectors to represent points on the real line, we could represent the point (1.5) using the homogeneous vector $[1.5 \ 1]^{\mathrm{T}}$, or any other point on the line $x = 1.5h$ in homogeneous space. (See Figure 7.10.)

In 2D homogeneous coordinates, in which we use 3-vectors to represent points in the plane, we could represent the point $(-1, -0.5)$ using the homogeneous vector $[-2; -1; 2]^{\mathrm{T}}$, or any other point on the line $\mathbf{x} = \alpha[-1 \ -0.5 \ 1]^{\mathrm{T}}$. Any homogeneous vector on the line can be mapped to the line's intersection with the plane $w = 1$ to obtain its Cartesian coordinates. (See Figure 7.11.)

It's fine to transform homogeneous vectors as many times as needed, without worrying about the value of the w-coordinate—in fact, it is fine if the w-coordinate is zero at some intermediate phase. It is only when we want the ordinary Cartesian coordinates of a point that we need to normalize to an equivalent point that has $w = 1$, which amounts to dividing all the coordinates by w. Once we've done this we are allowed to read off the (x, y, z)-coordinates from the first three components of the homogeneous vector.

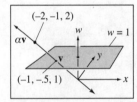

Figure 7.11. A point in homogeneous coordinates is equivalent to any other point on the line through it and the origin, and normalizing the point amounts to intersecting this line with the plane $w = 1$.

7.3 Perspective Projection

The mechanism of projective transformations makes it simple to implement the division by z required to implement perspective. In the 2D example shown in Figure 7.8, we can implement the perspective projection with a matrix transformation as follows:

$$\begin{bmatrix} y_s \\ 1 \end{bmatrix} \sim \begin{bmatrix} d & 0 & 0 \\ 0 & 1 & 0 \end{bmatrix} \begin{bmatrix} y \\ z \\ 1 \end{bmatrix}.$$

This transforms the 2D homogeneous vector $[y; z; 1]^{\mathrm{T}}$ to the 1D homogeneous vector $[dy\ z]^{\mathrm{T}}$, which represents the 1D point (dy/z) (because it is equivalent to the 1D homogeneous vector $[dy/z\ 1]^{\mathrm{T}}$. This matches Equation (7.5).

For the "official" perspective projection matrix in 3D, we'll adopt our usual convention of a camera at the origin facing in the $-z$ direction, so the distance of the point (x, y, z) is $-z$. As with orthographic projection, we also adopt the notion of near and far planes that limit the range of distances to be seen. In this context, we will use the near plane as the projection plane, so the image plane distance is $-n$.

Remember, $n < 0$.

The desired mapping is then $y_s = (n/z)y$, and similarly for x. This transformation can be implemented by the *perspective matrix*:

$$\mathbf{P} = \begin{bmatrix} n & 0 & 0 & 0 \\ 0 & n & 0 & 0 \\ 0 & 0 & n+f & -fn \\ 0 & 0 & 1 & 0 \end{bmatrix}.$$

The first, second, and fourth rows simply implement the perspective equation. The third row, as in the orthographic and viewport matrices, is designed to bring the z-coordinate "along for the ride" so that we can use it later for hidden surface removal. In the perspective projection, though, the addition of a non-constant denominator prevents us from actually preserving the value of z—it's actually impossible to keep z from changing while getting x and y to do what we need them to do. Instead we've opted to keep z unchanged for points on the near or far planes.

More on this later.

There are many matrices that could function as perspective matrices, and all of them non-linearly distort the z-coordinate. This specific matrix has the nice properties shown in Figures 7.12 and 7.13; it leaves points on the $(z = n)$-plane entirely alone, and it leaves points on the $(z = f)$-plane while "squishing" them in x and y by the appropriate amount. The effect of the matrix on a point (x, y, z) is

$$\mathbf{P} \begin{bmatrix} x \\ y \\ z \\ 1 \end{bmatrix} = \begin{bmatrix} x \\ y \\ z\frac{n+f}{n} - f \\ \frac{z}{n} \end{bmatrix} \sim \begin{bmatrix} \frac{nx}{z} \\ \frac{ny}{z} \\ n+f - \frac{fn}{z} \\ 1 \end{bmatrix}.$$

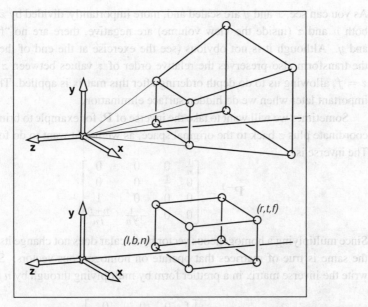

Figure 7.12. The perspective projection leaves points on the $z = n$ plane unchanged and maps the large $z = f$ rectangle at the back of the perspective volume to the small $z = f$ rectangle at the back of the orthographic volume.

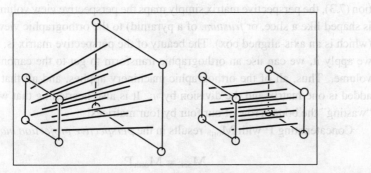

Figure 7.13. The perspective projection maps any line through the origin/eye to a line parallel to the z-axis and without moving the point on the line at $z = n$.

As you can see, x and y are scaled and, more importantly, divided by z. Because both n and z (inside the view volume) are negative, there are no "flips" in x and y. Although it is not obvious (see the exercise at the end of the chapter), the transform also preserves the relative order of z values between $z = n$ and $z = f$, allowing us to do depth ordering after this matrix is applied. This will be important later when we do hidden surface elimination.

Sometimes we will want to take the inverse of $\mathbf{P}$, for example to bring a screen coordinate plus z back to the original space, as we might want to do for picking. The inverse is

$$\mathbf{P}^{-1} = \begin{bmatrix} \frac{1}{n} & 0 & 0 & 0 \\ 0 & \frac{1}{n} & 0 & 0 \\ 0 & 0 & 0 & 1 \\ 0 & 0 & -\frac{1}{fn} & \frac{n+f}{fn} \end{bmatrix}.$$

Since multiplying a homogeneous vector by a scalar does not change its meaning, the same is true of matrices that operate on homogeneous vectors. So we can write the inverse matrix in a prettier form by multiplying through by nf:

This matrix is not literally the inverse of the matrix **P**, but the transformation it describes *is* the inverse of the transformation described by **P**.

$$\mathbf{P}^{-1} = \begin{bmatrix} f & 0 & 0 & 0 \\ 0 & f & 0 & 0 \\ 0 & 0 & 0 & fn \\ 0 & 0 & -1 & n+f \end{bmatrix}.$$

Taken in the context of the orthographic projection matrix $\mathbf{M}_{\text{orth}}$ in Equation (7.3), the perspective matrix simply maps the perspective view volume (which is shaped like a slice, or *frustum*, of a pyramid) to the orthographic view volume (which is an axis-aligned box). The beauty of the perspective matrix is, that once we apply it, we can use an orthographic transform to get to the canonical view volume. Thus, all of the orthographic machinery applies, and all that we have added is one matrix and the division by w. It is also heartening that we are not "wasting" the bottom row of our four by four matrices!

Concatenating $\mathbf{P}$ with $\mathbf{M}_{\text{orth}}$ results in the *perspective projection matrix*,

$$\mathbf{M}_{\text{per}} = \mathbf{M}_{\text{orth}}\mathbf{P}.$$

One issue, however, is: How are l,r,b,t determined for perspective? They identify the "window" through which we look. Since the perspective matrix does not change the values of x and y on the $(z = n)$-plane, we can specify (l, r, b, t) on that plane.

To integrate the perspective matrix into our orthographic infrastructure, we simply replace $\mathbf{M}_{\text{orth}}$ with $\mathbf{M}_{\text{per}}$, which inserts the perspective matrix $\mathbf{P}$ after the camera matrix $\mathbf{M}_{\text{cam}}$ has been applied but before the orthographic projection. So the full set of matrices for perspective viewing is

$$\mathbf{M} = \mathbf{M}_{vp}\mathbf{M}_{orth}\mathbf{P}\mathbf{M}_{cam}.$$

The resulting algorithm is:

compute $\mathbf{M}_{vp}$
compute $\mathbf{M}_{per}$
compute $\mathbf{M}_{cam}$
$\mathbf{M} = \mathbf{M}_{vp}\mathbf{M}_{per}\mathbf{M}_{cam}$
for each line segment $(\mathbf{a}_i, \mathbf{b}_i)$ **do**
$\quad \mathbf{p} = \mathbf{M}\mathbf{a}_i$
$\quad \mathbf{q} = \mathbf{M}\mathbf{b}_i$
$\quad \text{drawline}(x_p/w_p, y_p/w_p, x_q/w_q, y_q/w_q)$

Note that the only change other than the additional matrix is the divide by the homogeneous coordinate w.

Multiplied out, the matrix $\mathbf{M}_{per}$ looks like this:

$$\mathbf{M}_{per} = \begin{bmatrix} \frac{2n}{r-l} & 0 & \frac{l+r}{l-r} & 0 \\ 0 & \frac{2n}{t-b} & \frac{b+t}{b-t} & 0 \\ 0 & 0 & \frac{f+n}{n-f} & \frac{2fn}{f-n} \\ 0 & 0 & 1 & 0 \end{bmatrix}.$$

This or similar matrices often appear in documentation, and they are less mysterious when one realizes that they are usually the product of a few simple matrices.

Example. Many APIs such as *OpenGL* (Shreiner et al., 2004) use the same canonical view volume as presented here. They also usually have the user specify the absolute values of n and f. The projection matrix for *OpenGL* is

$$\mathbf{M}_{OpenGL} = \begin{bmatrix} \frac{2|n|}{r-l} & 0 & \frac{r+l}{r-l} & 0 \\ 0 & \frac{2|n|}{t-b} & \frac{t+b}{t-b} & 0 \\ 0 & 0 & \frac{|n|+|f|}{|n|-|f|} & \frac{2|f||n|}{|n|-|f|} \\ 0 & 0 & -1 & 0 \end{bmatrix}$$

Other APIs set n and f to 0 and 1, respectively. Blinn (J. Blinn, 1996) recommends making the canonical view volume $[0, 1]^3$ for efficiency. All such decisions will change the the projection matrix slightly.

7.4   Some Properties of the Perspective Transform

An important property of the perspective transform is that it takes lines to lines and planes to planes. In addition, it takes line segments in the view volume to line segments in the canonical volume. To see this, consider the line segment

$$\mathbf{q} + t(\mathbf{Q} - \mathbf{q}).$$

When transformed by a 4×4 matrix $\mathbf{M}$, it is a point with possibly varying homogeneous coordinate:

$$\mathbf{Mq} + t(\mathbf{MQ} - \mathbf{Mq}) \equiv \mathbf{r} + t(\mathbf{R} - \mathbf{r}).$$

The homogenized 3D line segment is

$$\frac{\mathbf{r} + t(\mathbf{R} - \mathbf{r})}{w_r + t(w_R - w_r)}. \tag{7.6}$$

If Equation (7.6) can be rewritten in a form

$$\frac{\mathbf{r}}{w_r} + f(t) \left(\frac{\mathbf{R}}{w_R} - \frac{\mathbf{r}}{w_r} \right), \tag{7.7}$$

then all the homogenized points lie on a 3D line. Brute force manipulation of Equation (7.6) yields such a form with

$$f(t) = \frac{w_R t}{w_r + t(w_R - w_r)}. \tag{7.8}$$

It also turns out that the line segments do map to line segments preserving the ordering of the points (Exercise 8), i.e., they do not get reordered or "torn."

A byproduct of the transform taking line segments to line segments is that it takes the edges and vertices of a triangle to the edges and vertices of another triangle. Thus, it takes triangles to triangles and planes to planes.

7.5   Field-of-View

While we can specify any window using the (l, r, b, t) and n values, sometimes we would like to have a simpler system where we look through the center of the window. This implies the constraint that

$$l = -r,$$
$$b = -t.$$

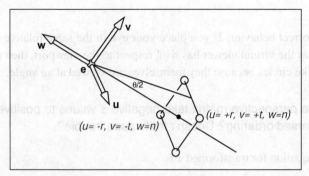

Figure 7.14. The field-of-view θ is the angle from the bottom of the screen to the top of the screen as measured from the eye.

If we also add the constraint that the pixels are square, i.e., there is no distortion of shape in the image, then the ratio of r to t must be the same as the ratio of the number of horizontal pixels to the number of vertical pixels:

$$\frac{n_x}{n_y} = \frac{r}{t}.$$

Once n_x and n_y are specified, this leaves only one degree of freedom. That is often set using the *field-of-view* shown as θ in Figure 7.14. This is sometimes called the vertical field-of-view to distinguish it from the angle between left and right sides or from the angle between diagonal corners. From the figure we can see that

$$\tan\frac{\theta}{2} = \frac{t}{|n|}.$$

If n and θ are specified, then we can derive t and use code for the more general viewing system. In some systems, the value of n is hard-coded to some reasonable value, and thus we have one fewer degree of freedom.

Frequently Asked Questions

• Is orthographic projection ever useful in practice?

It is useful in applications where relative length judgements are important. It can also yield simplifications where perspective would be too expensive as occurs in some medical visualization applications.

• The tessellated spheres I draw in perspective look like ovals. Is this a bug?

No. It is correct behavior. If you place your eye in the same relative position to the screen as the virtual viewer has with respect to the viewport, then these ovals will look like circles because they themselves are viewed at an angle.

• Does the perspective matrix take negative z values to positive z values with a reversed ordering? Doesn't that cause trouble?

Yes. The equation for transformed z is

$$z' = n + f - \frac{fn}{z}.$$

So $z = +\epsilon$ is transformed to $z' = -\infty$ and $z = -\epsilon$ is transformed to $z = \infty$. So any line segments that span $z = 0$ will be "torn" although all points will be projected to an appropriate screen location. This tearing is not relevant when all objects are contained in the viewing volume. This is usually assured by *clipping* to the view volume. However, clipping itself is made more complicated by the tearing phenomenon as is discussed in Chapter 8.

• The perspective matrix changes the value of the homogeneous coordinate. Doesn't that make the move and scale transformations no longer work properly?

Applying a translation to a homogeneous point we have

$$\begin{bmatrix} 1 & 0 & 0 & t_x \\ 0 & 1 & 0 & t_y \\ 0 & 0 & 1 & t_z \\ 0 & 0 & 0 & 1 \end{bmatrix} \begin{bmatrix} hx \\ hy \\ hz \\ h \end{bmatrix} = \begin{bmatrix} hx + ht_x \\ hy + ht_y \\ hz + ht_z \\ h \end{bmatrix} \xrightarrow{\text{homogenize}} \begin{bmatrix} x + t_x \\ y + t_y \\ z + t_z \\ 1 \end{bmatrix}.$$

Similar effects are true for other transforms (see Exercise 5).

Notes

Most of the discussion of viewing matrices is based on information in *Real-Time Rendering* (Akenine-Möller et al., 2008), the *OpenGL Programming Guide* (Shreiner et al., 2004), *Computer Graphics* (Hearn & Baker, 1986), and *3D Game Engine Design* (Eberly, 2000).

Exercises

1. Construct the viewport matrix required for a system in which pixel coordinates count down from the top of the image, rather than up from the bottom.

2. Multiply the viewport and orthographic projection matrices, and show that the result can also be obtained by a single application of Equation (6.7).

3. Derive the third row of Equation (7.3) from the constraint that z is preserved for points on the near and far planes.

4. Show algebraically that the perspective matrix preserves order of z values within the view volume.

5. For a 4×4 matrix whose top three rows are arbitrary and whose bottom row is $(0, 0, 0, 1)$, show that the points $(x, y, z, 1)$ and (hx, hy, hz, h) transform to the same point after homogenization.

6. Verify that the form of $\mathbf{M}_p^{-1}$ given in the text is correct.

7. Verify that the full perspective to canonical matrix $\mathbf{M}_{\text{projection}}$ takes (r, t, n) to $(1, 1, 1)$.

8. Write down a perspective matrix for $n = 1$, $f = 2$.

9. For the point $\mathbf{p} = (x, y, z, 1)$, what are the homogenized and unhomogenized result for that point transformed by the perspective matrix in Exercise 6?

10. For the eye position $\mathbf{e} = (0, 1, 0)$, a gaze vector $\mathbf{g} = (0, -1, 0)$, and a view-up vector $\mathbf{t} = (1, 1, 0)$, what is the resulting orthonormal $\mathbf{uvw}$ basis used for coordinate rotations?

11. Show, that for a perspective transform, line segments that start in the view volume do map to line segments in the canonical volume after homogenization. Further, show that the relative ordering of points on the two segments is the same. *Hint*: Show that the $f(t)$ in Equation (7.8) has the properties $f(0) = 0$, $f(1) = 1$, the derivative of f is positive for all $t \in [0, 1]$, and the homogeneous coordinate does not change sign.

8

The Graphics Pipeline

The previous several chapters have established the mathematical scaffolding we need to look at the second major approach to rendering: drawing objects one by one onto the screen, or *object-order rendering*. Unlike in ray tracing, where we consider each pixel in turn and find the objects that influence its color, we'll now instead consider each geometric object in turn and find the pixels that it could have an effect on. The process of finding all the pixels in an image that are occupied by a geometric primitive is called *rasterization*, so object-order rendering can also be called rendering by rasterization. The sequence of operations that is required, starting with objects and ending by updating pixels in the image, is known as the *graphics pipeline*.

Object-order rendering has enjoyed great success because of its efficiency. For large scenes, management of data access patterns is crucial to performance, and making a single pass over the scene visiting each bit of geometry once has significant advantages over repeatedly searching the scene to retrieve the objects required to shade each pixel.

The title of this chapter suggests that there is only one way to do object-order rendering. Of course this isn't true—two quite different examples of graphics pipelines with very different goals are the hardware pipelines used to support interactive rendering via APIs like OpenGL and Direct3D and the software pipelines used in film production, supporting APIs like RenderMan. Hardware pipelines must run fast enough to react in real time for games, visualizations, and user interfaces. Production pipelines must render the highest quality animation and visual effects possible and scale to enormous scenes, but may take much

Any graphics system has one or more types of "primitive object" that it can handle directly, and more complex objects are converted into these "primitives." Triangles are the most often used primitive.

Rasterization-based systems are also called *scanline renderers*.

more time to do so. Despite the different design decisions resulting from these divergent goals, a remarkable amount is shared among most, if not all, pipelines, and this chapter attempts to focus on these common fundamentals, erring on the side of following the hardware pipelines more closely.

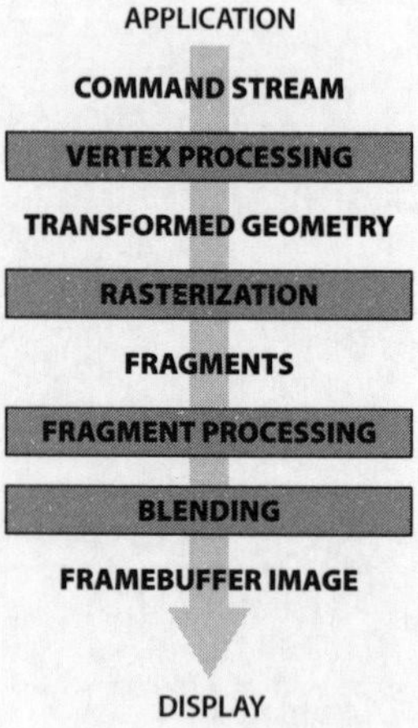

The work that needs to be done in object-order rendering can be organized into the task of rasterization itself, the operations that are done to geometry before rasterization, and the operations that are done to pixels after rasterization. The most common geometric operation is applying matrix transformations, as discussed in the previous two chapters, to map the points that define the geometry from object space to screen space, so that the input to the rasterizer is expressed in pixel coordinates, or *screen space*. The most common pixelwise operation is *hidden surface removal* which arranges for surfaces closer to the viewer to appear in front of surfaces farther from the viewer. Many other operations also can be included at each stage, thereby achieving a wide range of different rendering effects using the same general process.

For the purposes of this chapter we'll discuss the graphics pipeline in terms of four stages (Figure 8.1). Geometric objects are fed into the pipeline from an interactive application or from a scene description file, and they are always described by sets of vertices. The vertices are operated on in the *vertex-processing stage*, then the primitives using those vertices are sent to the *rasterization stage*. The rasterizer breaks each primitive into a number of *fragments*, one for each pixel covered by the primitive. The fragments are processed in the *fragment processing stage*, and then the various fragments corresponding to each pixel are combined in the *fragment blending stage*.

We'll begin by discussing rasterization, then illustrate the purpose of the geometric and pixel-wise stages by a series of examples.

8.1 Rasterization

Rasterization is the central operation in object-order graphics, and the *rasterizer* is central to any graphics pipeline. For each primitive that comes in, the rasterizer has two jobs: it *enumerates* the pixels that are covered by the primitive and it *interpolates* values, called attributes, across the primitive—the purpose for these attributes will be clear with later examples. The output of the rasterizer is a set of *fragments*, one for each pixel covered by the primitive. Each fragment "lives" at a particular pixel and carries its own set of attribute values.

In this chapter, we will present rasterization with a view toward using it to render three-dimensional scenes. The same rasterization methods are used to draw

APPLICATION

COMMAND STREAM

VERTEX PROCESSING

TRANSFORMED GEOMETRY

RASTERIZATION

FRAGMENTS

FRAGMENT PROCESSING

BLENDING

FRAMEBUFFER IMAGE

DISPLAY

Figure 8.1. The stages of a graphics pipeline.

lines and shapes in 2D as well—although it is becoming more and more common to use the 3D graphics system "under the covers" to do all 2D drawing.

8.1.1 Line Drawing

Most graphics packages contain a line drawing command that takes two endpoints in screen coodinates (see Figure 3.10) and draws a line between them. For example, the call for endpoints (1,1) and (3,2) would turn on pixels (1,1) and (3,2) and fill in one pixel between them. For general screen coordinate endpoints (x_0, y_0) and (x_1, y_1), the routine should draw some "reasonable" set of pixels that approximate a line between them. Drawing such lines is based on line equations, and we have two types of equations to choose from: implicit and parametric. This section describes the approach using implicit lines.

Even though we often use integer-valued endpoints for examples, it's important to properly support arbitrary endpoints.

Line Drawing Using Implicit Line Equations

The most common way to draw lines using implicit equations is the *midpoint* algorithm (Pitteway (1967); van Aken and Novak (1985)). The midpoint algorithm ends up drawing the same lines as the *Bresenham algorithm* (Bresenham, 1965) but it is somewhat more straightforward.

The first thing to do is find the implicit equation for the line as discussed in Section 2.5.2:

$$f(x, y) \equiv (y_0 - y_1)x + (x_1 - x_0)y + x_0y_1 - x_1y_0 = 0. \qquad (8.1)$$

We assume that $x_0 \leq x_1$. If that is not true, we swap the points so that it is true. The slope m of the line is given by

$$m = \frac{y_1 - y_0}{x_1 - x_0}.$$

The following discussion assumes $m \in (0, 1]$. Analogous discussions can be derived for $m \in (-\infty, -1]$, $m \in (-1, 0]$, and $m \in (1, \infty)$. The four cases cover all possibilities.

For the case $m \in (0, 1]$, there is more "run" than "rise," i.e., the line is moving faster in x than in y. If we have an API where the y-axis points downwards, we might have a concern about whether this makes the process harder, but, in fact, we can ignore that detail. We can ignore the geometric notions of "up" and "down," because the algebra is exactly the same for the two cases. Cautious readers can confirm that the resulting algorithm works for the y-axis downwards case. The key assumption of the midpoint algorithm is that we draw the thinnest line possible that has no gaps. A diagonal connection between two pixels is not considered a gap.

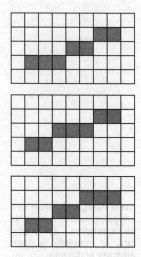

Figure 8.2. Three "reasonable" lines that go seven pixels horizontally and three pixels vertically.

As the line progresses from the left endpoint to the right, there are only two possibilities: draw a pixel at the same height as the pixel drawn to its left, or draw a pixel one higher. There will always be exactly one pixel in each column of pixels between the endpoints. Zero would imply a gap, and two would be too thick a line. There may be two pixels in the same row for the case we are considering; the line is more horizontal than vertical so sometimes it will go right, and sometimes up. This concept is shown in Figure 8.2, where three "reasonable" lines are shown, each advancing more in the horizontal direction than in the vertical direction.

The midpoint algorithm for $m \in (0, 1]$ first establishes the leftmost pixel and the column number (x-value) of the rightmost pixel and then loops horizontally establishing the row (y-value) of each pixel. The basic form of the algorithm is:

$y = y_0$
for $x = x_0$ to x_1 **do**
$\quad$ draw(x, y)
$\quad$ **if** (some condition) **then**
$\quad\quad y = y + 1$

Note that x and y are integers. In words this says, "keep drawing pixels from left to right and sometimes move upwards in the y-direction while doing so." The key is to establish efficient ways to make the decision in the *if* statement.

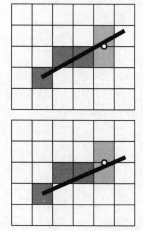

Figure 8.3. Top: the line goes above the midpoint so the top pixel is drawn. Bottom: the line goes below the midpoint so the bottom pixel is drawn.

An effective way to make the choice is to look at the *midpoint* of the line between the two potential pixel centers. More specifically, the pixel just drawn is pixel (x, y) whose center in real screen coordinates is at (x, y). The candidate pixels to be drawn to the right are pixels $(x+1, y)$ and $(x+1, y+1)$. The midpoint between the centers of the two candidate pixels is $(x + 1, y + 0.5)$. If the line passes below this midpoint we draw the bottom pixel, and otherwise we draw the top pixel (Figure 8.3).

To decide whether the line passes above or below $(x+1, y+0.5)$, we evaluate $f(x, y + 0.5)$ in Equation (8.1). Recall from Section 2.5.1 that $f(x, y) = 0$ for points (x, y) on the line, $f(x, y) > 0$ for points on one side of the line, and $f(x, y) < 0$ for points on the other side of the line. Because $-f(x, y) = 0$ and $f(x, y) = 0$ are both perfectly good equations for the line, it is not immediately clear whether $f(x, y)$ being positive indicates that (x, y) is above the line, or whether it is below. However, we can figure it out; the key term in Equation (8.1) is the y term $(x_1 - x_0)y$. Note that $(x_1 - x_0)$ is definitely positive because $x_1 > x_0$. This means that as y increases, the term $(x_1 - x_0)y$ gets larger (i.e., more positive or less negative). Thus, the case $f(x, +\infty)$ is definitely positive, and definitely above the line, implying points above the line are all positive. Another way to look at it is that the y component of the gradient vector is positive. So above the line, where y can increase arbitrarily, $f(x, y)$ must be positive. This means we can make our code more specific by filling in the *if* statement:

> **if** $f(x + 1, y + 0.5) < 0$ **then**
> $y = y + 1$

The above code will work nicely for lines of the appropriate slope (i.e., between zero and one). The reader can work out the other three cases which differ only in small details.

If greater efficiency is desired, using an *incremental* method can help. An incremental method tries to make a loop more efficient by reusing computation from the previous step. In the midpoint algorithm as presented, the main computation is the evaluation of $f(x + 1, y + 0.5)$. Note that inside the loop, after the first iteration, either we already evaluated $f(x - 1, y + 0.5)$ or $f(x - 1, y - 0.5)$ (Figure 8.4). Note also this relationship:

$$f(x + 1, y) = f(x, y) + (y_0 - y_1)$$
$$f(x + 1, y + 1) = f(x, y) + (y_0 - y_1) + (x_1 - x_0).$$

This allows us to write an incremental version of the code:

$y = y_0$
$d = f(x_0 + 1, y_0 + 0.5)$
for $x = x_0$ **to** x_1 **do**
   draw(x, y)
   if $d < 0$ **then**
      $y = y + 1$
      $d = d + (x_1 - x_0) + (y_0 - y_1)$
   else
      $d = d + (y_0 - y_1)$

This code should run faster since it has little extra setup cost compared to the non-incremental version (that is not always true for incremental algorithms), but it may accumulate more numeric error because the evaluation of $f(x, y + 0.5)$ may be composed of many adds for long lines. However, given that lines are rarely longer than a few thousand pixels, such an error is unlikely to be critical. Slightly longer setup cost, but faster loop execution, can be achieved by storing $(x_1 - x_0) + (y_0 - y_1)$ and $(y_0 - y_1)$ as variables. We might hope a good compiler would do that for us, but if the code is critical, it would be wise to examine the results of compilation to make sure.

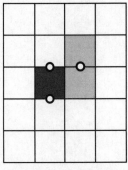

Figure 8.4. When using the decision point shown between the two light gray pixels, we just drew the dark gray pixel, so we evaluated *f* at one of the two left points shown.

8.1.2   Triangle Rasterization

We often want to draw a 2D triangle with 2D points $\mathbf{p}_0 = (x_0, y_0)$, $\mathbf{p}_1 = (x_1, y_1)$, and $\mathbf{p}_2 = (x_2, y_2)$ in screen coordinates. This is similar to the line drawing problem, but it has some of its own subtleties. As with line drawing, we may wish to interpolate color or other properties from values at the vertices. This is straightforward if we have the barycentric coordinates (Section 2.7). For example, if the vertices have colors $\mathbf{c}_0$, $\mathbf{c}_1$, and $\mathbf{c}_2$, the color at a point in the triangle with barycentric coordinates (α, β, γ) is

$$\mathbf{c} = \alpha \mathbf{c}_0 + \beta \mathbf{c}_1 + \gamma \mathbf{c}_2.$$

This type of interpolation of color is known in graphics as *Gouraud* interpolation after its inventor (Gouraud, 1971).

Another subtlety of rasterizing triangles is that we are usually rasterizing triangles that share vertices and edges. This means we would like to rasterize adjacent triangles so there are no holes. We could do this by using the midpoint algorithm to draw the outline of each triangle and then fill in the interior pixels. This would mean adjacent triangles both draw the same pixels along each edge. If the adjacent triangles have different colors, the image will depend on the order in which the two triangles are drawn. The most common way to rasterize triangles that avoids the order problem and eliminates holes is to use the convention that pixels are drawn if and only if their centers are inside the triangle, i.e., the barycentric coordinates of the pixel center are all in the interval $(0, 1)$. This raises the issue of what to do if the center is exactly on the edge of the triangle. There are several ways to handle this as will be discussed later in this section. The key observation is that barycentric coordinates allow us to decide whether to draw a pixel and what color that pixel should be if we are interpolating colors from the vertices. So our problem of rasterizing the triangle boils down to efficiently finding the barycentric coordinates of pixel centers (Pineda, 1988). The brute-force rasterization algorithm is:

> **for** all x **do**
>> **for** all y **do**
>>> compute (α, β, γ) for (x, y)
>>> **if** $(\alpha \in [0, 1]$ and $\beta \in [0, 1]$ and $\gamma \in [0, 1])$ **then**
>>>> $\mathbf{c} = \alpha \mathbf{c}_0 + \beta \mathbf{c}_1 + \gamma \mathbf{c}_2$
>>>> drawpixel (x, y) with color $\mathbf{c}$

The rest of the algorithm limits the outer loops to a smaller set of candidate pixels and makes the barycentric computation efficient.

We can add a simple efficiency by finding the bounding rectangle of the three vertices and only looping over this rectangle for candidate pixels to draw. We can compute barycentric coordinates using Equation (2.33). This yields the algorithm:

$x_{\min} = \text{floor}(x_i)$

$x_{\max} = \text{ceiling}(x_i)$

$y_{\min} = \text{floor}(y_i)$

$y_{\max} = \text{ceiling}(y_i)$

for $y = y_{\min}$ to $y_{\max}$ **do**

    for $x = x_{\min}$ to $x_{\max}$ **do**

        $\alpha = f_{12}(x, y)/f_{12}(x_0, y_0)$

        $\beta = f_{20}(x, y)/f_{20}(x_1, y_1)$

        $\gamma = f_{01}(x, y)/f_{01}(x_2, y_2)$

        if $(\alpha > 0$ and $\beta > 0$ and $\gamma > 0)$ **then**

            $\mathbf{c} = \alpha\mathbf{c}_0 + \beta\mathbf{c}_1 + \gamma\mathbf{c}_2$

            drawpixel (x, y) with color $\mathbf{c}$

Here f_{ij} is the line given by Equation (8.1) with the appropriate vertices:

$$f_{01}(x, y) = (y_0 - y_1)x + (x_1 - x_0)y + x_0 y_1 - x_1 y_0,$$

$$f_{12}(x, y) = (y_1 - y_2)x + (x_2 - x_1)y + x_1 y_2 - x_2 y_1,$$

$$f_{20}(x, y) = (y_2 - y_0)x + (x_0 - x_2)y + x_2 y_0 - x_0 y_2.$$

Note that we have exchanged the test $\alpha \in (0, 1)$ with $\alpha > 0$ etc., because if all of α, β, γ are positive, then we know they are all less than one because $\alpha + \beta + \gamma = 1$. We could also compute only two of the three barycentric variables

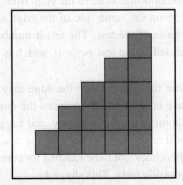
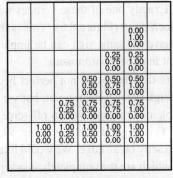

Figure 8.5. A colored triangle with barycentric interpolation. Note that the changes in color components are linear in each row and column as well as along each edge. In fact it is constant along every line, such as the diagonals, as well. (See also Plate II.)

and get the third from that relation, but it is not clear that this saves computation once the algorithm is made incremental, which is possible as in the line drawing algorithms; each of the computations of α, β, and γ does an evaluation of the form $f(x, y) = Ax + By + C$. In the inner loop, only x changes, and it changes by one. Note that $f(x + 1, y) = f(x, y) + A$. This is the basis of the incremental algorithm. In the outer loop, the evaluation changes for $f(x, y)$ to $f(x, y + 1)$, so a similar efficiency can be achieved. Because α, β, and γ change by constant increments in the loop, so does the color **c**. So this can be made incremental as well. For example, the red value for pixel $(x + 1, y)$ differs from the red value for pixel (x, y) by a constant amount that can be precomputed. An example of a triangle with color interpolation is shown in Figure 8.5.

Dealing with Pixels on Triangle Edges

We have still not discussed what to do for pixels whose centers are exactly on the edge of a triangle. If a pixel is exactly on the edge of a triangle, then it is also on the edge of the adjacent triangle if there is one. There is no obvious way to award the pixel to one triangle or the other. The worst decision would be to not draw the pixel because a hole would result between the two triangles. Better, but still not good, would be to have both triangles draw the pixel. If the triangles are transparent, this will result in a double-coloring. We would really like to award the pixel to exactly one of the triangles, and we would like this process to be simple; which triangle is chosen does not matter as long as the choice is well defined.

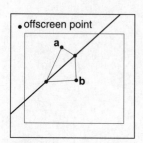

Figure 8.6. The off-screen point will be on one side of the triangle edge or the other. Exactly one of the non-shared vertices **a** and **b** will be on the same side.

One approach is to note that any off-screen point is definitely on exactly one side of the shared edge and that is the edge we will draw. For two non-overlapping triangles, the vertices not on the edge are on opposite sides of the edge from each other. Exactly one of these vertices will be on the same side of the edge as the off-screen point (Figure 8.6). This is the basis of the test. The test if numbers p and q have the same sign can be implemented as the test $pq > 0$, which is very efficient in most environments.

Note that the test is not perfect because the line through the edge may also go through the offscreen point, but we have at least greatly reduced the number of problematic cases. Which off-screen point is used is arbitrary, and $(x, y) = (-1, -1)$ is as good a choice as any. We will need to add a check for the case of a point exactly on an edge. We would like this check not to be reached for common cases, which are the completely inside or outside tests. This suggests:

$$x_{\min} = \text{floor}\,(x_i)$$
$$x_{\max} = \text{ceiling}\,(x_i)$$

$$y_{\min} = \text{floor}\,(y_i)$$
$$y_{\max} = \text{ceiling}\,(y_i)$$
$$f_\alpha = f_{12}(x_0, y_0)$$
$$f_\beta = f_{20}(x_1, y_1)$$
$$f_\gamma = f_{01}(x_2, y_2)$$
for $y = y_{\min}$ to $y_{\max}$ **do**
    for $x = x_{\min}$ to $x_{\max}$ **do**
       $\alpha = f_{12}(x, y)/f_\alpha$
       $\beta = f_{20}(x, y)/f_\beta$
       $\gamma = f_{01}(x, y)/f_\gamma$
       if ($\alpha \geq 0$ and $\beta \geq 0$ and $\gamma \geq 0$) **then**
         if ($\alpha > 0$ or $f_\alpha f_{12}(-1, -1) > 0$) and ($\beta > 0$ or $f_\beta f_{20}(-1, -1) > 0$)
         and ($\gamma > 0$ or $f_\gamma f_{01}(-1, -1) > 0$) **then**
           $\mathbf{c} = \alpha \mathbf{c}_0 + \beta \mathbf{c}_1 + \gamma \mathbf{c}_2$
           drawpixel (x, y) with color $\mathbf{c}$

We might expect that the above code would work to eliminate holes and double-draws only if we use exactly the same line equation for both triangles. In fact, the line equation is the same only if the two shared vertices have the same order in the draw call for each triangle. Otherwise the equation might flip in sign. This could be a problem depending on whether the compiler changes the order of operations. So if a robust implementation is needed, the details of the compiler and arithmetic unit may need to be examined. The first four lines in the pseudocode above must be coded carefully to handle cases where the edge exactly hits the pixel center.

In addition to being amenable to an incremental implementation, there are several potential early exit points. For example, if α is negative, there is no need to compute β or γ. While this may well result in a speed improvement, profiling is always a good idea; the extra branches could reduce pipelining or concurrency and might slow down the code. So as always, test any attractive-looking optimizations if the code is a critical section.

Another detail of the above code is that the divisions could be divisions by zero for degenerate triangles, i.e., if $f_\gamma = 0$. Either the floating point error conditions should be accounted for properly, or another test will be needed.

8.1.3 Clipping

Simply transforming primitives into screen space and rasterizing them does not quite work by itself. This is because primitives that are outside the view volume—

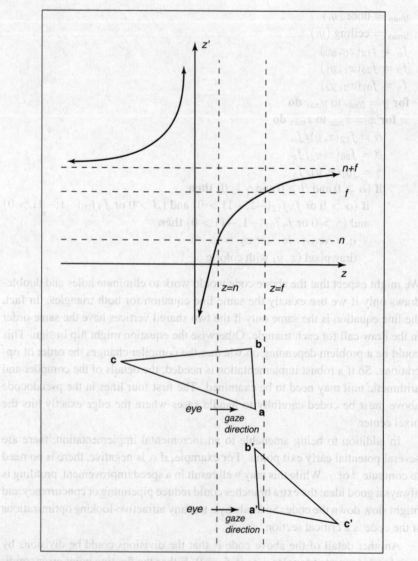

Figure 8.7. The depth z is transformed to the depth z' by the perspective transform. Note that when z moves from positive to negative, z' switches from negative to positive. Thus vertices behind the eye are moved in front of the eye beyond $z' = n + f$. This will lead to wrong results, which is why the triangle is first clipped to ensure all vertices are in front of the eye.

particularly, primitives that are behind the eye—can end up being rasterized, leading to incorrect results. For instance, consider the triangle shown in Figure 8.7. Two vertices are in the view volume, but the third is behind the eye. The projection transformation maps this vertex to a nonsensical location behind the far plane, and if this is allowed to happen the triangle will be rasterized incorrectly. For this reason, rasterization has to be preceded by a *clipping* operation that removes parts of primitives that could extend behind the eye.

Clipping is a common operation in graphics, needed whenever one geometric entity "cuts" another. For example, if you clip a triangle against the plane $x = 0$, the plane cuts the triangle into two parts if the signs of the x-coordinates of the vertices are not all the same. In most applications of clipping, the portion of the triangle on the "wrong" side of the plane is discarded. This operation for a single plane is shown in Figure 8.8.

In clipping to prepare for rasterization, the "wrong" side is the side outside the view volume. It is always safe to clip away all geometry outside the view volume—that is, clipping against all six faces of the volume—but many systems manage to get away with only clipping against the near plane.

This section discusses the basic implementation of a clipping module. Those interested in implementing an industrial-speed clipper should see the book by Blinn mentioned in the notes at the end of this chapter.

The two most common approaches for implementing clipping are

1. in world coordinates using the six planes that bound the truncated viewing pyramid,

2. in the 4D transformed space before the homogeneous divide.

Either possibility can be effectively implemented (J. Blinn, 1996) using the following approach for each triangle:

for each of six planes **do**
    if (triangle entirely outside of plane) **then**
        break (triangle is not visible)
    else if triangle spans plane **then**
        clip triangle
        if (quadrilateral is left) **then**
            break into two triangles

8.1.4 Clipping Before the Transform (Option 1)

Option 1 has a straightforward implementation. The only question is, "What are the six plane equations?" Because these equations are the same for all triangles

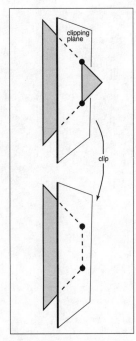

Figure 8.8. A polygon is clipped against a clipping plane. The portion "inside" the plane is retained.

rendered in the single image, we do not need to compute them very efficiently. For this reason, we can just invert the transform shown in Figure 5.11 and apply it to the eight vertices of the transformed view volume:

$$(x, y, z) = (l, b, n)$$
$$(r, b, n)$$
$$(l, t, n)$$
$$(r, t, n)$$
$$(l, b, f)$$
$$(r, b, f)$$
$$(l, t, f)$$
$$(r, t, f)$$

The plane equations can be inferred from here. Alternatively, we can use vector geometry to get the planes directly from the viewing parameters.

8.1.5 Clipping in Homogeneous Coordinates (Option 2)

Surprisingly, the option usually implemented is that of clipping in homogeneous coordinates before the divide. Here the view volume is 4D, and it is bounded by 3D volumes (hyperplanes). These are:

$$-x + lw = 0$$
$$x - rw = 0$$
$$-y + bw = 0$$
$$y - tw = 0$$
$$-z + nw = 0$$
$$z - fw = 0$$

These planes are quite simple, so the efficiency is better than for Option 1. They still can be improved by transforming the view volume $[l, r] \times [b, t] \times [f, n]$ to $[0, 1]^3$. It turns out that the clipping of the triangles is not much more complicated than in 3D.

8.1.6 Clipping against a Plane

No matter which option we choose, we must clip against a plane. Recall from Section 2.5.5 that the implicit equation for a plane through point **q** with normal

$\mathbf{n}$ is

$$f(\mathbf{p}) = \mathbf{n} \cdot (\mathbf{p} - \mathbf{q}) = 0.$$

This is often written

$$f(\mathbf{p}) = \mathbf{n} \cdot \mathbf{p} + D = 0. \tag{8.2}$$

Interestingly, this equation not only describes a 3D plane, but it also describes a line in 2D and the volume analog of a plane in 4D. All of these entities are usually called planes in their appropriate dimension.

If we have a line segment between points $\mathbf{a}$ and $\mathbf{b}$, we can "clip" it against a plane using the techniques for cutting the edges of 3D triangles in BSP tree programs described in Section 12.4.3. Here, the points $\mathbf{a}$ and $\mathbf{b}$ are tested to determine whether they are on opposite sides of the plane $f(\mathbf{p}) = 0$ by checking whether $f(\mathbf{a})$ and $f(\mathbf{b})$ have different signs. Typically $f(\mathbf{p}) < 0$ is defined to be "inside" the plane, and $f(\mathbf{p}) > 0$ is "outside" the plane. If the plane does split the line, then we can solve for the intersection point by substituting the equation for the parametric line,

$$\mathbf{p} = \mathbf{a} + t(\mathbf{b} - \mathbf{a}),$$

into the $f(\mathbf{p}) = 0$ plane of Equation (8.2). This yields

$$\mathbf{n} \cdot (\mathbf{a} + t(\mathbf{b} - \mathbf{a})) + D = 0.$$

Solving for t gives

$$t = \frac{\mathbf{n} \cdot \mathbf{a} + D}{\mathbf{n} \cdot (\mathbf{a} - \mathbf{b})}.$$

We can then find the intersection point and "shorten" the line.

To clip a triangle, we again can follow Section 12.4.3 to produce one or two triangles .

8.2   Operations Before and After Rasterization

Before a primitive can be rasterized, the vertices that define it must be in screen coordinates, and the colors or other attributes that are supposed to be interpolated across the primitive must be known. Preparing this data is the job of the *vertex-processing* stage of the pipeline. In this stage, incoming vertices are transformed by the modeling, viewing, and projection transformations, mapping them from their original coordinates into screen space (where, recall, position is measured in terms of pixels). At the same time, other information, such as colors, surface normals, or texture coordinates, is transformed as needed; we'll discuss these additional attributes in the examples below.

After rasterization, further processing is done to compute a color and depth for each fragment. This processing can be as simple as just passing through an interpolated color and using the depth computed by the rasterizer; or it can involve complex shading operations. Finally, the blending phase combines the fragments generated by the (possibly several) primitives that overlapped each pixel to compute the final color. The most common blending approach is to choose the color of the fragment with the smallest depth (closest to the eye).

The purposes of the different stages are best illustrated by examples.

8.2.1 Simple 2D Drawing

The simplest possible pipeline does nothing in the vertex or fragment stages, and in the blending stage the color of each fragment simply overwrites the value of the previous one. The application supplies primitives directly in pixel coordinates, and the rasterizer does all the work. This basic arrangement is the essence of many simple, older APIs for drawing user interfaces, plots, graphs, and other 2D content. Solid color shapes can be drawn by specifying the same color for all vertices of each primitive, and our model pipeline also supports smoothly varying color using interpolation.

8.2.2 A Minimal 3D Pipeline

To draw objects in 3D, the only change needed to the 2D drawing pipeline is a single matrix transformation: the vertex-processing stage multiplies the incoming vertex positions by the product of the modeling, camera, projection, and viewport matrices, resulting in screen-space triangles that are then drawn in the same way as if they'd been specified directly in 2D.

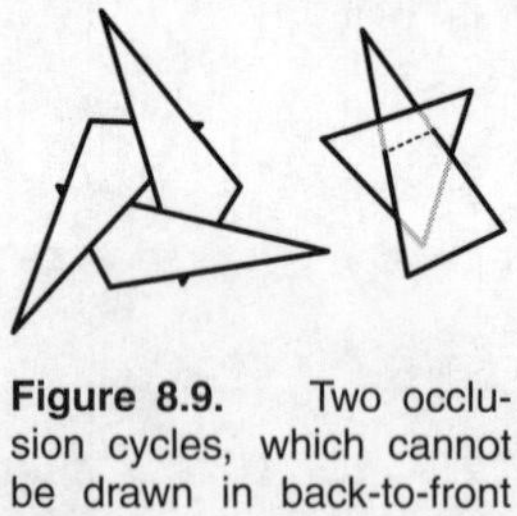

One problem with the minimal 3D pipeline is that in order to get occlusion relationships correct — to get nearer objects in front of farther away objects — primitives must be drawn in back-to-front order. This is known as the *painter's algorithm* for hidden surface removal, by analogy to painting the background of a painting first, then painting the foreground over it. The painter's algorithm is a perfectly valid way to remove hidden surfaces, but it has several drawbacks. It cannot handle triangles that intersect one another, because there is no correct order in which to draw them. Similarly, several triangles, even if they don't intersect, can still be arranged in an *occlusion cycle*, as shown in Figure 8.9, another case in which the back-to-front order does not exist. And most importantly, sorting the primitives by depth is slow, especially for large scenes, and disturbs the

Figure 8.9. Two occlusion cycles, which cannot be drawn in back-to-front order.

efficient flow of data that makes object-order rendering so fast. Figure 8.10 shows the result of this process when the objects are not sorted by depth.

Figure 8.10. The result of drawing two spheres of identical size using the minimal pipeline. The sphere that appears smaller is farther away but is drawn last, so it incorrectly overwrites the nearer one.

8.2.3 Using a z-Buffer for Hidden Surfaces

In practice the painter's algorithm is rarely used; instead a simple and effective hidden surface removal algorithm known as the *z-buffer* algorithm is used. The method is very simple: at each pixel we keep track of the distance to the closest surface that has been drawn so far, and we throw away fragments that are farther away than that distance. The closest distance is stored by allocating an extra value for each pixel, in addition to the red, green, and blue color values, which is known as the depth, or z-value. The *depth buffer*, or z-buffer, is the name for the grid of depth values.

The z-buffer algorithm is implemented in the fragment blending phase, by comparing the depth of each fragment with the current value stored in the z-buffer. If the fragment's depth is closer, both its color and its depth value overwrite the values currently in the color and depth buffers. If the fragment's depth is farther away, it is discarded. To ensure that the first fragment will pass the depth test, the z buffer is initialized to the maximum depth (the depth of the far plane). Irrespective of the order in which surfaces are drawn, the same fragment will win the depth test, and the image will be the same.

Of course there can be ties in the depth test, in which case the order may well matter.

The z-buffer algorithm requires each fragment to carry a depth. This is done simply by interpolating the z-coordinate as a vertex attribute, in the same way that color or other attributes are interpolated.

The z-buffer is such a simple and practical way to deal with hidden surfaces in object-order rendering that it is by far the dominant approach. It is much simpler than geometric methods that cut surfaces into pieces that can be sorted by depth, because it avoids solving any problems that don't need to be solved. The depth order only needs to be determined at the locations of the pixels, and that is all that the z-buffer does. It is universally supported by hardware graphics pipelines and is also the most commonly used method for software pipelines. Figure 8.11 shows an example result.

Figure 8.11. The result of drawing the same two spheres using the z-buffer.

Precision Issues

In practice, the z-values stored in the buffer are non-negative integers. This is preferable to true floats because the fast memory needed for the z-buffer is somewhat expensive and is worth keeping to a minimum.

The use of integers can cause some precision problems. If we use an integer range having B values $\{0, 1, \ldots, B - 1\}$, we can map 0 to the near clipping plane

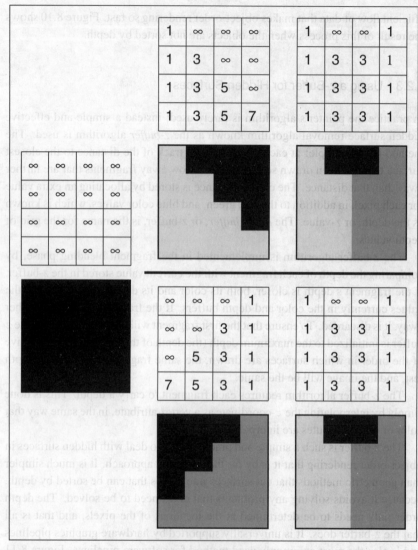

Figure 8.12. A z-buffer rasterizing two triangles in each of two possible orders. The first triangle is fully rasterized. The second triangle has every pixel computed, but for three of the pixels the depth-contest is lost, and those pixels are not drawn. The final image is the same regardless.

$z = n$ and $B - 1$ to the far clipping plane $z = f$. Note, that for this discussion, we assume z, n, and f are positive. This will result in the same results as the negative case, but the details of the argument are easier to follow. We send each z-value to a "bucket" with depth $\Delta z = (f - n)/B$. We would not use the integer z-buffer if memory were not a premium, so it is useful to make B as small as possible.

If we allocate b bits to store the z-value, then $B = 2^b$. We need enough bits to make sure any triangle in front of another triangle will have its depth mapped to distinct depth bins.

For example, if you are rendering a scene where triangles have a separation of at least one meter, then $\Delta z < 1$ should yield images without artifacts. There are two ways to make Δz smaller: move n and f closer together or increase b. If b is fixed, as it may be in APIs or on particular hardware platforms, adjusting n and f is the only option.

The precision of z-buffers must be handled with great care when perspective images are created. The value Δz above is used *after* the perspective divide. Recall from Section 7.3 that the result of the perspective divide is

$$z = n + f - \frac{fn}{z_w}.$$

The actual bin depth is related to z_w, the world depth, rather than z, the post-perspective divide depth. We can approximate the bin size by differentiating both sides:

$$\Delta z \approx \frac{fn\Delta z_w}{z_w^2}.$$

Bin sizes vary in depth. The bin size in world space is

$$\Delta z_w \approx \frac{z_w^2 \Delta z}{fn}.$$

Note that the quantity Δz is as discussed before. The biggest bin will be for $z' = f$, where

$$\Delta z_w^{\max} \approx \frac{f\Delta z}{n}.$$

Note that choosing $n = 0$, a natural choice if we don't want to lose objects right in front of the eye, will result in an infinitely large bin—a very bad condition. To make $\Delta z_w^{\max}$ as small as possible, we want to minimize f and maximize n. Thus, it is always important to choose n and f carefully.

8.2.4   Per-vertex Shading

So far the application sending triangles into the pipeline is responsible for setting the color; the rasterizer just interpolates the colors and they are written directly into the output image. For some applications this is sufficient, but in many cases we want 3D objects to be drawn with shading, using the same illumination equations that we used for image-order rendering in Chapter 4. Recall that these equations require a light direction, an eye direction, and a surface normal to compute the color of a surface.

One way to handle shading computations is to perform them in the vertex stage. The application provides normal vectors at the vertices, and the positions and colors of the lights are provided separately (they don't vary across the surface, so they don't need to be specified for each vertex). For each vertex, the direction to the viewer and the direction to each light are computed based on the positions of the camera, the lights, and the vertex. The desired shading equation is evaluated to compute a color, which is then passed to the rasterizer as the vertex color. Per-vertex shading is sometimes called *Gouraud shading*.

One decision to be made is the coordinate system in which shading computations are done. World space or eye space are good choices. It is important to choose a coordinate system that is orthonormal when viewed in world space, because shading equations depend on angles between vectors, which are not preserved by operations like nonuniform scale that are often used in the modeling transformation, or perspective projection, often used in the projection to the canonical view volume. Shading in eye space has the advantage that we don't need to keep track of the camera position, because the camera is always at the origin in eye space, in perspective projection, or the view direction is always $+z$ in orthographic projection.

Per-vertex shading has the disadvantage that it cannot produce any details in the shading that are smaller than the primitives used to draw the surface, because it only computes shading once for each vertex and never in between vertices. For instance, in a room with a floor that is drawn using two large triangles and illuminated by a light source in the middle of the room, shading will be evaluated only at the corners of the room, and the interpolated value will likely be much too dark in the center. Also, curved surfaces that are shaded with specular highlights must be drawn using primitives small enough that the highlights can be resolved.

Figure 8.13 shows our two spheres drawn with per-vertex shading.

Figure 8.13. Two spheres drawn using per-pixel (Gouraud) shading. Because the triangles are large, interpolation artifacts are visible.

Per-fragment shading is sometimes called Phong shading, which is confusing because the same name is attached to the Phong illumination model.

8.2.5 Per-fragment Shading

To avoid the interpolation artifacts associated with per-vertex shading, we can avoid interpolating colors by performing the shading computations *after* the interpolation, in the fragment stage. In per-fragment shading, the same shading equations are evaluated, but they are evaluated for each fragment using interpolated vectors, rather than for each vertex using the vectors from the application.

In per-fragment shading the geometric information needed for shading is passed through the rasterizer as attributes, so the vertex stage must coordinate with the fragment stage to prepare the data appropriately. One approach is to interpolate the eye-space surface normal and the eye-space vertex position, which then can be used just as they would in per-vertex shading.

Figure 8.14 shows our two spheres drawn with per-vertex shading.

Figure 8.14. Two spheres drawn using per-fragment shading. Because the triangles are large, interpolation artifacts are visible.

8.2.6 Texture Mapping

Textures (discussed in Chapter 11) are images that are used to add extra detail to the shading of surfaces that would otherwise look too homogeneous and artificial. The idea is simple: each time shading is computed, we read one of the values used in the shading computation—the diffuse color, for instance—from a texture instead of using the attribute values that are attached to the geometry being rendered. This operation is known as a *texture lookup*: the shading code specifies a *texture coordinate*, a point in the domain of the texture, and the texture-mapping system finds the value at that point in the texture image and returns it. The texture value is then used in the shading computation.

The most common way to define texture coordinates is simply to make the texture coordinate another vertex attribute. Each primitive then knows where it lives in the texture.

8.2.7 Shading Frequency

The decision about where to place shading computations depends on how fast the color changes—the *scale* of the details being computed. Shading with large-scale features, such as diffuse shading on curved surfaces, can be evaluated fairly infrequently and then interpolated: it can be computed with a low *shading frequency*. Shading that produces small-scale features, such as sharp highlights or detailed textures, needs to be evaluated at a high shading frequency. For details that need to look sharp and crisp in the image, the shading frequency needs to be at least one shading sample per pixel.

So large-scale effects can safely be computed in the vertex stage, even when the vertices defining the primitives are many pixels apart. Effects that require a high shading frequency can also be computed at the vertex stage, as long as the vertices are close together in the image; alternatively, they can be computed at the fragment stage when primitives are larger than a pixel.

For example, a hardware pipeline as used in a computer game, generally using primitives that cover several pixels to ensure high efficiency, normally does most shading computations per fragment. On the other hand, the PhotoRealistic RenderMan system does all shading computations per vertex, after first subdividing, or *dicing*, all surfaces into small quadrilaterals called *micropolygons* that are about the size of pixels. Since the primitives are small, per-vertex shading in this system achieves a high shading frequency that is suitable for detailed shading.

8.3 Simple Antialiasing

Just as with ray tracing, rasterization will produce jagged lines and triangle edges if we make an all-or-nothing determination of whether each pixel is inside the primitive or not. In fact, the set of fragments generated by the simple triangle rasterization algorithms described in this chapter, sometimes called standard or *aliased* rasterization, is exactly the same as the set of pixels that would be mapped to that triangle by a ray tracer that sends one ray through the center of each pixel. Also as in ray tracing, the solution is to allow pixels to be partly covered by a primitive (Crow, 1978). In practice this form of blurring helps visual quality, especially in animations. This is shown as the top line of Figure 8.15.

There are a number of different approaches to antialiasing in rasterization applications. Just as with a ray tracer, we can produce an antialiased image by setting each pixel value to the average color of the image over the square area belonging to the pixel, an approach known as *box filtering*. This means we have to think of all drawable entities as having well-defined areas. For example, the line in Figure 8.15 can be thought of as approximating a one-pixel-wide rectangle.

There are better filters than the box, but a box filter will suffice for all but the most demanding applications.

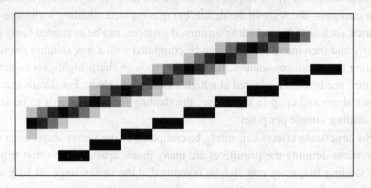

Figure 8.15. An antialiased and a jaggy line viewed at close range so individual pixels are visible.

The easiest way to implement box-filter antialiasing is by *supersampling*: create images at very high resolutions and then downsample. For example, if our goal is a 256×256 pixel image of a line with width 1.2 pixels, we could rasterize a rectangle version of the line with width 4.8 pixels on a 1024×1024 screen, and then average 4×4 groups of pixels to get the colors for each of the 256×256 pixels in the "shrunken" image. This is an approximation of the actual box-filtered image, but works well when objects are not extremely small relative to the distance between pixels.

Supersampling is quite expensive, however. Because the very sharp edges that cause aliasing are normally caused by the edges of primitives, rather than sudden variations in shading within a primitive, a widely used optimization is to sample visibility at a higher rate than shading. If information about coverage and depth is stored for several points within each pixel, very good antialiasing can be achieved even if only one color is computed. In systems like RenderMan that use per-vertex shading, this is achieved by rasterizing at high resolution: it is inexpensive to do so because shading is simply interpolated to produce colors for the many fragments, or visibility samples. In systems with per-fragment shading, such as hardware pipelines, *multisample antialiasing* is achieved by storing for each fragment a single color plus a coverage mask and a set of depth values.

8.4 Culling Primitives for Efficiency

The strength of object-order rendering, that it requires a single pass over all the geometry in the scene, is also a weakness for complex scenes. For instance, in a model of an entire city, only a few buildings are likely to be visible at any given time. A correct image can be obtained by drawing all the primitives in the scene, but a great deal of effort will be wasted processing geometry that is behind the visible buildings, or behind the viewer, and therefore doesn't contribute to the final image.

Identifying and throwing away invisible geometry to save the time that would be spent processing it is known as *culling*. Three commonly implemented culling strategies (often used in tandem) are:

- **view volume culling**—the removal of geometry that is outside the view volume;
- **occlusion culling**—the removal of geometry that may be within the view volume but is obscured, or occluded, by other geometry closer to the camera;
- **backface culling**—the removal of primitives facing away from the camera.

We will briefly discuss view volume culling and backface culling, but culling in high performance systems is a complex topic; see (Akenine-Möller et al., 2008) for a complete discussion and for information about occlusion culling.

8.4.1 View Volume Culling

When an entire primitive lies outside the view volume, it can be culled, since it will produce no fragments when rasterized. If we can cull many primitives with a quick test, we may be able to speed up drawing significantly. On the other hand, testing primitives individually to decide exactly which ones need to be drawn may cost more than just letting the rasterizer eliminate them.

View volume culling, also known as *view frustum culling*, is especially helpful when many triangles are grouped into an object with an associated bounding volume. If the bounding volume lies outside the view volume, then so do all the triangles that make up the object. For example, if we have 1000 triangles bounded by a single sphere with center $\mathbf{c}$ and radius r, we can check whether the sphere lies outside the clipping plane,

$$(\mathbf{p} - \mathbf{a}) \cdot \mathbf{n} = 0,$$

where $\mathbf{a}$ is a point on the plane, and $\mathbf{p}$ is a variable. This is equivalent to checking whether the signed distance from the center of the sphere $\mathbf{c}$ to the plane is greater than $+r$. This amounts to the check that

$$\frac{(\mathbf{c} - \mathbf{a}) \cdot \mathbf{n}}{\|\mathbf{n}\|} > r.$$

Note that the sphere may overlap the plane even in a case where all the triangles do lie outside the plane. Thus, this is a conservative test. How conservative the test is depends on how well the sphere bounds the object.

The same idea can be applied hierarchically if the scene is organized in one of the spatial data structures described in Chapter 12.

8.4.2 Backface Culling

When polygonal models are closed, i.e., they bound a closed space with no holes, then they are often assumed to have outward facing normal vectors as discussed in Chapter 10. For such models, the polygons that face away from the eye are certain to be overdrawn by polygons that face the eye. Thus, those polygons can be culled before the pipeline even starts. The test for this condition is the same one used for silhouette drawing given in Section 10.3.1.

Frequently Asked Questions

• I've often seen clipping discussed at length, and it is a much more involved process than that described in this chapter. What is going on here?

The clipping described in this chapter works, but lacks optimizations that an industrial-strength clipper would have. These optimizations are discussed in detail in Blinn's definitive work listed in the chapter notes.

• How are polygons that are not triangles rasterized?

These can either be done directly scan-line by scan-line, or they can be broken down into triangles. The latter appears to be the more popular technique.

• Is it always better to antialias?

No. Some images look crisper without antialiasing. Many programs use unantialiased "screen fonts" because they are easier to read.

• The documentation for my API talks about "scene graphs" and "matrix stacks." Are these part of the graphics pipeline?

The graphics pipeline is certainly designed with these in mind, and whether we define them as part of the pipeline is a matter of taste. This book delays their discussion until Chapter 12.

• Is a uniform distance z-buffer better than the standard one that includes perspective matrix non-linearities?

It depends. One "feature" of the non-linearities is that the z-buffer has more resolution near the eye and less in the distance. If a level-of-detail system is used, then geometry in the distance is coarser and the "unfairness" of the z-buffer can be a good thing.

• Is a software z-buffer ever useful?

Yes. Most of the movies that use 3D computer graphics have used a variant of the software z-buffer developed by Pixar (Cook et al., 1987) .

Notes

A wonderful book about designing a graphics pipeline is *Jim Blinn's Corner: A Trip Down the Graphics Pipeline* (J. Blinn, 1996). Many nice details of the pipeline and culling are in *3D Game Engine Design* (Eberly, 2000) and *Real-Time Rendering* (Akenine-Möller et al., 2008).

Exercises

1. Suppose that in the perspective transform we have $n = 1$ and $f = 2$. Under what circumstances will we have a "reversal" where a vertex before and after the perspective transform flips from in front of to behind the eye or vice-versa?

2. Is there any reason not to clip in x and y after the perspective divide (see Figure 11.2, stage 3)?

3. Derive the incremental form of the midpoint line-drawing algorithm with colors at endpoints for $0 < m \leq 1$.

4. Modify the triangle-drawing algorithm so that it will draw exactly one pixel for points on a triangle edge which goes through $(x, y) = (-1, -1)$.

5. Suppose you are designing an integer z-buffer for flight simulation where all of the objects are at least one meter thick, are never closer to the viewer than 4 meters, and may be as far away as 100 km. How many bits are needed in the z-buffer to ensure there are no visibility errors? Suppose that visibility errors only matter near the viewer, i.e., for distances less than 100 meters. How many bits are needed in that case?

9

Signal Processing

In graphics, we often deal with functions of a continuous variable: an image is the first example you have seen, but you will encounter many more as you continue your exploration of graphics. By their nature continuous functions can't be directly represented in a computer; we have to somehow represent them using a finite number of bits. One of the most useful approaches to representing continuous functions is to use *samples* of the function: just store the values of the function at many different points and *reconstruct* the values in between when and if they are needed.

You are by now familiar with the idea of representing an image using a two-dimensional grid of pixels—so you have already seen a sampled representation! Think of an image captured by a digital camera: the actual image of the scene that was formed by the camera's lens is a continuous function of the position on the image plane, and the camera converted that function into a two-dimensional grid of samples. Mathematically, the camera converted a function of type $\mathbb{R}^2 \to \mathbf{C}$ (where $\mathbf{C}$ is the set of colors) to a two-dimensional array of color samples, or a function of type $\mathbb{Z}^2 \to \mathbf{C}$.

Another example of a sampled representation is a 2D digitizing tablet such as the screen of a tablet computer or PDA. In this case the original function is the motion of the stylus, which is a time-varying 2D position, or a function of type $\mathbb{R} \to \mathbb{R}^2$. The digitizer measures the position of the stylus at many points in time, resulting in a sequence of 2D coordinates, or a function of type $\mathbb{Z} \to \mathbb{R}^2$. A *motion capture* system does exactly the same thing for a special marker attached to an actor's body: it takes the 3D position of the marker over time ($\mathbb{R} \to \mathbb{R}^3$) and makes it into a series of instantaneous position measurements ($\mathbb{Z} \to \mathbb{R}^3$).

Going up in dimension, a medical CT scanner, used to non-invasively examine the interior of a person's body, measures density as a function of position inside the body. The output of the scanner is a 3D grid of density values: it converts the density of the body ($\mathbb{R}^3 \to \mathbb{R}$) to a 3D array of real numbers ($\mathbb{Z}^3 \to \mathbb{R}$).

These examples seem different, but in fact they can all be handled using exactly the same mathematics. In all cases a function is being sampled at the points of a *lattice* in one or more dimensions, and in all cases we need to be able to reconstruct that original continuous function from the array of samples.

From the example of a 2D image, it may seem that the pixels are enough, and we never need to think about continuous functions again once the camera has discretized the image. But what if we want to make the image larger or smaller on the screen, particularly by non-integer scale factors? It turns out that the simplest algorithms to do this perform badly, introducing obvious visual artifacts known as *aliasing*. Explaining why aliasing happens and understanding how to prevent it requires the mathematics of sampling theory. The resulting algorithms are rather simple, but the reasoning behind them, and the details of making them perform well, can be subtle.

Representing continuous functions in a computer is, of course, not unique to graphics; nor is the idea of sampling and reconstruction. Sampled representations are used in applications from digital audio to computational physics, and graphics is just one (and by no means the first) user of the related algorithms and mathematics. The fundamental facts about how to do sampling and reconstruction have been known in the field of communications since the 1920s and were stated in exactly the form we use them by the 1940s (Shannon & Weaver, 1964).

This chapter starts by summarizing sampling and reconstruction using the concrete one-dimensional example of digital audio. Then we go on to present the basic mathematics and algorithms that underlie sampling and reconstruction in one and two dimensions. Finally we go into the details of the frequency-domain viewpoint, which provides many insights into the behavior of these algorithms.

9.1   Digital Audio: Sampling in 1D

Although sampled representations had already been in use for years in telecommunications, the introduction of the compact disc in 1982, following the increased use of digital recording for audio in the previous decade, was the first highly visible consumer application of sampling.

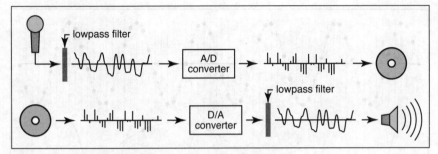

Figure 9.1. Sampling and reconstruction in digital audio.

In audio recording, a microphone converts sound, which exists as pressure waves in the air, into a time-varying voltage that amounts to a measurement of the changing air pressure at the point where the microphone is located. This electrical signal needs to be stored somehow so that it may be played back at a later time and sent to a loudspeaker that converts the voltage back into pressure waves by moving a diaphragm in synchronization with the voltage.

The digital approach to recording the audio signal (Figure 9.1) uses sampling: an *analog-to-digital converter* (*A/D converter*, or *ADC*) measures the voltage many thousand times per second, generating a stream of integers that can easily be stored on any number of media, say a disk on a computer in the recording studio, or transmitted to another location, say the memory in a portable audio player. At playback time, the data is read out at the appropriate rate and sent to a *digital-to-analog converter* (*D/A converter*, or *DAC*). The DAC produces a voltage according to the numbers it receives, and, provided we take enough samples to fairly represent the variation in voltage, the resulting electrical signal is, for all practical purposes, identical to the input.

It turns out that the number of samples per second required to end up with a good reproduction depends on how high-pitched the sounds are that we are trying to record. A sample rate that works fine for reproducing a string bass or a kick drum produces bizarre-sounding results if we try to record a piccolo or a cymbal; but those sounds are reproduced just fine with a higher sample rate. To avoid these *undersampling artifacts* the digital audio recorder *filters* the input to the ADC to remove high frequencies that cause problems.

Another kind of problem arises on the output side. The DAC produces a voltage that changes whenever a new sample comes in, but stays constant until the next sample, producing a stair-step shaped graph. These stair-steps act like noise, adding a high-frequency, signal-dependent buzzing sound. To remove this *reconstruction artifact*, the digital audio player filters the output from the DAC to smooth out the waveform.

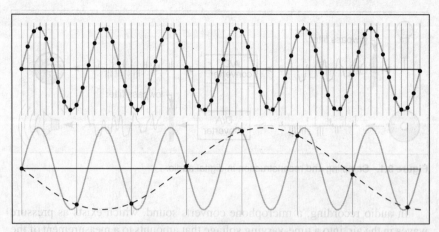

Figure 9.2. A sine wave (gray curve) sampled at two different rates. Top: at a high sample rate, the resulting samples (black dots) represent the signal well. Bottom: a lower sample rate produces an ambiguous result: the samples are exactly the same as would result from sampling a wave of much lower frequency (dashed curve).

9.1.1 Sampling Artifacts and Aliasing

The digital audio recording chain can serve as a concrete model for the sampling and reconstruction processes that happen in graphics. The same kind of under-sampling and reconstruction artifacts also happen with images or other sampled signals in graphics, and the solution is the same: filtering before sampling and filtering again during reconstruction.

A concrete example of the kind of artifacts that can arise from too-low sample frequencies is shown in Figure 9.2. Here we are sampling a simple sine wave using two different sample frequencies: 10.8 samples per cycle on the top and 1.2 samples per cycle on the bottom. The higher rate produces a set of samples that obviously capture the signal well, but the samples resulting from the lower sample rate are indistinguishable from samples of a low-frequency sine wave—in fact, faced with this set of samples the low-frequency sinusoid seems the more likely interpretation.

Once the sampling has been done, it is impossible to know which of the two signals—the fast or the slow sine wave—was the original, and therefore there is no single method that can properly reconstruct the signal in both cases. Because the high frequency signal is "pretending to be" a low-frequency signal, this phe-nomenon is known as *aliasing*.

Aliasing shows up whenever flaws in sampling and reconstruction lead to arti-facts at surprising frequencies. In audio, aliasing takes the form of odd-sounding extra tones—a bell ringing at 10KHz, after being sampled at 8KHz, turns into a

6KHz tone. In images, aliasing often takes the form of *moiré patterns* that result from the interaction of the sample grid with regular features in an image, for instance the window blinds in Figure 9.34.

Another example of aliasing in a synthetic image is the familiar stair-stepping on straight lines that are rendered with only black and white pixels (Figure 9.34). This is an example of small-scale features (the sharp edges of the lines) creating artifacts at a different scale (for shallow-slope lines the stair steps are very long).

The basic issues of sampling and reconstruction can be understood simply based on features being too small or too large, but some more quantitative questions are harder to answer:

- What sample rate is high enough to ensure good results?

- What kinds of filters are appropriate for sampling and reconstruction?

- What degree of smoothing is required to avoid aliasing?

Solid answers to these questions will have to wait until we have developed the theory fully in Section 9.5

9.2 Convolution

Before we discuss algorithms for sampling and reconstruction, we'll first examine the mathematical concept on which they are based—*convolution*. Convolution is a simple mathematical concept that underlies the algorithms that are used for sampling, filtering, and reconstruction. It also is the basis of how we will analyze these algorithms later in the chapter.

Convolution is an operation on functions: it takes two functions and combines them to produce a new function. In this book, the convolution operator is denoted by a star: the result of applying convolution to the functions f and g is $f \star g$. We say that f is convolved with g, and $f \star g$ is the convolution of f and g.

Convolution can be applied either to continuous functions (functions $f(x)$ that are defined for any real argument x) or to discrete sequences (functions $a[i]$ that are defined only for integer arguments i). It can also be applied to functions defined on one-dimensional, two-dimensional, or higher-dimensional domains (that is, functions of one, two, or more arguments). We will start with the discrete, one-dimensional case first, then continue to continuous functions and two- and three-dimensional functions.

For convenience in the definitions, we generally assume that the functions' domains go on forever, though of course in practice they will have to stop somewhere, and we have to handle the end points in a special way.

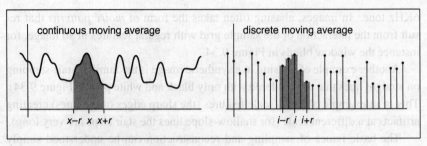

Figure 9.3. Smoothing using a moving average.

9.2.1 Moving Averages

To get a basic picture of convolution, consider the example of smoothing a 1D function using a moving average (Figure 9.3). To get a smoothed value at any point, we compute the average of the function over a range extending a distance r in each direction. The distance r, called the *radius* of the smoothing operation, is a parameter that controls how much smoothing happens.

We can state this idea mathematically for discrete or continuous functions. If we're smoothing a continuous function $g(x)$, averaging means integrating g over an interval and then dividing by the length of the interval:

$$h(x) = \frac{1}{2r} \int_{x-r}^{x+r} g(t)\, dt.$$

On the other hand, if we're smoothing a discrete function $b[i]$, averaging means summing b for a range of indices and dividing by the number of values:

$$c[i] = \frac{1}{2r+1} \sum_{j=i-r}^{i+r} b[j]. \tag{9.1}$$

In each case, the normalization constant is chosen so that if we smooth a constant function the result will be the same function.

This idea of a moving average is the essence of convolution; the only difference is that in convolution the moving average is a weighted average.

9.2.2 Discrete Convolution

We will start with the most concrete case of convolution: convolving a discrete sequence $a[i]$ with another discrete sequence $b[i]$. The result is a discrete sequence $(a \star b)[i]$. The process is just like smoothing b with a moving average, but this

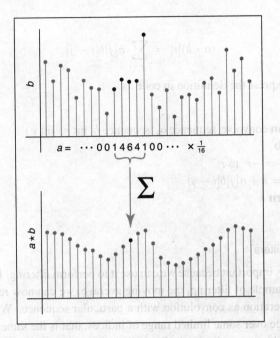

$$a = \cdots 0\,0\,1\,4\,6\,4\,1\,0\,0\,\cdots \times \tfrac{1}{16}$$

Figure 9.4. Computing one value in the discrete convolution of a sequence b with a filter a that has support five samples wide. Each sample in $a \star b$ is an average of nearby samples in b, weighted by the values of a.

time instead of equally weighting all samples within a distance r, we use a second sequence a to give a weight to each sample (Figure 9.4). The value $a[j]$ gives the weight for a sample that is a distance j from the index i where we are evaluating the convolution. Here is the definition of $(a \star b)$, expressed as a formula:

$$(a \star b)[i] = \sum_j a[j]b[i-j]. \tag{9.2}$$

By omitting bounds on j, we indicate that this sum runs over all integers (that is, from $-\infty$ to $+\infty$). Figure 9.4 illustrates how one output sample is computed, using the example of $a = \tfrac{1}{16}[\ldots, 0, 1, 4, 6, 4, 1, 0, \ldots]$—that is, $a[0] = \tfrac{6}{16}$, $a[\pm 1] = \tfrac{4}{16}$, etc.

In graphics, one of the two functions will usually have *finite support* (as does the example in Figure 9.4), which means that it is non-zero only over a finite interval of argument values. If we assume that a has finite support, there is some *radius* r such that $a[j] = 0$ whenever $|j| > r$. In that case, we can write the sum above as

$$(a \star b)[i] = \sum_{j=-r}^{r} a[j]b[i-j],$$

and we can express the definition in code as

```
function convolve(sequence a, sequence b, int r, int i)
    s = 0
    for j = −r to r
        s = s + a[j]b[i − j]
    return s
```

Convolution Filters

Convolution is important because we can use it to perform filtering. Looking back at our first example of filtering, the moving average, we can now reinterpret that smoothing operation as convolution with a particular sequence. When we compute an average over some limited range of indices, that is the same as weighting the points in the range all identically and weighting the rest of the points with zeros. This kind of filter, which has a constant value over the interval where it is non-zero, is known as a *box filter* (because it looks like a rectangle if you draw its graph—see Figure 9.5). For a box filter of radius r the weight is $1/(2r+1)$:

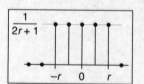

Figure 9.5. A discrete box filter.

$$a[j] = \begin{cases} \frac{1}{2r+1} & -r \le j \le r, \\ 0 & \text{otherwise.} \end{cases}$$

If you substitute this filter into Equation (9.2), you will find that it reduces to the moving average in Equation (9.1).

As in this example, convolution filters are usually designed so that they sum to 1. That way, they don't affect the overall level of the signal.

Example (Convolution of a box and a step). For a simple example of filtering, let the signal be the *step function*

$$b[i] = \begin{cases} 1 & i \ge 0, \\ 0 & i < 0, \end{cases}$$

and the filter be the five-point box filter centered at zero,

$$a[j] = \frac{1}{5} \begin{cases} 1 & -2 \le j \le 2, \\ 0 & \text{otherwise.} \end{cases}$$

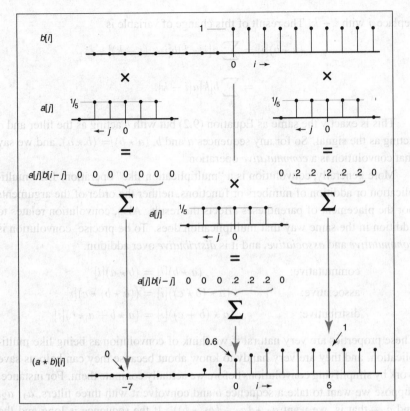

Figure 9.6. Discrete convolution of a box function with a step function.

What is the result of convolving a and b? At a particular index i, as shown in Figure 9.6, the result is the average of the step function over the range from $i - 2$ to $i + 2$. If $i < -2$, we are averaging all zeros and the result is zero. If $i \geq 2$, we are averaging all ones and the result is one. In between there are $i + 3$ ones, resulting in the value $\frac{i+3}{5}$. The output is a linear ramp that goes from 0 to 1 over five samples: $\frac{1}{5}[\ldots, 0, 0, 1, 2, 3, 4, 5, 5, \ldots]$.

Properties of Convolution

The way we've written it so far, convolution seems like an asymmetric operation: b is the sequence we're smoothing, and a provides the weights. But one of the nice properties of convolution is that it actually doesn't make any difference which is which: the filter and the signal are interchangeable. To see this, just rethink the sum in Equation (9.2) with the indices counting from the origin of the sequence b, rather than from the origin of a where we are computing the value. That is, we replace j with $i - k$. The result of this change of variable is

$$(a \star b)[i] = \sum_k a[i - k]b[i - (i - k)]$$

$$= \sum_k b[k]a[i - k].$$

This is exactly the same as Equation (9.2) but with b acting as the filter and a acting as the signal. So for any sequences a and b, $(a \star b) = (b \star a)$, and we say that convolution is a *commutative* operation.[1]

More generally, convolution is a "multiplication-like" operation. Like multiplication or addition of numbers or functions, neither the order of the arguments nor the placement of parentheses affects the result. Also, convolution relates to addition in the same way that multiplication does. To be precise, convolution is *commutative* and *associative*, and it is *distributive* over addition.

commutative: $(a \star b)[i] = (b \star a)[i]$

associative: $(a \star (b \star c))[i] = ((a \star b) \star c)[i]$

distributive: $(a \star (b + c))[i] = (a \star b + a \star c)[i]$

These properties are very natural if we think of convolution as being like multiplication, and they are very handy to know about because they can help us save work by simplifying convolutions before we actually compute them. For instance, suppose we want to take a sequence b and convolve it with three filters, a_1, a_2, and a_3—that is, we want $a_3 \star (a_2 \star (a_1 \star b))$. If the sequence is long and the filters are short (that is, they have small radii), it is much faster to first convolve the three filters together (computing $a_1 \star a_2 \star a_3$) and finally to convolve the result with the signal, computing $(a_1 \star a_2 \star a_3) \star b$, which we know from commutativity and associativity gives the same result.

A very simple filter serves as an *identity* for discrete convolution: it is the discrete filter of radius zero, or the sequence $d[i] = \ldots, 0, 0, 1, 0, 0, \ldots$ (Figure 9.7). If we convolve d with a signal b, there will be only one non-zero term in the sum:

$$(d \star b)[i] = \sum_{j=0}^{j=0} d[j]b[i - j]$$

$$= b[i].$$

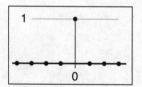

Figure 9.7. The discrete identity filter.

---

[1] You may have noticed that one of the functions in the convolution sum seems to be flipped over—that is, $a[j]$ gives the weight for the sample j units *earlier* in the sequence, while $a[-j]$ gives the weight for the sample j units *later* in the sequence. The reason for this has to do with ensuring associativity; see Exercise 4. Most of the filters we use are symmetric, so you hardly ever need to worry about this.

So clearly, convolving b with d just gives back b again. The sequence d is known as the *discrete impluse*. It is occasionally useful in expressing a filter: for instance, the process of smoothing a signal b with a filter a and then subtracting that from the original could be expressed as a single convolution with the filter $d - a$:

$$c = b - a \star b = d \star b - a \star b = (d - a) \star b.$$

9.2.3 Convolution as a Sum of Shifted Filters

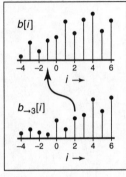

There is a second, entirely equivalent, way of interpreting Equation (9.2). Looking at the samples of $a \star b$ one at a time leads to the weighted-average interpretation that we have already seen. But if we omit the $[i]$, we can instead think of the sum as adding together entire sequences. One piece of notation is required to make this work: if b is a sequence, then the same sequence shifted to the right by j places is called $b_{\rightarrow j}$ (Figure 9.8):

$$b_{\rightarrow j}[i] = b[i - j].$$

Then, we can write Equation (9.2) as a statement about the whole sequence $(a \star b)$ rather than element-by-element:

$$(a \star b) = \sum_j a[j] b_{\rightarrow j}.$$

Figure 9.8. Shifting a sequence b to get $b_{\rightarrow j}$.

Looking at it this way, the convolution is a sum of shifted copies of b, weighted by the entries of a (Figure 9.9). Because of commutativity, we can pick either a

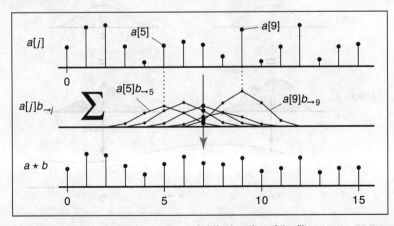

Figure 9.9. Discrete convolution as a sum of shifted copies of the filter.

or b as the filter; if we choose b, then we are adding up one copy of the filter for every sample in the input.

9.2.4 Convolution with Continuous Functions

While it is true that discrete sequences are what we actually work with in a computer program, these sampled sequences are supposed to represent continuous functions, and often we need to reason mathematically about the continuous functions in order to figure out what to do. For this reason it is useful to define convolution between continuous functions and also between continuous and discrete functions.

The convolution of two continuous functions is the obvious generalization of Equation (9.2), with an integral replacing the sum:

$$(f \star g)(x) = \int_{-\infty}^{+\infty} f(t)g(x-t)\,dt. \tag{9.3}$$

One way of interpreting this definition is that the convolution of f and g, evaluated at the argument x, is the area under the curve of the product of the two functions

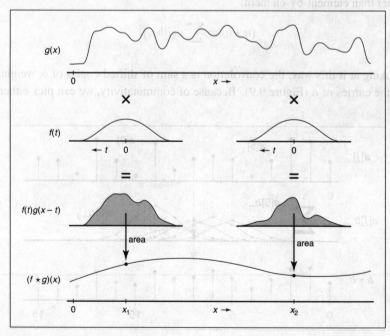

Figure 9.10. Continuous convolution.

after we shift f so that $f(0)$ lines up with $g(x)$. Just like in the discrete case, the convolution is a moving average, with the filter providing the weights for the average (See Figure 9.10).

Like discrete convolution, convolution of continuous functions is commutative and associative, and it is distributive over addition. Also as with the discrete case, the continuous convolution can be seen as a sum of copies of the filter rather than the computation of weighted averages. Except, in this case, there are infinitely many copies of the filter:

$$(f \star g) = \int_{-\infty}^{+\infty} f(t)g_{\to t}\, dt.$$

Example (Convolution of two box functions). Let f be a box function:

$$f(x) = \begin{cases} 1 & -\frac{1}{2} \le x < \frac{1}{2}, \\ 0 & \text{otherwise.} \end{cases}$$

Then what is $f \star f$? The definition (Equation (9.3)) gives

$$(f \star f)(x) = \int_{-\infty}^{\infty} f(t)f(x - t)\, dt.$$

Figure 9.11 shows the two cases of this integral. The two boxes might have zero overlap, which happens when $x \le -1$ or $x \ge 1$; in this case the result is zero. When $-1 < x < 1$, the overlap depends on the separation between the two boxes,

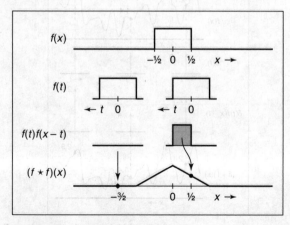

Figure 9.11. Convolving two boxes yields a tent function.

which is $|x|$; the result is $1 - |x|$. So

$$(f \star f)(x) = \begin{cases} 1 - |x| & -1 < x < 1, \\ 0 & \text{otherwise.} \end{cases}$$

This function, known as the *tent function*, is another common filter (see Section 9.3.1).

The Dirac Delta Function

In discrete convolution, we saw that the discrete impulse d acted as an identity: $d \star a = a$. In the continuous case, there is also an identity function, called the *Dirac impulse* or *Dirac delta* function, denoted $\delta(x)$.

Intuitively, the delta function is a very narrow, very tall spike that has infinitesimal width but still has area equal to 1 (Figure 9.12). The key defining property of the delta function is that multiplying it by a function selects out the value exactly at zero:

$$\int_{-\infty}^{\infty} \delta(x)f(x)dx = f(0).$$

The delta function does not have a well-defined value at 0 (you can think of its value loosely as $+\infty$), but it does have the value $\delta(x) = 0$ for all $x \neq 0$.

From this property of selecting out single values, it follows that the delta function is the identity for continuous convolution (Figure 9.13). The convolution of

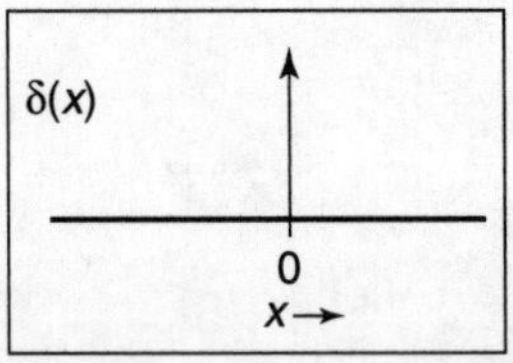

Figure 9.12. The Dirac delta function $\delta(x)$.

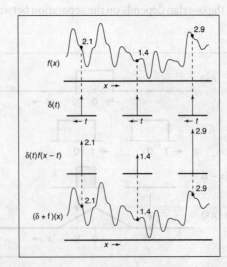

Figure 9.13. Convolving a function with $\delta(x)$ returns a copy of the same function.

δ with a function f is

$$(\delta \star f)(x) = \int_{-\infty}^{\infty} \delta(t)f(x - t)dt = f(x).$$

So $\delta \star f = f$.

9.2.5 Discrete-Continuous Convolution

There are two ways to connect the discrete and continuous worlds. One is sampling: we convert a continuous function into a discrete one by writing down the function's value at all integer arguments and forgetting about the rest. Given a continuous function $f(x)$, we can sample it to convert to a discrete sequence $a[i]$:

$$a[i] = f(i).$$

Going the other way, from a discrete function, or sequence, to a continuous function, is called *reconstruction*. This is accomplished using yet another form of convolution, the discrete-continuous form. In this case, we are filtering a discrete sequence $a[i]$ with a continuous filter $f(x)$:

$$(a \star f)(x) = \sum_i a[i]f(x - i).$$

The value of the reconstructed function $a \star f$ at x is a weighted sum of the samples $a[i]$ for values of i near x (Figure 9.14). The weights come from the filter f, which is evaluated at a set of points spaced one unit apart. For example, if $x = 5.3$ and

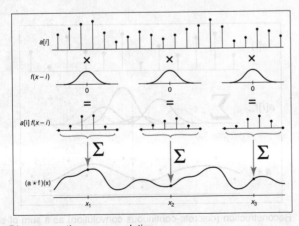

Figure 9.14. Discrete-continuous convolution.

f has radius 2, f is evaluated at $1.3, 0.3, -0.7,$ and -1.7. Note that for discrete-continuous convolution we generally write the sequence first and the filter second, so that the sum is over integers.

As with discrete convolution, we can put bounds on the sum if we know the filter's radius, r, eliminating all points where the difference between x and i is at least r:

$$(a \star f)(x) = \sum_{i=\lceil x-r \rceil}^{\lfloor x+r \rfloor} a[i]f(x-i).$$

Note, that if a point falls exactly at distance r from x (i.e., if $x - r$ turns out to be an integer), it will be left out of the sum. This is in contrast to the discrete case, where we included the point at $i - r$.

Expressed in code, this is:

function reconstruct(sequence a, filter f, real x)
$s = 0$
$r = f$.radius
for $i = \lceil x - r \rceil$ to $\lfloor x + r \rfloor$ **do**
$\quad s = s + a[i]f(x - i)$
return s

As with the other forms of convolution, discrete-continuous convolution may be seen as summing shifted copies of the filter (Figure 9.15):

$$(a \star f) = \sum_i a[i]f_{\to i}.$$

Discrete-continuous convolution is closely related to splines. For uniform splines (a uniform B-spline, for instance), the parameterized curve for the spline

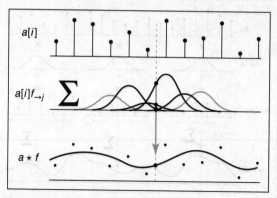

Figure 9.15. Reconstruction (discrete-continuous convolution) as a sum of shifted copies of the filter.

is exactly the convolution of the spline's basis function with the control point sequence (see Section 15.6.2).

9.2.6 Convolution in More Than One Dimension

So far, everything we have said about sampling and reconstruction has been one-dimensional: there has been a single variable x or a single sequence index i. Many of the important applications of sampling and reconstruction in graphics, though, are applied to two-dimensional functions—in particular, to 2D images. Fortunately, the generalization of sampling algorithms and theory from 1D to 2D, 3D, and beyond is conceptually very simple.

Beginning with the definition of discrete convolution, we can generalize it to two dimensions by making the sum into a double sum:

$$(a \star b)[i,j] = \sum_{i'} \sum_{j'} a[i',j']b[i-i',j-j'].$$

If a is a finitely supported filter of radius r (that is, it has $(2r+1)^2$ values), then we can write this sum with bounds (Figure 9.16):

$$(a \star b)[i,j] = \sum_{i'=-r}^{i'=r} \sum_{j'=-r}^{j'=r} a[i',j']b[i-i',j-j']$$

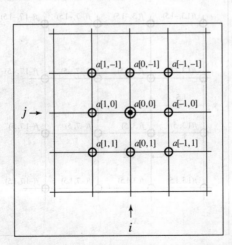

Figure 9.16. The weights for the nine input samples that contribute to the discrete convolution at point (i, j) with a filter a of radius 1.

and express it in code:

```
function convolve2d(sequence2d a, sequence2d b, int i, int j)
    s = 0
    r = a.radius
    for i' = -r to r do
        for j' = -r to r do
            s = s + a[i'][j']b[i - i'][j - j']
    return s
```

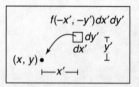

Figure 9.17. The weight for an infinitesimal area in the input signal resulting from continuous convolution at (x, y).

This definition can be interpreted in the same way as in the 1D case: each output sample is a weighted average of an area in the input, using the 2D filter as a "mask" to determine the weight of each sample in the average.

Continuing the generalization, we can write continuous-continuous (Figure 9.17) and discrete-continuous (Figure 9.18) convolutions in 2D as well:

$$(f \star g)(x, y) = \int \int f(x', y')g(x - x', y - y') \, dx' \, dy';$$
$$(a \star f)(x, y) = \sum_i \sum_j a[i, j]f(x - i, y - j).$$

In each case, the result at a particular point is a weighted average of the input near that point. For the continuous-continuous case, it is a weighted integral over a region centered at that point, and in the discrete-continuous case it is a weighted average of all the samples that fall near the point.

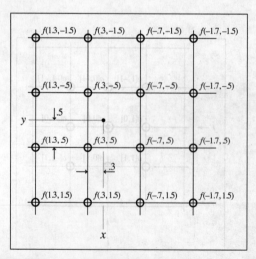

Figure 9.18. The weights for the 16 input samples that contribute to the discrete-continuous convolution at point (x, y) for a reconstruction filter of radius 2.

Once we have gone from 1D to 2D, it should be fairly clear how to generalize further to 3D or even to higher dimensions.

9.3   Convolution Filters

Now that we have the machinery of convolution, let's examine some of the particular filters commonly used in graphics.

9.3.1   A Gallery of Convolution Filters

The Box Filter

The box filter (Figure 9.19) is a piecewise constant function whose integral is equal to one. As a discrete filter, it can be written as

$$a_{\text{box},r}[i] = \begin{cases} 1/(2r+1) & |i| \leq r, \\ 0 & \text{otherwise.} \end{cases}$$

Note that for symmetry we include both endpoints.

As a continuous filter, we write

$$f_{\text{box},r}(x) = \begin{cases} 1/(2r) & -r \leq x < r, \\ 0 & \text{otherwise.} \end{cases}$$

In this case, we exclude one endpoint which makes the box of radius 0.5 usable as a reconstruction filter. It is because the box filter is discontinuous that these boundary cases are important, and so for this particular filter, we need to pay attention to them. We write just f_{box} for the common case of $r = \frac{1}{2}$.

The Tent Filter

The tent, or linear filter (Figure 9.20) is a continuous, piecewise linear function:

$$f_{\text{tent}}(x) = \begin{cases} 1 - |x| & |x| < 1, \\ 0 & \text{otherwise}; \end{cases}$$

$$f_{\text{tent},r}(x) = \frac{f_{\text{tent}}(x/r)}{r}.$$

For filters that are at least C^0 (that is, there are no sudden jumps in the value, as there are with the box), we no longer need to separate the definitions of the

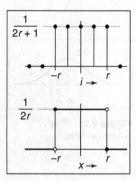

Figure 9.19. The discrete and continuous box filters.

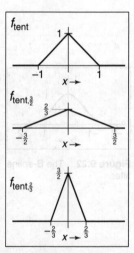

Figure 9.20. The tent filter and two scaled versions.

discrete and continuous filters: the discrete filter is just the continuous filter sampled at the integers. Also note that for simplicity we define $f_{\text{tent},r}$ by scaling the "standard size" tent filter f_{tent}. From now on, we'll take this scaling for granted: once we define a filter f, then we can use f_r to mean "the filter f stretched out by r and also scaled down by r." Note that f_r has the same integral as f, and we will always make sure that the value of the integral is equal to 1.0.

The Gaussian Filter

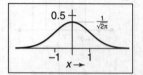

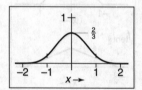

Figure 9.21. The Gaussian filter.

The Gaussian function (Figure 9.21), also known as the normal distribution, is an important filter theoretically and practically. We'll see more of its special properties as the chapter goes on:

$$f_g(x) = \frac{1}{\sqrt{2\pi}} e^{-x^2/2}.$$

The Gaussian does not have finite support, although because of the exponential decay, its values rapidly become small enough to ignore. When necessary, then, we can trim the tails from the function by setting it to zero outside some radius. The Gaussian makes a good sampling filter because it is very smooth; we'll make this statement more precise later in the chapter.

The B-spline Cubic Filter

Figure 9.22. The B-spline filter.

Many filters are defined as piecewise polynomials, and cubic filters with four pieces are often used as reconstruction filters. One such filter is known as the B-spline filter (Figure 9.22) because of its origins as a blending function for spline curves (see Chapter 15):

$$f_B(x) = \frac{1}{6} \begin{cases} -3(1-|x|)^3 + 3(1-|x|)^2 + 3(1-|x|) + 1 & -1 \le x \le 1, \\ (2-|x|)^3 & 1 \le |x| \le 2, \\ 0 & \text{otherwise.} \end{cases}$$

Among piecewise cubics, the B-spline is special because it has continuous first and second derivatives—that is, it is C^2. A more concise way of defining this filter is $F_B = f_{\text{box}} \star f_{\text{box}} \star f_{\text{box}} \star f_{\text{box}}$; proving that the longer form above is equivalent is a nice exercise in convolution (see Exercise 3).

The Catmull-Rom Cubic Filter

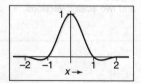

Figure 9.23. The Catmull-Rom filter.

Another piecewise cubic filter named for a spline, the Catmull-Rom filter (Figure 9.23), has the value zero at $x = -2, -1, 1$, and 2, which means it will *interpolate* the samples when used as a reconstruction filter (Section 9.3.2):

$$f_C(x) = \frac{1}{2} \begin{cases} -3(1 - |x|)^3 + 4(1 - |x|)^2 + (1 - |x|) & -1 \leq x \leq 1, \\ (2 - |x|)^3 - (2 - |x|)^2 & 1 \leq |x| \leq 2, \\ 0 & \text{otherwise.} \end{cases}$$

The Mitchell-Netravali Cubic Filter

For the all-important application of resampling images, Mitchell and Netravali (Mitchell & Netravali, 1988) made a study of cubic filters and recommended one part way between the previous two filters as the best all-around choice (Figure 9.24). It is simply a weighted combination of the previous two filters:

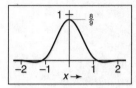

Figure 9.24. The Mitchell-Netravali filter.

$$f_M(x) = \frac{1}{3} f_B(x) + \frac{2}{3} f_C(x)$$

$$= \frac{1}{18} \begin{cases} -21(1 - |x|)^3 + 27(1 - |x|)^2 + 9(1 - |x|) + 1 & -1 \leq x \leq 1, \\ 7(2 - |x|)^3 - 6(2 - |x|)^2 & 1 \leq |x| \leq 2, \\ 0 & \text{otherwise.} \end{cases}$$

9.3.2 Properties of Filters

Filters have some traditional terminology that goes with them, which we use to describe the filters and compare them to one another.

The *impulse response* of a filter is just another name for the function: it is the response of the filter to a signal that just contains an impulse (and recall that convolving with an impulse just gives back the filter).

A continuous filter is *interpolating* if, when it is used to reconstruct a continuous function from a discrete sequence, the resulting function takes on exactly the values of the samples at the sample points— that is, it "connects the dots" rather than producing a function that only goes near the dots. Interpolating filters are exactly those filters f for which $f(0) = 1$ and $f(i) = 0$ for all non-zero integers i (Figure 9.25).

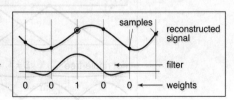

Figure 9.25. An interpolating filter reconstructs the sample points exactly because it has the value zero at all non-zero integer offsets from the center.

A filter that takes on negative values has *ringing* or *overshoot*: it will produce extra oscillations in the value around sharp changes in the value of the function being filtered.

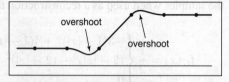

Figure 9.26.   A filter with negative lobes will always produce some overshoot when filtering or reconstructing a sharp discontinuity.

For instance, the Catmull-Rom filter has negative lobes on either side, and if you filter a step function with it, it will exaggerate the step a bit, resulting in function values that under-shoot 0 and overshoot 1 (Figure 9.26).

A continuous filter is *ripple free* if, when used as a reconstruction filter, it will reconstruct a constant sequence as a constant function (Figure 9.27). This is equivalent to the requirement that the filter sum to one on any integer-spaced grid:

$$\sum_i f(x + i) = 1 \quad \text{for all } x.$$

A continuous filter has a *degree of continuity*, which is the highest-order derivative that is defined everywhere. A filter, like the box filter, that has sudden jumps in its value is not continuous at all. A filter that is continuous but has sharp corners (discontinuities in the first derivative), such as the tent filter, has order of continuity zero, and we say it is C^0. A filter that has a continuous derivative (no sharp corners), such as the piecewise cubic filters in the previous section, is C^1; if its second derivative is also continuous, as is true of the B-spline filter, it is C^2. The order of continuity of a filter is particularly important for a reconstruction filter because the reconstructed function inherits the continuity of the filter.

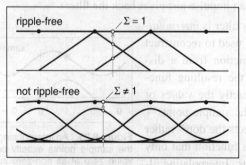

Figure 9.27.   The tent filter of radius 1 is a ripple-free reconstruction filter; the Gaussian filter with standard deviation 1/2 is not.

Separable Filters

So far we have only discussed filters for 1D convolution, but for images and other multidimensional signals we need filters too. In general, any 2D function could be a 2D filter, and occasionally it is useful to define them this way. But, in most cases, we can build suitable 2D (or higher-dimensional) filters from the 1D filters we have already seen.

The most useful way of doing this is by using a *separable* filter. The value of a separable filter $f_2(x, y)$ at a particular x and y is simply the product of f_1 (the 1D filter) evaluated at x and at y:

$$f_2(x, y) = f_1(x)f_1(y).$$

Similarly, for discrete filters,

$$a_2[i, j] = a_1[i]a_1[j].$$

Any horizontal or vertical slice through f_2 is a scaled copy of f_1. The integral of f_2 is the square of the integral of f_1, so in particular if f_1 is normalized, then so is f_2.

Example (The separable tent filter). If we choose the tent function for f_1, the resulting piecewise bilinear function (Figure 9.28) is

$$f_{2,\text{tent}}(x, y) = \begin{cases} (1 - |x|)(1 - |y|) & |x| < 1 \quad \text{and} \quad |y| < 1, \\ 0 & \text{otherwise.} \end{cases}$$

The profiles along the coordinate axes are tent functions, but the profiles along the diagonals are quadratics (for instance, along the line $x = y$ in the positive quadrant, we see the quadratic function $(1 - x)^2$).

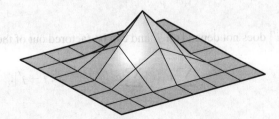

Figure 9.28. The separable 2D tent filter.

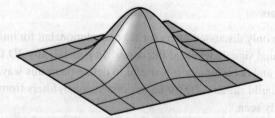

Figure 9.29. The 2D Gaussian filter, which is both separable and radially symmetric.

Example (The 2D Gaussian filter). If we choose the Gaussian function for f_1, the resulting 2D function (Figure 9.29) is

$$f_{2,g}(x, y) = \frac{1}{2\pi} \left(e^{-x^2/2} e^{-y^2/2} \right),$$

$$= \frac{1}{2\pi} \left(e^{-(x^2+y^2)/2} \right),$$

$$= \frac{1}{2\pi} e^{-r^2/2}.$$

Notice that this is (up to a scale factor) the same function we would get if we revolved the 1D Gaussian around the origin to produce a circularly symmetric function. The property of being both circularly symmetric and separable at the same time is unique to the Gaussian function. The profiles along the coordinate axes are Gaussians, but so are the profiles along any direction at any offset from the center.

The key advantage of separable filters over other 2D filters has to do with efficiency in implementation. Let's substitute the definition of a_2 into the definition of discrete convolution:

$$(a_2 \star b)[i, j] = \sum_{i'} \sum_{j'} a_1[i'] a_1[j'] b[i - i', j - j'].$$

Note that $a_1[i']$ does not depend on j' and can be factored out of the inner sum:

$$= \sum_{i'} a_1[i'] \sum_{j'} a_1[j'] b[i - i', j - j'].$$

Let's abbreviate the inner sum as $S[k]$:

$$S[k] = \sum_{j'} a_1[j']b[k, j - j'];$$

$$(a_2 \star b)[i, j] = \sum_{i'} a_1[i']S[i - i']. \qquad (9.4)$$

With the equation in this form, we can first compute and store $S[i - i']$ for each value of i', and then compute the outer sum using these stored values. At first glance this does not seem remarkable, since we still had to do work proportional to $(2r + 1)^2$ to compute all the inner sums. However, it's quite different if we want to compute the value at many points $[i, j]$.

Suppose we need to compute $a_2 \star b$ at $[2, 2]$ and $[3, 2]$, and a_1 has a radius of 2. Examining Equation (9.4), we can see that we will need $S[0], \ldots, S[4]$ to compute the result at $[2, 2]$, and we will need $S[1], \ldots, S[5]$ to compute the result at $[3, 2]$. So, in the separable formulation, we can just compute all six values of S and share $S[1], \ldots, S[4]$ (Figure 9.30).

This savings has great significance for large filters. Filtering an m by n 2D image with a filter of radius r in the general case requires computation of $(2r+1)^2$ products per pixel, while filtering the image with a separable filter of the same size requires $2(2r + 1)$ products (at the expense of some intermediate storage). This change in asymptotic complexity from $O(r^2)$ to $O(r)$ enables the use of much larger filters.

The algorithm is:

function filterImage(image I, filter f)
$r = f.\text{radius}$
$n_x = I.\text{width}$
$n_y = I.\text{height}$
allocate storage array $S[0, \ldots, n_x - 1]$
allocate image $I_{\text{out}}[r, \ldots, n_x - r - 1][r, \ldots, n_y - r - 1]$
initialize S and I_{out} to all zero
for $y = r$ to $n_y - r - 1$ **do**
  for $x = 0$ to $n_x - 1$ **do**
    $S[x] = 0$
    for $i = -r$ to r **do**
      $S[x] = S[x] + f[i]I[x][y - i]$
  for $x = r$ to $n_x - r - 1$ **do**
    for $i = -r$ to r **do**
      $I_{\text{out}}[x][y] = I_{\text{out}}[x][y] + f[i]S[x - i]$
return I_{out}

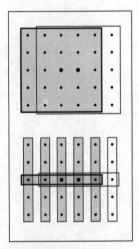

Figure 9.30. Computing two output points using separate 2D arrays of 25 samples (above) vs. filtering once along the columns, then using separate 1D arrays of five samples (below).

For simplicity, this function avoids all questions of boundaries by trimming r pixels off all four sides of the output image. In practice there are various ways to handle the boundaries; see Section 9.4.3.

9.4   Signal Processing for Images

We have discussed sampling, filtering, and reconstruction in the abstract so far, using mostly 1D signals for examples. But as we observed at the beginning of the chapter, the most important and most common application of signal processing in graphics is for sampled images. Let us look carefully at how all this applies to images.

9.4.1   Image Filtering Using Discrete Filters

Perhaps the simplest application of convolution is processing images using discrete convolution. Some of the most widely used features of image manipulation programs are simple convolution filters. Blurring of images can be achieved by convolving with many common lowpass filters, ranging from the box to the Gaus-

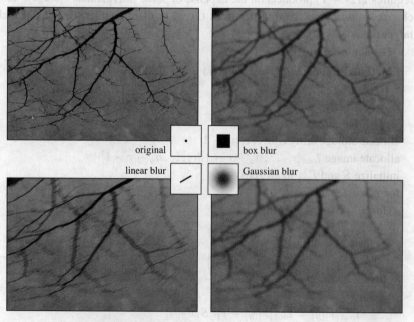

Figure 9.31. Blurring an image by convolution with each of three different filters.

Figure 9.32. Sharpening an image using a convolution filter.

sian (Figure 9.31). A Gaussian filter creates a very smooth-looking blur and is commonly used for this purpose.

The opposite of blurring is sharpening, and one way to do this is by using the "unsharp mask" procedure: subtract a fraction α of a blurred image from the original. With a rescaling to avoid changing the overall brightness, we have

$$
\begin{aligned}
I_{\text{sharp}} &= (1+\alpha)I - \alpha(f_{g,\sigma} \star I) \\
&= \big((1+\alpha)d - \alpha f_{g,\sigma}\big) \star I \\
&= f_{\text{sharp}}(\sigma, \alpha) \star I,
\end{aligned}
$$

where $f_{g,\sigma}$ is the Gaussian filter of width σ. Using the discrete impulse d and the distributive property of convolution, we were able to write this whole process as a single filter that depends on both the width of the blur and the degree of sharpening (Figure 9.32).

Another example of combining two discrete filters is a drop shadow. It's common to take a blurred, shifted copy of an object's outline to create a soft drop shadow (Figure 9.33). We can express the shifting operation as convolution with an off-center impulse:

Figure 9.33. A soft drop shadow.

$$
d_{m,n}(i,j) = \begin{cases} 1 & i=m \text{ and } j=n, \\ 0 & \text{otherwise.} \end{cases}
$$

Shifting, then blurring, is achieved by convolving with both filters:

$$
\begin{aligned}
I_{\text{shadow}} &= f_{g,\sigma} \star (d_{m,n} \star I) \\
&= (f_{g,\sigma} \star d_{m,n}) \star I \\
&= f_{\text{shadow}}(m,n,\sigma) \star I.
\end{aligned}
$$

Here we have used associativity to group the two operations into a single filter with three parameters.

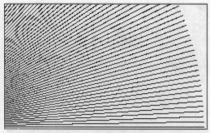

Figure 9.34. Two artifacts of aliasing in images: moiré patterns in periodic textures (left), and "jaggies" on straight lines (right).

9.4.2 Antialiasing in Image Sampling

In image synthesis, we often have the task of producing a sampled representation of an image for which we have a continuous mathematical formula (or at least a procedure we can use to compute the color at any point, not just at integer pixel positions). Ray tracing is a common example (see Chapter 4). In the language of signal processing, we have a continuous 2D signal (the image) that we need to sample on a regular 2D lattice. If we go ahead and sample the image without any special measures, the result will exhibit various aliasing artifacts (Figure 9.34). At sharp edges in the image, we see stair-step artifacts known as "jaggies." In areas where there are repeating patterns, we see wide bands known as *moiré patterns*.

The problem here is that the image contains too many small-scale features; we need to smooth it out by filtering it before sampling. Looking back at the definition of continuous convolution in Equation (9.3), we need to average the image over an area around the pixel location, rather than just taking the value at a single

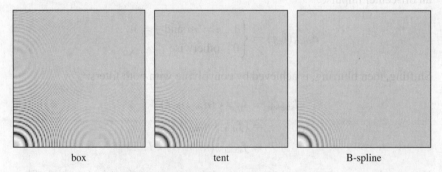

box   tent   B-spline

Figure 9.35. A comparison of three different sampling filters being used to antialias a difficult test image that contains circles that are spaced closer and closer as they get larger.

point. The specific methods for doing this are discussed in Chapter 4. A simple filter like a box will improve the appearance of sharp edges, but it still produces some moiré patterns (Figure 9.35). The Gaussian filter, which is very smooth, is much more effective against the moiré patterns, at the expense of overall somewhat more blurring. These two examples illustrate the tradeoff between sharpness and aliasing that is fundamental to choosing antialiasing filters.

9.4.3 Reconstruction and Resampling

One of the most common image operations where careful filtering is crucial is *resampling*—changing the sample rate, or changing the image size.

Suppose we have taken an image with a digital camera that is 3000 by 2000 pixels in size, and we want to display it on a monitor that has only 1280 by 1024 pixels. In order to make it fit, while maintaining the 3:2 aspect ratio, we need to resample it to 1278 by 852 pixels. How should we go about this?

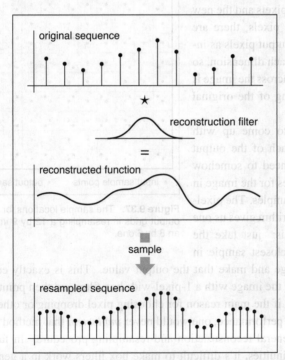

Figure 9.36. Resampling an image consists of two logical steps that are combined into a single operation in code. First, we use a reconstruction filter to define a smooth, continuous function from the input samples. Then, we sample that function on a new grid to get the output samples.

One way to approach this problem is to think of the process as dropping pixels: the size ratio is between 2 and 3, so we'll have to drop out one or two pixels between pixels that we keep. It's possible to shrink an image in this way, but the quality of the result is low—the images in Figure 9.34 were made using pixel dropping. Pixel dropping is very fast, however, and it is a reasonable choice to make a preview of the resized image during an interactive manipulation.

The way to think about resizing images is as a *resampling* operation: we want a set of samples of the image on a particular grid that is defined by the new image dimensions, and we get them by sampling a continuous function that is reconstructed from the input samples (Figure 9.36). Looking at it this way, it's just a sequence of standard image processing operations: first we reconstruct a continuous function from the input samples, and then we sample that function just as we would sample any other continuous image. To avoid aliasing artifacts, appropriate filters need to be used at each stage.

A small example is shown in Figure 9.37: if the original image is 12 × 9 pixels and the new one is 8 × 6 pixels, there are 2/3 as many output pixels as input pixels in each dimension, so their spacing across the image is 3/2 the spacing of the original samples.

In order to come up with a value for each of the output samples, we need to somehow compute values for the image in between the samples. The pixel-dropping algorithm gives us one way to do this: just take the value of the closest sample in

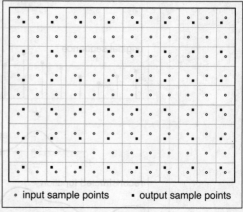

∘ input sample points   ▪ output sample points

Figure 9.37. The sample locations for the input and output grids in resampling a 12 by 9 image to make an 8 by 6 one.

the input image and make that the output value. This is exactly equivalent to reconstructing the image with a 1-pixel-wide box filter and then point sampling.

Of course, if the main reason for choosing pixel dropping or other very simple filtering is performance, one would never *implement* that method as a special case of the general reconstruction-and-resampling procedure. In fact, because of the discontinuities, it's difficult to make box filters work in a general framework. But, for high-quality resampling, the reconstruction/sampling framework provides valuable flexibility.

To work out the algorithmic details it's simplest to drop down to 1D and discuss resampling a sequence. The simplest way to write an implementation is in terms of the *reconstruct* function we defined in Section 9.2.5.

> **function** resample(sequence a, float x_0, float Δx, int n, filter f)
> create sequence b of length n
> **for** $i = 0$ to $n - 1$ **do**
> $\quad b[i] = \text{reconstruct}(a, f, x_0 + i\Delta x)$
> **return** b

The parameter x_0 gives the position of the first sample of the new sequence in terms of the samples of the old sequence. That is, if the first output sample falls midway between samples 3 and 4 in the input sequence, x_0 is 3.5.

This procedure reconstructs a continuous image by convolving the input sequence with a continuous filter and then point samples it. That's not to say that these two operations happen sequentially—the continuous function exists only in principle and its values are computed only at the sample points. But mathematically, this function computes a set of point samples of the function $a \star f$.

This point sampling seems wrong, though, because we just finished saying that a signal should be sampled with an appropriate smoothing filter to avoid aliasing. We should be convolving the reconstructed function with a sampling filter g and point sampling $g \star (f \star a)$. But since this is the same as $(g \star f) \star a$, we can roll the sampling filter together with the reconstruction filter; one convolution operation is all we need (Figure 9.38). This combined reconstruction and sampling filter is known as a *resampling filter*.

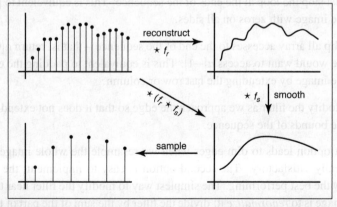

Figure 9.38. Resampling involves filtering for reconstruction and for sampling. Since two convolution filters applied in sequence can be replaced with a single filter, we only need one resampling filter, which serves the roles of reconstruction and sampling.

When resampling images, we usually specify a *source rectangle* in the units of the old image that specifies the part we want to keep in the new image. For example, using the pixel sample positioning convention from Chapter 3, the rectangle we'd use to resample the entire image is $(-0.5, n_x^{\text{old}} - 0.5) \times (-0.5, n_y^{\text{old}} - 0.5)$. Given a source rectangle $(x_l, x_h) \times (y_l, y_h)$, the sample spacing for the new image is $\Delta x = (x_h - x_l)/n_x^{\text{new}}$ in x and $\Delta y = (y_h - y_l)/n_y^{\text{new}}$ in y. The lower-left sample is positioned at $(x_l + \Delta x/2, y_l + \Delta y/2)$.

Modifying the 1D pseudocode to use this convention, and expanding the call to the reconstruct function into the double loop that is implied, we arrive at:

function resample(sequence a, float x_l, float x_h, int n, filter f)
   create sequence b of length n
   $r = f.\text{radius}$
   $x_0 = x_l + \Delta x/2$
   for $i = 0$ to $n - 1$ **do**
      $s = 0$
      $x = x_0 + i\Delta x$
      for $j = \lceil x - r \rceil$ to $\lfloor x + r \rfloor$ **do**
         $s = s + a[j]f(x - j)$
      $b[i] = s$
   return b

This routine contains all the basics of resampling an image. One last issue that remains to be addressed is what to do at the edges of the image, where the simple version here will access beyond the bounds of the input sequence. There are several things we might do:

- Just stop the loop at the ends of the sequence. This is equivalent to padding the image with zeros on all sides.

- Clip all array accesses to the end of the sequence—that is, return $a[0]$ when we would want to access $a[-1]$. This is equivalent to padding the edges of the image by extending the last row or column.

- Modify the filter as we approach the edge so that it does not extend beyond the bounds of the sequence.

The first option leads to dim edges when we resample the whole image, which is not really satisfactory. The second option is easy to implement; the third is probably the best performing. The simplest way to modify the filter near the edge of the image is to *renormalize* it: divide the filter by the sum of the part of the filter that falls within the image. This way, the filter always adds up to 1 over the actual image samples, so it preserves image intensity. For performance, it is desirable

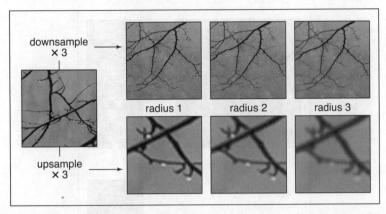

Figure 9.39. The effects of using different sizes of a filter for upsampling (enlarging) or downsampling (reducing) an image.

to handle the band of pixels within a filter radius of the edge (which require this renormalization) separately from the center (which contains many more pixels and does not require renormalization).

The choice of filter for resampling is important. There are two separate issues: the shape of the filter and the size (radius). Because the filter serves both as a reconstruction filter and a sampling filter, the requirements of both roles affect the choice of filter. For reconstruction, we would like a filter smooth enough to avoid aliasing artifacts when we enlarge the image, and the filter should be ripple-free. For sampling, the filter should be large enough to avoid undersampling and smooth enough to avoid moiré artifacts. Figure 9.39 illustrates these two different needs.

Generally we will choose one filter shape and scale it according to the relative resolutions of the input and output. The lower of the two resolutions determines the size of the filter: when the output is more coarsely sampled than the input (downsampling, or shrinking the image), the smoothing required for proper sampling is greater than the smoothing required for reconstruction, so we size the filter according to the output sample spacing (radius 3 in Figure 9.39). On the other hand, when the output is more finely sampled (upsampling, or enlarging the image) then the smoothing required for reconstruction dominates (the reconstructed function is already smooth enough to sample at a higher rate than it started), so the size of the filter is determined by the input sample spacing (radius 1 in Figure 9.39).

Choosing the filter itself is a tradeoff between speed and quality. Common choices are the box filter (when speed is paramount), the tent filter (moderate quality), or a piecewise cubic (excellent quality). In the piecewise cubic case, the

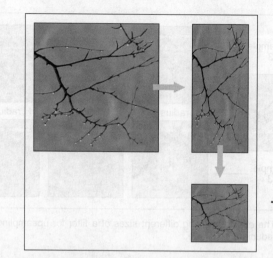

Figure 9.40. Resampling an image using a separable approach.

degree of smoothing can be adjusted by interpolating between f_B and f_C; the Mitchell-Netravali filter is a good choice.

Just as with image filtering, separable filters can provide a significant speed-up. The basic idea is to resample all the rows first, producing an image with changed width but not height, then to resample the columns of that image to produce the final result (Figure 9.40). Modifying the pseudocode given earlier so that it takes advantage of this optimization is reasonably straightforward.

9.5   Sampling Theory

If you are only interested in implementation, you can stop reading here; the algorithms and recommendations in the previous sections will let you implement programs that perform sampling and reconstruction and achieve excellent results. However, there is a deeper mathematical theory of sampling with a history reaching back to the first uses of sampled representations in telecommunications. Sampling theory answers many questions that are difficult to answer with reasoning based strictly on scale arguments.

But most important, sampling theory gives valuable insight into the workings of sampling and reconstruction. It gives the student who learns it an extra set of intellectual tools for reasoning about how to achieve the best results with the most efficient code.

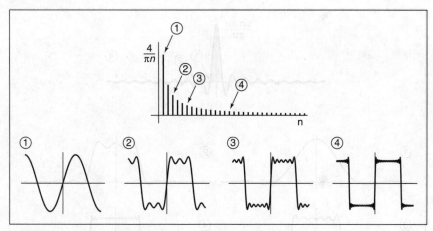

Figure 9.41. Approximating a square wave with finite sums of sines.

9.5.1 The Fourier Transform

The Fourier transform, along with convolution, is the main mathematical concept that underlies sampling theory. You can read about the Fourier transform in many math books on analysis, as well as in books on signal processing.

The basic idea behind the Fourier transform is to express any function by adding together sine waves (sinusoids) of all frequencies. By using the appropriate weights for the different frequencies, we can arrange for the sinusoids to add up to any (reasonable) function we want.

As an example, the square wave in Figure 9.41 can be expressed by a sequence of sine waves:

$$\sum_{n=1,3,5,\ldots}^{\infty} \frac{4}{\pi n} \sin 2\pi n x.$$

This *Fourier series* starts with a sine wave ($\sin 2\pi x$) that has frequency 1.0—same as the square wave—and the remaining terms add smaller and smaller corrections to reduce the ripples and, in the limit, reproduce the square wave exactly. Note that all the terms in the sum have frequencies that are integer multiples of the frequency of the square wave. This is because other frequencies would produce results that don't have the same period as the square wave.

A surprising fact is that a signal does not have to be periodic in order to be expressed as a sum of sinusoids in this way: a non-periodic signal just requires more sinusoids. Rather than summing over a discrete sequence of sinusoids, we will instead integrate over a continuous family of sinusoids. For instance, a box

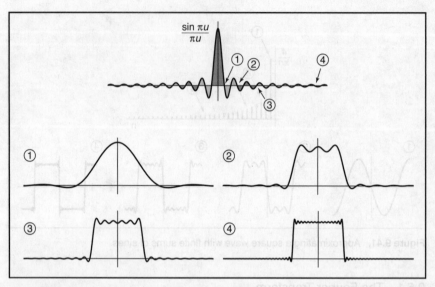

Figure 9.42. Approximating a box function with integrals of cosines up to each of four cutoff frequencies.

function can be written as the integral of a family of cosine waves:

$$\int_{-\infty}^{\infty} \frac{\sin \pi u}{\pi u} \cos 2\pi u x \, du. \qquad (9.5)$$

This integral in Equation (9.5) is adding up infinitely many cosines, weighting the cosine of frequency u by the weight $(\sin \pi u)/\pi u$. The result, as we include higher and higher frequencies, converges to the box function (see Figure 9.42). When a function f is expressed in this way, this weight, which is a function of the frequency u, is called the *Fourier transform* of f, denoted $\hat{f}$. The function $\hat{f}$ tells us how to build f by integrating over a family of sinusoids:

$$f(x) = \int_{-\infty}^{\infty} \hat{f}(u) e^{2\pi i u x} du. \qquad (9.6)$$

Equation (9.6) is known as the *inverse Fourier transform* (IFT) because it starts with the Fourier transform of f and ends up with f.[2]

Note that in Equation (9.6) the complex exponential $e^{2\pi i u x}$ has been substituted for the cosine in the previous equation. Also, $\hat{f}$ is a complex-valued function. The machinery of complex numbers is required to allow the phase, as well

---

[2]Note that the term "Fourier transform" is used both for the function $\hat{f}$ and for the operation that computes $\hat{f}$ from f. Unfortunately, this rather ambiguous usage is standard.

as the frequency, of the sinusoids to be controlled; this is necessary to represent any functions that are not symmetric across zero. The magnitude of $\hat{f}$ is known as the *Fourier spectrum*, and, for our purposes, this is sufficient—we won't need to worry about phase or use any complex numbers directly.

It turns out that computing $\hat{f}$ from f looks very much like computing f from $\hat{f}$:

$$\hat{f}(u) = \int_{-\infty}^{\infty} f(x)e^{-2\pi iux}\,dx. \tag{9.7}$$

Equation (9.7) is known as the (forward) *Fourier transform* (FT). The sign in the exponential is the only difference between the forward and inverse Fourier transforms, and it is really just a technical detail. For our purposes, we can think of the FT and IFT as the same operation.

Sometimes the f–$\hat{f}$ notation is inconvenient, and then we will denote the Fourier transform of f by $\mathcal{F}\{f\}$ and the inverse Fourier transform of $\hat{f}$ by $\mathcal{F}^{-1}\{\hat{f}\}$.

A function and its Fourier transform are related in many useful ways. A few facts (most of them easy to verify) that we will use later in the chapter are:

- A function and its Fourier transform have the same squared integral:

$$\int (f(x))^2\,dx = \int (\hat{f}(u))^2\,du.$$

The physical interpretation is that the two have the same energy (Figure 9.43).

In particular, scaling a function up by a also scales its Fourier transform by a. That is, $\mathcal{F}\{af\} = a\mathcal{F}\{f\}$.

- Stretching a function along the x-axis squashes its Fourier transform along the u-axis by the same factor (Figure 9.44):

$$\mathcal{F}\{f(x/b)\} = b\hat{f}(bx).$$

(The renormalization by b is needed to keep the energy the same.)

This means that if we are interested in a family of functions of different width and height (say all box functions centered at zero), then we only need to know the Fourier transform of one canonical function (say the box function with width and height equal to one), and we can easily know the Fourier transforms of all the scaled and dilated versions of that function.

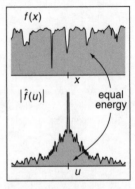

Figure 9.43. The Fourier transform preserves the squared integral of the signal.

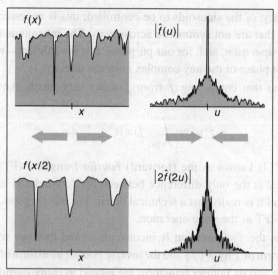

Figure 9.44. Scaling a signal along the *x*-axis in the space domain causes an inverse scale along the *u*-axis in the frequency domain.

For example, we can instantly generalize Equation (9.5) to give the Fourier transform of a box of width b and height a:

$$ab\frac{\sin \pi bu}{\pi bu}.$$

- The average value of f is equal to $\hat{f}(0)$. This makes sense since $\hat{f}(0)$ is supposed to be the zero-frequency component of the signal (the DC component if we are thinking of an electrical voltage).

- If f is real (which it always is for us), $\hat{f}$ is an even function—that is, $\hat{f}(u) = \hat{f}(-u)$. Likewise, if f is an even function then $\hat{f}$ will be real (this is not usually the case in our domain, but remember that we really are only going to care about the magnitude of $\hat{f}$).

9.5.2   Convolution and the Fourier Transform

One final property of the Fourier transform that deserves special mention is its relationship to convolution (Figure 9.45). Briefly,

$$\mathcal{F}\{f \star g\} = \hat{f}\hat{g}.$$

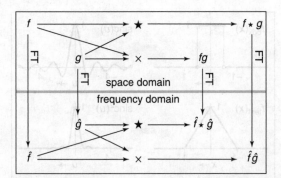

Figure 9.45. A commutative diagram to show visually the relationship between convolution and multiplication. If we multiply *f* and *g* in space, then transform to frequency, we end up in the same place as if we transformed *f* and *g* to frequency and then convolved them. Likewise, if we convolve *f* and *g* in space and then transform into frequency, we end up in the same place as if we transformed *f* and *g* to frequency, then multiplied them.

The Fourier transform of the convolution of two functions is the product of the Fourier transforms. Following the by now familiar symmetry,

$$\hat{f} \star \hat{g} = \mathcal{F}\{fg\}.$$

The convolution of two Fourier transforms is the Fourier transform of the product of the two functions. These facts are fairly straightforward to derive from the definitions.

This relationship is the main reason Fourier transforms are useful in studying the effects of sampling and reconstruction. We've seen how sampling, filtering, and reconstruction can be seen in terms of convolution; now the Fourier transform gives us a new domain—the frequency domain—in which these operations are simply products.

9.5.3 A Gallery of Fourier Transforms

Now that we have some facts about Fourier transforms, let's look at some examples of individual functions. In particular, we'll look at some filters from Section 9.3.1, which are shown with their Fourier transforms in Figure 9.46. We have already seen the box function:

$$\mathcal{F}\{f_{\text{box}}\} = \frac{\sin \pi u}{\pi u} = \text{sinc } \pi u.$$

The function[3] $\sin x / x$ is important enough to have its own name, sinc x.

---

[3] You may notice that $\sin \pi u / \pi u$ is undefined for $u = 0$. It is, however, continuous across zero, and we take it as understood that we use the limiting value of this ratio, 1, at $u = 0$.

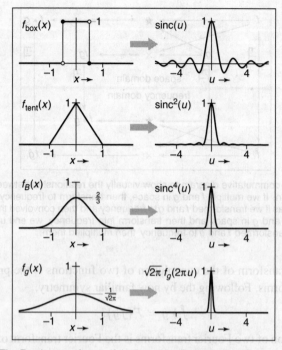

Figure 9.46. The Fourier transforms of the box, tent, B-spline, and Gaussian filters.

The tent function is the convolution of the box with itself, so its Fourier transform is just the square of the Fourier transform of the box function:

$$\mathcal{F}\{f_{\text{tent}}\} = \frac{\sin^2 \pi u}{\pi^2 u^2} = \text{sinc}^2 \pi u.$$

We can continue this process to get the Fourier transform of the B-spline filter (see Exercise 3):

$$\mathcal{F}\{f_{\text{B}}\} = \frac{\sin^4 \pi u}{\pi^4 u^4} = \text{sinc}^4 \pi u.$$

The Gaussian has a particularly nice Fourier transform:

$$\mathcal{F}\{f_{\text{G}}\} = e^{-(2\pi u)^2/2}.$$

It is another Gaussian! The Gaussian with standard deviation 1.0 becomes a Gaussian with standard deviation $1/2\pi$.

9.5.4 Dirac Impulses in Sampling Theory

The reason impulses are useful in sampling theory is that we can use them to talk about samples in the context of continuous functions and Fourier transforms. We represent a sample, which has a position and a value, by an impulse translated to that position and scaled by that value. A sample at position a with value b is represented by $b\delta(x - a)$. This way we can express the operation of sampling the function $f(x)$ at a as multiplying f by $\delta(x - a)$. The result is $f(a)\delta(x - a)$.

Sampling a function at a series of equally spaced points is therefore expressed as multiplying the function by the sum of a series of equally spaced impulses, called an *impulse train* (Figure 9.47). An impulse train with period T, meaning that the impulses are spaced a distance T apart is

$$s_T(x) = \sum_{i=-\infty}^{\infty} \delta(x - Ti).$$

The Fourier transform of s_1 is the same as s_1: a sequence of impulses at all integer frequencies. You can see why this should be true by thinking about what happens when we multiply the impulse train by a sinusoid and integrate. We wind up adding up the values of the sinusoid at all the integers. This sum will exactly cancel to zero for non-integer frequencies, and it will diverge to $+\infty$ for integer frequencies.

Because of the dilation property of the Fourier transform, we can guess that the Fourier transform of an impulse train with period T (which is like a dilation of s_1) is an impulse train with period $1/T$. Making the sampling finer in the space domain makes the impulses farther apart in the frequency domain.

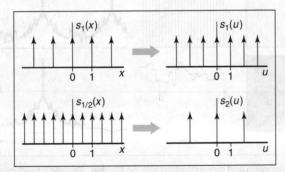

Figure 9.47. Impulse trains. The Fourier transform of an impulse train is another impulse train. Changing the period of the impulse train in space causes an inverse change in the period in frequency.

9.5.5 Sampling and Aliasing

Now we have built the mathematical machinery we need to understand the sampling and reconstruction process from the viewpoint of the frequency domian. The key advantage of introducing Fourier transforms is that it makes the effects of convolution filtering on the signal much clearer, and it provides more precise explanations of why we need to filter when sampling and reconstructing.

We start the process with the original, continuous signal. In general its Fourier transform could include components at any frequency, although for most kinds of signals (especially images), we expect the content to decrease as the frequency gets higher. Images also tend to have a large component at zero frequency—remember that the zero-frequency, or DC, component is the integral of the whole image, and since images are all positive values this tends to be a large number.

Let's see what happens to the Fourier transform if we sample and reconstruct without doing any special filtering (Figure 9.48). When we sample the signal, we model the operation as multiplication with an impulse train; the sampled signal is $f s_T$. Because of the multiplication-convolution property, the FT of the sampled signal is $\hat{f} \star \hat{s_T} = \hat{f} \star s_{1/T}$.

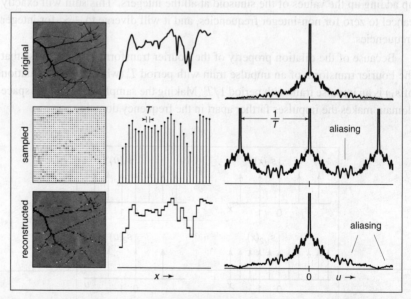

Figure 9.48. Sampling and reconstruction with no filtering. Sampling produces alias spectra that overlap and mix with the base spectrum. Reconstruction with a box filter collects even more information from the alias spectra. The result is a signal that has serious aliasing artifacts.

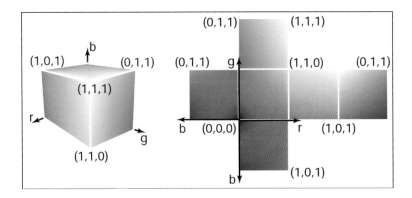
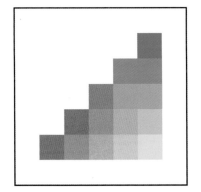
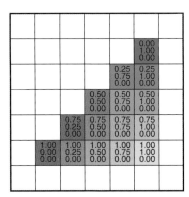

Plate I. The RGB color cube in 3D and its faces unfolded. Any RGB color is a point in the cube. (See also Figure 3.13.)

Plate II. A colored triangle with barycentric interpolation. Note that the changes in color components are linear in each row and column as well as along each edge. In fact it is constant along every line, such as the diagonals, as well. (See also Figure 8.5.)

Plate III. Left: a Phong-illuminated image. Middle: cool-to-warm shading is not useful without silhouettes. Right: cool-to-warm shading plus silhouettes. *Image courtesy Amy Gooch.* (See also Figure 10.9.)

Plate IV. The color of the glass is affected by total internal reflection and Beer's Law. The amount of light transmitted and reflected is determined by the Fresnel Equations. The complex lighting on the ground plane was computed using particle tracing as described in Chapter 24. (See also Figure 13.3.)

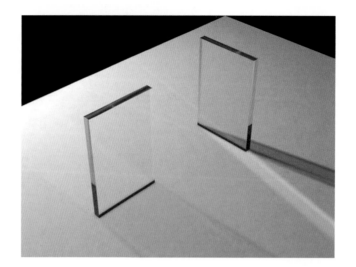

Plate V. An example of depth of field. The caustic in the shadow of the wine glass is computed using particle tracing (Chapter 24). (See also Figure 13.16.)

Plate VI. "Spiral Stairs." A complex BlobTree implicit model created in Erwin DeGroot's BlobTree.net system. (See also Figure 16.28.)

Plate VII. "The Next Step." A complex Blob-Tree implicit model created interactively in Ryan Schmidt's Shapeshop by artist, Corien Clapwijk (Andusan). (See also Figure 16.31.)

Plate VIII. Each sphere is rendered using only a vertex shader that computes Phong shading. Because the computation is being performed on a per-vertex basis, the Phong highlight only begins to appear accurate after the amount of geometry used to model the sphere is increased drastically. (See also Figure 18.7.)

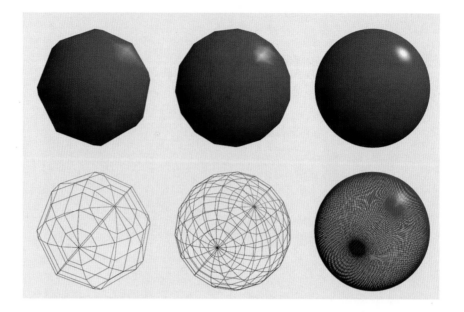

Plate IX. The results of running the fragment shader from Section 18.3.4. Note that the Phong highlight does appear on the left-most model which is represented by a single polygon. In fact, because lighting is calculated at the fragment, rather than at each vertex, the more coarsely tessellated sphere models also demonstrate appropriate Phong shading. (See also Figure 18.8.)

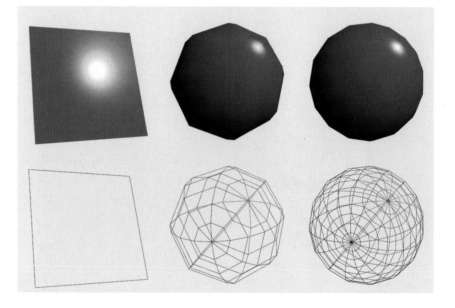

Plate X. The visible spectrum. Wavelengths are in nanometers.

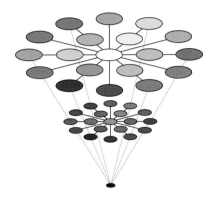

Plate XI. HSV color space. Hue varies around the circle, saturation varies with radius, and value varies with height.

Plate XII. Which color is closer to red: green or violet?

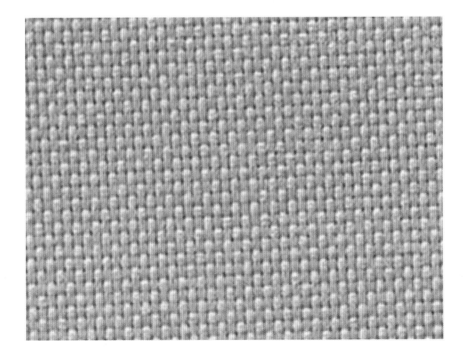

Plate XIII. The effect shown in Figure 22.29 is even more powerful when shown in color. *Figure courtesy Albert Yonas.*

Plate XIV. Per-channel gamma correction may desaturate the image. The left image was desaturated with a value of $s = 0.5$. The right image was not desaturated ($s = 1$). (See also Figure 23.11.)

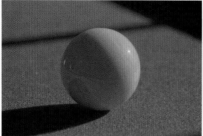

Plate XV. Image used for demonstrating the color transfer technique. Results are shown in Color Plates XVI and XVIII. (See also Figure 23.12 and Figure 23.30.)

Plate XVI. The image on the left is used to adjust the colors of the image shown in Color Plate XV. The result is shown on the right. (See also Figure 23.13.)

Plate XVII. Linear interpolation for color correction. The parameter c is set to 0.0 in the left image and to 1.0 in the right image. (See also Figure 23.24.)

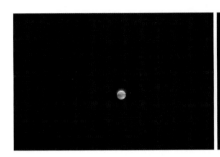 

Plate XVIII. The image on the left is used to transform the image of Color Plate XV into a night scene, shown here on the right. (See also Figure 23.31.)

Plate XIX. Simulated night scene using the image shown in Color Plate XV. (See also Figure 23.30.)

Plate XX. Aerial perspective, in which atmospheric effects reduce contrast and shift colors towards blue, provides a depth cue over long distances.

Plate XXI. A comparison between a rendering and a photo. *Figure courtesy Sumant Pattanaik and the Cornell Program of Computer Graphics.* (See also Figure 24.9.)

Plate XXII. The image shows extreme motion blur effects. The shadows use distribution ray tracing because they are moving during the image. *Model by Joseph Hamdorf and Young Song. Rendering by Eric Levin.*

Plate XXIII. Distribution ray-traced images with 1 sample per pixel, 16 samples per pixel, and 256 samples per pixel. *Images courtesy Jason Waltman.*

Plate XXIV. Top: A diffuse shading model is used. Bottom: Subsurface scattering is allowed using a technique from "A Practical Model for Sub-surface Light Transport," Jensen et al., Proceedings of SIGGRAPH 2001. *Images courtesy Henrik Jensen.*

Plate XXV. Ray-traced and photon-mapped image of an interior. Most of the lighting is indirect. *Image courtesy Henrik Jensen.*

Plate XXVI. The brightly colored pattern in the shadow is a "caustic" and is a product of light focused through the glass. It was computed using photon tracing. *Image courtesy Henrik Jensen.*

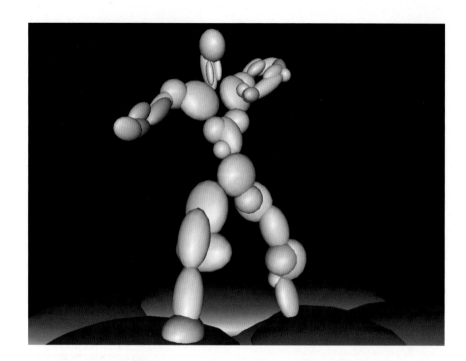

Plate XXVII. Top: A set of ellipsoids approximates the model. Bottom: The ellipsoids are used to create a gravity-like implicit function which is then displaced. *Image courtesy Eric Levin.*

Recall that δ is the identity for convolution. This means that

$$(\hat{f} \star s_{1/T})(u) = \sum_{i=-\infty}^{\infty} \hat{f}(u - i/T);$$

that is, convolving with the impulse train makes a whole series of equally spaced copies of the spectrum of f. A good intuitive interpretation of this seemingly odd result is that all those copies just express the fact (as we saw back in Section 9.1.1) that frequencies that differ by an integer multiple of the sampling frequency are indistinguishable once we have sampled—they will produce exactly the same set of samples. The original spectrum is called the *base spectrum* and the copies are known as *alias spectra*.

The trouble begins if these copies of the signal's spectrum overlap, which will happen if the signal contains any significant content beyond half the sample frequency. When this happens, the spectra add, and the information about different frequencies is irreversibly mixed up. This is the first place aliasing can occur, and if it happens here, it's due to undersampling—using too low a sample frequency for the signal.

Suppose we reconstruct the signal using the nearest-neighbor technique. This is equivalent to convolving with a box of width 1. (The discrete-continuous convolution used to do this is the same as a continuous convolution with the series of impulses that represent the samples.) The convolution-multiplication property means that the spectrum of the reconstructed signal will be the product of the spectrum of the sampled signal and the spectrum of the box. The resulting reconstructed Fourier transform contains the base spectrum (though somewhat attenuated at higher frequencies), plus attenuated copies of all the alias spectra. Because the box has a fairly broad Fourier transform, these attenuated bits of alias spectra are significant, and they are the second form of aliasing, due to an inadequate reconstruction filter. These alias components manifest themselves in the image as the pattern of squares that is characteristic of nearest-neighbor reconstruction.

Preventing Aliasing in Sampling

To do high quality sampling and reconstruction, we have seen that we need to choose sampling and reconstruction filters appropriately. From the standpoint of the frequency domain, the purpose of lowpass filtering when sampling is to limit the frequency range of the signal so that the alias spectra do not overlap the base spectrum. Figure 9.49 shows the effect of sample rate on the Fourier transform of the sampled signal. Higher sample rates move the alias spectra farther apart, and eventually whatever overlap is left does not matter.

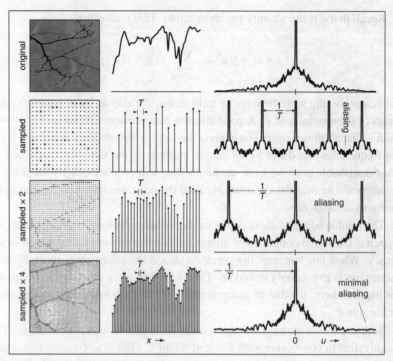

Figure 9.49. The effect of sample rate on the frequency spectrum of the sampled signal. Higher sample rates push the copies of the spectrum apart, reducing problems caused by overlap.

The key criterion is that the width of the spectrum must be less than the distance between the copies—that is, the highest frequency present in the signal must be less than half the sample frequency. This is known as the *Nyquist criterion*, and the highest allowable frequency is known as the *Nyquist frequency* or *Nyquist limit*. The *Nyquist-Shannon sampling theorem* states that a signal whose frequencies do not exceed the Nyquist limit (or, said another way, a signal that is bandlimited to the Nyquist frequency) can, in principle, be reconstructed exactly from samples.

With a high enough sample rate for a particular signal, we don't need to use a sampling filter. But if we are stuck with a signal that contains a wide range of frequencies (such as an image with sharp edges in it), we must use a sampling filter to bandlimit the signal before we can sample it. Figure 9.50 shows the effects of three lowpass (smoothing) filters in the frequency domain, and Figure 9.51 shows the effect of using these same filters when sampling. Even if the spectra overlap without filtering, convolving the signal with a lowpass filter can narrow the spectrum enough to eliminate overlap and produce a well-sampled

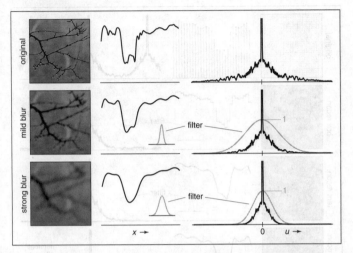

Figure 9.50.   Applying lowpass (smoothing) filters narrows the frequency spectrum of a signal.

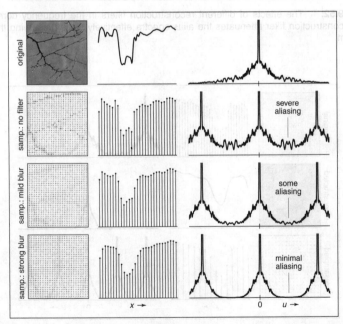

Figure 9.51.   How the lowpass filters from Figure 9.50 prevent aliasing during sampling. Lowpass filtering narrows the spectrum so that the copies overlap less, and the high frequencies from the alias spectra interfere less with the base spectrum.

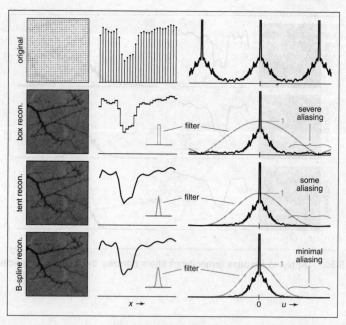

Figure 9.52. The effects of different reconstruction filters in the frequency domain. A good reconstruction filter attenuates the alias spectra effectively while preserving the base spectrum.

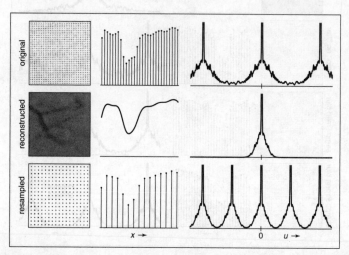

Figure 9.53. Resampling viewed in the frequency domain. The resampling filter both reconstructs the signal (removes the alias spectra) and bandlimits it (reduces its width) for sampling at the new rate.

representation of the filtered signal. Of course, we have lost the high frequencies, but that's better than having them get scrambled with the signal and turn into artifacts.

Preventing Aliasing in Reconstruction

From the frequency domain perspective, the job of a reconstruction filter is to remove the alias spectra while preserving the base spectrum. In Figure 9.48, we can see that the crudest reconstruction filter, the box, does attenuate the alias spectra. Most important, it completely blocks the DC spike for all the alias spectra. This is a characteristic of all reasonable reconstruction filters: they have zeroes in frequency space at all multiples of the sample frequency. This turns out to be equivalent to the ripple-free property in the space domain.

So a good reconstruction filter needs to be a good lowpass filter, with the added requirement of completely blocking all multiples of the sample frequency. The purpose of using a reconstruction filter different from the box filter is to more completely eliminate the alias spectra, reducing the leakage of high-frequency artifacts into the reconstructed signal, while disturbing the base spectrum as little as possible. Figure 9.52 illustrates the effects of different filters when used during reconstruction. As we have seen, the box filter is quite "leaky" and results in plenty of artifacts even if the sample rate is high enough. The tent filter, resulting in linear interpolation, attenuates high frequencies more, resulting in milder artifacts, and the B-spline filter is very smooth, controlling the alias spectra very effectively. It also smooths the base spectrum some—this is the tradeoff between smoothing and aliasing that we saw earlier.

Preventing Aliasing in Resampling

When the operations of reconstruction and sampling are combined in resampling, the same principles apply, but with one filter doing the work of both reconstruction and sampling. Figure 9.53 illustrates how a resampling filter must remove the alias spectra *and* leave the spectrum narrow enough to be sampled at the new sample rate.

9.5.6   Ideal Filters vs. Useful Filters

Following the frequency domain analysis to its logical conclusion, a filter that is exactly a box in the frequency domain is ideal for both sampling and reconstruction. Such a filter would prevent aliasing at both stages without diminishing the frequencies below the Nyquist frequency at all.

Recall that the inverse and forward Fourier transforms are essentially identical, so the spatial domain filter that has a box as its Fourier transform is the function $\sin \pi x / \pi x = \operatorname{sinc} \pi x$.

However, the sinc filter is not generally used in practice, either for sampling or for reconstruction, because it is impractical and because, even though it is optimal according to the frequency domain criteria, it doesn't produce the best results for many applications.

For sampling, the infinite extent of the sinc filter, and its relatively slow rate of decrease with distance from the center, is a liability. Also, for some kinds of sampling, the negative lobes are problematic. A Gaussian filter makes an excellent sampling filter even for difficult cases where high-frequency patterns must be removed from the input signal, because its Fourier transform falls off exponentially, with no bumps that tend to let aliases leak through. For less difficult cases, a tent filter generally suffices.

For reconstruction, the size of the sinc function again creates problems, but even more importantly, the many ripples create "ringing" artifacts in reconstructed signals.

Exercises

1. Show that discrete convolution is commutative and associative. Do the same for continuous convolution.

2. Discrete-continuous convolution can't be commutative, because its arguments have two different types. Show that it is associative, though.

3. Prove that the B-spline is the convolution of four box functions.

4. Show that the "flipped" definition of convolution is necessary by trying to show that convolution is commutative and associative using this (incorrect) definition (see the footnote on page 194):

$$(a \star b)[i] = \sum_j a[j]b[i+j]$$

5. Prove that $\mathcal{F}\{f \star g\} = \hat{f}\hat{g}$ and $\hat{f} \star \hat{g} = \mathcal{F}\{fg\}$.

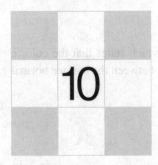

10

Surface Shading

To make objects appear to have more volume, it can help to use *shading*, i.e., the surface is "painted" with light. This chapter presents the most common heuristic shading methods. The first two, diffuse and Phong shading, were developed in the 1970s and are available in most graphics libraries. The last, artistic shading, uses artistic conventions to assign color to objects. This creates images reminiscent of technical drawings, which is desirable in many applications.

10.1 Diffuse Shading

Many objects in the world have a surface appearance loosely described as "matte," indicating that the object is not at all shiny. Examples include paper, unfinished wood, and dry unpolished stones. To a large degree, such objects do not have a color change with a change in viewpoint. For example, if you stare at a particular point on a piece of paper and move while keeping your gaze fixed on that point, the color at that point will stay relatively constant. Such matte objects can be considered as behaving as *Lambertian* objects. This section discusses how to implement the shading of such objects. A key point is that all formulas in this chapter should be evaluated in world coordinates and not in the warped coordinates after the perspective transform is applied. Otherwise, the angles between normals are changed and the shading will be inaccurate.

10.1.1   Lambertian Shading Model

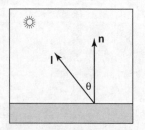

Figure 10.1. The geometry for Lambert's Law. Both **n** and **l** are unit vectors.

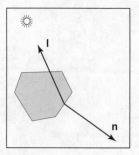

Figure 10.2. When a surface points away from the light, it should receive no light. This case can be verified by checking whether the dot product of **l** and **n** is negative.

A Lambertian object obeys *Lambert's cosine law*, which states that the color c of a surface is proportional to the cosine of the angle between the surface normal and the direction to the light source (Gouraud, 1971):

$$c \propto \cos\theta,$$

or in vector form,

$$c \propto \mathbf{n} \cdot \mathbf{l},$$

where $\mathbf{n}$ and $\mathbf{l}$ are shown in Figure 10.1. Thus, the color on the surface will vary according to the cosine of the angle between the surface normal and the light direction. Note that the vector $\mathbf{l}$ is typically assumed not to depend on the location of the object. That assumption is equivalent to assuming the light is "distant" relative to object size. Such a "distant" light is often called a *directional light*, because its position is specified only by a direction.

A surface can be made lighter or darker by changing the intensity of the light source or the reflectance of the surface. The diffuse reflectance c_r is the fraction of light reflected by the surface. This fraction will be different for different color components. For example, a surface is red if it reflects a higher fraction of red incident light than blue incident light. If we assume surface color is proportional to the light reflected from a surface, then the diffuse reflectance c_r—an RGB color—must also be included:

$$c \propto c_r \mathbf{n} \cdot \mathbf{l}. \tag{10.1}$$

The right-hand side of Equation (10.1) is an RGB color with all RGB components in the range $[0, 1]$. We would like to add the effects of light intensity while keeping the RGB components in the range $[0, 1]$. This suggests adding an RGB intensity term c_l which itself has components in the range $[0, 1]$:

$$c = c_r c_l \mathbf{n} \cdot \mathbf{l}. \tag{10.2}$$

This is a very convenient form, but it can produce RGB components for c that are outside the range $[0, 1]$, because the dot product can be negative. The dot product is negative when the surface is pointing away from the light as shown in Figure 10.2.

The "max" function can be added to Equation (10.2) to test for that case:

$$c = c_r c_l \max(0, \mathbf{n} \cdot \mathbf{l}). \tag{10.3}$$

Another way to deal with the "negative" light is to use an absolute value:

$$c = c_r c_l |\mathbf{n} \cdot \mathbf{l}|. \tag{10.4}$$

While Equation (10.4) may seem physically implausible, it actually corresponds to Equation (10.3) with two lights in opposite directions. For this reason it is often called *two-sided* lighting (Figure 10.3).

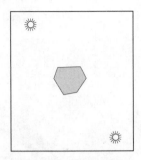

Figure 10.3. Using Equation (10.4), the two-sided lighting formula, is equivalent to assuming two opposing light sources of the same color.

10.1.2   Ambient Shading

One problem with the diffuse shading of Equation (10.3) is that any point whose normal faces away from the light will be black. In real life, light is reflected all over, and some light is incident from every direction. In addition, there is often skylight giving "ambient" lighting. One way to handle this is to use several light sources. A common trick is to always put a dim source at the eye so that all visible points will receive some light. Another way is to use two-sided lighting as described by Equation (10.4). A more common approach is to add an ambient term (Gouraud, 1971). This is just a constant color term added to Equation (10.3):

$$c = c_r \left(c_a + c_l \max \left(0, \mathbf{n} \cdot \mathbf{l} \right) \right).$$

Intuitively, you can think of the ambient color c_a as the average color of all surfaces in the scene. If you want to ensure that the computed RGB color stays in the range $[0, 1]^3$, then $c_a + c_l \leq (1, 1, 1)$. Otherwise your code should "clamp" RGB values above one to have the value one.

10.1.3   Vertex-Based Diffuse Shading

If we apply Equation (10.1) to an object made up of triangles, it will typically have a faceted appearance. Often, the triangles are an approximation to a smooth surface. To avoid the faceted appearance, we can place surface normal vectors at the vertices of the triangles (Phong, 1975), and apply Equation (10.3) at each of the vertices using the normal vectors at the vertices (see Figure 10.4). This will give a color at each triangle vertex, and this color can be interpolated using the barycentric interpolation described in Section 8.1.2.

One problem with shading at triangle vertices is that we need to get the normals from somewhere. Many models will come with normals supplied. If you tessellate your own smooth model, you can create normals when you create the triangles. If you are presented with a polygonal model that does not have normals at vertices and you want to shade it smoothly, you can compute normals by a variety of heuristic methods. The simplest is to just average the normals of the triangles that share each vertex and use this average normal at the vertex. This

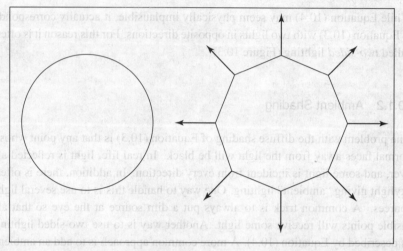

Figure 10.4. A circle (left) is approximated by an octagon (right). Vertex normals record the surface normal of the original curve.

average normal will not automatically be of unit length, so you should convert it to a unit vector before using it for shading.

10.2   Phong Shading

Some surfaces are essentially like matte surfaces, but they have *highlights*. Examples of such surfaces include polished tile floors, gloss paint, and whiteboards. Highlights move across a surface as the viewpoint moves. This means that we must add a unit vector e toward the eye into our equations. If you look carefully at highlights, you will see that they are really reflections of the light; sometimes these reflections are blurred. The color of these highlights is the color of the light—the surface color seems to have little effect. This is because the reflection occurs at the object's surface, and the light that penetrates the surface and picks up the object's color is scattered diffusely.

10.2.1   Phong Lighting Model

We want to add a fuzzy "spot" the same color as the light source in the right place. The center of the dot should be drawn where the direction e to the eye "lines" up with the natural direction of reflection r as shown in Figure 10.5. Here "lines up" is mathematically equivalent to "where σ is zero." We would like to have the

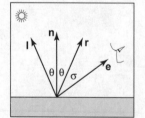

Figure 10.5. The geometry for the Phong illumination model. The eye should see a highlight if σ is small.

highlight have some non-zero area, so that the eye sees some highlight wherever σ is small.

Given $\mathbf{r}$, we'd like a heuristic function that is bright when $\mathbf{e} = \mathbf{r}$ and falls off gradually when $\mathbf{e}$ moves away from $\mathbf{r}$. An obvious candidate is the cosine of the angle between them:

$$c = c_l(\mathbf{e} \cdot \mathbf{r}),$$

There are two problems with using this equation. The first is that the dot product can be negative. This can be solved computationally with an "if" statement that sets the color to zero when the dot product is negative. The more serious problem is that the highlight produced by this equation is much wider than that seen in real

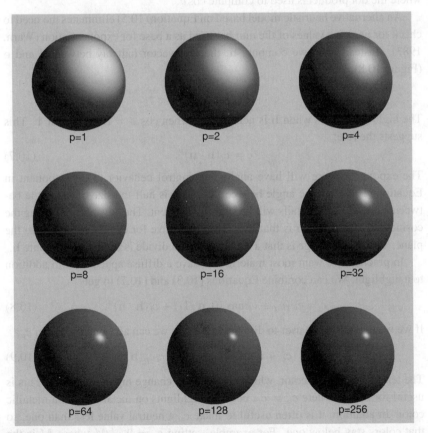

Figure 10.6. The effect of the Phong exponent on highlight characteristics. This uses Equation (10.5) for the highlight. There is also a diffuse component, giving the objects a shiny but non-metallic appearance. *Image courtesy Nate Robins.*

life. The maximum is in the right place and it is the right color, but it is just too big. We can narrow it without reducing its maximum color by raising to a power:

$$c = c_l \max(0, \mathbf{e} \cdot \mathbf{r})^p. \tag{10.5}$$

Here p is called the *Phong exponent*; it is a positive real number (Phong, 1975). The effect that changing the Phong exponent has on the highlight can be seen in Figure 10.6.

To implement Equation (10.5), we first need to compute the unit vector $\mathbf{r}$. Given unit vectors $\mathbf{l}$ and $\mathbf{n}$, $\mathbf{r}$ is the vector $\mathbf{l}$ reflected about $\mathbf{n}$. Figure 10.7 shows that this vector can be computed as

$$\mathbf{r} = -\mathbf{l} + 2(\mathbf{l} \cdot \mathbf{n})\mathbf{n}, \tag{10.6}$$

where the dot product is used to compute $\cos \theta$.

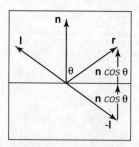

Figure 10.7. The geometry for calculating the vector **r**.

An alternative heuristic model based on Equation (10.5) eliminates the need to check for negative values of the number used as a base for exponentiation (Warn, 1983). Instead of $\mathbf{r}$, we compute $\mathbf{h}$, the unit vector halfway between $\mathbf{l}$ and $\mathbf{e}$ (Figure 10.8):

$$\mathbf{h} = \frac{\mathbf{e} + \mathbf{l}}{\|\mathbf{e} + \mathbf{l}\|}.$$

The highlight occurs when $\mathbf{h}$ is near $\mathbf{n}$, i.e., when $\cos \omega = \mathbf{h} \cdot \mathbf{n}$ is near 1. This suggests the rule:

$$c = c_l (\mathbf{h} \cdot \mathbf{n})^p. \tag{10.7}$$

The exponent p here will have analogous control behavior to the exponent in Equation (10.5), but the angle between $\mathbf{h}$ and $\mathbf{n}$ is half the size of the angle between $\mathbf{e}$ and $\mathbf{r}$, so the details will be slightly different. The advantage of using the cosine between $\mathbf{n}$ and $\mathbf{h}$ is that it is always positive for eye and light above the plane. The disadvantage is that a square root and divide is needed to compute $\mathbf{h}$.

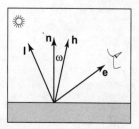

Figure 10.8. The unit vector **h** is halfway between **l** and **e**.

In practice, we want most materials to have a diffuse appearance in addition to a highlight. We can combine Equations (10.3) and (10.7) to get

$$c = c_r (c_a + c_l \max(0, \mathbf{n} \cdot \mathbf{l})) + c_l (\mathbf{h} \cdot \mathbf{n})^p. \tag{10.8}$$

If we want to allow the user to dim the highlight, we can add a control term c_p:

$$c = c_r (c_a + c_l \max(0, \mathbf{n} \cdot \mathbf{l})) + c_l c_p (\mathbf{h} \cdot \mathbf{n})^p. \tag{10.9}$$

The term c_p is a RGB color, which allows us to change highlight colors. This is useful for metals where $c_p = c_r$, because highlights on metal take on a metallic color. In addition, it is often useful to make c_p a neutral value less than one, so that colors stay below one. For example, setting $c_p = 1 - M$ where M is the maximum component of c_r will keep colors below one for one light source and no ambient term.

10.2.2 Surface Normal Vector Interpolation

Smooth surfaces with highlights tend to change color quickly compared to Lambertian surfaces with the same geometry. Thus, shading at the normal vectors can generate disturbing artifacts.

These problems can be reduced by interpolating the normal vectors across the polygon and then applying Phong shading at each pixel. This allows you to get good images without making the size of the triangles extremely small. Recall from Chapter 3, that when rasterizing a triangle, we compute barycentric coordinates (α, β, γ) to interpolate the vertex colors c_0, c_1, c_2:

$$c = \alpha c_0 + \beta c_1 + \gamma c_2. \tag{10.10}$$

We can use the same equation to interpolate surface normals $\mathbf{n}_0$, $\mathbf{n}_1$, and $\mathbf{n}_2$:

$$\mathbf{n} = \alpha \mathbf{n}_0 + \beta \mathbf{n}_1 + \gamma \mathbf{n}_2. \tag{10.11}$$

And Equation (10.9) can then be evaluated for the $\mathbf{n}$ computed at each pixel. Note that the $\mathbf{n}$ resulting from Equation (10.11) is usually not a unit normal. Better visual results will be achieved if it is converted to a unit vector before it is used in shading computations. This type of normal interpolation is often called *Phong normal interpolation* (Phong, 1975).

10.3 Artistic Shading

The Lambertian and Phong shading methods are based on heuristics designed to imitate the appearance of objects in the real world. Artistic shading is designed to mimic drawings made by human artists (Yessios, 1979; Dooley & Cohen, 1990; Saito & Takahashi, 1990; L. Williams, 1991). Such shading seems to have advantages in many applications. For example, auto manufacturers hire artists to draw diagrams for car owners' manuals. This is more expensive than using much more "realistic" photographs, so there is probably some intrinsic advantage to the techniques of artists when certain types of communication are needed. In this section, we show how to make subtly shaded line drawings reminiscent of human-drawn images. Creating such images is often called *non-photorealistic rendering*, but we will avoid that term because many non-photorealistic techniques are used for efficiency that are not related to any artistic practice.

10.3.1 Line Drawing

The most obvious thing we see in human drawings that we don't see in real life is *silhouettes*. When we have a set of triangles with shared edges, we should draw

an edge as a silhouette when one of the two triangles sharing an edge faces toward
the viewer, and the other triangle faces away from the viewer. This condition can
be tested for two normals $\mathbf{n}_0$ and $\mathbf{n}_1$ by

$$\text{draw silhouette if } (\mathbf{e} \cdot \mathbf{n}_0)(\mathbf{e} \cdot \mathbf{n}_1) \leq 0.$$

Here $\mathbf{e}$ is a vector from the edge to the eye. This can be any point on the edge or
either of the triangles. Alternatively, if $f_i(\mathbf{p}) = 0$ are the implicit plane equations
for the two triangles, the test can be written

$$\text{draw silhouette if } f_0(\mathbf{e})f_1(\mathbf{e}) \leq 0.$$

We would also like to draw visible edges of a polygonal model. To do this, we
can use either of the hidden surface methods of Chapter 12 for drawing in the
background color and then draw the outlines of each triangle in black. This, in
fact, will also capture the silhouettes. Unfortunately, if the polygons represent a
smooth surface, we really don't want to draw most of those edges. However, we
might want to draw all *creases* where there really is a corner in the geometry. We
can test for creases by using a heuristic threshold:

$$\text{draw crease if } (\mathbf{n}_0 \cdot \mathbf{n}_1) \leq \text{threshold}.$$

This combined with the silhouette test will give nice-looking line drawings.

10.3.2   Cool-to-Warm Shading

When artists shade line drawings, they often use low intensity shading to give
some impression of curve to the surface and to give colors to objects (Gooch et
al., 1998). Surfaces facing in one direction are shaded with a cool color, such
as a blue, and surfaces facing in the opposite direction are shaded with a warm
color, such as orange. Typically these colors are not very saturated and are also
not dark. That way, black silhouettes show up nicely. Overall this gives a cartoon-
like effect. This can be achieved by setting up a direction to a "warm" light $\mathbf{l}$ and
using the cosine to modulate color, where the warmth constant k_w is defined on
$[0, 1]$:

$$k_w = \frac{1 + \mathbf{n} \cdot \mathbf{l}}{2}.$$

The color c is then just a linear blend of the cool color c_c and the warm color c_w:

$$c = k_w c_w + (1 - k_w)c_c.$$

Figure 10.9. Left: a Phong-illuminated image. Middle: cool-to-warm shading is not useful without silhouettes. Right: cool-to-warm shading plus silhouettes. *Image courtesy Amy Gooch.* (See also Plate III.)

There are many possible c_w and c_b that will produce reasonable looking results. A good starting place for a guess is

$$c_c = (0.4, 0.4, 0.7),$$
$$c_c = (0.8, 0.6, 0.6).$$

Figure 10.9 shows a comparison between traditional Phong lighting and this type of artistic shading.

Frequently Asked Questions

• All of the shading in this chapter seems like enormous hacks. Is that true?

Yes. However, they are carefully designed hacks that have proven useful in practice. In the long run, we will probably have better-motivated algorithms that include physics, psychology, and tone-mapping. However, the improvements in image quality will probably be incremental.

• I hate calling pow(). Is there a way to avoid it when doing Phong lighting?

A simple way is to only have exponents that are themselves a power of two, i.e., 2, 4, 8, 16, ... In practice, this is not a problematic restriction for most applications. A look-up table is also possible, but will often not give a large speed-up.

Exercises

1. The moon is poorly approximated by diffuse or Phong shading. What observations tell you that this is true?

2. Velvet is poorly approximated by diffuse or Phong shading. What observations tell you that this is true?

3. Why do most highlights on plastic objects look white, while those on gold metal look gold?

11

Texture Mapping

The shading models presented in Chapter 10 assume that a diffuse surface has uniform reflectance c_r. This is fine for surfaces such as blank paper or painted walls, but it is inefficient for objects such as a printed sheet of paper. Such objects have an appearance whose complexity arises from variation in reflectance properties. While we could use such small triangles that the variation is captured by varying the reflectance properties of the triangles, this would be inefficient.

The common technique to handle variations of reflectance is to store the reflectance as a function or a a pixel-based image and "map" it onto a surface (Catmull, 1975). The function or image is called a *texture map*, and the process of controlling reflectance properties is called *texture mapping*. This is not hard to implement once you understand the coordinate systems involved. Texture mapping can be classified by several different properties:

1. the dimensionality of the texture function,

2. the correspondences defined between points on the surface and points in the texture function, and

3. whether the texture function is primarily procedural or primarily a table look-up.

These items are usually closely related, so we will somewhat arbitrarily classify textures by their dimension. We first cover 3D textures, often called *solid* textures or *volume* textures. We will then cover 2D textures, sometimes called *image*

243

textures. When graphics programmers talk about textures without specifying dimension, they usually mean 2D textures. However, we begin with 3D textures because, in many ways, they are easier to understand and implement. At the end of the chapter we discuss bump mapping and displacement mapping which use textures to change surface normals and position, respectively. Although those methods modify properties other than reflectance, the images/functions they use are still called textured. This is consistent with common usage where any image used to modify object appearance is called a texture.

11.1   3D Texture Mapping

In previous chapters we used c_r as the diffuse reflectance at a point on an object. For an object that does not have a solid color, we can replace this with a function $c_r(\mathbf{p})$ which maps 3D points to RGB colors (Peachey, 1985; Perlin, 1985). This function might just return the reflectance of the object that contains $\mathbf{p}$. But for objects with *texture*, we should expect $c_r(\mathbf{p})$ to vary as $\mathbf{p}$ moves across a surface. One way to do this is to create a 3D texture that defines an RGB value at every point in 3D space. We will only call it for points $\mathbf{p}$ on the surface, but it is usually easier to define it for all 3D points than a potentially strange 2D subset of points that are on an arbitrary surface. Such a strategy is clearly suitable for surfaces that are "carved" from a solid medium, such as a marble sculpture.

Note that in a ray-tracing program, we have immediate access to the point $\mathbf{p}$ seen through a pixel. However, for a z-buffer or BSP-tree program, we only know the point after projection into device coordinates. We will show how to resolve this problem in Section 11.3.1.

11.1.1   3D Stripe Textures

There are a surprising number of ways to make a striped texture. Let's assume we have two colors c_0 and c_1 that we want to use to make the stripe color. We need some oscillating function to switch between the two colors. An easy one is a sine:

RGB stripe(point $\mathbf{p}$)
if $(\sin(x_p) > 0)$ **then**
    return c_0
else
    return c_1

We can also make the stripe's width w controllable:

RGB stripe(point **p**, real w)
if $(\sin(\pi x_p/w) > 0)$ **then**
   return c_0
else
   return c_1

If we want to interpolate smoothly between the stripe colors, we can use a parameter t to vary the color linearly:

RGB stripe(point **p**, real w)
$t = (1 + \sin(\pi p_x/w))/2$
return $(1 - t)c_0 + tc_1$

These three possibilities are shown in Figure 11.1.

11.1.2 Texture Arrays

Another way we can specify texture in space is to store a 3D array of color values and to associate a spatial position to each of these values. We first discuss this for 2D arrays in 2D space. Such textures can be applied in 3D by using two of the dimensions, e.g. x and y, to determine what texture values are used. We then extend those 2D results to 3D.

We will assume the two dimensions to be mapped are called u and v. We also assume we have an n_x by n_y image that we use as the texture. Somehow we need every (u, v) to have an associated color found from the image. A fairly standard way to make texturing work for (u, v) is to first remove the integer portion of (u, v) so that it lies in the unit square. This has the effect of "tiling" the entire uv plane with copies of the now-square texture (Figure 11.2). We then use one of three interpolation strategies to compute the image color for that coordinate. The simplest strategy is to treat each image pixel as a constant colored rectangular tile (Figure 11.3 (a). To compute the colors, we apply $c(u, v) = c_{ij}$, where $c(u, v)$ is the texture color at (u, v) and c_{ij} is the pixel color for pixel indices:

$$i = \lfloor un_x \rfloor,$$
$$j = \lfloor vn_y \rfloor; \tag{11.1}$$

$\lfloor x \rfloor$ is the floor of x, (n_x, n_y) is the size of the image being textured, and the indices start at $(i, j) = (0, 0)$. This method for a simple image is shown in Figure 11.3 (b).

Figure 11.1. Various stripe textures result from drawing a regular array of *xy* points while keeping *z* constant.

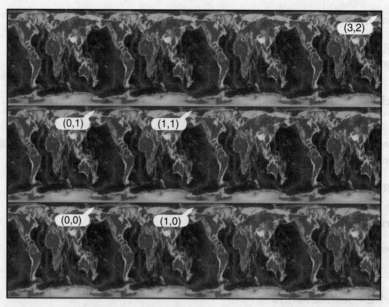

Figure 11.2. The tiling of an image onto the (u,v) plane. Note that the input image is rectangular, and that this rectangle is mapped to a unit square on the (u,v) plane.

For a smoother texture, a bilinear interpolation can be used as shown in Figure 11.3 (c). Here we use the formula

$$c(u,v) = (1 - u')(1 - v')c_{ij}$$
$$+ u'(1 - v')c_{(i+1)j}$$
$$+ (1 - u')v'c_{i(j+1)}$$
$$+ u'v'c_{(i+1)(j+1)}$$

where

$$u' = n_x u - \lfloor n_x u \rfloor,$$
$$v' = n_y v - \lfloor n_y v \rfloor.$$

The discontinuities in the derivative in intensity can cause visible mach bands, so hermite smoothing can be used:

$$c(u,v) = (1 - u'')(1 - v'')c_{ij} +$$
$$+ u''(1 - v'')c_{(i+1)j}$$
$$+ (1 - u'')v''c_{i(j+1)}$$
$$+ u''v''c_{(i+1)(j+1)},$$

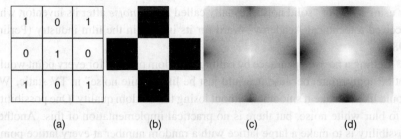

Figure 11.3. (a) The image on the left has nine pixels that are all either black or white. The three interpolation strategies are (b) nearest-neighbor, (c) bilinear, and (d) hermite.

where

$$u'' = 3(u')^2 - 2(u')^3,$$
$$v'' = 3(v')^2 - 2(v')^3,$$

which results in Figure 11.3 (d).

In 3D, we have a 3D array of values. All of the ideas from 2D extend naturally. As an example, let's assume that we will do *trilinear* interpolation between values. First, we compute the texture coordinates (u', v', w') and the lower indices (i, j, k) of the array element to be interpolated:

$$
\begin{aligned}
c(u, v, w) = {}& (1 - u')(1 - v')(1 - w')c_{ijk} \\
& + u'(1 - v')(1 - w')c_{(i+1)jk} \\
& + (1 - u')v'(1 - w')c_{i(j+1)k} \\
& + (1 - u')(1 - v')w'c_{ij(k+1)} \\
& + u'v'(1 - w')c_{(i+1)(j+1)k} \\
& + u'(1 - v')w'c_{(i+1)j(k+1)} \\
& + (1 - u')v'w'c_{i(j+1)(k+1)} \\
& + u'v'w'c_{(i+1)(j+1)(k+1)},
\end{aligned}
\tag{11.2}
$$

where

$$
\begin{aligned}
u' &= n_x u - \lfloor n_x u \rfloor, \\
v' &= n_y v - \lfloor n_y v \rfloor, \\
w' &= n_z w - \lfloor n_z w \rfloor.
\end{aligned}
\tag{11.3}
$$

11.1.3 Solid Noise

Although regular textures such as stripes are often useful, we would like to be able to make "mottled" textures such as we see on birds' eggs. This is usually done by using a sort of "solid noise," usually called *Perlin noise* after its inventor, who received a technical Academy Award for its impact in the film industry (Perlin, 1985).

Getting a noisy appearance by calling a random number for every point would not be appropriate, because it would just be like "white noise" in TV static. We would like to make it smoother without losing the random quality. One possibility is to blur white noise, but there is no practical implementation of this. Another possibility is to make a large lattice with a random number at every lattice point, and then interpolate these random points for new points between lattice nodes; this is just a 3D texture array as described in the last section with random numbers in the array. This technique makes the lattice too obvious. Perlin used a variety of tricks to improve this basic lattice technique so the lattice was not so obvious. This results in a rather baroque-looking set of steps, but essentially there are just three changes from linearly interpolating a 3D array of random values. The first change is to use Hermite interpolation to avoid mach bands, just as can be done with regular textures. The second change is the use of random vectors rather than values, with a dot product to derive a random number; this makes the underlying grid structure less visually obvious by moving the local minima and maxima off the grid vertices. The third change is to use a 1D array and hashing to create a virtual 3D array of random vectors. This adds computation to lower memory use. Here is his basic method:

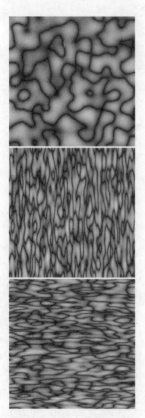

$$n(x, y, z) = \sum_{i=\lfloor x \rfloor}^{\lfloor x \rfloor + 1} \sum_{j=\lfloor y \rfloor}^{\lfloor y \rfloor + 1} \sum_{k=\lfloor z \rfloor}^{\lfloor z \rfloor + 1} \Omega_{ijk}(x - i, y - j, z - k),$$

where (x, y, z) are the Cartesian coordinates of $\mathbf{x}$, and

$$\Omega_{ijk}(u, v, w) = \omega(u)\omega(v)\omega(w) \left(\Gamma_{ijk} \cdot (u, v, w) \right),$$

and $\omega(t)$ is the cubic weighting function:

$$\omega(t) = \begin{cases} 2|t|^3 - 3|t|^2 + 1 & \text{if } |t| < 1, \\ 0 & \text{otherwise.} \end{cases}$$

Figure 11.4. Absolute value of solid noise, and noise for scaled *x* and *y* values.

The final piece is that Γ_{ijk} is a random unit vector for the lattice point $(x, y, z) = (i, j, k)$. Since we want any potential ijk, we use a pseudorandom table:

$$\Gamma_{ijk} = \mathbf{G} \left(\phi(i + \phi(j + \phi(k))) \right),$$

where $\mathbf{G}$ is a precomputed array of n random unit vectors, and $\phi(i) = P[i \mod n]$ where P is an array of length n containing a permutation of the integers 0 through $n - 1$. In practice, Perlin reports $n = 256$ works well. To choose a random unit vector (v_x, v_y, v_z) first set

$$v_x = 2\xi - 1,$$
$$v_y = 2\xi' - 1,$$
$$v_z = 2\xi'' - 1,$$

where ξ, ξ', ξ'' are canonical random numbers (uniform in the interval $[0, 1)$). Then, if $(v_x^2 + v_y^2 + v_z^2) < 1$, make the vector a unit vector. Otherwise keep setting it randomly until its length is less than one, and then make it a unit vector. This is an example of a *rejection method*, which will be discussed more in Chapter 14. Essentially, the "less than" test gets a random point in the unit sphere, and the vector for the origin to that point is uniformly random. That would not be true of random points in the cube, so we "get rid" of the corners with the test.

Because solid noise can be positive or negative, it must be transformed before being converted to a color. The absolute value of noise over a ten by ten square is shown in Figure 11.4, along with stretched versions. There versions are stretched by scaling the points input to the noise function.

The dark curves are where the original noise function changed from positive to negative. Since noise varies from -1 to 1, a smoother image can be achieved by using $(\text{noise} + 1)/2$ for color. However, since noise values close to 1 or -1 are rare, this will be a fairly smooth image. Larger scaling can increase the contrast (Figure 11.5).

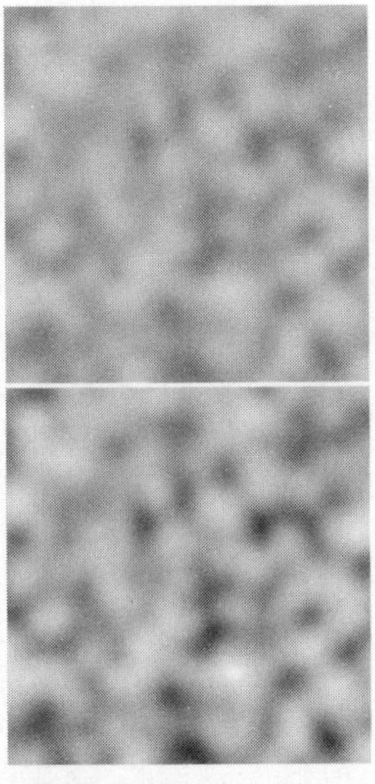

Figure 11.5. Using 0.5(noise+1) (top) and 0.8(noise+1) (bottom) for intensity.

11.1.4 Turbulence

Many natural textures contain a variety of feature sizes in the same texture. Perlin uses a pseudofractal "turbulence" function:

$$n_t(\mathbf{x}) = \sum_i \frac{|n(2^i \mathbf{x})|}{2^i}$$

This effectively repeatedly adds scaled copies of the noise function on top of itself as shown in Figure 11.6.

The turbulence can be used to distort the stripe function:

RGB turbstripe(point **p**, double w)
    double $t = (1 + \sin(k_1 z_p + \text{turbulence}(k_2 \mathbf{p}))/w)/2$
    return $t * s0 + (1 - t) * s1$

Various values for k_1 and k_2 were used to generate Figure 11.7.

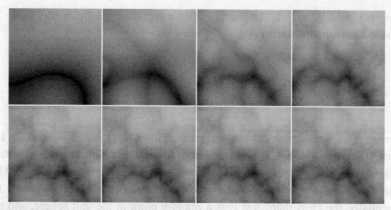

Figure 11.6. Turbulence function with (from top left to bottom right) one through eight terms in the summation.

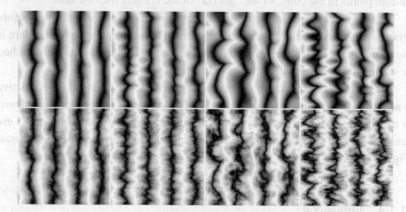

Figure 11.7. Various turbulent stripe textures with different k_1, k_2. The top row has only the first term of the turbulence series.

11.2   2D Texture Mapping

For 2D texture mapping, we use a 2D coordinate, often called uv, which is used to create a reflectance $R(u, v)$. The key is to take an image and associate a (u, v) coordinate system on it so that it can, in turn, be associated with points on a 3D surface. For example, if the latitudes and longitudes on the world map are associated with a polar coordinate system on the sphere, we get a globe (Figure 11.8).

It is crucial that the coordinates on the image and the object match in "just the right way." As a convention, the coordinate system on the image is set to be the unit square $(u, v) \in [0, 1]^2$. For (u, v) outside of this square, only the fractional parts of the coordinates are used resulting in a tiling of the plane (Figure 11.2).

Figure 11.8. A Miller cylindrical projection map world map and its placement on the sphere. The distortions in the texture map (i.e., Greenland being so large) exactly correspond to the shrinking that occurs when the map is applied to the sphere.

Note that the image has a different number of pixels horizontally and vertically, so the image pixels have a non-uniform aspect ratio in (u, v) space.

To map this $(u, v) \in [0, 1]^2$ image onto a sphere, we first compute the polar coordinates. Recall the spherical coordinate system described by Equation (2.25). For a sphere of radius R with center (c_x, c_y, c_z), the parametric equation of the sphere is

$$x = x_c + R \cos \phi \sin \theta,$$
$$y = y_c + R \sin \phi \sin \theta,$$
$$z = z_c + R \cos \theta.$$

We can find (θ, ϕ):

$$\theta = \arccos \left(\frac{z - z_c}{R} \right),$$

$$\phi = \arctan2(y - y_c, x - x_c),$$

where $\arctan2(a, b)$ is the the *atan2* of most math libraries which returns the arctangent of a/b. Because $(\theta, \phi) \in [0, \pi] \times [-\pi, \pi]$, we convert to (u, v) as follows, after first adding 2π to ϕ if it is negative:

$$u = \frac{\phi}{2\pi},$$

$$v = \frac{\pi - \theta}{\pi}.$$

This mapping is shown in Figure 11.8. There is a similar, although likely more complicated way, to generate coordinates for most 3D shapes.

11.3   Texture Mapping for Rasterized Triangles

For surfaces represented by triangle meshes, texture coordinates are defined by storing (u, v) texture coordinates at each vertex of the mesh (see Section 12.1). So, if a triangle is intersected at barycentric coordinates (β, γ), you interpolate the (u, v) coordinates the same way you interpolate points. Recall that the point at barycentric coordinate (β, γ) is

$$\mathbf{p}(\beta, \gamma) = \mathbf{a} + \beta(\mathbf{b} - \mathbf{a}) + \gamma(\mathbf{c} - \mathbf{a}).$$

A similar equation applies for (u, v):

$$u(\beta, \gamma) = u_a + \beta(u_b - u_a) + \gamma(u_c - u_a),$$
$$v(\beta, \gamma) = v_a + \beta(v_b - v_a) + \gamma(v_c - v_a).$$

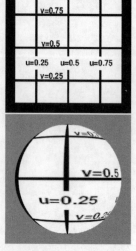

Figure 11.9. Top: a calibration texture map. Bottom: the sphere viewed along the y-axis.

Several ways a texture can be applied by changing the (u, v) at triangle vertices are shown in Figure 11.10. This sort of calibration texture map makes it easier to understand the texture coordinates of your objects during debugging (Figure 11.9).

We would like to get the same texture images whether we use a ray tracing program or a rasterization method, such as a z-buffer. There are some subtleties in achieving this with correct-looking perspective, but we can address this at the rasterization stage. The reason things are not straightforward is that just interpolating

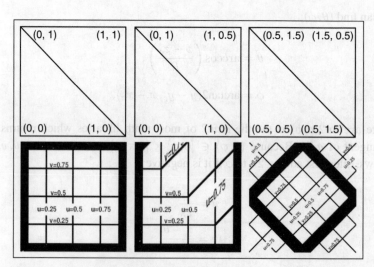

Figure 11.10.   Various mesh textures obtained by changing (u,v) coordinates stored at vertices.

texture coordinates in screen space results in incorrect images, as shown for the grid texture shown in Figure 11.11. Because things in perspective get smaller as the distance to the viewer increases, the lines that are evenly spaced in 3D should compress in 2D image space. More careful interpolation of texture coordinates is needed to accomplish this.

11.3.1 Perspective Correct Textures

We can implement texture mapping on triangles by interpolating the (u, v) coordinates, modifying the rasterization method of Section 8.1.2, but this results in the problem shown at the right of Figure 11.11. A similar problem occurs for triangles if screen space barycentric coordinates are used as in the following rasterization code:

for all x **do**
  for all y **do**
    compute (α, β, γ) for (x, y)
    if $\alpha \in (0, 1)$ and $\beta \in (0, 1)$ and $\gamma \in (0, 1)$ **then**
      $\mathbf{t} = \alpha \mathbf{t}_0 + \beta \mathbf{t}_1 + \gamma \mathbf{t}_2$
      drawpixel (x, y) with color texture($\mathbf{t}$) for a solid texture
      or with texture(β, γ) for a 2D texture.

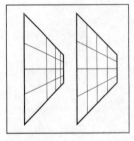

Figure 11.11. Left: correct perspective. Right: interpolation in screen space.

This code will generate images, but there is a problem. To unravel the basic problem, let's consider the progression from world space $\mathbf{q}$ to homogeneous point $\mathbf{r}$ to homogenized point $\mathbf{s}$:

$$\begin{bmatrix} x_q \\ y_q \\ z_q \\ 1 \end{bmatrix} \xrightarrow{\text{transform}} \begin{bmatrix} x_r \\ y_r \\ z_r \\ h_r \end{bmatrix} \xrightarrow{\text{homogenize}} \begin{bmatrix} x_r/h_r \\ y_r/h_r \\ z_r/h_r \\ 1 \end{bmatrix} \equiv \begin{bmatrix} x_s \\ y_s \\ z_s \\ 1 \end{bmatrix}.$$

If we use screen space, we are interpolating in $\mathbf{s}$. However, we would like to be interpolating in space $\mathbf{q}$ or $\mathbf{r}$, where the homogeneous division has not yet nonlinearly distorted the barycentric coordinates of the triangle.

The key observation is that $1/h_r$ is interpolated with no distortion. Likewise, so is u/h_r and v/h_r. In fact, so is k/h_r, where k is any quantity that varies linearly across the triangle. Recall from Section 7.4 that if we transform all points along the line segment between points $\mathbf{q}$ and $\mathbf{Q}$ and homogenize, we have

$$\mathbf{s} + \frac{h_R t}{h_r + t(h_R - h_r)}(\mathbf{S} - \mathbf{s}),$$

but if we linearly interpolate in the homogenized space we have

$$\mathbf{s} + a(\mathbf{S} - \mathbf{s}).$$

Although those lines sweep out the same points, typically $a \neq t$ for the same points on the line segment. However, if we interpolate $1/h$, we *do* get the same answer regardless of which space we interpolate in. To see this is true, confirm (Exercise 2):

$$\frac{1}{h_r} + \frac{h_R t}{h_r + t(h_R - h_r)} \left(\frac{1}{h_R} - \frac{1}{h_r} \right) = \frac{1}{h_r} + t \left(\frac{1}{h_R} - \frac{1}{h_r} \right) \quad (11.4)$$

This ability to interpolate $1/h$ linearly with no error in the transformed space allows us to correctly texture triangles. Perhaps the least confusing way to deal with this distortion is to compute the world space barycentric coordinates of the triangle (β_w, γ_w) in terms of screen space coordinates (β, γ). We note that β_s/h and γ_s/h can be interpolated linearly in screen space. For example, at the screen space position associated with screen space barycentric coordinates (β, γ), we can interpolate β_w/h without distortion. Because $\beta_w = 0$ at vertex 0 and vertex 2, and $\beta_w = 1$ at vertex 1, we have

$$\frac{\beta_s}{h} = \frac{0}{h_0} + \beta \left(\frac{1}{h_1} - \frac{0}{h_0} \right) + \gamma \left(\frac{0}{h_2} - \frac{0}{h_0} \right). \quad (11.5)$$

Because of all the zero terms, Equation (11.5) is fairly simple. However, to get β_w from it, we must know h. Because we know $1/h$ is linear in screen space, we have

$$\frac{1}{h} = \frac{1}{h_0} + \beta \left(\frac{1}{h_1} - \frac{1}{h_0} \right) + \gamma \left(\frac{1}{h_2} - \frac{1}{h_0} \right). \quad (11.6)$$

Dividing Equation (11.5) by Equation (11.6) gives

$$\beta_w = \frac{\frac{\beta}{h_1}}{\frac{1}{h_0} + \beta \left(\frac{1}{h_1} - \frac{1}{h_0} \right) + \gamma \left(\frac{1}{h_2} - \frac{1}{h_0} \right)}.$$

Multiplying numerator and denominator by $h_0 h_1 h_2$ and doing a similar set of manipulations for the analogous equations in γ_w gives

$$\beta_w = \frac{h_0 h_2 \beta}{h_1 h_2 + h_2 \beta (h_0 - h_1) + h_1 \gamma (h_0 - h_2)},$$

$$\gamma_w = \frac{h_0 h_1 \gamma}{h_1 h_2 + h_2 \beta (h_0 - h_1) + h_1 \gamma (h_0 - h_2)}. \quad (11.7)$$

Note that the two denominators are the same.

For triangles that use the perspective matrix from Chapter 7, recall that $w = z/n$ where z is the distance from the viewer perpendicular to the screen. Thus, for that matrix $1/z$ also varies linearly. We can use this fact to modify our scan-conversion code for three points $\mathbf{t}_i = (x_i, y_i, z_i, h_i)$ that have been passed through the viewing matrices, but have not been homogenized:

> Compute bounds for $x = x_i/h_i$ and $y = y_i/h_i$
> **for** all x **do**
>   **for** all y **do**
>   compute (α, β, γ) for (x, y)
>   **if** $(\alpha \in [0, 1]$ and $\beta \in [0, 1]$ and $\gamma \in [0, 1])$ **then**
> $d = h_1 h_2 + h_2 \beta (h_0 - h_1) + h_1 \gamma (h_0 - h_2)$
> $\beta_w = h_0 h_2 \beta / d$
> $\gamma_w = h_0 h_1 \gamma / d$
> $\alpha_w = 1 - \beta_w - \gamma_w$
> $u = \alpha_w u_0 + \beta_w u_1 + \gamma_w u_2$
> $v = \alpha_w v_0 + \beta_w v_1 + \gamma_w v_2$
>   drawpixel (x, y) with color texture(u, v)

For solid textures, just recall that by the definition of barycentric coordinates

$$\mathbf{p} = (1 - \beta_w - \gamma_w)\mathbf{p}_0 + \beta_w \mathbf{p}_1 + \gamma_w \mathbf{p}_2,$$

where $\mathbf{p}_i$ are the world space vertices. Then, just call a solid texture routine for point $\mathbf{p}$.

11.4 Bump Textures

Although we have only discussed changing reflectance using texture, you can also change the surface normal to give an illusion of fine-scale geometry on the surface. We can apply a *bump map* that perturbs the surface normal (J. F. Blinn, 1978).
One way to do this is:

> vector3 n = surfaceNormal(x)
> n += k_1 * vectorTurbulence$(k_2 * x)$
> **return** $t * s0 + (1 - t) * s1$

This is shown in Figure 11.12.
To implement *vectorTurbulence*, we first need *vectorNoise* which produces a simple spatially-varying 3D vector:

$$n_v(x, y, z) = \sum_{i=\lfloor x \rfloor}^{\lfloor x \rfloor + 1} \sum_{j=\lfloor y \rfloor}^{\lfloor y \rfloor + 1} \sum_{k=\lfloor z \rfloor}^{\lfloor z \rfloor + 1} \Gamma_{ijk} \omega(x) \omega(y) \omega(z).$$

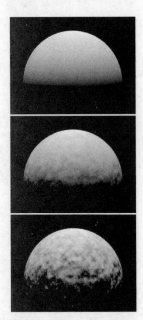

Figure 11.12. Vector turbulence on a sphere of radius 1.6. Lighting directly from above. Top: $k_1 = 0$. Middle: $k_1 = 0.08$, $k_2 = 8$. Bottom: $k_1 = 0.24$, $k_2 = 8$.

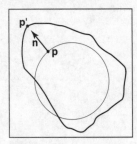

Figure 11.13. The points **p** on the circle are each displaced in the direction of **n** by the function $f(\mathbf{p})$. If f is continuous, then the resulting points **p**′ form a continuous surface.

Then, *vectorTurbulence* is a direct analog of turbulence: sum a series of scaled versions of *vectorNoise*.

11.5 Displacement Mapping

One problem with Figure 11.12 is that the bumps neither cast shadows nor affect the silhouette of the object. These limitations occur because we are not really changing any geometry. If we want more realism, we can apply a *displacement map* (Cook et al., 1987). A displacement map actually changes the geometry using a texture. A common simplification is that the displacement will be in the direction of the surface normal.

If we take all points **p** on a surface, with associated surface normal vectors **n**, then we can make a new surface using a 3D texture $d(\mathbf{p})$:

$$\mathbf{p}' = \mathbf{p} + f(\mathbf{p})\mathbf{n}.$$

This concept is shown in Figure 11.13.

Displacement mapping is straightforward to implement in a z-buffer code by storing the surface to be displaced as a fine mesh of many triangles. Each vertex in the mesh can then be displaced along the normal vector direction. This results in large models, but it is quite robust.

11.6 Environment Maps

Often we would like to have a texture-mapped background and for objects to have specular reflections of that background. This can be accomplished using *environment maps* (J. F. Blinn, 1976). An environment map can be implemented as a background function that takes in a viewing direction **b** and returns a RGB color from a texture map. There are many ways to store environment maps. For example, we can use a spherical table indexed by spherical coordinates. In this section, we will instead describe a cube-based table with six square texture maps, often called a *cube map*.

The basic idea of a cube map is that we have an infinitely large cube with a texture on each face. Because the cube is large, the origin of a ray does not change what the ray "sees." This is equivalent to an arbitrarily-sized cube that is queried by a ray whose origin is at the Cartesian origin. As an example of how a given direction **b** is converted to (u, v) coordinates, consider the right face of

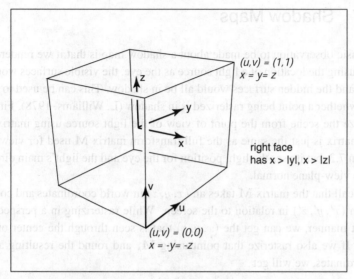

right face
has x > |y|, x > |z|

(u,v) = (1,1)
x = y= z

(u,v) = (0,0)
x = -y= -z

Figure 11.14. The cube map has six axis-aligned textures that store the background. The right face contains a single texture.

Figure 11.14. Here we have x_b as the maximum magnitude component. In that case, we can compute (u, v) for that texture to be

$$u = \frac{y + x}{2x},$$

$$v = \frac{z + x}{2x}.$$

There are analogous formulas for the other five faces.

So for any reflection ray $\mathbf{a} + t\mathbf{b}$ we return *cubemap*($\mathbf{b}$) for the background color. In a z-buffer implementation, we need to perform this calculation on a pixel-by-pixel basis. If at a given pixel we know the viewing direction $\mathbf{c}$ and the surface normal vector $\mathbf{n}$, we can compute the reflected direction $\mathbf{b}$ (Figure 11.15). We can do this by modifying Equation (10.6) to get

$$\mathbf{b} = -\mathbf{c} + \frac{2(\mathbf{c} \cdot \mathbf{n})\mathbf{n}}{\|\mathbf{c}\|^2}. \qquad (11.8)$$

Here the denominator of the fraction accounts for the fact that $\mathbf{c}$ may not be a unit vector. Because we need to know $\mathbf{b}$ at each pixel, we can either compute $\mathbf{b}$ at each triangle vertex and interpolate $\mathbf{b}$ in a perspective correct manner, or we can interpolate $\mathbf{n}$ and compute $\mathbf{b}$ for each pixel. This will allow us to call *cubemap*($\mathbf{b}$) at each pixel.

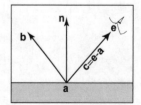

Figure 11.15. The vector $\mathbf{b}$ is the reflection of vector $\mathbf{c}$ with respect to the surface normal $\mathbf{n}$.

11.7   Shadow Maps

The basic observation to be made about a shadow map is that if we rendered the scene using the location of a light source as the eye, the visible surfaces would all be lit, and the hidden surfaces would all be in shadow. This can be used to determine whether a point being rasterized is in shadow (L. Williams, 1978). First, we rasterize the scene from the point of view of the light source using matrix $\mathbf{M}_s$. This matrix is just the same as the full transform matrix $\mathbf{M}$ used for viewing in Section 7.3, but it uses the light position for the eye and the light's main direction for the view-plane normal.

Recall that the matrix $\mathbf{M}$ takes an (x, y, z) in world coordinates and converts it to an (x', y', z') in relation to the screen. While rasterizing in a perspectively correct manner, we can get the (x, y, z) that is seen through the center of each pixel. If we also rasterize that point using $\mathbf{M}_s$ and round the resulting x- and y-coordinates, we will get

$$(i, j, \text{depth}).$$

We can compare this depth with the z-value in the shadow depth map at pixel (i, j). If it is the same, then the point is lit, and otherwise it is in shadow. Because of computational inaccuracies, we should actually test whether the points are the same to within a small constant.

Because we typically don't want the light to only be within a square window, often a *spot light* is used. This attenuates the value of the light source based on closeness to the sides of the shadow buffer. For example, if the shadow buffer is $n \times n$ pixels, then for pixel (i, j) in the shadow buffer, we can apply the attenuation coefficient based on the fractional radius r:

$$r = \sqrt{\left(\frac{2i - n}{n}\right)^2 + \left(\frac{2j - n}{n}\right)^2}.$$

Any radially decreasing function will then give a spot-like look.

Frequently Asked Questions

• How do I implement displacement mapping in ray tracing?

There is no ideal way to do it. Generating all the triangles and caching the geometry when necessary will prevent memory overload (Pharr & Hanrahan, 1996; Pharr et al., 1997). Trying to intersect the displaced surface directly is possible when the displacement function is restricted (Patterson et al., 1991; Heidrich & Seidel, 1998; Smits et al., 2000).

• Why don't my images with textures look realistic?

Humans are good at seeing small imperfections in surfaces. Geometric imperfections are typically absent in computer-generated images that use texture maps for details, so they look "too smooth."

• My textured animations look bad when there are many texels visible inside a pixel. What should I do?

The problem is that the texture resolution is too high for that image. We would like a smaller down-sampled version of the texture. However, if we move closer, such a down-sampled texture would look too blurry. What we really need is to be able to dynamically choose the texture resolution based on viewing conditions so that about one texel is visible through each pixel. A common way to do that is to use *MIP-mapping* (L. Williams, 1983). That technique establishes a multi-resolution set of textures and chooses one of the textures for each polygon or pixel. Typically the resolutions vary by a factor of two, e.g., 512^2, 256^2, 128^2, etc.

Notes

The discussion of perspective-correct textures is based on *Fast Shadows and Lighting Effects Using Texture Mapping* (Segal et al., 1992) and on *3D Game Engine Design* (Eberly, 2000).

Exercises

1. Find several ways to implement an infinite 2D checkerboard using surface and solid techniques. Which is best?

2. Verify that Equation (11.4) is a valid equality using brute-force algebra.

3. How could you implement solid texturing by using the z-buffer depth and a matrix transform?

12

Data Structures for Graphics

Certain data structures seem to pop up repeatedly in graphics applications, perhaps because they address fundamental underlying ideas like surfaces, space, and scene structure. This chapter talks about several basic and unrelated categories of data structures that are among the most common and useful: mesh structures, spatial data structures, scene graphs, and tiled multidimensional arrays.

For meshes, we discuss the basic storage schemes used for storing static meshes and for transferring meshes to graphics APIs. We also discuss the winged-edge data structure (Baumgart, 1974) and the related half-edge structure, which are useful for managing models where the tessellation changes, such as in subdivision or model simplification. Although these methods generalize to arbitrary polygon meshes, we focus on the simpler case of triangle meshes here.

Next, the scene-graph data structure is presented. Various forms of this data structure are ubiquitous in graphics applications because they are so useful in managing objects and transformations. All new graphics APIs are designed to support scene graphs well.

For spatial data structures, we discuss three approaches to organizing models in 3D space—bounding volume hierarchies, hierarchical space subdivision, and uniform space subdivision—and the use of hierarchical space subdivision (BSP trees) for hidden surface removal. The same methods are also used for other purposes including geometry culling and collision detection.

Finally, the tiled multidimensional array is presented. Originally developed to help paging performance in applications where graphics data needed to be swapped in from disk, such structures are now crucial for memory locality on machines regardless of whether the array fits in main memory.

12.1 Triangle Meshes

Most real-world models are composed of complexes of triangles with shared vertices. These are usually known as *triangular meshes*, *triangle meshes*, or *triangular irregular networks* (TINs) and handling them efficiently is crucial to the performance of many graphics programs. The kind of efficiency that is important depends on the application. Meshes are stored on disk and in memory, and we'd like to minimize the amount of storage consumed. When meshes are transmitted across networks or from the CPU to the graphics system, they consume bandwidth, which is often even more precious than storage. In applications that perform operations on meshes, besides simply storing and drawing them—such as subdivision, mesh editing, mesh compression, or other operations—efficient access to adjacency information is crucial.

Triangle meshes are generally used to represent surfaces, so a mesh is not just a collection of unrelated triangles, but rather a network of triangles that connect to one another through shared vertices and edges to form a single continuous surface. This is a key insight about meshes: a mesh can be handled more efficiently than a collection of the same number of unrelated triangles.

The minimum information required for a triangle mesh is a set of triangles (triples of vertices) and the positions (in 3D space) of their vertices. But many, if not most, programs require the ability to store additional data at the vertices, edges, or faces to support texture mapping, shading, animation, and other operations. Vertex data is the most common: each vertex can have material parameters, texture coordinates, irradiances—any parameters whose values change across the surface. These parameters are then linearly interpolated across each triangle to define a continuous function over the whole surface of the mesh. However, it is also occasionally important to be able to store data per edge or per face.

12.1.1 Mesh Topology

The idea that meshes are surface-like can be formalized as constraints on the *mesh topology*—the way the triangles connect together, without regard for the vertex positions. Many algorithms will only work, or are much easier to implement, on a mesh with predictable connectivity. The simplest and most restrictive requirement on the topology of a mesh is for the surface to be a *manifold*. A manifold mesh is "watertight"—it has no gaps and separates the space on the inside of the surface from the space outside. It also looks like a surface everywhere on the mesh.

We'll leave the precise definitions to the mathematicians; see the chapter notes.

The term *manifold* comes from the mathematical field of topology: roughly speaking, a manifold (specifically a two-dimensional manifold, or 2-manifold) is a surface in which a small neighborhood around any point could be smoothed out into a bit of flat surface. This idea is most clearly explained by counterexample: if an edge on a mesh has three triangles connected to it, the neighborhood of a point on the edge is different from the neighborhood of one of the points in the interior of one of the triangles, because it has an extra "fin" sticking out of it (Figure 12.1). If the edge has exactly two triangles attached to it, points on the edge have neighborhoods just like points in the interior, only with a crease down the middle. Similarly, if the triangles sharing a vertex are in a configuration like the left one in Figure 12.2, the neighborhood is like two pieces of surface glued together at the center, which can't be flattened without doubling it up. The vertex with the simpler neighborhood shown at right is just fine.

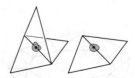

Figure 12.1. Non-manifold (left) and manifold (right) interior edges.

Many algorithms assume that meshes are manifold, and it's always a good idea to verify this property to prevent crashes or infinite loops if you are handed a malformed mesh as input. This verification boils down to checking that all edges are manifold and checking that all vertices are manifold by verifying the following conditions:

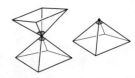

Figure 12.2. Non-manifold (left) and manifold (right) interior vertices.

- Every edge is shared by exactly two triangles.

- Every vertex has a single, complete loop of triangles around it.

Figure 12.1 illustrates how an edge can fail the first test by having too many triangles, and Figure 12.2 illustrates how a vertex can fail the second test by having two separate loops of triangles attached to it.

Manifold meshes are convenient, but sometimes it's necessary to allow meshes to have edges, or *boundaries*. Such meshes are not manifolds—a point on the boundary has a neighborhood that is cut off on one side. They are not necessarily watertight. However, we can relax the requirements of a manifold mesh to those for a *manifold with boundary* without causing problems for most mesh processing algorithms. The relaxed conditions are:

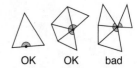

Figure 12.3. Conditions at the edge of a manifold with boundary.

- Every edge is used by either one or two triangles.

- Every vertex connects to a single edge-connected set of triangles.

Figure 12.3 illustrates these conditions: from left to right, there is an edge with one triangle, a vertex whose neighboring triangles are in a single edge-connected set, and a vertex with two disconnected sets of triangles attached to it.

Finally, in many applications it's important to be able to distinguish the "front" or "outside" of a surface from the "back" or "inside"—this is known as the *orientation* of the surface. For a single triangle we define orientation based on the order in which the vertices are listed: the front is the side from which the triangle's three vertices are arranged in counterclockwise order. A connected mesh is

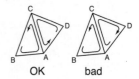

Figure 12.4. Triangles (B,A,C) and (D,C,A) are consistently oriented, whereas (B,A,C) and (A,C,D) are inconsistently oriented.

consistently oriented if its triangles all agree on which side is the front—and this is true if and only if every pair of adjacent triangles is consistently oriented.

In a consistently oriented pair of triangles, the two shared vertices appear in opposite orders in the two triangles' vertex lists (Figure 12.4). What's important is consistency of orientation—some systems define the front using clockwise rather than counterclockwise order.

Any mesh that has non-manifold edges can't be oriented consistently. But it's also possible for a mesh to be a valid manifold with boundary (or even a manifold), and yet have no consistent way to orient the triangles—they are not *orientable* surfaces. An example is the Möbius band shown in Figure 12.5. This is rarely an issue in practice, however.

Figure 12.5. A triangulated Mobius band, which is not orientable.

12.1.2 Indexed Mesh Storage

A simple triangular mesh is shown in Figure 12.6. You could store these three triangles as independent entities, each of this form:

```
Triangle {
    vector3 vertexPosition[3]
}
```

This would result in storing vertex **b** three times and the other vertices twice each for a total of nine stored points (three vertices for each of three triangles). Or you could instead arrange to share the common vertices and store only four, re-

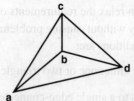

separate triangles:

#	vertex 0	vertex 1	vertex 2
0	(a_x, a_y, a_z)	(b_x, b_y, b_z)	(c_x, c_y, c_z)
1	(b_x, b_y, b_z)	(d_x, d_y, d_z)	(c_x, c_y, c_z)
2	(a_x, a_y, a_z)	(d_x, d_y, d_z)	(b_x, b_y, b_z)

shared vertices:

triangles		vertices	
#	vertices	#	position
0	(0, 1, 2)	0	(a_x, a_y, a_z)
1	(1, 3, 2)	1	(b_x, b_y, b_z)
2	(0, 3, 1)	2	(c_x, c_y, c_z)
		3	(d_x, d_y, d_z)

Figure 12.6. A three-triangle mesh with four vertices, represented with separate triangles (left) and with shared vertices (right).

sulting in a *shared-vertex mesh*. Logically, this data structure has triangles which
point to vertices which contain the vertex data:

```
Triangle {
  Vertex v[3]
}

Vertex {
  vector3 position   // or other vertex data
}
```

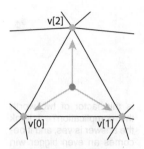

Figure 12.7. The triangle-to-vertex references in a shared-vertex mesh.

Note that the entries in the v array are references, or pointers, to Vertex objects;
the vertices are not contained in the triangle.

In implementation, the vertices and triangles are normally stored in arrays,
with the triangle-to-vertex references handled by storing array indices:

```
IndexedMesh {
  int tInd[nt][3]
  vector3 verts[nv]
}
```

The index of the kth vertex of the ith triangle is found in tInd[i][k], and the
position of that vertex is stored in the corresponding row of the verts array; see
Figure 12.8 for an example. This way of storing a shared-vertex mesh is an *indexed triangle mesh.*

Separate triangles or shared vertices will both work well. Is there a space
advantage for sharing vertices? If our mesh has n_v vertices and n_t triangles, and
if we assume that the data for floats, pointers, and ints all require the same storage
(a dubious assumption), the space requirements are:

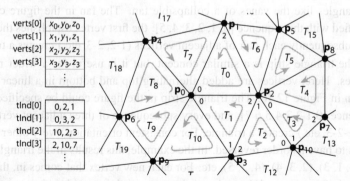

Figure 12.8. A larger triangle mesh, with part of its representation as an indexed triangle
mesh.

- **Triangle.** Three vectors per triangle, for $9n_t$ units of storage;

- **IndexedMesh.** One vector per vertex and three ints per triangle, for $3n_v + 3n_t$ units of storage.

The relative storage requirements depend on the ratio of n_t to n_v.

As a rule of thumb, a large mesh has each vertex connected to about six triangles (although there can be any number for extreme cases). Since each triangle connects to three vertices, this means that there are generally twice as many triangles as vertices in a large mesh: $n_t \approx 2n_v$. Making this substitution, we can conclude that the storage requirements are $18n_v$ for the Triangle structure and $9n_v$ for IndexedMesh. Using shared vertices reduces storage requirements by about a factor of two; and this seems to hold in practice for most implementations.

12.1.3 Triangle Strips and Fans

Indexed meshes are the most common in-memory representation of triangle meshes, because they achieve a good balance of simplicity, convenience, and compactness. They are also commonly used to transfer meshes over networks and between the application and graphics pipeline. In applications where even more compactness is desirable, the triangle vertex indices (which take up two-thirds of the space in an indexed mesh with only positions at the vertices) can be expressed more efficiently using *triangle strips* and *triangle fans*.

A triangle fan is shown in Figure 12.9. In an indexed mesh, the triangles array would contain [(0, 1, 2), (0, 2, 3), (0, 3, 4), (0, 4, 5)]. We are storing 12 vertex indices, although there are only six distinct vertices. In a triangle fan, all the triangles share one common vertex, and the other vertices generate a set of triangles like the vanes of a collapsible fan. The fan in the figure could be specified with the sequence [0, 1, 2, 3, 4, 5]: the first vertex establishes the center, and subsequently each pair of adjacent vertices (1-2, 2-3, etc.) creates a triangle.

The triangle strip is a similar concept, but it is useful for a wider range of meshes. Here, vertices are added alternating top and bottom in a linear strip as shown in Figure 12.10. The triangle strip in the figure could be specified by the sequence [0 1 2 3 4 5 6 7], and every subsequence of three adjacent vertices (0-1-2, 1-2-3, etc.) creates a triangle. For consistent orientation, every other triangle needs to have its order reversed. In the example, this results in the triangles (0, 1, 2), (2, 1, 3), (2, 3, 4), (4, 3, 5), etc. For each new vertex that comes in, the oldest vertex is forgotten and the order of the two remaining vertices is swapped. See Figure 12.11 for a larger example.

Is this factor of two worth the complication? I think the answer is yes, and it becomes an even bigger win as soon as you start adding "properties" to the vertices.

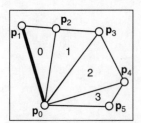

Figure 12.9. A triangle fan.

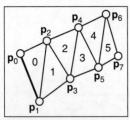

Figure 12.10. A triangle strip.

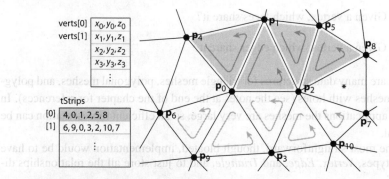

Figure 12.11. Two triangle strips in the context of a larger mesh. Note that neither strip can be extended to include the triangle marked with an asterisk.

In both strips and fans, $n + 2$ vertices suffice to describe n triangles—a substantial savings over the $3n$ vertices required by a standard indexed mesh. Long triangle strips will save approximately a factor of three if the program is vertex-bound.

It might seem that triangle strips are only useful if the strips are very long, but even relatively short strips already gain most of the benefits. The savings in storage space (for only the vertex indices) are as follows:

strip length	1	2	3	4	5	6	7	8	16	100	∞
relative size	1.00	0.67	0.56	0.50	0.47	0.44	0.43	0.42	0.38	0.34	0.33

So, in fact, there is a rather rapid diminishing return as the strips grow longer. Thus, even for an unstructured mesh, it is worthwhile to use some greedy algorithm to gather them into short strips.

12.1.4 Data Structures for Mesh Connectivity

Indexed meshes, strips, and fans are all good, compact representations for static meshes. However, they do not readily allow for meshes to be modified. In order to efficiently edit meshes, more complicated data structures are needed to efficiently answer queries such as:

- Given a triangle, what are the three adjacent triangles?
- Given an edge, which two triangles share it?

- Given a vertex, which faces share it?

- Given a vertex, which edges share it?

There are many data structures for triangle meshes, polygonal meshes, and polygonal meshes with holes (see the notes at the end of the chapter for references). In many applications the meshes are very large, so an efficient representation can be crucial.

The most straightforward, though bloated, implementation would be to have three types, *Vertex*, *Edge*, and *Triangle*, and to just store all the relationships directly:

```
Triangle {
  Vertex v[3]
  Edge e[3]
}

Edge {
  Vertex v[2]
  Triangle t[2]
}

Vertex {
  Triangle t[]
  Edge e[]
}
```

This lets us directly look up answers to the connectivity questions above, but because this information is all inter-related, it stores more than is really needed. Also, storing connectivity in vertices makes for variable-length data structures (since vertices can have arbitrary numbers of neighbors), which are generally less efficient to implement. Rather than committing to store all these relationships explicitly, it is best to define a class interface to answer these questions, behind which a more efficient data structure can hide. It turns out we can store only some of the connectivity and efficiently recover the other information when needed.

The fixed-size arrays in the Edge and Triangle classes suggest that it will be more efficient to store the connectivity information there. In fact, for polygon meshes, in which polygons have arbitrary numbers of edges and vertices, only edges have fixed-size connectivity information, which leads to many traditional mesh data structures being based on edges. But for triangle-only meshes, storing connectivity in the (less numerous) faces is appealing.

A good mesh data structure should be reasonably compact and allow efficient answers to all adjacency queries. Efficient means constant-time: the time to find neighbors should not depend on the size of the mesh. We'll look at three data structures for meshes, one based on triangles and two based on edges.

The Triangle-Neighbor Structure

We can create a compact mesh data structure based on triangles by augmenting the basic shared-vertex mesh with pointers from the triangles to the three neighboring triangles, and a pointer from each vertex to one of the adjacent triangles (it doesn't matter which one); see Figure 12.12:

```
Triangle {
    Triangle nbr[3];
    Vertex v[3];
}

Vertex {
    // ... per-vertex data ...
    Triangle t; // any adjacent tri
}
```

In the array Triangle.nbr, the kth entry points to the neighboring triangle that shares vertices k and $k + 1$. We call this structure the *triangle-neighbor struc-ture*. Starting from standard indexed mesh arrays, it can be implemented with two additional arrays: one that stores the three neighbors of each triangle, and one that stores a single neighboring triangle for each vertex. (See Figure 12.13 for an example):

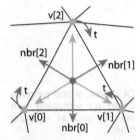

Figure 12.12. The ref-erences between triangles and vertices in the triangle neighbor structure.

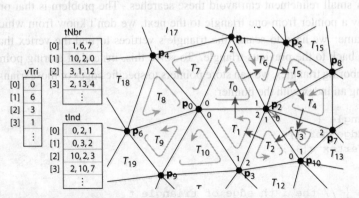

Figure 12.13. The triangle neighbor structure as encoded in arrays, and the sequence that is followed in traversing the neighboring triangles of vertex 2.

```
Mesh {
    // ... per-vertex data ...
    int tInd[nt][3]; // vertex indices
    int tNbr[nt][3]; // indices of neighbor triangles
    int vTri[nv]; // index of any adjacent triangle
}
```

Clearly the neighboring triangles and vertices of a triangle can be found directly in the data structure, but by using this triangle adjacency information carefully it is also possible to answer connectivity queries about vertices in constant time. The idea is to move from triangle to triangle, visiting only the triangles adjacent to the relevant vertex. If triangle t has vertex v as its kth vertex, then the triangle t.nbr[k] is the next triangle around v in the clockwise direction. This observation leads to the following algorithm to traverse all the triangles adjacent to a given vertex:

```
TrianglesOfVertex(v) {
    t = v.t
    do {
        find i such that (t.v[i] == v)
        t = t.nbr[i]
    } while (t != v.t)
}
```

Of course, a real program would *do* something with the triangles as it found them.

This operation finds each subsequent triangle in constant time—even though a search is required to find the position of the central vertex in each triangle's vertex list, the vertex lists have constant size so the search takes constant time. However, that search is awkward and requires extra branching.

A small refinement can avoid these searches. The problem is that once we follow a pointer from one triangle to the next, we don't know from which way we came: we have to search the triangle's vertices to find the vertex that connects back to the previous triangle. To solve this, instead of storing pointers to neighboring triangles, we can store pointers to specific edges of those triangles by storing an index with the pointer:

```
Triangle {
    Edge nbr[3];
    Vertex v[3];
}
```

```
Edge { // the i-th edge of triangle t
    Triangle t;
    int i;   // in {0,1,2}
}
```

```
Vertex {
    // ... per-vertex data ...
    Edge e;  // any edge leaving vertex
}
```

In practice the `Edge` is stored by borrowing two bits of storage from the triangle index t to store the edge index i, so that the total storage requirements remain the same.

In this structure the neighbor array for a triangle tells *which* of the neighboring triangles' edges are shared with the three edges of that triangle. With this extra information, we always know where to find the original triangle, which leads to an invariant of the data structure: for any jth edge of any triangle t,

$$t.\text{nbr}[j].t.\text{nbr}[t.\text{nbr}[j].i].t == t.$$

Knowing which edge we came in through lets us know immediately which edge to leave through in order to continue traversing around a vertex, leading to a stream-lined algorithm:

```
TrianglesOfVertex(v) {
    {t, i} = v.e;
    do {
        {t, i} = t.nbr[i];
    } while (t != v.t);
}
```

The triangle-neighbor structure is quite compact. For a mesh with only vertex positions, we are storing four numbers (three coordinates and an edge) per vertex and six (three vertex indices and three edges) per face, for a total of $4n_v + 6n_t \approx 16n_v$ units of storage per vertex, compared with $9n_v$ for the basic indexed mesh.

The triangle neighbor structure as presented here works only for manifold meshes, because it depends on returning to the starting triangle to terminate the traversal of a vertex's neighbors, which will not happen at a boundary vertex that doesn't have a full cycle of triangles. However, it is not difficult to generalize it to manifolds with boundary, by introducing a suitable sentinel value (such as -1) for the neighbors of boundary triangles and taking care that the boundary vertices point to the most counterclockwise neighboring triangle, rather than to any arbitrary triangle.

The Winged-Edge Structure

One widely used mesh data structure that stores connectivity information at the edges instead of the faces is the *winged-edge* data structure. This data struc-

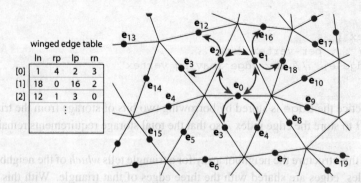

Figure 12.14. An example of a winged-edge mesh structure, stored in arrays.

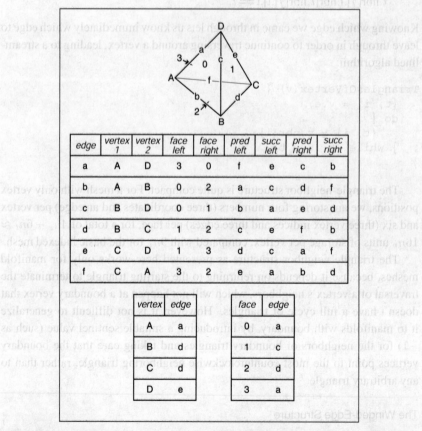

Figure 12.15. A tetrahedron and the associated elements for a winged-edge data structure. The two small tables are not unique; each vertex and face stores any one of the edges with which it is associated.

ture makes edges the first-class citizen of the data structure, as illustrated in Figures 12.14 and 12.15.

In a winged-edge mesh, each edge stores pointers to the two vertices it connects (the *head* and *tail* vertices), the two faces it is part of (the *left* and *right* faces), and, most importantly, the next and previous edges in the counterclockwise traversal of its left and right faces (Figure 12.16). Each vertex and face also stores a pointer to a single, arbitrary edge that connects to it:

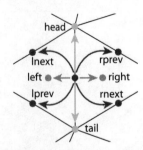

Figure 12.16. The references from an edge to the neighboring edges, faces, and vertices in the winged-edge structure.

```
Edge {
    Edge lprev, lnext, rprev, rnext;
    Vertex head, tail;
    Face left, right;
}

Face {
    // ... per-face data ...
    Edge e;  // any adjacent edge
}

Vertex {
    // ... per-vertex data ...
    Edge e;  // any incident edge
}
```

The winged-edge data structure supports constant-time access to the edges of a face or of a vertex, and from those edges the adjoining vertices or faces can be found:

```
EdgesOfVertex(v) {
    e = v.e;
    do {
        if (e.tail == v)
            e = e.lprev;
        else
            e = e.rprev;
    } while (e != v.e);
}

EdgesOfFace(f) {
    e = f.e;
    do {
        if (e.left == f)
            e = e.lnext;
        else
            e = e.rnext;
```

```
    } while (e != f.e);
}
```

These same algorithms and data structures will work equally well in a polygon mesh that isn't limited to triangles; this is one important advantage of edge-based structures.

As with any data structure, the winged-edge data structure makes a variety of time/space trade-offs. For example, we can eliminate the *prev* references. This makes it more difficult to traverse clockwise around faces or counterclockwise around vertices, but when we need to know the previous edge, we can always follow the successor edges in a circle until we get back to the original edge. This saves space, but it makes some operations slower. (See the chapter notes for more information on these tradeoffs).

The Half-Edge Structure

The winged-edge structure is quite elegant, but it has one remaining awkwardness — the need to constantly check which way the edge is oriented before moving to the next edge. This check is directly analogous to the search we saw in the basic version of the triangle neighbor structure: we are looking to find out whether we entered the present edge from the head or from the tail. The solution is also almost indistinguishable: rather than storing data for each edge, we store data for each *half-edge*. There is one half-edge for each of the two triangles that share an edge, and the two half-edges are oriented oppositely, each oriented consistently with its own triangle.

The data normally stored in an edge is split between the two half-edges. Each half-edge points to the face on its side of the edge and to the vertex at its head, and each contains the edge pointers for its face. It also points to its neighbor on the

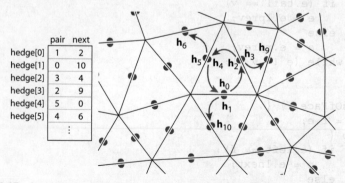

Figure 12.17. An example of a half-edge mesh structure, stored in arrays.

other side of the edge, from which the other half of the information can be found. Like the winged-edge, a half-edge can contain pointers to both the previous and next half-edges around its face, or only to the next half-edge. We'll show the example that uses a single pointer.

```
HEdge {
    HEdge pair, next;
    Vertex v;
    Face f;
}

Face {
    // ... per-face data ...
    HEdge h;  // any h-edge of this face
}

Vertex {
    // ... per-vertex data ...
    HEdge h;  // any h-edge pointing toward this vertex
}
```

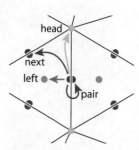

Figure 12.18. The references from a half-edge to its neighboring mesh components.

Traversing a half-edge structure is just like traversing a winged-edge structure except that we no longer need to check orientation, and we follow the *pair* pointer to access the edges in the opposite face.

```
EdgesOfVertex(v) {
    h = v.h;
    do {
        h = h.pair.next;
    } while (h != v.h);
}


EdgesOfFace(f) {
    h = f.h;
    do {
        h = h.next;
    } while (h != f.h);
}
```

The vertex traversal here is clockwise, which is necessary because of omitting the *prev* pointer from the structure.

Because half-edges are generally allocated in pairs (at least in a mesh with no boundaries), many implementations can do away with the *pair* pointers. For instance, in an implementation based on array indexing (such as shown in Figure 12.17), the array can be arranged so that an even-numbered edge i always pairs with edge $i + 1$ and an odd-numbered edge j always pairs with edge $j - 1$.

In addition to the simple traversal algorithms shown in this chapter, all three of these mesh topology structures can support "mesh surgery" operations of various sorts, such as splitting or collapsing vertices, swapping edges, adding or removing triangles, etc.

12.2   Scene Graphs

A triangle mesh manages a collection of triangles that constitute an object in a scene, but another universal problem in graphics applications is arranging the objects in the desired positions. As we saw in Chapter 6, this is done using transformations, but complex scenes can contain a great many transformations and organizing them well makes the scene much easier to manipulate. Most scenes admit to a hierarchical organization, and the transformations can be managed according to this hierarchy using a *scene graph*.

To motivate the scene-graph data structure, we will use the hinged pendulum shown in Figure 12.19. Consider how we would draw the top part of the pendulum:

$M_1 = \text{rotate}(\theta)$
$M_2 = \text{translate}(p)$
$M_3 = M_2 M_1$
Apply M_3 to all points in upper pendulum

The bottom is more complicated, but we can take advantage of the fact that it is attached to the bottom of the upper pendulum at point b in the local coordinate system. First, we rotate the lower pendulum so that it is at an angle ϕ relative to

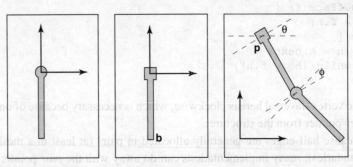

Figure 12.19. A hinged pendulum. On the left are the two pieces in their "local" coordinate systems. The hinge of the bottom piece is at point **b** and the attachment for the bottom piece is at its local origin. The degrees of freedom for the assembled object are the angles (θ, ϕ) and the location **p** of the top hinge.

its initial position. Then, we move it so that its top hinge is at point **b**. Now it is at the appropriate position in the local coordinates of the upper pendulum, and it can then be moved along with that coordinate system. The composite transform for the lower pendulum is:

$$\mathbf{M}_a = \text{rotate}(\phi)$$
$$\mathbf{M}_b = \text{translate}(\mathbf{b})$$
$$\mathbf{M}_c = \mathbf{M}_b\mathbf{M}_a$$
$$\mathbf{M}_d = \mathbf{M}_3\mathbf{M}_c$$

Apply $\mathbf{M}_d$ to all points in lower pendulum

Thus, we see that the lower pendulum not only lives in its own local coordinate system, but also that coordinate system itself is moved along with that of the upper pendulum.

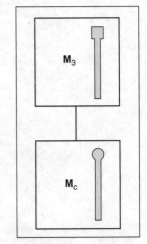

Figure 12.20. The scene graph for the hinged pendulum of Figure 12.19.

We can encode the pendulum in a data structure that makes management of these coordinate system issues easier, as shown in Figure 12.20. The appropriate matrix to apply to an object is just the product of all the matrices in the chain from the object to the root of the data structure. For example, consider the model of a ferry that has a car that can move freely on the deck of the ferry, and wheels that each move relative to the car as shown in Figure 12.21.

As with the pendulum, each object should be transformed by the product of the matrices in the path from the root to the object:

- **ferry** transform using M_0

- **car body** transform using M_0M_1

- **left wheel** transform using $M_0M_1M_2$

- **left wheel** transform using $M_0M_1M_3$

An efficient implementation can be achieved using a *matrix stack*, a data structure supported by many APIs. A matrix stack is manipulated using *push* and *pop* operations that add and delete matrices from the right-hand side of a matrix product. For example, calling:

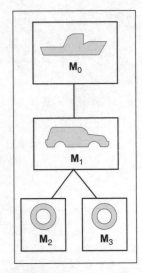

Figure 12.21. A ferry, a car on the ferry, and the wheels of the car (only two shown) are stored in a scene-graph.

push($\mathbf{M}_0$)
push($\mathbf{M}_1$)
push($\mathbf{M}_2$)

creates the active matrix $\mathbf{M} = \mathbf{M}_0\mathbf{M}_1\mathbf{M}_2$. A subsequent call to *pop()* strips the last matrix added so that the active matrix becomes $\mathbf{M} = \mathbf{M}_0\mathbf{M}_1$. Combining the matrix stack with a recursive traversal of a scene graph gives us:

```
function traverse(node)
push(M_local)
draw object using composite matrix from stack
traverse(left child)
traverse(right child)
pop()
```

There are many variations on scene graphs but all follow the basic idea above.

12.3   Spatial Data Structures

In many, if not all, graphics applications, the ability to quickly locate geometric objects in particular regions of space is important. Ray tracers need to find objects that intersect rays; interactive applications navigating an environment need to find the objects visible from any given viewpoint; games and physical simulations require detecting when and where objects collide. All these needs can be supported by various *spatial data structures* designed to organize objects in space so they can be looked up efficiently.

In this section we will discuss examples of three general classes of spatial data structures. Structures that group objects together into a hierarchy are *object partitioning* schemes: objects are divided into disjoint groups, but the groups may end up overlapping in space. Structures that divide space into disjoint regions are *space partitioning* schemes: space is divided into separate partitions, but one object may have to intersect more than one partition. Space partitioning schemes can be regular, in which space is divided into uniformly shaped pieces, or irregular, in which space is divided adaptively into irregular pieces, with smaller pieces where there are more and smaller objects.

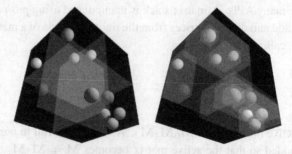

Figure 12.22.   Left: a uniform partitioning of space. Right: adaptive bounding-box hierarchy. *Image courtesy David DeMarle.*

We will use ray tracing as the primary motivation while discussing these structures, though they can all also be used for view culling or collision detection. In Chapter 4, all objects were looped over while checking for intersections. For N objects, this is an $O(N)$ linear search and is thus slow for large scenes. Like most search problems, the ray-object intersection can be computed in sub-linear time using "divide and conquer" techniques, provided we can create an ordered data structure as a preprocess. There are many techniques to do this.

This section discusses three of these techniques in detail: bounding volume hierarchies (Rubin & Whitted, 1980; Whitted, 1980; Goldsmith & Salmon, 1987), uniform spatial subdivision (Cleary et al., 1983; Fujimoto et al., 1986; Amanatides & Woo, 1987), and binary space partitioning (Glassner, 1984; Jansen, 1986; Havran, 2000). An example of the first two strategies is shown in Figure 12.22.

12.3.1 Bounding Boxes

A key operation in most intersection-acceleration schemes is computing the intersection of a ray with a bounding box (Figure 12.23). This differs from conventional intersection tests in that we do not need to know where the ray hits the box; we only need to know whether it hits the box.

To build an algorithm for ray-box intersection, we begin by considering a 2D ray whose direction vector has positive x and y components. We can generalize this to arbitrary 3D rays later. The 2D bounding box is defined by two horizontal and two vertical lines:

$$x = x_{\min},$$
$$x = x_{\max},$$
$$y = y_{\min},$$
$$y = y_{\max}.$$

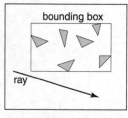

Figure 12.23. The ray is only tested for intersection with the surfaces if it hits the bounding box.

The points bounded by these lines can be described in interval notation:

$$(x, y) \in [x_{\min}, x_{\max}] \times [y_{\min}, y_{\max}].$$

As shown in Figure 12.24, the intersection test can be phrased in terms of these intervals. First, we compute the ray parameter where the ray hits the line $x = x_{\min}$:

$$t_{x\min} = \frac{x_{\min} - x_e}{x_d}.$$

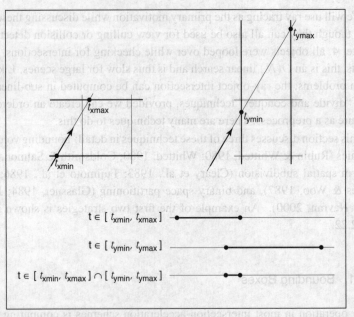

Figure 12.24. The ray will be inside the interval $x \in [x_{min}, x_{max}]$ for some interval in its parameter space $t \in [t_{xmin}, t_{xmax}]$. A similar interval exists for the y interval. The ray intersects the box if it is in both the x interval and y interval at the same time, i.e., the intersection of the two one-dimensional intervals is not empty.

We then make similar computations for t_{xmax}, t_{ymin}, and t_{ymax}. The ray hits the box if and only if the intervals $[t_{xmin}, t_{xmax}]$ and $[t_{ymin}, t_{ymax}]$ overlap, i.e., their intersection is non-empty. In pseudocode this algorithm is:

$$t_{xmin} = (x_{min} - x_e)/x_d$$
$$t_{xmax} = (x_{max} - x_e)/x_d$$
$$t_{ymin} = (y_{min} - y_e)/y_d$$
$$t_{ymax} = (y_{max} - y_e)/y_d$$
if $(t_{xmin} > t_{ymax})$ or $(t_{ymin} > t_{xmax})$ **then**
    return false
else
    return true

The if statement may seem non-obvious. To see the logic of it, note that there is no overlap if the first interval is either entirely to the right or entirely to the left of the second interval.

The first thing we must address is the case when x_d or y_d is negative. If x_d is negative, then the ray will hit x_{max} before it hits x_{min}. Thus the code for computing

t_{xmin} and t_{xmax} expands to:

if $(x_d \geq 0)$ **then**
$$t_{xmin} = (x_{min} - x_e)/x_d$$
$$t_{xmax} = (x_{max} - x_e)/x_d$$
else
$$t_{xmin} = (x_{max} - x_e)/x_d$$
$$t_{xmax} = (x_{min} - x_e)/x_d$$

A similar code expansion must be made for the y cases. A major concern is that horizontal and vertical rays have a zero value for y_d and x_d, respectively. This will cause divide by zero which may be a problem. However, before addressing this directly, we check whether IEEE floating point computation handles these cases gracefully for us. Recall from Section 1.5 the rules for divide by zero: for any positive real number a,

$$+a/0 = +\infty;$$
$$-a/0 = -\infty.$$

Consider the case of a vertical ray where $x_d = 0$ and $y_d > 0$. We can then calculate

$$t_{xmin} = \frac{x_{min} - x_e}{0};$$
$$t_{xmax} = \frac{x_{max} - x_e}{0}.$$

There are three possibilities of interest:

1. $x_e \leq x_{min}$ (no hit);

2. $x_{min} < x_e < x_{max}$ (hit);

3. $x_{max} \leq x_e$ (no hit).

For the first case we have

$$t_{xmin} = \frac{\text{positive number}}{0};$$
$$t_{xmax} = \frac{\text{positive number}}{0}.$$

This yields the interval $(t_{xmin}, t_{xmin}) = (\infty, \infty)$. That interval will not overlap with any interval, so there will be no hit, as desired. For the second case, we have

$$t_{xmin} = \frac{\text{negative number}}{0};$$
$$t_{xmax} = \frac{\text{positive number}}{0}.$$

This yields the interval $(t_{xmin}, t_{xmin}) = (-\infty, \infty)$ which will overlap with all intervals and thus will yield a hit as desired. The third case results in the interval $(-\infty, -\infty)$ which yields no hit, as desired. Because these cases work as desired, we need no special checks for them. As is often the case, IEEE floating point conventions are our ally. However, there is still a problem with this approach.

Consider the code segment:

if $(x_d \geq 0)$ **then**
$\quad t_{min} = (x_{min} - x_e)/x_d$
$\quad t_{max} = (x_{max} - x_e)/x_d$
else
$\quad t_{min} = (x_{max} - x_e)/x_d$
$\quad t_{max} = (x_{min} - x_e)/x_d$

This code breaks down when $x_d = -0$. This can be overcome by testing on the reciprocal of x_d (A. Williams et al., 2005):

$a = 1/x_d$
if $(a \geq 0)$ **then**
$\quad t_{min} = a(x_{min} - x_e)$
$\quad t_{max} = a(x_{max} - x_e)$
else
$\quad t_{min} = a(x_{max} - x_e)$
$\quad t_{max} = a(x_{min} - x_e)$

12.3.2 Hierarchical Bounding Boxes

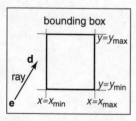

Figure 12.25. A 2D ray **e** + t**d** is tested against a 2D bounding box.

The basic idea of hierarchical bounding boxes can be seen by the common tactic of placing an axis-aligned 3D bounding box around all the objects as shown in Figure 12.25. Rays that hit the bounding box will actually be more expensive to compute than in a brute force search, because testing for intersection with the box is not free. However, rays that miss the box are cheaper than the brute force search. Such bounding boxes can be made hierarchical by partitioning the set of objects in a box and placing a box around each partition as shown in Figure 12.26. The data structure for the hierarchy shown in Figure 12.27 might be a tree with the large bounding box at the root and the two smaller bounding boxes as left and right subtrees. These would in turn each point to a list of three triangles. The intersection of a ray with this particular hard-coded tree would be:

$\quad$**if** (ray hits root box) **then**
$\quad\quad$**if** (ray hits left subtree box) **then**

      check three triangles for intersection
if (ray intersects right subtree box) **then**
      check other three triangles for intersection
if (an intersections returned from each subtree) **then**
      return the closest of the two hits
else if (a intersection is returned from exactly one subtree) **then**
      return that intersection
else
      return false
else
    return false

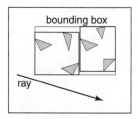

Figure 12.26. The bounding boxes can be nested by creating boxes around subsets of the model.

Some observations related to this algorithm are that there is no geometric ordering between the two subtrees, and there is no reason a ray might not hit both subtrees. Indeed, there is no reason that the two subtrees might not overlap.

A key point of such data hierarchies is that a box is guaranteed to bound all objects that are below it in the hierarchy, but they are *not* guaranteed to contain all objects that overlap it spatially, as shown in Figure 12.27. This makes this geometric search somewhat more complicated than a traditional binary search on strictly ordered one-dimensional data. The reader may note that several possible optimizations present themselves. We defer optimizations until we have a full hierarchical algorithm.

If we restrict the tree to be binary and require that each node in the tree have a bounding box, then this traversal code extends naturally. Further, assume that all nodes are either leaves in the tree and contain a primitive, or that they contain one or two subtrees.

The *bvh-node* class should be of type surface, so it should implement *surface::hit*. The data it contains should be simple:

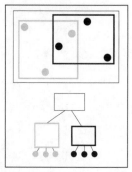

Figure 12.27. The gray box is a tree node that points to the three gray spheres, and the thick black box points to the three black spheres. Note that not all spheres enclosed by the box are guaranteed to be pointed to by the corresponding tree node.

class bvh-node subclass of surface
    virtual bool hit(ray $\mathbf{e} + t\mathbf{d}$, real t_0, real t_1, hit-record rec)
    virtual box bounding-box()
    surface-pointer left
    surface-pointer right
    box bbox

The traversal code can then be called recursively in an object-oriented style:

function bool bvh-node::hit(ray $\mathbf{a} + t\mathbf{b}$, real t_0, real t_1, hit-record rec)
    if (bbox.hitbox($\mathbf{a} + t\mathbf{b}$, t_0, t_1)) **then**
      hit-record lrec, rrec

left-hit = (left $\neq$ NULL) and (left $\rightarrow$ hit($\mathbf{a} + t\mathbf{b}, t_0, t_1$, lrec))
right-hit = (right $\neq$ NULL) and (right $\rightarrow$ hit($\mathbf{a} + t\mathbf{b}, t_0, t_1$, rrec))
if (left-hit and right-hit) **then**
   if (lrec.t < rrec.t) **then**
     rec = lrec
   else
     rec = rrec
   return true
else if (left-hit) **then**
   rec = lrec
   return true
else if (right-hit) **then**
   rec = rrec
   return true
else
     return false
  else
     return false

Note that because *left* and *right* point to surfaces rather than bvh-nodes specifically, we can let the virtual functions take care of distinguishing between internal and leaf nodes; the appropriate hit function will be called. Note that if the tree is built properly, we can eliminate the check for left being NULL. If we want to eliminate the check for right being NULL, we can replace NULL right pointers with a redundant pointer to left. This will end up checking left twice, but will eliminate the check throughout the tree. Whether that is worth it will depend on the details of tree construction.

There are many ways to build a tree for a bounding volume hierarchy. It is convenient to make the tree binary, roughly balanced, and to have the boxes of sibling subtrees not overlap too much. A heuristic to accomplish this is to sort the surfaces along an axis before dividing them into two sublists. If the axes are defined by an integer with $x = 0$, $y = 1$, and $z = 2$ we have:

```
function bvh-node::create(object-array A, int AXIS)
  N = A.length
  if (N= 1) then
    left = A[0]
    right = NULL
    bbox = bounding-box(A[0])
```

```
else if (N= 2) then
    left-node = A[0]
    right-node = A[1]
    bbox = combine(bounding-box(A[0]), bounding-box(A[1]))
else
    sort A by the object center along AXIS
    left= new bvh-node(A[0..N/2 − 1], (AXIS +1) mod 3)
    right = new bvh-node(A[N/2..N−1], (AXIS +1) mod 3)
    bbox = combine(left → bbox, right → bbox)
```

The quality of the tree can be improved by carefully choosing AXIS each time. One way to do this is to choose the axis such that the sum of the volumes of the bounding boxes of the two subtrees is minimized. This change compared to rotating through the axes will make little difference for scenes composed of isotopically distributed small objects, but it may help significantly in less well-behaved scenes. This code can also be made more efficient by doing just a partition rather than a full sort.

Another, and probably better, way to build the tree is to have the subtrees contain about the same amount of space rather than the same number of objects. To do this we partition the list based on space:

```
function bvh-node::create(object-array A, int AXIS)
    N = A.length
    if (N = 1) then
        left = A[0]
        right = NULL
        bbox = bounding-box(A[0])
    else if (N = 2) then
        left = A[0]
        right = A[1]
        bbox = combine(bounding-box(A[0]), bounding-box(A[1]))
    else
        find the midpoint m of the bounding box of A along AXIS
        partition A into lists with lengths k and (N-k) surrounding m
        left = new bvh-node(A[0..k], (AXIS +1) mod 3)
        right = new bvh-node(A[k+1..N−1], (AXIS +1) mod 3)
        bbox = combine(left → bbox, right → bbox)
```

Although this results in an unbalanced tree, it allows for easy traversal of empty space and is cheaper to build because partitioning is cheaper than sorting.

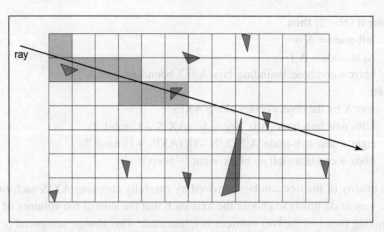

Figure 12.28.   In uniform spatial subdivision, the ray is tracked forward through cells until an object in one of those cells is hit. In this example, only objects in the shaded cells are checked.

12.3.3   Uniform Spatial Subdivision

Another strategy to reduce intersection tests is to divide space. This is fundamentally different from dividing objects as was done with hierarchical bounding volumes:

- In hierarchical bounding volumes, each object belongs to one of two sibling nodes, whereas a point in space may be inside both sibling nodes.
- In spatial subdivision, each point in space belongs to exactly one node, whereas objects may belong to many nodes.

In uniform spatial subdivision, the scene is partitioned into axis-aligned boxes. These boxes are all the same size, although they are not necessarily cubes. The ray traverses these boxes as shown in Figure 12.28. When an object is hit, the traversal ends.

The grid itself should be a subclass of surface and should be implemented as a 3D array of pointers to surface. For empty cells these pointers are NULL. For cells with one object, the pointer points to that object. For cells with more than one object, the pointer can point to a list, another grid, or another data structure, such as a bounding volume hierarchy.

This traversal is done in an incremental fashion. The regularity comes from the way that a ray hits each set of parallel planes, as shown in Figure 12.29. To see how this traversal works, first consider the 2D case where the ray direction has positive x and y components and starts outside the grid. Assume the grid is bounded by points $(x_{\min}, y_{\min})$ and $(x_{\max}, y_{\max})$. The grid has $n_x \times n_y$ cells.

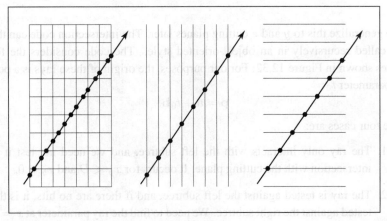

Figure 12.29. Although the pattern of cell hits seems irregular (left), the hits on sets of parallel planes are very even.

Our first order of business is to find the index (i, j) of the first cell hit by the ray $\mathbf{e} + t\mathbf{d}$. Then, we need to traverse the cells in an appropriate order. The key parts to this algorithm are finding the initial cell (i, j) and deciding whether to increment i or j (Figure 12.30). Note that when we check for an intersection with objects in a cell, we restrict the range of t to be within the cell (Figure 12.31). Most implementations make the 3D array of type "pointer to surface." To improve the locality of the traversal, the array can be tiled as discussed in Section 12.5.

12.3.4 Axis-Aligned Binary Space Partitioning

We can also partition space in a hierarchical data structure such as a *binary space partitioning tree* (BSP tree). This is similar to the BSP tree used for visibility sorting in Section 12.4, but it's most common to use axis-aligned, rather than polygon-aligned, cutting planes for ray intersection.

A node in this structure contains a single cutting plane and a left and right subtree. Each subtree contains all the objects on one side of the cutting plane. Objects that pass through the plane are stored in in both subtrees. If we assume the cutting plane is parallel to the yz plane at $x = D$, then the node class is:

class bsp-node subclass of surface
    virtual bool hit(ray $\mathbf{e} + t\mathbf{d}$, real t_0, real t_1, hit-record rec)
    virtual box bounding-box()
    surface-pointer left
    surface-pointer right
    real D

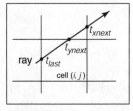

Figure 12.30. To decide whether we advance right or upwards, we keep track of the intersections with the next vertical and horizontal boundary of the cell.

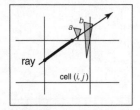

Figure 12.31. Only hits within the cell should be reported. Otherwise the case above would cause us to report hitting object b rather than object a.

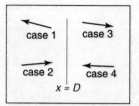

Figure 12.32. The four cases of how a ray relates to the BSP cutting plane $x = D$.

We generalize this to y and z cutting planes later. The intersection code can then be called recursively in an object-oriented style. The code considers the four cases shown in Figure 12.32. For our purposes, the origin of these rays is a point at parameter t_0:

$$\mathbf{p} = \mathbf{a} + t_0 \mathbf{b}.$$

The four cases are:

1. The ray only interacts with the left subtree, and we need not test it for intersection with the cutting plane. It occurs for $x_p < D$ and $x_b < 0$.

2. The ray is tested against the left subtree, and if there are no hits, it is then tested against the right subtree. We need to find the ray parameter at $x = D$, so we can make sure we only test for intersections within the subtree. This case occurs for $x_p < D$ and $x_b > 0$.

3. This case is analogous to case 1 and occurs for $x_p > D$ and $x_b > 0$.

4. This case is analogous to case 2 and occurs for $x_p > D$ and $x_b < 0$.

The resulting traversal code handling these cases in order is:

function bool bsp-node::hit(ray $\mathbf{a} + t\mathbf{b}$, real t_0, real t_1, hit-record rec)
$\quad x_p = x_a + t_0 x_b$
$\quad$**if** $(x_p < D)$ **then**
$\quad\quad$**if** $(x_b < 0)$ **then**
$\quad\quad\quad$**return** (left $\neq$ NULL) and (left$\rightarrow$hit($\mathbf{a} + t\mathbf{b}$, t_0, t_1, rec))
$\quad\quad t = (D - x_a)/x_b$
$\quad\quad$**if** $(t > t_1)$ **then**
$\quad\quad\quad$**return** (left $\neq$ NULL) and (left$\rightarrow$hit($\mathbf{a} + t\mathbf{b}$, t_0, t_1, rec))
$\quad\quad$**if** (left $\neq$ NULL) and (left$\rightarrow$hit($\mathbf{a} + t\mathbf{b}$, t_0, t, rec)) **then**
$\quad\quad\quad$**return** true
$\quad\quad$**return** (right $\neq$ NULL) and (right$\rightarrow$hit($\mathbf{a} + t\mathbf{b}$, t, t_1, rec))
$\quad$**else**
$\quad\quad$analogous code for cases 3 and 4

This is very clean code. However, to get it started, we need to hit some root object that includes a bounding box so we can initialize the traversal, t_0 and t_1. An issue we have to address is that the cutting plane may be along any axis. We can add an integer index *axis* to the *bsp-node* class. If we allow an indexing operator for points, this will result in some simple modifications to the code above, for example,

$$x_p = x_a + t_0 x_b$$

would become

$$u_p = a[\text{axis}] + t_0 b[\text{axis}]$$

which will result in some additional array indexing, but will not generate more branches.

While the processing of a single bsp-node is faster than processing a bvh-node, the fact that a single surface may exist in more than one subtree means there are more nodes and, potentially, a higher memory use. How "well" the trees are built determines which is faster. Building the tree is similar to building the BVH tree. We can pick axes to split in a cycle, and we can split in half each time, or we can try to be more sophisticated in how we divide.

12.4   BSP Trees for Visibility

Another geometric problem in which spatial data structures can be used is determining the visibility ordering of objects in a scene with changing viewpoint.

If we are making many images of a fixed scene composed of planar polygons, from different viewpoints—as is often the case for applications such as games— we can use a *binary space partitioning* scheme closely related to the method for ray intersection discussed in the previous section. The difference is that for visibility sorting we use non–axis-aligned splitting planes, so that the planes can be made coincident with the polygons. This leads to an elegant algorithm known as the BSP tree algorithm to order the surfaces from front to back. The key aspect of the BSP tree is that it uses a preprocess to create a data structure that is useful for any viewpoint. So, as the viewpoint changes, the same data structure is used without change.

12.4.1   Overview of BSP Tree Algorithm

The BSP tree algorithm is an example of a *painter's algorithm*. A painter's algorithm draws every object from back-to-front, with each new polygon potentially overdrawing previous polygons, as is shown in Figure 12.33. It can be implemented as follows:

    sort objects back to front relative to viewpoint
    for each object **do**
        draw object on screen

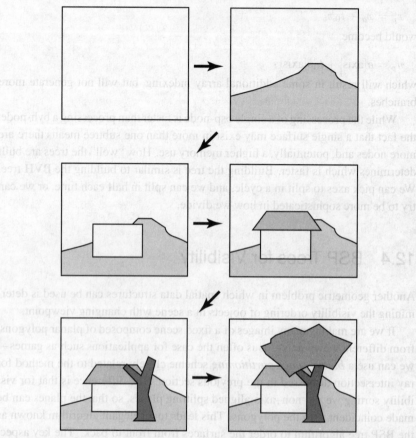

Figure 12.33. A painter's algorithm starts with a blank image and then draws the scene one object at a time from back-to-front, overdrawing whatever is already there. This automatically eliminates hidden surfaces.

Figure 12.34. A cycle occurs if a global back-to-front ordering is not possible for a particular eye position.

The problem with the first step (the sort) is that the relative order of multiple objects is not always well defined, even if the order of every pair of objects is. This problem is illustrated in Figure 12.34 where the three triangles form a *cycle*.

The BSP tree algorithm works on any scene composed of polygons where no polygon crosses the plane defined by any other polygon. This restriction is then relaxed by a preprocessing step. For the rest of this discussion, triangles are assumed to be the only primitive, but the ideas extend to arbitrary polygons.

The basic idea of the BSP tree can be illustrated with two triangles, T_1 and T_2. We first recall (see Section 2.5.3) the implicit plane equation of the plane containing T_1: $f_1(\mathbf{p}) = 0$. The key property of implicit planes that we wish to take advantage of is that for all points $\mathbf{p}^+$ on one side of the plane, $f_1(\mathbf{p}^+) > 0$;

and for all points $\mathbf{p}^-$ on the other side of the plane, $f_1(\mathbf{p}^-) < 0$. Using this property, we can find out on which side of the plane T_2 lies. Again, this assumes all three vertices of T_2 are on the same side of the plane. For discussion, assume that T_2 is on the $f_1(\mathbf{p}) < 0$ side of the plane. Then, we can draw T_1 and T_2 in the right order for any eyepoint $\mathbf{e}$:

if $(f_1(\mathbf{e}) < 0)$ **then**
    draw T_1
    draw T_2
else
    draw T_2
    draw T_1

The reason this works is that if T_2 and $\mathbf{e}$ are on the same side of the plane containing T_1, there is no way for T_2 to be fully or partially blocked by T_1 as seen from $\mathbf{e}$, so it is safe to draw T_1 first. If $\mathbf{e}$ and T_2 are on opposite sides of the plane containing T_1, then T_2 cannot fully or partially block T_1, and the opposite drawing order is safe (Figure 12.35).

This observation can be generalized to many objects provided none of them span the plane defined by T_1. If we use a binary tree data structure with T_1 as root, the *negative* branch of the tree contains all the triangles whose vertices have $f_i(\mathbf{p}) < 0$, and the *positive* branch of the tree contains all the triangles whose vertices have $f_i(\mathbf{p}) > 0$. We can draw in proper order as follows:

function draw(bsptree tree, point e)
  if (tree.empty) **then**
    return

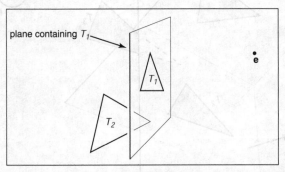

Figure 12.35. When $\mathbf{e}$ and T_2 are on opposite sides of the plane containing T_1, then it is safe to draw T_2 first and T_1 second. If $\mathbf{e}$ and T_2 are on the same side of the plane, then T_1 should be drawn before T_2. This is the core idea of the BSP tree algorithm.

if $(f_{\text{tree.root}}(\mathbf{e}) < 0)$ **then**
    draw(tree.plus, **e**)
    rasterize tree.triangle
    draw(tree.minus, **e**)
else
    draw(tree.minus, **e**)
    rasterize tree.triangle
    draw(tree.plus, **e**)

The nice thing about that code is that it will work for any viewpoint **e**, so the tree can be precomputed. Note that, if each subtree is itself a tree, where the root triangle divides the other triangles into two groups relative to the plane containing it, the code will work as is. It can be made slightly more efficient by terminating the recursive calls one level higher, but the code will still be simple. A tree illustrating this code is shown in Figure 12.36. As discussed in Section 2.5.5, the implicit equation for a point **p** on a plane containing three non-colinear points **a**, **b**, and **c** is

$$f(\mathbf{p}) = ((\mathbf{b} - \mathbf{a}) \times (\mathbf{c} - \mathbf{a})) \cdot (\mathbf{p} - \mathbf{a}) = 0. \qquad (12.1)$$

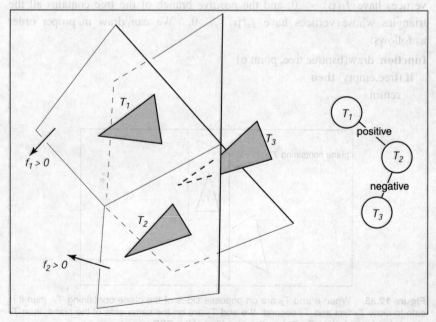

Figure 12.36. Three triangles and a BSP tree that is valid for them. The "positive" and "negative" are encoded by right and left subtree position, respectively.

It can be faster to store the (A, B, C, D) of the implicit equation of the form

$$f(x, y, z) = Ax + By + Cz + D = 0. \qquad (12.2)$$

Equations (12.1) and (12.2) are equivalent, as is clear when you recall that the gradient of the implicit equation is the normal to the triangle. The gradient of Equation (12.2) is $\mathbf{n} = (A, B, C)$ which is just the normal vector

$$\mathbf{n} = (\mathbf{b} - \mathbf{a}) \times (\mathbf{c} - \mathbf{a}).$$

We can solve for D by plugging in any point on the plane, e.g., $\mathbf{a}$:

$$D = -Ax_a - By_a - Cz_a$$

$$= -\mathbf{n} \cdot \mathbf{a}.$$

This suggests the form:

$$f(\mathbf{p}) = \mathbf{n} \cdot \mathbf{p} - \mathbf{n} \cdot \mathbf{a}$$

$$= \mathbf{n} \cdot (\mathbf{p} - \mathbf{a})$$

$$= 0,$$

which is the same as Equation (12.1) once you recall that $\mathbf{n}$ is computed using the cross product. Which form of the plane equation you use and whether you store only the vertices, $\mathbf{n}$ and the vertices, or $\mathbf{n}$, D, and the vertices, is probably a matter of taste—a classic time-storage tradeoff that will be settled best by profiling. For debugging, using Equation (12.1) is probably the best.

The only issue that prevents the code above from working in general is that one cannot guarantee that a triangle can be uniquely classified on one side of a plane or the other. It can have two vertices on one side of the plane and the third on the other. Or it can have vertices on the plane. This is handled by splitting the triangle into smaller triangles using the plane to "cut" them.

12.4.2   Building the Tree

If none of the triangles in the dataset cross each other's planes, so that all triangles are on one side of all other triangles, a BSP tree that can be traversed using the code above can be built using the following algorithm:

> tree-root = node(T_1)
> **for** $i \in \{2, \ldots, N\}$ **do**
>   tree-root.add(T_i)

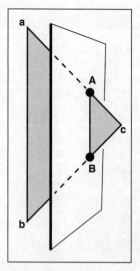

Figure 12.37. When a triangle spans a plane, there will be one vertex on one side and two on the other.

```
function  add ( triangle T )
    if (f(a) < 0 and f(b) < 0 and f(c) < 0) then
        if (negative subtree is empty) then
            negative-subtree = node(T)
        else
            negative-subtree.add (T)
    else if (f(a) > 0 and f(b) > 0 and f(c) > 0) then
        if positive subtree is empty then
            positive-subtree = node(T)
        else
            positive-subtree.add (T)
    else
        we have assumed this case is impossible
```

The only thing we need to fix is the case where the triangle crosses the dividing plane, as shown in Figure 12.37. Assume, for simplicity, that the triangle has vertices $\mathbf{a}$ and $\mathbf{b}$ on one side of the plane, and vertex $\mathbf{c}$ is on the other side. In this case, we can find the intersection points $\mathbf{A}$ and $\mathbf{B}$ and cut the triangle into three new triangles with vertices

$$T_1 = (\mathbf{a}, \mathbf{b}, \mathbf{A}),$$
$$T_2 = (\mathbf{b}, \mathbf{B}, \mathbf{A}),$$
$$T_3 = (\mathbf{A}, \mathbf{B}, \mathbf{c}),$$

as shown in Figure 12.38. This order of vertices is important so that the direction of the normal remains the same as for the original triangle. If we assume that $f(\mathbf{c}) < 0$, the following code could add these three triangles to the tree assuming the positive and negative subtrees are not empty:

```
positive-subtree = node (T_1)
positive-subtree = node (T_2)
negative-subtree = node (T_3)
```

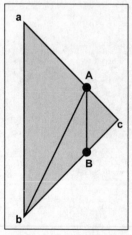

Figure 12.38. When a triangle is cut, we break it into three triangles, none of which span the cutting plane.

A precision problem that will plague a naive implementation occurs when a vertex is very near the splitting plane. For example, if we have two vertices on one side of the splitting plane and the other vertex is only an extremely small distance on the other side, we will create a new triangle almost the same as the old one, a triangle that is a sliver, and a triangle of almost zero size. It would be better to detect this as a special case and not split into three new triangles. One might expect this case to be rare, but because many models have tessellated planes and triangles with shared vertices, it occurs frequently, and thus must be handled carefully. Some simple manipulations that accomplish this are:

function add(triangle T)
   fa = $f(\mathbf{a})$
   fb = $f(\mathbf{b})$
   fc = $f(\mathbf{c})$
   if $(abs(fa) < \epsilon)$ **then**
     fa = 0
   if $(abs(fb) < \epsilon)$ **then**
     fb = 0
   if $(abs(fc) < \epsilon)$ **then**
     fc = 0
   if $(fa \leq 0$ and fb ≤ 0 and fc $\leq 0)$ **then**
     if (negative subtree is empty) **then**
       negative-subtree = node(T)
     else
       negative-subtree.add(T)
   else if $(fa \geq 0$ and fb ≥ 0 and fc $\geq 0)$ **then**
     if (positive subtree is empty) **then**
       positive-subtree = node(T)
     else
       positive-subtree.add(T)
   else
     cut triangle into three triangles and add to each side

This takes any vertex whose f value is within ϵ of the plane and counts it as positive or negative. The constant ϵ is a small positive real chosen by the user. The technique above is a rare instance where testing for floating-point equality is useful and works because the zero value is set rather than being computed. Comparing for equality with a computed floating-point value is almost never advisable, but we are not doing that.

12.4.3   Cutting Triangles

Filling out the details of the last case "cut triangle into three triangles and add to each side" is straightforward, but tedious. We should take advantage of the BSP tree construction as a preprocess where highest efficiency is not key. Instead, we should attempt to have a clean compact code. A nice trick is to force many of the cases into one by ensuring that **c** is on one side of the plane and the other two vertices are on the other. This is easily done with swaps. Filling out the details in the final else statement (assuming the subtrees are non-empty for simplicity) gives:

if $(fa * fc \geq 0)$ **then**
    swap(fb, fc)
    swap$(\mathbf{b}, \mathbf{c})$
    swap(fa, fb)
    swap$(\mathbf{a}, \mathbf{b})$
else if $(fb * fc \geq 0)$ **then**
    swap(fa, fc)
    swap$(\mathbf{a}, \mathbf{c})$
    swap(fa, fb)
    swap$(\mathbf{a}, \mathbf{b})$
compute $\mathbf{A}$
compute $\mathbf{B}$
$T_1 = (\mathbf{a}, \mathbf{b}, \mathbf{A})$
$T_2 = (\mathbf{b}, \mathbf{B}, \mathbf{A})$
$T_3 = (\mathbf{A}, \mathbf{B}, \mathbf{c})$
if $(fc \geq 0)$ **then**
    negative-subtree.add(T_1)
    negative-subtree.add(T_2)
    positive-subtree.add(T_3)
else
    positive-subtree.add(T_1)
    positive-subtree.add(T_2)
    negative-subtree.add(T_3)

This code takes advantage of the fact that the product of a and b are positive if they have the same sign—thus, the first if statement. If vertices are swapped, we must do two swaps to keep the vertices ordered counterclockwise. Note that exactly one of the vertices may lie exactly on the plane, in which case the code above will work, but one of the generated triangles will have zero area. This can be handled by ignoring the possibility, which is not that risky, because the rasterization code must handle zero-area triangles in screen space (i.e., edge-on triangles). You can also add a check that does not add zero-area triangles to the tree. Finally, you can put in a special case for when exactly one of fa, fb, and fc is zero which cuts the triangle into two triangles.

To compute $\mathbf{A}$ and $\mathbf{B}$, a line segment and implicit plane intersection is needed. For example, the parametric line connecting $\mathbf{a}$ and $\mathbf{c}$ is

$$\mathbf{p}(t) = \mathbf{a} + t(\mathbf{c} - \mathbf{a}).$$

The point of intersection with the plane $\mathbf{n} \cdot \mathbf{p} + D = 0$ is found by plugging $\mathbf{p}(t)$ into the plane equation:

$$\mathbf{n} \cdot (\mathbf{a} + t(\mathbf{c} - \mathbf{a})) + D = 0,$$

and solving for t:

$$t = -\frac{\mathbf{n} \cdot \mathbf{a} + D}{\mathbf{n} \cdot (\mathbf{c} - \mathbf{a})}.$$

Calling this solution t_A, we can write the expression for $\mathbf{A}$:

$$\mathbf{A} = \mathbf{a} + t_A(\mathbf{c} - \mathbf{a}).$$

A similar computation will give $\mathbf{B}$.

12.4.4   Optimizing the Tree

The efficiency of tree creation is much less of a concern than tree traversal because it is a preprocess. The traversal of the BSP tree takes time proportional to the number of nodes in the tree. (How well balanced the tree is does not matter.) There will be one node for each triangle, including the triangles that are created as a result of splitting. This number can depend on the order in which triangles are added to the tree. For example, in Figure 12.39, if T_1 is the root, there will be two nodes in the tree, but if T_2 is the root, there will be more nodes, because T_1 will be split.

It is difficult to find the "best" order of triangles to add to the tree. For N triangles, there are $N!$ orderings that are possible. So trying all orderings is not usually feasible. Alternatively, some predetermined number of orderings can be tried from a random collection of permutations, and the best one can be kept for the final tree.

The splitting algorithm described above splits one triangle into three triangles. It could be more efficient to split a triangle into a triangle and a convex quadrilateral. This is probably not worth it if all input models have only triangles, but would be easy to support for implementations that accommodate arbitrary polygons.

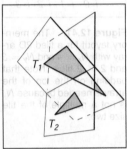

Figure 12.39.   Using T_1 as the root of a BSP tree will result in a tree with two nodes. Using T_2 as the root will require a cut and thus make a larger tree.

12.5   Tiling Multidimensional Arrays

Effectively utilizing the memory hierarchy is a crucial task in designing algorithms for modern architectures. Making sure that multidimensional arrays have

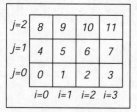

Figure 12.40. The memory layout for an untiled 2D array with $N_x = 4$ and $N_y = 3$.

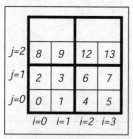

Figure 12.41. The memory layout for a tiled 2D array with $N_x = 4$ and $N_y = 3$ and 2×2 tiles. Note that padding on the top of the array is needed because N_y is not a multiple of the tile size two.

data in a "nice" arrangement is accomplished by *tiling*, sometimes also called *bricking*. A traditional 2D array is stored as a 1D array together with an indexing mechanism; for example, an N_x by N_y array is stored in a 1D array of length $N_x N_y$ and the 2D index (x, y) (which runs from $(0, 0)$ to $(N_x - 1, N_y - 1)$) maps to the 1D index (running from 0 to $N_x N_y - 1$) using the formula

$$\text{index} = x + N_x y.$$

An example of how that memory lays out is shown in Figure 12.40. A problem with this layout is that although two adjacent array elements that are in the same row are next to each other in memory, two adjacent elements in the same column will be separated by N_x elements in memory. This can cause poor memory locality for large N_x. The standard solution to this is to use *tiles* to make memory locality for rows and columns more equal. An example is shown in Figure 12.41 where 2×2 tiles are used. The details of indexing such an array are discussed in the next section. A more complicated example, with two levels of tiling on a 3D array, is covered after that.

A key question is what size to make the tiles. In practice, they should be similar to the memory-unit size on the machine. For example, if we are using 16-bit (2-byte) data values on a machine with 128-byte cache lines, 8×8 tiles fit exactly in a cache line. However, using 32-bit floating-point numbers, which fit 32 elements to a cache line, 5×5 tiles are a bit too small and 6×6 tiles are a bit too large. Because there are also coarser-sized memory units such as pages, hierarchical tiling with similar logic can be useful.

12.5.1 One-Level Tiling for 2D Arrays

If we assume an $N_x \times N_y$ array decomposed into square $n \times n$ tiles (Figure 12.42), then the number of tiles required is

$$B_x = N_x/n,$$
$$B_y = N_y/n.$$

Here, we assume that n divides N_x and N_y exactly. When this is not true, the array should be *padded*. For example, if $N_x = 15$ and $n = 4$, then N_x should be changed to 16. To work out a formula for indexing such an array, we first find the tile indices (b_x, b_y) that give the row/column for the tiles (the tiles themselves form a 2D array):

$$b_x = x \div n,$$
$$b_y = y \div n,$$

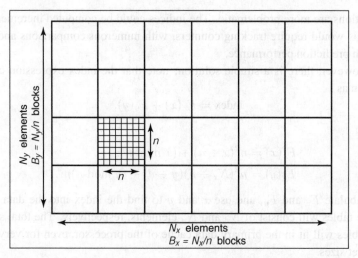

Figure 12.42. A tiled 2D array composed of $B_x \times B_y$ tiles each of size n by n.

where $\div$ is integer division, e.g., $12 \div 5 = 2$. If we order the tiles along rows as shown in Figure 12.40, then the index of the first element of the tile (b_x, b_y) is

$$\text{index} = n^2 (B_x b_y + b_x).$$

The memory in that tile is arranged like a traditional 2D array as shown in Figure 12.41. The partial offsets (x', y') inside the tile are

$$x' = x \bmod n,$$
$$y' = y \bmod n,$$

where mod is the remainder operator, e.g., $12 \bmod 5 = 2$. Therefore, the offset inside the tile is

$$\text{offset} = y'n + x'.$$

Thus the full formula for finding the 1D index element (x, y) in an $N_x \times N_y$ array with $n \times n$ tiles is

$$\text{index} = n^2 (B_x b_y + b_x) + y'n + x',$$
$$= n^2 ((N_x \div n)(y \div n) + x \div n) + (y \bmod n)n + (x \bmod n).$$

This expression contains many integer multiplication, divide and modulus operations, which are costly on some processors. When n is a power of two, these operations can be converted to bitshifts and bitwise logical operations. However, as noted above, the ideal size is not always a power of two. Some of the multiplications can be converted to shift/add operations, but the divide and modulus operations are more problematic. The indices could be computed incrementally, but this would require tracking counters, with numerous comparisons and poor branch prediction performance.

However, there is a simple solution; note that the index expression can be written as

$$\text{index} = F_x(x) + F_y(y),$$

where

$$F_x(x) = n^2(x \div n) + (x \bmod n),$$
$$F_y(y) = n^2(N_x \div n)(y \div n) + (y \bmod n)n.$$

We tabulate F_x and F_y, and use x and y to find the index into the data array. These tables will consist of N_x and N_y elements, respectively. The total size of the tables will fit in the primary data cache of the processor, even for very large data set sizes.

12.5.2 Example: Two-Level Tiling for 3D Arrays

Effective TLB utilization is also becoming a crucial factor in algorithm performance. The same technique can be used to improve TLB hit rates in a 3D array by creating $m \times m \times m$ bricks of $n \times n \times n$ cells. For example, a $40 \times 20 \times 19$ volume could be decomposed into $4 \times 2 \times 2$ macrobricks of $2 \times 2 \times 2$ bricks of $5 \times 5 \times 5$ cells. This corresponds to $m = 2$ and $n = 5$. Because 19 cannot be factored by $mn = 10$, one level of padding is needed. Empirically useful sizes are $m = 5$ for 16 bit datasets and $m = 6$ for float datasets.

The resulting index into the data array can be computed for any (x, y, z) triple with the expression

$$
\begin{aligned}
\text{index} = \ & ((x \div n) \div m)n^3 m^3((N_z \div n) \div m)((N_y \div n) \div m) \\
& + ((y \div n) \div m)n^3 m^3((N_z \div n) \div m) \\
& + ((z \div n) \div m)n^3 m^3 \\
& + ((x \div n) \bmod m)n^3 m^2 \\
& + ((y \div n) \bmod m)n^3 m \\
& + ((z \div n) \bmod m)n^3 \\
& + (x \bmod (n^2))n^2 \\
& + (y \bmod n)n \\
& + (z \bmod n),
\end{aligned}
$$

where N_x, N_y and N_z are the respective sizes of the dataset.

TLB: translation lookaside buffer, a cache that is part of the virtual memory system.

Note that, as in the simpler 2D one-level case, this expression can be written as

$$index = F_x(x) + F_y(y) + F_z(z),$$

where

$$
\begin{aligned}
F_x(x) &= ((x \div n) \div m)n^3 m^3 ((N_z \div n) \div m)((N_y \div n) \div m) \\
&\quad + ((x \div n) \bmod m)n^3 m^2 \\
&\quad + (x \bmod n)n^2, \\
F_y(y) &= ((y \div n) \div m)n^3 m^3 ((N_z \div n) \div m) \\
&\quad + ((y \div n) \bmod m)n^3 m + \\
&\quad + (y \bmod n)n, \\
F_z(z) &= ((z \div n) \div m)n^3 m^3 \\
&\quad + ((z \div n) \bmod m)n^3 \\
&\quad + (z \bmod n).
\end{aligned}
$$

Frequently Asked Questions

• Does tiling really make that much difference in performance?

On some volume rendering applications, a two-level tiling strategy made as much as a factor-of-ten performance difference. When the array does not fit in main memory, it can effectively prevent thrashing in some applications such as image editing.

• How do I store the lists in a winged-edge structure?

For most applications it is feasible to use arrays and indices for the references. However, if many delete operations are to be performed, then it is wise to use linked lists and pointers.

Notes

The discussion of the winged-edge data structure is based on the course notes of *Ching-Kuang Shene* (Shene, 2003). There are smaller mesh data structures than winged-edge. The trade-offs in using such structures is discussed in *Directed Edges—A Scalable Representation for Triangle Meshes* (Campagna et al., 1998).

The tiled-array discussion is based on *Interactive Ray Tracing for Volume Visualization* (Parker, Martin, et al., 1999). A structure similar to the triangle neighbor structure is discussed in a technical report by Charles Loop (Loop, 2000). A discussion of manifolds can be found in an introductory topology text (Munkres, 2000).

Exercises

1. What is the memory difference for a simple tetrahedron stored as four independent triangles and one stored in a winged-edge data structure?

2. Diagram a scene graph for a bicycle.

3. How many look-up tables are needed for a single-level tiling of an n-dimensional array?

4. Given N triangles, what is the minimum number of triangles that could be added to a resulting BSP tree? What is the maximum number?

13

More Ray Tracing

A ray tracer is a great substrate on which to build all kinds of advanced rendering effects. Many effects that take significant work to fit into the object-order rasterization framework, including basics like the shadows and reflections already presented in Chapter 4, are simple and elegant in a ray tracer. In this chapter we discuss some fancier techniques that can be used to ray-trace a wider variety of scenes and to include a wider variety of effects. Some extensions allow more general geometry: instancing and constructive solid geometry (CSG) are two ways to make models more complex with minimal complexity added to the program. Other extensions add to the range of materials we can handle: refraction through transparent materials, like glass and water, and glossy reflections on a variety of surfaces are essential for realism in many scenes.

This chapter also discusses the general framework of *distribution ray tracing* (Cook et al., 1984), a powerful extension to the basic ray-tracing idea in which multiple random rays are sent through each pixel in an image to produce images with smooth edges and to simply and elegantly (if slowly) produce a wide range of effects from soft shadows to camera depth-of-field.

The price of the elegance of ray tracing is exacted in terms of computer time: most of these extensions will trace a very large number of rays for any non-trivial scene. Because of this, it's crucial to use the methods described in Chapter 12 to accelerate the tracing of rays.

If you start with a brute-force ray intersection loop, you'll have ample time to implement an acceleration structure while you wait for images to render.

13.1 Transparency and Refraction

In Chapter 4 we discussed the use of recursive ray tracing to compute specular, or mirror, reflection from surfaces. Another type of specular object is a *dielectric*—a transparent material that refracts light. Diamonds, glass, water, and air are dielectrics. Dielectrics also filter light; some glass filters out more red and blue light than green light, so the glass takes on a green tint. When a ray travels from a medium with refractive index n into one with a refractive index n_t, some of the light is transmitted, and it bends. This is shown for $n_t > n$ in Figure 13.1. Snell's law tells us that

$$n \sin \theta = n_t \sin \phi.$$

Example values of n:
air: 1.00;
water: 1.33–1.34;
window glass: 1.51;
optical glass: 1.49–1.92;
diamond: 2.42.

Computing the sine of an angle between two vectors is usually not as convenient as computing the cosine, which is a simple dot product for the unit vectors such as we have here. Using the trigonometric identity $\sin^2 \theta + \cos^2 \theta = 1$, we can derive a refraction relationship for cosines:

$$\cos^2 \phi = 1 - \frac{n^2 \left(1 - \cos^2 \theta\right)}{n_t^2}.$$

Note that if n and n_t are reversed, then so are θ and ϕ as shown on the right of Figure 13.1.

To convert $\sin \phi$ and $\cos \phi$ into a 3D vector, we can set up a 2D orthonormal basis in the plane of the surface normal, $\mathbf{n}$, and the ray direction, $\mathbf{d}$.

From Figure 13.2, we can see that $\mathbf{n}$ and $\mathbf{b}$ form an orthonormal basis for the plane of refraction. By definition, we can describe the direction of the transformed

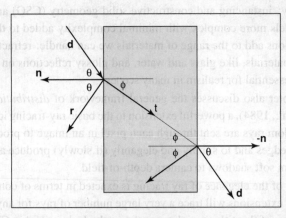

Figure 13.1. Snell's Law describes how the angle ϕ depends on the angle θ and the refractive indices of the object and the surrounding medium.

ray, $\mathbf{t}$, in terms of this basis:

$$\mathbf{t} = \sin\phi\,\mathbf{b} - \cos\phi\,\mathbf{n}.$$

Since we can describe $\mathbf{d}$ in the same basis, and $\mathbf{d}$ is known, we can solve for $\mathbf{b}$:

$$\mathbf{d} = \sin\theta\,\mathbf{b} - \cos\theta\,\mathbf{n},$$
$$\mathbf{b} = \frac{\mathbf{d} + \mathbf{n}\cos\theta}{\sin\theta}.$$

This means that we can solve for $\mathbf{t}$ with known variables:

$$\mathbf{t} = \frac{n\,(\mathbf{d} + \mathbf{n}\cos\theta))}{n_t} - \mathbf{n}\cos\phi$$
$$= \frac{n\,(\mathbf{d} - \mathbf{n}(\mathbf{d}\cdot\mathbf{n}))}{n_t} - \mathbf{n}\sqrt{1 - \frac{n^2\,(1 - (\mathbf{d}\cdot\mathbf{n})^2)}{n_t^2}}.$$

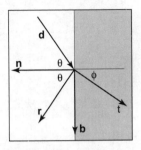

Figure 13.2. The vectors $\mathbf{n}$ and $\mathbf{b}$ form a 2D orthonormal basis that is parallel to the transmission vector $\mathbf{t}$.

Note that this equation works regardless of which of n and n_t is larger. An immediate question is, "What should you do if the number under the square root is negative?" In this case, there is no refracted ray and all of the energy is reflected. This is known as *total internal reflection*, and it is responsible for much of the rich appearance of glass objects.

The reflectivity of a dielectric varies with the incident angle according to the *Fresnel equations*. A nice way to implement something close to the Fresnel equations is to use the *Schlick approximation* (Schlick, 1994a),

$$R(\theta) = R_0 + (1 - R_0)\,(1 - \cos\theta)^5,$$

where R_0 is the reflectance at normal incidence:

$$R_0 = \left(\frac{n_t - 1}{n_t + 1}\right)^2.$$

Note that the $\cos\theta$ terms above are always for the angle in air (the larger of the internal and external angles relative to the normal).

For homogeneous impurities, as is found in typical colored glass, a light-carrying ray's intensity will be attenuated according to *Beer's Law*. As the ray travels through the medium it loses intensity according to $dI = -CI\,dx$, where dx is distance. Thus, $dI/dx = -CI$. We can solve this equation and get the exponential $I = k\exp(-Cx) + k'$. The degree of attenuation is described by the RGB attenuation constant a, which is the amount of attenuation after one unit of distance. Putting in boundary conditions, we know that $I(0) = I_0$, and

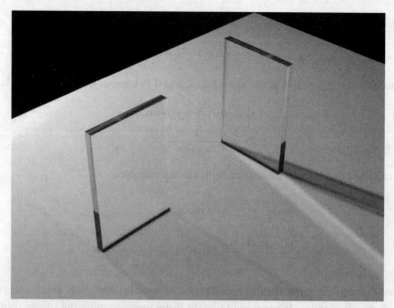

Figure 13.3. The color of the glass is affected by total internal reflection and Beer's Law. The amount of light transmitted and reflected is determined by the Fresnel equations. The complex lighting on the ground plane was computed using particle tracing as described in Chapter 24. (See also Plate IV.)

$I(1) = aI(0)$. The former implies $I(x) = I_0 \exp(-Cx)$. The latter implies $I_0 a = I_0 \exp(-C)$, so $-C = \ln(a)$. Thus, the final formula is

$$I(s) = I(0)e^{-\ln(a)s},$$

where $I(s)$ is the intensity of the beam at distance s from the interface. In practice, we reverse-engineer a by eye, because such data is rarely easy to find. The effect of Beer's Law can be seen in Figure 13.3, where the glass takes on a green tint.

To add transparent materials to our code, we need a way to determine when a ray is going "into" an object. The simplest way to do this is to assume that all objects are embedded in air with refractive index very close to 1.0, and that surface normals point "out" (toward the air). The code segment for rays and dielectrics with these assumptions is:

if (**p** is on a dielectric) **then**
    r = reflect(**d**, **n**)
    if (**d** · **n** < 0) **then**
        refract(**d**, **n**, n, **t**)
        $c = -\mathbf{d} \cdot \mathbf{n}$
        $k_r = k_g = k_b = 1$

else
$$k_r = \exp(-a_r t)$$
$$k_g = \exp(-a_g t)$$
$$k_b = \exp(-a_b t)$$
if refract$(\mathbf{d}, -\mathbf{n}, 1/n, \mathbf{t})$ **then**
$$c = \mathbf{t} \cdot \mathbf{n}$$
else
    return $k * \text{color}(\mathbf{p} + t\mathbf{r})$
$$R_0 = (n-1)^2/(n+1)^2$$
$$R = R_0 + (1 - R_0)(1 - c)^5$$
return $k(R\,\text{color}(\mathbf{p} + t\mathbf{r}) + (1 - R)\,\text{color}(\mathbf{p} + t\mathbf{t}))$

The code above assumes that the natural log has been folded into the constants (a_r, a_g, a_b). The *refract* function returns false if there is total internal reflection, and otherwise it fills in the last argument of the argument list.

13.2 Instancing

An elegant property of ray tracing is that it allows very natural *instancing*. The basic idea of instancing is to distort all points on an object by a transformation matrix before the object is displayed. For example, if we transform the unit circle (in 2D) by a scale factor $(2, 1)$ in x and y, respectively, then rotate it by $45°$, and move one unit in the x-direction, the result is an ellipse with an eccentricity of 2 and a long axis along the $(x = -y)$-direction centered at $(0, 1)$ (Figure 13.4). The key thing that makes that entity an "instance" is that we store the circle and the composite transform matrix. Thus, the explicit construction of the ellipse is left as a future operation at render time.

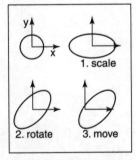

Figure 13.4. An instance of a circle with a series of three transforms is an ellipse.

The advantage of instancing in ray tracing is that we can choose the space in which to do intersection. If the base object is composed of a set of points, one of which is $\mathbf{p}$, then the transformed object is composed of that set of points transformed by matrix $\mathbf{M}$, where the example point is transformed to $\mathbf{Mp}$. If we have a ray $\mathbf{a} + t\mathbf{b}$ that we want to intersect with the transformed object, we can instead intersect an *inverse-transformed ray* with the untransformed object (Figure 13.5). There are two potential advantages to computing in the untransformed space (i.e., the right-hand side of Figure 13.5):

1. the untransformed object may have a simpler intersection routine, e.g., a sphere versus an ellipsoid;

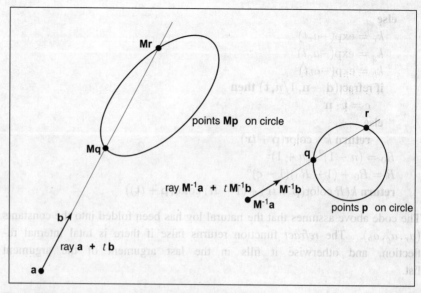

Figure 13.5. The ray intersection problem in the two spaces are just simple transforms of each other. The object is specified as a sphere plus matrix **M**. The ray is specified in the transformed (world) space by location **a** and direction **b**.

2. many transformed objects can share the same untransformed object thus reducing storage, e.g., a traffic jam of cars, where individual cars are just transforms of a few base (untransformed) models.

As discussed in Section 6.2.2, surface normal vectors transform differently. With this in mind and using the concepts illustrated in Figure 13.5, we can determine the intersection of a ray and an object transformed by matrix **M**. If we create an instance class of type *surface*, we need to create a *hit* function:

instance::hit(ray $\mathbf{a} + t\mathbf{b}$, real t_0, real t_1, hit-record rec)
ray $\mathbf{r}' = \mathbf{M}^{-1}\mathbf{a} + t\mathbf{M}^{-1}\mathbf{b}$
if (base-object$\rightarrow$hit($\mathbf{r}'$, t_0, t_1, rec)) **then**
    rec.n = $(\mathbf{M}^{-1})^{\mathrm{T}}$rec.n
    return true
else
    return false

An elegant thing about this function is that the parameter rec.t does not need to be changed, because it is the same in either space. Also note that we need not compute or store the matrix **M**.

This brings up a very important point: the ray direction **b** must *not* be restricted to a unit-length vector, or none of the infrastructure above works. For this reason, it is useful not to restrict ray directions to unit vectors.

13.3 Constructive Solid Geometry

One nice thing about ray tracing is that any geometric primitive whose intersection with a 3D line can be computed can be seamlessly added to a ray tracer. It turns out to also be straightforward to add *constructive solid geometry* (CSG) to a ray tracer (Roth, 1982). The basic idea of CSG is to use set operations to combine solid shapes. These basic operations are shown in Figure 13.6. The operations can be viewed as *set* operations. For example, we can consider C the set of all points in the circle and S the set of all points in the square. The intersection operation $C \cap S$ is the set of all points that are both members of C and S. The other operations are analogous.

Although one can do CSG directly on the model, if all that is desired is an image, we do not need to explicitly change the model. Instead, we perform the set operations directly on the rays as they interact with a model. To make this natural, we find all the intersections of a ray with a model rather than just the closest. For example, a ray $\mathbf{a} + t\mathbf{b}$ might hit a sphere at $t = 1$ and $t = 2$. In the context of CSG, we think of this as the ray being inside the sphere for $t \in [1, 2]$. We can compute these "inside intervals" for all of the surfaces and do set operations on those intervals (recall Section 2.1.2). This is illustrated in Figure 13.7, where the hit intervals are processed to indicate that there are two intervals inside the difference object. The first hit for $t > 0$ is what the ray actually intersects.

In practice, the CSG intersection routine must maintain a list of intervals. When the first hitpoint is determined, the material property and surface normal is that associated with the hitpoint. In addition, you must pay attention to precision issues because there is nothing to prevent the user from taking two objects that abut and taking an intersection. This can be made robust by eliminating any interval whose thickness is below a certain tolerance.

13.4 Distribution Ray Tracing

For some applications, ray-traced images are just too "clean." This effect can be mitigated using *distribution ray tracing* (Cook et al., 1984) . The conventionally ray-traced images look clean, because everything is crisp; the shadows are per-

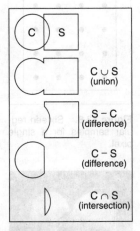

Figure 13.6. The basic CSG operations on a 2D circle and square.

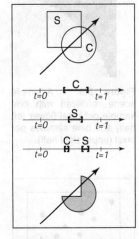

Figure 13.7. Intervals are processed to indicate how the ray hits the composite object.

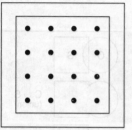

Figure 13.8. Sixteen regular samples for a single pixel.

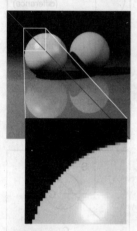

Figure 13.9. A simple scene rendered with one sample per pixel (lower left half) and nine samples per pixel (upper right half).

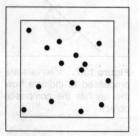

Figure 13.10. Sixteen random samples for a single pixel.

fectly sharp, the reflections have no fuzziness, and everything is in perfect focus. Sometimes we would like to have the shadows be soft (as they are in real life), the reflections be fuzzy as with brushed metal, and the image have variable degrees of focus as in a photograph with a large aperture. While accomplishing these things from first principles is somewhat involved (as is developed in Chapter 24), we can get most of the visual impact with some fairly simple changes to the basic ray tracing algorithm. In addition, the framework gives us a relatively simple way to antialias (recall Section 8.3) the image.

13.4.1 Antialiasing

Recall that a simple way to antialias an image is to compute the average color for the area of the pixel rather than the color at the center point. In ray tracing, our computational primitive is to compute the color at a point on the screen. If we average many of these points across the pixel, we are approximating the true average. If the screen coordinates bounding the pixel are $[i, i+1] \times [j, j+1]$, then we can replace the loop:

for each pixel (i, j) **do**
$\quad c_{ij} = \text{ray-color}(i + 0.5, j + 0.5)$

with code that samples on a regular $n \times n$ grid of samples within each pixel:

for each pixel (i, j) **do**
$\quad c = 0$
$\quad$ **for** $p = 0$ to $n - 1$ **do**
$\quad\quad$ **for** $q = 0$ to $n - 1$ **do**
$\quad\quad\quad c = c + \text{ray-color}(i + (p + 0.5)/n, j + (q + 0.5)/n)$
$\quad c_{ij} = c/n^2$

This is usually called *regular sampling*. The 16 sample locations in a pixel for $n = 4$ are shown in Figure 13.8. Note that this produces the same answer as rendering a traditional ray-traced image with one sample per pixel at $n_x n$ by $n_y n$ resolution and then averaging blocks of n by n pixels to get a n_x by n_y image.

One potential problem with taking samples in a regular pattern within a pixel is that regular artifacts such as moiré patterns can arise. These artifacts can be turned into noise by taking samples in a random pattern within each pixel as shown in Figure 13.10. This is usually called *random sampling* and involves just a small change to the code:

```
for each pixel (i, j) do
    c = 0
    for p = 1 to n² do
        c = c+ ray-color(i + ξ, j + ξ)
    cᵢⱼ = c/n²
```

Here ξ is a call that returns a uniform random number in the range $[0, 1)$. Unfortunately, the noise can be quite objectionable unless many samples are taken. A compromise is to make a hybrid strategy that randomly perturbs a regular grid:

```
for each pixel (i, j) do
    c = 0
    for p = 0 to n − 1 do
        for q = 0 to n − 1 do
            c = c + ray-color(i + (p + ξ)/n, j + (q + ξ)/n)
    cᵢⱼ = c/n²
```

That method is usually called *jittering* or *stratified sampling* (Figure 13.11).

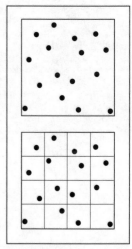

Figure 13.11. Sixteen stratified (jittered) samples for a single pixel shown with and without the bins highlighted. There is exactly one random sample taken within each bin.

13.4.2 Soft Shadows

The reason shadows are hard to handle in standard ray tracing is that lights are infinitesimal points or directions and are thus either visible or invisible. In real life, lights have non-zero area and can thus be partially visible. This idea is shown in 2D in Figure 13.12. The region where the light is entirely invisible is called the *umbra*. The partially visible region is called the *penumbra*. There is not a commonly used term for the region not in shadow, but it is sometimes called the *anti-umbra*.

The key to implementing soft shadows is to somehow account for the light being an area rather than a point. An easy way to do this is to approximate the light with a distributed set of N point lights each with one Nth of the intensity of the base light. This concept is illustrated at the left of Figure 13.13 where nine lights are used. You can do this in a standard ray tracer, and it is a common trick to get soft shadows in an off-the-shelf renderer. There are two potential problems with this technique. First, typically dozens of point lights are needed to achieve visually smooth results, which slows down the program a great deal. The second problem is that the shadows have sharp transitions inside the penumbra.

Distribution ray tracing introduces a small change in the shadowing code. Instead of representing the area light at a discrete number of point sources, we represent it as an infinite number and choose one at random for each viewing ray.

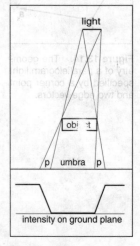

Figure 13.12. A soft shadow has a gradual transition from the unshadowed to shadowed region. The transition zone is the "penumbra" denoted by *p* in the figure.

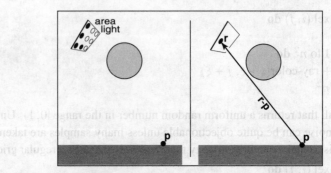

Figure 13.13. Left: an area light can be approximated by some number of point lights; four of the nine points are visible to **p** so it is in the penumbra. Right: a random point on the light is chosen for the shadow ray, and it has some chance of hitting the light or not.

This amounts to choosing a random point on the light for any surface point being lit as is shown at the right of Figure 13.13.

If the light is a parallelogram specified by a corner point **c** and two edge vectors **a** and **b** (Figure 13.14), then choosing a random point **r** is straightforward:

$$\mathbf{r} = \mathbf{c} + \xi_1 \mathbf{a} + \xi_2 \mathbf{b},$$

where ξ_1 and ξ_2 are uniform random numbers in the range $[0, 1)$.

We then send a shadow ray to this point as shown at the right in Figure 13.13. Note that the direction of this ray is not unit length, which may require some modification to your basic ray tracer depending upon its assumptions.

We would really like to jitter points on the light. However, it can be dangerous to implement this without some thought. We would not want to always have the ray in the upper left-hand corner of the pixel generate a shadow ray to the upper left-hand corner of the light. Instead we would like to scramble the samples, such that the pixel samples and the light samples are each themselves jittered, but so that there is no correlation between pixel samples and light samples. A good way to accomplish this is to generate two distinct sets of n^2 jittered samples and pass samples into the light source routine:

for each pixel (i, j) **do**
    $c = 0$
    generate $N = n^2$ jittered 2D points and store in array r[ ]
    generate $N = n^2$ jittered 2D points and store in array s[ ]
    shuffle the points in array s[ ]
    for $p = 0$ to $N - 1$ **do**
        $c = c + \text{ray-color}(i + \text{r}[p].\text{x}(), j + \text{r}[p].\text{y}(), \text{s}[p])$
    $c_{ij} = c/N$

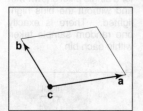

Figure 13.14. The geometry of a parallelogram light specified by a corner point and two edge vectors.

This shuffle routine eliminates any coherence between arrays r and s. The shadow routine will just use the 2D random point stored in $s[p]$ rather than calling the random number generator. A shuffle routine for an array indexed from 0 to $N - 1$ is:

for $i = N - 1$ downto 1 **do**

 choose random integer j between 0 and i inclusive

 swap array elements i and j

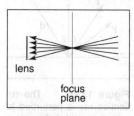

13.4.3 Depth of Field

The soft focus effects seen in most photos can be simulated by collecting light at a non-zero size "lens" rather than at a point. This is called *depth of field*. The lens collects light from a cone of directions that has its apex at a distance where everything is in focus (Figure 13.15). We can place the "window" we are sampling on the plane where everything is in focus (rather than at the $z = n$ plane as we did previously) and the lens at the eye. The distance to the plane where everything is in focus we call the *focus plane*, and the distance to it is set by the user, just as the distance to the focus plane in a real camera is set by the user or range finder.

Figure 13.15. The lens averages over a cone of directions that hit the pixel location being sampled.

Figure 13.16. An example of depth of field. The caustic in the shadow of the wine glass is computed using particle tracing as described in Chapter 24. (See also Plate V.)

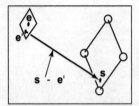

Figure 13.17. To create depth-of-field effects, the eye is randomly selected from a square region.

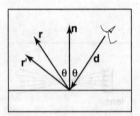

Figure 13.18. The reflection ray is perturbed to a random vector $\mathbf{r}'$.

To be most faithful to a real camera, we should make the lens a disk. However, we will get very similar effects with a square lens (Figure 13.17). So we choose the side-length of the lens and take random samples on it. The origin of the view rays will be these perturbed positions rather than the eye position. Again, a shuffling routine is used to prevent correlation with the pixel sample positions. An example using 25 samples per pixel and a large disk lens is shown in Figure 13.16.

13.4.4   Glossy Reflection

Some surfaces, such as brushed metal, are somewhere between an ideal mirror and a diffuse surface. Some discernible image is visible in the reflection but it is blurred. We can simulate this by randomly perturbing ideal specular reflection rays as shown in Figure 13.18.

Only two details need to be worked out: how to choose the vector $\mathbf{r}'$ and what to do when the resulting perturbed ray is below the surface from which the ray is reflected. The latter detail is usually settled by returning a zero color when the ray is below the surface.

To choose $\mathbf{r}'$, we again sample a random square. This square is perpendicular to $\mathbf{r}$ and has width a which controls the degree of blur. We can set up the square's orientation by creating an orthonormal basis with $\mathbf{w} = \mathbf{r}$ using the techniques in Section 2.4.6. Then, we create a random point in the 2D square with side length a centered at the origin. If we have 2D sample points $(\xi, \xi') \in [0, 1]^2$, then the analogous point on the desired square is

$$u = -\frac{a}{2} + \xi a,$$

$$v = -\frac{a}{2} + \xi' a.$$

Because the square over which we will perturb is parallel to both the $\mathbf{u}$ and $\mathbf{v}$ vectors, the ray $\mathbf{r}'$ is just

$$\mathbf{r}' = \mathbf{r} + u\mathbf{u} + v\mathbf{v}.$$

Note that $\mathbf{r}'$ is not necessarily a unit vector and should be normalized if your code requires that for ray directions.

13.4.5   Motion Blur

We can add a blurred appearance to objects as shown in Figure 13.19. This is called *motion blur* and is the result of the image being formed over a non-zero

Figure 13.19. The bottom right sphere is in motion, and a blurred appearance results. *Image courtesy Chad Barb.*

span of time. In a real camera, the aperture is open for some time interval during which objects move. We can simulate the open aperture by setting a time variable ranging from T_0 to T_1. For each viewing ray we choose a random time,

$$T = T_0 + \xi(T_1 - T_0).$$

We may also need to create some objects to move with time. For example, we might have a moving sphere whose center travels from c_0 to c_1 during the interval. Given T, we could compute the actual center and do a ray–intersection with that sphere. Because each ray is sent at a different time, each will encounter the sphere at a different position, and the final appearance will be blurred. Note that the bounding box for the moving sphere should bound its entire path so an efficiency structure can be built for the whole time interval (Glassner, 1988).

Notes

There are many, many other advanced methods that can be implemented in the ray-tracing framework. Some resources for further information are Glassner's *An Introduction to Ray Tracing* and *Principles of Digital Image Synthesis*, Shirley's *Realistic Ray Tracing*, and Pharr and Humphreys's *Physically Based Rendering: From Theory to Implementation*.

Frequently Asked Questions

- What is the best ray-intersection efficiency structure?

The most popular structures are binary space partitioning trees (BSP trees), uniform subdivision grids, and bounding volume hierarchies. Most people who use BSP trees make the splitting planes axis-aligned, and such trees are usually called k-d trees. There is no clear-cut answer for which is best, but all are much, much better than brute-force search in practice. If I were to implement only one, it would be the bounding volume hierarchy because of its simplicity and robustness.

- Why do people use bounding boxes rather than spheres or ellipsoids?

Sometimes spheres or ellipsoids are better. However, many models have polygonal elements that are tightly bounded by boxes, but they would be difficult to tightly bind with an ellipsoid.

14

Sampling

Many applications in graphics require "fair" sampling of unusual spaces, such as the space of all possible lines. For example, we might need to generate random edges within a pixel, or random sample points on a pixel that vary in density according to some density function. This chapter provides the machinery for such probability operations. These techniques will also prove useful for numerically evaluating complicated integrals using *Monte Carlo integration*, also covered in this chapter.

14.1   Integration

Although the words "integral" and "measure" often seem intimidating, they relate to some of the most intuitive concepts found in mathematics, and they should not be feared. For our very non-rigorous purposes, a *measure* is just a function that maps subsets to $\mathbb{R}^+$ in a manner consistent with our intuitive notions of length, area, and volume. For example, on the 2D real plane $\mathbb{R}^2$, we have the area measure A which assigns a value to a set of points in the plane. Note that A is just a function that takes pieces of the plane and returns area. This means the domain of A is all possible subsets of $\mathbb{R}^2$, which we denote as the *power set* $\mathcal{P}(\mathbb{R}^2)$. Thus, we can characterize A in arrow notation:

$$A : \mathcal{P}(\mathbb{R}^2) \to \mathbb{R}^+.$$

An example of applying the area measure shows that the area of the square with side length one is one:

$$A([a, a + 1] \times [b, b + 1]) = 1,$$

where (a, b) is just the lower left-hand corner of the square. Note that a single point such as $(3, 7)$ is a valid subset of $\mathbb{R}^2$ and has zero area: $A((3, 7)) = 0$. The same is true of the set of points S on the x-axis, $S = (x, y)$ such that $(x, y) \in \mathbb{R}^2$ and $y = 0$, i.e., $A(S) = 0$. Such sets are called *zero measure sets*.

To be considered a measure, a function has to obey certain area-like properties. For example, we have a function $\mu : \mathcal{P}(\mathbb{S}) \to \mathbb{R}^+$. For μ to be a measure, the following conditions must be true:

1. The measure of the empty set is zero: $\mu(\emptyset) = 0$,

2. The measure of two distinct sets together is the sum of their measure alone. This rule with possible intersections is

$$\mu(A \cup B) = \mu(A) + \mu(B) - \mu(A \cap B),$$

where $\cup$ is the set union operator and $\cap$ is the set intersection operator.

When we actually compute measures, we usually use *integration*. We can think of integration as really just notation:

$$A(S) \equiv \int_{x \in S} dA(\mathbf{x}).$$

You can informally read the right-hand side as "take all points $\mathbf{x}$ in the region S, and sum their associated differential areas." The integral is often written other ways including

$$\int_S dA, \quad \int_{\mathbf{x} \in S} d\mathbf{x}, \quad \int_{\mathbf{x} \in S} dA_{\mathbf{x}}, \quad \int_{\mathbf{x}} d\mathbf{x}.$$

All of the above formulas represent "the area of region S." We will stick with the first one we used, because it is so verbose it avoids ambiguity. To evaluate such integrals analytically, we usually need to lay down some coordinate system and use our bag of calculus tricks to solve the equations. But have no fear if those skills have faded, as we usually have to numerically approximate integrals, and that requires only a few simple techniques which are covered later in this chapter.

Given a measure on a set $\mathbb{S}$, we can always create a new measure by weighting with a non-negative function $w : \mathbb{S} \to \mathbb{R}^+$. This is best expressed in integral notation. For example, we can start with the example of the simple area measure on $[0, 1]^2$:

$$\int_{\mathbf{x} \in [0,1]^2} dA(\mathbf{x}),$$

and we can use a "radially weighted" measure by inserting a weighting function of radius squared:

$$\int_{\mathbf{x} \in [0,1]^2} \|\mathbf{x}\|^2 dA(\mathbf{x}).$$

To evaluate this analytically, we can expand using a Cartesian coordinate system with $dA \equiv dx\, dy$:

$$\int_{\mathbf{x} \in [0,1]^2} \|\mathbf{x}\|^2 dA(\mathbf{x}) = \int_{x=0}^{1} \int_{y=0}^{1} (x^2 + y^2) \ dx\, dy.$$

The key thing here is that if you think of the $\|\mathbf{x}\|^2$ term as married to the dA term, and that these together form a new measure, we can call that measure ν. This would allow us to write $\nu(S)$ instead of the whole integral. If this strikes you as just a bunch of notation and bookkeeping, you are right. But it does allow us to write down equations that are either compact or expanded depending on our preference.

14.1.1 Measures and Averages

Measures really start paying off when taking averages of a function. You can only take an average with respect to a particular measure, and you would like to select a measure that is "natural" for the application or domain. Once a measure is chosen, the average of a function f over a region S with respect to measure μ is

$$\text{average}(f) \equiv \frac{\int_{x \in S} f(\mathbf{x})\, d\mu(\mathbf{x})}{\int_{x \in S} d\mu(\mathbf{x})}.$$

For example, the average of the function $f(x, y) = x^2$ over $[0, 2]^2$ with respect to the area measure is

$$\text{average}(f) \equiv \frac{\int_{x=0}^{2} \int_{y=0}^{2} x^2 \, dx\, dy}{\int_{x=0}^{2} \int_{y=0}^{2} dx\, dy} = \frac{4}{3}.$$

This machinery helps solve seemingly hard problems where choosing the measure is the tricky part. Such problems often arise in *integral geometry*, a field that studies measures on geometric entities, such as lines and planes. For example, one might want to know the average length of a line through $[0, 1]^2$. That is, by definition,

$$\text{average(length)} = \frac{\int_{\text{lines } L \text{ through } [0,\,1]^2} \text{length}(L) d\mu(L)}{\int_{\text{lines } L \text{ through } [0,\,1]^2} d\mu(L)}.$$

All that is left, once we know that, is choosing the appropriate μ for the application. This is dealt with for lines in the next section.

14.1.2 Example: Measures on the Lines in the 2D Plane

What measure μ is "natural"?

If you parameterize the lines as $y = mx + b$, you might think of a given line as a point (m, b) in "slope-intercept" space. An easy measure to use would be $dm\, db$, but this would not be a "good" measure in that not all equal size "bundles" of lines would have the same measure. More precisely, the measure would not be invariant with respect to change of coordinate system. For example, if you took all lines through the square $[0, 1]^2$, the measure of lines through it would not be the same as the measure through a unit square rotated forty-five degrees. What we would really like is a "fair" measure that does not change with rotation or translation of a set of lines. This idea is illustrated in Figures 14.1 and 14.2.

To develop a natural measure on the lines, we should first start thinking of them as points in a dual space. This is a simple concept: the line $y = mx + b$ can be specified as the point (m, b) in a slope-intercept space. This concept is illustrated in Figure 14.3. It is more straightforward to develop a measure in (ϕ, b) space. In that space b is the y-intercept, while ϕ is the angle the line makes with the x-axis, as shown in Figure 14.4. Here, the differential measure $d\phi\, db$ almost works, but it would not be fair due to the effect shown in Figure 14.1. To account for the larger span b that a constant width bundle of lines makes, we must add a cosine factor:

$$d\mu = \cos \phi \, d\phi \, db.$$

It can be shown that this measure, up to a constant, is the only one that is invariant with respect to rotation and translation.

This measure can be converted into an appropriate measure for other parameterizations of the line. For example, the appropriate measure for (m, b) space is

$$d\mu = \frac{dm\, db}{(1 + m^2)^{\frac{3}{2}}}.$$

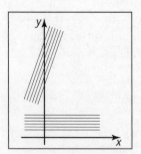

Figure 14.1. These two bundles of lines should have the same measure. They have different intersection lengths with the y-axis so using db would be a poor choice for a differential measure.

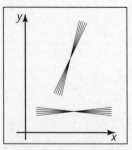

Figure 14.2. These two bundles of lines should have the same measure. Since they have different values for change in slope, using dm would be a poor choice for a differential measure.

For the space of lines parameterized in (u, v) space,

$$ux + vy + 1 = 0,$$

the appropriate measure is

$$d\mu = \frac{du\ dv}{(u^2 + v^2)^{\frac{3}{2}}}.$$

For lines parameterized in terms of (a, b), the x-intercept and y-intercept, the measure is

$$d\mu = \frac{ab\ da\ db}{(a^2 + b^2)^{\frac{3}{2}}}.$$

Note that any of those spaces are equally valid ways to specify lines, and which is best depends upon the circumstances. However, one might wonder whether there exists a coordinate system where the measure of a set of lines is just an area in the dual space. In fact, there is such a coordinate system, and it is delightfully simple; it is the *normal coordinates* which specify a line in terms of the normal distance from the origin to the line, and the angle the normal of the line makes with respect to the x-axis (Figure 14.5). The implicit equation for such lines is

$$x \cos \theta + y \sin \theta - p = 0.$$

And, indeed, the measure in that space is

$$d\mu = dp\ d\theta.$$

We shall use these measures to choose fair random lines in a later section.

14.1.3   Example: Measure of Lines in 3D

In 3D there are many ways to parameterize lines. Perhaps, the simplest way is to use their intersection with a particular plane along with some specification of their orientation. For example, we could chart the intersection with the xy plane along with the spherical coordinates of its orientation. Thus, each line would be specified as a (x, y, θ, ϕ) quadruple. This shows that lines in 3D are 4D entities, i.e., they can be described as points in a 4D space.

The differential measure of a line should not vary with (x, y), but bundles of lines with equal cross section should have equal measure. Thus, a fair differential measure is

$$d\mu = dx\ dy\ \sin \theta\ d\theta\ d\phi.$$

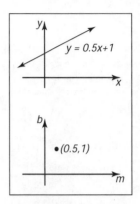

Figure 14.3. The set of points on the line $y = mx + b$ in (x, y) space can also be represented by a single point in (m, b) space so the top line and the bottom point represent the same geometric entity: a 2D line.

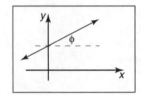

Figure 14.4. In angle-intercept space we parameterize the line by angle $\phi \in [-\pi/2, \pi/2)$ rather than slope.

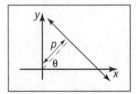

Figure 14.5. The normal coordinates of a line use the normal distance to the origin and an angle to specify a line.

Another way to parameterize lines is to chart the intersection with two parallel planes. For example, if the line intersects the plane $z = 0$ at $(x = u, y = v)$ and the plane $z = 1$ at $(x = s, y = t)$, then the line can be described by the quadruple (u, v, s, t). Note, that like the previous parameterization, this one is degenerate for lines parallel to the xy plane. The differential measure is more complicated for this parameterization although it can be approximated as

$$d\mu \approx du\,dv\,a\,ds\,dt,$$

for bundles of lines nearly parallel to the z-axis. This is the measure often implicitly used in image-based rendering.

For sets of lines that intersect a sphere, we can use the parameterization of the two points where the line intersects the sphere. If these are in spherical coordinates, then the point can be described by the quadruple $(\theta_1, \phi_1, \theta_2, \phi_2)$ and the measure is just the differential area associated with each point:

$$d\mu = \sin\theta_1\,d\theta_1\,d\phi_1\,\sin\theta_2\,d\theta_2\,d\phi_2.$$

This implies that picking two uniform random endpoints on the sphere results in a line with uniform density. This observation was used to compute form-factors by Mateu Sbert in his dissertation (Sbert, 1997).

Note that sometimes we want to parameterize directed lines, and sometimes we want the order of the endpoints not to matter. This is a bookkeeping detail that is especially important for rendering applications where the amount of light flowing along a line is different in the two directions along the line.

14.2   Continuous Probability

Many graphics algorithms use probability to construct random samples to solve integration and averaging problems. This is the domain of applied continuous probability which has basic connections to measure theory.

14.2.1   One-Dimensional Continuous Probability Density Functions

Loosely speaking, a *continuous random variable* x is a scalar or vector quantity that "randomly" takes on some value from the real line $\mathbb{R} = (-\infty, +\infty)$. The behavior of x is entirely described by the distribution of values it takes. This distribution of values can be quantitatively described by the *probability density function* (pdf), p, associated with x (the relationship is denoted $x \sim p$). The probability that x assumes a particular value in some interval $[a, b]$ is given by the following integral:

$$\text{Probability}(x \in [a, b]) = \int_a^b p(x) dx. \tag{14.1}$$

Loosely speaking, the probability density function p describes the relative likelihood of a random variable taking a certain value; if $p(x_1) = 6.0$ and $p(x_2) = 3.0$, then a random variable with density p is twice as likely to have a value "near" x_1 than it it to have a value near x_2. The density p has two characteristics:

$$p(x) \geq 0 \quad \text{(probability is non-negative)}, \tag{14.2}$$

$$\int_{-\infty}^{+\infty} p(x) dx = 1 \quad (\text{Probability}(x \in \mathbb{R}) = 1). \tag{14.3}$$

As an example, the *canonical* random variable ξ takes on values between zero (inclusive) and one (non-inclusive) with uniform probability (here *uniform* simply means each value for ξ is equally likely). This implies that the probability density function q for ξ is

$$q(\xi) = \begin{cases} 1 & \text{if } 0 \leq \xi < 1, \\ 0 & \text{otherwise}, \end{cases}$$

The space over which ξ is defined is simply the interval $[0, 1)$. The probability that ξ takes on a value in a certain interval $[a, b] \in [0, 1)$ is

$$\text{Probability}(a \leq \xi \leq b) = \int_a^b 1 \, dx = b - a.$$

14.2.2   One-Dimensional Expected Value

The average value that a real function f of a one-dimensional random variable with underlying pdf p will take on is called its *expected value*, $E(f(x))$ (sometimes written $Ef(x)$):

$$E(f(x)) = \int f(x)p(x)dx.$$

The expected value of a one-dimensional random variable can be calculated by setting $f(x) = x$. The expected value has a surprising and useful property: the expected value of the sum of two random variables is the sum of the expected values of those variables:

$$E(x + y) = E(x) + E(y),$$

for random variables x and y. Because functions of random variables are themselves random variables, this linearity of expectation applies to them as well:

$$E(f(x) + g(y)) = E(f(x)) + E(g(y)).$$

An obvious question to ask is whether this property holds if the random variables being summed are correlated (variables that are not correlated are called *independent*). This linearity property in fact does hold *whether or not* the variables are independent! This summation property is vital for most Monte Carlo applications.

14.2.3 Multi-Dimensional Random Variables

The discussion of random variables and their expected values extends naturally to multi-dimensional spaces. Most graphics problems will be in such higher-dimensional spaces. For example, many lighting problems are phrased on the surface of the hemisphere. Fortunately, if we define a measure μ on the space the random variables occupy, everything is very similar to the one-dimensional case. Suppose the space S has associated measure μ; for example S is the surface of a sphere and μ measures area. We can define a pdf $p : S \mapsto \mathbb{R}$, and if x is a random variable with $x \sim p$, then the probability that x will take on a value in some region $S_i \subset S$ is given by the integral

$$\text{Probability}(x \in S_i) = \int_{S_i} p(x) d\mu.$$

Here *Probability* (*event*) is the probability that *event* is true, so the integral is the probability that x takes on a value in the region S_i.

In graphics, S is often an area ($d\mu = dA = dxdy$) or a set of directions (points on a unit sphere: $d\mu = d\omega = \sin\theta \, d\theta \, d\phi$). As an example, a two-dimensional random variable α is a uniformly distributed random variable on a disk of radius R. Here *uniformly* means uniform with respect to area, e.g., the way a bad dart player's hits would be distributed on a dart board. Since it is uniform, we know that $p(\alpha)$ is some constant. From the fact that the area of the disk is πr^2 and that the total probability is one, we can deduce that

$$p(\alpha) = \frac{1}{\pi R^2}.$$

This means that the probability that α is in a certain subset S_1 of the disk is just

$$\text{Probability}(\alpha \in S_1) = \int_{S_1} \frac{1}{\pi R^2} dA.$$

This is all very abstract. To actually use this information, we need the integral in a form we can evaluate. Suppose S_i is the portion of the disk closer to the center than the perimeter. If we convert to polar coordinates, then α is represented as a (r, ϕ) pair, and S_1 is the region where $r < R/2$. Note, that just because α is uniform, it does not imply that ϕ or r are necessarily uniform (in fact, ϕ is uniform, and r is not uniform). The differential area dA is just $r\, dr\, d\phi$. Thus,

$$\text{Probability}\left(r < \frac{R}{2}\right) = \int_0^{2\pi} \int_0^{\frac{R}{2}} \frac{1}{\pi R^2} r\, dr\, d\phi = 0.25.$$

The formula for expected value of a real function applies to the multi-dimensional case:

$$E(f(x)) = \int_S f(x)p(x)d\mu,$$

where $x \in S$ and $f : S \mapsto \mathbb{R}$, and $p : S \mapsto \mathbb{R}$. For example, on the unit square $S = [0,1] \times [0,1]$ and $p(x, y) = 4xy$, the expected value of the x coordinate for $(x, y) \sim p$ is

$$E(x) = \int_S f(x, y)p(x, y)dA$$
$$= \int_0^1 \int_0^1 4x^2 y\, dx\, dy$$
$$= \frac{2}{3}.$$

Note that here $f(x, y) = x$.

14.2.4 Variance

The *variance*, $V(x)$, of a one-dimensional random variable is, by definition, the expected value of the square of the difference between x and $E(x)$:

$$V(x) \equiv E([x - E(x)]^2).$$

Some algebraic manipulation gives the non-obvious expression:

$$V(x) = E(x^2) - [E(x)]^2.$$

The expression $E([x - E(x)]^2)$ is more useful for thinking intuitively about variance, while the algebraically equivalent expression $E(x^2) - [E(x)]^2$ is usually convenient for calculations. The variance of a sum of random variables is the sum of the variances *if the variables are independent*. This summation property of variance is one of the reasons it is frequently used in analysis of probabilistic models. The square root of the variance is called the *standard deviation, σ*, which gives some indication of expected absolute deviation from the expected value.

14.2.5   Estimated Means

Many problems involve sums of independent random variables x_i, where the variables share a common density p. Such variables are said to be *independent identically distributed* (iid) random variables. When the sum is divided by the number of variables, we get an estimate of $E(x)$:

$$E(x) \approx \frac{1}{N} \sum_{i=1}^{N} x_i.$$

As N increases, the variance of this estimate decreases. We want N to be large enough so that we have confidence that the estimate is "close enough." However, there are no sure things in Monte Carlo; we just gain statistical confidence that our estimate is good. To be sure, we would have to have $N = \infty$. This confidence is expressed by the *Law of Large Numbers*:

$$\text{Probability} \left[E(x) = \lim_{N \to \infty} \frac{1}{N} \sum_{i=1}^{N} x_i \right] = 1.$$

14.3   Monte Carlo Integration

In this section, the basic Monte Carlo solution methods for definite integrals are outlined. These techniques are then straightforwardly applied to certain integral problems. All of the basic material of this section is also covered in several of the classic Monte Carlo texts. (See the Notes section at the end of this chapter.)

As discussed earlier, given a function $f : S \mapsto \mathbb{R}$ and a random variable $x \sim p$, we can approximate the expected value of $f(x)$ by a sum:

$$E(f(x)) = \int_{x \in S} f(x)p(x)d\mu \approx \frac{1}{N} \sum_{i=1}^{N} f(x_i). \tag{14.4}$$

Because the expected value can be expressed as an integral, the integral is also approximated by the sum. The form of Equation (14.4) is a bit awkward; we would usually like to approximate an integral of a single function g rather than a product fp. We can accomplish this by substituting $g = fp$ as the integrand:

$$\int_{x \in S} g(x)d\mu \approx \frac{1}{N} \sum_{i=1}^{N} \frac{g(x_i)}{p(x_i)}. \tag{14.5}$$

For this formula to be valid, p must be positive when g is nonzero.

So to get a good estimate, we want as many samples as possible, and we want the g/p to have a low variance (g and p should have a similar shape). Choosing p intelligently is called *importance sampling*, because if p is large where g is large, there will be more samples in important regions. Equation (14.4) also shows the fundamental problem with Monte Carlo integration: *diminishing return*. Because the variance of the estimate is proportional to $1/N$, the standard deviation is proportional to $1/\sqrt{N}$. Since the error in the estimate behaves similarly to the standard deviation, we will need to quadruple N to halve the error.

Another way to reduce variance is to partition S, the domain of the integral, into several smaller domains S_i, and evaluate the integral as a sum of integrals over the S_i. This is called *stratified sampling*, the technique that jittering employs in pixel sampling (Chapter 4). Normally only one sample is taken in each S_i (with density p_i), and in this case the variance of the estimate is:

$$var\left(\sum_{i=1}^{N} \frac{g(x_i)}{p_i(x_i)}\right) = \sum_{i=1}^{N} var\left(\frac{g(x_i)}{p_i(x_i)}\right). \tag{14.6}$$

It can be shown that the variance of stratified sampling is never higher than unstratified if all strata have equal measure:

$$\int_{S_i} p(x)d\mu = \frac{1}{N} \int_S p(x)d\mu.$$

The most common example of stratified sampling in graphics is jittering for pixel sampling as discussed in Section 13.4.

As an example of the Monte Carlo solution of an integral I, set $g(x)$ equal to x over the interval $(0, 4)$:

$$I = \int_0^4 x\, dx = 8. \tag{14.7}$$

The impact of the shape of the function p on the variance of the N sample estimates is shown in Table 14.1. Note that the variance is reduced when the shape of p is similar to the shape of g. The variance drops to zero if $p = g/I$, but

Method	Sampling function	Variance	Samples needed for standard error of 0.008
importance	$(6-x)/(16)$	$56.8N^{-1}$	887,500
importance	$1/4$	$21.3N^{-1}$	332,812
importance	$(x+2)/16$	$6.3N^{-1}$	98,437
importance	$x/8$	0	1
stratified	$1/4$	$21.3N^{-3}$	70

Table 14.1. Variance for Monte Carlo estimate of $\int_0^4 x\,dx$.

I is not usually known or we would not have to resort to Monte Carlo. One important principle illustrated in Table 14.1 is that stratified sampling is often *far* superior to importance sampling (Mitchell, 1996). Although the variance for this stratification on I is inversely proportional to the cube of the number of samples, there is no general result for the behavior of variance under stratification. There are some functions for which stratification does no good. One example is a white noise function, where the variance is constant for all regions. On the other hand, most functions will benefit from stratified sampling, because the variance in each subcell will usually be smaller than the variance of the entire domain.

14.3.1 Quasi–Monte Carlo Integration

A popular method for quadrature is to replace the random points in Monte Carlo integration with *quasi-random* points. Such points are deterministic, but are in some sense uniform. For example, on the unit square $[0,1]^2$, a set of N quasi-random points should have the following property on a region of area A within the square:

$$\text{number of points in the region} \approx AN.$$

For example, a set of regular samples in a lattice has this property.

Quasi-random points can improve performance in many integration applications. Sometimes care must be taken to make sure that they do not introduce aliasing. It is especially nice that, in any application where calls are made to random or stratified points in $[0,1]^d$, one can substitute d-dimensional quasi-random points with no other changes.

The key intuition motivating quasi–Monte Carlo integration is that when estimating the average value of an integrand, any set of sample points will do, provided they are "fair."

14.4 Choosing Random Points

We often want to generate sets of random or pseudorandom points on the unit square for applications such as distribution ray tracing. There are several methods for doing this, e.g., jittering (see Section 13.4). These methods give us a set of N reasonably equidistributed points on the unit square $[0, 1]^2 : (u_1, v_1)$ through (u_N, v_N).

Sometimes, our sampling space may not be square (e.g., a circular lens), or may not be uniform (e.g, a filter function centered on a pixel). It would be nice if we could write a mathematical transformation that would take our equidistributed points (u_i, v_i) as input and output a set of points in our desired sampling space with our desired density. For example, to sample a camera lens, the transformation would take (u_i, v_i) and output (r_i, ϕ_i) such that the new points are approximately equidistributed on the disk of the lens. While we might be tempted to use the transform

$$\phi_i = 2\pi u_i,$$
$$r_i = v_i R,$$

it has a serious problem. While the points do cover the lens, they do so non-uniformly (Figure 14.6). What we need in this case is a transformation that takes equal-area regions to equal-area regions—one that takes uniform sampling distributions on the square to uniform distributions on the new domain.

There are several ways to generate such non-uniform points or uniform points on non-rectangular domains, and the following sections review the three most often used: function inversion, rejection, and Metropolis.

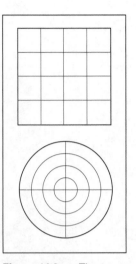

Figure 14.6. The transform that takes the horizontal and vertical dimensions uniformly to (r, ϕ) does not preserve relative area; not all of the resulting areas are the same.

14.4.1 Function Inversion

If the density $f(x)$ is one-dimensional and defined over the interval $x \in [x_{\min}, x_{\max}]$, then we can generate random numbers α_i that have density f from a set of uniform random numbers ξ_i, where $\xi_i \in [0, 1]$. To do this, we need the cumulative probability distribution function $P(x)$:

$$\text{Probability}(\alpha < x) = P(x) = \int_{x_{\min}}^{x} f(x')d\mu.$$

To get α_i, we simply transform ξ_i:

$$\alpha_i = P^{-1}(\xi_i),$$

where P^{-1} is the inverse of P. If P is not analytically invertible, then numerical methods will suffice, because an inverse exists for all valid probability distribution functions.

Note that analytically inverting a function is more confusing than it should be due to notation. For example, if we have the function

$$y = x^2,$$

for $x > 0$, then the inverse function is expressed in terms of y as a function of x:

$$x = \sqrt{y}.$$

When the function is analytically invertible, it is almost always that simple. However, things are a little more opaque with the standard notation:

$$f(x) = x^2,$$
$$f^{-1}(x) = \sqrt{x}.$$

Here x is just a dummy variable. You may find it easier to use the less standard notation:

$$y = x^2,$$
$$x = \sqrt{y},$$

while keeping in mind that these are inverse functions of each other.

For example, to choose random points x_i that have density

$$p(x) = \frac{3x^2}{2}$$

on $[-1, 1]$, we see that

$$P(x) = \frac{x^3 + 1}{2},$$

and

$$P^{-1}(x) = \sqrt[3]{2x - 1},$$

so we can "warp" a set of canonical random numbers $(\xi_1, \cdots, \xi_N)$ to the properly distributed numbers

$$(x_1, \cdots, x_N) = (\sqrt[3]{2\xi_1 - 1}, \cdots, \sqrt[3]{2\xi_N - 1}).$$

Of course, this same warping function can be used to transform "uniform" jittered samples into nicely distributed samples with the desired density.

If we have a random variable $\alpha = (\alpha_x, \alpha_y)$ with two-dimensional density (x, y) defined on $[x_{\min}, x_{\max}] \times [y_{\min}, y_{\max}]$, then we need the two-dimensional distribution function:

$$\text{Probability}(\alpha_x < x \text{ and } \alpha_y < y) = F(x, y) = \int_{y_{\min}}^{y} \int_{x_{\min}}^{x} f(x', y') d\mu(x', y').$$

We first choose an x_i using the marginal distribution $F(x, y_{\max})$ and then choose y_i according to $F(x_i, y)/F(x_i, y_{\max})$. If $f(x, y)$ is separable (expressible as $g(x)h(y)$), then the one-dimensional techniques can be used on each dimension.

Returning to our earlier example, suppose we are sampling uniformly from the disk of radius R, so $p(r, \phi) = 1/(\pi R^2)$. The two-dimensional distribution function is

$$\text{Probability}(r < r_0 \text{ and } \phi < \phi_0) = F(r_0, \phi_0) = \int_{0}^{\phi_0} \int_{0}^{r_0} \frac{r \, dr \, d\phi}{\pi R^2} = \frac{\phi r^2}{2\pi R^2}.$$

This means that a canonical pair (ξ_1, ξ_2) can be transformed to a uniform random point on the disk:

$$\phi = 2\pi \xi_1,$$
$$r = R\sqrt{\xi_2}.$$

This mapping is shown in Figure 14.7.

To choose reflected ray directions for some realistic rendering applications, we choose points on the unit hemisphere according to the density:

$$p(\theta, \phi) = \frac{n + 1}{2\pi} \cos^n \theta.$$

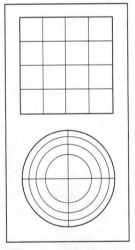

Figure 14.7. A mapping that takes equal area regions in the unit square to equal area regions in the disk.

Where n is a Phong-like exponent, θ is the angle from the surface normal and $\theta \in [0, \pi/2]$ (is on the upper hemisphere) and ϕ is the azimuthal angle ($\phi \in [0, 2\pi]$). The cumulative distribution function is

$$P(\theta, \phi) = \int_{0}^{\phi} \int_{0}^{\theta} p(\theta', \phi') \sin \theta' d\theta' d\phi'. \tag{14.8}$$

The $\sin \theta'$ term arises because, on the sphere, $d\omega = \cos \theta d\theta d\phi$. When the marginal densities are found, p (as expected) is separable, and we find that a (ξ_1, ξ_2) pair of canonical random numbers can be transformed to a direction by

$$\theta = \arccos \left((1 - \xi_1)^{\frac{1}{n+1}} \right),$$
$$\phi = 2\pi \xi_2.$$

Again, a nice thing about this is that a set of jittered points on the unit square can be easily transformed to a set of jittered points on the hemisphere with the desired distribution. Note that if n is set to 1, we have a diffuse distribution, as is often needed.

Often we must map the point on the sphere into an appropriate direction with respect to a *uvw* basis. To do this, we can first convert the angles to a unit vector $\vec{a}$:

$$\mathbf{a} = (\cos\phi\sin\theta, \; \sin\phi\sin\theta, \; \cos\theta)$$

As an efficiency improvement, we can avoid taking trigonometric functions of inverse trigonometric functions (e.g., $\cos(\arccos\theta)$). For example, when $n = 1$ (a diffuse distribution), the vector $\mathbf{a}$ simplifies to

$$\mathbf{a} = \left(\cos(2\pi\xi_1)\sqrt{\xi_2}, \sin(2\pi\xi_1)\sqrt{\xi_2}, \sqrt{1 - \xi_2} \right)$$

14.4.2 Rejection

A *rejection* method chooses points according to some simple distribution and rejects some of them that are in a more complex distribution. There are several scenarios where rejection is used, and we show some of these by example.

Suppose we want uniform random points within the unit circle. We can first choose uniform random points $(x, y) \in [-1, 1]^2$ and reject those outside the circle. If the function $r()$ returns a canonical random number, then the procedure is:

done = false
while (not done) **do**
    $x = -1 + 2r()$
    $y = -1 + 2r()$
    if $(x^2 + y^2 < 1)$ **then**
        done = true

If we want a random number $x \sim p$ and we know that $p : [a, b] \mapsto \mathbb{R}$, and that for all x, $p(x) < m$, then we can generate random points in the rectangle $[a, b] \times [0, m]$ and take those where $y < p(x)$:

done = false
while (not done) **do**
    $x = a + r()(b - a)$
    $y = r()m$
    if $(y < p(x))$ **then**
        done = true

This same idea can be applied to take random points on the surface of a sphere. To pick a random unit vector with uniform directional distribution, we first pick a random point in the unit sphere and then treat that point as a direction vector by taking the unit vector in the same direction:

> done = false
> **while** (not done) **do**
> $\qquad x = -1 + 2r()$
> $\qquad y = -1 + 2r()$
> $\qquad z = -1 + 2r()$
> $\qquad$ **if** $((l = \sqrt{x^2 + y^2 + z^2}) < 1)$ **then**
> $\qquad\qquad$ done = true
> $x = x/l$
> $y = y/l$
> $z = z/l$

Although the rejection method is usually simple to code, it is rarely compatible with stratification. For this reason, it tends to converge more slowly and should thus be used mainly for debugging, or in particularly difficult circumstances.

14.4.3 Metropolis

The *Metropolis* method uses random *mutations* to produce a set of samples with a desired density. This concept is used extensively in the *Metropolis Light Transport* algorithm referenced in the chapter notes. Suppose we have a random point x_0 in a domain S. Further, suppose for any point x, we have a way to generate random $y \sim p_x$. We use the marginal notation $p_x(y) \equiv p(x \rightarrow y)$ to denote this density function. Now, suppose we let x_1 be a random point in S selected with underlying density $p(x_0 \rightarrow x_1)$. We generate x_2 with density $p(x_1 \rightarrow x_0)$ and so on. In the limit, where we generate an infinite number of samples, it can be proved that the samples will have some underlying density determined by p regardless of the initial point x_0.

Now, suppose we want to choose p such that the underlying density of samples to which we converge is proportional to a function $f(x)$ where f is a non-negative function with domain S. Further, suppose we can evaluate f, but we have little or no additional knowledge about its properties (such functions are common in graphics). Also, suppose we have the ability to make "transitions" from x_i to x_{i+1} with underlying density function $t(x_i \rightarrow x_{i+1})$. To add flexibility, further suppose we add the potentially non-zero probability that x_i transitions to itself, i.e., $x_{i+1} = x_i$. We phrase this as generating a potential candidate $y \sim t(x_i \rightarrow y)$ and "accepting" this candidate (i.e., $x_{i+1} = y$) with probability $a(x_i \rightarrow y)$ and rejecting it (i.e., $x_{i+1} = x_i$) with probability $1 - a(x_i \rightarrow y)$. Note that the sequence $x_0, x_1, x_2, \ldots$ will be a random set, but there will be some correlation among samples. They will still be suitable for Monte Carlo integration or density estimation, but analyzing the variance of those estimates is much more challenging.

Now, suppose we are given a transition function $t(x \rightarrow y)$ and a function $f(x)$ of which we want to mimic the distribution, can we use $a(y \rightarrow x)$ such that the points are distributed in the shape of f? Or more precisely,

$$\{x_0, x_1, x_2, \ldots\} \sim \frac{f}{\int_s f}.$$

It turns out this can be forced by making sure the x_i are *stationary* in some strong sense. If you visualize a huge collection of sample points x, you want the "flow" between two points to be the same in each direction. If we assume the density of points near x and y are proportional to $f(x)$ and $f(y)$, respectively, then the flow in the two directions should be the same:

$$\text{flow}(x \rightarrow y) = k f(x) t(x \rightarrow y) a(x \rightarrow y),$$
$$\text{flow}(y \rightarrow x) = k f(y) t(y \rightarrow x) a(y \rightarrow x),$$

where k is some positive constant. Setting these two flows constant gives a constraint on a:

$$\frac{a(y \rightarrow x)}{a(x \rightarrow y)} = \frac{f(x) t(x \rightarrow y)}{f(y) t(y \rightarrow x)}.$$

Thus, if either $a(y \rightarrow x)$ or $a(x \rightarrow y)$ is known, so is the other. Making them larger improves the chance of acceptance, so the usual technique is to set the larger of the two to 1.

A difficulty in using the Metropolis sample generation technique is that it is hard to estimate how many points are needed before the set of points is "good." Things are accelerated if the first n points are discarded, although choosing n wisely is non-trivial.

14.4.4   Example: Choosing Random Lines in the Square

As an example of the full process of designing a sampling strategy, consider the problem of finding random lines that intersect the unit square $[0, 1]^2$. We want this process to be fair; that is, we would like the lines to be uniformly distributed within the square. Intuitively, we can see that there is some subtlety to this problem; there are "more" lines at an oblique angle than in horizontal or vertical directions. This is because the cross section of the square is not uniform.

Our first goal is to find a function-inversion method, if one exists, and then to fall back on rejection or Metropolis if that fails. This is because we would like to have stratified samples in line space. We try using normal coordinates first, because the problem of choosing random lines in the square is just the problem of finding uniform random points in whatever part of (r, θ) space corresponds to lines in the square.

Consider the region where $-\pi/2 < \theta < 0$. What values of r correspond to lines that hit the square? For those angles, $r < \cos\theta$ are all the lines that hit the square as shown in Figure 14.8. Similar reasoning in the other four quadrants finds the region in (r, θ) space that must be sampled, as shown in Figure 14.9. The equation of the boundary of that region $r_{\max}(\theta)$ is

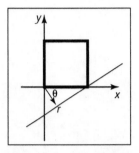

Figure 14.8. The largest distance r corresponds to a line hitting the square for $\theta \in [-\pi/2, 0]$. Because the square has sidelength one, $r = \cos\theta$.

$$r_{\max}(\theta) = \begin{cases} 0 & \text{if } \theta \in [-\pi, -\frac{\pi}{2}], \\ \cos\theta & \text{if } \theta \in [-\frac{\pi}{2}, 0], \\ \sqrt{2}\cos(\theta - \frac{\pi}{4}) & \text{if } \theta \in [0, \frac{\pi}{2}], \\ \sin\theta & \text{if } \theta \in [\frac{\pi}{2}, \pi]. \end{cases}$$

Because the region under $r_{\max}(\theta)$ is a simple function bounded below by $r = 0$, we can sample it by first choosing θ according to the density function:

$$p(\theta) = \frac{r_{\max}(\theta)}{\int_{-\pi}^{\pi} r_{\max}(\theta)d\theta}.$$

The denominator here is 4. Now, we can compute the cumulative probability distribution function:

$$P(\theta) = \begin{cases} 0 & \text{if } \theta \in [-\pi, -\frac{\pi}{2}], \\ (1 + \sin\theta)/4 & \text{if } \theta \in [-\frac{\pi}{2}, 0], \\ (1 + \frac{\sqrt{2}}{2}\sin(\theta - \frac{\pi}{4}))/2 & \text{if } \theta \in [0, \frac{\pi}{2}], \\ (3 - \cos\theta)/4 & \text{if } \theta \in [\frac{\pi}{2}, \pi]. \end{cases}$$

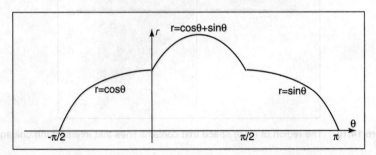

Figure 14.9. The maximum radius for lines hitting the unit square $[0,1]^2$ as a function of θ.

We can invert this by manipulating $\xi_1 = P(\theta)$ into the form $\theta = g(\xi_1)$. This yields

$$\theta = \begin{cases} \arcsin(4\xi_1 - 1) & \text{if } \xi_1 < \frac{1}{4}, \\ \arcsin(\frac{\sqrt{2}}{2}(2\xi_1 - 1)) + \frac{\pi}{4} & \text{if } \xi_1 \in [\frac{1}{4}, \frac{3}{4}], \\ \arccos(3 - 4\xi_1) & \text{if } \xi_1 > \frac{3}{4}. \end{cases}$$

Once we have θ, then r is simply:

$$r = \xi_2 r_{\max}(\theta).$$

As discussed earlier, there are many parameterizations of the line, and each has an associated "fair" measure. We can generate random lines in any of these spaces as well. For example, in slope-intercept space, the region that hits the square is shown in Figure 14.10. By similar reasoning to the normal space, the density function for the slope is

$$p(m) = \frac{1 + |m|}{4}$$

with respect to the differential measure

$$d\mu = \frac{dm}{(1 + m^2)^{\frac{3}{2}}}.$$

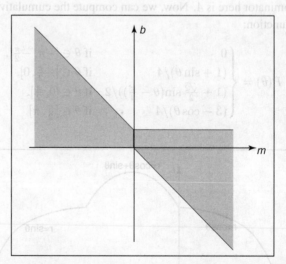

Figure 14.10. The region of (m,b) space that contains lines that intersect the unit square $[0,1]^2$.

This gives rise to the cumulative distribution function:

$$P(m) = \begin{cases} \frac{1}{4} + \frac{m+1}{4\sqrt{1+m^2}} & \text{if } m < 0, \\ \frac{3}{4} + \frac{m-1}{4\sqrt{1+m^2}} & \text{if } m \geq 0. \end{cases}$$

These can be inverted by solving two quadratic equations. Given an m generated using ξ_1, we then have

$$b = \begin{cases} (1-m)\xi_2 & \text{if } \xi < \frac{1}{2}, \\ -m + (1+m)\xi_2 & \text{otherwise.} \end{cases}$$

This is not a better way than using normal coordinates; it is just an alternative way.

Frequently Asked Questions

• This chapter discussed probability but not statistics. What is the distinction?

Probability is the study of how likely an event is. Statistics infers characteristics of large, but finite, populations of random variables. In that sense, statistics could be viewed as a specific type of applied probability.

• Is Metropolis sampling the same as the Metropolis Light Transport Algorithm?

No. The *Metropolis Light Transport* (Veach & Guibas, 1997) algorithm uses Metropolis sampling as part of its procedure, but it is specifically for rendering, and it has other steps as well.

Notes

The classic reference for geometric probability is *Geometric Probability* (Solomon, 1978). Another method for picking random edges in a square is given in *Random–Edge Discrepancy of Supersampling Patterns* (Dobkin & Mitchell, 1993). More information on quasi-Monte Carlo methods for graphics can be found in *Efficient Multidimensional Sampling* (Kollig & Keller, 2002). Three classic and very readable books on Monte Carlo methods are *Monte Carlo Methods* (Hammersley & Handscomb, 1964), *Monte Carlo Methods, Basics* (Kalos & Whitlock, 1986), and *The Monte Carlo Method* (Sobel et al., 1975).

Exercises

1. What is the average value of the function xyz in the unit cube $(x, y, z) \in [0, 1]^3$?

2. What is the average value of r on the unit-radius disk: $(r, \phi) \in [0, 1] \times [0, 2\pi)$?

3. Show that the uniform mapping of canonical random points (ξ_1, ξ_2) to the barycentric coordinates of any triangle is: $\beta = 1 - \sqrt{1 - \xi_1}$, and $\gamma = (1 - u)\xi_2$.

4. What is the average length of a line inside the unit square? Verify your answer by generating ten million random lines in the unit square and averaging their lengths.

5. What is the average length of a line inside the unit cube? Verify your answer by generating ten million random lines in the unit cube and averaging their lengths.

6. Show from the definition of variance that $V(x) = E(x^2) - [E(x)]^2$.

Michael Gleicher

15

Curves

15.1 Curves

Intuitively, think of a *curve* as something you can draw with a pen. The curve is the set of points that the pen traces over an interval of time. While we usually think of a pen writing on paper (e.g., a curve that is in a 2D space), the pen could move in 3D to generate a *space curve*, or you could imagine the pen moving in some other kind of space.

Mathematically, definitions of curve can be seen in at least two ways:

1. The continuous image of some interval in an n-dimensional space.

2. A continuous map from a one-dimensional space to an n-dimensional space.

Both of these definitions start with the idea of an interval range (the time over which the pen traces the curve). However, there is a significant difference: in the first definition, the curve is the set of points the pen traces (the image), while in the second definition, the curve is the mapping between time and that set of points. For this chapter, we use the first definition.

A curve is an infinitely large set of points. The points in a curve have the property that any point has two neighbors, except for a small number of points that have one neighbor (these are the endpoints). Some curves have no endpoints, either because they are infinite (like a line) or they are *closed* (loop around and connect to themselves).

Because the "pen" of the curve is thin (infinitesimally), it is difficult to create filled regions. While space-filling curves are possible (by having them fold over themselves infinitely many times), we do not consider such mathematical oddities here. Generally, we think of curves as the outlines of things, not the "insides."

The problem that we need to address is how to specify a curve—to give a name or representation to a curve so that we can represent it on a computer. For some curves, the problem of naming them is easy since they have known shapes: line segments, circles, elliptical arcs, etc. A general curve that does not have a "named" shape is sometimes called a *free-form* curve. Because a free-form curve can take on just about any shape, they are much harder to specify.

There are three main ways to specify curves mathematically:

1. *Implicit* curve representations define the set of points on a curve by giving a procedure that can test to see if a point in on the curve. Usually, an implicit curve representation is defined by an *implicit function* of the form

$$f(x, y) = 0,$$

   so that the curve is the set of points for which this equation is true. Note that the implicit function f is a scalar function (it returns a single real number).

2. *Parametric* curve representations provide a mapping from a *free parameter* to the set of points on the curve. That is, this free parameter provides an index to the points on the curve. The parametric form of a curve is a function that assigns positions to values of the free parameter. Intuitively, if you think of a curve as something you can draw with a pen on a piece of paper, the free parameter is time, ranging over the interval from the time that we began drawing the curve to the time that we finish. The *parametric function* of this curve tells us where the pen is at any instant in time:

$$(x, y) = \mathbf{f}(t).$$

   Note that the parametric function is a vector-valued function. This example is a 2D curve, so the output of the function is a 2-vector; in 3D it would be a 3-vector.

3. *Generative or procedural* curve representations provide procedures that can generate the points on the curve that do not fall into the first two categories. Examples of generative curve descriptions include subdivision schemes and fractals.

Remember that a curve is a set of points. These representations give us ways to specify those sets. Any curve has many possible representations. For this reason, mathematicians typically are careful to distinguish between a curve and its representations. In computer graphics we are often sloppy, since we usually only refer to the representation, not the actual curve itself. So when someone says "an implicit curve," they are either referring to the curve that is represented by some implicit function or to the implicit function that is one of the representations of some curve. Such distinctions are not usually important, unless we need to consider different representations of the same curve. We will consider different curve representations in this chapter, so we will be more careful. When we use a term like "polynomial curve," we will mean the curve that can be represented by the polynomial.

By the definition given at the beginning of the chapter, for something to be a curve it must have a parametric representation. However, many curves have other representations. For example, a circle in 2D with its center at the origin and radius equal to 1 can be written in implicit form as

$$f(x, y) = x^2 + y^2 - 1 = 0,$$

or in parametric form as

$$(x, y) = \mathbf{f}(t) = (\cos t, \sin t), \quad t \in [0, 2\pi).$$

The parametric form need not be the most convenient representation for a given curve. In fact, it is possible to have curves with simple implicit or generative representations for which it is difficult to find a parametric representation.

Different representations of curves have advantages and disadvantages. For example, parametric curves are much easier to draw, because we can sample the free parameter. Generally, parametric forms are the most commonly used in computer graphics since they are easier to work with. Our focus will be on parametric representations of curves.

15.1.1   Parameterizations and Re-Parameterizations

A *parametric curve* refers to the curve that is given by a specific parametric function over some particular interval. To be more precise, a parametric curve has a given function that is a mapping from an interval of the parameters. It is often convenient to have the parameter run over the unit interval from 0 to 1. When the free parameter varies over the unit interval, we often denote the parameter as u.

If we view the parametric curve to be a line drawn with a pen, we can consider $u = 0$ as the time when the pen is first set down on the paper and the unit of time to be the amount of time it takes to draw the curve ($u = 1$ is the end of the curve).

The curve can be specified by a function that maps time (in these unit coordinates) to positions. Basically, the specification of the curve is a function that can answer the question, "Where is the pen at time u?"

If we are given a function $\mathbf{f}(t)$ that specifies a curve over interval $[a, b]$, we can easily define a new function $\mathbf{f}_2(u)$ that specifies the same curve over the unit interval. We can first define

$$g(u) = a + (b - a)u,$$

and then

$$\mathbf{f}_2(u) = \mathbf{f}(g(u)).$$

The two functions, $\mathbf{f}$ and $\mathbf{f}_2$ both represent the same curve; however, they provide different *parameterizations* of the curve. The process of creating a new parameterization for an existing curve is called *re-parameterization*, and the mapping from old parameters to the new ones (g, in this example) is called the *re-parameterization function*.

If we have defined a curve by some parameterization, infinitely many others exist (because we can always re-parameterize). Being able to have multiple parameterizations of a curve is useful, because it allows us to create parameterizations that are convenient. However, it can also be problematic, because it makes it difficult to compare two functions to see if they represent the same curve.

The essence of this problem is more general: the existence of the free parameter (or the element of time) adds an invisible, potentially unknown element to our representation of the curves. When we look at the curve after it is drawn, we don't necessarily know the timing. The pen might have moved at a constant speed over the entire time interval, or it might have started slowly and sped up. For example, while $u = 0.5$ is halfway through the parameter space, it may not be half-way along the curve if the motion of the pen starts slowly and speeds up at the end. Consider the following representations of a very simple curve:

$$
\begin{aligned}
(x, y) &= \mathbf{f}(u) = & (u, u), \\
(x, y) &= \mathbf{f}(u) = & (u^2, u^2), \\
(x, y) &= \mathbf{f}(u) = & (u^5, u^5).
\end{aligned}
$$

All three functions represent the same curve on the unit interval; however when u is not 0 or 1, $\mathbf{f}(u)$ refers to a different point depending on the representation of the curve.

If we are given a parameterization of a curve, we can use it directly as our specification of the curve, or we can develop a more convenient parameterization. Usually, the *natural parameterization* is created in a way that is convenient (or natural) for specifying the curve, so we don't have to know about how the speed changes along the curve.

If we know that the pen moves at a constant velocity, then the values of the free parameters have more meaning. Halfway through parameter space is halfway along the curve. Rather than measuring time, the parameter can be thought to measure length along the curve. Such parameterizations are called *arc-length* parameterizations because they define curves by functions that map from the distance along the curve (known as the arc length) to positions. We often use the variable s to denote an arc length parameter.

Technically, a parameterization is an arc-length parameterization if the magnitude of its *tangent* (that is, the derivative of the parameterization with respect to the parameter) has constant magnitude. Expressed as an equation,

$$\left| \frac{d\mathbf{f}(s)}{ds} \right|^2 = c.$$

Computing the length along a curve can be tricky. In general, it is defined by the integral of the magnitude of the derivative (intuitively, the magnitude of the derivative is the velocity of the pen as it moves along the curve). So, given a value for the parameter v, you can compute s (the arc-length distance along the curve from the point $\mathbf{f}(0)$ to the point $\mathbf{f}(v)$) as

$$s = \int_0^v \left| \frac{d\mathbf{f}(t)}{dt} \right|^2 dt, \tag{15.1}$$

where $\mathbf{f}(t)$ is a function that defines the curve with a natural parameterization.

Using the arc-length parameterization requires being able to solve Equation (15.1) for t, given s. For many of the kinds of curves we examine, it cannot be done in a closed-form (simple) manner and must be done numerically.

Generally, we use the variable u to denote free parameters that range over the unit interval, s to denote arc-length free parameters, and t to represent parameters that aren't one of the other two.

15.1.2 Piecewise Parametric Representations

For some curves, defining a parametric function that represents their shape is easy. For example, lines, circles, and ellipses all have simple functions that define the points they contain in terms of a parameter. For many curves, finding a function that specifies their shape can be hard. The main strategy that we use to create complex curves is divide-and-conquer: we break the curve into a number of simpler smaller pieces, each of which has a simple description.

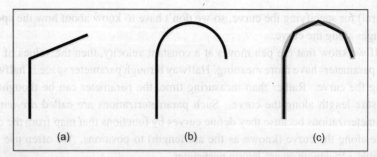

(a)   (b)   (c)

Figure 15.1. (a) A curve that can be easily represented as two lines; (b) a curve that can be easily represented as a line and a circular arc; (c) a curve approximating curve (b) with five line segments

For example, consider the curves in Figure 15.1. The first two curves are easily specified in terms of two pieces. In the case of the curve in Figure 15.1(b), we need two different kinds of pieces: a line segment and a circle.

To create a parametric representation of a compound curve (like the curve in Figure 15.1(b)), we need to have our parametric function switch between the functions that represent the pieces. If we define our parametric functions over the range $0 \le u \le 1$, then the curve in Figures 15.1(a) or (b) might be defined as

$$\mathbf{f}(u) = \begin{cases} \mathbf{f}_1(2u) & \text{if } u \le 0.5, \\ \mathbf{f}_2(2u - 1) & \text{if } u > 0.5, \end{cases} \tag{15.2}$$

where $\mathbf{f}_1$ is a parameterization of the first piece, $\mathbf{f}_2$ is a parameterization of the second piece, and both of these functions are defined over the unit interval.

We need to be careful in defining the functions $\mathbf{f}_1$ and $\mathbf{f}_2$ to make sure that the pieces of the curve fit together. If $\mathbf{f}_1(1) \ne \mathbf{f}_2(0)$, then our curve pieces will not connect and will not form a single continuous curve.

To represent the curve in Figure 15.1(b), we needed to use two different types of pieces: a line segment and a circular arc. For simplicity's sake, we may prefer to use a single type of piece. If we try to represent the curve in Figure 15.1(b) with only one type of piece (line segments), we cannot exactly recreate the curve (unless we use an infinite number of pieces). While the new curve made of line segments (as in Figure 15.1(c)) may not be exactly the same shape as in Figure 15.1(b), it might be close enough for our use. In such a case, we might prefer the simplicity of using the simpler line segment pieces to having a curve that more accurately represents the shape.

Also, notice that as we use an increasing number of pieces, we can get a better approximation. In the limit (using an infinite number of pieces), we can exactly represent the original shape.

One advantage to using a piecewise representation is that it allows us to make a tradeoff between

1. how well our represented curve approximates the real shape we are trying to represent;

2. how complicated the pieces that we use are;

3. how many pieces we use.

So, if we are trying to represent a complicated shape, we might decide that a crude approximation is acceptable and use a small number of simple pieces. To improve the approximation, we can choose between using more pieces and using more complicated pieces.

In computer graphics practice, we tend to prefer using relatively simple curve pieces (either line segments, arcs, or polynomial segments).

15.1.3   Splines

Before computers, when draftsmen wanted to draw a smooth curve, one tool they employed was a stiff piece of metal that they would bend into the desired shape for tracing. Because the metal would bend, not fold, it would have a smooth shape. The stiffness meant that the metal would bend as little as possible to make the desired shape. This stiff piece of metal was called a *spline.*

Mathematicians found that they could represent the curves created by a draftman's spline with piecewise polynomial functions. Initially, they used the term spline to mean a smooth, piecewise polynomial function. More recently, the term spline has been used to describe any piecewise polynomial function. We prefer this latter definition.

For us, a *spline* is a piecewise polynomial function. Such functions are very useful for representing curves.

15.2   Curve Properties

To describe a curve, we need to give some facts about its properties. For "named" curves, the properties are usually specific according to the type of curve. For example, to describe a circle, we might provide its radius and the position of its center. For an ellipse, we might also provide the orientation of its major axis and the ratio of the lengths of the axes. For free-form curves however, we need to have a more general set of properties to describe individual curves.

Some properties of curves are attributed to only a single location on the curve, while other properties require knowledge of the whole curve. For an intuition of the difference, imagine that the curve is a train track. If you are standing on the track on a foggy day you can tell that the track is straight or curved and whether or not you are at an end point. These are *local* properties. You cannot tell whether or not the track is a closed curve, or crosses itself, or how long it is. We call this type of property, a *global* property.

The study of local properties of geometric objects (curves and surfaces) is known as *differential geometry*. Technically, to be a differential property, there are some mathematical restrictions about the properties (roughly speaking, in the train-track analogy, you would not be able to have a GPS or a compass). Rather than worry about this distinction, we will use the term *local* property rather than differential property.

Local properties are important tools for describing curves because they do not require knowledge about the whole curve. Local properties include

- continuity,

- position at a specific place on the curve,

- direction at a specific place on the curve,

- curvature (and other derivatives).

Often, we want to specify that a curve includes a particular point. A curve is said to *interpolate* a point if that point is part of the curve. A function f interpolates a value v if there is some value of the parameter u for which $f(t) = v$. We call the place of interpolation, that is the value of t, the *site*.

15.2.1 Continuity

It will be very important to understand the local properties of a curve where two parametric pieces come together. If a curve is defined using an equation like Equation (15.2), then we need to be careful about how the pieces are defined. If $f_1(1) \neq f_2(0)$, then the curve will be "broken"—we would not be able to draw the curve in a continuous stroke of a pen. We call the condition that the curve pieces fit together *continuity* conditions because if they hold, the curve can be drawn as a continuous piece. Because our definition of "curve" at the beginning of the chapter requires a curve to be continuous, technically a "broken curve" is not a curve.

In addition to the positions, we can also check that the derivatives of the pieces match correctly. If $\mathbf{f}_1'(1) \neq \mathbf{f}_2'(0)$, then the combined curve will have an abrupt change in its first derivative at the switching point; the first derivative will not be continuous. In general, we say that a curve is C^n continuous if all of its derivatives up to n match across pieces. We denote the position itself as the zeroth derivative, so that the C^0 continuity condition means that the positions of the curve are continuous, and C^1 continuity means that positions and first derivatives are continuous. The definition of curve requires the curve to be C^0.

An illustration of some continuity conditions is shown in Figure 15.2. A discontinuity in the first derivative (the curve is C^0 but not C^1) is usually noticeable because it displays a sharp corner. A discontinuity in the second derivative is sometimes visually noticeable. Discontinuities in higher derivatives might matter, depending on the application. For example, if the curve represents a motion, an abrupt change in the second derivative is noticeable, so third derivative continuity is often useful. If the curve is going to have a fluid flowing over it (for example, if it is the shape for an airplane wing or boat hull), a discontinuity in the fourth or fifth derivative might cause turbulence.

The type of continuity we have just introduced (C^n) is commonly referred to as *parametric continuity* as it depends on the parameterization of the two curve pieces. If the "speed" of each piece is different, then they will not be continuous. For cases where we care about the shape of the curve, and not its parameterization, we define *geometric continuity* that requires that the derivatives of the curve pieces match when the curves are parameterized equivalently (for example, using an arc-length parameterization). Intuitively, this means that the corresponding derivatives must have the same direction, even if they have different magnitudes.

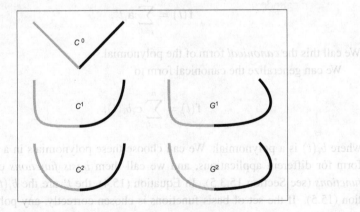

Figure 15.2. An illustration of various types of continuity between two curve segments.

So, if the C^1 continuity condition is

$$\mathbf{f}_1'(1) = \mathbf{f}_2'(0),$$

the G^1 continuity condition would be

$$\mathbf{f}_1'(1) = k\,\mathbf{f}_2'(0),$$

for some value of scalar k. Generally, geometric continuity is less restrictive than parametric continuity. A C^n curve is also G^n except when the parametric derivatives vanish.

15.3 Polynomial Pieces

The most widely used representations of curves in computer graphics is done by piecing together basic elements that are defined by polynomials and called polynomial pieces. For example, a line element is given by a linear polynomial. In Section 15.3.1, we give a formal definition and explain how to put pieces of polynomial together.

15.3.1 Polynomial Notation

Polynomials are functions of the form

$$f(t) = a_0 + a_1 t + a_2 t^2 + \ldots + a_n t^n. \tag{15.3}$$

The a_i are called the *coefficients.* and n is called the degree of the polynomial if $a_n \neq 0$. We also write Equation (15.3) in the form

$$\mathbf{f}(t) = \sum_{i=0}^{n} \mathbf{a}_i t^i. \tag{15.4}$$

We call this the *canonical* form of the polynomial.

We can generalize the canonical form to

$$\mathbf{f}(t) = \sum_{i=0}^{n} \mathbf{c}_i b_i(t), \tag{15.5}$$

where $b_i(t)$ is a polynomial. We can choose these polynomials in a convenient form for different applications, and we call them *basis functions* or *blending functions* (see Section 15.3.5). In Equation (15.4), the t^i are the $b_i(t)$ of Equation (15.5). If the set of basis functions is chosen correctly, any polynomial of degree $n + 1$ can be represented by an appropriate choice of $\mathbf{c}$.

The canonical form does not always have convenient coefficients. For practical purposes, throughout this chapter, we will find sets of basis functions such that the coefficients are convenient ways to control the curves represented by the polynomial functions.

To specify a curve embedded in two dimensions, one can either specify two polynomials in t: one for how x varies with t and one for how y varies with t; or specify a single polynomial where each of the $\mathbf{a}_i$ is a 2D point. An analogous situation exists for any curve in an n-dimensional space.

15.3.2 A Line Segment

To introduce the concepts of piecewise polynomial curve representations, we will discuss line segments. In practice, line segments are so simple that the mathematical derivations will seem excessive. However, by understanding this simple case, things will be easier when we move on to more complicated polynomials.

Consider a line segment that connects point $\mathbf{p}_0$ to $\mathbf{p}_1$. We could write the parametric function over the unit domain for this line segment as

$$\mathbf{f}(u) = (1 - u)\mathbf{p}_0 + u\mathbf{p}_1 \tag{15.6}$$

By writing this in vector form, we have hidden the dimensionality of the points and the fact that we are dealing with each dimension separately. For example, were we working in 2D, we could have created separate equations:

$$f_x(u) = (1 - u)x_0 + ux_1,$$
$$f_y(u) = (1 - u)y_0 + uy_1.$$

The line that we specify is determined by the two end points, but from now on we will stick to vector notation since it is cleaner. We will call the vector of control parameters, $\mathbf{p}$, the *control points*, and each element of $\mathbf{p}$, a *control point*.

While describing a line segment by the positions of its endpoints is obvious and usually convenient, there are other ways to describe a line segment. For example,

1. the position of the center of the line segment, the orientation, and the length;

2. the position of one endpoint and the position of the second point relative to the first;

3. the position of the middle of the line segment and one endpoint.

It is obvious that given one kind of a description of a line segment, we can switch to another one.

A different way to describe a line segment is using the canonical form of the polynomial (as discussed in Section 15.3.1),

$$\mathbf{f}(u) = \mathbf{a}_0 + u\mathbf{a}_1. \tag{15.7}$$

Any line segment can be represented either by specifying $\mathbf{a}_0$ and $\mathbf{a}_1$ or the endpoints ($\mathbf{p}_0$ and $\mathbf{p}_1$). It is usually more convenient to specify the endpoints, because we can compute the other parameters from the endpoints.

To write the canonical form as a vector expression, we define a vector $\mathbf{u}$ that is a vector of the powers of u:

$$\mathbf{u} = \begin{bmatrix} 1 \ u \ u^2 \ u^3 \ \dots \ u^n \end{bmatrix},$$

so that Equation (15.4) can be written as

$$\mathbf{f}(u) = \mathbf{u} \cdot \mathbf{a}. \tag{15.8}$$

This vector notation will make transforming between different forms of the curve easier.

Equation (15.8) describes a curve segment by the set of polynomial coefficients for the simple form of the polynomial. We call such a representation the *canonical* form. We will denote the parameters of the canonical form by $\mathbf{a}$.

While it is mathematically simple, the canonical form is not always the most convenient way to specify curves. For example, we might prefer to specify a line segment by the positions of its endpoints. If we want to define $\mathbf{p}_0$ to be the beginning of the segment (where the segment is when $u = 0$) and $\mathbf{p}_1$ to be the end of the line segment (where the line segment is at $u = 1$), we can write

$$\begin{aligned} \mathbf{p}_0 &= \mathbf{f}(0) &= [1 \ 0] \cdot [\mathbf{a}_0 \ \mathbf{a}_1], \\ \mathbf{p}_1 &= \mathbf{f}(1) &= [1 \ 1] \cdot [\mathbf{a}_0 \ \mathbf{a}_1]. \end{aligned} \tag{15.9}$$

We can solve these equations for $\mathbf{a}_0$ and $\mathbf{a}_1$:

$$\begin{aligned} \mathbf{a}_0 &= \mathbf{p}_0, \\ \mathbf{a}_1 &= \mathbf{p}_1 - \mathbf{p}_0. \end{aligned}$$

Matrix Form for Polynomials

While this first example was easy enough to solve, for more complicated examples it will be easier to write Equation (15.9) in the form

$$\begin{bmatrix} \mathbf{p}_0 \\ \mathbf{p}_1 \end{bmatrix} = \begin{bmatrix} 1 & 0 \\ 1 & 1 \end{bmatrix} \begin{bmatrix} \mathbf{a}_0 \\ \mathbf{a}_1 \end{bmatrix}.$$

Alternatively, we can write

$$\mathbf{p} = \mathbf{C}\,\mathbf{a}, \tag{15.10}$$

where we call $\mathbf{C}$, the *constraint matrix*.[1] If having vectors of points bothers you, you can consider each dimension independently (so that $\mathbf{p}$ is $[x_0 \; x_1]$ or $[y_0 \; y_1]$) and $\mathbf{a}$ is handled correspondingly).

We can solve Equation (15.10) for $\mathbf{a}$ by finding the inverse of $\mathbf{C}$. This inverse matrix which we will denote by $\mathbf{B}$ is called the *basis* matrix. The basis matrix is very handy since it tells us how to convert between the convenient parameters $\mathbf{p}$ and the canonical form $\mathbf{a}$, and, therefore, gives us an easy way to evaluate the curve

$$\mathbf{f}(u) = \mathbf{u}\,\mathbf{B}\,\mathbf{p}.$$

We can find a basis matrix for whatever form of the curve that we want, providing that there are no non-linearities in the definition of the parameters. Examples of non-linearly defined parameters include the length and angle of the line segment.

Now, suppose we want to parameterize the line segment so that $\mathbf{p}_0$ is the half-way point ($u = 0.5$), and $\mathbf{p}_1$ is the ending point ($u = 1$). To derive the basis matrix for this parameterization, we set

$$\mathbf{p}_0 = \mathbf{f}(0.5) = 1\,\mathbf{a}_0 + 0.5\,\mathbf{a}_1,$$
$$\mathbf{p}_1 = \mathbf{f}(1) = 1\,\mathbf{a}_0 + 1\,\mathbf{a}_1.$$

So

$$\mathbf{C} = \begin{bmatrix} 1 & .5 \\ 1 & 1 \end{bmatrix},$$

and therefore

$$\mathbf{B} = \mathbf{C}^{-1} = \begin{bmatrix} 2 & -1 \\ -2 & 2 \end{bmatrix}.$$

15.3.3 Beyond Line Segments

Line segments are so simple that finding a basis matrix is trivial. However, it was good practice for curves of higher degree. First, let's consider quadratics (curves of degree two). The advantage of the canonical form (Equation (15.4)) is that it works for these more complicated curves, just by letting n be a larger number.

---

[1] We assume the form of a vector (row or column) is obvious from the context, and we will skip all of the transpose symbols for vectors.

A quadratic (a degree-two polynomial) has three coefficients, $\mathbf{a}_0$, $\mathbf{a}_1$, and $\mathbf{a}_2$. These coefficients are not convenient for describing the shape of the curve. However, we can use the same basis matrix method to devise more convenient parameters. If we know the value of u, Equation (15.4) becomes a linear equation in the parameters, and the linear algebra from the last section still works.

Suppose that we wanted to describe our curves by the position of the beginning ($u = 0$), middle[2] ($u = 0.5$), and end ($u = 1$). Entering the appropriate values into Equation (15.4):

$$
\begin{aligned}
\mathbf{p}_0 &= \mathbf{f}(0)   &&= \mathbf{a}_0 + 0^1 && \mathbf{a}_1 + 0^2 && \mathbf{a}_2, \\
\mathbf{p}_1 &= \mathbf{f}(0.5) &&= \mathbf{a}_0 + 0.5^1 && \mathbf{a}_1 + 0.5^2 && \mathbf{a}_2, \\
\mathbf{p}_2 &= \mathbf{f}(1)   &&= \mathbf{a}_0 + 1^1 && \mathbf{a}_1 + 1^2 && \mathbf{a}_2.
\end{aligned}
$$

So the constraint matrix is

$$
\mathbf{C} = \begin{bmatrix} 1 & 0 & 0 \\ 1 & .5 & .25 \\ 1 & 1 & 1 \end{bmatrix},
$$

and the basis matrix is

$$
\mathbf{B} = \mathbf{C}^{-1} = \begin{bmatrix} 1 & 0 & 0 \\ -3 & 4 & -1 \\ 2 & -4 & 2 \end{bmatrix}.
$$

There is an additional type of constraint (or parameter) that is sometimes convenient to specify: the derivative of the curve (with respect to its free parameter) at a particular value. Intuitively, the derivatives tell us how the curve is changing, so that the first derivative tells us what direction the curve is going, the second derivative tells us how quickly the curve is changing direction, etc. We will see examples of why it is useful to specify derivatives later.

For the quadratic,

$$
\mathbf{f}(u) = \mathbf{a}_0 + \mathbf{a}_1 u + \mathbf{a}_2 u^2,
$$

the derivatives are simple:

$$
\mathbf{f}'(u) = \frac{d\mathbf{f}}{du} = \mathbf{a}_1 + 2\mathbf{a}_2 u,
$$

and

$$
\mathbf{f}''(u) = \frac{d^2\mathbf{f}}{du^2} = \frac{d\mathbf{f}'}{du} = 2\mathbf{a}_2.
$$

---

[2]Notice that this is the middle of the parameter space, which might not be the middle of the curve itself.

Or, more generally,

$$\mathbf{f}'(u) = \sum_{i=1}^{n} iu^{i-1}\mathbf{a}_i,$$
$$\mathbf{f}''(u) = \sum_{i=2}^{n} i(i-1)u^{i-2}\mathbf{a}_i.$$

For example, consider a case where we want to specify a quadratic curve segment by the position, first, and second derivative at its middle ($u = 0.5$).

$$
\begin{array}{llllllll}
\mathbf{p}_0 & = \mathbf{f}(0.5) & = \mathbf{a}_0+ & 0.5^1 & \mathbf{a}_1+ & & 0.5^2 & \mathbf{a}_2, \\
\mathbf{p}_1 & = \mathbf{f}'(0.5) & = & & \mathbf{a}_1+ & 2 & 0.5 & \mathbf{a}_2, \\
\mathbf{p}_2 & = \mathbf{f}''(0.5) & = & & & & 2 & \mathbf{a}_2.
\end{array}
$$

The constraint matrix is

$$\mathbf{C} = \begin{bmatrix} 1 & .5 & .25 \\ 0 & 1 & 1 \\ 0 & 0 & 2 \end{bmatrix},$$

and the basis matrix is

$$\mathbf{B} = \mathbf{C}^{-1} = \begin{bmatrix} 1 & -.5 & .125 \\ 0 & 1 & -.5 \\ 0 & 0 & .5 \end{bmatrix}.$$

15.3.4 Basis Matrices for Cubics

Cubic polynomials are popular in graphics (See Section 15.5). The derivations for the various forms of cubics are just like the derivations we've seen already in this section. We will work through one more example for practice.

A very useful form of a cubic polynomial is the *Hermite* form, where we specify the position and first derivative at the beginning and end, that is,

$$
\begin{array}{lllllllll}
\mathbf{p}_0 & = & \mathbf{f}(0) & = \mathbf{a}_0 + & 0^1 \, \mathbf{a}_1 & + & 0^2 \, \mathbf{a}_2+ & & 0^3 \, \mathbf{a}_3, \\
\mathbf{p}_1 & = & \mathbf{f}'(0) & = & \mathbf{a}_1 & +2 & 0^1 \, \mathbf{a}_2+ & 3 & 0^2 \, \mathbf{a}_3, \\
\mathbf{p}_2 & = & \mathbf{f}(1) & = \mathbf{a}_0 + & 1^1 \, \mathbf{a}_1 & + & 1^2 \, \mathbf{a}_2+ & & 1^3 \, \mathbf{a}_3, \\
\mathbf{p}_3 & = & \mathbf{f}'(1) & = & \mathbf{a}_1 & +2 & 1^1 \, \mathbf{a}_2+ & 3 & 1^2 \, \mathbf{a}_3.
\end{array}
$$

Thus, the constraint matrix is

$$
\mathbf{C} = \begin{bmatrix} 1 & 0 & 0 & 0 \\ 0 & 1 & 0 & 0 \\ 1 & 1 & 1 & 1 \\ 0 & 1 & 2 & 3 \end{bmatrix},
$$

and the basis matrix is

$$
\mathbf{B} = \mathbf{C}^{-1} = \begin{bmatrix} 1 & 0 & 0 & 0 \\ 0 & 1 & 0 & 0 \\ -3 & -2 & 3 & -1 \\ 2 & 1 & -2 & 1 \end{bmatrix}.
$$

We will discuss Hermite cubic splines in Section 15.5.2.

15.3.5 Blending Functions

If we know the basis matrix, $\mathbf{B}$, we can multiply it by the parameter vector, $\mathbf{u}$, to get a vector of functions

$$
\mathbf{b}(u) = \mathbf{u}\,\mathbf{B}.
$$

Notice that we denote this vector by $\mathbf{b}(u)$ to emphasize the fact that its value depends on the free parameter u. We call the elements of $\mathbf{b}(u)$ the *blending functions*, because they specify how to blend the values of the control point vector together:

$$
\mathbf{f}(u) = \sum_{i=0}^{n} b_i(u)\mathbf{p}_i. \tag{15.11}
$$

It is important to note that for a chosen value of u, Equation (15.11) is a *linear* equation specifying a *linear blend* (or weighted average) of the control points. This is true no matter what degree polynomials are "hidden" inside of the b_i functions.

Blending functions provide a nice abstraction for describing curves. Any type of curve can be represented as a linear combination of its control points, where those weights are computed as some arbitrary functions of the free parameter.

15.3.6 Interpolating Polynomials

In general, a polynomial of degree n can interpolate a set of $n + 1$ values. If we are given a vector $\mathbf{p} = (p_0, \ldots, p_n)$ of points to interpolate and a vector

$\mathbf{t} = (t_0, \ldots, t_n)$ of increasing parameter values, $t_i \neq t_j$, we can use the methods described in the previous sections to determine an $n + 1 \times n + 1$ basis matrix that gives us a function $f(t)$ such that $f(t_i) = p_i$. For any given vector $\mathbf{t}$, we need to set up and solve an $n = 1 \times n + 1$ linear system. This provides us with a set of $n + 1$ basis functions that perform interpolation:

$$\mathbf{f}(t) = \sum_{i=0}^{n} \mathbf{p}_i b_i(t).$$

These interpolating basis functions can be derived in other ways. One particularly elegant way to define them is the *Lagrange form:*

$$b_i = \prod_{j=0, j \neq i}^{n} \frac{x - t_j}{t_i - t_j}. \tag{15.12}$$

There are more computationally efficient ways to express the interpolating basis functions than the Lagrange form (see De Boor (1978) for details).

Interpolating polynomials provide a mechanism for defining curves that interpolate a set of points. Figure 15.3 shows some examples. While it is possible to create a single polynomial to interpolate any number of points, we rarely use high-order polynomials to represent curves in computer graphics. Instead, interpolating splines (piecewise polynomial functions) are preferred. Some reasons for this are considered in Section 15.5.3.

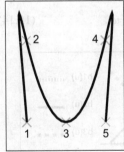

(a) Interpolating polynomial through five points

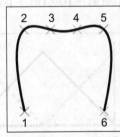

(b) Interpolating polynomial through six points

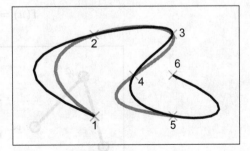

(c) Interpolating polynomial through five and six points

Figure 15.3. Interpolating polynomials through multiple points. Notice the extra wiggles and over-shooting between points. In (c), when the sixth point is added, it completely changes the shape of the curve due to the non-local nature of interpolating polynomials.

15.4　Putting Pieces Together

Now that we've seen how to make individual pieces of polynomial curves, we can consider how to put these pieces together.

15.4.1　Knots

The basic idea of a piecewise parametric function is that each piece is only used over some parameter range. For example, if we want to define a function that has two piecewise linear segments that connect three points (as shown in Figure 15.4(a)), we might define

$$\mathbf{f}(u) = \begin{cases} \mathbf{f}_1(2u) & \text{if } 0 \le u < \frac{1}{2}, \\ \mathbf{f}_2(2u - 1) & \text{if } \frac{1}{2} \le u < 1, \end{cases} \tag{15.13}$$

where $\mathbf{f}_1$ and $\mathbf{f}_2$ are functions for each of the two line segments. Notice that we have re-scaled the parameter for each of the pieces to facilitate writing their equations as

$$\mathbf{f}_1(u) = (1 - u)\mathbf{p}_1 + u\mathbf{p}_2.$$

For each polynomial in our piecewise function, there is a site (or parameter value) where it starts and ends. Sites where a piece function begins or ends are called *knots*. For the example in Equation (15.13), the values of the knots are 0, 0.5, and 1.

We may also write piecewise polynomial functions as the sum of basis functions, each scaled by a coefficient. For example, we can re-write the two line segments of Equation (15.13) as

$$\mathbf{f}(u) = \mathbf{p}_1 b_1(u) + \mathbf{p}_2 b_2(u) + \mathbf{p}_3 b_3(u), \tag{15.14}$$

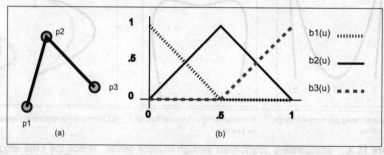

Figure 15.4. (a) Two line segments connect three points; (b) the blending functions for each of the points are graphed at right.

where the function $b_1(u)$ is defined as

$$b_1(u) = \begin{cases} 1 - 2u & \text{if } 0 \le u < \frac{1}{2}, \\ 0 & \text{otherwise,} \end{cases}$$

and b_2 and b_3 are defined similarly. These functions are plotted in Figure 15.4(b).

The knots of a polynomial function are the combination of the knots of all of the pieces that are used to create it. The *knot vector* is a vector that stores all of the knot values in ascending order.

Notice that in this section we have used two different mechanisms for combining polynomial pieces: using independent polynomial pieces for different ranges of the parameter and blending together piecewise polynomial functions.

15.4.2   Using Independent Pieces

In Section 15.3, we defined pieces of polynomials over the unit parameter range. If we want to assemble these pieces, we need to convert from the parameter of the overall function to the value of the parameter for the piece. The simplest way to do this is to define the overall curve over the parameter range $[0, n]$ where n is the number of segments. Depending on the value of the parameter, we can shift it to the required range.

15.4.3   Putting Segments Together

If we want to make a single curve from two line segments, we need to make sure that the end of the first line segment is at the same location as the beginning of the next. There are three ways to connect the two segments (in order of simplicity):

1. Represent the line segment as its two endpoints, and then use the same point for both. We call this a *shared-point* scheme.

2. Copy the value of the end of the first segment to the beginning of the second segment every time that the parameters of the first segment change. We call this a *dependency* scheme.

3. Write an explicit equation for the connection, and enforce it through numerical methods as the other parameters are changed.

While the simpler schemes are preferable since they require less work, they also place more restrictions on the way the line segments are parameterized. For example, if we want to use the center of the line segment as a parameter (so that the user can specify it directly), we will use the beginning of each line segment and the center of the line segment as their parameters. This will force us to use the dependency scheme.

Notice that if we use a shared point or dependency scheme, the total number of control points is less than $n * m$, where n is the number of segments and m is the number of control points for each segment; many of the control points of the independent pieces will be computed as functions of other pieces. Notice that if we use either the shared-point scheme for lines (each segment uses its two

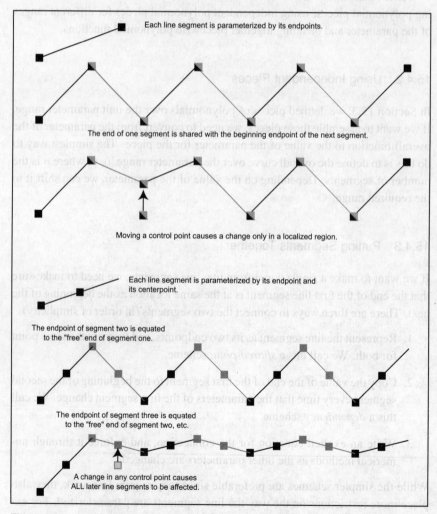

Figure 15.5. A chain of line segments with local control and one with non-local control.

endpoints as parameters and shares interior points with its neighbors), or if we use the dependency scheme (such as the example one with the first endpoint and midpoint), we end up with $n + 1$ controls for an n-segment curve.

Dependency schemes have a more serious problem. A change in one place in the curve can propagate through the entire curve. This is called a lack of *locality*. Locality means that if you move a point on a curve it will only effect a local region. The local region might be big, but it will be finite. If a curve's controls do not have locality, changing a control point may effect points infinitely far away.

To see locality, and the lack thereof, in action, consider two chains of line segments, as shown in Figure 15.5. One chain has its pieces parameterized by their endpoints and uses point-sharing to maintain continuity. The other has its pieces parameterized by an endpoint and midpoint and uses dependency propagation to keep the segments together. The two segment chains can represent the same curves: they are both a set of n connected line segments. However, because of locality issues, the endpoint-shared form is likely to be more convenient for the user. Consider changing the position of the first control point in each chain. For the endpoint-shared version, only the first segment will change, while all of the segments will be affected in the midpoint version, as in Figure 15.5. In fact, for any point moved in the endpoint-shared version, at most two line segments will change. In the midpoint version, all segments after the control point that is moved will change, even if the chain is infinitely long.

In this example, the dependency propagation scheme was the one that did not have local control. This is not always true. There are direct sharing schemes that are not local and propagation schemes that are local.

We emphasize that locality is a convenience of control issue. While it is inconvenient to have the entire curve change every time, the same changes can be made to the curve. It simply requires moving several points in unison.

15.5 Cubics

In graphics, when we represent curves using piecewise polynomials we usually use either line segments or cubic polynomials for the pieces. There are a number of reasons why cubics are popular in computer graphics:

- Piecewise cubic polynomials allow for C^2 continuity, which is generally sufficient for most visual tasks. The C^1 smoothness that quadratics offer is often insufficient. The greater smoothness offered by higher-order polynomials is rarely important.

- Cubic curves provide the minimum-curvature interpolants to a set of points. That is, if you have a set of $n + 3$ points and define the "smoothest" curve that passes through them (that is the curve that has the minimum curvature over its length), this curve can be represented as a piecewise cubic with n segments.

- Cubic polynomials have a nice symmetry where position and derivative can be specified at the beginning and end.

- Cubic polynomials have a nice tradeoff between the numerical issues in computation and the smoothness.

Notice that we do not have to use cubics. They just tend to be a good tradeoff between the amount of smoothness and complexity. Different applications may have different tradeoffs. We focus on cubics since they are the most commonly used.

The canonical form of a cubic polynomial is

$$\mathbf{f}(u) = \mathbf{a}_0 + \mathbf{a}_1\, u + \mathbf{a}_2\, u^2 + \mathbf{a}_3\, u^3.$$

As we discussed in Section 15.3, these canonical form coefficients are not a convenient way to describe a cubic segment.

We seek forms of cubic polynomials for which the coefficients are a convenient way to control the resulting curve represented by the cubic. One of the main conveniences will be to provide ways to insure the connectedness of the pieces and the continuity between the segments.

Each cubic polynomial piece requires four coefficients or control points. That means for a piecewise polynomial with n pieces, we may require up to $4n$ control points if no sharing between segments is done or dependencies used. More often, some part of each segment is either shared or depends on an adjacent segment, so the total number of control points is much lower. Also, note that a control point might be a position or a derivative of the curve.

Unfortunately, there is no single "best" representation for a piecewise cubic. It is not possible to have a piecewise polynomial curve representation that has all of the following desirable properties:

1. each piece of the curve is a cubic;

2. the curve interpolates the control points;

3. the curve has local control;

4. the curve has C^2 continuity.

We can have any three of these properties, but not all four; there are representations that have any combination of three. In this book, we will discuss cubic B-splines that do not interpolate their control points (but have local control and are C^2); Cardinal splines and Catmull-Rom splines that interpolate their control points and offer local control, but are not C^2; and natural cubics that interpolate and are C^2, but do not have local control.

The continuity properties of cubics refer to the continuity between the segments (at the knot points). The cubic pieces themselves have infinite continuity in their derivatives (the way we have been talking about continuity so far). Note that if you have a lot of control points (or knots), the curve can be wiggly, which might not seem "smooth."

15.5.1   Natural Cubics

With a piecewise cubic curve, it is possible to create a C^2 curve. To do this, we need to specify the position and first and second derivative at the beginning of each segment (so that we can make sure that it is the same as at the end of the previous segment). Notice, that each curve segment receives three out of its four parameters from the previous curve in the chain. These C^2 continuous chains of cubics are sometimes referred to as *natural* cubic splines.

For one segment of the natural cubic, we need to parameterize the cubic by the positions of its endpoints and the first and second derivative at the beginning point. The control points are therefore

$$\begin{aligned}
\mathbf{p}_0 &= \mathbf{f}(0) &= \mathbf{a}_0 &+ 0^1\mathbf{a}_1 &+ &\ 0^2\,\mathbf{a}_2 &+ &\ 0^3\,\mathbf{a}_3, \\
\mathbf{p}_1 &= \mathbf{f}'(0) &= &\ 1^1\mathbf{a}_1 &+2 &\ 0^1\,\mathbf{a}_2 &+3 &\ 0^2\,\mathbf{a}_3, \\
\mathbf{p}_2 &= \mathbf{f}''(0) &= & &2 &\ 1^1\mathbf{a}_2 &+6 &\ 0^1\,\mathbf{a}_3, \\
\mathbf{p}_3 &= \mathbf{f}(1) &= \mathbf{a}_0 &+ 1^1\,\mathbf{a}_1 &+ &\ 1^2\,\mathbf{a}_2 &+ &\ 1^3\,\mathbf{a}_3.
\end{aligned}$$

Therefore, the constraint matrix is

$$\mathbf{C} = \begin{bmatrix} 1 & 0 & 0 & 0 \\ 0 & 1 & 0 & 0 \\ 0 & 0 & 2 & 0 \\ 1 & 1 & 1 & 1 \end{bmatrix},$$

and the basis matrix is

$$\mathbf{B} = \mathbf{C}^{-1} = \begin{bmatrix} 1 & 0 & 0 & 0 \\ 0 & 1 & 0 & 0 \\ 0 & 0 & .5 & 0 \\ -1 & -1 & -.5 & 1 \end{bmatrix}.$$

Given a set of n control points, a natural cubic spline has $n-1$ cubic segments. The first segment uses the control points to define its beginning position, ending position, and first and second derivative at the beginning. A dependency scheme copies the position, and first and second derivative of the end of the first segment for use in the second segment.

A disadvantage of natural cubic splines is that they are not local. Any change in any segment may require the entire curve to change (at least the part after the change was made). To make matters worse, natural cubic splines tend to be ill-conditioned: a small change at the beginning of the curve can lead to large changes later. Another issue is that we only have control over the derivatives of the curve at its beginning. Segments after the beginning of the curve determine their derivatives from their beginning point.

15.5.2 Hermite Cubics

Hermite cubic polynomials were introduced in Section 15.3.4. A segment of a cubic Hermite spline allows the positions and first derivatives of both of its end points to be specified. A chain of segments can be linked into a C^1 spline by using the same values for the position and derivative of the end of one segment and for the beginning of the next.

Given a set of n control points, where every other control point is a derivative value, a cubic Hermite spline contains $(n-2)/2$ cubic segments. The spline interpolates the points, as shown in Figure 15.6, but can guarantee only C^1 continuity.

Hermite cubics are convenient because they provide local control over the shape, and provide C^1 continuity. However, since the user must specify both positions and derivatives, a special interface for the derivatives must be provided. One possibility is to provide the user with points that represent where the derivative vectors would end if they were "placed" at the position point.

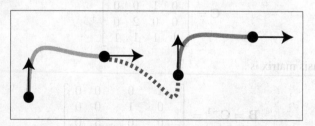

Figure 15.6. A Hermite cubic spline made up of three segments.

15.5.3 Cardinal Cubics

A *cardinal cubic spline* is a type of C^1 interpolating spline made up of cubic polynomial segments. Given a set of n control points, a cardinal cubic spline uses $n - 2$ cubic polynomial segments to interpolate all of its points except for the first and last.

Cardinal splines have a parameter called *tension* that controls how "tight" the curve is between the points it interpolates. The tension is a number in the range $[0, 1)$ that controls how the curve bends towards the next control point. For the important special case of $t = 0$, the splines are called *Catmull-Rom* splines.

Each segment of the cardinal spline uses four control points. For segment i, the points used are i, $i + 1$, $i + 2$, and $i + 3$ as the segments share three points with their neighbors. Each segment begins at its second control point and ends at its third control point. The derivative at the beginning of the curve is determined by the vector between the first and third control points, while the derivative at the end of the curve is given by the vector between the second and forth points, as shown in Figure 15.7.

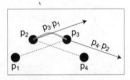

Figure 15.7. A segment of a cardinal cubic spline interpolates its second and third control points ($\mathbf{p}_2$ and $\mathbf{p}_3$), and uses its other points to determine the derivatives at the beginning and end.

The tension parameter adjusts how much the derivatives are scaled. Specifically, the derivatives are scaled by $(1 - t)/2$. The constraints on the cubic are therefore

$$
\begin{aligned}
\mathbf{f}(0) &= \mathbf{p}_2, \\
\mathbf{f}(1) &= \mathbf{p}_3, \\
\mathbf{f}'(0) &= \tfrac{1}{2}(1 - t)(\mathbf{p}_3 - \mathbf{p}_1), \\
\mathbf{f}'(1) &= \tfrac{1}{2}(1 - t)(\mathbf{p}_4 - \mathbf{p}_2).
\end{aligned}
$$

Solving these equations for the control points (defining $s = (1 - t)/2$) gives

$$
\begin{aligned}
\mathbf{p}_0 &= \mathbf{f}(1) - \tfrac{2}{1-t}\mathbf{f}'(0) &&= \mathbf{a}_0 &&+ (1 - \tfrac{1}{s})\ \mathbf{a}_1 &&+\ \mathbf{a}_2 &&+\ \mathbf{a}_3, \\
\mathbf{p}_1 &= \mathbf{f}(0) &&= \mathbf{a}_0, \\
\mathbf{p}_2 &= \mathbf{f}(1) &&= \mathbf{a}_0 &&+\ \mathbf{a}_1 &&+\ \mathbf{a}_2 &&+\ \mathbf{a}_3, \\
\mathbf{p}_3 &= \mathbf{f}(0) + \tfrac{1}{s}\mathbf{f}'(1) &&= \mathbf{a}_0 &&+ \tfrac{1}{s}\ \mathbf{a}_1 &&+ 2\tfrac{1}{s}\ \mathbf{a}_2 &&+ 3\tfrac{1}{s}\ \mathbf{a}_3.
\end{aligned}
$$

This yields the cardinal matrix

$$
\mathbf{B} = \mathbf{C}^{-1} = \begin{bmatrix} 0 & 1 & 0 & 0 \\ -s & 0 & s & 0 \\ 2s & s - 3 & 3 - 2s & -s \\ -s & 2 - s & s - 2 & s \end{bmatrix}.
$$

Since the third point of segment i is the second point of segment $i+1$, adjacent segments of the cardinal spline connect. Similarly, the same points are used to specify the first derivative of each segment, providing C^1 continuity.

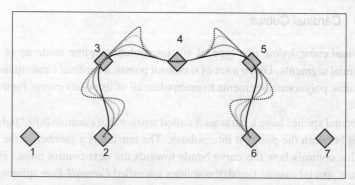

Figure 15.8. Cardinal splines through seven control points with varying values of tension parameter *t*.

Cardinal splines are useful, because they provide an easy way to interpolate a set of points with C^1 continuity and local control. They are only C^1, so they sometimes get "kinks" in them. The tension parameter gives some control over what happens between the interpolated points, as shown in Figure 15.8, where a set of cardinal splines through a set of points is shown. The curves use the same control points, but they use different values for the tension parameters. Note that the first and last control points are not interpolated.

Given a set of n points to interpolate, you might wonder why we might prefer to use a cardinal cubic spline (that is a set of $n - 2$ cubic pieces) rather than a single, order n polynomial as described in Section 15.3.6. Some of the disadvantages of the interpolating polynomial are:

- The interpolating polynomial tends to overshoot the points, as seen in Figure 15.9. This overshooting gets worse as the number of points grows larger. The cardinal splines tend to be well behaved in between the points.

- Control of the interpolating polynomial is not local. Changing a point at the beginning of the spline affects the entire spline. Cardinal splines are local: any place on the spline is affected by its four neighboring points at most.

- Evaluation of the interpolating polynomial is not local. Evaluating a point on the polynomial requires access to all of its points. Evaluating a point on the piecewise cubic requires a fixed small number of computations, no matter how large the total number of points is.

There are a variety of other numerical and technical issues in using interpolating splines as the number of points grows larger. See (De Boor, 2001) for more information.

A cardinal spline has the disadvantage that it does not interpolate the first or last point, which can be easily fixed by adding an extra point at either end of

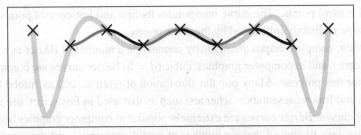

Figure 15.9. Splines interpolating nine control points (marked with small crosses). The thick gray line shows an interpolating polynomial. The thin, dark line shows a Catmull-Rom spline. The latter is made of seven cubic segments, which are each shown in alternating gray tones.

the sequence. The cardinal spline also is not as continuous—providing only C^1 continuity at the knots.

15.6 Approximating Curves

It might seem like the easiest way to control a curve is to specify a set of points for it to interpolate. In practice, however, interpolation schemes often have undesirable properties because they have less continuity and offer no control of what happens between the points. Curve schemes that only approximate the points are often preferred. With an approximating scheme, the control points influence the shape of the curve, but do not specify it exactly. Although we give up the ability to directly specify points for the curve to pass through, we gain better behavior of the curve and local control. Should we need to interpolate a set of points, the positions of the control points can be computed such that the curve passes through these interpolation points.

The two most important types of approximating curves in computer graphics are Bézier curves and B-spline curves.

15.6.1 Bézier Curves

Bézier curves are one of the most common representations for free-form curves in computer graphics. The curves are named for Pierre Bézier, one of the people who was instrumental in their development. Bézier curves have an interesting history where they were concurrently developed by several independent groups.

A Bézier curve is a polynomial curve that approximates its control points. The curves can be a polynomial of any degree. A curve of degree d is controlled by

$d + 1$ control points. The curve interpolates its first and last control points, and the shape is directly influenced by the other points.

Often, complex shapes are made by connecting a number of Bézier curves of low degree, and in computer graphics, cubic ($d = 3$) Bézier curves are commonly used for this purpose. Many popular illustration programs, such as Adobe Illustrator, and font representation schemes, such as that used in Postscript, use cubic Bézier curves. Bézier curves are extremely popular in computer graphics because they are easy to control, have a number of useful properties, and there are very efficient algorithms for working with them.

Bézier curves are constructed such that:

- The curve interpolates the first and last control points, with $u = 0$ and 1, respectively.

- The first derivative of the curve at its beginning (end) is determined by the vector between the first and second (next to last and last) control points. The derivatives are given by the vectors between these points scaled by the degree of the curve.

- Higher derivatives at the beginning (end) of the curve depend on the points at the beginning (end) of the curve. The nth derivative depends on the first (last) $n + 1$ points.

For example, consider the Bézier curve of degree 3 as in Figure 15.10. The curve has four ($d + 1$) control points. It begins at the first control point ($\mathbf{p}_0$) and ends at the last ($\mathbf{p}_1$). The first derivative at the beginning is proportional to the vector between the first and second control points ($\mathbf{p}_1 - \mathbf{p}_0$). Specifically, $\mathbf{f}'(0) = 3(\mathbf{p}_1 - \mathbf{p}_0)$. Similarly, the first derivative at the end of the curve is given

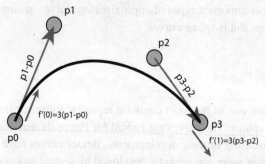

Figure 15.10. A cubic Bézier curve is controlled by four points. It interpolates the first and last, and the beginning and final derivatives are three times the vectors between the first two (or last two) points.

by $\mathbf{f}'(1) = 3(\mathbf{p}_3 - \mathbf{p}_2)$. The second derivative at the beginning of the curve can be determined from control points $\mathbf{p}_0$, $\mathbf{p}_1$ and $\mathbf{p}_2$.

Using the facts about Bézier cubics in the preceding paragraph, we can use the methods of Section 15.5 to create a parametric function for them. The definitions of the beginning and end interpolation and derivatives give

$$
\begin{aligned}
\mathbf{p}_0 = & \ \mathbf{f}(0) & = \mathbf{a}_3 0^3 + \mathbf{a}_2 0^2 + \mathbf{a}_1 0 + \mathbf{a}_0, \\
\mathbf{p}_3 = & \ \mathbf{f}(1) & = \mathbf{a}_3 1^3 + \mathbf{a}_2 1^2 + \mathbf{a}_1 1 + \mathbf{a}_0, \\
3(\mathbf{p}_1 - \mathbf{p}_0) = & \ \mathbf{f}'(0) & = 3\mathbf{a}_3 0^2 + 2\mathbf{a}_2 0 + \mathbf{a}_1, \\
3(\mathbf{p}_3 - \mathbf{p}_2) = & \ \mathbf{f}'(1) & = 3\mathbf{a}_3 1^2 + 2\mathbf{a}_2 1 + \mathbf{a}_1.
\end{aligned}
$$

This can be solved for the basis matrix

$$
\mathbf{B} = \mathbf{C}^{-1} = \begin{bmatrix} 1 & 0 & 0 & 0 \\ -3 & 3 & 0 & 0 \\ 3 & -6 & 3 & 0 \\ -1 & 3 & -3 & 1 \end{bmatrix},
$$

and then written as

$$
\mathbf{f}(u) = (1 - 3u + 3u^2 - u^3)\mathbf{p}_0 + (3u - 6u^2 + 3u^3)\mathbf{p}_1 + (3u^2 - 3u^3)\mathbf{p}_2 + (u^3)\mathbf{p}_3,
$$

or

$$
\mathbf{f}(u) = \sum_{i=0}^{d} b_{i,3}\mathbf{p}_i,
$$

where the $b_{i,3}$ are the Bézier blending functions of degree 3:

$$
\begin{aligned}
b_{0,3} = & \ (1 - u)^3, \\
b_{1,3} = & \ 3u(1 - u)^2, \\
b_{2,3} = & \ 3u^2(1 - u), \\
b_{3,3} = & \ u^3.
\end{aligned}
$$

Fortunately, the blending functions for Bézier curves have a special form that works for all degrees. These functions are known as the *Bernstein basis polynomials* and have the general form

$$
b_{k,n}(u) = C(n, k) \, u^k \, (1 - u)^{(n-k)},
$$

where n is the order of the Bézier curve, and k is the blending function number between 0 and n (inclusive). $C(n, k)$ are the binomial coefficients:

$$
C(n, k) = \frac{n!}{k! \, (n - k)!}.
$$

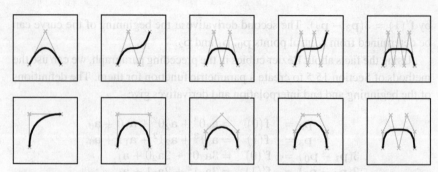

Figure 15.11. Various Bézier segments of degree 2–6. The control points are shown with crosses, and the control polygons (line segments connecting the control points) are also shown.

Given the positions of the control points $\mathbf{p}_k$, the function to evaluate the Bézier curve of order n (with $n + 1$ control points) is

$$\mathbf{p}(u) = \sum_{k=0}^{n} p_k C(n, k) \, u^k \, (1 - u)^{(n-k)}.$$

Some Bézier segments are shown in Figure 15.11.

Bézier segments have several useful properties:

- The curve is bounded by the convex hull of the control points.

- Any line intersects the curve no more times than it intersects the set of line segments connecting the control points. This is called the *variation diminishing* property. This property is illustrated in Figure 15.12.

- The curves are symmetric: reversing the order of the control points yields the same curve, with a reversed parameterization.

- The curves are *affine invariant*. This means that translating, scaling, rotating, or skewing the control points is the same as performing those operations on the curve itself.

- There are good simple algorithms for evaluating and subdividing Bézier curves into pieces that are themselves Bézier curves. Because subdivision can be done effectively using the algorithm described later, a divide and conquer approach can be used to create effective algorithms for important tasks such as rendering Bézier curves, approximating them with line segments, and determining the intersection between two curves.

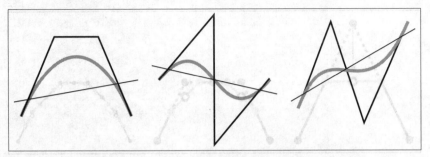

Figure 15.12. The *variation diminishing* property of Bézier curves means that the curve does not cross a line more than its control polygon does. Therefore, if the control polygon has no "wiggles," the curve will not have them either. B-splines (Section 15.6.2) also have this property.

When Bézier segments are connected together to make a spline, connectivity between the segments is created by sharing the endpoints. However, continuity of the derivatives must be created by positioning the other control points. This provides the user of a Bézier spline with control over the smoothness. For G^1 continuity, the second-to-last point of the first curve and the second point of the second curve must be collinear with the equated endpoints. For C^1 continuity, the distances between the points must be equal as well. This is illustrated in Figure 15.13. Higher degrees of continuity can be created by properly positioning more points.

Figure 15.13. Two Bézier segments connect to form a C^1 spline, because the vector between the last two points of the first segment is equal to the vector between the first two points of the second segment.

Geometric Intuition for Bezier Curves

Bézier curves can be derived from geometric principles, as well as from the algebraic methods described above. We outline the geometric principles because they provides intuition on how Bézier curves work.

Imagine that we have a set of control points from which we want to create a smooth curve. Simply connecting the points with lines (to form the control polygon) will lead to something that is non-smooth. It will have sharp corners. We could imagine "smoothing" this polygon by cutting off the sharp corners, yielding a new polygon that is smoother, but still not "smooth" in the mathematical sense (since the curve is still a polygon, and therefore only C^1. We can repeat this process, each time yielding a smoother polygon, as shown in Figure 15.14. In the limit, that is if we repeated the process infinitely many times, we would obtain a C^1 smooth curve.

What we have done with corner cutting is defining a *subdivision* scheme. That is, we have defined curves by a process for breaking a simpler curve into smaller pieces (e.g., subdividing it). The resulting curve is the *limit curve* that is achieved

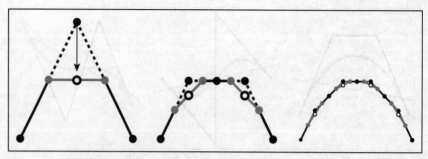

Figure 15.14. Subdivision procedure for quadratic Béziers. Each line segment is divided in half and these midpoints are connected (gray points and lines). The interior control point is moved to the midpoint of the new line segment (white circle).

by applying the process infinitely many times. If the subdivision scheme is defined correctly, the result will be a smooth curve, and it will have a parametric form.

Let us consider applying corner cutting to a single corner. Given three points $(\mathbf{p}_0, \mathbf{p}_1, \mathbf{p}_2)$, we repeatedly "cut off the corners" as shown in Figure 15.15. At each step, we divide each line segment in half, connect the midpoints, and then move the corner point to the midpoint of the new line segment. Note that in this process, new points are introduced, moved once, and then remain in this position for any remaining iterations. The endpoints never move.

If we compute the "new" position for $\mathbf{p}_2$ as the midpoint of the midpoints, we get the expression

$$\mathbf{p}_2' = \frac{1}{2}(\frac{1}{2}\mathbf{p}_0 + \frac{1}{2}\mathbf{p}_1) + \frac{1}{2}(\frac{1}{2}\mathbf{p}_1 + \frac{1}{2}\mathbf{p}_2).$$

The construction actually works for other proportions of distance along each segment. If we let u be the distance between the beginning and the end of each

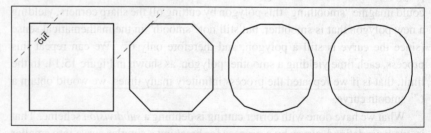

Figure 15.15. By repeatedly cutting the corners off a polygon, we approach a smooth curve.

segment where we place the middle point, we can re-write this expression as

$$\mathbf{p}(u) = (1-u)((1-u)\mathbf{p}_0 + u\mathbf{p}_1) + u((1-u)\mathbf{p}_1 + u\mathbf{p}_2).$$

Regrouping terms gives the quadratic Bézier function:

$$\mathbf{B}_2(u) = (1-u)^2\mathbf{p}_0 + 2u(1-u)\mathbf{p}_1 + u^2\mathbf{p}_2.$$

The De Casteljau Algorithm

One nice feature of Bézier curves is that there is a very simple and general method for computing and subdividing them. The method, called the *de Casteljau algorithm,* uses a sequence of linear interpolations to compute the positions along the Bézier curve of arbitrary order. It is the generalization of the subdivision scheme described in the previous section.

The de Casteljau algorithm begins by connecting every adjacent set of points with lines, and finding the point on these lines that is the u interpolation, giving a set of $n-1$ points. These points are then connected with straight lines, those lines are interpolated (again by u), giving a set of $n-2$ points. This process is repeated until there is one point. An illustration of this process is shown in Figure 15.16.

The process of computing a point on a Bézier segment also provides a method for dividing the segment at the point. The intermediate points computed during the de Casteljau algorithm form the new control points of the new, smaller segments, as shown in Figure 15.17.

The existence of a good algorithm for dividing Bézier curves makes divide-and-conquer algorithms possible. For example, when drawing a Bézier curve segment, it is easy to check if the curve is close to being a straight line because it is bounded by its convex hull. If the control points of the curve are all close to being co-linear, the curve can be drawn as a straight line. Otherwise, the curve can be

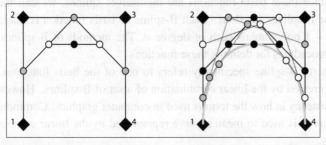

Figure 15.16. An illustration of the de Casteljau algorithm for a cubic Bézier. The left-hand image shows the construction for $u = 0.5$. The right-hand image shows the construction for 0.25, 0.5, and 0.75.

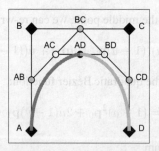

Figure 15.17. The de Casteljau algorithm is used to subdivide a cubic Bézier segment. The initial points (black diamonds A, B, C, and D) are linearly interpolated to yield gray circles (AB, BC, CD), which are linearly interpolated to yield white circles (AC, BD), which are linearly interpolated to give the point on the cubic AD. This process also has subdivided the Bézier segment with control points A,B,C,D into two Bézier segments with control points A, AB, AC, AD and AD, BD, CD, D.

divided into smaller pieces, and the process can be repeated. Similar algorithms can be used for determining the intersection between two curves. Because of the existence of such algorithms, other curve representations are often converted to Bézier form for processing.

15.6.2 B-splines

B-splines provide a method for approximating a set of n points with a curve made up of polynomials of degree d that gives $C^{(d-1)}$ continuity. Unlike the Bézier splines of the previous section, B-splines allow curves to be generated for any desired degree of continuity (almost up to the number of points). Because of this, B-splines are a preferred way to specify very smooth curves (high degrees of continuity) in computer graphics. If we want a C^2 or higher curve through an arbitrary number of points, B-splines are probably the right method.

We can represent a curve using a linear combination of B-spline basis functions. Since these basis functions are themselves splines, we call them basis splines or B-splines for short. Each B-spline or basis function is made up of a set of $d + 1$ polynomials each of degree d. The methods of B-splines provide general procedures for defining these functions.

The term B-spline specifically refers to one of the basis functions, not the function created by the linear combination of a set of B-splines. However, there is inconsistency in how the term is used in computer graphics. Commonly, a "B-spline curve" is used to mean a curve represented by the linear combination of B-splines.

The idea of representing a polynomial as the linear combination of other polynomials has been discussed in Section 15.3.1 and 15.3.5. Representing a spline as a linear combination of other splines was shown in Section 15.4.1. In fact, the example given is a simple case of a B-spline.

The general notation for representing a function as a linear combination of other functions is

$$\mathbf{f}(t) = \sum_{i=1}^{n} \mathbf{p}_i b_i(t), \qquad\qquad (15.15)$$

where the $\mathbf{p}_i$ are the coefficients and the b_i are the basis functions. If the coefficients are points (e.g. 2 or 3 vectors), we refer to them as control points. The key to making such a method work is to define the b_i appropriately. B-splines provide a very general way to do this.

A set of B-splines can be defined for a number of coefficients n and a parameter value k.[3] The value of k is one more than the degree of the polynomials used to make the B-splines ($k = d + 1$.)

B-splines are important because they provide a very general method for creating functions (that will be useful for representing curves) that have a number of useful properties. A curve with n points made with B-splines with parameter value k:

- is $C^{(k-2)}$ continuous;

- is made of polynomials of degree $k - 1$;

- has local control—any site on the curve only depends on k of the control points;

- is bounded by the convex hull of the points;

- exhibits the variation diminishing property illustrated in Figure 15.12.

A curve created using B-splines does not necessarily interpolate its control points.

We will introduce B-splines by first looking at a specific, simple case to introduce the concepts. We will then generalize the methods and show why they are interesting. Because the method for computing B-splines is very general, we delay introducing it until we have shown what these generalizations are.

---

[3]The B-spline parameter is actually the *order* of the polynomials used in the B-splines. While this terminology is not uniform in the literature, the use of the B-spline parameter k as a value one greater than the polynomial degree is widely used, although some texts (see the chapter notes) write all of the equations in terms of polynomial degree.

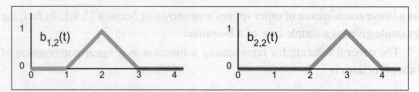

Figure 15.18. B-splines with $d = 1$ or $k = 2$.

Uniform Linear B-splines

Consider a set of basis functions of the following form:

$$b_{i,2}(t) = \begin{cases} t - i & \text{if } i \leq t < i + 1, \\ 2 - t + i & \text{if } i + 1 \leq t \leq i + 2, \\ 0 & \text{otherwise.} \end{cases} \qquad (15.16)$$

Each of these functions looks like a little triangular "hat" between i and $i+2$ with its peak at $i+1$. Each is a piecewise polynomial, with knots at i, $i+1$, and $i+2$. Two of them are graphed in Figure 15.18.

Each of these functions $b_{i,2}$ is a first degree (linear) B-spline. Because we will consider B-splines of other parameter values later, we denote these with the 2 in the subscript.

Notice that we have chosen to put the lower edge of the B-spline (its first knot) at i. Therefore the first knot of the first B-spline ($i = 1$) is at 1. Iteration over the B-splines or elements of the coefficient vector is from 1 to n (see Equation 15.15). When B-splines are implemented, as well as in many other discussions of them, they often are numbered from 0 to $n - 1$.

We can create a function from a set of n control points using Equation 15.15, with these functions used for the b_i to create an "overall function" that was influenced by the coefficients. If we were to use these ($k = 2$) B-splines to define the overall function, we would define a piecewise polynomial function that linearly interpolates the coefficients $\mathbf{p}_i$ between $t = k$ and $t = n + 1$. Note that while ($k = 2$) B-splines interpolate all of their coefficients, B-splines of higher degree do this under some specific conditions that we will discuss in Section 15.6.3.

Some properties of B-splines can be seen in this simple case. We will write these in the general form using k, the parameter, and n for the number of coefficients or control points.

- Each B-spline has $k + 1$ knots.

- Each B-spline is zero before its first knot and after its last knot.

- The overall spline has local control because each coefficient is only multiplied by one B-spline, and this B-spline is non-zero only between $k + 1$ knots.

- The overall spline has $n + k$ knots.

- Each B-spline is $C^{(k-2)}$ continuous, therefore the overall spline is $C^{(k-2)}$ continuous.

- The set of B-splines sums to 1 for all parameter values between knots k and $n + 1$. This range is where there are k B-splines that are non-zero. Summing to 1 is important because it means that the B-splines are shift invariant: translating the control points will translate the entire curve.

- Between each of its knots, the B-spline is a single polynomial of degree $d = k - 1$. Therefore, the overall curve (that sums these together) can also be expressed as a single, degree d polynomial between any adjacent knots.

In this example, we have chosen the knots to be uniformly spaced. We will consider B-splines with non-uniform spacing later. When the knot spacing is uniform, each of the B-splines are identical except for being shifted. B-splines with uniform knot spacing are sometimes called *uniform B-splines* or *periodic B-splines*.

Uniform Quadratic B-splines

The properties of B-splines listed in the previous section were intentionally written for arbitrary n and k. A general procedure for constructing the B-splines will be provided later, but first, lets consider another specific case with $k = 3$.

The B-spline $b_{2,3}$ is shown in Figure 15.19. It is made of quadratic pieces (degree 2), and has 3 of them. It is C^1 continuous and is non-zero only within the 4 knots that it spans. Notice that a quadratic B-spline is made of 3 pieces, one between knot 1 and 2, one between knot 2 and 3, and one between knot 3

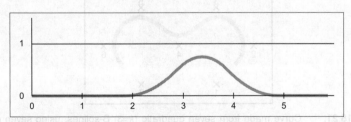

Figure 15.19. The B-spline $b_{2,3}$ with uniform knot spacing.

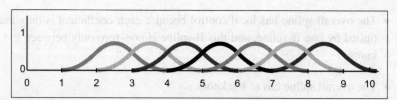

Figure 15.20. The set of seven B-splines with $k = 3$ and uniform knot spacing [1, 2, 3, 4, 5, 6, 7, 8, 10].

and 4. In Section 15.6.3 we will see a general procedure for building these functions. For now, we simply examine these functions:

$$b_{i,3}(t) = \begin{cases} \frac{1}{2}u^2 & \text{if } i \leq t < i+1 & u = t - i, \\ -u^2 + u + \frac{1}{2} & \text{if } i+1 \leq t < i+2 & u = t - (i+1), \\ \frac{1}{2}(1-u)^2 & \text{if } i+2 \leq t < i+3 & u = t - (i+2), \\ 0 & \text{otherwise.} \end{cases} \quad (15.17)$$

In order to make the expressions simpler, we wrote the function for each part as if it applied over the range 0 to 1.

If we evaluate the overall function made from summing together the B-splines, at any time only k (3 in this case) of them are non-zero. One of them will be in the first part of Equation 15.17, one will be in the second part, and one will be in the third part. Therefore, we can think of any piece of the overall function as being made up of a degree $d = k - 1$ polynomial that depends on k coefficients. For the $k = 3$ case, we can write

$$\mathbf{f}(u) = \frac{1}{2}(1-u)^2\mathbf{p}_i + (-u^2 + u + \frac{1}{2})\mathbf{p}_{i+1} + \frac{1}{2}u^2\mathbf{p}_{i+2}$$

where $u = t - i$. This defines the piece of the overall function when $i \leq t < i+1$.

If we have a set of n points, we can use the B-splines to create a curve. If we have seven points, we will need a set of seven B-splines. A set of seven B-splines

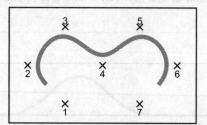

Figure 15.21. Curve made from seven quadratic ($k=3$) B-splines, using seven control points.

for $k = 3$ is shown in Figure 15.20. Notice that there are $n + k$ (10) knots, that the sum of the B-splines is 1 over the range k to $n + 1$ (knots 3 through 8). A curve specified using these B-splines and a set of points is shown in Figure 15.21.

Uniform Cubic B-splines

Because cubic polynomials are so popular in computer graphics, the special case of B-splines with $k = 4$ is sufficiently important that we consider it before discussing the general case. A B-spline of third degree is defined by 4 cubic polynomial pieces. The general process by which these pieces are determined is described later, but the result is

$$b_{i,4}(t) = \begin{cases} \frac{1}{6}u^3 & \text{if } i \le t < i+1 \quad u = t - i, \\ \frac{1}{6}(-3u^3 + 3u^2 + 3u + 1) & \text{if } i+1 \le t < i+2 \quad u = t - (i+1), \\ \frac{1}{6}(3u^3 - 6u^2 + 4) & \text{if } i+2 \le t < i+3 \quad u = t - (i+2), \\ \frac{1}{6}(-u^3 + 3u^2 - 3u + 1) & \text{if } i+3 \le t < i+4 \quad u = t - (i+3), \\ 0 & \text{otherwise.} \end{cases}$$

(15.18)

This degree 3 B-spline is graphed for $i = 1$ in Figure 15.22.

We can write the function for the overall curve between knots $i + 3$ and $i + 4$ as a function of the parameter u between 0 and 1 and the four control points that influence it:

$$\mathbf{f}(u) = \frac{1}{6}(-u^3 + 3u^2 - 3u + 1)\mathbf{p}_i + \frac{1}{6}(3u^3 - 6u^2 + 4)\mathbf{p}_{i+1}$$
$$+ \frac{1}{6}(-3u^3 + 3u^2 + 3u + 1)\mathbf{p}_{i+2} + \frac{1}{6}u^3\mathbf{p}_{i+3}.$$

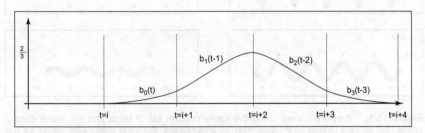

Figure 15.22. The cubic ($k = 4$) B-spline with uniform knots.

This can be re-written using the matrix notation of the previous sections, giving a basis matrix for cubic B-splines of

$$\mathbf{M_b} = \frac{1}{6} \begin{bmatrix} -1 & 3 & -3 & 1 \\ 3 & -6 & 3 & 0 \\ -3 & 0 & 3 & 0 \\ 1 & 4 & 1 & 0 \end{bmatrix}.$$

Unlike the matrices that were derived from constraints in Section 15.5, this matrix is created from the polynomials that are determined by the general B-spline procedure defined in the next section.

15.6.3   Non-uniform B-splines

One nice feature of B-splines is that they can be defined for any $k > 1$. So if we need a smoother curve, we can simply increase the value of k. This is illustrated in Figure 15.1.

So far, we have said that B-splines generalize to any $k > 1$ and any $n \geq d$. There is one last generalization to introduce before we show how to actually compute these B-splines. B-splines are defined for any non-decreasing knot vector.

For a given n and k, the set of B-splines (and the function created by their linear combination) has $n + k$ knots. We can write the value of these knots as a vector, that we will denote as $\mathbf{t}$. For the uniform B-splines, the knot vector is $[1, 2, 3, \ldots, n + k]$. However, B-splines can be generated for any knot vector of length $n + k$, providing the values are non-decreasing (e.g., $t_{i+1} \geq t_i$).

There are two main reasons why non-uniform knot spacing is useful: it gives us control over what parameter range of the overall function each coefficient af-

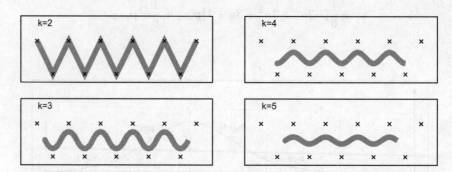

Figure 15.1.   B-spline curves using the same uniform set of knots and the same control points, for various values of k. Note that as k increases, the valid parameter range for the curve shrinks.

fects, and it allows us to repeat knots (e.g., create knots with no spacing in between) in order to create functions with different properties around these points. The latter will be considered later in this section.

The ability to specify knot values for B-splines is similar to being able to specify the interpolation sites for interpolating spline curves. It allows us to associate curve features with parameter values. By specifying a non-uniform knot vector, we specify what parameter range each coefficient of a B-spline curve affects. Remember that B-spline i is non-zero only between knot i and knot $i + k$. Therefore, the coefficient associated with it only affects the curve between these parameter values.

One place where control over knot values is particularly useful is in inserting or deleting knots near the beginning of a sequence. To illustrate this, consider a curve defined using linear B-splines ($k = 2$) as discussed in Section 15.6.2. For $n = 4$, the uniform knot vector is $[1, 2, 3, 4, 5, 6]$. This curve is controlled by a set of four points and spans the parameter range $t = 2$ to $t = 5$. The "end" of the curve ($t = 5$) interpolates the last control point. If we insert a new point in the middle of the point set, we would need a longer knot vector. The locality properties of the B-splines prevent this insertion from affecting the values of the curve at the ends. The longer curve would still interpolate its last control point at its end. However, if we chose to keep the uniform knot spacing, the new knot vector would be $[1, 2, 3, 4, 5, 6, 7]$. The end of the curve would be at $t = 6$, and the parameter value at which the last control point is interpolated will be a different parameter value than before the insertion. With non-uniform knot spacing, we can use the knot vector $[1, 2, 3, 3.5, 4, 5, 6]$ so that the ends of the curve are unaffected by the change. The abilities to have non-uniform knot spacing makes the locality property of B-splines an algebraic property, as well as a geometric one.

We now introduce the general method for defining B-splines. Given values for the number of coefficients n, the B-spline parameter k, and the knot vector $\mathbf{t}$ (which has length $n + k$), the following recursive equations define the B-splines:

$$b_{i,1,\mathbf{t}}(t) = \begin{cases} 1 & \text{if } \mathbf{t}_i \leq t < \mathbf{t}_{i+1}, \\ 0 & \text{otherwise.} \end{cases} \tag{15.19}$$

$$b_{i,k,\mathbf{t}}(t) = \frac{t - \mathbf{t}_i}{\mathbf{t}_{i+k-1} - \mathbf{t}_i} b_{i,k-1}(t) + \frac{\mathbf{t}_{i+k} - t}{\mathbf{t}_{i+k} - \mathbf{t}_{i+1}} b_{i+1,k-1}(t). \tag{15.20}$$

This equation is know as the *Cox-de Boor recurrence*. It may be used to compute specific values for specific B-splines. However, it is more often applied algebraically to derive equations such as Equation 15.17 or 15.18.

As an example, consider how we would have derived Equation 15.17. Using a uniform knot vector $[1, 2, 3, \ldots]$, $t_i = i$, and the value $k = 3$ in Equation 15.20

yields

$$b_{i,3}(t) = \frac{t-i}{(i+2)-i}b_{i,2} + \frac{(i+3)-t}{(i+3)-(i+1)}b_{i+1,2} \quad (15.21)$$

$$= \frac{1}{2}(t-i)b_{i,2} + \frac{1}{2}(i+3-t)b_{i+1,2}.$$

Continuing the recurrence, we must evaluate the recursive expressions:

$$b_{i,2}(t) = \frac{t-i}{(i+2-1)-i}b_{i,1} + \frac{(i+2)-t}{(i+2)-(i+1)}b_{i+1,1}$$

$$= (t-i)b_{i,1} + (i+2-t)b_{i+1,1}$$

$$b_{i+1,2}(t) = \frac{t-(i+1)}{((i+1)+2-1)-(i+1)}b_{i+1,1}$$

$$+ \frac{((i+1)+2)-t}{((i+1)+2)-((i+1)+1)}b_{(i+1)+1,1}$$

$$= (t-i+1)b_{i+1,1} + (i+3-t)b_{i+2,1}.$$

Inserting these results into Equation 15.22 gives:

$$b_{i,3}(t) = \frac{1}{2}(t-i)((t-i)b_{i,1} + (i+2-t)b_{i+1,1})$$

$$+ \frac{1}{2}(i+3-t)(t-i+1)b_{i+1,1} + (i+3-t)b_{i+2,1}.$$

To see that this expression is equivalent to Equation 15.17, we note that each of the $(k=1)$ B-splines is like a switch, turning on only for a particular parameter range. For instance, $b_{i,1}$ is only non-zero between i and $i+1$. So, if $i \leq t < i+1$, only the first of the $(k=1)$ B-splines in the expression is non-zero, so

$$b_{i,3}(t) = \frac{1}{2}(t-i)^2 \text{ if } i \leq t < i+1.$$

Similar manipulations give the other parts of Equation 15.17.

Repeated Knots and B-spline Interpolation

While B-splines have many nice properties, functions defined using them generally do not interpolate the coefficients. This can be inconvenient if we are using them to define a curve that we want to interpolate a specific point. We give a brief overview of how to interpolate a specific point using B-splines here. A more complete discussion can be found in the books listed in the chapter notes.

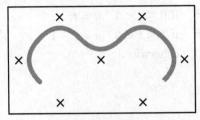
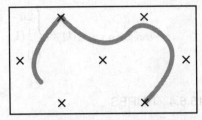

(a) Uniform knots   (b) Non-uniform knots

Figure 15.23. A curve parameterized by quadratic B-splines ($k = 3$) with seven control points. On the left, uniform knots vector [1,2,3,4,5,6,7,8,9,10] is used. On the right, the non-uniform knot spacing [1,2,3,4,4,6,7,8,8,10] is used. The duplication of the 4th and 8th knot means that all interior knots of the 3rd and 7th B-spline are equal, so the curve interpolates the control point associated with those points.

One way to cause B-splines to interpolate their coefficients is to repeat knots. If all of the interior knots for a particular B-spline have the same value, then the overall function will interpolate this B-spline's coefficient. An example of this is shown in Figure 15.23.

Interpolation by repeated knots comes at a high cost: it removes the smoothness of the B-spline and the resulting overall function and represented curve. However, at the beginning and end of the spline, where continuity is not an issue, knot repetition is useful for creating *endpoint interpolating B-splines*. While the first (or last) knot's value is not important for interpolation, for simplicity, we make the first (or last) k knots have the same value to achieve interpolation.

Endpoint interpolating quadratic B-splines are shown in Figure 15.24. The first two and last two B-splines are different than the uniform ones. Their expressions can be derived through the use of the Cox-de Boor recurrence:

$$b_{1,3,[0,0,0,1,2,...]}(t) = \begin{cases} (1-t)^2 & \text{if } 0 \leq t < 1, \\ 0 & \text{otherwise.} \end{cases}$$

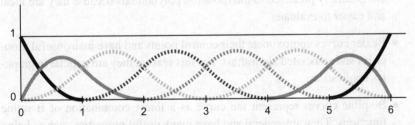

Figure 15.24. Endpoint-interpolating quadratic ($k =3$) B-splines, for $n = 8$. The knot vector is [0,0,0,1,2,3,4,5,6,6,6]. The first and last two B-splines are aperiodic, while the middle four (shown as dotted lines) are periodic and identical to the ones in Figure 15.20.

$$b_{2,3,[0,0,0,1,2,\dots]}(t) = \begin{cases} 2u - \frac{3}{2}u^2 & \text{if } 0 \le t < 1 \quad u = t, \\ \frac{1}{2}(1-u)^2 & \text{if } 1 \le t < 2 \quad u = t-1, \\ 0 & \text{otherwise.} \end{cases}$$

15.6.4 NURBS

Despite all of the generality B-splines provide, there are some functions that cannot be exactly represented using them. In particular, B-splines cannot represent conic sections. To represent such curves, a ratio of two polynomials is used. Non-uniform B-splines are used to represent both the numerator and the denominator. The most general form of these are non-uniform rational B-splines, or NURBS for short.

NURBS associate a scalar weight h_i with every control point $\mathbf{p_i}$ and use the same B-splines for both:

$$\mathbf{f}(u) = \frac{\sum_{i=1}^{n} h_i \mathbf{p}_i b_{i,k,\mathbf{t}}}{\sum_{i=1}^{n} h_i b_{i,k,\mathbf{t}}},$$

where $b_{i,k,\mathbf{t}}$ are the B-splines with parameter k and knot vector $\mathbf{t}$.

NURBS are very widely used to represent curves and surfaces in geometric modeling because of the amazing versatility they provide, in addition to the useful properties of B-splines.

15.7 Summary

In this chapter, we have discussed a number of representations for free-form curves. The most important ones for computer graphics are:

- Cardinal splines use a set of cubic pieces to interpolate control points. They are generally preferred to interpolating polynomials because they are local and easier to evaluate.

- Bézier curves approximate their control points and have many useful properties and associated algorithms. For this reason, they are popular in graphics applications.

- B-spline curves represent the curve as a linear combination of B-spline functions. They are general and have many useful properties such as being bounded by their convex hull and being variation diminishing. B-splines are often used when smooth curves are desired.

Notes

The problem of representing shapes mathematically is an entire field unto itself, generally known as Geometric Modeling. Representing curves is just the beginning and is generally a precursor to modeling surfaces and solids. A more thorough discussion of curves can be found in most geometric modeling texts, see for example *Geometric Modeling* (Mortenson, 1985) for a text that is accessible to computer graphics students. Many geometric modeling books specifically focus on smooth curves and surfaces. Texts such as *An Introduction to Splines for Use in Computer Graphics* (Bartels et al., 1987), *Curves and Surfaces for CAGD: A Practical Guide* (Farin, 2002) and *Geometric Modeling with Splines: An Introduction* (E. Cohen et al., 2001) provide considerable detail about curve and surface representations. Other books focus on the mathematics of splines; *A Practical Guide to Splines* (De Boor, 2001) is a standard reference.

The history of the development of curve and surface representations is complex, see the chapter by Farin in *Handbook of Computer Aided Geometric Design* (Farin et al., 2002) or the book on the subject *An Introduction to NURBS: With Historical Perspective* (D. F. Rogers, 2000) for a discussion. Many ideas were independently developed by multiple groups who approached the problems from different disciplines. Because of this, it can be difficult to attribute ideas to a single person or to point at the "original" sources. It has also led to a diversity of notation, terminology, and ways of introducing the concepts in the literature.

15.7.1 Exercises

For Exercises 1–4, find the constraint matrix, the basis matrix, and the basis functions. To invert the matrices you can use a program such as MATLAB or OCTAVE (a free MATLAB-like system).

1. A line segment: parameterized with p_0 located 25% of the way along the segment ($u = 0.25$), and p_1 located 75% of the way along the segment.

2. A quadratic: parameterized with p_0 as the position of the beginning point ($u = 0$), p_1, the first derivative at the beginning point, and p_2, the second derivative at the beginning point.

3. A cubic: its control points are equally spaced (p_0 has $u = 0$, p_1 has $u = 1/3$, p_2 has $u = 2/3$, and p_3 has $u = 1$).

4. A quintic: (a degree five polynomial, so the matrices will be 6×6) where p_0 is the beginning position, p_1 is the beginning derivative, p_2 is the middle

($u = 0.5$) position, $\mathbf{p}_3$ is the first derivative at the middle, $\mathbf{p}_4$ is the position at the end, and $\mathbf{p}_5$ is the first derivative at the end.

5. The Lagrange Form (Equation (15.12)) can be used to represent the interpolating cubic of Exercise 3. Use it at several different parameter values to confirm that it does produce the same results as the basis functions derived in Exercise 3.

6. Devise an arc-length parameterization for the curve represented by the parametric function

$$f(u) = (u, u^2).$$

7. Given the four control points of a segment of a Hermite spline, compute the control points of an equivalent Bézier segment.

8. Use the de Castijeau algorithm to evaluate the position of the cubic Bézier curve with its control points at (0,0), (0,1), (1,1) and (1,0) for parameter values $u = 0.5$ and $u = 0.75$. Drawing a sketch will help you do this.

9. Use the Cox / de Boor recurrence to derive Equation (15.16).

Brian Wyvill

16

Implicit Modeling

Implicit modeling (also known as implicit surfaces) in computer graphics covers many different methods for defining models. These include *skeletal implicit modeling*, *offset surfaces*, *level sets*, *variational surfaces*, and *algebraic surfaces*. In this chapter we briefly touch on these methods and describe how to build skeletal implicit models in more detail. Curves can be defined by implicit equations of the form

$$f(x, y) = 0.$$

If we consider a closed curve, such as a circle, with radius r, then the implicit equation can be written as

$$f(x, y) = x^2 + y^2 - r^2 = 0. \tag{16.1}$$

The value of $f(x, y)$ can be positive (outside the circle), negative (inside the circle), or zero for points precisely on the circle. The equivalent in three dimensions is a closed surface around a set of points that occupy a given volume or region of space. The volume forms a scalar field, i.e., we can compute a value for every point and as can be seen for the circle, the negative values are bounded by the implicit curve or surface. The surface can be visualized as a contour in the field, connecting points with a particular value such as zero (see Equation (16.1)). To compute such a surface implies searching through space to find the points that satisfy the implicit equation; this method is unlikely to lead to an efficient algorithm for circle drawing (and even less likely in three dimensions). This was perhaps the reason that algorithmic methods for modeling with parametric curves and surfaces were investigated before implicit methods; however, there are some good reasons to develop algorithms to visualize implicit surfaces. Chapter 28 mentions scalar fields in the context of volume visualization. In this chapter we explore the implications of deriving the data from a modeling process rather than from a scanner.

Despite the computational overhead of finding the implicit surface, designing with implicit modeling techniques offers some advantages over other modeling methods. Many geometric operations are simplified using implicit methods including:

- the definition of blends;

- the standard set operations (union, intersection, difference, etc.) of constructive solid geometry (CSG);

- functional composition with other implicit functions (e.g., R-functions, Barthe blends, Ricci blends, and warping);

- inside/outside tests, (e.g., for collision detection).

Visualizing the surfaces can be done either by direct ray tracing using an algorithm as described in (Kalra & Barr, 1989; Mitchell, 1990; Hart & Baker, 1996; deGroot & Wyvill, 2005) or by first converting to polygons (Wyvill et al., 1986).

One of the first methods was proposed by Ricci as far back as 1973 (Ricci, 1973), who also introduced CSG in the same paper. Jim Blinn's algorithm for finding contours in electron density fields, known as *Blobby molecules* (J. Blinn, 1982), Nishimura's *Metaballs* (Nishimura et al., 1985) and Wyvills' *Soft Objects* (Wyvill et al., 1986) were all early examples of implicit modeling methods. Jim Blinn's *Blobby Man* (see Figure 16.1) was the first rendering of a non-algebraic implicit model.

Figure 16.1. Blinn's Blobby Man 1980. *Image courtesy Jim Blinn.*

16.1 Implicit Functions, Skeletal Primitives and Summation Blending

In the context of modeling an *implicit* function is defined as a function f applied to a point $\mathbf{p} \in \mathbb{E}^3$ yielding a scalar value $\in \mathbb{R}$.

The implicit function $f_i(x, y, z)$ may be split into a distance function $d_i(x, y, z)$ and a *fall-off filter function*[1] $g_i(r)$, where r stands for the distance from the skeleton and the subscript refers to the ith skeletal element.

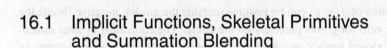

[1]These functions have been given many names by researchers in the past, e.g., *filter, potential, radial-basis, kernel,* but we use *fall-off filter* as a simple term to describe their appearance.

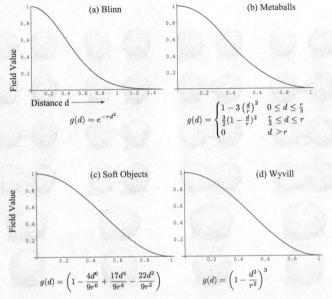

Figure 16.2. Fall-off filter functions ($0 \leq r \leq 1$). (a) Blinn's Gaussian or "blobby" function; (b) Nishimura's "metaball" function; (c) Wyvill et al.'s "soft objects" function; (d) the Wyvill function.

We will use the following notation:

$$f_i(x, y, z) = g_i \circ d_i(x, y, z) \tag{16.2}$$

A simple example is a point primitive, and we take the analogy of a star radiating heat into space. The field value (temperature in this example) may be measured at any point p and can be found by taking the distance from p to the center of the star and supplying the value to a fall-off filter function similar to one of those given in Figure 16.2. In these sample functions, the field is given a value of 1 at the center of the star; the value falls off with distance. The surface of a model may be derived from the implicit function $f(x, y, z)$ as the points of space whose values are equal to some desired *iso-value* (iso); in the star example, a spherical shell for values of iso $\in (0, 1)$.

In general, filter functions (g_i) are chosen so that the field values are maximized on the skeleton and fall off to zero at some chosen distance from the skeleton. In the simple case where the resulting surfaces are blended together, the global field $f(x, y, z)$ of an object, the implicit function, may be defined as

$$f(x, y, z) = \sum_{i=1}^{i=n} f_i(x, y, z), \tag{16.3}$$

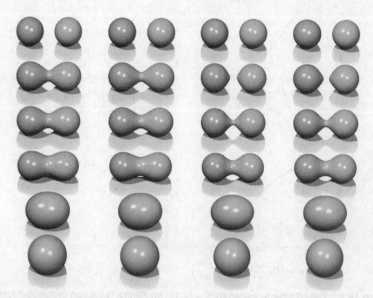

Figure 16.3. Each column shows two point primitives approaching each other. From left to right: the fall-off filter functions used are Blobby, Metaball, soft objects, and Wyvill. *Image courtesy Erwin DeGroot.*

where n skeletal elements contribute to the resulting field value. An example is shown in (Figure 16.3) in which the field at any point (x, y, z) is calculated as in Equation (16.3).

In this case, two point primitives are placed in close proximity. As the two points are brought together, the surfaces bulge and then blend together. The term *filter* function is used because the function causes the primitives to be blurred together somewhat akin to a filter function for images. The summation blend is the most compact and efficient blending operation that can be applied to implicit surfaces (see Equation (16.3)).

One advantage of using filter functions with finite support is that primitives that are far from p will have zero contribution and thus need not be considered (Wyvill et al., 1986).

16.1.1 C^1 Continuity and the Gradient

The most basic form of continuity is C^0 continuity, which ensures that there are no "jumps" in a function. Higher-order continuity is defined in terms of derivatives of functions (see Chapter 15).

In the case of a 3D scalar field f, the first derivative is a vector function known as the *gradient*, written ∇f and defined as

$$\nabla f(\mathbf{p}) = \left\{ \frac{\partial f(\mathbf{p})}{\partial x}, \frac{\partial f(\mathbf{p})}{\partial y}, \frac{\partial f(\mathbf{p})}{\partial z} \right\}.$$

If ∇f is defined at all points, and the three one-dimensional partial derivatives are each C^0, then f is C^1. Informally, C^1 surface continuity means that the *surface normal* varies smoothly over the surface. The surface normal is the unit vector perpendicular to the surface. If no unique surface normal can be defined on the edge of a cube, for example, then the surface is not C^1. For points on an implicit surface the surface normal can be computed by normalizing the gradient vector ∇f. In the example of the circle, points inside have a negative value and those on the outside have a positive one. For many types of implicit surfaces, the sense of inside and outside is inverted, and since the normal vector must always point outwards, it can be opposite to the gradient direction.

Skeletal implicit primitives are created by applying a fall-off filter function to an unsigned distance field as in Equation (16.2). Although the distance field is never C^1 at the skeleton, these discontinuities can be removed by using a suitable fall-off function (Akleman & Chen, 1999). If an operator, g, combines implicit functions, f_1 and f_2, where all points are C^1, then $g(f_1, f_2)$ is not necessarily C^1. For example it is possible to make a sharp CSG junction using the min and max operators. The combination is *not* C^1 continuous because the min and max operators don't have that property (see Section 16.5).

The analysis of operators is complicated by the fact that it is sometimes desirable to create a C^1 discontinuity. This case occurs whenever a crease in the surface is desired. For example, a cube is not C^1 because tangent discontinuities occur at each edge. To create creases using C^1 primitives, the operator must introduce C^1 discontinuities, and hence cannot be C^1 itself.

16.1.2   Distance Fields, R-Functions, and F-Reps

The *distance field* is defined with respect to some geometric object T:

$$\mathbf{F}(\mathsf{T}, \mathbf{p}) = \min_{\mathbf{q} \in \mathsf{T}} |\mathbf{q} - \mathbf{p}|.$$

Visually, $\mathbf{F}(\mathsf{T}, \mathbf{p})$ is the shortest distance from $\mathbf{p}$ to T. Hence, when $\mathbf{p}$ lies on T, $\mathbf{F}(\mathsf{T}, \mathbf{p}) = 0$ and the surface created by the implicit function is the object T. Outside of T, a non-zero distance is returned. The function T can be any geometric entity embedded in 3D—a point, curve, surface, or solid. Procedural modeling with distance fields started with Ricci (Ricci, 1973); *R-functions* (Rvachev, 1963) were first applied to shape modeling more than 20 years later (see (Shapiro, 1994) and (A. Pasko et al., 1995)).

An R-function or Rvachev function is a function whose sign can change if and only if the sign of one of its arguments changes; that is, its sign is determined solely by its arguments. R-functions provide a robust theoretical framework for boolean composition of real functions, permitting the construction of C^n CSG operators (Shapiro, 1988). These CSG operators can be used to create blending operators simply by adding a fixed offset to the result (A. Pasko et al., 1995). Although these blending functions are no longer technically R-functions, they have most of the desirable properties and can be mixed freely with R-functions to create complex hierarchical models (Shapiro, 1988). These R-function-based blending and CSG operators are referred to as *R-operators* (see Section 16.4). The Hyperfun system (Adzhiev et al., 1999) is based on *F-reps* (function representation), another name for an implicit surface. The system uses a procedural C-like language to describe many types of implicit surfaces.

16.1.3   Level Sets

It is useful to represent an implicit field discretely via a regular grid (Barthe et al., 2002) or an adaptive grid (Frisken et al., 2000). This is exactly what the polygonization algorithm does in the case of *level sets*; moreover, the grid can be used for various other purposes beside building polygons. Discrete representations of f are commonly obtained by sampling a continuous function at regular intervals. For example, the sampled function may be defined by other volume model representations (V. V. Savchenko et al., 1998). The data may also be a physical object sampled using three-dimensional imaging techniques. Discrete volume data has most often been used in conjunction with the *level sets* method (Osher & Sethian, 1988), which defines a means for dynamically modifying the data structure using curvature-dependent speed functions. Interactive modeling environments based on *level sets* have been defined (Museth et al., 2002), although level sets are only one method employing a discrete representation of the implicit field. Methods for interactively defining discrete representations using standard implicit surfaces techniques have also been explored (Baerentzen & Christensen, 2002).

A key advantage to employing a discrete data structure is its ability to act as a unifying approach for all of the various volume models defined by potential fields (discrete or not) (V. V. Savchenko et al., 1998). The conversion of any continuous function to a discrete representation introduces the problem of how to reconstruct a continuous function, needed for the combined purposes of additional modeling operations and visualization of the resulting potential field. A well known solution to this problem is to apply a filter g using the convolution operator (see Chapter 9). The choice of a filter is guided by the desired properties of the reconstruction, and many filters have been explored (Marschner & Lobb, 1994). The salient point is that there is typically a trade-off between the efficiency of the chosen filter and the smoothness of the resulting reconstruction; see also Section 16.9.

To be interactive, a discrete system must restrict the size of the grid relative to the available computing power. This, in turn, limits the ability of the modeler to include high-frequency details. Additionally, the smoothing triquadratic filter makes it impossible to include sharp edges should they be desired. A partial solution to this problem is the use of adaptive grids, although with any discrete representation there will be limitations. A discrete grid is used in (Schmidt, Wyvill, & Galin, 2005) to act as a cache representing a *BlobTree* node. The grid in this work is used for fast prototyping and uses trilinear interpolation for position and the slower, more accurate triquadratic interpolation to calculate gradient values, because the eye is more discerning in observing gradient errors than position errors.

16.1.4 Variational Implicit Surfaces

It is often required to convert sampled data to an implicit representation. Variational implicit surfaces interpolate or approximate a set of points using a weighted sum of globally-supported basis functions (V. Savchenko et al., 1995; Turk & O'Brien, 1999; J. C. Carr et al., 2001; Turk & O'Brien, 2002). These radially symmetric basis functions are applied at each sample point. The continuity of such a surface depends on the choice of basis function. The C^2 thin-plate spline is most commonly used (Turk & O'Brien, 2002; J. C. Carr et al., 2001). Like Blinn's exponential function (see Figure 16.2), this function is unbounded as is the resulting variational implicit surface.

If the field is is globally C^2, creases cannot be defined;[2] however, anisotropic basis functions can be used to produce fields which change more rapidly and may appear to have creases (Dinh et al., 2001). At the appropriate scale, the surface is still smooth. The smooth field implies that self-intersections do not occur, and hence volumes are always well-defined. The thin-plate spline guarantees that global curvature is minimized (Duchon, 1977). Variational interpolation has many properties which are desirable for 3D modeling, however controlling the resulting surfaces can be difficult.

---

[2]Except see Section 15.2.

Variational implicit surfaces can also be based on compactly-supported radial basis functions (CS-RBFs) to reduce the computational cost of variational interpolation techniques (Morse et al., 2001). Each CS-RBF only influences a local region, so computing $f(\mathbf{p})$ requires only evaluation of basis functions within some small neighborhood of $\mathbf{p}$. As with the globally-supported counterpart, the resulting field is C^k, creases are not supported, and self-intersections cannot occur.[3] The local support of each basis function results in a bounded global field. This also guarantees that additional iso-contours will be present, as noted by various researchers (Ohtake et al., 2003; Reuter, 2003).

16.1.5   Convolution Surfaces

Convolution surfaces, introduced by Bloomenthal and Shoemake (Bloomenthal & Shoemake, 1991) are produced by convolving a geometric skeleton S with a *kernel* function h. Hence, the value at any position in space is defined by an integral over the skeleton:

$$f(\mathbf{p}) = \int_S g(\mathbf{r})\, h(\mathbf{p} - \mathbf{r})\, d\mathbf{r}.$$

Any finitely-supported function can be used as h; see (Sherstyuk, 1999) for a detailed analysis of different kernels.

Like skeletal primitives, convolution surfaces have bounded fields. Blinn's "blobby molecules" is the simplest form of a convolution surface (J. Blinn, 1982); in this case, the skeleton consists of points only. This idea was extended by Bloomenthal to include line, arc, triangle, and polygon skeletons (Bloomenthal & Shoemake, 1991). These represent $1D$ and $2D$ primitives; $3D$ primitives were later described by Bloomenthal (Bloomenthal, 1995).

Figure 16.4. Two blended cylinders. Left: summation blend; right: convolution surface with barely discernible bulge (Bloomenthal, 1997). *Image courtesy Erwin DeGroot.*

Combination of convolution surfaces is defined by composition of the underlying geometric skeletons and has the advantage of eliminating the bulges that tend to occur when composing multiple skeletal primitives with additive blending. The surface resulting from convolution of the combined skeleton does not have bulges, as in Figure 16.4, and the field is continuous even if the combined skeleton is non-convex. Convolution surfaces are offset a fixed distance from convex portions of a skeleton, but produce a fillet along concave portions of a skeleton.

An example of skeletal elements convolved to build a complex model is shown in Figure 16.5. The hand model contains fourteen primitives.

---

[3]Note, $k > 0$ depending on the RBF (see Section 15.2).

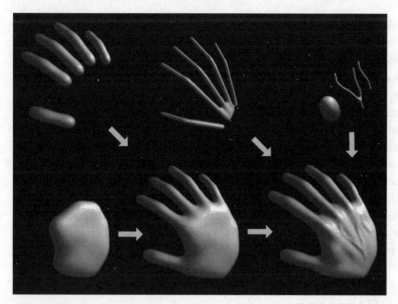

Figure 16.5. Skeletal elements convolved to build a hand model. *Image courtesy Jules Bloomenthal.*

16.1.6 Defining Skeletal Primitives

As we will see in the following sections rendering the implicit models requires finding the field value and gradient for a large number of points. We need the distance to supply to Equation (16.2) and the gradient is useful for root finding as well as lighting calculations. Supplying the distance to the fall-off filter functions of Figure 16.2 is a matter of calculating the nearest distance to the skeletal primitive, simple for point primitives but a little trickier for more complex geometrical shapes. A line segment primitive (AB) can be defined as a cylinder around a line with hemispherical end caps (see Figure 16.6). Point P_0 lies on the surface where $f(P_0) = $ iso and $f(P_1) = 0$ since it lies outside of the influence of the line primitive. The distance from some P_i to the line is found by simply projecting onto the line AB and calculating the perpendicular distance, e.g., $|CP_0|$; this can be found from AC, since A, P_0, and B, are all known:

$$\vec{AC} = \vec{AB}\frac{\vec{AP_0} \cdot \vec{AB}}{\|AB\|^2}.$$

In Figure 16.6 the field value of $P_2 > 0$, since P_2 is in the hemispherical end-cap, which can be checked separately. Variations of this idea can define primitives

Figure 16.6. Line primitive *ab* and example points p_0, p_1, p_2 showing distance calculation.

Figure 16.7. Cylinder primitive blended with a sphere. *Image courtesy Erwin DeGroot.*

Figure 16.8. Implicit models from various skeletal primitives. *Image courtesy Erwin DeGroot.*

Figure 16.9. A ray-traced dinosaur model showing the underlying skeletal primitives. *Image courtesy Erwin DeGroot.*

with endcaps of different radii producing interesting cone shapes. An example is shown in Figure 16.7.

A great variety of geometrical skeletons have been described, and, in principle, it is simply a matter of defining the distance to the skeleton from some point **p** and also the gradient at **p**. For example, an offset surface of a triangle can be defined from the vertices of the triangle and a radius r. A simple way to implement this is to use line segment primitives to describe bounding cylinders connecting the vertices (radius r). The distance from a point **q** within the triangle that does not fall within the bounding fields of one of the line segment primitives is returned as the perpendicular distance to the plane of the triangle. Other examples include an implicit disk, defined by a circle and a thickness parameter, a torus also defined by a circle and the radius of the cross section (or inner and outer circle radii), a circular cone from a disk and a height, a cube with rounded corners, etc. (see Figure 16.8).

16.2 Rendering

Modeling methods, such as parametric surfaces, lend themselves to visualization, since it is easy to iterate over points on the surface that can be found directly from the defining equations; for example $(x, y) = (\cos \theta, \sin \theta), \ \theta \in [0, 2\pi)$ produces a circle.

There are two techniques that are commonly used to render implicit surfaces: ray tracing and surface tiling. In practice, a designer wants to visualize an implicit surface model quickly, sacrificing quality for speed for interaction purposes. Prototyping algorithms have been concerned with producing a polygon mesh that can be rendered in real time on modern workstations. Finding the polygonal mesh which best approximates the desired surface is referred to as *polygonization* or *surface tiling*. For animation or for a final visualization, where quality is preferred over speed, ray tracing implicit surfaces directly without first polygonizing produces excellent results.

As previously mentioned, finding an implicit surface requires searching through space to find the points that satisfy, $f(\mathbf{p}) = 0$. There are two main approaches to executing such a search: space partitioning—partitioning space into manageable units such as cubes, and non-space partitioning, e.g., marching triangles (Hartmann, 1998; Akkouche & Galin, 2001) and the shrinkwrap algorithm (Overveld & Wyvill, 2004).

In this chapter we describe the original space partitioning algorithm and leave it to the reader to explore the more advanced methods. This algorithm together with post-processing for mesh refinement (see Chapter 12) and caching provide a method for interactive viewing of implicit models on modern workstations.

16.3 Space Partitioning

16.3.1 Exhaustive Search

The basic cubic space partitioning algorithm for tiling implicit surfaces was first published in (Wyvill et al., 1986) and a similar algorithm oriented towards volume visualization, called marching cubes in (W. Lorensen & Cline, 1987). Since then there have been many refinements and extensions.

A first approach to finding the implicit surface might be to subdivide space uniformly into a regular lattice of cubic cells and calculate a value for every vertex. Each cell is replaced with a set of polygons that best approximates the part of the surface contained within that cell. The problem with this method is that many of the cells will be completely outside or completely inside the volume; thus, many cells that contain no part of the surface are processed. For large grids of data this can be very time consuming and memory intensive.

To avoid storing the whole grid, a hash table is used to store only the cubes that contain a piece of the surface, based on the data structures used in (Wyvill et al., 1986). Working software was published in *Graphics Gems IV* (Bloomenthal, 1990). The algorithm is based on *numerical continuation*; it starts with a seed cube that intersects part of the surface and builds neighboring cubes as necessary to follow the surface.

The algorithm has two parts. In the first part, cubic cells are found that contain the surface and in the second part, each cube is replaced by triangles. The first part of the algorithm is driven by a queue of cubes, each of which contains part of the surface; the second part of the algorithm is table-driven.

16.3.2 Algorithm Description

A fast overview of the algorithm is as follows:

- divide space into cubic voxels;
- search for surface, starting from a skeletal element;
- add voxel to queue, mark it visited;
- search neighbors;
- when done, replace voxel with polygons.

First, space is subdivided into a cubic lattice, and the next task is to find a seed cube containing part of the surface. A cube vertex v_i inside the surface will have a field value $v_i >=$ iso and a vertex outside the surface will have a field value $v_i <$ iso; thus, an edge with one of each type of vertex will intersect the surface. We call this an *intersecting* edge. The field value at the nearest cube vertex to the first primitive can be evaluated by summing the contributions of the primitives as per Equation (16.3), although other operators can also be used as will be seen later. We will assume that $f(v_0) >$ iso, which indicates that v_0 lies within the solid. The value of iso is chosen by the user; an example is iso $= 0.5$ when using the *soft* fall-off function, which has some symmetry properties that lead to nice blending (see Figure 16.3). The vertices along one axis are evaluated in turn until a value $v_i <$ iso is found. The cube containing the *intersecting* edge is the seed cube.

The neighbors of the seed cube are examined, and those that contain at least one *intersecting* edge are added to the queue ready for processing. To process a cube we examine each face. If any of the bounding edges have oppositely signed

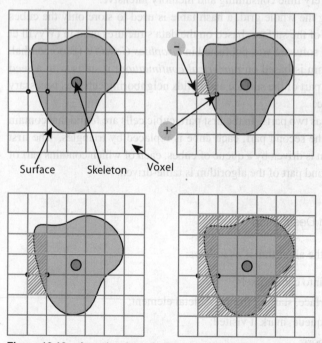

Figure 16.10. A section through the cubic lattice. The + sign indicates a vertex inside the surface ($f(v_i \geq$ iso) and - is outside $f(v_i <$ iso).

vertices, the surface will pass through that face and the face neighbor must be processed. When this process has been completed for all the faces, the second phase of the algorithm is applied to the cube. If the surface is closed, eventually a cube will be re-visited and no more unmarked neighbors found, and the search algorithm will terminate. Processing a cube involves marking it as processed and processing its unmarked neighbors. Those that contain *intersecting* edges are processed until the entire surface has been covered (see Figure 16.10).

Each cube is indexed by an *identifying vertex* which we define to be the lower-left far corner (i.e., the vertex with the lowest (x, y, z)-coordinate values (see Figure 16.11)). For each vertex that is inside the surface, the corresponding bit will be set to form the address in an 8-bit table (see Figure 16.11 and Section 16.3.3).

The identifying vertex is addressed by integers i, j, k, computed from the (x, y, z)-coordinate location of the cube such that $x = \text{side} * i$, etc., where side is the size of the cube. The identifying vertex of each cube may appear in as many as eight other cubes, and it would be inefficient to store these vertices more than once. Thus, the vertices are stored uniquely in a chained hash table. Since most of the space does not contain any part of the surface, only those cubes that are visited will be stored. The implicit function value is found for each vertex as it is stored in the hash table.

Nothing is known about the topology of the surface so a search must be started from every primitive to avoid any disconnected parts of the surface being missed. A scalar can be used to scale the influence of a primitive. If the scalar can be less than zero, then it is possible to search along an axis without finding an intersecting edge. In this case, a more sophisticated search must be done to find a seed cube (Galin & Akkouche, 1999).

Data Structures

The hash table entry holds five values:

- the i, j, k lattice indices of the identifying vertex (see Figure 16.11);

- f, the implicit function value of the identifying vertex;

- Boolean to indicate whether this cube has been visited.

The hash function computes an address in the hash table by selecting a few bits out of each of i, j, k and combining them arithmetically. For example, the five least significant bits produces a 15-bit address for a table, which must have a length of 2^{15}. Such a hash function can be neatly implemented in the C-preprocessor as follows:

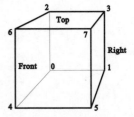

Vertex		If (+)
0	0	00000001
1	01	00000010
2	010	00000100
3	011	00001000
4	100	00010000
5	101	00100000
6	110	01000000
7	111	10000000

Figure 16.11. Vertex numbering.

```
#define NBITS    5
#define BMASK    037
#define HASH(a,b,c) (((a&BMASK)<<NBITS|b&BMASK)
                                   <<NBITS|c&BMASK)
#define HSIZE    1<<NBITS*3
```

The queue (FIFO list) is used as temporary storage to identify the neighbors for processing. The algorithm begins with a seed cube that is marked as visited and placed on the queue. The first cube on the queue is dequeued and all its unvisited neighbors are added to the queue. Each cube is processed and passed to the second phase of the algorithm if it contains part of the surface. The queue is then processed until empty.

16.3.3 Polygonization Algorithm

The second phase of the algorithm treats each cube independently. The cell is replaced by a set of triangles that best matches the shape of the part of the surface that passes through the cell. The algorithm must decide how to polygonize the cell given the implicit function values at each vertex. These values will be positive or negative (i.e., less than or greater than the iso-value), giving 256 combinations

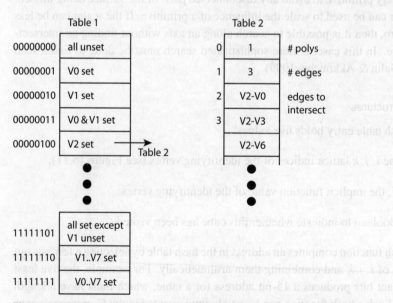

Figure 16.12. Table 2 contains the edges intersected by the surface. Table 1 points to the appropriate entry in Table 2.

of positive or negative vertices for the eight vertices of the cube. A table of 256
entries provides the right vertices to use in each triangle (Figure 16.12). For example, entry 4(00000100) points to a second table that records the vertices that
bound the *intersecting* edges. In this example, vertex number 2 is inside the surface ($f(V2) >=$ iso) and, therefore, we wish to draw a triangle that connects the
points on the surface that intersect with edges bounded by $(V2, V0)$, $(V2, V3)$,
and $(V2, V6)$ as shown in Figure 16.13.

Finding Cube-Surface Intersections

Figure 16.13 shows a cube where vertex V_2 is inside the surface and all other
vertices are outside. Intersections with the surface occur on three edges as shown.
The surface intersects edge $V_2 - V_6$ at the point A. The fastest but inaccurate way
to calculate A is to use linear interpolation:

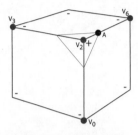

Figure 16.13. Finding the
intersection of the surface
with a cube edge.

$$\frac{f(A) - f(V_2)}{f(V_6) - f(V_2)} = \frac{|A - V_2|}{\text{side}}.$$

If the cube side is 1 and the iso-value sought for $f(A)$ is 0.5, then

$$A = V_3 + \frac{0.5 - f(V_2)}{f(V_6) - f(V_2)}.$$

This works well for a static image but in animation error differences between
frames will be very noticeable. A root-finding method such as *regula falsi* should
be employed. This becomes more computationally costly as the gradient is needed
to evaluate the point of intersection. The gradient is also needed at surface points
for rendering. For many types of primitives it is simpler to find a numerical approximation using sample points around p, as in

$$\nabla f(\mathbf{p}) = \left(\frac{f(\mathbf{p} + \Delta x) - f(\mathbf{p})}{\Delta x}, \frac{f(\mathbf{p} + \Delta y) - f(\mathbf{p})}{\Delta y}, \frac{f(\mathbf{p} + \Delta z) - f(\mathbf{p})}{\Delta z} \right).$$

A reasonable value for Δ has been found empirically to be $0.01 * \text{side}$ where side
is the length of a cube edge.

For manufacturing a mesh, as opposed to a set of independent triangles, a
second hash table can maintain a list of all the *intersecting edges*. Since each cube
edge is shared by up to four neighbors, the edge hash table prevents repetition of
the surface-cube edge intersection calculation. The hash address can be derived
from the same hash function as for vertices (applied to the edge endpoints).

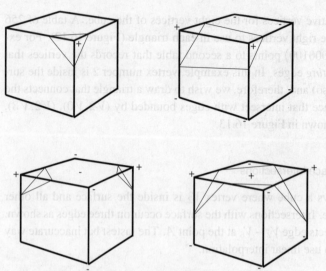

Figure 16.14. Examples of vertices inside (+) and outside (-) the surface. Note the extra sample gives a clue to avoid ambiguous cases.

16.3.4 Sampling Problems

Ambiguities occur when opposite corners of a face (or the cube) have the same sign and the other pair of vertices on the face have the opposite sign (see Figure 16.14). A sample taken in the center of the face will give a clue as to whether the cube represents the meeting of two surfaces or a saddle. It should be made clear that a spatial grid stores a sample of the implicit function at every vertex. If the function happens to vary considerably within a cell the polygonal representation will not show such variations (see Figure 16.15). The surface cannot be resolved by sampling alone unless something is known about the curvature of the surface. A good discussion of this topic appears in (Kalra & Barr, 1989).

This ambiguity problem (not the under-sampling problem) is avoided by subdividing the cubic cell into tetrahedra. The tetrahedra can then be polygonized unambiguously. Since there are four vertices in each tetrahedron, a table of sixteen entries will provide the correct triangle information. The disadvantage is that approximately twice the number of polygons will be generated.

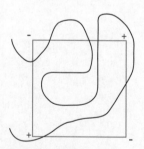

Figure 16.15. Cube too large to capture small variation in implicit function.

Subdividing a Cube

Without requiring additional cell vertices, a cube may be decomposed into five or six tetrahedra as shown in Figure 16.16. These decompositions introduce diagonals on the cube faces, and to maintain a consistent diagonal direction between

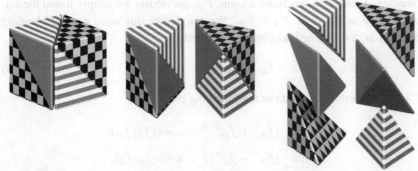

Figure 16.16. Decomposing a cube into six tetrahedra. *Image courtesy Erwin DeGroot.*

neighbors, the six decomposition is preferable. The introduction of diagonal edges produces a higher-resolution surface than replacing each cube directly with triangles. The decomposition into tetrahedra and the replacement of the tetrahedra with triangles are fast, table-driven algorithms, which produce topologically consistent meshes.

16.3.5   Cell Polygonization

Two obvious problems emerge from the use of uniform space subdivision. The size of triangles output by this algorithm do not adapt to the curvature of the surface and a further sample is required to solve the ambiguities, in which cubic cells are replaced by polygons. A space subdivision algorithm based on an octree was developed by Bloomenthal (Bloomenthal, 1988), which does adapt to the curvature of the surface. Cells are subdivided into eight octants and cracks are avoided by using a restricted octree scheme, i.e., neighboring cells cannot differ by more than one level of subdivision. This indeed reduces the number of polygons generated, but full advantage of large cells can only be taken if the flat regions of the surface happen to fall entirely within the appropriate octants. The algorithm proves in practice to be considerably slower than the uniform voxel algorithm and is more complicated to implement.

16.4   More on Blending

Section 16.1 showed that blending can be made to occur when field values are summed. Ricci, in his landmark paper (Ricci, 1973), describes super-elliptic blending. Given two functions F_A and F_B, previously we simply found the implicit value as $F_{\text{total}} = F_A + F_B$. We can denote this more general blending operator as $A \diamond B$. The Ricci blend is defined as:

$$f_{A \diamond B} = (f_A{}^n + f_B{}^n)^{\frac{1}{n}}. \tag{16.4}$$

It is interesting to point out the following properties:

$$\lim_{n \to +\infty} (f_A{}^n + f_B{}^n)^{\frac{1}{n}} = \max(f_A, f_B),$$
$$\lim_{n \to -\infty} (f_A{}^n + f_B{}^n)^{\frac{1}{n}} = \min(f_A, f_B).$$

Moreover, this generalized blending is associative, i.e., $f_{(A \diamond B) \diamond C} = f_{A \diamond (B \diamond C)}$. The standard blending operator $+$ proves to be a special case of the super-elliptic blend with $n = 1$. When n varies from 1 to infinity, it creates a set of blends interpolating between blending $A + B$ and union $A \cup B$ (see Figure 16.17). Figure 16.27 shows the nodes to be binary or unary; in fact the binary nodes can easily be extended using the above formulation to n-ary nodes.

The power of Ricci's operators is that they are *closed* under the operations on the space of all possible implicit volumes, meaning that an application of an operator simply produces another scalar field defining another implicit volume. This new field can be composed with other fields, again using Ricci's operators. Equation (16.4) will always produce the exact union of two implicit volumes, regardless of how complex they are. Compared with the difficulties involved in applying boolean CSG operations to B-rep surfaces, solid modeling with implicit volumes is incredibly simple.

Following Pasko's functional representation (A. Pasko et al., 1995), another generalized blending function may be defined:

$$f_{A \diamond B} = \left(f_A + f_B + \alpha \sqrt{f_A{}^2 + f_B{}^2} \right) \left(f_A{}^2 + f_B{}^2 \right)^{\frac{n}{2}}.$$

When $\alpha \in [-1, 1]$ varies from -1 to 1, it creates a set of blends interpolating the union and the intersection operators. However, this operator is no longer associative which is incompatible with the definition of n-ary operators.

Figure 16.17. By varying *n*, the Ricci blend may be made to change smoothly from blend to union. *Image courtesy Erwin DeGroot.*

16.5   Constructive Solid Geometry

Implicit models are frequently termed *implicit surfaces*; however, they are inherently volume models and useful for *solid modeling* operations. Ricci introduced a *constructive geometry* for defining complex shapes from operations such as union, intersection, difference, and blend upon primitives (Ricci, 1973). The surface was considered as the boundary between the half spaces $f(\mathbf{p}) < 1$, defining the inside, and $f(\mathbf{p}) > 1$ defining the outside. This initial approach to solid modeling evolved into *constructive solid geometry* or CSG (Ricci, 1973; Requicha, 1980). CSG is typically evaluated bottom-up according to a binary tree, with low-degree polynomial primitives as the leaf nodes and internal nodes representing Boolean set operations. These methods are readily adapted for use in implicit modeling, and in the case of skeletal implicit surfaces, the Boolean set operations union $\cup_{max}$, intersection $\cap_{min}$ and difference $\backslash_{minmax}$ are defined as follows (Wyvill et al., 1999):

$$\cup_{max} \quad f = \max_{i=0}^{k-1}(f_i), \quad\quad\quad (16.5)$$

$$\cap_{min} \quad f = \min_{i=0}^{k-1}(f_i),$$

$$\backslash_{minmax} \quad f = \min\left(f_0, 2 * \text{iso} - \max_{j=1}^{k-1}(f_j)\right).$$

The Ricci operators are illustrated in Figure 16.18 for point primitives A and B. For union (bottom left) the field at all points inside the union will be the greater of $f_A()$ and $f_B()$. For intersection (center), points in the region marked as P_1 will have value $\min(f_A(P_1), f_B(P_1)) = 0$, since the contribution of B will be zero outside of its range of influence. Similarly, for the region marked as P_2, (influence of A is zero, i.e., the minimum) leaving only the intersection region with positive values. Difference works similarly using the iso-value in the three marked regions (P_i) as follows:

$$f(P_0) = \min(f_B(P_0), 2 * \text{iso} - f_A(P_0))$$
$$= \min([\text{iso}, 1], [2 * \text{iso} - 1, \text{iso}])$$
$$= [2 * \text{iso} - 1, \text{iso}] < \text{iso}$$
$$f(P_1) = \min(f_B(P_1), 2 * \text{iso} - f_A(P_1))$$
$$= \min([0, \text{iso}], [2 * \text{iso} - 1, \text{iso}]) < \text{iso}$$
$$f(P_2) = \min(f_B(P_2), 2 * \text{iso} - f_A(P_2))$$
$$= \min([\text{iso}, 1], [\text{iso}, 2 * \text{iso}]) >= \text{iso}$$

CSG operators create creases, i.e., C^1 discontinuities. For example, the $\min()$ operator (Equation (16.5)) creates C^1 discontinuities at all points where $f_1(\mathbf{p}) = f_2(\mathbf{p})$. When applied to two spheres, the discontinuities produced by this union operator result in a crease on the surface, as shown in Figure 16.18, which is the desired result. Discontinuities unfortunately extend into the field outside of

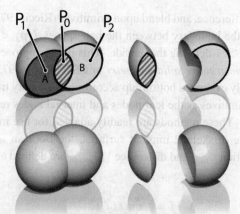

P_1 P_0 P_2

Figure 16.18. Ricci operators for CSG. *Image courtesy Erwin DeGroot.*

the surface, which is not visible in this image. If a blend is then applied to the result of the union, the C^1-discontinuous plane in the field produces a shading discontinuity (Figure 16.19).

The problem can be avoided to an extent (G. Pasko et al., 2002), and CSG operators have been developed that are C^1 at all points except those where $f_1(\mathbf{p}) = f_2(\mathbf{p}) = $ iso (Barthe et al., 2003).

16.6 Warping

The ability to distort the shape of a surface by warping the space in its neighborhood is a useful modeling tool. A warp is a continuous function $w(x, y, z)$ that maps $\mathbb{R}^3$ onto $\mathbb{R}^3$. Sederberg provides a good analogy for warping when describing free form deformations (Sederberg & Parry, 1986). He suggests that the warped space can be likened to a clear, flexible, plastic parallelepiped in which the objects to be warped are embedded. A warped element may be defined by simply applying some warp function $w(\mathbf{p})$ to the implicit equation:

$$f_i(x, y, z) = g_i \circ d_i \circ w_i(x, y, z). \tag{16.6}$$

A warped element may be fully characterized by the distance to its skeleton $d_i(x, y, z)$, its fall-off filter function $g_i(r)$, and eventually its warp function $w_i(x, y, z)$. To render or perform operations on an implicit surface, the implicit value of many points $f(P)$ must be found. First, P is transformed by the warp function to some new point Q, and $f(Q)$ is returned in place of $f(P)$. In Figure 16.20, instead of returning the implicit value of some point $f(Q)$, the value

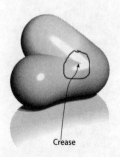

Crease

Figure 16.19. Two point primitives on the left are connected by the Ricci union. A third primitive is blended to the result, creating an unwanted crease in the field. *Image courtesy Erwin DeGroot.*

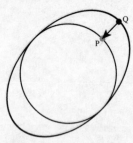

Q

P

Figure 16.20. Point Q returns the field value for point P.

for $f(P)$ is returned. In this case, the iso-value is returned and the implicit surface (curve in 2D) passes through Q instead of P. Thus, the circle is warped into an ellipse.

Barr introduced the notion of global and local deformations using the operations of *twist*, *taper*, and *bend* applied to parametric surfaces (Barr, 1984). The deformations can be nested to produce models such as the one shown in Figure 16.27. Conceptually, these are easy to apply to an implicit surface, as indicated in Equation (16.6).

Note that the normal cannot be calculated in a similar manner to warping a point. This problem is similar to the problem outlined in Section 13.2 on instancing. In this case, the normal can most easily be approximated using Equation (16.3.3) although the use of the Jacobian, as suggested in (Barr, 1984), yields precise results. The Barr warps are described in the following sections.

16.6.1 Twist

In this example, the twist is around the z-axis by θ (see Figure 16.21) for three blended implicit cylinders with a twist warp applied to them.

The twist around z is expressed as

$$w(x,y,z) = \left\{ \begin{array}{c} x * \cos(\theta(z)) - y * \sin(\theta(z)) \\ x * \sin(\theta(z)) + y * \cos(\theta(z)) \\ z \end{array} \right\}.$$

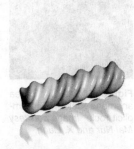

Figure 16.21. Three blended implicit cylinders twisted together. *Image courtesy Erwin DeGroot.*

16.6.2 Taper

Taper is applied along one major axis. A linear taper has proved to be the most useful although quadratic and cubic tapers are easily implemented. For example a linear taper along the y-axis involves changing both x- and z-coordinates. A linear scale is applied to y between $y_{\max}$ and $y_{\min}$:

$$s(y) = \frac{y_{\max} - y}{y_{\max} - y_{\min}} \qquad w(x,y,z) = \left\{ \begin{array}{c} s(y)x \\ y \\ s(y)z \end{array} \right\}$$

Figure 16.22. Three blended implicit cylinders, twisted then tapered. *Image courtesy Erwin DeGroot.*

16.6.3 Bend

Bend is also applied along one major axis. For the bend example below, the bending rate is k measured in radians per unit length, the axis of the bend is

Figure 16.23. Three blended implicit cylinders, twisted together, tapered and bent. *Image courtesy Erwin DeGroot.*

Figure 16.24. Sea anemone deforms to implicit rock. *Image courtesy Mai Nur and X. Liang.*

$(x_0, 1/k)$, and the angle θ is defined as $(x - x_0) * k$. The bend around z is

$$w(x,y,z) = \left\{ \begin{array}{c} -\sin(\theta) * (y - 1/k) + x_0 \\ \cos(\theta) * (y - 1/k) + 1/k \\ z \end{array} \right\}$$

16.7   Precise Contact Modeling

Precise contact modeling (PCM) is a method of deforming implicit surface primitives in contact situations while maintaining a precise contact surface with C^1 continuity (Gascuel, 1993). PCM is important in that it is a simple and automatic way of showing how a model can react to its environment. This cannot be so easily done with non-implicit methods (see Figure 16.24).

PCM is implemented by the inclusion of a deforming function $s(p)$ that modifies the field value returned for each point. For each pair of objects, collision is first detected using a bounding-box test. Once it is established that a collision is likely, PCM is applied. A local, geometric deformation term s_i is computed and added to the implicit function f_i. The volume of the colliding objects is divided into an interpenetration region and a deformation region. The result of applying s_i is that the interpenetration region is compressed so that contact is maintained without interpenetration occurring (see Figure 16.25). The effect of s_i is attenuated to zero within the propagation region so that the volume outside of the two regions is not deformed.

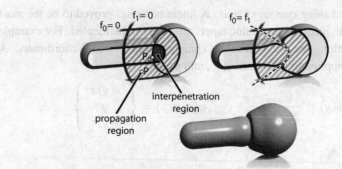

Figure 16.25. A 2D slice through objects in collision showing the various regions and PCM deformation. *Image courtesy Erwin DeGroot.*

Given two skeletal elements generating fields $f_1(p)$ and $f_2(p)$, the surface around each one is calculated as

$$f_1(p) + s_1(p) = 0,$$
$$f_2(p) + s_2(p) = 0.$$

We need to generate a surface common to both elements (dotted line in Figure 16.25), i.e., where they share a solution in the interpenetration region for some p in that region:

$$s_1(p) - f_1(p) = \text{iso}, \qquad (16.7)$$
$$s_2(p) - f_2(p) = \text{iso}.$$

Intuitively, the deeper within object 1 that object 2 penetrates, the higher the implicit value of object 1 and thus the more that object 2 will be compressed.

The function, s_i is defined to produce a smooth junction at the boundary of the interpenetration region, in other words where $s_i = 0$ but its derivative is greater than zero. From here to the boundary of the propagation region, s_i is used to attenuate the propagation to zero. The *nearest* point on the interpenetration region boundary p_0 is found by following the gradient.

Within the propagation region $s_i(p) = h_i(r)$, where $p = (x, y, z)$ is the point whose implicit value is being calculated and $r = \|p - p_0\|$ (see Figure 16.26). The value of r_i, set by the user, defines the size of the propagation region; no deformation occurs beyond this region. To control how much the objects inflate in the propagation region, the user provides a value for the parameter α. The maximum value of h_i is M_i. The current minimum of s_i is negative in the interpenetration region and is given as $s_{i\min}$, where $M_i = -\alpha_i s_{i\min}$. Thus an object will

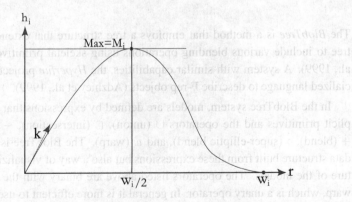

Figure 16.26. The function, $h_i(r)$ is the value of the deformation function w_i in the propagation region.

be compressed in the interpenetration region and will inflate in the propagation region. The equation for h_i is formed in two parts by two cubic polynomials that are designed to join at $r = r_i/2$, where the slope is zero:

$$c = \frac{4(w_i k - 4M_i)}{w_i^3},$$

$$d = \frac{4(3M_i - w_i k)}{w_i^2},$$

$$h_i(r) = cr^3 + dr^2 + kr \quad \text{if } r \in [0, w_i/2],$$

$$h_i(r) = \frac{4M_i}{w_i^3}(r - w_i)^2(4r - w_i)^3 \quad \text{if } r \in [w_i/2, w_i].$$

It is desirable that we have C^1-continuity as we move from the interpenetration to the propagation region. Thus, $h_i'(0) = k$ in Figure 16.26, is the directional derivative of s_i at the junction (marked as p_0 in Figure 16.25). As indicated in Equation (16.7), $s_i = -f_i$ in the interpenetration region, thus:

$$k = \|\nabla(f_i, p_0)\|$$

PCM is only an approximation to a properly deformed surface, but it is an attractive algorithm due to its simplicity.

16.8   The BlobTree

The *BlobTree* is a method that employs a tree structure that extended the CSG tree to include various blending operations using skeletal primitives (Wyvill et al., 1999). A system with similar capabilities, the *Hyperfun* project, used a specialized language to describe F-rep objects (Adzhiev et al., 1999).

In the BlobTree system, models are defined by expressions that combine implicit primitives and the operators ∪ (union), ∩ (intersection), − (difference), + (blend), ◇ (super-elliptic blend), and w (warp). The BlobTree is not only the data structure built from these expressions but also a way of visualizing the structure of the models. The operators listed above are binary with the exception of warp, which is a unary operator. In general it is more efficient to use n-ary rather than binary operators. The BlobTree incorporates affine transformations as nodes so that it is also a scene graph and primitives (e.g., skeletons) form the leaf nodes.

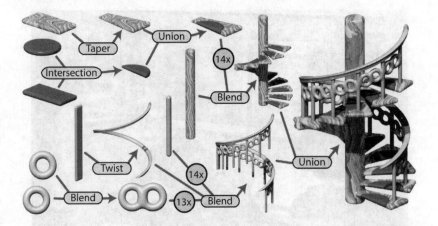

Figure 16.27. BlobTree. The spiral staircase is built from a central textured cylinder to which the stairs and the railing are blended. The railing is comprised of a series of cylinders blended with two circle (torus) primitives, blended together and further blended with a vertical cylinder. The BlobTree is also a scene graph and instancing nodes repeat the various parts transformed by the appropriate matrices. Each stair is made from a tapered polygon primitive (that becomes an offset surface); intersection and union nodes combine the inflated disk with the stair.

16.8.1 Traversing the BlobTree

An example of a BlobTree including the Barr warps and CSG operations is shown in Figure 16.27. Other nodes can include 2D texturing (Schmidt et al., 2006), precise contact modeling, as well as animation and other attributes. The traversal of the BlobTree is in essence very simple. All that is required to render the object either by polygonizing or ray tracing is to find the implicit value of any point (and the corresponding gradient). This can be done by traversing the tree. Polygonization and ray-tracing algorithms need to evaluate the implicit field function at a large number of points in space. The function $f(\mathcal{N}, M)$ returns the field value for the node $\mathcal{N}$ at the point M, which depends on the type of the node. The values $\mathcal{L}$ and $\mathcal{R}$ indicate that the left or right branch of the tree is explored.The algorithm below is written (for simplicity) as if the tree were binary:

function $f(\mathcal{N}, M)$:

- primitive: $f(M)$;

- warp: $f(\mathcal{L}(\mathcal{N}), w(M))$;

- blend: $f(\mathcal{L}(\mathcal{N}), M) + f(\mathcal{R}(\mathcal{N}), M))$;

Figure 16.28.   "Spiral Stairs." A complex BlobTree implicit model created in Erwin DeGroot's BlobTree.net system. (See also Plate VI.)

- union: $\max(f(\mathcal{L}(\mathcal{N}), M), f(\mathcal{R}(\mathcal{N}), M))$;

- intersection: $\min(f(\mathcal{L}(\mathcal{N}), M), f(\mathcal{R}(\mathcal{N}), M))$;

- difference: $\min(f(\mathcal{L}(\mathcal{N}), M), -f(\mathcal{R}(\mathcal{N}), M))$.

A complex BlobTree model showing many of the features that have been integrated is shown in Figure 16.28.

16.9   Interactive Implicit Modeling Systems

Figure 16.29.   Outlines are inflated. *Image courtesy Erwin DeGroot.*

Early sketch-based modeling systems, such as Teddy (Igarashi et al., 1999), used a few drawn strokes from the user to infer a polygonal model in 3-space. With better hardware and improved algorithms, sketch-based implicit modeling systems are now possible. Shapeshop uses implicit sweep surfaces to manufacture 3D strokes from 2D user strokes and also preserves the hierarchy of the BlobTree unlike the early systems that produced homogeneous meshes (Schmidt, Wyvill, Sousa, & Jorge, 2005). This enables a user to produce complex models of arbitrary topology from a few simple strokes. The margin figures show a closed drawn stroke (Figure 16.29) inflated into a an implicit sweep and a second sweep (Figure 16.30) that has a smaller sweep object subtracted using CSG.

One of the improvements that made this possible is a caching system that uses a fixed 3D grid of implicit values at each node of the BlobTree representing the values found by traversing the tree below the node (Schmidt, Wyvill, & Galin, 2005). If the value of some point p is required at node N, a value may be returned without traversing the tree below N, provided that part of the tree is unaltered. Instead, an interpolation scheme (see Chapter 28) is used to find a value for p. This scheme speeds up traversal for complex BlobTrees and is one factor in enabling a system to run at interactive rates.

The next generation of implicit modeling systems will exploit hardware and software advances to be able to handle more and more complex hierarchical models interactively. A more complex Shapeshop example is shown in Figure 16.31.

Figure 16.30. BlobTree operations can be applied, e.g., CSG difference. *Image courtesy Erwin DeGroot.*

Figure 16.31. "The Next Step." A complex BlobTree implicit model created interactively in Ryan Schmidt's Shapeshop by artist, Corien Clapwijk (Andusan). (See also Plate VII.)

Exercises

1. In an implicit surface modeling system the fall-off filter function is defined
   as
   $$f(r) = \begin{cases} 0, & r > R, \\ 1 - r/R, & \text{otherwise}, \end{cases}$$

   where R is a constant. A point primitive placed at $(-1,0)$ and another
   at $(1,0)$ are rendered to show the $f = 0.5$ iso-surface. The value R, the
   distance where the potential due to the point falls to zero in both cases, is
   1.5.

   Calculate the potential at the point $(0,0)$ and at $+0.5$ intervals until the
   point $(2.5,0)$. Sketch the 0.5 contour and the contour at which the field
   falls to zero.

2. Why are the ambiguous cases in the polygonization algorithm considered
   to be a sampling problem?

3. Calculate the error involved in using linear interpolation to estimate the
   intersection of an implicit surface and a cubic voxel.

4. Design an implicit primitive function using the skeleton of your choice. The
   function must take as input a point and return an implicit value and also the
   gradient at that point.

Michael Ashikhmin

17

Computer Animation

Animation is derived from the Latin *anima* and means the act, process, or result of imparting life, interest, spirit, motion, or activity. Motion is a defining property of life and much of the true art of animation is about how to tell a story, show emotion, or even express subtle details of human character through motion. A computer is a secondary tool for achieving these goals—it is a tool which a skillful animator can use to help get the result he wants faster and without concentrating on technicalities in which he is not interested. Animation without computers, which is now often called "traditional" animation, has a long and rich history of its own which is continuously being written by hundreds of people still active in this art. As in any established field, some time-tested rules have been crystallized which give general high-level guidance to how certain things should be done and what should be avoided. These principles of traditional animation apply equally to computer animation, and we will discuss some of them below.

The computer, however, is more than just a tool. In addition to making the animator's main task less tedious, computers also add some truly unique abilities that were simply not available or were extremely difficult to obtain before. Modern modeling tools allow the relatively easy creation of detailed three-dimensional models, rendering algorithms can produce an impressive range of appearances, from fully photorealistic to highly stylized, powerful numerical simulation algorithms can help to produce desired physics-based motion for particularly hard to animate objects, and motion capture systems give the ability to record and use real-life motion. These developments led to an exploding use of computer animation techniques in motion pictures and commercials, automotive design and architecture, medicine and scientific research among many other areas. Completely new domains and applications have also appeared including fully computer-animated feature films, virtual/augmented reality systems and, of course, computer games.

Other chapters of this book cover many of the developments mentioned above (for example, geometric modeling and rendering) more directly. Here, we will provide an overview only of techniques and algorithms directly used to create and manipulate motion. In particular, we will loosely distinguish and briefly describe four main computer animation approaches:

- *Keyframing* gives the most direct control to the animator who provides necessary data at some moments in time and the computer fills in the rest.

- *Procedural* animation involves specially designed, often empirical, mathematical functions and procedures whose output resembles some particular motion.

- *Physics-based* techniques solve differential equation of motion.

- *Motion capture* uses special equipment or techniques to record real-world motion and then transfers this motion into that of computer models.

We do not touch upon the artistic side of the field at all here. In general, we can not possibly do more here than just scratch the surface of the fascinating subject of creating motion with a computer. We hope that readers truly interested in the subject will continue their journey well beyond the material of this chapter.

17.1   Principles of Animation

In his seminal 1987 SIGGRAPH paper (Lasseter, 1987), John Lasseter brought key principles developed as early as the 1930's by traditional animators of Walt Disney studios to the attention of the then-fledgling computer animation community. Twelve principles were mentioned: *squash and stretch; timing; anticipation; follow through and overlapping action; slow-in and slow-out; staging; arcs; secondary action; straight-ahead and pose-to-pose action; exaggeration; solid drawing skill; appeal.* Almost two decades later, these time-tested rules, which can make a difference between a natural and entertaining animation and a mechanistic-looking and boring one, are as important as ever. For computer animation, in addition, it is very important to *balance* control and flexibility given to the animator with the full advantage of the computer's abilities. Although these principles are widely known, many factors affect how much attention is being paid to these rules in practice. While a character animator working on a feature film might spend many hours trying to follow some of these suggestions (for example, tweaking his timing to be just right), many game designers tend to believe that their time is better spent elsewhere.

17.1.1 Timing

Timing, or the speed of action, is at the heart of any animation. How fast things happen affects the meaning of action, emotional state, and even perceived weight of objects involved. Depending on its speed, the same action, a turn of a character's head from left to right, can mean anything from a reaction to being hit by a heavy object to slowly seeking a book on a bookshelf or stretching a neck muscle. It is very important to set timing appropriate for the specific action at hand. Action should occupy enough time to be noticed while avoiding too slow and potentially boring motions. For computer animation projects involving recorded sound, the sound provides a natural timing anchor to be followed. In fact, in most productions, the actor's voice is recorded first and the complete animation is then synchronized to this recording. Since large and heavy objects tend to move slower than small and light ones (with less acceleration, to be more precise), timing can be used to provide significant information about the weight of an object.

17.1.2 Action Layout

At any moment during an animation, it should be clear to the viewer what idea (action, mood, expression) is being presented. Good *staging*, or high-level planning of the action, should lead a viewer's eye to where the important action is currently concentrated, effectively telling him "look at this, and now, look at this" without using any words. Some familiarity with human perception can help us with this difficult task. Since human visual systems react mostly to relative changes rather than absolute values of stimuli, a sudden motion in a still environment or lack of motion in some part of a busy scene naturally draws attention. The same action presented so that the silhouette of the object is changing can often be much more noticeable compared with a frontal arrangement (see Figure 17.1(a)).

On a slightly lower level, each action can be split into three parts: *anticipation* (preparation for the action), the action itself and *follow-through* (termination of the action). In many cases the action itself is the shortest part and, in some sense, the least interesting. For example, kicking a football might involve extensive preparation on the part of the kicker and long "visual tracking" of the departing

Figure 17.1. Action layout. Left: Staging action properly is crucial for bringing attention to currently important motion. The act of raising a hand would be prominent on the top but harder to notice on the bottom. A change in nose length, on the contrary, might be completely invisible in the first case. Note that this might be intentionally hidden, for example, to be suddenly revealed later. Neither arrangement is particularly good if both motions should be attended to. Middle: The amount of anticipation can tell much about the following action. The action which is about to follow (throwing a ball) is very short but it is clear what is about to happen. The more wound up the character is, the faster the following action is perceived to be. Right: The follow-through phase is especially important for secondary appendages (hair) whose motion follows the leading part (head). The motion of the head is very simple, but leads to non-trivial follow-through behavior of the hair itself. It is impossible to create a natural animation without a follow-through phase and overlapping action in this case. *Figure courtesy Peter Shirley and Christina Villarruel.*

ball with ample opportunities to show the stress of the moment, emotional state of the kicker, and even the reaction to the expected result of the action. The action itself (motion of the leg to kick the ball) is rather plain and takes just a fraction of a second in this case.

The goal of anticipation is to prepare the viewer to what is about to happen. This becomes especially important if the action itself is very fast, greatly important, or extremely difficult. Creating a more extensive anticipation for such actions serves to underscore these properties and, in case of fast events, makes sure the action will not be missed (see Figure 17.1(b)).

In real life, the main action often causes one or more other *overlapping actions*. Different appendages or loose parts of the object typically drag behind the main leading section and keep moving for a while in the follow-through part of the main action as shown in Figure 17.1(c). Moreover, the next action often starts before the previous one is completely over. A player might start running while he is still tracking the ball he just kicked. Ignoring such natural flow is generally perceived as if there are pauses between actions and can result in robot-like mechanical motion. While overlapping is necessary to keep the motion natural, *secondary action* is often added by the animator to make motion more interesting and achieve realistic complexity of the animation. It is important not to allow secondary action to dominate the main action.

17.1.3   Animation Techniques

Several specific techniques can be used to make motion look more natural. The most important one is probably *squash and stretch* which suggests to change the shape of a moving object in a particular way as it moves. One would generally stretch an object in the direction of motion and squash it when a force is applied to it, as demonstrated in Figure 17.2 for a classic animation of a bouncing ball. It is important to preserve the total volume as this happens to avoid the illusion of growing or shrinking of the object. The greater the speed of motion (or the force), the more stretching (or squashing) is applied. Such deformations are used for several reasons. For very fast motion, an object can move between two sequential frames so quickly that there is no overlap between the object at the time of the current frame and at the time of the previous frame which can lead to strobing (a variant of aliasing). Having the object elongated in the direction of motion can ensure better overlap and helps the eye to fight this unpleasant effect. Stretching/squashing can also be used to show flexibility of the object with more deformation applied for more pliable materials. If the object is intended to appear as rigid, its shape is purposefully left the same when it moves.

Natural motion rarely happens along straight lines, so this should generally be avoided in animation and *arcs* should be used instead. Similarly, no real-world motion can instantly change its speed—this would require an infinite amount of force to be applied to an object. It is desirable to avoid such situations in animation as well. In particular, the motion should start and end gradually (*slow in and out*). While hand-drawn animation is sometimes done via *straight-ahead action* with an animator starting at the first frame and drawing one frame after another in

Figure 17.2. Classic example of applying the squash and stretch principle. Note that the volume of the bouncing ball should remain roughly the same throughout the animation.

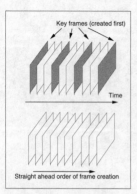

Figure 17.3. Keyframing (top) encourages detailed action planning while straight-ahead action (bottom) leads to a more spontaneous result.

sequence until the end, *pose-to-pose action*, also known as *keyframing*, is much more suitable for computer animation. In this technique, animation is carefully planned through a series of relatively sparsely spaced key frames with the rest of the animation (in-between frames) filled in only after the keys are set (Figure 17.3). This allows more precise timing and allows the computer to take over the most tedious part of the process—the creation of the in-between frames—using algorithms presented in the next section.

Almost any of the techniques outlined above can be used with some reasonable amount of *exaggeration* to achieve greater artistic effect or underscore some specific property of an action or a character. The ultimate goal is to achieve something the audience will want to see, something which is *appealing*. Extreme complexity or too much symmetry in a character or action tends to be less appealing. To create good results, a traditional animator needs *solid drawing skills*. Analogously, a computer animator should certainly understand computer graphics and have a solid knowledge of the tools he uses.

17.1.4 Animator Control vs. Automatic Methods

In traditional animation, the animator has complete control over all aspects of the production process and nothing prevents the final product to be as it was planned in every detail. The price paid for this flexibility is that every frame is created by hand, leading to an extremely time- and labor-consuming enterprise. In computer animation, there is a clear tradeoff between, on the one hand, giving an animator more direct control over the result, but asking him to contribute more work and, on the other hand, relying on more automatic techniques which might require setting just a few input parameters but offer little or no control over some of the properties of the result. A good algorithm should provide sufficient flexibility while asking an animator only the information which is intuitive, easy to provide, and which he himself feels is necessary for achieving the desired effect. While perfect compliance with this requirement is unlikely in practice since it would probably take something close to a mind-reading machine, we do encourage the reader to evaluate any computer-animation technique from the point of view of providing such *balance*.

17.2 Keyframing

The term keyframing can be misleading when applied to 3D computer animation since no actual completed frames (i.e., images) are typically involved. At any given moment, a 3D scene being animated is specified by a set of numbers: the

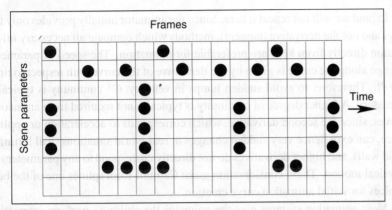

Figure 17.4. Different patterns of setting keys (black circles above) can be used simultaneously for the same scene. It is assumed that there are more frames before as well as after this portion.

positions of centers of all objects, their RGB colors, the amount of scaling applied to each object in each axis, modeling transformations between different parts of a complex object, camera position and orientation, light sources intensity, etc. To animate a scene, some subset of these values have to change with time. One can, of course, directly set these values at every frame, but this will not be particularly efficient. Short of that, some number of important moments in time (key frames t_k) can be chosen along the timeline of animation for each of the parameters and values of this parameter (key values f_k) are set only for these selected frames. We will call a combination (t_k, f_k) of key frame and key value simply a key. Key frames do not have to be the same for different parameters, but it is often logical to set keys at least for some of them simultaneously. For example, key frames chosen for x-, y- and z-coordinates of a specific object might be set at exactly the same frames forming a single position vector key $(t_k, \mathbf{p_k})$. These key frames, however, might be completely different from those chosen for the object's orientation or color. The closer key frames are to each other, the more control the animator has over the result; however the cost of doing more work of setting the keys has to be assessed. It is, therefore, typical to have large spacing between keys in parts of the animation which are relatively simple, concentrating them in intervals where complex action occurs as shown in Figure 17.4.

Once the animator sets the key (t_k, f_k), the system has to compute values of f for all other frames. Although we are ultimately interested only in a discrete set of values, it is convenient to treat this as a classical interpolation problem which fits a continuous *animation curve* $f(t)$ through a provided set of data points (Figure 17.5). Extensive discussion of curve fitting algorithms can be found in Chap-

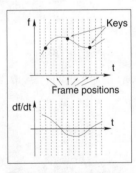

Figure 17.5. A continuous curve *f(t)* is fit through the keys provided by the animator even though only values at frame positions are of interest. The derivative of this function gives the speed of parameter change and is at first determined automatically by the fitting procedure.

ter 15, and we will not repeat it here. Since the animator initially provides only the keys and not the derivative (tangent), methods which compute all necessary information directly from keys are preferable for animation. The speed of parameter change along the curve is given by the derivative of the curve with respect to time df/dt. Therefore, to avoid sudden jumps in velocity, C^1 continuity is typically necessary. A higher degree of continuity is typically not required from animation curves, since the second derivative, which corresponds to acceleration or applied force, can experience very sudden changes in real-world situations (ball hitting a solid wall), and higher derivatives do not directly correspond to any parameters of physical motion. These consideration make Catmull-Rom splines one of the best choices for initial animation curve creation.

Most animation systems give the animator the ability to perform interactive fine editing of this initial curve, including inserting more keys, adjusting existing keys, or modifying automatically computed tangents. Another useful technique which can help to tweak the shape of the curve is called TCB control (TCB stands for tension, continuity and bias). The idea is to introduce three new parameters which can be used to modify the shape of the curve near a key through coordinated adjustment of incoming and outgoing tangents at this point. For keys uniformly spaced in time with distance Δt between them, the standard Catmull-Rom expression for incoming T_i^{in} and outgoing T_i^{out} tangents at an internal key (t_k, f_k) can be rewritten as

$$T_k^{in} = T_k^{out} = \frac{1}{2\Delta t}(f_{k+1} - f_k) + \frac{1}{2\Delta t}(f_k - f_{k-1}).$$

Modified tangents of a TCB spline are

$$T_k^{in} = \frac{(1-t)(1-c)(1+b)}{2\Delta t}(f_{k+1} - f_k) + \frac{(1-t)(1+c)(1-b)}{2\Delta t}(f_k - f_{k-1}),$$

$$T_k^{out} = \frac{(1-t)(1+c)(1+b)}{2\Delta t}(f_{k+1} - f_k) + \frac{(1-t)(1-c)(1-b)}{2\Delta t}(f_k - f_{k-1}).$$

The tension parameter t controls the sharpness of the curve near the key by scaling both incoming and outgoing tangents. Larger tangents (lower tension) lead to a flatter curve shape near the key. Bias b allows the animator to selectively increase the weight of a key's neighbors locally pulling the curve closer to a straight line connecting the key with its left (b near 1, "overshooting" the action) or right (b near -1, "undershooting" the action) neighbors. A non-zero value of continuity c makes incoming and outgoing tangents different allowing the animator to create kinks in the curve at the key value. Practically useful values of TCB parameters are typically confined to the interval $[-1; 1]$ with defaults $t = c = b = 0$ corresponding to the original Catmull-Rom spline. Examples of possible curve shape adjustments are shown in Figure 17.6.

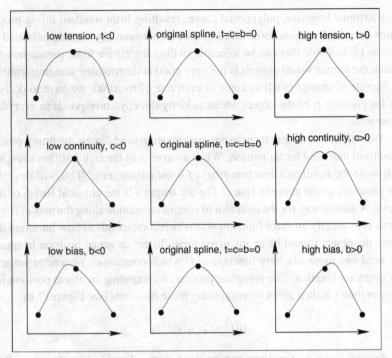

Figure 17.6. Editing the default interpolating spline (middle column) using TCB controls. Note that all keys remain at the same positions.

17.2.1   Motion Controls

So far, we have described how to control the shape of the animation curve through key positioning and fine tweaking of tangent values at the keys. This, however, is generally not sufficient when one would like to have control both over where the object is moving, i.e., its path, and how fast it moves along this path. Given a set of positions in space as keys, automatic curve-fitting techniques can fit a curve through them, but resulting motion is only constrained by forcing the object to arrive at a specified key position $\mathbf{p_k}$ at the corresponding key frame t_k, and nothing is directly said about the speed of motion between the keys. This can create problems. For example, if an object moves along the x-axis with velocity 11 meters per second for 1 second and then with 1 meter per second for 9 seconds, it will arrive at position $x = 20$ after 10 seconds thus satisfying animator's keys (0,0) and (10, 20). It is rather unlikely that this jerky motion was actually desired, and uniform motion with speed 2 meters/second is probably closer to what the animator wanted when setting these keys. Although typically not displaying

such extreme behavior, polynomial curves resulting from standard fitting procedures do exhibit non-uniform speed of motion between keys as demonstrated in
Figure 17.7. While this can be tolerable (within limits) for some parameters for
which the human visual system is not very good at determining non-uniformities
in the rate of change (such as color or even rate of rotation), we have to do better for position **p** of the object where velocity directly corresponds to everyday
experience.

We will first distinguish curve parameterization used during the fitting procedure from that used for animation. When a curve is fit through position keys, we
will write the result as a function $\mathbf{p}(u)$ of some parameter u. This will describe
the geometry of the curve in space. The arc length s is the physical length of the
curve. A natural way for the animator to control the motion along the now existing
curve is to specify an extra function $s(t)$ which corresponds to how far along the
curve the object should be at any given time. To get an actual position in space,
we need one more auxiliary function $u(s)$ which computes a parameter value u
for given arc length s. The complete process of computing an object position for
a given time t is then given by composing these functions (see Figure 17.8):

$$\mathbf{p}(t) = \mathbf{p}(u(s(t))).$$

Several standard functions can be used as the distance-time function $s(t)$.
One of the simplest is the linear function corresponding to constant velocity:
$s(t) = vt$ with $v = \text{const}$. Another common example is the motion with constant acceleration a (and initial speed v_0) which is described by the parabolic
$s(t) = v_0 t + a t^2 / 2$. Since velocity is changing gradually here, this function
can help to model desirable ease-in and ease-out behavior. More generally, the

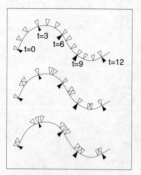

Figure 17.7. All three
motions are along the same
2D path and satisfy the set
of keys at the tips of the
black triangles. The tips of
the white triangles show object position at $\Delta t = 1$ intervals. Uniform speed of
motion between the keys
(top) might be closer to
what the animator wanted
but automatic fitting procedures could result in either
of the other two motions.

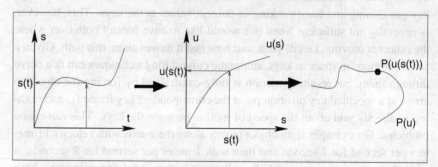

Figure 17.8. To get position in space at a given time t, one first utilizes user-specified motion
control to obtain the distance along the curve $s(t)$ and then compute the corresponding curve
parameter value $u(s(t))$. Previously fitted curve $\mathbf{P}(u)$ can now be used to find the position
$\mathbf{P}(u(s(t)))$.

slope of $s(t)$ gives the velocity of motion with negative slope corresponding to the motion backwards along the curve. To achieve most flexibility, the ability to interactively edit $s(t)$ is typically provided to the animator by the animation system. The distance-time function is not the only way to control motion. In some cases it might be more convenient for the user to specify a velocity-time function $v(t)$ or even an acceleration-time function $a(t)$. Since these are correspondingly first and second derivatives of $s(t)$, to use these type of controls, the system first recovers the distance-time function by integrating the user input (twice in the case of $a(t)$).

The relationship between the curve parameter u and arc length s is established automatically by the system. In practice, the system first determines arc length dependance on parameter u (i.e., the inverse function $s(u)$). Using this function, for any given S it is possible to solve the equation $s(u) - S = 0$ with unknown u obtaining $u(S)$. For most curves, the function $s(u)$ can not be expressed in closed analytic form and numerical integration is necessary (see Chapter 14). Standard numerical root-finding procedures (such as the Newton-Raphson method, for example) can then be directly used to solve the equation $s(u) - S = 0$ for u.

An alternative technique is to approximate the curve itself as a set of linear segments between points $\mathbf{p}_i$ computed at some set of sufficiently densely spaced parameter values u_i. One then creates a table of approximate arc lengths

$$s(u_i) \approx \sum_{j=1}^{i} ||\mathbf{p_j} - \mathbf{p_{j-1}}|| = s(u_{i-1}) + ||\mathbf{p_i} - \mathbf{p_{i-1}}||.$$

Since $s(u)$ is a non-decreasing function of u, one can then find the interval containing the value S by simple searching through the table (see Figure 17.9). Linear interpolation of the interval's u end values is then performed to finally find u(S). If greater precision is necessary, a few steps of the Newton-Raphson algorithm with this value as the starting point can be applied.

17.2.2 Interpolating Rotation

The techniques presented above can be used to interpolate the keys set for most of the parameters describing the scene. Three-dimensional rotation is one important motion for which more specialized interpolation methods and representations are common. The reason for this is that applying standard techniques to 3D rotations often leads to serious practical problems. Rotation (a change in orientation of an object) is the only motion other than translation which leaves the shape of the object intact. It therefore plays a special role in animating rigid objects.

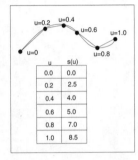

u	s(u)
0.0	0.0
0.2	2.5
0.4	4.0
0.6	5.0
0.8	7.0
1.0	8.5

Figure 17.9. To create a tabular version of $s(u)$, the curve can be approximated by a number of line segments connecting points on the curve positioned at equal parameter increments. The table is searched to find the u-interval for a given S. For the curve above, for example, the value of u corresponding to the position of $S = 6.5$ lies between $u = 0.6$ and $u = 0.8$.

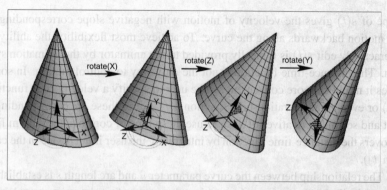

Figure 17.10. Three Euler angles can be used to specify arbitrary object orientation through a sequence of three rotations around coordinate axes embedded into the object (axis Y always points to the tip of the cone). Note that each rotation is given in a new coordinate system. Fixed angle representation is very similar but the coordinate axes it uses are fixed in space and do not rotate with the object.

There are several ways to specify the orientation of an object. First, transformation matrices as described in Chapter 6 can be used. Unfortunately, naive (element-by-element) interpolation of rotation matrices does not produce a correct result. For example, the matrix "half-way" between 2D clock- and counterclockwise 90 degree rotation is the null matrix:

$$\frac{1}{2}\begin{bmatrix} 0 & 1 \\ -1 & 0 \end{bmatrix} + \frac{1}{2}\begin{bmatrix} 0 & -1 \\ 1 & 0 \end{bmatrix} = \begin{bmatrix} 0 & 0 \\ 0 & 0 \end{bmatrix}.$$

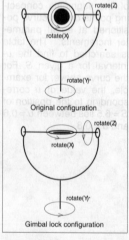

Figure 17.11. In this example, gimbal lock occurs when a 90 degree turn around axis Z is made. Both X and Y rotations are now performed around the same axis leading to the loss of one degree of freedom.

The correct result is, of course, the unit matrix corresponding to no rotation. Second, one can specify arbitrary orientation as a sequence of exactly three rotations around coordinate axes chosen in some specific order. These axes can be fixed in space (*fixed-angle* representation) or embedded into the object therefore changing after each rotation (*Euler-angle* representation as shown in Figure 17.10). These three angles of rotation can be animated directly through standard keyframing, but a subtle problem known as gimbal lock arises. Gimbal lock occurs if during rotation one of the three rotation axes is by accident aligned with another, thereby reducing by one the number of available degrees of freedom as shown in Figure 17.11 for a physical device. This effect is more common than one might think—a single 90 degree turn to the right (or left) can potentially put an object into a gimbal lock. Finally, any orientation can be specified by choosing an appropriate axis in space and angle of rotation around this axis. While animating in this representation is relatively straightforward, combining two rotations, i.e., finding the axis and angle corresponding to a sequence of two rotations both represented by axis and angle, is non-trivial. A special mathematical apparatus, *quaternions* has been developed to make this representation suitable both for combining several rotations into a single one and for animation.

Given a 3D vector $\mathbf{v} = (x, y, z)$ and a scalar s, a quaternion q is formed by combining the two into a four component object: $q = [s\ x\ y\ z] = [s;\ \mathbf{v}]$. Several new operations are then defined for quaternions. Quaternion addition simply sums scalar and vector parts separately:

$$q_1 + q_2 \equiv [s_1 + s_2;\ \mathbf{v_1} + \mathbf{v_2}].$$

Multiplication by a scalar a gives a new quaternion

$$aq \equiv [as;\ a\mathbf{v}].$$

More complex quaternion multiplication is defined as

$$q_1 \cdot q_2 \equiv [s_1 s_2 - \mathbf{v_1 v_2};\ s_1 \mathbf{v_2} + s_2 \mathbf{v_1} + \mathbf{v_1} \times \mathbf{v_2}],$$

where $\times$ denotes a vector cross product. It is easy to see that, similar to matrices, quaternion multiplication is associative, but not commutative. We will be interested mostly in normalized quaternions—those for which the quaternion norm $|q| = \sqrt{s^2 + \mathbf{v}^2}$ is equal to one. One final definition we need is that of an inverse quaternion:

$$q^{-1} = (1/|q|)[s;\ -\mathbf{v}].$$

To represent a rotation by angle ϕ around an axis passing through the origin whose direction is given by the normalized vector $\mathbf{n}$, a normalized quaternion

$$q = [\cos(\phi/2);\ \sin(\phi/2)\mathbf{n}]$$

is formed. To rotate point $\mathbf{p}$, one turns it into the quaternion $q_p = [0;\ \mathbf{p}]$ and computes the quaternion product

$$q_p' = q \cdot q_p \cdot q^{-1}$$

which is guaranteed to have a zero scalar part and the rotated point as its vector part. Composite rotation is given simply by the product of quaternions representing each of the separate rotation steps. To animate with quaternions, one can treat them as points in a four-dimensional space and set keys directly in this space. To keep quaternions normalized, one should, strictly speaking, restrict interpolation procedures to a unit sphere (a 3D object) in this 4D space. However, a spherical version of even linear interpolation (often called *slerp*) already results in rather unpleasant math. Simple 4D linear interpolation followed by projection onto the unit sphere shown in Figure 17.12 is much simpler and often sufficient in practice. Smoother results can be obtained via repeated application of a linear interpolation procedure using the de Casteljau algorithm.

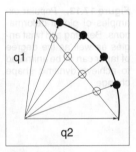

Figure 17.12. Interpolating quaternions should be done on the surface of a 3D unit sphere embedded in 4D space. However, much simpler interpolation along a 4D straight line (open circles) followed by re-projection of the results onto the sphere (black circles) is often sufficient.

17.3   Deformations

Although techniques for object deformation might be more properly treated as modeling tools, they are traditionally discussed together with animation methods. Probably the simplest example of an operation which changes object shape is a non-uniform scaling. More generally, some function can be applied to local co-ordinates of all points specifying the object (i.e., vertices of a triangular mesh or control polygon of a spline surface), repositioning these points and creating a new shape: $\mathbf{p}' = f(\mathbf{p}, \gamma)$ where γ is a vector of parameters used by the deformation function. Choosing different f (and combining them by applying one after another) can help to create very interesting deformations. Examples of useful simple functions include bend, twist, and taper which are shown in Figure 17.13. Animating shape change is very easy in this case by keyframing the parameters of the deformation function. Disadvantages of this technique include difficulty of choosing the mathematical function for some non-standard deformations and the fact that the resulting deformation is *global* in the sense that the complete object, and not just some part of it, is reshaped.

To deform an object locally while providing more direct control over the re-sult, one can choose a single vertex, move it to a new location and adjust vertices within some neighborhood to follow the seed vertex. The area affected by the de-formation and the specific amount of displacement in different parts of the object are controlled by an attenuation function which decreases with distance (typically computed over the object's surface) to the seed vertex. Seed vertex motion can be keyframed to produce animated shape change.

A more general deformation technique is called free-form deformation (FFD) (Sederberg & Parry, 1986). A local (in most cases rectilinear) coordinate grid is first established to encapsulate the part of the object to be deformed, and co-ordinates (s, t, u) of all relevant points are computed with respect to this grid. The user then freely reshapes the grid of lattice points $\mathbf{P_{ijk}}$ into a new distorted lattice $\mathbf{P'_{ijk}}$ (Figure 17.14). The object is reconstructed using coordinates com-puted in the original undistorted grid in the trivariate analog of Bézier interpolants (see Chapter 15) with distorted lattice points $\mathbf{P'_{ijk}}$ serving as control points in this expression:

$$P(s, u, t) = \sum_{i=0}^{L} \binom{i}{L} (1-s)^{L-i} s^i \sum_{j=0}^{M} \binom{j}{M} (1-t)^{M-j} t^j \sum_{k=0}^{N} \binom{k}{N} (1-u)^{N-k} u^k \mathbf{P'_{ijk}},$$

where L, M, N are maximum indices of lattice points in each dimension. In ef-fect, the lattice serves as a low resolution version of the object for the purpose of deformation, allowing for a smooth shape change of an arbitrarily complex ob-

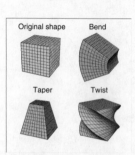

Figure 17.13. Popular ex-amples of global deforma-tions. Bending and twist an-gles as well as the degree of taper can all be animated to achieve dynamic shape change.

ject through a relatively small number of intuitive adjustments. FFD lattices can themselves be treated as regular objects by the system and can be transformed, animated, and even further deformed if necessary, leading to corresponding changes in the object to which the lattice is attached. For example, moving a *deformation tool* consisting of the original lattice and distorted lattice representing a bulge across an object results in a bulge moving across the object.

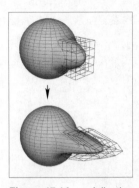

Figure 17.14. Adjusting the FFD lattice results in the deformation of the object.

17.4 Character Animation

Animation of articulated figures is most often performed through a combination of keyframing and specialized deformation techniques. The character model intended for animation typically consists of at least two main layers as shown in Figure 17.15. The motion of a highly detailed surface representing the outer shell or *skin* of the character is what the viewer will eventually see in the final product. The *skeleton* underneath it is a hierarchical structure (a tree) of joints which provides a kinematic model of the figure and is used exclusively for animation. In some cases, additional intermediate layer(s) roughly corresponding to muscles are inserted between the skeleton and the skin.

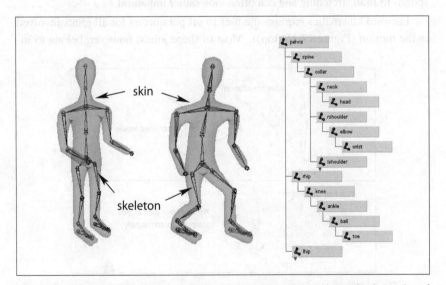

Figure 17.15. (Left) A hierarchy of joints, a skeleton, serves as a kinematic abstraction of the character; (middle) repositioning the skeleton deforms a separate skin object attached to it; (right) a tree data structure is used to represent the skeleton. For compactness, the internal structure of several nodes is hidden (they are identical to a corresponding sibling).

Each of the skeleton's joints acts as a parent for the hierarchy below it. The root represents the whole character and is positioned directly in the world coordinate system. If a local transformation matrix which relates a joint to its parent in the hierarchy is available, one can obtain a transformation which relates local space of any joint to the world system (i.e., the system of the root) by simply concatenating transformations along the path from the root to the joint. To evaluate the whole skeleton (i.e., find position and orientation of all joints), a depth-first traversal of the complete tree of joints is performed. A transformation stack is a natural data structure to help with this task. While traversing down the tree, the current composite matrix is pushed on the stack and new one is created by multiplying the current matrix with the one stored at the joint. When backtracking to the parent, this extra transformation should be undone before another branch is visited; this is easily done by simply popping the stack. Although this general and simple technique for evaluating hierarchies is used throughout computer graphics, in animation (and robotics) it is given a special name—*forward kinematics* (FK). While general representations for all transformations can be used, it is common to use specialized sets of parameters, such as link lengths or joint angles, to specify skeletons. To animate with forward kinematics, rotational parameters of all joints are manipulated directly. The technique also allows the animator to change the distance between joints (link lengths), but one should be aware that this corresponds to limb stretching and can often look rather unnatural.

Forward kinematics requires the user to set parameters for all joints involved in the motion (Figure 17.16 (top)). Most of these joints, however, belong to in-

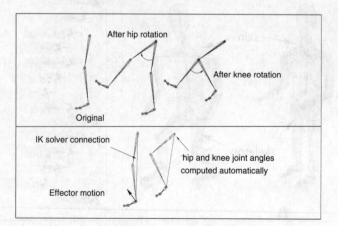

Figure 17.16. Forward kinematics (top) requires the animator to put all joints into correct position. In inverse kinematic (bottom), parameters of some internal joints are computed based on desired end effector motion.

ternal nodes of the hierarchy, and their motion is typically not something the animator wants to worry about. In most situations, the animator just wants them to move naturally "on their own," and one is much more interested in specifying the behavior of the end point of a joint chain, which typically corresponds to something performing a specific action, such as an ankle or a tip of a finger. The animator would rather have parameters of all internal joints be determined from the motion of the end effector automatically by the system. *Inverse kinematics* (IK) allows us to do just that (see Figure 17.16 (bottom)).

Let $\mathbf{x}$ be the position of the end effector and α be the vector of parameters needed to specify all internal joints along the chain from the root to the final joint. Sometimes the orientation of the final joint is also directly set by the animator, in which case we assume that the corresponding variables are included in the vector $\mathbf{x}$. For simplicity, however, we will write all specific expressions for the vector:

$$\mathbf{x} = (x_1, x_2, x_3)^T.$$

Since each of the variables in $\mathbf{x}$ is a function of α, it can be written as a vector equation $\mathbf{x} = \mathbf{F}(\alpha)$. If we change the internal joint parameters by a small amount $\delta\alpha$, a resulting change $\delta\mathbf{x}$ in the position of the end effector can be approximately written as

$$\delta\mathbf{x} = \frac{\partial \mathbf{F}}{\partial \alpha} \delta\alpha, \tag{17.1}$$

where $\frac{\partial \mathbf{F}}{\partial \alpha}$ is the matrix of partial derivatives called the Jacobian:

$$\frac{\partial \mathbf{F}}{\partial \alpha} = \begin{bmatrix} \frac{\partial f_1}{\partial \alpha_1} & \frac{\partial f_1}{\partial \alpha_2} & \cdots & \frac{\partial f_1}{\partial \alpha_n} \\ \frac{\partial f_2}{\partial \alpha_1} & \frac{\partial f_2}{\partial \alpha_2} & \cdots & \frac{\partial f_2}{\partial \alpha_n} \\ \frac{\partial f_3}{\partial \alpha_1} & \frac{\partial f_3}{\partial \alpha_2} & \cdots & \frac{\partial f_3}{\partial \alpha_n} \end{bmatrix}.$$

At each moment in time, we know the desired position of the end effector (set by the animator) and, of course, the effector's current position. Subtracting the two, we will get the desired adjustment $\delta\mathbf{x}$. Elements of the Jacobian matrix are related to changes in a coordinate of the end effector when a particular internal parameter is changed while others remain fixed (see Figure 17.17). These elements can be computed for any given skeleton configuration using geometric relationships. The only remaining unknowns in the system of equations (17.1) are the changes in internal parameters α. Once we solve for them, we update $\alpha = \alpha + \delta\alpha$ which gives all the necessary information for the FK procedure to reposition the skeleton.

Unfortunately, the system (17.1) can not usually be solved analytically and, moreover, it is in most cases underconstrained, i.e., the number of unknown internal joint parameters α exceeds the number of variables in vector $\mathbf{x}$. This means that different motions of the skeleton can result in the same motion of the end

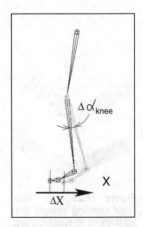

Figure 17.17. Partial derivative $\partial x / \partial \alpha_{knee}$ is given by the limit of $\Delta x / \Delta \alpha_{knee}$. Effector displacement is computed while all joints, except the knee, are kept fixed.

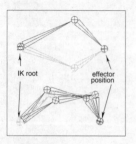

Figure 17.18. Multiple configurations of internal joints can result in the same effector position. (Top) disjoint "flipped" solutions; (bottom) a continuum of solutions.

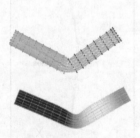

Figure 17.20. Top: Rigid skinning assigns skin vertices to a specific joint. Those belonging to the elbow joint are shown in black; Bottom: Soft skinning can blend the influence of several joints. Weights for the elbow joint are shown (lighter = greater weight). Note smoother skin deformation of the inner part of the skin near the joint.

effector. Some examples are shown on Figure 17.18. Many ways of obtaining specific solution for such systems are available, including those taking into account natural *constraints* needed for some real-life joints (bending a knee only in one direction, for example). One should also remember that the computed Jacobian matrix is valid only for one specific configuration, and it has to be updated as the skeleton moves. The complete IK framework is presented in Figure 17.19. Of course, the root joint for IK does not have to be the root of the whole hierarchy, and multiple IK solvers can be applied to independent parts of the skeleton. For example, one can use separate solvers for right and left feet and yet another one to help animate grasping with the right hand, each with its own root.

A combination of FK and IK approaches is typically used to animate the skeleton. Many common motions (walking or running cycles, grasping, reaching, etc.) exhibit well-known patterns of mutual joint motion making it possible to quickly create naturally looking motion or even use a library of such "clips." The animator then adjusts this generic result according to the physical parameters of the character and also to give it more individuality.

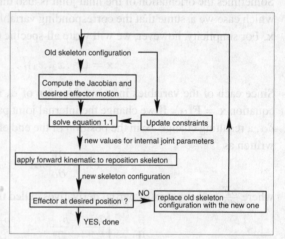

Figure 17.19. A diagram of the inverse kinematic algorithm.

When a skeleton changes its position, it acts as a special type of deformer applied to the skin of the character. The motion is transferred to this surface by assigning each skin vertex one (*rigid skinning*) or more (*smooth skinning*) joints as drivers (see Figure 17.20). In the first case, a skin vertex is simply frozen into the local space of the corresponding joint, which can be the one nearest in space or one chosen directly by the user. The vertex then repeats whatever motion this joint experiences, and its position in world coordinates is determined by standard FK procedure. Although it is simple, rigid skinning makes it difficult to obtain sufficiently smooth skin deformation in areas near the joints or also for more subtle effects resembling breathing or muscle action. Additional specialized deformers called *flexors* can be used for this purpose. In smooth skinning, several joints can influence a skin vertex according to some weight assigned by the animator, providing more detailed control over the results. Displacement vectors, $\mathbf{d_i}$, suggested by different joints affecting a given skin vertex (each again computed with standard FK) are averaged according to their weights w_i to compute the final displacement of the vertex $\mathbf{d} = \sum w_i \mathbf{d_i}$. Normalized weights ($\sum w_i = 1$) are the most common but not fundamentally necessary. Setting smooth skinning weights to achieve the desired effect is not easy and requires significant skill from the animator.

17.4.1 Facial Animation

Skeletons are well suited for creating most motions of a character's body, but they are not very convenient for realistic facial animation. The reason is that the skin of a human face is moved by muscles directly attached to it contrary to other parts of the body where the primary objective of the muscles is to move the bones of the skeleton and any skin deformation is a secondary outcome. The result of this facial anatomical arrangement is a very rich set of dynamic facial expressions humans use as one of the main instruments of communication. We are all very well trained to recognize such facial variations and can easily notice any unnatural appearance. This not only puts special demands on the animator but also requires a high-resolution geometric model of the face and, if photorealism is desired, accurate skin reflection properties and textures.

While it is possible to set key poses of the face vertex-by-vertex and interpolate between them or directly simulate the behavior of the underlying muscle structure using physics-based techniques (see Section 17.5 below), more specialized high-level approaches also exist. The static shape of a specific face can be characterized by a relatively small set of so-called *conformational parameters* (overall scale, distance from the eye to the forehead, length of the nose, width of the jaws, etc.) which are used to morph a generic face model into one with individual features. An additional set of *expressive parameters* can be used to describe the dynamic shape of the face for animation. Examples include rigid rotation of the head, how wide the eyes are open, movement of some feature point from its static position, etc. These are chosen so that most of the interesting expressions can be obtained through some combination of parameter adjustments, therefore, allowing a face to be animated via standard keyframing. To achieve a higher level of control, one can use expressive parameters to create a set of expressions corresponding to common emotions (neutral, sadness, happiness, anger, surprise, etc.) and then blend these key poses to obtain a "slightly sad" or "angrily surprised" face. Similar techniques can be used to perform lip-synch animation, but key poses in this case correspond to different phonemes. Instead of using a sequence of static expressions to describe a dynamic one, the Facial Action Coding System (FACS) (Eckman & Friesen, 1978) decomposes dynamic facial expressions directly into a sum of elementary motions called action units (AUs). The set of AUs is based on extensive psychological research and includes such movements as raising the inner brow, wrinkling the nose, stretching lips, etc. Combining AUs can be used to synthesize a necessary expression.

17.4.2 Motion Capture

Even with the help of the techniques described above, creating realistic-looking character animation from scratch remains a daunting task. It is therefore only natural that much attention is directed towards techniques which record an actor's motion in the real world and then apply it to computer-generated characters. Two main classes of such *motion capture* (MC) techniques exist: electromagnetic and optical.

In electromagnetic motion capture, an electromagnetic sensor directly measures its position (and possibly orientation) in 3D often providing the captured results in real time. Disadvantages of this technique include significant equipment cost, possible interference from nearby metal objects, and noticeable size of sensors and batteries which can be an obstacle in performing high-amplitude motions. In optical MC, small colored markers are used instead of active sensors making it a much less intrusive procedure. Figure 17.21 shows the operation of such a system. In the most basic arrangement, the motion is recorded by two calibrated video cameras, and simple triangulation is used to extract the marker's 3D position. More advanced computer vision algorithms used for accurate tracking of multiple markers from video are computationally expensive, so, in most cases, such processing is done offline. Optical tracking is generally less robust than electromagnetic. Occlusion of a given marker in some frames, possible misidentification of markers, and noise in images are just a few of the common problem which have to be addressed. Introducing more cameras observing the motion from different directions improves both accuracy and robustness, but this approach is more expensive and it takes longer to process such data. Optical MC becomes more attractive as available computational power increases and better computer vision algorithms are developed. Because of low impact nature of markers, optical methods are suitable for delicate facial motion capture and can also be used with objects other than humans—for example, animals or even tree branches in the wind.

With several sensors or markers attached to a performer's body, a set of time-dependant 3D positions of some collection of points can be recorded. These track-

Figure 17.21. Optical motion capture: markers attached to a performer's body allow skeletal motion to be extracted. *Image courtesy of Motion Analysis Corp.*

ing locations are commonly chosen near joints, but, of course, they still lie on skin surface and not at points where actual bones meet. Therefore, some additional care and a bit of extra processing is necessary to convert recorded positions into those of the physical skeleton joints. For example, putting two markers on opposite sides of the elbow or ankle allows the system to obtain better joint position by averaging locations of the two markers. Without such extra care, very noticeable artifacts can appear due to offset joint positions as well as inherent noise and insufficient measurement accuracy. Because of physical inaccuracy during motion, for example, character limbs can loose contact with objects they are supposed to touch during walking or grasping, problems like foot-sliding (skating) of the skeleton can occur. Most of these problems can be corrected by using inverse kinematics techniques which can explicitly force the required behavior of the limb's end.

Recovered joint positions can now be directly applied to the skeleton of a computer-generated character. This procedure assumes that the physical dimensions of the character are identical to those of the performer. Retargeting recorded motion to a different character and, more generally, editing MC data, requires significant care to satisfy necessary constraints (such as maintaining feet on the ground or not allowing an elbow to bend backwards) and preserve an overall natural appearance of the modified motion. Generally, the greater the desired change from the original, the less likely it will be possible to maintain the quality of the result. An interesting approach to the problem is to record a large collection of motions and stich together short clips from this library to obtain desired movement. Although this topic is currently a very active research area, limited ability to adjust the recorded motion to the animator's needs remains one of the main disadvantages of motion capture technique.

17.5 Physics-Based Animation

The world around us is governed by physical laws many of which can be formalized as sets of partial or, in some simpler cases, ordinary differential equations. One of the original applications of computers was (and remains) solving such equations. It is therefore only natural to attempt to use numerical techniques developed over the several past decades to obtain realistic motion for computer animation.

Because of its relative complexity and significant cost, physics-based animation is most commonly used in situations when other techniques are either unavailable or do not produce sufficiently realistic results. Prime examples include

Figure 17.22. Realistic cloth simulation is often performed with physics-based methods. In this example, forces are due to collisions and gravity.

animation of fluids (which includes many gaseous phase phenomena described by the same equations—smoke, clouds, fire, etc.), cloth simulation (an example is shown in Figure 17.22), rigid body motion, and accurate deformation of elastic objects. Governing equations and details of commonly used numerical approaches are different in each of these cases, but many fundamental ideas and difficulties remain applicable across applications. Many methods for numerically solving ODEs and PDEs exist but discussing them in details is far beyond the scope of this book. To give the reader a flavor of physics-based techniques and some of the issues involved, we will briefly mention here only the finite difference approach—one of the conceptually simplest and most popular families of algorithms which has been applied to most, if not all, differential equations encountered in animation.

The key idea of this approach is to replace a differential equation with its discrete analog—a difference equation. To do this, the continuous domain of interest is represented by a finite set of points at which the solution will be computed. In the simplest case, these are defined on a uniform rectangular grid as shown in Figure 17.23. Every derivative present in the original ODE or PDE is then replaced by its approximation through function values at grid points. One way of doing this is to subtract the function value at a given point from the function value for its neighboring point on the grid:

$$\frac{df(t)}{dt} \approx \frac{\Delta f}{\Delta t} = \frac{f(t + \Delta t) - f(t)}{\Delta t} \text{ or } \frac{\partial f(x,t)}{\partial x} \approx \frac{\Delta f}{\Delta x} = \frac{f(x + \Delta x, t) - f(x,t)}{\Delta x}.$$

$$(17.2)$$

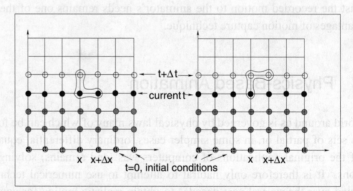

Figure 17.23. Two possible difference schemes for an equation involving derivatives $\partial f/\partial x$ and $\partial f/\partial t$. (Left) An explicit scheme expresses unknown values (open circles) only through known values at the current (black circles) and possibly past (gray circles) time; (Right) Implicit schemes mix known and unknown values in a single equation making it necessary to solve all such equations as a system. For both schemes, information about values on the right boundary is needed to close the process.

These expressions are, of course, not the only way. One can, for example, use $f(t - \Delta t)$ instead of $f(t)$ above and divide by $2\Delta t$. For an equation containing a time derivative, it is now possible to propagate values of an unknown function forward in time in a sequence of Δt-size steps by solving the system of difference equations (one at each spatial location) for unknown $f(t + \Delta t)$. Some initial conditions, i.e., values of the unknown function at $t = 0$, are necessary to start the process. Other information, such as values on the boundary of the domain, might also be required depending on the specific problem.

The computation of $f(t+\Delta t)$ can be done easily for so called *explicit* schemes when all other values present are taken at the current time and the only unknown in the corresponding difference equation $f(t + \Delta t)$ is expressed through these known values. *Implicit* schemes mix values at current and future times and might use, for example,

$$\frac{f(x + \Delta x, t + \Delta t) - f(x, t + \Delta t)}{\Delta x}$$

as an approximation of $\frac{\partial f}{\partial x}$. In this case one has to solve a system of algebraic equations at each step.

The choice of difference scheme can dramatically affect all aspects of the algorithm. The most obvious among them is *accuracy*. In the limit $\Delta t \to 0$ or $\Delta x \to 0$, expressions of the type in Equation (17.2) are exact, but for finite step size some schemes allow better approximation of the derivative than others. *Stability* of a difference scheme is related to how fast numerical errors, which are always present in practice, can grow with time. For stable schemes this growth is bounded, while for unstable ones it is exponential and can quickly overwhelm the solution one seeks (see Figure 17.24). It is important to realize that while some inaccuracy in the solution is tolerable (and, in fact, accuracy demanded in physics and engineering is rarely needed for animation), an unstable result is completely meaningless, and one should avoid using unstable schemes. Generally, explicit schemes are either unstable or can become unstable at larger step sizes while implicit ones are unconditionally stable. Implicit schemes allows greater step size (and, therefore, fewer steps) which is why they are popular despite the need to solve a system of algebraic equations at each step. Explicit schemes are attractive because of their simplicity if their stability conditions can be satisfied. Developing a good difference scheme and corresponding algorithm for a specific problem is not easy, and for most standard situations it is well advised to use an existing method. Ample literature discussing details of these techniques is available.

One should remember that, in many cases, just computing all necessary terms in the equation is a difficult and time-consuming task on its own. In rigid body or cloth simulation, for example, most of the forces acting on the system are due

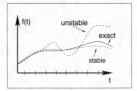

Figure 17.24. An unstable solution might follow the exact one initially, but can deviate arbitrarily far from it with time. Accuracy of a stable solution might still be insufficient for a specific application.

to collisions among objects. At each step during animation, one therefore has to solve a purely geometric, but very non-trivial, problem of collision detection. In such conditions, schemes which require fewer evaluations of such forces might provide significant computational savings.

Although the result of solving appropriate time-dependant equations gives very realistic motion, this approach has its limitations. First of all, it is very hard to control the result of physics-based animation. Fundamental mathematical properties of these equations state that once the initial conditions are set, the solution is uniquely defined. This does not leave much room for animator input and, if the result is not satisfactory for some reason, one has only a few options. They are mostly limited to adjusting initial condition used, changing physical properties of the system, or even modifying the equations themselves by introducing artificial terms intended to "drive" the solution in the direction the animator wants. Making such changes requires significant skill as well as understanding of the underlying physics and, ideally, numerical methods. Without this knowledge, the realism provided by physics-based animation can be destroyed or severe numerical problems might appear.

17.6   Procedural Techniques

Imagine that one could write (and implement on a computer) a mathematical function which outputs precisely the desired motion given some animator guidance. Physics-based techniques outlined above can be treated as a special case of such an approach when the "function" involved is the procedure to solve a particular differential equation and "guidance" is the set of initial and boundary conditions, extra equation terms, etc.

However, if we are only concerned with the final result, we do not have to follow a physics-based approach. For example, a simple constant amplitude wave on the surface of a lake can be directly created by applying the function $f(\mathbf{x}, t) = A\cos(\omega t - \mathbf{k}\mathbf{x} + \phi)$ with constant frequency ω, wave vector $\mathbf{k}$ and phase ϕ to get displacement at the 2D point $\mathbf{x}$ at time t. A collection of such waves with random phases and appropriately chosen amplitudes, frequencies, and wave vectors can result in a very realistic animation of the surface of water without explicitly solving any fluid dynamics equations. It turns out that other rather simple mathematical functions can also create very interesting patterns or objects. Several such functions, most based on lattice noises, have been described in Chapter 11. Adding time dependance to these functions allows us to animate certain complex phenomena much easier and cheaper than with physics-based techniques while maintaining very high visual quality of the results. If $noise(\mathbf{x})$ is the underlying pattern-generating function, one can create a time-dependant variant of it by moving the argument position through the lattice. The simplest case is motion with constant speed: $timenoise(\mathbf{x}, t) = noise(\mathbf{x} + \mathbf{v}t)$, but more complex motion through the lattice is, of course, also possible and, in fact, more common. One such path, a spiral, is shown in Figure 17.25. Another approach is to animate parameters used to generate the *noise* function. This is especially appropriate if the appearance changes significantly with time—a cloud becoming more turbulent, for example. In this way one can animate the dynamic process of formation of clouds using the function which generates static ones.

For some procedural techniques, time dependance is a more integral component. The simplest *cellular automata* operate on a 2D rectangular grid where a binary value is stored at each location (cell). To create a time varying pattern, some user-provided rules for modifying these values are repeatedly applied. Rules typically involve some set of conditions on the current value and that of the cell's neighbors. For example, the rules of the popular 2D *Game of Life* cellular automaton invented in 1970 by British mathematician John Conway are the following:

1. A dead cell (i.e., binary value at a given location is 0) with exactly three live neighbors becomes a live cell (i.e., its value set to 1).

2. A live cell with two or three live neighbors stays alive.

3. In all other cases, a cell dies or remains dead.

Once the rules are applied to all grid locations, a new pattern is created and a new evolution cycle can be started. Three sample snapshots of the live cell distribution at different times are shown in Figure 17.26. More sophisticated automata

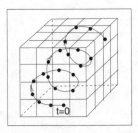

Figure 17.25. A path through the cube defining procedural noise is traversed to animate the resulting pattern.

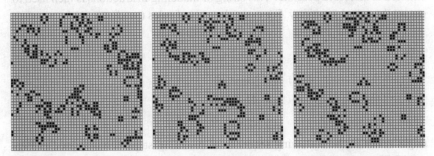

Figure 17.26. Several (non-consecutive) stages in the evolution of a *Game of Life* automaton. Live cells are shown in black. Stable objects, oscillators, travelling patterns, and many other interesting constructions can result from the application of very simple rules. *Figure created using a program by Alan Hensel.*

simultaneously operate on several 3D grids of possibly floating point values and can be used for modeling dynamics of clouds and other gaseous phenomena or biological systems for which this apparatus was originally invented (note the terminology). Surprising pattern complexity can arise from just a few well-chosen rules, but how to write such rules to create the desired behavior is often not obvious. This is a common problem with procedural techniques: there is only limited, if any, guidance on how to create new procedures or even adjust parameters of existing ones. Therefore, a lot of tweaking and learning by trial-and-error ("by experience") is usually needed to unlock the full potential of procedural methods.

Another interesting approach which was also originally developed to describe biological objects is the technique called *L-systems* (after the name of their original inventor, Astrid Lindenmayer). This approach is based on *grammars* or sets of recursive rules for rewriting strings of symbols. There are two types of symbols: *terminal symbols* stand for elements of something we want to represent with a grammar. Depending on their meaning, grammars can describe structure of trees and bushes, buildings and whole cities, or programming and natural languages. In animation, L-systems are most popular for representing plants and corresponding terminals are instructions to the geometric modeling system: put a leaf (or a branch) at a current position—we will use the symbol @ and just draw a circle, move current position forward by some number of units (symbol f), turn current direction 60 degrees around world Z-axis (symbol $+$), pop (symbol $[$) or push (symbol $]$) current position/orientation, etc. Auxiliary *nonterminal symbols* (denoted by capital letters) have only semantic rather than any direct meaning. They are intended to be eventually rewritten through terminals. We start from the special nonterminal start symbol S and keep applying grammar rules to the current string in parallel, i.e., replace all nonterminals currently present to get the new string, until we end up with a string containing only terminals and no more substitution is therefore possible. This string of modeling instructions is then used to output the actual geometry. For example, a set of rules (productions)

$$S \to A$$
$$A \to [+B]fA$$
$$A \to B$$
$$B \to fB$$
$$B \to f@$$

might result in the following sequence of rewriting steps demonstrated in Figure 17.27

$$S \longmapsto A \longmapsto [+B]fA \longmapsto [+fB]f[+B]fA \longmapsto$$
$$[+ff@]f[+fB]fB \longmapsto [+ff@]f[+ff@]ff@$$

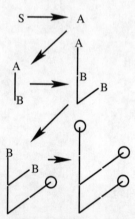

Figure 17.27. Consecutive derivation steps using a simple L-system. Capital letters denote non-terminals and illustrate positions at which corresponding non-terminal will be expanded. They are not part of the actual output.

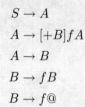

As shown above, there are typically many different productions for the same non-terminal allowing the generation of many different objects with the same grammar. The choice of which rule to apply can depend on which symbols are located next to the one being replaced (context-sensitivity) or can be performed at random with some assigned probability for each rule (stochastic L-systems). More complex rules can model interaction with the environment, such as pruning to a particular shape, and parameters can be associated with symbols to control geometric commands issued.

L-systems already capture plant topology changes with time: each intermediate string obtained in the rewriting process can be interpreted as a "younger" version of the plant (see Figure 17.27). For more significant changes, different productions can be in effect at different times allowing the structure of the plant to change significantly as it grows. A young tree, for example, produces a lot of new branches while an older one branches only moderately.

Very realistic plant models have been created with L-systems. However, as with most procedural techniques, one needs some experience to meaningfully apply existing L-systems, and writing new grammars to capture some desired effect is certainly not easy.

17.7 Groups of Objects

To animate multiple objects one can, of course, simply apply standard techniques outlined above to each of them. This works reasonably well for a moderate number of independent objects whose desired motion is known in advance. However, in many cases, some kind of coordinated action in a dynamic environment is necessary. If only a few objects are involved, the animator can use an artificial intelligence (AI)-based system to automatically determine immediate tasks for each object based on some high-level goal, plan necessary motion, and execute the plan. Many modern games use such *autonomous objects* to create smart monsters or player's collaborators.

Interestingly, as the number of objects in a group grows from just a few to several dozens, hundreds, and thousands, individual members of a group must have only very limited "intelligence" in order for the group as a whole to exhibit what looks like coordinated goal-driven motion. It turns out that this *flocking* is *emergent behavior* which can arise as a result of limited interaction of group members with just a few of their closest neighbors (Reynolds, 1987). Flocking should be familiar to anyone who has observed the fascinatingly synchronized motion of a flock of birds or a school of fish. The technique can also be used to control groups of animals moving over terrain or even a human crowd.

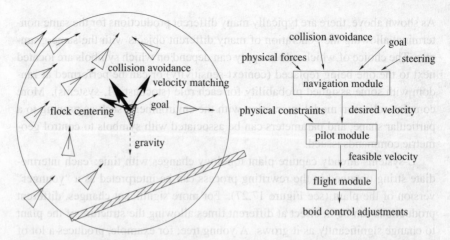

Figure 17.28. (Left) Individual flock member (boid) can experience several urges of different importance (shown by line thickness) which have to be negotiated into a single velocity vector. A boid is aware of only its limited neighborhood (circle). (Right) Boid control is commonly implemented as three separate modules.

At any given moment, the motion of a member of a group, often called boid when applied to flocks, is the result of balancing several often contradictory tendencies, each of which suggests its own velocity vector (see Figure 17.28). First, there are external physical forces F acting on the boid, such as gravity or wind. New velocity due to those forces can be computed directly through Newton's law as

$$\mathbf{v}_{new}^{physics} = \mathbf{v}_{old} + \mathbf{F}\Delta t/m.$$

Second, a boid should react to global environment and to the behavior of other group members. Collision avoidance is one of the main results of such interaction. It is crucial for flocking that each group member has only limited field of view, and therefore is aware only of things happening within some neighborhood of its current position. To avoid objects in the environment, the simplest, if imperfect, strategy is to set up a limited extent repulsive force field around each such object. This will create a second desired velocity vector $\mathbf{v}_{new}^{col\_avoid}$, also given by Newton's law. Interaction with other group members can be modeled by simultaneously applying different steering behaviors resulting in several additional desired velocity vectors $\mathbf{v}_{new}^{steer}$. Moving away from neighbors to avoid crowding, steering towards flock mates to ensure flock cohesion and adjusting a boid's speed to align with average heading of neighbors are most common. Finally, some additional desired velocity vectors $\mathbf{v}_{new}^{goal}$ are usually applied to achieve needed global goals. These can be vectors along some path in space, following some specific designated leader of the flock, or simply representing migratory urge of a flock member.

Once all $\mathbf{v}_{new}$ are determined, the final desired vector is negotiated based on priorities among them. Collision avoidance and velocity matching typically have higher priority. Instead of simple averaging of desired velocity vectors which can lead to cancellation of urges and unnatural "moving nowhere" behavior, an acceleration allocation strategy is used. Some fixed total amount of acceleration is made available for a boid and fractions of it are being given to each urge in order of priority. If the total available acceleration runs out, some lower priority urges will have less effect on the motion or be completely ignored. The hope is that once the currently most important task (collision avoidance in most situations) is accomplished, other tasks can be taken care of in near future. It is also important to respect some physical limitations of real objects, for example, clamping too high accelerations or speeds to some realistic values. Depending on the internal complexity of the flock member, the final stage of animation might be to turn the negotiated velocity vector into a specific set of parameters (bird's wing positions, orientation of plane model in space, leg skeleton bone configuration) used to control a boid's motion. A diagram of a system implementing flocking is shown on Figure 17.28 (right).

A much simpler, but still very useful, version of group control is implemented by *particle systems* (Reeves, 1983). The number of particles in a system is typically much larger than number of boids in a flock and can be in the tens or hundreds of thousands, or even more. Moreover, the exact number of particles can fluctuate during animation with new particles being born and some of the old ones destroyed at each step. Particles are typically completely independent from each other, ignoring one's neighbors and interacting with the environment only by experiencing external forces and collisions with objects, *not* through collision avoidance as was the case for flocks. At each step during animation, the system first creates new particles with some initial parameters, terminates old ones, and then computes necessary forces and updates velocities and positions of the remaining particles according to Newton's law.

All parameters of a particle system (number of particles, particle life span, initial velocity, and location of a particle, etc.) are usually under the direct control of the animator. Prime applications of particle systems include modeling fireworks, explosions, spraying liquids, smoke and fire, or other fuzzy objects and phenomena with no sharp boundaries. To achieve a realistic appearance, it is important to introduce some randomness to all parameters, for example, having a random number of particles born (and destroyed) at each step with their velocities generated according to some distribution. In addition to setting appropriate initial

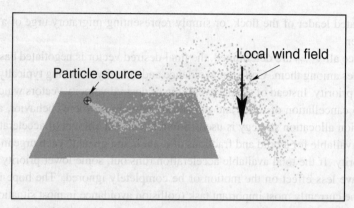

Figure 17.29. After being emitted by a directional source, particles collide with an object and then are blown down by a local wind field once they clear the obstacle.

parameters, controlling the motion of a particle system is commonly done by creating a specific force pattern in space — blowing a particle in a new direction once it reaches some specific location or adding a center of attraction, for example. One should remember that with all their advantages, simplicity of implementation and ease of control being the prime ones, particle systems typically do not provide the level of realism characteristic of true physics-based simulation of the same phenomena.

Notes

In this chapter we have concentrated on techniques used in 3D animation. There also exist a rich set of algorithms to help with 2D animation production and post-processing of images created by computer graphics rendering systems. These include techniques for cleaning up scanned-in artist drawings, feature extraction, automatic 2D in-betweening, colorization, image warping, enhancement and compositing, and many others.

One of the most significant developments in the area of computer animation has been the increasing power and availability of sophisticated animation systems. While different in their specific set of features, internal structure, details of user interface, and price, most such systems include extensive support not only for animation, but also for modeling and rendering turning them into complete production platforms. It is also common to use these systems to create still images. For example, many images for figures in this section were produced using Maya software generously donated by Alias.

Large-scale animation production is an extremely complex process which typically involves a combined effort by dozens of people with different backgrounds spread across many departments or even companies. To better coordinate this activity, a certain production pipeline is established which starts with a story and character sketches, proceeds to record necessary sound, build models, and rig characters for animation. Once actual animation commences, it is common to go back and revise the original designs, models, and rigs to fix any discovered motion and appearance problems. Setting up lighting and material properties is then necessary, after which it is possible to start rendering. In most sufficiently complex projects, extensive postprocessing and compositing stages bring together images from different sources and finalize the product.

We conclude this chapter by reminding the reader that in the field of computer animation any technical sophistication is secondary to a good story, expressive characters, and other artistic factors, most of which are hard or simply impossible to quantify. It is safe to say that Snow White and her seven dwarfs will always share the screen with green ogres and donkeys, and most of the audience will be much more interested in the characters and the story rather than in which, if any, computers (and in what exact way) helped to create either of them.

Peter Willemsen

18

Using Graphics Hardware

Throughout most of this book, the focus has been on the fundamentals underlying computer graphics rather than on implementation details. This chapter takes a slightly different route and blends the details of using graphics hardware with the practical issues associated with programming that hardware.

This chapter, however, is not written to teach you OpenGL,[TM] other graphics APIs, or even the nitty gritty specifics of graphics hardware programming. The purpose of this chapter is to introduce the basic concepts and thought processes that are necessary when writing programs that use graphics hardware.

18.1 What Is Graphics Hardware

Graphics hardware describes the hardware components necessary to quickly render 3D objects as pixels on your computer's screen using specialized rasterization-based hardware architectures. The use of this term is meant to elicit a sense of the physical components necessary for performing these computations. In other words, we're talking about the chipsets, transistors, buses, and processors found on many current video cards. As we will see in this chapter, current graphics hardware is very good at processing descriptions of 3D objects and transforming them into the colored pixels that fill your monitor.

One thing has been certain with graphics hardware: it changes very *quickly* with new extensions and features being added continually! One explanation for the fast pace is the video game industry and its economic momentum. Essentially

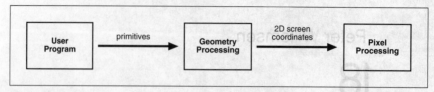

Figure 18.1.   The basic graphics hardware pipeline consists of stages that transform 3D data into 2D screen objects ready for rasterizing and coloring by the pixel processing stages.

Real-Time Graphics: By real-time graphics, we generally mean that the graphics-related computations are being carried out fast enough that the results can be viewed immediately. Being able to conduct operations at 60Hz is considered real time. Once the time to refresh the display (*frame rate*) drops below 15Hz, the speed is considered more interactive than it is real-time, but this distinction is not critical. Because the computations need to be fast, the equations used to render the graphics are often approximations to what could be done if more time were available.

what this means is that each new graphics card provides better performance and processing capabilities. As a result, graphics hardware is being used for tasks that support a much richer use of 3D graphics. For instance, researchers are performing computation on graphics hardware to perform ray-tracing (Purcell et al., 2002) and even solve the Navier-Stokes equations to simulate fluid flow (Harris, 2004).

Most graphics hardware has been built to perform a set of fixed operations organized as a pipeline designed to push vertices and pixels through different stages. The fixed functionality of the pipeline ensures that basic coloring, lighting, and texturing can occur very quickly—often referred to as *real-time graphics*.

Figure 18.1 illustrates the real-time graphics pipeline. The important things to note about the pipeline follow:

- The user program, or application, supplies the data to the graphics hardware in the form of *primitives*, such as points, lines, or polygons describing the 3D geometry. Images or bitmaps are also supplied for use in texturing surfaces.

- Geometric primitives are processed on a per-vertex basis and are transformed from 3D coordinates to 2D screen triangles.

- Screen objects are passed to the pixel processors, rasterized, and then colored on a per-pixel basis before being output to the frame buffer, and eventually to the monitor.

18.2   Describing Geometry for the Hardware

As a graphics programmer, you need to be concerned with how the data associated with your 3D objects is transferred onto the memory cache of the graphics hardware. Unfortunately (or maybe fortunately), as a programmer you don't have complete control over this process. There are a variety of ways to place your data on the graphics hardware, and each has its own advantages which will be discussed in this section. Any of the APIs you might use to program your video card will provide different methods to load data onto the graphics hardware memory. The examples that follow are presented in pseudocode that is based loosely on the C function syntax of OpenGL,™ but semantically the examples should be applicable to other graphics APIs.

Most graphics hardware work with specific sets of geometric primitives. The primitive types leverage primitive complexity for processing speed on the graphics hardware. Simpler primitives can be processed very fast. The caveat is that the primitive types need to be general purpose so as to model a wide range of geometry from very simple to very complex. On typical graphics hardware, the primitive types are limited to one or more of the following:

- **points**—single vertices used to represent points or particle systems;

- **lines**—pairs of vertices used to represent lines, silhouettes, or edge-highlighting;

- **polygons**—triangles, triangle strips, indexed triangles, indexed triangle strips, quadrilaterals, general convex polygons, etc., used for describing triangle meshes, geometric surfaces, and other solid objects, such as spheres, cones, cubes, or cylinders.

These three primitives form the basic building blocks for most geometry you will define. (An example of a triangle mesh is shown in Figure 18.2.) Using these primitives, you can build descriptions of your geometry using one of the graphics APIs and send the geometry to the graphics hardware for rendering. For instance,

Primitives: The three primitives (points, lines, and polygons) are the only primitives available! Even when creating spline-based surfaces, such as NURBs, the surfaces are tessellated into triangle primitives by the graphics hardware.

Point Rendering: Point and line primitives may initially appear to be limited in use, but researchers have used points to render very complex geometry (Rusinkiewicz & Levoy, 2000; Dachsbacher et al., 2003).

Figure 18.2. How your geometry is organized will affect the performance of your application. This wireframe depiction of the Little Cottonwood Canyon terrain dataset shows tens of thousands of triangles organized in a triangle mesh running at real-time rates. *The image is rendered using the VTerrain Project terrain system courtesy of Ben Discoe.*

to transfer the description of a line to the graphics hardware, we might use the following:

```
beginLine();
    vertex( x1, y1, z1 );
    vertex( x2, y2, z2 );
endLine();
```

In this example, two things occur. First, one of the primitive types is declared and made active by the `beginLine()` function call. The line primitive is then made inactive by the `endLine()` function call. Second, all vertices declared between these two functions are copied directly to the graphics card for processing with the `vertex` function calls.

A second example creates a set of triangles grouped together in a strip (refer to Figure 18.3); we could use the following code:

```
beginTriangleStrip();
    vertex( x0, y0, z0 );
    vertex( x1, y1, z1 );
    vertex( x2, y2, z2 );
    vertex( x3, y3, z3 );
    vertex( x4, y4, z4 );
endTriangleStrip();
```

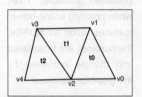

Figure 18.3. A triangle strip composed of five vertices defining three triangles.

In this example, the primitive type, `TriangleStrip`, is made active and the set of vertices that define the triangle strip are copied to the graphics card memory for processing. Note that ordering does matter when describing geometry. In the triangle strip example, connectivity between adjacent triangles is embedded within the ordering of the vertices. Triangle $t0$ is constructed from vertices $(v0, v1, v2)$, triangle $t1$ from vertices $(v1, v3, v2)$, and triangle $t2$ from vertices $(v2, v3, v4)$.

The key point to learn from these simple examples is that geometry is defined for rendering on the graphics hardware using a primitive type along with a set of vertices. The previous examples are simple and push the vertices directly onto the graphics hardware. However, in practice, you will need to make conscious decisions about how you will push your data to the graphics hardware. These issues will be discussed shortly.

As geometry is passed to the graphics hardware, additional data can be specified for each vertex. This extra data is useful for defining *state* attributes, that might represent the color of the vertex, the normal direction at the vertex, texture coordinates at the vertex, or other per-vertex data. For instance, to set the color and normal state parameters at each vertex of a triangle strip, we might use the following code:

```
beginTriangleStrip();
  color( r0, g0, b0 ); normal( n0x, n0y, n0z );
  vertex( x0, y0, z0 );
  color( r1, g1, b1 ); normal( n1x, n1y, n1z );
  vertex( x1, y1, z1 );
  color( r2, g2, b2 ); normal( n2x, n2y, n2z );
  vertex( x2, y2, z2 );
  color( r3, g3, b3 ); normal( n3x, n3y, n3z );
  vertex( x3, y3, z3 );
  color( r4, g4, b4 ); normal( n4x, n4y, n4z );
  vertex( x4, y4, z4 );
endTriangleStrip();
```

Here, the color and normal direction at each vertex are specified just prior to the vertex being defined. Each vertex in this example has a unique color and normal direction. The color function sets the active color state using a RGB 3-tuple. The normal direction state at each vertex is set by the normal function. Both the color and normal function affect the current rendering state on the graphics hardware. Any vertices defined after these state attributes are set will be bound with those state attributes.

This is a good moment to mention that the graphics hardware maintains a fairly elaborate set of state parameters that determine how vertices and other components are rendered. Some state is bound to vertices, such as color, normal direction, and texture coordinates, while another state may affect pixel level rendering. The *graphics state* at any particular moment describes a large set of internal hardware parameters. This aspect of graphics hardware is important to consider when you write 3D applications. As you might suspect, making frequent changes to the graphics state affects performance at least to some extent. However, attempting to minimize graphics state changes is only one of many areas where thoughtful programming should be applied. You should attempt to minimize state changes when you can, but it is unlikely that you can group all of your geometry to completely reduce state context switches. One data structure that can help minimize state changes, especially on static scenes, is the scene graph data structure. Prior to rendering any geometry, the scene graph can re-organize the geometry and associated graphics state in an attempt to minimize state changes. Scene graphs are described in Chapter 12.

```
color( r, g, b );
normal( nx, ny, nz );
beginTriangleStrip();
  vertex( x0, y0, z0 );
  vertex( x1, y1, z1 );
  vertex( x2, y2, z2 );
```

```
        vertex( x3, y3, z3 );
        vertex( x4, y4, z4 );
    endTriangleStrip();
```

All vertices in this `TriangleStrip` have the same color and normal direction, so these state parameters can be set prior to defining the vertices. This minimizes both function call overhead and changes to the internal graphics state.

Many things can affect the performance of a graphics program, but one of the potentially large contributors to performance (or lack thereof) is how your geometry is organized and whether it is stored in the memory cache of the graphics card. In the pseudocode examples provided so far, geometry has been pushed onto the graphics hardware in what is often called *immediate mode* rendering. As vertices are defined, they are sent directly to the graphics hardware. The primary disadvantage of immediate mode rendering is that the geometry is sent to the graphics hardware each iteration of your application. If your geometry is static (i.e., it doesn't change), then there is no real need to resend the data each time you redraw a frame. In these and other circumstances, it is more desirable to store the geometry in the graphics card's memory.

The graphics hardware in your computer is connected to the rest of the system via a data bus, such as the PCI, AGP, or PCI-Express buses. When you send data to the graphics hardware, it is sent by the CPU on your machine across one of these buses, eventually being stored in the memory on your graphics hardware. If you have very large triangle meshes representing complex geometry, passing all this data across the bus can end up resulting in a large hit to performance. This is especially true if the geometry is being rendered in immediate mode, as the previous examples have illustrated.

There are various ways to organize geometry; some can help reduce the overall bandwidth needed for transmitting the geometry across the graphics bus. Some possible organization approaches include:

- **triangles**. Triangles are specified with three vertices. A triangle mesh created in this manner requires that each triangle in the mesh be defined separately with many vertices potentially duplicated. For a triangle mesh containing m triangles, $3m$ vertices will be sent to the graphics hardware.

- **triangle strips**. Triangles are organized in strips; the first three vertices specify the first triangle in the strip and each additional vertex adds a triangle. If you create a triangle mesh with m triangles organized as a single triangle strip, you send three vertices to the graphics hardware for the first triangle followed by a single vertex for each additional triangle in the strip for a total of $m + 2$ vertices.

- **indexed triangles**. Triangle vertices are arranged as an array of vertices with a separate array defining the triangles using indices into the vertex array. Vertex arrays are sent to the graphics card with very few function calls.

- **indexed triangle strips**. Similar to indexed triangles, triangle vertices are stored in a vertex array. However, triangles are organized in strips with the index array defining the strip layout. This is the most compact of the organizational structures for defining triangle meshes as it combines the benefits of triangles strips with the compactness of vertex arrays.

Of the different organizational structures, the use of vertex arrays, either through indexed triangles or indexed triangle strips, provides a good option for increasing the performance of your application. The tight encapsulation of the organization means that many fewer function calls need to be made as well. Once the vertices and indices are stored in an array, only a few function calls need to be made to transfer the data to the graphics hardware, whereas with the pseudocode examples illustrated previously, a function is called for each vertex.

At this point, you may be wondering how the graphics state such as colors, normals, or texture coordinates are defined when vertex arrays are used. In the immediate-mode rendering examples earlier in the chapter, interleaving the graphics state with the associated vertices is obvious based on the order of the function calls. When vertex arrays are used, graphics state can either be interleaved in the vertex array or specified in separate arrays that are passed to the graphics hardware.

Even if the geometry is organized efficiently when it is sent to the graphics hardware, you can achieve higher performance gains if you can store your geometry in the graphics hardware's memory for the duration of your application. A somewhat unfortunate fact about current graphics hardware is that many of the specifications describing the layout of the graphics hardware memory and cache structure are often not widely publicized. Fortunately though, there are ways using graphics APIs that allow programmers to place geometry into the graphics hardware memory resulting in applications that run faster.

Two commonly used methods to store geometry and graphics state in the graphics hardware cache involve creating *display lists* or *vertex buffer objects*.

Display lists compile a compact list representation of the geometry and the state associated with the geometry and store the list in the memory on the graphics hardware. The benefits of display lists are that they are general purpose and good at storing a static geometric representation plus associated graphics state on the hardware. They do not work well at all for continuously changing geometry and graphics state, since the display list must be recompiled and then stored *again* in the graphics hardware memory for every iteration in which the display list changes.

```
displayID = createDisplayList();
color( r, g, b );
normal( nx, ny, nz );
beginTriangleStrip();
    vertex( x0, y0, z0 );
    vertex( x1, y1, z1 );
    ...
    vertex( xN, yN, zN );
endTriangleStrip();
endDisplayList();
```

In the above example, a display list is created that contains the definition of a triangle strip with its associated color and normal information. The commands between the `createDisplayList` and `endDisplayList` function calls provide the elements that define the display list. Display lists are most often created during an initialization phase of an application. After the display list is created, it is stored in the memory of the graphics hardware and can be referenced for later use by the identifier assigned to the list.

```
// draw the display list created earlier
drawDisplayList(displayID);
```

When it is time to draw the contents of the display list, a single function call will instruct the graphics hardware to access the memory indexed through the display list identifier and display the contents.

Optimal Organization:
Much research effort has gone into looking at ways to optimize triangle meshes for maximum performance on graphics hardware. A good place to start reading if you want to delve further into understanding how triangle mesh organization affects performance is the SIGGRAPH 1999 paper on the optimization of mesh locality (Hoppe, 1999).

A second method to store geometry on the graphics hardware for the duration of your application is through vertex buffer objects (VBOs). VBOs are specialized buffers that reside in high-performance memory on the graphics hardware and store vertex arrays and associated graphics state. They can also provide a mapping from your application to the memory on the graphics hardware to allow for fast access and updating to the contents of the VBO.

The chief advantage of VBOs is that they provide a mapping into the graphics hardware memory. With VBOs, geometry can be modified during an application with a minimal loss of performance as compared with using immediate mode rendering or display lists. This is extremely useful if portions of your geometry change during each iteration of your application or if the indices used to organize your geometry change.

VBOs are created in much the same way indexed triangles and indexed triangle strips are built. A buffer object is first created on the graphics card to make room for the vertex array containing the vertices of the triangle mesh. Next, the vertex array and index array are copied over to the graphics hardware. When it is time to render the geometry, the vertex buffer object identifier can be used to instruct the graphics hardware to draw your geometry. If you are already using vertex arrays in your application, modifying your code to use VBOs should likely require a minimal change.

18.3   Processing Geometry into Pixels

After the geometry has been placed in the graphics hardware memory, each vertex must be lit as well as transformed into screen coordinates during the geometry processing stage. In the fixed-function graphics pipeline illustrated in Figure 18.1, vertices are transformed from a model coordinate system to a screen coordinate frame of reference. This process and the matrices involved are described in Chapters 7 and 8. The modelview and projection matrices needed for this transformation are defined using functions provided with the graphics API you decide to use.

Lighting is calculated on a per-vertex basis. Depending on the global shading parameters, the triangle face will either have a flat-shaded look or the face color will be diffusely shaded (Gouraud shading) by linearly interpolating the color at each triangle vertex across the face of the triangle. The latter method produces a much smoother appearance. The color at each vertex is computed based on the assigned material properties, the lights in the scene, and various lighting parameters.

The lighting model in the fixed-function graphics pipeline is good for fast lighting of vertices; we make a tradeoff for increased speed over accurate illumination. As a result, Phong shaded surfaces are not supported with this fixed-function framework.

In particular, the diffuse shading algorithm built into the graphics hardware often fails to compute the appropriate illumination since the lighting is only being calculated at each vertex. For example, when the distance to the light source is small, as compared with the size of the face being shaded, the illumination on the face will be incorrect. Figure 18.4 illustrates this situation. The center of the triangle will not be illuminated brightly despite being very close to the light source, since the lighting on the vertices, which are far from the light source, are used to interpolate the shading across the face.

With the fixed-function pipeline, this issue can only be remedied by increasing the tessellation of the geometry. This solution works but is of limited use in real-

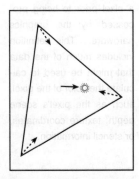

Figure 18.4. The distance to the light source is small relative to the size of the triangle.

time graphics as the added geometry required for more accurate illumination can result in slower rendering.

However, with current hardware, the problem of obtaining better approximations for illumination can be solved without necessarily increasing the geometric complexity of the objects. The solution involves replacing the fixed-function routines embedded within the graphics hardware with your own programs. These small programs run on the graphics hardware and perform a part of the geometry processing and pixel-processing stages of the graphics pipeline.

18.3.1   Programming the Pipeline

Fairly recent changes to the organization of consumer graphics hardware has generated a substantial buzz from game developers, graphics researchers, and many others. It is quite likely that you have heard about *GPU programming*, *graphics hardware programming*, or even *shader programming*. These terms and the changes in consumer hardware that have spawned them primarily have to do with how the graphics hardware rendering pipeline can now be programmed.

Definition: *Fragment* is a term that describes the information associated with a pixel prior to being processed by the graphics hardware. This definition includes much of the data that might be used to calculate the color of the pixel, such as the pixel's scene depth, texture coordinates, or stencil information.

Specifically, the changes have opened up two specific aspects of the graphics hardware pipeline. Programmers now have the ability to modify how the hardware processes vertices and shades pixels by writing *vertex shaders* and *fragment shaders* (also sometimes referred to as *vertex programs* or *fragment programs*). Vertex shaders are programs that perform the vertex and normal transformations, texture coordinate generation, and per-vertex lighting computations normally computed in the geometry processing stage. Fragment shaders are programs that perform the computations in the pixel processing stage of the graphics pipeline and determine exactly how each pixel is shaded, how textures are applied, and if a pixel should be drawn or not. These small shader programs are sent to the graphics hardware from the user program (see Figure 18.5), but they are executed on the graphics hardware.   What this programmability means for

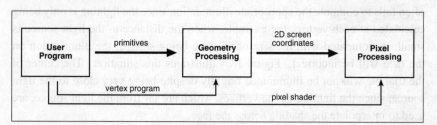

Figure 18.5. The programmable graphics hardware pipeline. The user program supplies primitives, vertex programs, and fragment programs to the hardware.

you is that you essentially have a multi-processor machine. This turns out to be a good way to think about your graphics hardware, since it means that you may be able to use the graphics hardware processor to relieve the load on the CPU in some of your applications. The graphics hardware processors are often referred to as *GPUs*. GPU stands for graphics processing unit and highlights the fact that graphics hardware components now contain a separate processor dedicated to graphics-related computations.

Interestingly, modern GPUs contain more transistors than modern CPUs. For the time being, GPUs are utilizing most of these transistors for computations and less for memory or cache management operations.

However, this will not always be the case as graphics hardware continues to advance. And just because the computations are geared towards 3D graphics, it does not mean that you cannot perform computations unrelated to computer graphics on the GPU. The manner in which the GPU is programmed is different from your general purpose CPU and will require a slightly modified way of thinking about how to solve problems and program the graphics hardware.

The GPU is a stream processor that excels at 3D vector operations such as vector multiplication, vector addition, dot products, and other operations necessary for basic lighting of surfaces and texture mapping. As stream processors, both the vertex and fragment processing components include the ability to process multiple primitives at the same time. In this regard, the GPU acts as a SIMD (Single Instruction, Multiple Data) processor, and in certain hardware implementations of the fragment processor, up to 16 pixels can be processed at a time. When you write programs for these processing components, it will be helpful, at least conceptually, to think of the computations being performed concurrently on your data. In other words, the vertex shader program will run for all vertices at the same time. The vertex computations will then be followed by a stage in which your fragment shader program will execute simultaneously on all fragments. It is important to note that while the computations on vertices or fragments occur concurrently, the staging of the pipeline components still occur in the same order.

The manner in which vertex and fragment shaders work is simple. You write a vertex shader program and a fragment shader program and send it to the graphics hardware. These programs can be used on specific geometry, and when your geometry is processed, the vertex shader is used to transform and light the vertices, while the fragment shader performs the final shading of the geometry on a per-pixel basis. Just as you can texture map different images onto different pieces of geometry, you can also write different shader programs to act upon different objects in your application. Shader programs are a part of the graphics state so you do need to be concerned with how your shader programs might get swapped in and out based on the geometry being rendered.

Historical: Programming the pipeline is not entirely new. One of the first introductions of a graphics hardware architecture designed for programming flexibility were the PixelFlow architectures and shading languages from UNC (Molnar et al., 1992; Lastra et al., 1995; Olano & Lastra, 1998). Additional efforts to provide custom shading techniques have included shade trees (Cook, 1984), RenderMan (Pixar, 2000), accelerated multi-pass rendering using OpenGL^{TM} (Peercy et al., 2000), and other real-time shading languages (Proudfoot et al., 2001; McCool et al., 2004).

The details tend to be a bit more complicated, however. Vertex shaders usually perform two basic actions: set the color at the vertex and transform the vertex into screen coordinates by multiplying the vertex by the modelview and projection matrices. The perspective divide and clipping steps are not performed in a vertex program. Vertex shaders are also often used to set the stage for a fragment shader. In particular, you may have vertex attributes, such as texture coordinates or other application-dependent data, that the vertex shader calculates or modifies and then sends to the fragment processing stage for use in your fragment shader. It may seem strange at first, but vertex shaders can be used to manipulate the positions of the vertices. This is often useful for generating simulated ocean wave motion entirely on the GPU.

In a fragment shader, it is required that the program outputs the fragment color. This may involve looking up texture values and combining them in some manner with values obtained by performing a lighting calculation at each pixel; or, it may involve killing the fragment from being drawn entirely. Because operations in the fragment shader operate at the fragment level, the real power of the programmable graphics hardware is in the fragment shader. This added processing power represents one of the key differences between the fixed function pipeline and the programmable pipeline. In the fixed pipeline, fragment processing used illumination values interpolated between the vertices of the triangle to compute the fragment color. With the programmable pipeline, the color at each fragment can be computed independently. For instance, in the example situation posed in Figure 18.4, Gouraud shading of a triangle face fails to produce a reasonable solution because lighting only occurs at the vertices which are farther away from the light than the center of the triangle. In a fragment shader, the lighting equation can be evaluated at each fragment, rather than at each vertex, resulting in a more accurate rendering of the face.

18.3.2   Basic Execution Model

When writing vertex or fragment shaders, there are a few important things to understand in terms of how vertex and fragment programs execute and access data on the GPU. Because these programs run entirely on the GPU, the first details you will need to figure out are which data your shaders will use and how to get that data to them. There are several characteristics associated with the data types used in shader programs. The following terms, which come primarily from the OpenGL^{TM} Shading Language framework, are used to describe the conceptual aspects of these data characteristics. The concepts are the same across different shading language frameworks. In the shaders you write, variables are characterized using one of the following terms:

- **attributes**. Attribute variables represent data that changes frequently, often on a per-vertex basis. Attribute variables are often tied to the changing graphics state associated with each vertex. For instance, normal vectors or texture coordinates are considered to be attribute data since they are part of the graphics state associated with each vertex.

- **uniforms**. Uniform variables represent data that cannot change during the execution of a shader program. However, uniform variables can be modified by your application between executions of a shader. This provides another way for your application to communicate data to a shader. Uniform data often represent the graphics state associated with an application. For instance, the modelview and projection matrices can be accessed through uniform variables. Information about light sources in your application can also be obtained through uniform variables. In these examples, the data does not change while the shader is executing, but could (e.g., the light could move) prior to the next iteration of the application.

- **varying**. Varying data is used to pass data between a vertex shader and a fragment shader. The reason the data is considered *varying* is because it is written by vertex shaders on a per-vertex basis, but read by fragment shaders as value interpolated across the face of the primitive between neighboring vertices.

Variables defined using one of these three characteristics can either be built-in variables or user-defined variables. In addition to accessing the built-in graphics state, attribute and uniform variables are one of the ways to communicate user-defined data to your vertex and fragment programs. Varying data is the only means to pass data from a vertex shader to a fragment shader. Figure 18.6 illustrates the basic execution of the vertex and fragment processors in terms of the inputs and outputs used by the shaders.

Another way to pass data to vertex and fragment shaders is by using texture maps as sources and sinks of data. This may come as a surprise if you have been thinking of texture maps solely as images that are applied to the outside surface of geometry. The reason texture maps are important is because they give you access to the memory on the graphics hardware. When you write applications that run on the CPU, you control the memory your application requires and have direct access to it when necessary. On graphics hardware, memory is not accessed in the same manner. In fact, you are not directly able to allocate and deallocate general purpose memory chunks, and this particular aspect usually requires a slight change in thinking.

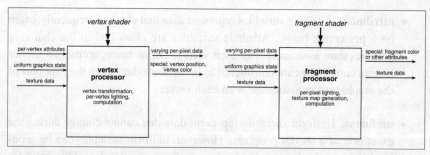

Figure 18.6. The execution model for shader programs. Input, such as per-vertex attributes, graphics state-related uniform variables, varying data, and texture maps are provided to vertex and fragment programs within the shader processor. Shaders output special variables used in later parts of the graphics pipeline.

Note: The shader language examples used in this chapter are presented using GLSL (OpenGL™ Shading Language). This language was chosen since it is being developed by the OpenGL™ Architecture Review Board and will likely become a standard shading language for OpenGL™ with the release of OpenGL™ 2.0. As of this writing, GLSL can be used on most modern graphics cards with updated graphics hardware drivers.

Texture maps on graphics hardware, however, can be created, deleted, and controlled through the graphics API you use. In other words, for general data used by your shader, you will create texture maps that contain that data and then use texture access functions to look up the data in the texture map. Technically, textures can be accessed by both vertex and fragment shaders. However, in practice, texture lookups from the vertex shader are not currently supported on all graphics cards. An example that utilizes a texture map as a data source is bump mapping. Bump mapping uses a normal map which defines how the normal vectors change across a triangle face. A bump mapping fragment shader would look up the normal vector in the normal map "texture data" and use it in the shading calculations at that particular fragment.

You need to be concerned about the types of data you put into your texture maps. Not all numerical data types are well supported and only recently has graphics hardware included floating point textures with 16-bit components. Moreover, *none* of the computation being performed on your GPU is done with double-precision math! If numerical precision is important for your application, you will need to think through these issues very carefully to determine if using the graphics hardware for computation is useful.

So what do these shader programs look like? One way to write vertex and fragment shaders is through assembly language instructions. For instance, performing a matrix multiplication in shader assembly language looks something like this:

```
DP4 p[0].x, M[0], v[0];
DP4 p[0].y, M[1], v[0];
DP4 p[0].z, M[2], v[0];
DP4 p[0].w, M[3], v[0];
```

In this example, the DP4 instruction is a 4-component dot product function. It stores the result of the dot product in the first register and performs the dot product between the last two registers. In shader programming, registers hold 4-components corresponding to the x, y, z, and w components of a homogeneous coordinate, or the r, g, b, and a components of a RGBA tuple. So, in this example, a simple matrix multiplication,

$$\mathbf{p} = \mathbf{M}\mathbf{v}$$

is computed by four DP4 instructions. Each instruction computes one element of the final result.

Fortunately though, you are not forced to program in assembly language. The good news is that higher-level languages are available to write vertex and fragment shaders. NVIDIA's Cg, the OpenGL™ Shading Language (GLSL), and Microsoft's High Level Shading Language (HLSL) all provide similar interfaces to the programmable aspects of graphics hardware. Using the notation of GLSL, the same matrix multiplication performed above looks like this:

```
p = M * v;
```

where **p** and **v** are vertex data types and **M** is a matrix data type. As evidenced here, one advantage of using a higher-level language over assembly language is that various data types are available to the programmer. In all of these languages, there are built-in data types for storing vectors and matrices, as well as arrays and constructs for creating structures. Many different functions are also built in to these languages to help compute trigonometric values (sin, cos, etc...), minimum and maximum values, exponential functions (log2, sqrt, pow, etc...), and other math or geometric-based functions.

18.3.3 Vertex Shader Example

Vertex shaders give you control over how your vertices are lit and transformed. They are also used to set the stage for fragment shaders. An interesting aspect to vertex shaders is that you still are able to use geometry-caching mechanisms, such as display lists or VBOs, and thus, benefit from their performance gains while using vertex shaders to do computation on the GPU. For instance, if the vertices represent particles and you can model the movement of the particles using a vertex shader, you have nearly eliminated the CPU from these computations. Any bottleneck in performance that may have occurred due to data being passed between the CPU and the GPU will be minimized. Prior to the introduction of vertex shaders, the computation of the particle movement would have been performed on the CPU and each vertex would have been re-sent to the graphics hardware on each iteration of your application. The ability to perform computations on the vertices already stored in the graphics hardware memory is a big performance win.

One of the simplest vertex shaders transforms a vertex into clip coordinates and assigns the front-facing color to the color attribute associated with the vertex.

```
void main(void)
{
    gl_Position = gl_ModelViewProjectionMatrix *
                    gl_Vertex;
    gl_FrontColor = gl_Color;
}
```

In this example, gl_ModelViewProjectionMatrix is a built-in uniform variable supplied by the GLSL run-time environment. The variables gl_Vertex and gl_Color are built-in vertex attributes; the special output variables, gl_Position and gl_FrontColor are used by the vertex shader to set the transformed position and the vertex color.

A more interesting vertex shader that implements the surface-shading equations developed in Chapter 10 illustrates the effect of per-vertex shading using the Phong shading algorithm.

```
void main(void)
{
    vec4 v = gl_ModelViewMatrix * gl_Vertex;
    vec3 n = normalize(gl_NormalMatrix * gl_Normal);
    vec3 l = normalize(gl_LightSource[0].position - v);
    vec3 h = normalize(l - normalize(v));

    float p = 16;
    vec4 cr = gl_FrontMaterial.diffuse;
    vec4 cl = gl_LightSource[0].diffuse;
    vec4 ca = vec4(0.2, 0.2, 0.2, 1.0);

    vec4 color;
    if (dot(h,n) > 0)
        color = cr * (ca + cl * max(0,dot(n,l))) +
                        cl * pow(dot(h,n), p);
    else
        color = cr * (ca + cl * max(0,dot(n,l)));

    gl_FrontColor = color;
    gl_Position = ftransform();
}
```

From the code presented in this shader, you should be able to gain a sense of shader programming and how it resembles C-style programming. Several things are happening with this shader. First, we create a set of variables to hold the vectors necessary for computing Phong shading: $\mathbf{v}, \mathbf{n}, \mathbf{l}$, and $\mathbf{h}$. Note that the computation in the vertex shader is performed in *eye-space*. This is done for a variety of reasons, but one reason is that the light-source positions accessible within a shader have already been transformed into the eye coordinate frame. When you create shaders, the coordinate system that you decide to use will likely depend on the types of computations being performed; this is an important factor to consider. Also, note the use of built-in functions and data structures in the example. In particular, there are several functions used in this shader: `normalize`, `dot`, `max`, `pow`, and `ftransform`. These functions are provided with the shader language. Additionally, the graphics state associated with materials and lighting can be accessed through built-in uniform variables: `gl_FrontMaterial` and `gl_LightSource[0]`. The diffuse component of the material and light is accessed through the `diffuse` member of these variables. The color at the vertex is computed using Equation (10.8) and then stored in the special output variable `gl_FrontColor`. The vertex position is transformed using the func-

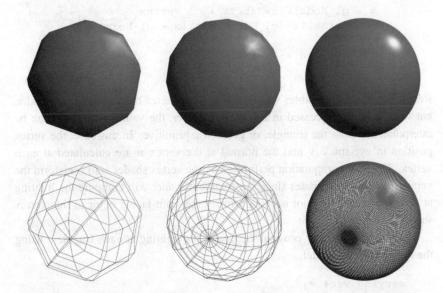

Figure 18.7. Each sphere is rendered using only a vertex shader that computes Phong shading. Because the computation is being performed on a per-vertex basis, the Phong highlight only begins to appear accurate after the amount of geometry used to model the sphere is increased drastically. (See also Plate VIII.)

tion `ftransform` which is a convenience function that performs the multiplication with the modelview and projection matrices. Figure 18.7 shows the results from running this vertex shader with differently tessellated spheres. Because the computations are performed on a per-vertex basis, a large amount of geometry is required to produce a Phong highlight on the sphere that appears correct.

18.3.4 Fragment Shader Example

Fragment shaders are written in a manner very similar to vertex shaders, and to emphasize this, Equation (10.8) from will be implemented with a fragment shader. In order to do this, we first will need to write a vertex shader to set the stage for the fragment shader.

The vertex shader required for this example is fairly simple, but introduces the use of *varying* variables to communicate data to the fragment shader.

```
varying vec4 v;
varying vec3 n;

void main(void)
{
    v = gl_ModelViewMatrix * gl_Vertex;
    n = normalize(gl_NormalMatrix * gl_Normal);

    gl_Position = ftransform();
}
```

Recall that varying variables will be set on a per-vertex basis by a vertex shader, but when they are accessed in a fragment shader, the values will *vary* (i.e., be interpolated) across the triangle, or geometric primitive. In this case, the vertex position in eye-space **v** and the normal at the vertex **n** are calculated at each vertex. The final computation performed by the vertex shader is to transform the vertex into clip coordinates since the fragment shader will compute the lighting at each fragment. It is not necessary to set the front-facing color in this vertex shader.

The fragment shader program computes the lighting at each fragment using the Phong shading model.

```
varying vec4 v;
varying vec3 n;

void main(void)
{
```

```
      vec3 l = normalize(gl_LightSource[0].position - v);
      vec3 h = normalize(l - normalize(v));

      float p = 16;
      vec4 cr = gl_FrontMaterial.diffuse;
      vec4 cl = gl_LightSource[0].diffuse;
      vec4 ca = vec4(0.2, 0.2, 0.2, 1.0);

      vec4 color;
      if (dot(h,n) > 0)
          color = cr * (ca + cl * max(0,dot(n,l))) +
                        cl * pow(dot(h,n),p);
      else
          color = cr * (ca + cl * max(0,dot(n,l)));

      gl_FragColor = color;
}
```

The first thing you should notice is the similarity between the fragment shader code in this example and the vertex shader code presented in Section 18.3.3. The

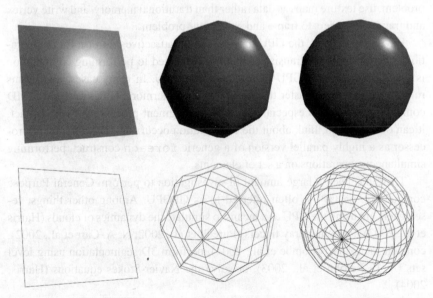

Figure 18.8. The results of running the fragment shader from Section 18.3.4. Note that the Phong highlight does appear on the left-most model which is represented by a single polygon. In fact, because lighting is calculated at the fragment, rather than at each vertex, the more coarsely tessellated sphere models also demonstrate appropriate Phong shading. (See also Plate IX.)

main difference is in the use of the varying variables, **v** and **n**. In the fragment shader, the view vectors and normal values are interpolated across the surface of the model between neighboring vertices. The results are shown in Figure 18.8. Immediately, you should notice the Phong highlight on the quadrilateral, which only contains four vertices. Because the shading is being calculated at the fragment level using the Phong equation with the interpolated (i.e., varying) data, more consistent and accurate Phong shading is produced with far less geometry.

18.3.5   General Purpose Computing on the GPU

After studying the vertex and fragment shader examples, you may be wondering if you can write programs to perform other types of computations on the GPU. Obviously, the answer is yes, as many problems can be coded to run on the GPU given the various languages available for programming on the GPU. However, a few facts are important to remember. Foremost, floating point math processing on graphics hardware is not currently double-precision. Secondly, you will likely need to transform your problem into a form that fits within a graphics-related framework. In other words, you will need to use the graphics APIs to set up the problem, use texture maps as data rather than traditional memory, and write vertex and fragment shaders to frame and solve your problem.

Having stated that, the GPU may still be an attractive platform for computation, since the ratio of transistors that are dedicated to performing computation is much higher on the GPU than it is on the CPU. In many cases, algorithms running on GPUs run faster than on a CPU. Furthermore, GPUs perform SIMD computation, which is especially true at the fragment-processing level. In fact, it can often help to think about the computation occurring on the fragment processor as a highly parallel version of a generic `foreach` construct, performing simultaneous operations on a set of elements.

There has been a large amount of investigation to perform General Purpose computation on GPUs, often referred to as GPGPU. Among other things, researchers are using the GPU as a means to simulate the dynamics of clouds (Harris et al., 2003), implement ray tracers (Purcell et al., 2002; N. A. Carr et al., 2002), compute radiosity (Coombe et al., 2004), perform 3D segmentation using level sets (A. E. Lefohn et al., 2003), or solve the Navier-Stokes equations (Harris, 2004).

General purpose computation is often performed on the GPU using multiple rendering "passes," and most computation is done using the fragment processor due to its highly data-parallel setup. Each pass, called a *kernel*, completes a portion of the computation. Kernels work on streams of data with several kernels strung together to form the overall computation. The first kernel completes the first part of the computation, the second kernel works on the first kernel's data, and so on, until the calculation is complete. In this style of programming, working with data and data structures on the GPU is different than conventional programming and does require a bit of thought. Fortunately, recent efforts are providing abstractions and information for creating efficient data structures for GPU programming (A. Lefohn et al., 2005).

Using the GPU for general purpose programming does require that you understand how to program the graphics hardware. For instance, most applications that perform GPGPU will render a simple quadrilateral, or sets of quadrilaterals, with vertex and fragment shaders operating on that geometry. The geometry doesn't have to be visible, or drawn to the screen, but it is necessary to allow the vertex and fragment operations to occur. This focus on graphics does make the learning curve for general purpose computing on this hardware an adventure. Fortunately, recent efforts are working to make the interface to the GPU more like traditional programming. The Brook for GPUs project (Buck et al., n.d.) is a system that provides a C-like interface to afford stream computations on the GPU, which should allow more people to take advantage of the computational power on modern graphics hardware.

Frequently Asked Questions

- How do I debug shader programs?

On most platforms, debugging both vertex shaders and fragment shaders is not simple. There is very little runtime support for debugging graphics applications in general, and even less available for runtime debugging of shader programs. However, this is starting to change. In the latest versions of Mac OS X, Linux, and Windows, support for shader programming is incorporated. A good solution for debugging shader programs is to use one of the shader development tools available from various graphics hardware manufacturers.

Notes

There are many good resources available to learn more about the technical details involved with programming graphics hardware. A good starting point might be the OpenGL™ Programming Guide (Shreiner et al., 2004). The OpenGL™ Shading Language (Rost, 2004) and The Cg Tutorial (Fernando & Killgard, 2003) provide details on how to program using a shading language. More advanced technical information and examples for programming the vertex and fragment processors can be found in the GPU Gems series of books (Fernando, 2004; Pharr & Fernando, 2005). A source of information for learning more about general purpose computation on GPUs (GPGPU) can be found on the GPGPU.org web site (http://www.gpgpu.org).

Exercises

1. How fast is the GPU as compared to performing the operations on the CPU? Write a program in which you can parameterize how much data is processed on the GPU, ranging from no computation using a shader program to all of the computation being performed using a shader program. How does the performance of you application change when the computation is being performed solely on the GPU?

2. Are there sizes of triangle strip lengths that work better than others? Try to determine the maximum size of a triangle strip that maximizes performance. What does this tell you about the memory, or cache structure, on the graphics hardware?

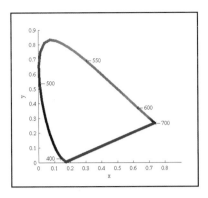

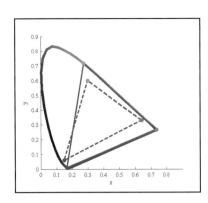

Plate XXVIII. The spectrum locus for the CIE 1931 standard observer. (See also Figure 21.6).

Plate XXIX. The chromaticity boundaries of the CIE RGB primaries at 435.8, 546.1, and 700 nm (solid) and a typical HDTV (dashed). (See also Figure 21.7.)

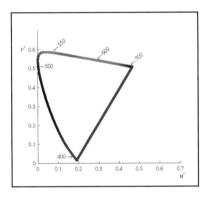

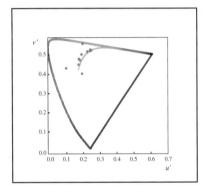

Plate XXX. The CIE $u'v'$ chromaticity diagram. (See also Figure 21.8.)

Plate XXXI. A series of light sources plotted in the CIE $u'v'$ chromaticity diagram. A white piece of paper illuminated by any of these light sources maintains a white color appearance. (See also Figure 21.11.)

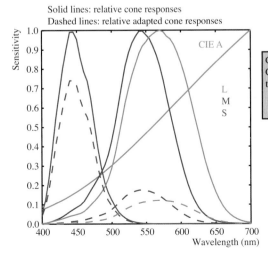

Plate XXXII. An example of von Kries–style independent photoreceptor gain control. The relative cone responses (solid line) and the relative adapted cone responses to CIE illuminant A (dashed) are shown. The separate patch of color represents CIE illuminant A rendered into the sRGB color space. (See also Figure 21.12.)

Plate XXXIII. *Crysis* exemplifies the realistic and detailed graphics expected of first-person shooters. *Image courtesy Crytek.* (See also Figure 26.2.)

Plate XXXIV. An example of highly stylized, non-photorealistic rendering from the game *Okami*. *Image courtesy Capcom Entertainment, Inc.* (See also Figure 26.3.)

Plate XXXV. The *LittleBig-Planet* developers took care to choose techniques that fit the game's constraints, combining them in unusual ways to achieve stunning results. *LittleBigPlanet* © *2007 Sony Computer Entertainment Europe. Developed by Media Molecule. LittleBigPlanet is a trademark of Sony Computer Entertainment Europe.* (See also Figure 26.4.)

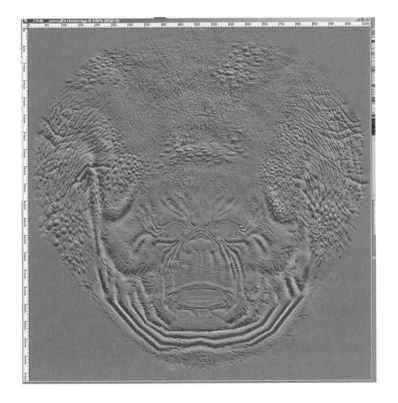

Plate XXXVI. The normal map used in Figure 26.8. In this image, the red, green and blue channels of the texture contain the X, Y, and Z coordinates of the surface normals. *Image courtesy Keith Bruns.* (See also Figure 26.9.)

Plate XXXVII. An early version of a diffuse color texture for the mesh from Figure 26.8, shown in Photoshop. *Image courtesy Keith Bruns.* (See also Figure 26.10.)

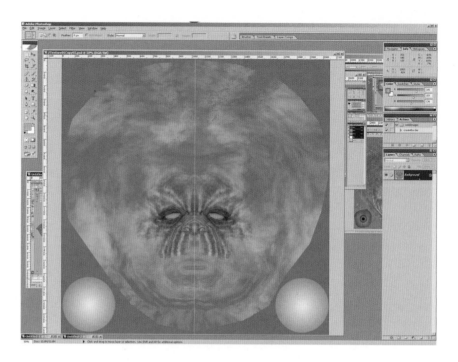

Plate XXXVIII. A rendering (in ZBrush) of the mesh with normal map and early diffuse color texture (from Plate XXXVII) applied. *Image courtesy Keith Bruns.* (See also Figure 26.11.)

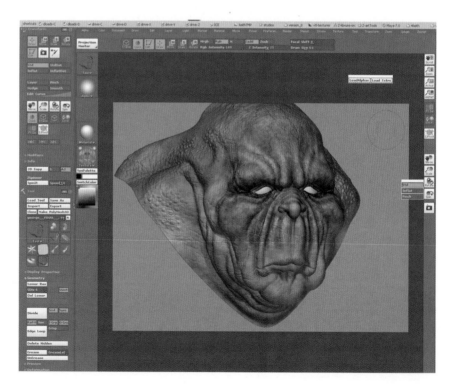

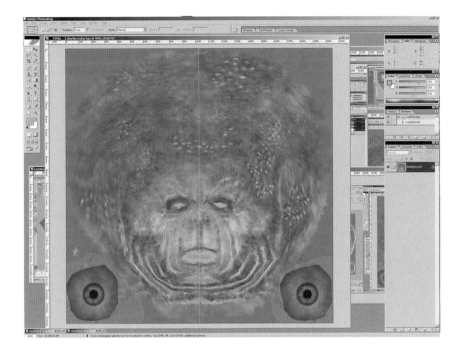

Plate XXXIX. Final version of the color texture from Plate XXXVII. *Image courtesy Keith Bruns.* (See also Figure 26.12.)

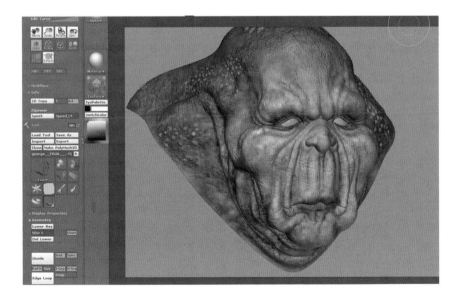

Plate XL. Rendering of the mesh with normal map and final color texture (from Figure 26.12) applied. *Image courtesy Keith Bruns.* (See also Figure 26.13.)

Plate XLI. Shader configuration in Maya. The interface on the right is used to select the shader, assign textures to shader inputs, and set the values of non-texture shader inputs (such as the "Specular Color" and "Specular Power" sliders). The rendering on the left is updated dynamically while these properties are modified, enabling immediate visual feedback. *Image courtesy Keith Bruns.* (See also Figure 26.14.)

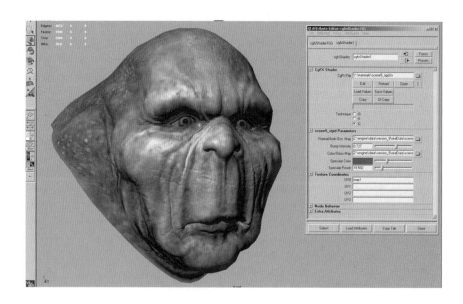

Plate XLII. The Tableau/Polaris system default mappings for four visual channels according to data type. *Image courtesy Chris Stolte* (Stolte et al., 2008), © 2008 IEEE. (See also Figure 27.6.)

Property	Ordinal/nominal mapping	Quantitative mapping
Shape	○ □ + × ✳ ◇ △	
Size	• • ● ●	•••••●●●●●
Orientation	— ╱ / ∣ \ ＼	— ╱ ╱ ⁄ ⁄ / / / ∣ ∣
Color		

Plate XLIII. Complex glyphs require significant display area so that the encoded information can be read. *Image courtesy Matt Ward, created with the SpiralGlyphics software* (M. O. Ward, 2002). (See also Figure 27.14.)

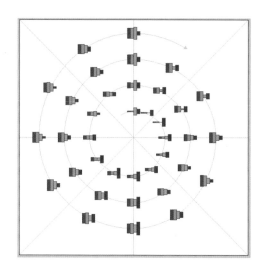

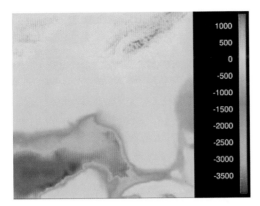
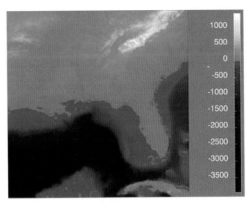

Plate XLIV. Left: The standard rainbow colormap has two defects: it uses hue to denote ordering, and it is not perceptually isolinear. (See also Figure 27.8.) Right: The structure of the same dataset is far more clear with a colormap where monotonically increasing lightness is used to show ordering and hue is used instead for segmenting into categorical regions. (See also Figure 27.9.) *Courtesy Bernice Rogowitz.*

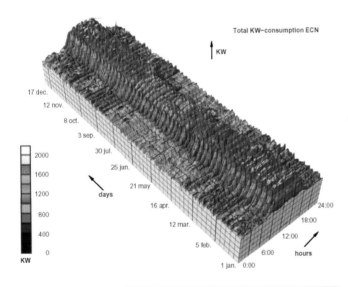

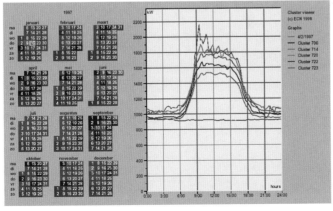

Plate XLV. Top: A 3D representation of this time series dataset introduces the problems of occlusion and perspective distortion. Bottom: The linked 2D views of derived aggregate curves and the calendar allow direct comparison and show more fine-grained patterns. *Image courtesy Jarke van Wijk* (van Wijk & van Selow, 1999), © 1999 IEEE. (See also Figure 27.10.)

Plate XLVI. Tarantula shows an overview of source code using one-pixel lines color coded by execution status of a software test suite. *Image courtesy John Stasko* (Jones et al., 2002), © 2002 ACM, Inc. Included here by permission. (See also Figure 27.11.)

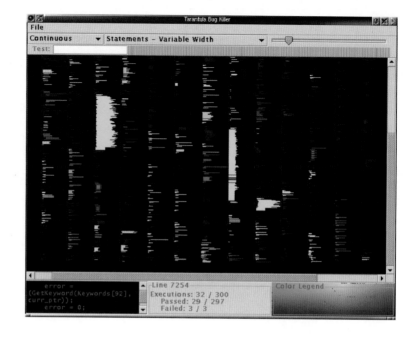

Plate XLVII. Visual layering with size, saturation, and brightness in the Constellation system (Munzner, 2000). (See also Figure 27.12.)

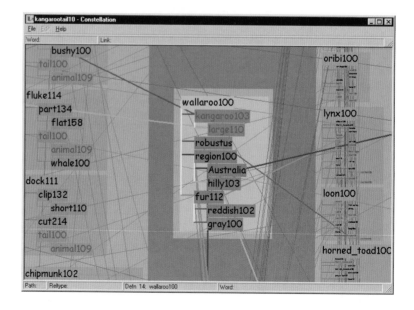

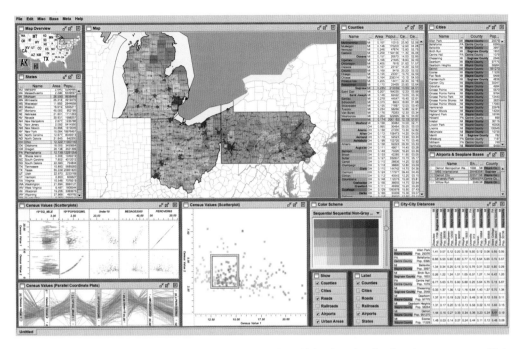

Plate XLVIII. The Improvise toolkit was used to create this multiple-view visualization. *Image courtesy Chris Weaver.* (See also Figure 27.16.)

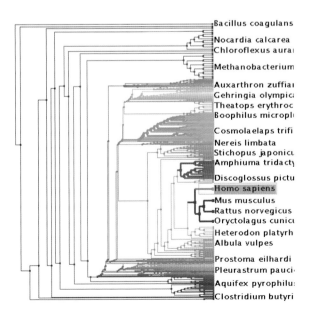

Plate XLIX. The Tree-Juxtaposer system features stretch and squish navigation and guaranteed visibility of regions marked with colors (Munzner et al., 2003). (See also Figure 27.17).

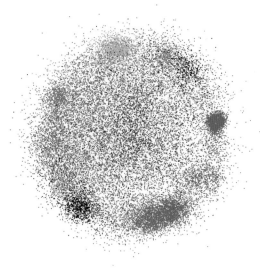

Plate L. Dimensionality reduction with the Glimmer multidimensional scaling approach shows clusters in a document dataset (Ingram et al., 2009), ⓒ 2009 IEEE. (See also Figure 27.19.)

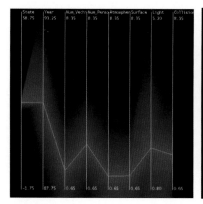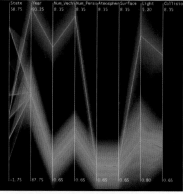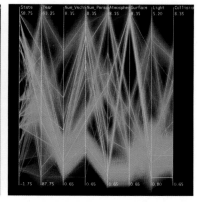

Plate LI. Hierarchical parallel coordinates show high-dimensional data at multiple levels of detail. *Image courtesy Matt Ward* (Fua et al., 1999), ⓒ 1999 IEEE. (See also Figure 27.21).

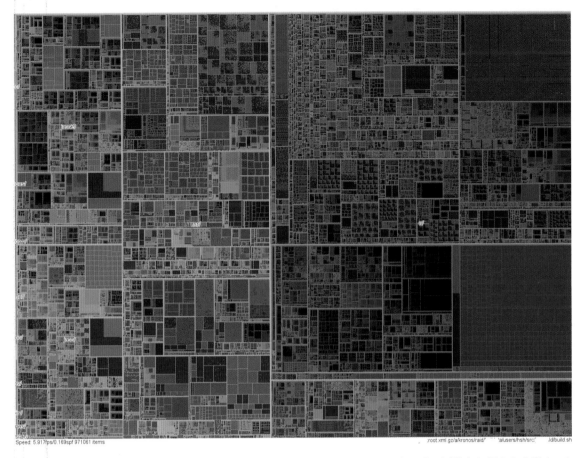

Speed: 5.917fps/0.169spf 971061 items — :root.xml.gz/a/kronos/raid/" 'a/users/hsh/src/' .ld/build.sh

Plate LII. Treemap showing a filesystem of nearly one million files. *Image courtesy Jean-Daniel Fekete* (Fekete & Plaisant, 2002), © 2002 IEEE. (See also Figure 27.25.)

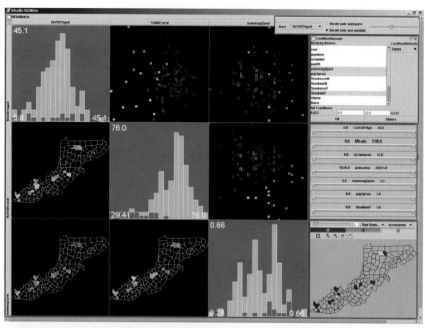

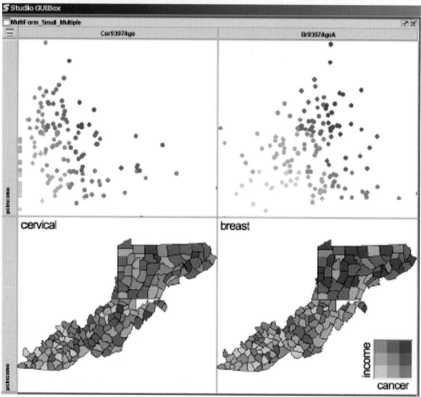

Plate LIII. Two matrices of linked small multiples showing cancer demographic data (MacEachren et al., 2003), © 2003 IEEE. (See also Figure 27.26).

Kelvin Sung

19

Building Interactive Graphics Applications

While most of the other chapters in this book discuss the fundamental algorithms in the field of computer graphics, this chapter treats the integration of these algorithms into applications. This is an important topic since the knowledge of fundamental graphics algorithms does not always easily lead to an understanding of the best practices in implementing these algorithms in real applications.

We start with a simple example: a program that allows the user to simulate the shooting of a ball (under the influence of gravity). The user can specify initial velocity, create balls of different sizes, shoot the ball, and examine the parabolic free fall of the ball. Some fundamental concepts we will need include mesh structure for the representation of the ball (sphere); texture mapping, lighting, and shading for the aesthetic appearance of the ball; transformations for the trajectories of the ball; and rasterization techniques for the generation of the images of the balls.

To implement the simple ball shooting program, one also needs knowledge of

- graphical user interface (GUI) systems for efficient and effective user interaction;

- software architecture and design patterns for crafting an implementation framework that is easy to maintain and expand;

- application program interfaces (APIs) for choosing the appropriate support and avoiding a massive amount of unnecessary coding.

467

To gain an appreciation for these three important aspects of building the application, we will complete the following steps:

- analyze interactive applications;

- understand different programming models and recognize important functional components in these models;

- define the interaction of the components;

- design solution frameworks for integrating the components; and

- demonstrate example implementations based on different sets of existing APIs.

We will use the ball shooting program as our example and begin by refining the detailed specifications. For clarity, we avoid graphics-specific complexities in 3D space and confine our example to 2D space. Obviously, our simple program is neither sophisticated nor representative of real applications. However, with slightly refined specifications, this example contains all the essential components and behavioral characteristics of more complex real-world interactive systems.

We will continue to build complexity into our simple example, adding new concepts until we arrive at a software architecture framework that is suitable for building general interactive graphics applications. We will examine the validity of our results and discuss how the lessons learned from this simple example can be applied to other familiar real-world applications (e.g., PowerPoint, Maya, etc.).

19.1   The Ball Shooting Program

Our simple program has the following elements and behaviors.

- **The balls (objects).** The user can left-mouse-button-click and drag-out a new ball (circle) anywhere on the screen (see Figure 19.1). Dragging-out a ball includes:

  - **(A).** Initial mouse-button-click position defines the center of the circle;

  - **(B).** Mouse button down and moving the mouse is the dragging action;

  - **(C).** Current mouse position while dragging allows us to define the radius and the initial velocity. The radius R (in pixel units) is the distance to the center defined in (A). The vector from the current position to the center is the initial velocity V (in units of pixel per second).

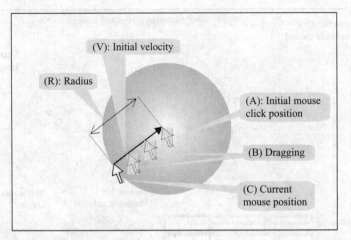

Figure 19.1. Dragging out a ball.

Once created, the ball will begin traveling with the defined initial velocity.

- **HeroBall (Hero/active object).** The user can also right-mouse-button-click to select a ball to be the current HeroBall. The HeroBall's velocity can be controlled by the slider bars (discussed below) where its velocity is displayed. (A newly created ball is by default the current HeroBall.) A right-mouse-button-click on unoccupied space indicates that no current HeroBall exists.

- **Velocity slider bars (GUI elements).** The user can monitor and control two slider bars (x- and y-directions with magnitudes) to change the velocity of the HeroBall. When there is no HeroBall, the slider bar values are undefined.

- **The simulation.**

  - **Ball traveling/collisions (object intrinsic behaviors).** A ball knows how to travel based on its current velocity and one ball can potentially collide with another. For simplicity, we will assume all balls have identical mass and all collisions are perfectly elastic.

  - **Gravity (external effects on objects).** The velocity of a ball is constantly changing due to the defined gravitational force.

  - **Status bar (application state echo).** The user can monitor the application state by examining the information in the status bar. In our application, the number of balls currently on the screen is updated in the status bar.

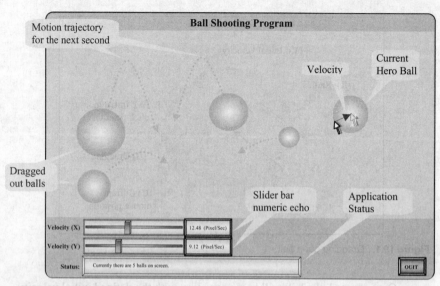

Figure 19.2. The ball shooting program.

Our application starts with an empty screen. The user clicks and drags to create new balls with different radii and velocities. Once a ball travels off of the screen, it is removed. To avoid unnecessary details, we do not include the drawing of the motion trajectories or the velocity vector in our solutions. Notice that a slider bar communicates its current state to the user in two ways: the position of the slider knob and the numeric echo (see Figure 19.2).

We have now described the behavior of a simple interactive graphics application. In the rest of this chapter, we will learn the concepts that support the implementation of this type of application.

19.2   Programming Models

For many of us, when we were first introduced to computer programming, we learned that the program should always start and end with the *main*() function— when the *main*() function returns, all the work must have been completed and the program terminates. Since the overall control remains internal to the *main*() function during the entire life time of the program, the type of model for this approach to solving problems is called an *internal control model,* or *control-driven programming*. As we will see, an alternative paradigm, *event-driven programming* or an *external control model* approach, is the more appropriate way to design solutions to interactive programs.

In this section, we will first formulate a solution to the 2D ball shooting program based on the, perhaps more familiar, control-driven programming model. We will then analyze the solution, identify shortcomings, and describe the motivation for the external control model or event-driven programming approach.

The pseudocode which follows is C++/Java-like. We assume typical functionality from the operating System (*OperatingSystem::*) and from a graphical user interface API (*GUISystem::*). The purpose of the pseudocode is to assist us in analyzing the foundation control structure (i.e., if/while/case) of the solution. For this reason, the details of application- and graphics-specific operations are intentionally glossed over. For example, the details of how to *UpdateSimulation*() is purposely omitted.

19.2.1 Control-Driven Programming

The main advantage of control-driven programming is that it is fairly straightforward to translate a verbal description of a solution to a program control structure. In this case, we verbalize our solution as follows:

> while the user does not want to quit (A);
>
> parse and execute the user's command (B);
>
> update the velocities and positions of the balls (C);
>
> then draw all the balls (D);
>
> and finally before we poll the user for another command,
>
> tell the user what is going on by echoing current application state to
> the status bar (E).

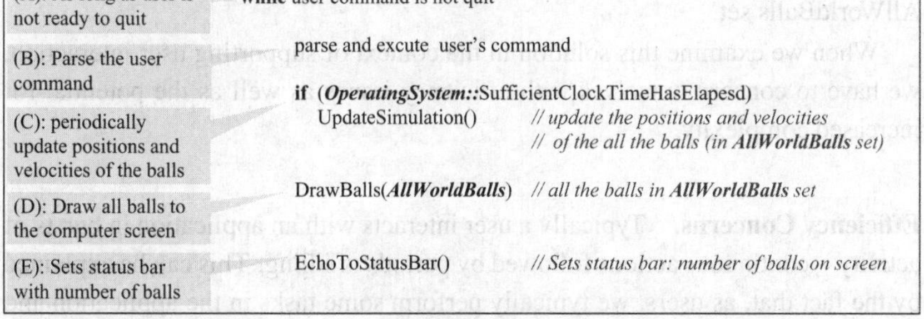

(A): As long as user is not ready to quit	**while** user command is not quit
(B): Parse the user command	parse and excute user's command

(C): periodically update positions and velocities of the balls	**if** (*OperatingSystem::*SufficientClockTimeHasElapesd)
	    UpdateSimulation() *// update the positions and velocities*
	                                      *// of the all the balls (in **AllWorldBalls** set)*

(D): Draw all balls to the computer screen	DrawBalls(***AllWorldBalls***) *// all the balls in **AllWorldBalls** set*
(E): Sets status bar with number of balls	EchoToStatusBar() *// Sets status bar: number of balls on screen*

Figure 19.3. Programming structure from a verbalized solution.

Figure 19.3 shows a translation from this verbal solution into a simple programming structure. We introduce the set of *AllWorldBalls* to represent all the balls that are currently on the computer screen. The only other difference between the pseudocode in Figure 19.3 and our verbalized solution is in the added elapsed time check in Step (C): *SufficientClockTimeHasElapsed*. (Recall that the velocities are defined in pixels per second.) To support proper pixel displacements, we must know real elapsed time between updates.

As we add additional details to parse and execute the user's commands (B), the solution must be expanded. The revised solution in Figure 19.4 shows the details of a central parsing switch statement (B) and the support for all three commands a user can issue: defining a new HeroBall (B1); selecting a HeroBall (B2); and adjusting current HeroBall velocity with the slider bars (B3). Undefined user actions (e.g., mouse movement with no button pressed) are simply ignored (B4).

Notice that HeroBall creation (B1) involves three user actions: mouse down (B1), followed by mouse drag (B1-1), and finally mouse up (B1-2). The parsing of this operation is performed in multiple consecutive passes through the outer while-loop (A): the first time through, we create the new HeroBall (B1); in the subsequent passes, we perform the actual *dragging* operation (B1-1). We assume that mouse drag (B1-1) will never be invoked without mouse button down (B1) action, and thus the HeroBall is always defined during the dragging operation.

The *LeftMouseButtonUp* action (B1-2) is an implicit action not defined in the original specification. In our implementation, we choose this implicit action to activate the insertion of the new HeroBall into the AllWorldBalls set. In this way the HeroBall is not a member of the AllWorldBalls set until after the user has completed the dragging operation. This delay ensures that the HeroBall's velocity and position will not be affected when the *UpdateSimulation*() procedure updates all the balls in AllWorldBalls set (C). This means a user can take the time to drag out a new HeroBall without worrying that the ball will free fall before the release of the mouse button. The simple amendment in the drawing operation (D1) ensures a proper drawing of the new HeroBall before it is inserted into the AllWorldBalls set.

When we examine this solution in the context of supporting user interaction, we have to concern ourselves with efficiency issues as well as the potential for increased complexity.

Efficiency Concerns.   Typically a user interacts with an application in bursts of activity—continuous actions followed by periods of idling. This can be explained by the fact that, as users, we typically perform some tasks in the application and then spend time examining the results. For example, when working with a word

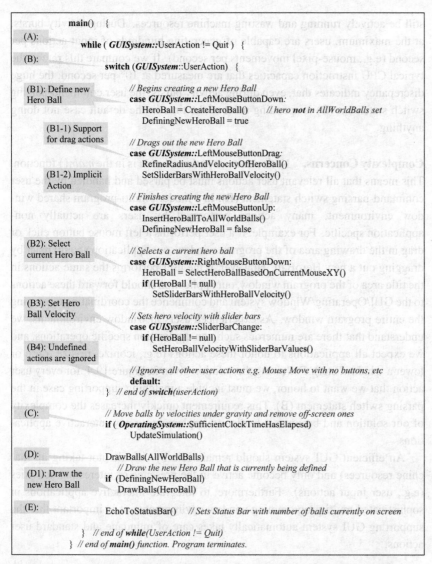

```
          main() {
(A):
                    while ( GUISystem::UserAction != Quit ) {
(B):
                         switch (GUISystem::UserAction) {

(B1): Define new                // Begins creating a new Hero Ball
Hero Ball                       case GUISystem::LeftMouseButtonDown:
                                     HeroBall = CreateHeroBall()    // hero not in AllWorldBalls set
                                     DefiningNewHeroBall = true

       (B1-1) Support           // Drags out the new Hero Ball
       for drag actions         case GUISystem::LeftMouseButtonDrag:
                                     RefineRadiusAndVelocityOfHeroBall()
       (B1-2) Implicit          SetSliderBarsWithHeroBallVelocity()
       Action
                                // Finishes creating the new Hero Ball
                                case GUISystem::LeftMouseButtonUp:
                                     InsertHeroBallToAllWorldBalls()
                                     DefiningNewHeroBall = false

(B2): Select                    // Selects a current hero ball
current Hero Ball               case GUISystem::RightMouseButtonDown:
                                     HeroBall = SelectHeroBallBasedOnCurrentMouseXY()
                                     if (HeroBall != null)
                                          SetSliderBarsWithHeroBallVelocity()

(B3): Set Hero
Ball Velocity                   // Sets hero velocity with slider bars
                                case GUISystem::SliderBarChange:
                                     if (HeroBall != null)
(B4): Undefined                       SetHeroBallVelocityWithSliderBarValues()
actions are ignored
                                // Ignores all other user actions e.g. Mouse Move with no buttons, etc
                                default:
                         } // end of switch(userAction)

(C):                            // Move balls by velocities under gravity and remove off-screen ones
                                if ( OperatingSystem::SufficientClockTimeHasElapesd)
                                     UpdateSimulation()

(D):                            DrawBalls(AllWorldBalls)
(D1): Draw the                  // Draw the new Hero Ball that is currently being defined
new Hero Ball                   if (DefiningNewHeroBall)
                                     DrawBalls(HeroBall)

(E):                            EchoToStatusBar()    // Sets Status Bar with number of balls currently on screen

                    } // end of while(UserAction != Quit)
          } // end of main() function. Program terminates.
```

Figure 19.4. Programming solution based on the control-driven programming model.

processor, our typical work pattern consists of bursts of typing/editing followed by periods of reading (with no input action). In our example application, we can expect the user to drag out some circles and then observe the free-falling of the circles. The continuous while-loop polling of user commands in the *main()* function means that when the user is not performing any action, our program will still be actively running and wasting machine resources. During activity bursts, at the maximum, users are capable of generating hundreds of input actions per second (e.g., mouse-pixel movements per second). If we compare this rate to the typical CPU instruction capacities that are measured at 10^9 per second, the huge discrepancy indicates that, even during activity bursts, the user command-parsing switch statement (B) is spending most of the time in the default case not doing anything.

Complexity Concerns.   Notice that our *entire solution* is in the *main*() function. This means that all relevant user actions must be parsed and handled by the user command-parsing switch statement (B). In a modern multi-program shared window environment, many actions performed by users are actually non-application specific. For example, if a user performs a left mouse button click or drag in the drawing area of the program window, our application should react by dragging out a new HeroBall. However, if the user performs the same actions in the title area of the program window, our application should forward these actions to the GUI/Operating/Window system and commence the coordination of moving the entire program window. As experienced users in window environments, we understand that there are numerous such non-application specific operations, and we expect all applications to honor these actions (e.g., iconize, re-size, raise or lower a window, etc.). Following the solution given in Figure 19.4, for every user action that we want to honor, we must include a matching supporting case in the parsing switch statement (B). This requirement quickly increases the complexity of our solution and becomes a burden to implementing any interactive applications.

An efficient GUI system should remain idle by default (not taking up machine resources) and only become active in the presence of interesting activities (e.g., user input actions). Furthermore, to integrate interactive applications in sophisticated multi-programming window environments, it is important that the supporting GUI system automatically takes care of mundane and standard user actions.

19.2.2   Event-Driven Programming

Event-driven programming remedies the efficiency and complexity concerns with a default *MainEventLoop*() function defined in the GUI system. For event-driven programs, the *MainEventLoop*() replaces the *main*() function, because all programs start and end in this function. Just as in the case of the *main*() function for control-driven programming, when the *MainEventLoop*() function re-

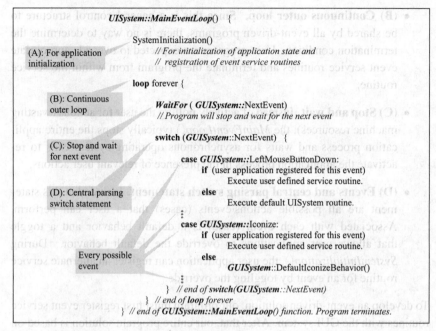

Figure 19.5. The default *MainEventLoop* function.

turns, all work should have been completed, and the program terminates. The *MainEventLoop()* function defines the central control structure for all event-driven programming solutions and typically cannot be changed by a user application. In this way, the overall control of an application is actually external to the user's program code. For this reason, event-driven programming is also referred to as the external control model.

Figure 19.5 depicts a typical *MainEventLoop()* implementation. In this case, our program is the user application that is based on the *MainEventLoop()* function. Structurally, the *MainEventLoop()* is very similar to the *main()* function of Figure 19.4: with a continuous loop (B) containing a central parsing switch statement (D). The important differences between the two functions include:

- **(A) SystemInitialization().** Recall that event-driven programs start and end in the *MainEventLoop()* function. *SystemInitialization()* is a mechanism defined to invoke the user program from within the *MainEventLoop()*. It is expected that user programs implement *SystemInitialization()* to initialize the application state and to register event service routines (refer to the discussion in (D)).

- **(B) Continuous outer loop.** Since this is a general control structure to be shared by all event-driven programs, there is no way to determine the termination condition. User program are expected to override appropriate event service routines and terminate the program from within the service routine.

- **(C) Stop and wait.** Instead of actively polling the user for actions (wasting machine resources), the *MainEventLoop*() typically stops the entire application process and waits for asynchronous operating system calls to re-activate the application process in the presence of relevant user actions.

- **(D) Events and central parsing switch statement.** Included in this statement are all possible actions/events (cases) that a user can perform. Associated with each event (case) is a default behavior and a toggle that allows user applications to override the default behavior. During *SystemInitialization*(), the user application can register an alternate service routine for an event by toggling the override.

To develop an event-driven solution, our program must first register event service routines with the GUI system. After that, our entire program solution is based on waiting and servicing user events. While control-driven programming solutions are based on an algorithmic organization of control structures in the *main*() function, an event-driven programming solution is based on the specification of events that cause changes to a defined application state. This is a different paradigm for designing programming solutions. The key difference here is that, as programmers, we have no explicit control over the algorithmic organization of the events: over which, when, or how often an event should occur.

The program in Figure 19.6 implements the left mouse button operations for our ball shooting program. We see that during system initialization (A), the program defines an appropriate application state (A1) and registers left mouse button (LMB) down/drag/up events (A2). The corresponding event service routines (D1, D2, and D3) are also defined. At the end of each event service routine, we redraw all the balls to ensure that the user can see an up-to-date display at all times. Notice the absence of any control structure organizing the initialization and service routines. Recall that this is an event-driven program: the overall control structure is defined in the MainEventLoop which is external to our solution.

Figure 19.7 shows how our program from Figure 19.6 is linked with the pre-defined *MainEventLoop*() from the GUI system. The *MainEventLoop*() calls the *SystemInitialization*() function defined in our solution (A). As described, after the initialization, our entire program is essentially the three event service routines (D1, D2, and D3). However, we have no control over the invocation of

```
(A) System Initialization:
    (A1): Define Application State:
          AllWorldBalls: A set of defined Balls, initialze to empty
          HeroBall: current active ball, initialize to null

    (A2): Register Event Service Routines
          Register for:  Left Mouse Button Down Event
          Register for:  Left Mouse Button Drag Event
          Register for:  Left Mouse Button Up Event
                           // We care about these events, inform us if these events happen
(D) Events Services:
    (D1): Left Mouse Button Down// service routine for this event
          HeroBall = Create a new ball at current mouse position
          DrawAllBalls(AllWorldBalls, HeroBall)  // Draw all balls (including HeroBall)

    (D2): Left Mouse Button Drag  // service routine for this event
          RefineRadiusAndVelocityOfHeroBall()
          DrawAllBalls(AllWorldBalls, HeroBall)  // Draw all balls (inlucding HeroBall)

    (D3): Left Mouse Button Up    // service routine for this event
          InsertHeroBallToAllWorldBalls()
          DrawAllBalls(AllWorldBalls, null)      // Draw all balls
```

Figure 19.6. A simple event-driven program specification.

these routines. Instead, a user performs actions that trigger events which drive these routines. These routines in turn change the application state. In this way, an event-driven programming solution is based on specification of events (LMB events) that cause changes to a defined application state (AllWorldBalls and HeroBall). Since the user command parsing switch statement (D in Figure 19.7) in the *MainEventLoop*() contains a case and the corresponding default behavior for every possible user actions, without any added complexity, our solution honors the non-application specific actions in the environment (e.g., iconize, moving, etc).

In the context of event-driven programming, an event can be perceived as an asynchronous notification that something interesting has happened. The messenger for the *notification* is the underlying GUI system. The mechanism for receiving an event is via overriding the corresponding event service routine.

For these reasons, when discussing event-driven programming, there is always a supporting GUI system. This GUI system is generally referred to as the graphical user interface (GUI) application programming interface (API). Examples of GUI APIs include: *Java Swing Library*, *OpenGL Utility ToolKit (GLUT)*, *The Fast Light ToolKit (FLTK)*, *Microsoft Foundation Classes (MFC)*, etc.

From the above discussion, we see that the registration for services of appropriate events is the core of designing and developing solutions for event-driven programs. Before we begin developing a complete solution for our ball shooting program, let us spend some time understanding *events*.

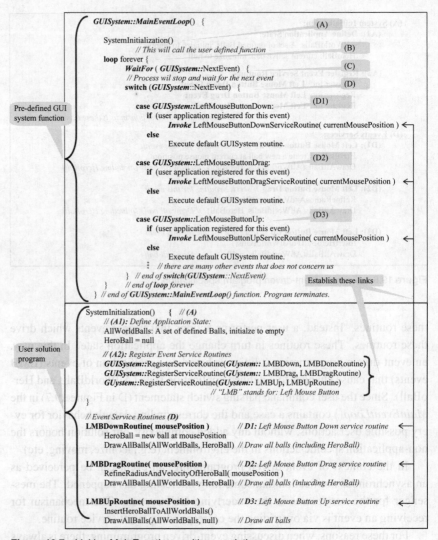

Figure 19.7. Linking MainEventLoop with our solution.

Graphical User Interface (GUI) Events

In general, an application may receive events generated by the user, the application itself, or by the GUI system. In this section, we describe each of these event sources and discuss the application's role in servicing these events.

S1: The User. These are events triggered by the actions a user performs on the input devices. Notice that input devices include actual hardware devices (e.g., mouse, keyboard, etc.) and/or software-simulated GUI elements (e.g., slider bars, combo boxes, etc.). Typically, a user performs actions for two very different reasons:

- **S1a: Application specific.** These are input actions that are part of the application. Clicking and dragging in the application screen area to create a HeroBall is an example of an action performed on a hardware input device. Changing the slider bars to control the HeroBall's velocity is an example of an action performed on a software-simulated GUI element. Both of these actions and the resulting events are application specific; the application (our program) is solely responsible for servicing these events.

- **S1b: General.** These are input actions defined by the operating environment. For example, a user clicks and drags in the window title-bar area expecting to move the entire application window. The servicing of these types of events requires collaboration between our application and the GUI system. We will discuss the servicing of these types of events in more detail when explaining events that originate from the GUI system in S3c.

Notice that the meaning of a user's action is *context sensitive*. It depends on where the action is performed: click and drag in the application screen area vs. slider bar vs. application window title-bar area. In any case, the underlying GUI system is responsible for parsing the context and determining which application element receives a particular event.

S2: The Application.   These are events defined by the application, typically depending on some run-time conditions. During run time, if and when the condition is favorable, the supporting GUI system triggers the event and conveys the favorable conditions to the application. A straightforward example is a periodic alarm. Modern GUI systems typically allow an application to define (sometimes multiple) *timer events* . Once defined, the GUI system will trigger an event to wake up the application when the timer expires. As we will see, this timer event is essential for supporting real-time simulations. Since the application (our program) requested the generation of these types of events, our program is solely responsible for serving them. The important distinction between application-defined and user-generated events is that application-defined events can be *spontaneous*: when properly defined, even when the user is not doing anything, these types of events may trigger.

S3: The GUI System.   These are events that originate from within the GUI system in order to convey state information to the application. There are typically three reasons for these events:

- **S3a: Internal GUI states change.** These are events signaling an internal
  state change of the GUI system. The GUI system typically generates an
  event before the creation of the application's main window. This provides
  an opportunity for the application to perform the corresponding initialization. In some GUI systems (e.g., MFC) the *SystemInitialization*() functionality is accomplished with these types of events: user applications are
  expected to override the appropriate windows' creation event and initialize
  the application state. Modern, general purpose commercial GUI systems
  typically define a large number of events signaling detailed state changes in
  anticipation of supporting different types of applications and requirements.
  For example, for the creation of the application's main window, the GUI
  system may define events for the following states:

    - before resource allocation;
    - after resource allocation but before initialization;
    - after initialization but before initial drawing, etc.

  A GUI system usually defines meaningful default behaviors for such events.
  To program an effective application based on a GUI system, one must understand the different groups of events and only service the appropriate
  selections.

- **S3b: External environment requests attention.** These are events indicating that there are changes in the operating environment that potentially
  require application attention. For example, a user has moved another application window to cover a portion of our application window, or a user
  has minimized our application window. The GUI system and the window
  environment typically have appropriate service routines for these types of
  events. An application would only choose to service these events when
  special actions must be performed. For example, in a real-time simulation
  program, the application may choose to suspend the simulation if the application window is minimized. In this situation, an application must service
  the minimized and the maximized events.

- **S3c: External environment requests application collaboration.** These
  are typically events requesting the application's collaboration to complete
  the service of *general user actions* (please refer to S1b). For example, if
  a user click-drags the application window's title bar, the GUI system reacts by letting the user "drag" the entire application window. This "drag"

operation is implemented by continuously erasing and redrawing the entire application window at the current mouse pointer position on the computer display. The GUI system has full knowledge of the appearance of the application window (e.g., the window frames, the menus, etc.), but it has no knowledge of the application window content (e.g., how many free falling balls traveling at what velocity, etc.). In this case, the GUI system redraws the application window frame and generates a Redraw/Paint event for the application, requesting assistance in completing the service of the user's "drag" operation. As an application in a shared window environment, our application is expected to honor and service these types of events. The most common events in this category include: Redraw/Paint and Resize. Redraw/Paint is the single most important event an application must service, because it supports the most common operations a user may perform in a shared window environment. Resize is also an important event to which the application must respond because the application is in charge of GUI element placement policy (e.g., if window size is increased, how should the GUI elements be placed in the larger window).

19.2.3 The Event-Driven Ball Shooting Program

In Section 19.2.1, we started a control-driven programming solution to the ball shooting program based on verbalizing the conditions (controls) under which the appropriate actions should be taken:

> while favorable condition, parse the input ...

As we have seen, with appropriate modifications, we were able to detail the control structures for our solution.

From the discussion in Section 19.2.2, we see that to design an event-driven programming solution we must

1. define the application state;

2. describe how user actions change the application state;

3. map the user actions to events that the GUI system supports; and

4. override corresponding event service routines to implement user actions.

The specification in Section 19.1 detailed the behaviors of our ball shooting program. The description is based on actions performed on familiar input devices (e.g., slider bars and mouse) that change the appearance on the display screen. Thus, the specification from Section 19.1 describes items (2) and (3) from the above list without explicitly defining what the application state is. Our job in designing a solution is to derive the implicitly defined application state and design the appropriate service routines.

Figure 19.8 presents our event-driven programming solution. As expected, the application state (A1) is defined in *SystemInitialization*(). The AllWorldBalls set and HeroBall can be derived from the specification in Section 19.1. The *DefiningNewHeroBall* flag is a transient (temporary) application state designed to support user actions across multiple events (click-and-drag). Using *transient* application states is a common approach to support consecutive inter-related events.

Figure 19.8 shows the registration of three types of service routines (A2):

- user-generated application specific events (S1a);

- an application defined event (S2);

- a GUI system-generated event requesting collaboration (S3c).

The timer event definition (A2S2) sets up a periodic alarm for the application to update the simulation of the free falling balls. The service routines of the user-generated application specific events (D1-D5) are remarkably similar to the corresponding case statements in the control-driven solution presented in Figure 19.4 (B1-B3). It should not be surprising that this is so, because we are implementing the exact same user actions based on the same specification. Line 3 of the *LMBDownRoutine*() (D1L3) demonstrates that, when necessary, our application can request the GUI system to initiate events. In this case, we signal the GUI system that an application redraw is necessary. Notice that event service routines are simply functions in our program. This means, at D1L3 we could also call *RedrawRoutine*() (D7) directly. The difference is that a call to *RedrawRoutine*() will force a redraw immediately while requesting the generation of a redraw event allows the GUI system to optimize the number of redraws. For example, if the user performs a LMB click and starts dragging immediately, with our D1 and D2 implementation, the GUI system can gather the many *GenerateRedrawEvent* requests in a short period of time and only generate one re-draw event. In this way, we can avoid performing more redraws than necessary.

In order to achieve a smooth animation, we should perform about 20–40 updates per second. It follows that the *SimulationUpdateInterval* should be no more than 50 milliseconds so that the *ServiceTimer*() routine can be invoked more than 20 times per second. (Notice that a redraw event is requested at the end of the *ServiceTimer*() routine.) This means, at the very least, our application is guaranteed to receive more than 20 redraw events in one second. For this reason, the

```
SystemInitialization() {    // (A)
    // (A1): Define Application State
        AllWorldBalls: A set of defined Balls, initialze to empty
        HeroBall = null
        DefiningNewHeroBall = false

    // (A2): Register Event Service Routines
        // S1a: Application Specific User Events
            GUISystem::RegisterServiceRoutine(GUISystem:: LMBDown, LMBDownRoutine)
            GUISystem::RegisterServiceRoutine(GUISystem:: LMBDrag, LMBDragRoutine)
            GUISystem::RegisterServiceRoutine(GUISystem:: LMBUp, LMBUpRoutine)
            GUISystem::RegisterServiceRoutine(GUISystem:: RMBDown, RMBDownRoutine)
            GUISystem::RegisterServiceRoutine(GUISystem:: SliderBar, SliderBarRoutine)
        // S2: Application Define Event
            GUISystem::DefineTimerPeriod(SimulationUpdateInterval)
            GUISystem::RegisterServiceRoutine(GUISystem:: TimerEvent, ServiceTimer)
                        // Triggers TimerEvent every: SimulationUpdateInterval period
        // S3c: Honor collaboration request from the GUI system
            GUISystem::RegisterServiceRoutine(GUISystem:: RedrawEvent, RedrawRoutine)
}

// Event Service Routines (D)
LMBDownRoutine( mousePosition )    // D1: Left Mouse Button Down service routine
    HeroBall = CreateHeroBall (mousePosition)
    DefiningNewHeroBall = true
    GUISystem::GenerateRedrawEvent

LMBDragRoutine( mousePosition )    // D2: Left Mouse Button Drag service routine
    RefineRadiusAndVelocityOfHeroBall( mousePosition )
    SetSliderBarsWithHeroBallVelocity()
    GUISystem::GenerateRedrawEvent    // Generates a redraw event

LMBUpRoutine( mousePosition )    // D3: Left Mouse Button Up service routine
    InsertHeroBallToAllWorldBalls()
    DefiningNewHeroBall = false

RMBDownRoutine ( mousePosition )    // D4: Right Mouse Button Down service routine
    HeroBall = SelectHeroBallBasedOn (mousePosition )
    if (HeroBall != null)  SetSliderBarsWithHeroBallVelocity()

SliderBarRoutine ( sliderBarValues )    // D5: Slider Bar changes service routine
    if (HeroBall != null)
        SetSliderBarsWithHeroBallVelocity( sliderBarValues )

ServiceTimer ( )                    // D6: Timer expired service routine
    UpdateSimulation( )                // Move balls by velocities  and remove off-screen ones
    EchoToStatusBar( )                 // Sets status bar with number of balls on screen
    GUISystem:: GenerateRedrawEvent    // Generates a redraw event
    if (HeroBall != null)              // Reflect propoer HeroBall velocity
        SetSliderBarsWithHeroBallVelocity( sliderBarValues )

RedrawRoutine ( )                  // D7:Redraw event service routine
    DrawBalls(AllWorldBalls)
    if (DefiningNewHeroBall)
        DrawBalls(HeroBall)            // Draw the new Hero Ball that is being defined
```

A1: Application State

A2S2: Defines a Timer Event

D1L3: Force a Redraw Event

Figure 19.8. Programming solution based on the event-driven programming model.

GenerateRedrawEvent requests in D1 and D2 are really not necessary. The servicing of our timer events will guarantee us an up-to-date display screen at all times.

19.2.4   Implementation Notes

The application state of an event-driven program must persist over the entire life time of the program. In terms of implementation, this means that the application state must be defined based on variables that are dynamically allocated during run time and that reside on the heap memory. These are in contrast to local variables that reside on the stack memory and which do not persist over different function invocations.

The mapping of user actions to events in the GUI system often results in *implicit* and/or undefined events. In our ball shooting program, the actions to define a HeroBall involve left mouse button down and drag. When mapping these actions to events in our implementation (in Figure 19.4 and Figure 19.8), we realize that we should also pay attention to the implicit mouse button up event. Another example is the HeroBall selection action: right mouse button down. In this case, right mouse button drag and up events are not serviced by our application, and thus, they are undefined (to our application).

When one user action (e.g., *"drag out the HeroBall"*) is mapped to a group of consecutive events (e.g., mouse button down, then drag, then up) a finite state diagram can usually be derived to help design the solution. Figure 19.9 depicts the finite state diagram for defining the HeroBall in our ball shooting program.

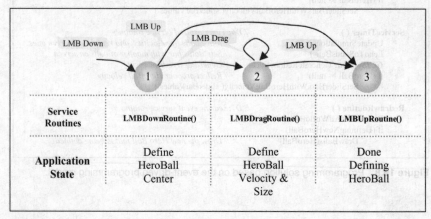

Figure 19.9. State diagram for defining the HeroBall.

The left mouse button down event puts the program into State 1 where, in our solution from Figure 19.8, *LMBDownRoutine*() implements this state and defines the center of the HeroBall, etc. In this case the transition between states is triggered by the mouse events, and we see that it is physically impossible to move from State 2 back to State 1. However, we do need to handle the case where the user action causes a transition from State 1 to State 3 directly (mouse button down and release without any dragging actions). This state diagram helps us analyze possible combinations of state transitions and perform appropriate initializations.

Event-driven applications interface with the user through physical (e.g., mouse clicks) or simulated GUI elements (e.g., quit button, slider bars). An input GUI element (e.g., the quit button) is an artifact (e.g., an icon) for the user to direct changes to the application state, while an output GUI element (e.g., the status bar) is an avenue for the application to present application state information to the user as feedback. For both types of elements, information only flows in one direction—either from the user to the application (input) or from the application to the user (output). When working with GUI elements that serve both input and output purposes, special care is required. For example, after the user selects or defines a HeroBall, the slider bars reflects the velocity of the free falling HeroBall (output), while at any time, the user can manipulate the slider bar to alter the HeroBall velocity (input). In this case, the GUI element's displayed state and the application's internal state are connected. The application must ensure that these two states are consistent. Notice that in the solution shown in Figure 19.4, this state consistency is not maintained. When a user clicks the RMB (B2 in Figure 19.4) to select a HeroBall, the slider bar values are updated properly; however, as the HeroBall free falls under gravity, the slider bar values are not updated. The solution presented in Figure 19.8 fixes this problem by using the *ServiceTimer*() function.

Event service routines are functions defined in our program that cause a *callback* from the MainEventLoop in the presence of relevant events. For this reason, these service routines are also referred to as *callback* functions. The application program registers callback functions with the GUI system by passing the address of the function to the GUI system. This is the registration mechanism implied in Figure 19.7 and Figure 19.8. Simple GUI systems (e.g., GLUT or FLTK) usually support this form of registration mechanism. The advantage of this mechanism is that it is easy to understand, straightforward to program, and often contributes to a small memory footprint in the resulting program. The main disadvantage of this mechanism is the lack of organizational structure for the callback functions.

In commercial GUI systems, there are a large numbers of events with which user applications must deal, and a structured organization of the service routines can assist the programmability of the GUI system. Modern commercial GUI systems are often implemented based on object-oriented languages (e.g., C++ for MFC, Java for Java Swing). For these systems, many event service registrations are implemented as sub-classes of an appropriate GUI system class, and they override corresponding virtual functions. In this way, the event service routines are organized according to the functionality of GUI elements. The details of different registration mechanisms will be explained in Section 19.4.1 when we describe the implementation details.

Event service routines (or callback functions) are simply functions in our program. However, these functions also serve the important role as the server of external asynchronous events. The following are guidelines one should take into account when implementing event service routines:

1. An event service routine should only service the triggering event and immediately return the control back to the *MainEventLoop*(). This may seem to be a "no-brainer." However, because of our familiarity with control-driven programming, it is often tempting to anticipate/poll subsequent events with a control structure in the service routine. For example, when servicing the left mouse button down event, we know that the mouse drag event will happen next. After allocating and defining the circle center, we have properly initialized data to work with the HeroBall object. It may seem easier to simply include a while loop to poll and service mouse drag events. However, with all the other external events that may happen (e.g., timer event, external redraw events, etc.), this monopolizing of control in one service routine is not only a bad design decision, but also it may cause the program to malfunction.

2. An event service routine should be *stateless*, and individual invocations should be independent. In terms of implementation, this essentially means event service routines should not define local *static* variables that record data from previous invocations. Because we have no control over when, or how often, events are triggered, when these variables are used as data, or conditions for changing application states, it can easily lead to disastrously and unnecessarily complex solutions. We can always define extra state variables in the application state to record temporary state information that must persist over multiple event services. The *DefiningNewHeroBall* flag in Figure 19.8 is one such example.

3. An event service routine should check for invocation conditions regardless of common sense *logical* sequence. For example, although logically, a mouse drag event can never happen unless a mouse down event has already occurred, in reality, a user may depress a mouse button from outside

of our application window and then drag the mouse into our application window. In this case, we will receive a mouse drag event without the corresponding mouse down event. For this reason, the mouse drag service routine should check the *invocation condition* that the proper initialization has indeed happened. Notice in Figure 19.8, we do not include proper invocation condition checking. For example, in the *LMBDragRoutine*(), we do not verify that *LMBDownRotine*() has been invoked (by checking the *DefiningNewHeroBall* flag). In a real system, this may causes the program to malfunction and/or crash.

19.2.5 Summary

In this section we have discussed *programming models* or *strategies for organizing statements of our program.* We have seen that for *interactive* applications, where an application continuously waits and reacts to a user's input actions, organizing the program statements based on designing control structures results in complex and inefficient programs. Existing GUI systems analyze all possible user actions, design control structures to interact with the user, implement default behaviors for all user actions, and provide this functionality in GUI APIs. To develop interactive applications, we take advantage of the existing control structure in the GUI API (i.e., the *MainEventLoop*()) and modify the default behaviors (via event service routines) of user actions. In order to properly collaborate with existing GUI APIs, the strategy for organizing the program statements should be based on specifying user actions that cause changes to the application state.

Now that we understand how to organize the statements of our program, let's examine strategies for organizing functional modules of our solution.

19.3   The Modelview-Controller Architecture

The event-driven ball shooting program presented in Section 19.2.3 and Figure 19.8 addresses programmability and efficiency issues when interacting with a user. In the development of that model, we glossed over many supporting functions (e.g., *UpdateSimulation*()) needed in our solution. In this section, we develop strategies for organizing these functions. Notice that we are not interested in the implementation details of these functions. Instead, we are interested in grouping related functions into components. We then pay attention to how the different *components* collaborate to support the functionality of our application.

In this way, we derive a framework that is suitable for implementing general interactive graphics applications. With a proper framework guiding our design and implementation, we will be better equipped to develop programs that are easier to understand, maintain, modify, and expand.

19.3.1 The Modelview-Controller Framework

Based on our experience developing solutions in Section 19.2, we understand that *interactive graphics applications* can be described as applications that allow users to interactively update their internal states. These applications provide real-time visualization of their internal states (e.g., the free-falling balls) with computer graphics (e.g., drawing circles). The *modelview-controller (MVC)* framework provides a convenient structure for discussing this type of application. In the MVC framework, the *model* is the application state, the *view* is responsible for setting up support for the model to present itself to the user, and the *controller* is responsible for providing the support for the user to interact with the model. Within this framework, our solution from Figure 19.8 is simply the implementation of a controller. In this section, we will develop the understanding of the other two components in the MVC framework and how these components collaborate to support interactive graphics applications.

Figure 19.10 shows the details of a MVC framework to describe the behavior of a typical interactive graphics application. We continue to use the ball shooting program as our example to illustrate the details of the components. The top-right rectangular box is the model, the bottom-right rectangular box is the view, and the rectangular box on the left is the controller component. These three boxes represent program code we, as application developers, must develop. The two dotted rounded boxes represent external graphics and GUI APIs. These are *the external libraries* that we will use as a base for building our system. Examples of popular Graphics APIs include OpenGL, Microsoft Direct-3D (D3D), Java 3D, among others. As mentioned in Section 19.2.2, examples of popular GUI APIs include GLUT, FLTK, MFC, and Java Swing Library.

The model component defines the persistent application state (e.g., AllWorld-Balls, HeroBalls, etc.) and implements interface functions for this application state (e.g., *UpdateSimulation*()). Since we are working with a "graphics" application, we expect graphical primitives to be part of the representation for the application state (e.g., CirclePrimitives). This fact is represented in Figure 19.10 by the application state (the ellipse) partially covering the Graphics API box. In the rest of this section, we will use the terms model and persistent application state interchangeably.

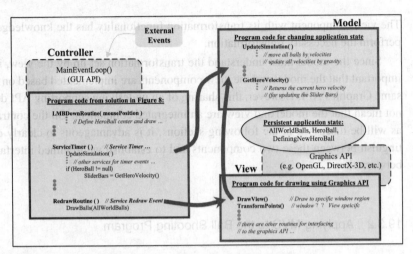

Figure 19.10. Components of an interactive graphics application.

The view component is in charge of *drawing* to the *drawing area* on the application window (e.g., drawing the free falling balls). More specifically, the view component is responsible for initializing the graphics API transformation such that drawing of the model's graphical primitives will appear in the appropriate drawing area. The arrow from the view to the model component signifies that the actual application state redraw must be performed by the model component. Only the model component knows the details of the entire application state (e.g., size and location of the free falling circles) so only the model component can redraw the entire application. The view component is also responsible for transforming user mouse click positions to a coordinate system that the model understands (e.g., mouse button clicks for dragging out the hero ball).

The top left *external events* arrow in Figure 19.10 shows that all external events are handled by the *MainEventLoop()*. The relevant events will be forwarded to the event service routines in the controller component. Since the controller component is responsible for interacting with the user, the design is typically based on event-driven programming techniques. The solution presented in Section 19.2.3 and Figure 19.8 is an example of a controller component implementation. The arrow from the controller to the model indicates that most external events eventually change the model component (e.g., creating a new HeroBall or changing the current HeroBall velocity). The arrow from the controller to the view component indicates that the user input point transformation is handled by the view component. Controllers typically return mouse click positions in the device coordinate with the origin at the top-left corner. In the application model, it is more convenient for us to work with a coordinate system with a lower-left origin.

The view component with its transformation functionality has the knowledge to perform the necessary transformation.

Since the model must understand the transformation set up by the view, it is important that the model and the view components are implemented based on the same Graphics API. However, this sharing of an underlying supporting API does not mean that the model and view are an integrated component. On the contrary, as will be discussed in the following sections, it is advantageous to clearly distinguish between these two components and to establish well-defined interfaces between them.

19.3.2   Applying MVC to the Ball Shooting Program

With the described MVC framework and the understanding of how responsibilities are shared among the components, we can now extend the solution presented in Figure 19.8 and complete the design of the ball shooting program.

The Model

The model is the application state and thus this is the core of our program. When describing approaches to designing an event-driven program in Section 19.2.3, the first two points mentioned were:

1. define the application state, and

2. describe how a user changes this application state.

These two points are the guidelines for designing the model component. In an object-oriented environment, the model component can be implemented as classes, and *state of the application* can be implemented as instance variables, with "*how a user changes this application state*" implemented as methods of the classes.

Figure 19.11 shows that the instance variables representing the state are typically private to the model component. As expected, we have a "very graphical" application state. To properly support this state, we define the CirclePrimitive class based on the underlying graphics API. The CirclePrimitive class supports the definition of center, radius, drawing, and moving of the circle, etc. Figure 19.11 also shows the four categories of methods that a typical model component must support.

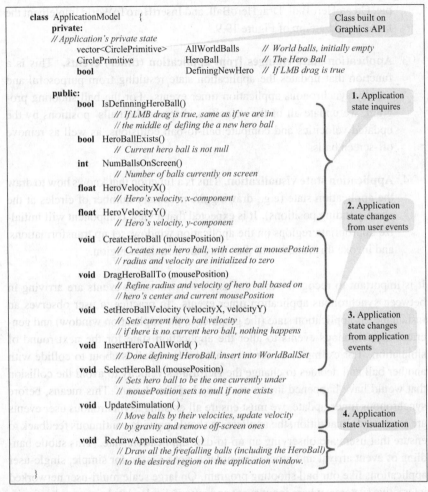

```
class ApplicationModel    {                              Class built on
      private:                                           Graphics API
      // Application's private state
            vector<CirclePrimitive>    AllWorldBalls    // World balls, initially empty
            CirclePrimitive            HeroBall          // The Hero Ball
            bool                       DefiningNewHero   // If LMB drag is true

      public:                                                1. Application
            bool    IsDefinningHeroBall()                        state inquires
                    // If LMB drag is true, same as if we are in
                    // the middle of defing the a new hero ball

            bool    HeroBallExists()
                    // Current hero ball is not null

            int     NumBallsOnScreen()
                    // Number of balls currently on screen

            float   HeroVelocityX()
                    // Hero's velocity, x-component

            float   HeroVelocityY()                          2. Application
                    // Hero's velocity, y-component             state changes
                                                               from user events
            void    CreateHeroBall (mousePosition)
                    // Creates new hero ball, with center at mousePosition
                    // radius and velocity are initialized to zero

            void    DragHeroBallTo (mousePosition)
                    // Refine radius and velocity of hero ball based on
                    // hero's center and current mousePosition

            void    SetHeroBallVelocity (velocityX, velocityY)   3. Application
                    // Sets current hero ball velocity               state changes
                    // if there is no current hero ball, nothing happens  from application
                                                                    events
            void    InsertHeroToAllWorld( )
                    // Done defining HeroBall, insert into WorldBallSet

            void    SelectHeroBall (mousePosition)
                    // Sets hero ball to be the one currently under
                    // mousePosition sets to null if none exists

            void    UpdateSimulation( )
                    // Move balls by their velocities, update velocity   4. Application
                    // by gravity and remove off-screen ones              state visualization

            void    RedrawApplicationState( )
                    // Draw all the freefalling balls (including the HeroBall)
                    // to the desired region on the application window.
}
```

Figure 19.11. The model component of the ball shooting program.

1. **Application state inquiries.** These are functions that return the application state. These functions are important for maintaining up-to-date GUI elements (e.g., status echo or velocity slider bars).

2. **Application state changes from user events.** These are functions that change the application state according to a user's input actions. Notice that the function names should reflect the functionality (e.g., CreateHeroBall) and not the user event actions (e.g., ServiceLMBDown). It is common for a group of functions to support a defined finite state transition. For exam-

ple, CreateHeroBall, DragHeroBall, and InsertHeroToWorld implement the finite state diagram of Figure 19.9.

3. **Application state changes from application (timer) events.** This is a function that updates the application state resulting from purposeful and usually synchronous application timer events. For the ball shooting program, we update all of the velocities, displace the balls' positions by the updated velocities and compute ball-to-ball collisions, as well as remove off-screen balls.

4. **Application state visualization.** This is a function that knows how to draw the application state (e.g., drawing the necessary number of circles at the corresponding positions). It is expected that a view component will initialize appropriate regions on the application window, set up transformations, and invoke this function to draw into the initialized region.

It is important to recognize that the user's asynchronous events are arriving in between synchronous application timer events. In practice, a user observes an instantaneous application state (the graphics in the application window) and generates asynchronous events to alter the application state for the next round of simulation. For example, a user sees that the HeroBall is about to collide with another ball and decides to change the HeroBall's velocity to avoid the collision that would have happened in the next round of simulation. This means, before synchronous timer update, we must ensure all existing asynchronous user events are processed. In addition, the application should provide continuous feedback to ensure that users are observing an up-to-date application state. This subtle handling of event arrival and processing order is not an issue for simple, single-user applications like our ball shooting program. On large scale multi-user networked interactive systems, where input event and output display latencies may be significant, the *UpdateSimulation*() function is often divided into pre-update, update, and post-update.

The View

Figure 19.12 shows the ApplicationView class supporting the two main functionalities of a view component: coordinate space transformation and initialization for redraw. As discussed earlier, the controller is responsible for calling the *DeviceToWorldXform*() to communicate user input points to the model component. The viewport class is introduced to encapsulate the highly API-dependent device initialization and transformation procedures.

```
class Viewport {
        private:
            // An area on application window for drawing.
            // Actual implemenation of the viewport is GraphicsAPI dependent.
        public:
            void        EraseViewport()
                        // Erase the area on the application window
            void        ActivateViewportForDrawing()
                        // All subsequent Graphics API draw commands
                        // will show up on this viewport
}
class ApplicationView {
        private:
        // a view's private state information
        Viewport    TargetDrawArea
                    // An area of the application main window that
                    // this view will be drawing to
        public:
            void        DeviceToWorldXform( inputDevicePoint, outputModelPoint)
                        // transform the input device coordinate point to
                        // output point in a coordinate system that the model understands

            void        DrawView( ApplicationModel TheModel)
                        // Erase and activate the TargetDrawArea and then
                        // Sets up transformation for TheModel
                        // calls TheModel.DrawApplicationState() to draw all the balls.
}
```

Figure 19.12.   The view component of the ball shooting program.

The Controllers

We can improve the solution of Figure 19.8 to better support the specified functionality of the ball shooting program. Recall that the application window depicted in Figure 19.2 has two distinct regions for interpreting events: the upper
application drawing area where mouse button events are associated with defin-
ing/selecting the HeroBall and the lower GUI element area where mouse button
events on the GUI elements have different meanings (e.g., mouse button events
on the slider bars generate SliderBarChange events, etc.). We also notice that the
upper application drawing area is the exact same area where the ApplicationView
must direct the drawings of the ApplicationModel state.

Figure 19.13 introduces two types of controller classes: a *ViewController* and
a *GenericController*. Each controller class is dedicated to receiving input events
from the corresponding region on the application window. The ViewController
creates an ApplicationView during initialization such that the view can be tightly
paired for drawing of the ApplicationModel state in the same area. In addition,
the ViewController class also defines the appropriate mouse event service routines
to support the interaction with the HeroBall. The GenericController is meant to
contain GUI elements for interacting with the application state.

```
        class ViewController {
            private:
                ApplicationModel      TheModel = null        // Reference to the application state
                ApplicationView       TheView = null         // for drawing to the desirable region
            public:
                void InitializeController(ApplicationMode aModel, anArea) {
                    // Define and initialize the Application State
                    TheModel = aModel
                    TheView = new ApplicationView( anArea )

                    // Register Event Service Routines
                    GUISystem::RegisterServiceRoutine(GUISystem:: LMBDown, LMBDownRoutine)
                    GUISystem::RegisterServiceRoutine(GUISystem:: LMBDrag, LMBDragRoutine)
                    GUISystem::RegisterServiceRoutine(GUISystem:: LMBUp, LMBUpRoutine)
                    GUISystem::RegisterServiceRoutine(GUISystem:: RMBDown, RMBDownRoutine)
                    GUISystem::RegisterServiceRoutine(GUISystem:: RedrawEvent, RedrawRoutine)
                }

                // Event Service Routines
                // ... define the 5 event routines similar to the ones in Figure 8 ...
        }
        class GenericController {
            private:
                ApplicationModel      TheModel = null        // Reference to the application state
            public:
                void InitializeController(ApplicationModel aModel, anArea) {
                    TheModel = aModel

                    // Register Event Service Routines
                    GUISystem::RegisterServiceRoutine(GUISystem:: SliderBar, SliderBarRoutine)
                    GUISystem::DefineTimerPeriod(SimulationUpdateInterval)
                    GUISystem::RegisterServiceRoutine(GUISystem:: TimerEvent, ServiceTimer)
                }

                // Event Service Routines
                // ... define the 2 event routines similar to the ones in Figure 8 ...
        }
        //
        // GUI API: MainEventLoop will call this function to initialize our applicaiton
        SystemInitialization() {
            ApplicationModel aModel = new ApplicationModel();
            ViewController    aViewController = new ViewController()
            GenericController aGenericController = new GenericController()

            aViewController.InitializeController(aModel,  drawingAreaOfWindow)
            aGenericController.InitializeController(aModel, uiAreaOfWindow)
        }
```

Figure 19.13. The controller component of the ball shooting program.

The bottom of Figure 19.13 illustrates that the GUI API MainEventLoop will still call the *SystemInitialization*() function to initialize the application. In this case, we create one instance each of ViewController and GenericController. The ViewController is initialized to monitor mouse button events in the drawing area of the application window (e.g., LMB click to define HeroBall), while the GenericController is initialized to monitor the GUI element state changes (e.g., LMB dragging of a slider bar). Notice that the service of the timer event is global to the entire application and should be defined in only one of the controllers (either one will do).

In practice, the GUI API MainEventLoop *dispatches* events to the controllers based on the *context of the event*. The context of an event is typically defined by the location of the mouse pointer or the current *focus* of the GUI element (i.e., which element is active). The application is responsible for creating a controller for any region on the window that it will receive events directly from the GUI API.

19.3.3   Using the MVC to Expand the Ball Shooting Program

One interesting characteristic of the MVC solution presented in Section 19.3.2 is that the model component does not have any knowledge of the view or the controller components. This clean interface allows us to expand our solution by inserting additional view/controller pairs.

For example, Figure 19.14 shows an extension to the ball shooting program given in Figure 19.2. It has an additional small view in the UI (user interface) area next to the quit button. The small view is exactly the same as the *original large view*, except that it covers a smaller area on the application window.

Figure 19.15 shows that, with our MVC solution design, we can implement the small view by creating a new instance of ViewController (an additional ApplicaitonView will be created by the ViewController) for the desired application window area. Notice that the GenericController's window area actually contains

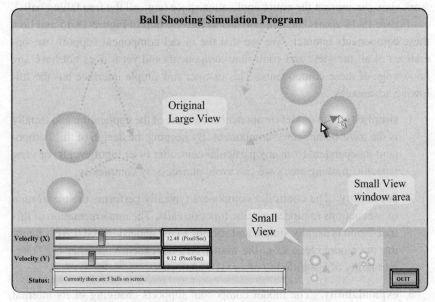

Figure 19.14. The ball shooting program with large and small views.

```
//
// GUI API: MainEventLoop will call this function to initialize our applicaiton
SystemInitialization() {
    ApplicationModel  aModel = new ApplicationModel();
    ViewController     aLargeViewController = new ViewController()
    GenericController  aGenericController = new GenericController()

    aLargeViewController.InitializeController(aModel,  drawingAreaOfWindow)
    aGenericController.InitializeController(aModel, uiAreaOfWindow)

    ViewController aSmallViewController = new ViewController()
    aSmallViewController.InitializeController(aModel,  smallViewDrawingArea)
}
```

New instance of
ViewController (and
ApplicationView)

Figure 19.15. Implementing the small view for the ball shooting program.

the area of the small ViewController. When a user event is triggered in this area, the "top-layer" controller (the visible one) will receive the event. After the initialization, the new small view will behave in exactly the same manner as the original large view.

For simplicity, Figure 19.14 shows two identical view/controller pairs. In general, a new view/controller pair is created to present a different visualization of the application state. For example, with slight modifications to the view component's transformation functionality, the large view of Figure 19.14 can be configured into a *zoom view* and the small view can be configured into a *work view*, where the zoom view can zoom into different regions (e.g., around the HeroBall) and the work view can present the entire application space (e.g., all the free falling balls).

Figure 19.16 shows the components of the solution in Figure 19.15 and how these components interact. We see that the model component supports the operations of all the view and controller components and yet it does not have any knowledge of these components. This distinct and simple interface has the following advantages:

1. **simplicity.** The model component is the core of the application and usually is the most complicated component. By keeping the design of this component independent from any particular controller (user input/events) or view (specific drawing area), we can avoid unnecessary complexity.

2. **portability.** The controller component typically performs the *translation* of user actions to model-specific function calls. The implementation of this translation is usually simple and specific to the underlying GUI API. Keeping the model clean from the highly API-dependent controller facilitates portability of a solution to other GUI platforms.

3. **expandability.** The model component supports changing of its internal state and understands how to draw its contents. As we have seen (Fig-

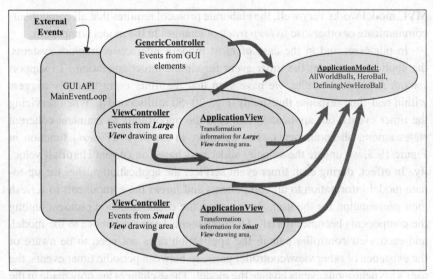

Figure 19.16. Components of the ball shooting program with small view.

ures 19.15 and 19.16), this means that it is straightforward to add new view/controller pairs to increase the interactivity of the application.

19.3.4 Interaction among the MVC Components

The MVC framework is a tool for describing general interactive systems. One of the beauties of the framework is that it is straightforward to support multiple view/controller pairs. Each view/controller pair shares responsibilities in exactly the same way: the view *presents* the model and the controller allows the events (user-generated or otherwise) to change the model component.

For an application with multiple view/controller pairs, like the one depicted in Figure 19.16, we see that a user can change the model component via any of the three controllers. In addition, the application itself is also capable of changing the model state. All components must however, ensure that a coherent and up-to-date presentation is maintained for the user. For example, when a user drags out a new HeroBall, both the large and small view components must display the dragging of the ball, while the GenericController component must ensure that the slider bars properly echo the implicitly defined HeroBall velocity. In the classical MVC model, the coherency among different components is maintained with an elaborate protocol (e.g., via the observer design pattern). Although the classical

MVC model works very well, the elaborate protocol requires that all components communicate or otherwise to *keep track* of changes in the model component.

In our case, and in the case of most modern interactive graphics systems, the application defines the timer event for simulation computation. To support *smooth* simulation results, we have seen that the timer event typically triggers within real-time response thresholds (e.g., 20–50 milliseconds). When servicing the timer events, our application can take the opportunity to maintain coherent states among all components. For example, in the *ServiceTimer*() function in Figure 19.8, we update the velocity slider bars based on current HeroBall velocity. In effect, during each timer event service, the application *pushes* the up-to-date model information to all components and *forces* the components to refresh their presentation for the user. In this way, the communication protocol among the components becomes trivial. All components keep a reference to the model, and each view/controller pair in the application does not need to be aware of the existence of other view/controller pairs. In between periodic timer events, the user's asynchronous events change the model. These changes are only made in the model component, and no other components in the application need to be aware of the changes. During the periodic timer service, besides computing the model's simulation update, all components poll the model for up-to-date state information. For example, when the user clicks and drags with the left mouse button pressed, a new HeroBall will be defined in the model component. During this time, the large and small view components will not display the new HeroBall, and the velocity slider bars will not show the new HeroBall's velocity. These components will get and display up-to-date HeroBall information only during the application timer event servicing. Since the timer event is triggered more than 30 times per second, the user will observe a smooth and up-to-date application state in all components at all times.

19.3.5   Applying the MVC Concept

The MVC framework is applicable to general interactive systems. As we have seen in this section, interactive systems with the MVC framework result in clearly defined component behaviors. In addition, with clearly defined interfaces among the components, it becomes straightforward to expand the system with additional view/controller pairs.

An *interactive system* does not need to be an elaborate software application. For example, the slider bar is a fully functional interactive system. The model component contains a current *value* (typically a floating point number), the view component presents this value to the user, and the controller allows the user to interactively change this value. A typical view component draws rectangular icons (bar and knobs) representing the current value in the model component, while the controller component typically supports mouse down and drag events to interactively change the value in the model component. With this understanding, it becomes straightforward to expand the system with additional view/controller pairs. For example, in our ball shooting program, the slider bars have an additional view component where the numeric value of the model is displayed. In this case, there is no complementary controller component defined for the numeric view; an example complementary controller would allow the user to type in numeric values.

19.4 Example Implementations

Figure 19.17 shows two implementations of the solution presented in Section 19.3.3. The version on the left is based on OpenGL and FLTK, while the version to the right is based on D3D and MFC. In this section, we present the details of these two implementations. The lessons we want to learn are that (a) a proper MVC solution framework should be independent from any implementation and (b) a well designed implementation should be realizable based on and/or easily ported to any suitable API.

Before examining the details of each implementation, we will develop some understanding for working with modern GUI and graphics APIs.

19.4.1 Working with GUI APIs

Building the graphical user interface (GUI) of an application involves two distinct steps. The first step is to *design the layout* of the user interface system. In this step, an application developer places GUI elements (e.g., buttons, slider bars, etc.)

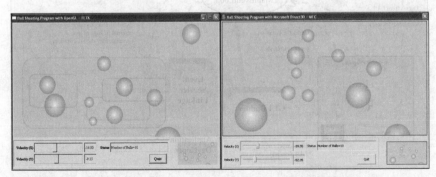

Figure 19.17. Ball shooting programs with OpenGL+FLTK and D3D+MFC.

in an area that represents the application window. The GUI elements are typically two-dimensional graphical artifacts (e.g., a 3D looking icon representing a slider bar). The goal of this first step is to arrange these graphical artifacts to achieve user friendliness and maximum usability (e.g., what is the best place/color/size for the slider bar, etc.). The second step in building a GUI for an application is to *semantically link* the GUI elements to the functionality of the application (e.g., update HeroBall velocity when the slider bar is dragged). In this step, an application developer builds the code for the necessary functionality (e.g., code for changing HeroBall velocity) and *registers* this code with the on-screen graphical artifacts (e.g., the slider bar). This is precisely the *event service registration* described in Section 19.2.2.

Modern GUI APIs support the building of a graphical user interface with a *GUI builder*. A GUI builder is an interactive graphical editor that allows its user to interactively place and manipulate the appearances of GUI elements. In addition, the GUI builder assists the application developer to compose or generate service routines and links those service routines to the events generated by the GUI elements.

Figure 19.18 illustrates the mechanism by which the GUI builder (in the middle of the figure) links the graphical user interface front-end (left side of the the figure) to the user-developed program code (right side of the figure). The patterned ellipse, the GUI Builder, is shown in the middle of Figure 19.18 The arrow pointing left towards the application (*A Simple Program*) indicates that the application developer works with the GUI builder to design the layout of the application (e.g., where to place the button or the status echo area). The arrows pointing from the GUI builder toward the *MainEventLoop* and *Event Service Linkage* mod-

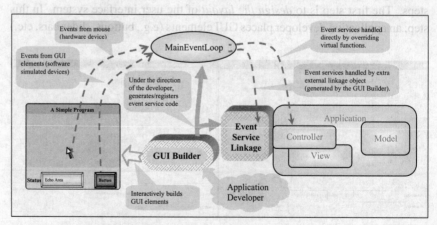

Figure 19.18. Working with a GUI API.

ules indicate that the GUI builder is capable of generating programming code to register event services. In Figure 19.18, there are two dotted connections between the mouse and the button GUI element through the MainEventLoop module to the event service linkage and the application controller modules. These two connections represent the two different mechanisms with which GUI APIs support event services:

1. **External Service Linkage.** Some GUI builders generate extra program modules (e.g., in the form of source code files) with code fragments supplied by the application developer to semantically link the GUI elements to the application functionality. For example, when the "button" of "A Simple Program" is clicked, the GUI builder ensures that a function in the "Event Service Linkage" module will be called. It is the application developer's responsibility to insert code fragments into this function to implement the required action.

2. **Internal Direct Code Modification.** Some GUI builders insert linkage programming code directly into the application source code. For example, the GUI builder modifies the source code of the application's controller class and inserts a new function to be called when the "button" of "A Simple Program" is clicked. Notice that the GUI Builder only inserts an empty function; the application developer is still responsible for filling in the details of this new function.

The advantage of an external service linkage mechanism is that the GUI builder only has minimal knowledge of the application source code. This provides a simple and flexible development environment where the developer is free to organize the source code structure, variable names, etc., in any appropriate way. However, the externally generated programming module implies a loosely integrated environment. For example, to modify the "button" behavior of "A Simple Program," the application developer must invoke the GUI builder, modify code fragments, and re-generate the external program module. The Internal Direct Code Modification mechanism in contrast provides a better integrated environment where the GUI builder modifies the application program source code directly. However, to support proper "direct code modification," the GUI builder must have intimate knowledge of, and often places severe constraints on, the application source code system (e.g., source code organization, file names, variable names, etc.).

19.4.2 Working with Graphics APIs

Figure 19.19 illustrates that one way to understand a modern graphics API is by considering the API as a functional interface to the underlying graphics hardware.

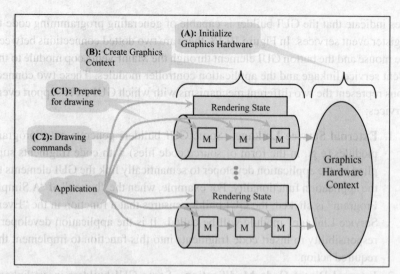

Figure 19.19. Working with a graphics API.

It is convenient to consider this functional interface as consisting of two stages: *Graphics Hardware Context (GHC)* and *Graphics Device Context (GDC)*.

1. **Graphics Hardware Context (GHC).** This stage is depicted as the vertical ellipse on the right of Figure 19.19. We consider the GHC as a configuration which wraps over the hardware video display card. An application creates a GHC for each unique configuration (e.g., depth of frame buffer or z-buffer, etc.) of the hardware video card(s). Many Graphics Device Contexts (see below) can be connected to each GHC to support drawing to multiple on-screen areas from the same application.

2. **Graphics Device Context (GDC).** This stage is depicted as a cylindrical *pipe* in Figure 19.19. The multiple pipes in the figure illustrates that an application can create multiple GDCs to connect to the same GHC. Through each GDC, an application can draw to distinct areas on the application window. To properly support this functionality, each GDC represents a complete *rendering state*. A rendering state encompasses all the information that affects the final appearance of an image. This includes primitive attributes, illumination parameters, coordinate transformations, etc. Examples of primitive attributes are color, size, pattern, etc., while examples of illumination parameters include light position, light color, surface material properties, etc. Graphics APIs typically support coordinate transformation with a series of two or three matrix processors. In Figure 19.19, the "M"

boxes inside the GDC pipes are the matrix processors. Each matrix processor has a transformation matrix and transforms input vertices using this matrix. Since these processors operate in series, together they are capable of implementing multi-stage coordinate space transformations (e.g., object to world, world to eye, and eye to projected space). The application must load these matrix processors with appropriate matrices to implement a desired transformation.

With this understanding, Figure 19.19 illustrates that to work with a graphics API, an application will

(A) **initialize one or more GHCs.** Each GHC represents a unique configuration of the graphics video card(s). In typical cases, one GHC is initialized and configured to be shared by the entire application.

(B) **create one or more GDCs.** Each GDC supports drawing to distinct areas on the application window. For example, an application might create a GDC for each view component in an application.

(C) **draw using a GDC.** An application draws to a desired window area via the corresponding GDC. Referring to Figure 19.19, an application sets the rendering state (C1) and then issues drawing commands to the GDC (C2). Setting of the rendering state involves setting of all relevant primitive and illumination attributes and computing/loading appropriate transformation matrices into the matrix processors. A drawing command is typically a series of vertex positions accompanied by instructions on how to interpret the vertices (e.g., two vertex positions and an instruction that these are end points of a line).

In practice, modern graphics APIs are highly configurable and support many abstract programming modes. For example, Microsoft's Direct3D supports a drawing mode where the matrix processors can be by-passed entirely (e.g., when vertices are pre-transformed).

19.4.3 Implementation Details

Figure 19.20 shows the design of our implementation for the solution presented in Section 19.3.3.[1] Here, the MainUIWindow object represents the entire ball shooting program. This object contains the GUI elements (slider bars, quit button,

---

[1] Source code for this section can be found at http://faculty.washington.edu/ksung/fcg3/ball.tar.zip

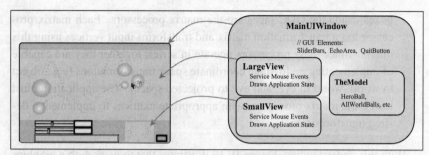

Figure 19.20.   Implementation of the ball shooting program with two views.

etc.), the model (application state), and two instances of view/controller pairs (one each for LargeView and SmallView).

OpenGL with FLTK

Figure 19.21 shows a screen shot of *Fluid*, FLTK's GUI builder, during the construction of the GUI for the ball shooting program. In the lower-right corner of Figure 19.21, we see that (A) Fluid allows an application developer to interactively place graphical representations of GUI elements (3D-looking icons); (B) is an area representing the application window. In addition (C), the application developer can interactively select each GUI element to define its physical appearances (color, shape, size, etc.). In the lower-left corner of Figure 19.21, we see that (D) the application developer has the option to type in program fragments to service events generated by the corresponding GUI element. In this case, we can see that the developer must type in the program fragment for handling the X velocity slider bar events. Notice that this program fragment is separated from

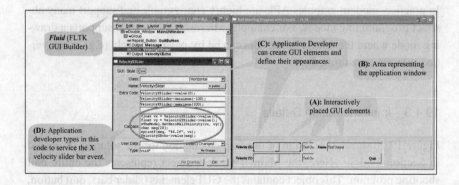

Figure 19.21.   Fluid: FLTK's GUI Builder.

```
    // Forward declaration of mouse event service routines
        void ServiceMouse(int button, int state, int x, int y); // service mouse button click
        void ServiceActiveMouse(int x, int y);              // service mouse drag
class MainUIWindow {
        UserInterface        UI;            // This is Linkage Code generated by Fluid (GUI Builder)
                                            //    This object services events geneated by GUI  elements
        Model               *TheModel;     // The application State (Figure 11)
        FlGlutWindow        *LargeView;    // These are View/Controller pairs that understand graphics
        FlGlutWindow        *SmallView;    //    outputs (GDC) and mouse events (controller)

        MainUIWindow(Model *m)   {                              // The constructor
            TheModel = m;                               // Sets the model ...
            LargeView = new FlGlutWindow(TheModel);     // Create LargeView
            LargeView->mouse = ServiceMouse;            // callback functions for service mouse events
            LargeView->motion = ServiceActiveMouse;
            // Create SmallView ... exactly the same as LargeView (not shown)
            glutTimeFunc( // set up timer and services )      // Set up timer ...
        }
};
```

Figure 19.22.   MainUIWindow based on OpenGL and FLTK.

the rest of the program source code system and is associated with Fluid (the GUI builder). At the conclusion of the GUI layout design, Fluid generates new source code files to be included with the rest of the application development environment. Since these source code files are controlled and generated by the GUI builder, the application developer must invoke the GUI builder in order to update/maintain the event service routines. In this way, FLTK implements external service linkage as described in Section 19.4.1. In our implementation, we instruct *Fluid* to create a *UserInterface* class (.h and .cpp files) for the integration with the rest of our application development environment.

Figure 19.22 shows the *MainUIWindow* implementation with OpenGL and FLTK. In this case, graphics operations are performed through OpenGL and user interface operations are supported by FLTK. As described, the *UserInterface* object in the MainUIWindow is created by Fluid for servicing GUI events. The Model is the application state as detailed in Figure 19.11. The two FlGlutWindow objects are based on a predefined FLTK class designed specifically for supporting drawing with OpenGL. The constructor of MainUIWindow shows that the mouse event services are registered via a callback mechanism. As discussed in Section 19.2.4, the FLTK (Fast Light ToolKit) is an example of a light weight GUI API. Here, we see examples of using callback as a registration mechanism for receiving user events.

FlGlutWindow is a FLTK pre-defined Fl_Glut_Window class object (see Figure 19.23) designed specifically to support drawing with OpenGL. Each instance of a FlGlutWindow object is a combination of a controller (e.g., to receive mouse events) and a Graphics Device Context (GDC). We see that the *draw*() function

```
// Fl_Glut_Window is a pure virtual class supplied by FLTK specifically for supporting
// windows with OpenGL output and for receiving mouse events.
class FlGlutWindow : public Fl_Glut_Window {
  FlGlutWindow(Model *m);                    // Constructor
  Model      *TheModel;                      // The application state: initialized during construction time.
  float      WorldWidth, WorldHeight;        // World Space Dimension

  void HardwareToWorldPoint(int hwX, int hwY, float &wcX, float &wcY);
                                 // Transform mouse clicks (hwX, hwY) to World Cooridnate (wcX, wcY)

  virtual void draw() {                          // virtual function from Fl_Glut_Window for drawing
    glClearColor( 0.8f, 0.8f, 0.95f, 0.0f );
    glClear(GL_COLOR_BUFFER_BIT);               // Clearing the background color
    glMatrixMode(GL_PROJECTION);                // Programming the OpenGL's GL_PROJECTION
      glLoadIdentity();                         //     Matrix Processor to the propoer transfrotm
      gluOrtho2D(0.0f, WorldWidth, 0.0f, WorldHeight);
    TheModel->DrawApplicaitonState();           // Drawing of the application state
  }
};
```

Figure 19.23. FlGlutWindow: OpenGL/FLTK view/controller pair.

first sets the rendering state (e.g., clear color and matrix values), including computing and programming the matrix processor (e.g., GL_PROJECTION), before calling TheModel to re-draw the application state.

Direct3D with MFC

Figure 19.24 shows a screen shot of the MFC resource editor, MFC's GUI builder, during the construction of the ball shooting program. Similar to Fluid (Figure 19.21), in the middle of Figure 19.24, (A) we see that the resource editor

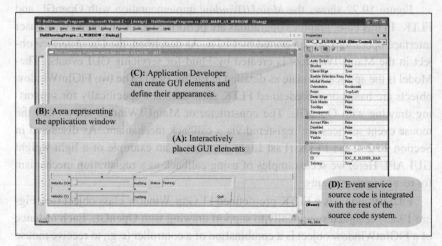

Figure 19.24. The MFC resource editor.

```
class MainUIWindow : public CDialog {
       Model            *TheModel;       // The application State (Figure 11)
       LPDIRECT3D9       TheGHC;         // This is the Graphics Hardware Context
       CWndD3D           *LargeView;     // These are View/Controller pairs that understand drawing
       CWndD3D           *SmallView;     //     with D3D (GDC) and UI element events (controller)

       CSliderCtrl       XSlider, YSlider;   // These are the GUI  elements
       CStringEcho       StatusEcho;

       void      OnTimer();              // Override the Timer service function
       void      OnHScroll( ...);        // Override the Scroll bar service function
};
```

Figure 19.25. MainUIWindow based on Microsoft Direct3D and MFC.

also supports interactive designing of the GUI element layout in (B), an area representing the application window. Although the GUI builder interfaces operate differently, we observe that in (C), the MFC resource editor also supports the definition/modification of the physical appearance of GUI elements. However, unlike Fluid, the MFC resource editor is tightly integrated with the rest of the development environment. In this case, a developer can register for event services by inheriting or overriding appropriate service routines. The MFC resource editor automatically inserts code fragments into the application source code system. To support this functionality, the application source code organization is governed/shared with the GUI builder; the application developer is not entirely free to rename files/classes and/or to re-organize implementation source code file system structure. MFC implements internal direct code modification for event service linkage, as described in Section 19.4.1.

Figure 19.25 shows the *MainUIWindow* implementation with Direct3D and MFC. In this implementation, graphics operations are performed through Direct3D while user interface operations are supported by MFC. Once again, TheModel is the application state as detailed in Figure 19.11. *LPDIRECT3D9* is the Graphics Hardware Context (GHC) interface object. This object is created and initialized in the MainUIWindow constructor (not shown here). The two CWndD3D objects are defined to support drawing with Direct3D. We notice that one major difference between Figure 19.25 and Figure 19.22 is in the GUI element support. In Figure 19.25, we see that the GUI element objects (e.g., XSlider) and the corresponding service routines (e.g., OnHScroll()) are integrated into the MainUIWindow object. This is in contrast to the solution shown in Figure 19.22 where GUI elements are grouped into a separate object (e.g., the UserInterface object) with callback event service registrations. As discussed in Section 19.2.4, MFC is an example of a large commercial GUI API, where many event services are registered based on object-oriented function overrides (e.g., the OnHScroll() and OnTimer() functions).

```
// CWnd is the MFC base class for all window objects. Here we subclass to create a D3D output
// window by including a D3D Graphics Device Context.
class CWndD3D: public CWnd {
    LPDIRECT3DDEVICE9  D3DDevice;       // This is the D3D Graphics Device Context (GDC)
    Model             *TheModel;        // The application state
    void InitD3D(LPDIRECT3D9);          // Create D3DDevice (GDC) to connect to GHC

    void RedrawView()    {              // Draws the Application State
            // Compute world coordinate to device transform
            D3DMATRIX transform = ComputeTransformation();
            D3DDevice->SetTransform(D3DTS_WORLD, &transform);
                // Programming the D3D_WORLD matrix with the computed transform matrix

            D3DDevice->Clear( bgColor, D3DCLEAR_TARGET);
            D3DDevice->BeginScene();
                TheModel->DrawApplicationState(D3DDevice);
            D3DDevice->EndScene();
            D3DDevice->Present();
    }

    void HardwareToWorldPoint(CPoint hwPt, float &wcX, float &wcY);
                // Transform mouse clicks (hwPt) to world coordinate (wcX, wcY)

    void OnLButtonDown(CPoint hwPt);  // Override mouse button/drag service functions
        ⋮
};
```

Figure 19.26. CWndD3D: Direct3D/MFC view/controller pair.

CWndD3D is a sub-class of the MFC CWnd class (see Figure 19.26). CWnd is the base class designed for a generic MFC window. By sub-classing from this base class, CWndD3D can support all default window-related events (e.g., mouse events). The *LPDIRECT3DDEVICE*9 object is the D3D Graphics Device Context (GDC) interface object. The *InitD3D*() function creates and initializes the GDC object and connects this object to the *LPDIRECT3D*9 (GHC). In this way, a CWndD3D sub-class is a basic view/controller pair: it supports the view functionality with drawing via the D3D GDC and controller functionality with input via MFC. The *RedrawView*() function is similar to the *draw*() function of Figure 19.23 where we first set up the rendering state (e.g., bgColor and matrix), including programming the matrix processor (e.g., *D3DTS_WORLD*), before calling the model to draw itself.

In conclusion, we see that Figure 19.20 represents an implementation of the solution presented in Section 19.3.3 while Section 19.4.3 presented two versions of the implementation for Figure 19.20. Although the GUI Builder, event service registration, and actual API function calls are very different, the final programming source code structures are remarkably similar. In fact, the two versions share the exact same source code files for the *Model* class. In addition, although the drawing functions for *CirclePrimitive* are different for OpenGL and D3D, we were able to share the source code files for the rest of the primitive behaviors (e.g., set center/radius, travel with velocity, collide, etc.). We reaffirm our assertion that software framework, solution structures, and event implementations should be designed independent of any APIs.

19.5   Applying Our Results

We have seen that the event-driven programming model is well suited for designing and implementing programs that interact with users. In addition, we have seen that the modelview-controller framework is a convenient and powerful structure for organizing functional modules in an interactive graphics application. In developing a solution to the ball shooting program, we have demonstrated that knowledge from event-driven programming helps us design the controller component (e.g., handling of mouse events, etc.), computer graphics knowledge helps us design the view component (e.g., transformation and drawing of circles, etc.), while the model component is highly dependent upon the specific application (e.g., free falling and colliding circles). Our discussion so far has been based on a very simple example. We will now explore the applicability of the MVC framework and its implementation in real-world applications.

19.5.1   Example 1: PowerPoint

Figure 19.27 shows how we can apply our knowledge in analyzing and gaining insights into Microsoft PowerPoint,[2] a popular interactive graphics application. A screen shot of a slide creation session using the PowerPoint application is shown at the left of Figure 19.27. The right side of Figure 19.27 shows how we can apply the implementation framework to gain insights into the PowerPoint application. The MainUIWindow at the right of Figure 19.27 is the GUI window of the entire application, and it contains the GUI elements that affect/echo the entire application state (e.g., main menu, status area, etc.). We can consider the MainUI-Window as the module that contains TheModel component and includes the four view/controller pairs.

Recall that TheModel is the state of the application and that this component contains all the data that the user interactively creates. In the case of PowerPoint, the user creates a collection of presentation slides, and thus TheModel contains all the information about these slides (e.g. layout design style, content of the slides,

---

[2]Powerpoint is a registered trademark of Microsoft.

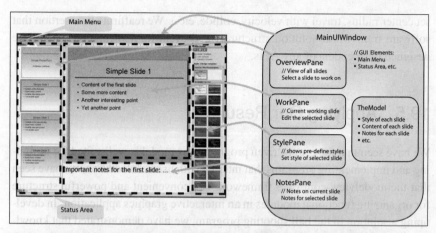

Figure 19.27. Understanding PowerPoint using the MVC implementation framework.

notes associated with each slide, etc.). With this understanding of TheModel component, the rest of the application can be considered as a convenient tool for presenting TheModel (the view) to the user and changing TheModel (the controller) by the user. In this way, these convenient tools are precisely the view/controller pairs (e.g., ViewController components from Figure 19.16).

In Figure 19.27, each of the four view/controller pairs (i.e., OverviewPane, WorkPane, StylePane, and NotesPane) presents, and supports changing of different aspects of TheModel component:

- **OverviewPane.** The view component displays multiple consecutive slides from all the slides that the user has created; the controller component supports user scrolling through all these slides and selecting one for editing.

- **WorkPane.** The view component displays the details of the slide that is currently being edited; the controller supports selecting and editing the content of this slide.

- **StylePane.** The view component displays the layout design of the slide that is currently being edited; the controller supports selecting and defining a new layout design for this slide.

- **NotesPane.** The view component displays the notes that the user has created for the slide that is currently being edited; the controller supports editing of this notes.

As is the case with most modern interactive applications, PowerPoint defines an application timer event to support user-defined animations (e.g., animated se-

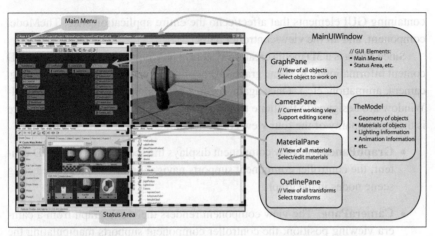

Figure 19.28. Understanding Maya with the MVC implementation framework.

quences between slide transitions). The coherency of the four view/controller pairs can be maintained during the servicing of this application timer event. For example, the user works with the StylePane to change the layout of the current slide in TheModel component. In the meantime, before servicing the next timer event, OverviewPane and WorkPane are not aware of the changes and display an out-of-date design for the current slide. During the servicing of the timer event, the MainUIWindow forces all view/controller pairs to poll TheModel and refresh their contents. As discussed in Section 19.3.4, since the timer events are typically triggered more than 30 times in a second, the user is not be able to detect the brief out-of-date display and observes a consistent display at all times. In this way, the four view/controller pairs only need to keep a reference to TheModel component and do not need to have any knowledge of each other. Thus, it is straightforward to insert and delete view/controller pairs into/from the application.

19.5.2   Example 2: Maya

We now apply our knowledge in analyzing and understanding Maya[3], an inter-active 3D modeling/animation/rendering system. The left side of Figure 19.28 shows a screen shot of Maya in a simple 3D content creation session. As in the case of Figure 19.27, the right side of Figure 19.28 shows how we can apply the implementation framework to gain insights into the Maya application. Once again we see that the MainUIWindow is the GUI window of the entire application

---

[3]Maya is a registered trademark of Alias.

containing GUI elements that affect/echo the entire application state, TheModel component, and all the view/controller pairs.

Since Maya is a 3D media creation system, TheModel component contains 3D content information (e.g. scene graph, 3D geometry, material properties, lighting, camera, animation, etc.). Once again, the rest of the components in the MainUI-Window are designed to facilitate the user's view and to change TheModel. Here is the functionality of the four view/controller pairs:

- **GraphPane.** The view component displays the scene graph of the 3D content; the controller component supports navigating the graph and selecting scene nodes in the graph.

- **CameraPane.** The view component renders the scene graph from a camera viewing position; the controller component supports manipulating the camera view and selecting objects in the scene.

- **MaterialPane.** The view component displays all the defined materials; the controller component supports selecting and editing materials.

- **OutlinePane.** The view component displays all the transform nodes in the scene; the controller component supports manipulating the transforms (e.g. create/change parent-child relationships, etc.).

Once again, the coherency among the different view/controller pairs can be maintained while servicing the application timer events.

We do not speculate that PowerPoint or Maya is implemented according to our framework. These are highly sophisticated commercial applications and the underlying implementation is certainly much more complex. However, based on the knowledge we have gained from this chapter, we can begin to understand how to approach discussing, designing, and building such interactive graphics applications. Remember that the important lesson we want to learn from this chapter is how to organize the functionality of an interactive graphics application into components and understand how the components interact so that we can better understand, maintain, modify, and expand an interactive graphics application.

Notes

I first learned about the model view controller framework and event-driven programming from SmallTalk (Goldberg & Robson, 1989) (You may also want to refer to the SmallTalk web site (http://www.smalltalk.org/main/).) Both *Design Patterns—Elements of Reusable Object-Oriented Design* (Gamma et al., 1995) and *Pattern-Oriented Software Architecture* (Buschmann et al., 1996) are excellent sources for finding out more about design patterns and software architecture frameworks in general. I recommend *3D Game Engine Architecture* (Eberly, 2004) as a good source for discussions on issues relating to implementing real-time graphics systems. I learned MFC and Direct3D mainly by referring to the online Microsoft Developer Network pages (http://msdn.microsoft.com). In addition, I find Prosise's book *Programming Windows with MFC* (Prosise, 1999) to be very helpful. I refer to the *OpenGL Programming Guide* (Shreiner et al., 2004), *Reference Manual* (Shreiner, 2004), and FLTK on-line help (http://www.fltk.org/) when developing my OpenGL/FLTK programs.

Exercises

1. Here is the specification for dragging out a line:

   - Left mouse button (LMB) clicks define the center of the line.

   - LMB drags out a line such that the line extends in two directions. The first direction extends from the center (LMB click) position toward the current mouse position. The second direction extends in the opposite direction from the first with exactly the same length.

   - Right mouse button (RMB) click-drag moves the line such that the center of the line follows the current mouse position.

   (a) Follow the steps outlined in Section 19.2.3 and design an event-driven programming solution for this specification.

   (b) Implement your design with FLTK and OpenGL.

   (c) Implement your design with MFC and Direct-3D.

   Notice that in this case the useful application internal state information (the center position of the line) and the drawing presentation requirements (end points of the line) do not coincide exactly. When defining the application state, we should pay attention to what is the most important and convenient information to store in order to support the specified functionality.

2. For the line defined in Exercise 1, define a velocity that is the same as the slope of the line: once created, the line will travel along the direction defined by its slope. Use the length of the line as the speed. (Note that longer lines travel faster than shorter lines).

3. Here is the specification for dragging out a rectangle:

   - LMB click defines the center of the rectangle.
   - LMB drag out a rectangle such that the rectangle extends from the center position and one of the corner positions of the rectangle always follows the current mouse position.
   - RMB click-drag moves the rectangle such that the center of the rectangle follows the current mouse position.

   (a) Follow the steps outlined in Section 19.2.3 and design an event-driven programming solution for this specification.

   (b) Implement your design with FLTK and OpenGL.

   (c) Implement your design with MFC and Direct-3D.

4. For the rectangle in Exercise 3:

   (a) Support the definition of a velocity similar to that of HeroBall velocity in Section 19.1: once created, the rectangle will travel along a direction that is the vector defined from its center towards the LMB release position.

   (b) Design and implement collision between two rectangles (this is a simple 2D bound intersection check).

5. With results from Exercise 4, we can approximate a simple Pong game:

   - The paddles are rectangles;
   - A pong-ball is drawn as a circle but we will use the bounding square (a square that centers at the center of the circle, with dimension defined by the diameter of the circle) to approximate collision with the paddle.

   Design and implement a single-player pong-game where a ball (circle) drops under gravitational force and the user must manipulate a paddle to bounce the ball upward to prevent it from dropping below the application window. You should:

   (a) design a specification (similar to that of Section 19.1) for this pong game;

   (b) follow the steps outlined in Section 19.2.3 to design an event-driven programming solution;

   (c) implement your design either with OpenGL or Direct-3D.

6. Extend the ApplicationView in Figure 19.12 to include functionality for setting a world coordinate window bound. The world coordinate window bound defines a rectangular region in the world for displaying in the Viewport. Define a method for setting the world coordinate window bound and modify the *ApplicaitonView::DeviceToWorldXform()* function to support transforming mouse clicks to world coordinate space.

7. Integrate your results from Exercise 6 into the two-view ball shooting program from Figure 19.14 such that the small view can be focused around the current HeroBall. When there is no current HeroBall, the small view should display nothing. When user LMB click-drags, or when user RMB selects a HeroBall, the small view's world coordinate window bound should center at the HeroBall center and include a region that is 1.5 times the HeroBall diameter.

20

Light

In this chapter, we discuss the practical issues of measuring light, usually called *radiometry*. The terms that arise in radiometry may at first seem strange and have terminology and notation that may be hard to keep straight. However, because radiometry is so fundamental to computer graphics, it is worth studying radiometry until it sinks in. This chapter also covers *photometry*, which takes radiometric quantities and scales them to estimate how much "useful" light is present. For example, a green light may seem twice as bright as a blue light of the same power because the eye is more sensitive to green light. Photometry attempts to quantify such distinctions.

20.1 Radiometry

Although we can define radiometric units in many systems, we use *SI* (International System of Units) units. Familiar SI units include the metric units of *meter* (m) and *gram* (g). Light is fundamentally a propagating form of energy, so it is useful to define the SI unit of energy, which is the *joule* (J).

20.1.1 Photons

To aid our intuition, we will describe radiometry in terms of collections of large numbers of *photons*, and this section establishes what is meant by a photon in this context. For the purposes of this chapter, a photon is a quantum of light that has a position, direction of propagation, and a wavelength λ. Somewhat strangely, the SI unit used for wavelength is *nanometer* (nm). This is mainly for historical reasons, and $1\,\text{nm} = 10^{-9}$ m. Another unit, the *angstrom*, is sometimes used, and one nanometer is ten angstroms. A photon also has a speed c that depends only on the refractive index n of the medium through which it propagates. Sometimes the frequency $f = c/\lambda$ is also used for light. This is convenient because unlike λ and c, f does not change when the photon refracts into a medium with a new refractive index. Another invariant measure is the amount of energy q carried by a photon, which is given by the following relationship:

$$q = hf = \frac{hc}{\lambda}, \tag{20.1}$$

where $h = 6.63 \times 10^{-34}\,\text{J}\,\text{s}$ is Plank's Constant. Although these quantities can be measured in any unit system, we will use SI units whenever possible.

20.1.2 Spectral Energy

If we have a large collection of photons, their total energy Q can be computed by summing the energy q_i of each photon. A reasonable question to ask is "How is the energy distributed across wavelengths?" An easy way to answer this is to partition the photons into bins, essentially histogramming them. We then have an energy associated with an interval. For example, we can count all the energy between $\lambda = 500$ nm and $\lambda = 600$ nm and have it turn out to be 10.2 J, and this might be denoted $q[500, 600] = 10.2$. If we divided the wavelength interval into two 50 nm intervals, we might find that $q[500, 550] = 5.2$ and $q[550, 600] = 5.0$. This tells us there was a little more energy in the short wavelength half of the interval $[500, 600]$. If we divide into 25 nm bins, we might find $q[500, 525] = 2.5$, and so on. The nice thing about the system is that it is straightforward. The bad thing about it is that the choice of the interval size determines the number.

A more commonly used system is to divide the energy by the size of the interval. So instead of $q[500, 600] = 10.2$ we would have

$$Q_\lambda[500, 600] = \frac{10.2}{100} = 0.12\,\text{J}(\text{nm})^{-1}.$$

This approach is nice, because the size of the interval has much less impact on the overall size of the numbers. An immediate idea would be to drive the interval size $\Delta\lambda$ to zero. This could be awkward, because for a sufficiently small $\Delta\lambda$, Q_λ will either be zero or huge depending on whether there is a single photon or no photon in the interval. There are two schools of thought to solve that dilemma. The first is to assume that $\Delta\lambda$ is small, but not so small that the quantum nature of light comes into play. The second is to assume that the light is a continuum rather than individual photons, so a true derivative $dQ/d\lambda$ is appropriate. Both ways of thinking about it are appropriate and lead to the same computational machinery. In practice, it seems that most people who measure light prefer small, but finite, intervals, because that is what they can measure in the lab. Most people who do theory or computation prefer infinitesimal intervals, because that makes the machinery of calculus available.

The quantity Q_λ is called *spectral energy*, and it is an *intensive* quantity as opposed to an *extensive* quantity such as energy, length, or mass. Intensive quantities can be thought of as density functions that tell the density of an extensive quantity at an infinitesimal point. For example, the energy Q at a specific wavelength is probably zero, but the spectral energy (energy density) Q_λ is a meaningful quantity. A probably more familiar example is that the population of a country may be 25 million, but the population at a point in that country is meaningless. However, the population *density* measured in people per square meter is meaningful, provided it is measured over large enough areas. Much like with photons, population density works best if we pretend that we can view population as a continuum where population density never becomes granular even when the area is small.

We will follow the convention of graphics where spectral energy is almost always used, and energy is rarely used. This results in a proliferation of λ subscripts if "proper" notation is used. Instead, we will drop the subscript and use Q to denote spectral energy. This can result in some confusion when people outside of graphics read graphics papers, so be aware of this standards issue. Your intuition about spectral power might be aided by imagining a measurement device with an energy sensor that measures light energy q. If you place a colored filter in front of the sensor that allows only light in the interval $[\lambda - \Delta\lambda/2, \lambda + \Delta\lambda/2]$, then the spectral power at λ is $Q = \Delta q/\Delta\lambda$.

20.1.3   Power

It is useful to estimate a rate of energy production for light sources. This rate is called *power*, and it is measured in *watts*, W, which is another name for *joules per second*. This is easiest to understand in a *steady state*, but because power is an intensive quantity (a density over time), it is well defined even when energy production is varying over time. The units of power may be more familiar, e.g., a 100-watt light bulb. Such bulbs draw approximately 100 J of energy each second. The power of the light produced will actually be less than 100 W because of heat loss, etc., but we can still use this example to help understand more about photons. For example, we can get a feel for how many photons are produced in a second by a 100 W light. Suppose the average photon produced has the energy of a $\lambda = 500$ nm photon. The frequency of such a photon is

$$f = \frac{c}{\lambda} = \frac{3 \times 10^8 \text{ ms}^{-1}}{500 \times 10^{-9} \text{ m}} = 6 \times 10^{14} \text{ s}^{-1}.$$

The energy of that photon is $hf \approx 4 \times 10^{-19}$ J. That means a staggering 10^{20} photons are produced each second, even if the bulb is not very efficient. This explains why simulating a camera with a fast shutter speed and directly simulated photons is an inefficient choice for producing images.

As with energy, we are really interested in *spectral power* measured in W(nm)^{-1}. Again, although the formal standard symbol for spectral power is Φ_λ, we will use Φ with no subscript for convenience and consistency with most of the graphics literature. One thing to note is that the spectral power for a light source is usually a smaller number than the power. For example, if a light emits a power of 100 W evenly distributed over wavelengths 400 nm to 800 nm, then the spectral power will be 100 W/400 nm = 0.25 W(nm)^{-1}. This is something to keep in mind if you set the spectral power of light sources by hand for debugging purposes.

The measurement device for spectral energy in the last section could be modified by taking a reading with a shutter that is open for a time interval Δt centered at time t. The spectral power would then be $\Delta Q/(\Delta t \Delta \lambda)$.

20.1.4   Irradiance

The quantity *irradiance* arises naturally if you ask the question "How much light hits this point?" Of course the answer is "none," and again we must use a density function. If the point is on a surface, it is natural to use area to define our density function. We modify the device from the last section to have a finite ΔA area sensor that is smaller than the light field being measured. The spectral irradiance H is just the power per unit area $\Delta \Phi/\Delta A$. Fully expanded this is

$$H = \frac{\Delta q}{\Delta A \, \Delta t \Delta \lambda}. \tag{20.2}$$

Thus, the full units of irradiance are $\text{Jm}^{-2}\text{s}^{-1}(\text{nm})^{-1}$. Note that the SI units for radiance include inverse-meter-squared for area and inverse-nanometer for wavelength. This seeming inconsistency (using both nanometer and meter) arises because of the natural units for area and visible light wavelengths.

When the light is leaving a surface, e.g., when it is reflected, the same quantity as irradiance is called *radiant exitance*, E. It is useful to have different words for incident and exitant light, because the same point has potentially different irradiance and radiant exitance.

20.1.5 Radiance

Although irradiance tells us how much light is arriving at a point, it tells us little about the direction that light comes from. To measure something analogous to what we see with our eyes, we need to be able to associate "how much light" with a specific direction. We can imagine a simple device to measure such a quantity (Figure 20.1). We use a small irradiance meter and add a conical "baffler" which limits light hitting the counter to a range of angles with solid angle $\Delta\sigma$. The response of the detector is as follows:

$$
\text{response} = \frac{\Delta H}{\Delta\sigma}
$$

$$
= \frac{\Delta q}{\Delta A \, \Delta\sigma \, \Delta t \, \Delta\lambda}.
$$

This is the spectral *radiance* of light travelling in space. Again, we will drop the "spectral" in our discussion and assume that it is implicit.

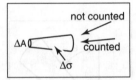

Figure 20.1. By adding a blinder that shows only a small solid angle $\Delta\sigma$ to the irradiance detector, we measure radiance.

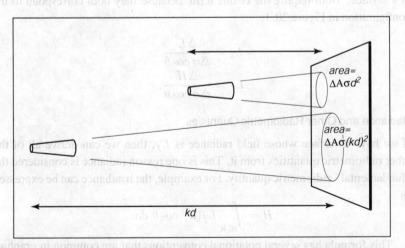

Figure 20.2. The signal a radiance detector receives does not depend on the distance to the surface being measured. This figure assumes the detectors are pointing at areas on the surface that are emitting light in the same way.

Radiance is what we are usually computing in graphics programs. A wonderful property of radiance is that it does not vary along a line in space. To see why this is true, examine the two radiance detectors both looking at a surface as shown in Figure 20.2. Assume the lines the detectors are looking along are close enough together that the surface is emitting/reflecting light "the same" in both of the areas being measured. Because the area of the surface being sampled is proportional to squared distance, and because the light reaching the detector is *inversely* proportional to squared distance, the two detectors should have the same reading.

It is useful to measure the radiance hitting a surface. We can think of placing the cone baffler from the radiance detector at a point on the surface and measuring the irradiance H on the surface originating from directions within the cone (Figure 20.3). Note that the surface "detector" is not aligned with the cone. For this reason we need to add a cosine correction term to our definition of radiance:

$$\text{response} = \frac{\Delta H}{\Delta \sigma \cos \theta}$$
$$= \frac{\Delta q}{\Delta A \cos \theta \, \Delta \sigma \, \Delta t \, \Delta \lambda}.$$

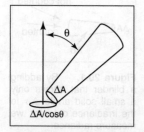

Figure 20.3. The irradiance at the surface as masked by the cone is smaller than that measured at the detector by a cosine factor.

As with irradiance and radiant exitance, it is useful to distinguish between radiance incident at a point on a surface and exitant from that point. Terms for these concepts sometimes used in the graphics literature are *surface radiance* L_s for the radiance of (leaving) a surface, and *field radiance* L_f for the radiance incident at a surface. Both require the cosine term, because they both correspond to the configuration in Figure 20.3:

$$L_s = \frac{\Delta E}{\Delta \sigma \cos \theta}$$
$$L_f = \frac{\Delta H}{\Delta \sigma \cos \theta}.$$

Radiance and Other Radiometric Quantities

If we have a surface whose field radiance is L_f, then we can derive all of the other radiometric quantities from it. This is one reason radiance is considered the "fundamental" radiometric quantity. For example, the irradiance can be expressed as

$$H = \int_{\text{all } \mathbf{k}} L_f(\mathbf{k}) \, \cos \theta \, d\sigma.$$

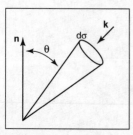

Figure 20.4. The direction **k** has a differential solid angle $d\sigma$ associated with it.

This formula has several notational conventions that are common in graphics that make such formulae opaque to readers not familiar with them (Figure 20.4). First, **k** is an incident direction and can be thought of as a unit vector, a direction, or a (θ, ϕ) pair in spherical coordinates with respect to the surface normal. The direction has a differential solid angle $d\sigma$ associated with it. The field radiance is potentially different for every direction, so we write it as a function $L(\mathbf{k})$.

As an example, we can compute the irradiance H at a surface that has constant field radiance L_f in all directions. To integrate, we use a classic spherical coordinate system and recall that the differential solid angle is

$$d\sigma \equiv \sin\theta \, d\theta \, d\phi,$$

so the irradiance is

$$H = \int_{\phi=0}^{2\pi} \int_{\theta=0}^{\frac{\pi}{2}} L_f \, \cos\theta \sin\theta \, d\theta \, d\phi$$
$$= \pi L_f.$$

This relation shows us our first occurrence of a potentially surprising constant π. These factors of π occur frequently in radiometry and are an artifact of how we chose to measure solid angles, i.e., the area of a unit sphere is a multiple of π rather than a multiple of one.

Similarly, we can find the power hitting a surface by integrating the irradiance across the surface area:

$$\Phi = \int_{\text{all } \mathbf{x}} H(\mathbf{x}) dA,$$

where $\mathbf{x}$ is a point on the surface, and dA is the differential area associated with that point. Note that we don't have special terms or symbols for incoming versus outgoing power. That distinction does not seem to come up enough to have encouraged the distinction.

20.1.6 BRDF

Because we are interested in surface appearance, we would like to characterize how a surface reflects light. At an intuitive level, for any incident light coming from direction $\mathbf{k}_i$, there is some fraction scattered in a small solid angle near the outgoing direction $\mathbf{k}_o$. There are many ways we could formalize such a concept, and not surprisingly, the standard way to do so is inspired by building a simple measurement device. Such a device is shown in Figure 20.5, where a small light source is positioned in direction $\mathbf{k}_i$ as seen from a point on a surface, and a detector is placed in direction $\mathbf{k}_o$. For every directional pair $(\mathbf{k}_i, \mathbf{k}_o)$, we take a reading with the detector.

Now we just have to decide how to measure the strength of the light source and make our reflection function independent of this strength. For example, if we

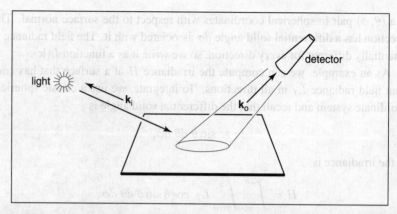

Figure 20.5. A simple measurement device for directional reflectance. The positions of light and detector are moved to each possible pair of directions. Note that both $\mathbf{k}_i$ and $\mathbf{k}_o$ point away from the surface to allow reciprocity.

replaced the light with a brighter light, we would not want to think of the surface as reflecting light differently. We could place a radiance meter at the point being illuminated to measure the light. However, for this to get an accurate reading that would not depend on the $\Delta\sigma$ of the detector, we would need the light to subtend a solid angle bigger than $\Delta\sigma$. Unfortunately, the measurement taken by our roving radiance detector in direction $\mathbf{k}_o$ will also count light that comes from points outside the new detector's cone. So this does not seem like a practical solution.

Alternatively, we can place an irradiance meter at the point on the surface being measured. This will take a reading that does not depend strongly on subtleties of the light source geometry. This suggests characterizing reflectance as a ratio:

$$\rho = \frac{L_s}{H},$$

where this fraction ρ will vary with incident and exitant directions $\mathbf{k}_i$ and $\mathbf{k}_o$, H is the irradiance for light position $\mathbf{k}_i$, and L_s is the surface radiance measured in direction $\mathbf{k}_o$. If we take such a measurement for all direction pairs, we end up with a 4D function $\rho(\mathbf{k}_i, \mathbf{k}_o)$. This function is called the *bidirectional reflectance distribution function* (BRDF). The BRDF is all we need to know to characterize the directional properties of how a surface reflects light.

Directional Hemispherical Reflectance

Given a BRDF it is straightforward to ask "What fraction of incident light is reflected?" However, the answer is not so easy; the fraction reflected depends on the directional distribution of incoming light. For this reason, we typically only set a fraction reflected for a fixed incident direction $\mathbf{k}_i$. This fraction is called the *directional hemispherical reflectance*. This fraction, $R(\mathbf{k}_i)$ is defined by

$$R(\mathbf{k}_i) = \frac{\text{power in all outgoing directions } \mathbf{k}_o}{\text{power in a beam from direction } \mathbf{k}_i}.$$

Note that this quantity is between zero and one for reasons of energy conservation. If we allow the incident power Φ_i to hit on a small area ΔA, then the irradiance is $\Phi_i/\Delta A$. Also, the ratio of the incoming power is just the ratio of the radiance exitance to irradiance:

$$R(\mathbf{k}_i) = \frac{E}{H}.$$

The radiance in a particular direction resulting from this power is by the definition of BRDF:

$$L(\mathbf{k}_o) = H\rho(\mathbf{k}_i, \mathbf{k}_o)$$
$$= \frac{\Phi_i}{\Delta A}.$$

And from the definition of radiance, we also have

$$L(\mathbf{k}_o) = \frac{\Delta E}{\Delta \sigma_o \cos \theta_o},$$

where E is the radiant exitance of the small patch in direction $\mathbf{k}_o$. Using these two definitions for radiance we get

$$H\rho(\mathbf{k}_i, \mathbf{k}_o) = \frac{\Delta E}{\Delta \sigma_o \cos \theta_o}.$$

Rearranging terms, we get

$$\frac{\Delta E}{H} = \rho(\mathbf{k}_i, \mathbf{k}_o)\Delta \sigma_o \cos \theta_o.$$

This is just the small contribution to E/H that is reflected near the particular $\mathbf{k}_o$. To find the total $R(\mathbf{k}_i)$, we sum over all outgoing $\mathbf{k}_o$. In integral form this is

$$R(\mathbf{k}_i) = \int_{\text{all } \mathbf{k}_o} \rho(\mathbf{k}_i, \mathbf{k}_o) \cos \theta_o \, d\sigma_o.$$

Ideal Diffuse BRDF

An idealized diffuse surface is called *Lambertian*. Such surfaces are impossible in nature for thermodynamic reasons, but mathematically they do conserve energy. The Lambertian BRDF has ρ equal to a constant for all angles. This means the surface will have the same radiance for all viewing angles, and this radiance will be proportional to the irradiance.

If we compute $R(\mathbf{k}_i)$ for a a Lambertian surface with $\rho = C$ we get

$$
\begin{aligned}
R(\mathbf{k}_i) &= \int_{\text{all } \mathbf{k}_o} C \cos\theta_o \, d\sigma_o \\
&= \int_{\phi_o=0}^{2\pi} \int_{\theta_o=0}^{\pi/2} k \cos\theta_o \sin\theta_o \, d\theta_o \, d\phi_o \\
&= \pi C.
\end{aligned}
$$

Thus, for a perfectly reflecting Lambertian surface ($R = 1$), we have $\rho = 1/\pi$, and for a Lambertian surface where $R(\mathbf{k}_i) = r$, we have

$$
\rho(\mathbf{k}_i, \mathbf{k}_o) = \frac{r}{\pi}.
$$

This is another example where the use of a steradian for the solid angle determines the normalizing constant and thus introduces factors of π.

20.2 Transport Equation

With the definition of BRDF, we can describe the radiance of a surface in terms of the incoming radiance from all different directions. Because in computer graphics we can use idealized mathematics that might be impractical to instantiate in the lab, we can also write the BRDF in terms of radiance only. If we take a small part of the light with solid angle $\Delta\sigma_i$ with radiance L_i and "measure" the reflected radiance in direction $\mathbf{k}_o$ due to this small piece of the light, we can compute a BRDF (Figure 20.6). The irradiance due to the small piece of light is $H =$

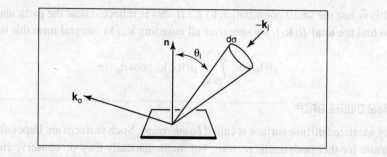

Figure 20.6. The geometry for the transport equation in its directional form.

$L_i \cos \theta_i \Delta \sigma_i$. Thus the BRDF is

$$\rho = \frac{L_o}{L_i \cos \theta_i \Delta \sigma_i}.$$

This form can be useful in some situations. Rearranging terms, we can write down the part of the radiance that is due to light coming from direction $\mathbf{k}_i$:

$$\Delta L_o = \rho(\mathbf{k}_i, \mathbf{k}_o) L_i \cos \theta_i \Delta \sigma_i.$$

If there is light coming from many directions $L_i(\mathbf{k}_i)$, we can sum all of them. In integral form, with notation for surface and field radiance, this is

$$L_s(\mathbf{k}_o) = \int_{\text{all } \mathbf{k}_i} \rho(\mathbf{k}_i, \mathbf{k}_o) L_f(\mathbf{k}_i) \cos \theta_i d\sigma_i.$$

This is often called the *rendering equation* in computer graphics (Immel et al., 1986).

Sometimes it is useful to write the transport equation in terms of surface radiances only (Kajiya, 1986). Note, that in a closed environment, the field radiance $L_f(\mathbf{k}_i)$ comes from some surface with surface radiance $L_s(-\mathbf{k}_i) = L_f(\mathbf{k}_i)$ (Figure 20.7). The solid angle subtended by the point $\mathbf{x}'$ in the figure is given by

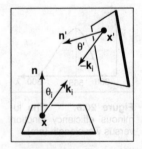

$$\Delta \sigma_i = \frac{\Delta A' \cos \theta'}{\|\mathbf{x} - \mathbf{x}'\|^2},$$

where $\Delta A'$ the the area we associate with $\mathbf{x}'$. Substituting for $\Delta \sigma_i$ in terms of $\Delta A'$ suggests the following transport equation:

Figure 20.7. The light coming into one point comes from another point.

$$L_s(\mathbf{x}, \mathbf{k}_o) = \int_{\text{all } \mathbf{x}' \text{ visible to } \mathbf{x}} \frac{\rho(\mathbf{k}_i, \mathbf{k}_o) L_s(\mathbf{x}', \mathbf{x} - \mathbf{x}') \cos \theta_i \cos \theta'}{\|\mathbf{x} - \mathbf{x}'\|^2} dA'.$$

Note that we are using a non-normalized vector $\mathbf{x} - \mathbf{x}'$ to indicate the direction from $\mathbf{x}'$ to $\mathbf{x}$. Also note that we are writing L_s as a function of position and direction.

The only problem with this new transport equation is that the domain of integration is awkward. If we introduce a visibility function, we can trade off complexity in the domain with complexity in the integrand:

$$L_s(\mathbf{x}, \mathbf{k}_o) = \int_{\text{all } \mathbf{x}'} \frac{\rho(\mathbf{k}_i, \mathbf{k}_o) L_s(\mathbf{x}', \mathbf{x} - \mathbf{x}') v(\mathbf{x}, \mathbf{x}') \cos \theta_i \cos \theta'}{\|\mathbf{x} - \mathbf{x}'\|^2} dA',$$

where

$$v(\mathbf{x}, \mathbf{x}') = \begin{cases} 1 & \text{if } \mathbf{x} \text{ and } \mathbf{x}' \text{ are mutually visible,} \\ 0 & \text{otherwise.} \end{cases}$$

20.3 Photometry

For every spectral radiometric quantity there is a related *photometric quantity* that measures how much of that quantity is "useful" to a human observer. Given a spectral radiometric quantity $f_r(\lambda)$, the related photometric quantity f_p is

$$f_p = 683\frac{\text{lm}}{\text{W}} \int_{\lambda=380\text{ nm}}^{800\text{ nm}} \bar{y}(\lambda)f_r(\lambda)\ d\lambda,$$

where $\bar{y}$ is the *luminous efficiency function* of the human visual system. This function is zero outside the limits of integration above, so the limits could be 0 and ∞ and f_p would not change. The luminous efficiency function will be discussed in more detail in Chapter 21, but we discuss its general properties here. The leading constant is to make the definition consistent with historical absolute photometric quantities.

The luminous efficiency function is not equally sensitive to all wavelengths (Figure 20.8). For wavelengths below 380 nm (the *ultraviolet range*), the light is not visible to humans and thus has a $\bar{y}$ value of zero. From 380 nm it gradually increases until $\lambda = 555$ nm where it peaks. This is a pure green light. Then, it gradually decreases until it reaches the boundary of the infrared region at 800 nm.

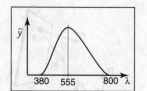

Figure 20.8. The luminous efficiency function versus wavelength (nm).

The photometric quantity that is most commonly used in graphics is *luminance*, the photometric analog of radiance:

$$Y = 683\frac{\text{lm}}{\text{W}} \int_{\lambda=380\text{ nm}}^{800\text{ nm}} \bar{y}(\lambda)L(\lambda)\ d\lambda.$$

The symbol Y for luminance comes from colorimetry. Most other fields use the symbol L; we will not follow that convention because it is too confusing to use L for both luminance and spectral radiance. Luminance gives one a general idea of how "bright" something is independent of the adaptation of the viewer. Note that the black paper under noonday sun is subjectively darker than the lower luminance white paper under moonlight; reading too much into luminance is dangerous, but it is a very useful quantity for getting a quantitative feel for relative perceivable light output. The unit lm stands for *lumens*. Note that most light bulbs are rated in terms of the power they consume in watts, and the useful light they produce in lumens. More efficient bulbs produce more of their light where $\bar{y}$ is large and thus produce more lumens per watt. A "perfect" light would convert all power into 555 nm light and would produce 683 lumens per watt. The units of luminance are thus $(\text{lm/W})(\text{W}/(\text{m}^2\text{sr})) = \text{lm}/(\text{m}^2\text{sr})$. The quantity one lumen per steradian is defined to be one *candela* (cd), so luminance is usually described in units cd/m^2.

Frequently Asked Questions

- What is "intensity"?

The term *intensity* is used in a variety of contexts and its use varies with both era and discipline. In practice, it is no longer meaningful as a specific radiometric quantity, but it is useful for intuitive discussion. Most papers that use it do so in place of radiance.

- What is "radiosity"?

The term *radiosity* is used in place of radiant exitance in some fields. It is also sometimes used to describe world-space light transport algorithms.

Notes

A common radiometric quantity not described in this chapter is *radiant intensity* (I), which is the spectral power per steradian emitted from an infinitesimal point source. It should usually be avoided in graphics programs because point sources cause implementation problems. A more rigorous treatment of radiometry can be found in *Analytic Methods for Simulated Light Transport* (Arvo, 1995). The radiometric and photometric terms in this chapter are from the *Illumination Engineering Society's* standard that is increasingly used by all fields of science and engineering (American National Standard Institute, 1986). A broader discussion of radiometric and appearance standards can be found in *Principles of Digital Image Synthesis* (Glassner, 1995).

Exercises

1. For a diffuse surface with outgoing radiance L, what is the radiant exitance?

2. What is the total power exiting a diffuse surface with an area of 4 m^2 and a radiance of L?

3. If a fluorescent light and an incandescent light both consume 20 watts of power, why is the fluorescent light usually preferred?

Erik Reinhard and Garrett Johnson

21

Color

Photons are the carriers of optical information. They propagate through media taking on properties associated with waves. At surface boundaries they interact with matter, behaving more as particles. They can also be absorbed by the retina, where the information they carry is transcoded into electrical signals that are subsequently processed by the brain. It is only there that a sensation of color is generated.

As a consequence, the study of color in all its guises touches upon several different fields: physics for the propagation of light through space; chemistry for its interaction with matter; neuroscience and psychology for aspects relating to perception and cognition of color (Reinhard et al., 2008).

In computer graphics, we traditionally take a simplified view of how light propagates through space. Photons travel along straight paths until they hit a surface boundary and are then reflected according to a reflection function of some sort. A single photon will carry a certain amount of energy, which is represented by its wavelength. Thus, a photon will have only one wavelength. The relationship between its wavelength λ and the amount of energy it carries (ΔE) is given by

$$\lambda \, \Delta E = 1239.9,$$

where ΔE is measured in electron volts (eV).

In computer graphics, it is not very efficient to simulate single photons; instead large collections of them are simulated at the same time. If we take a very large number of photons, each carrying a possibly different amount of energy,

531

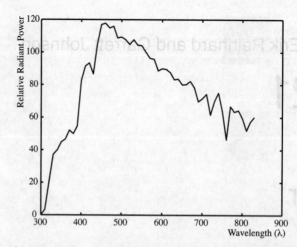

Figure 21.1.   A spectrum describes how much energy is available at each wavelength λ, here measured as relative radiant power. This specific spectrum represents average daylight.

then together they represent a spectrum. A spectrum can be thought of as a graph where the number of photons is plotted against wavelength. Because two photons of the same wavelength carry twice as much energy as a single photon of that wavelength, this graph can also be seen as a plot of energy against wavelength. An example of a spectrum is shown in Figure 21.1. The range of wavelengths to which humans are sensitive is roughly between 380 and 800 nanometers (nm).

When simulating light, it would therefore be possible to trace rays that each carry a spectrum. A renderer that accomplishes this is normally called a *spectral renderer*. From preceding chapters it should be clear that we are not normally going through the expense of building spectral renderers. Instead, we replace spectra with representations that typically use red, green, and blue components. The reason that this is possible at all has to do with human vision and will be discussed later in this chapter.

Simulating light by tracing rays takes care of the physics of light, although it should be noted that several properties of light, including for instance polarization, diffraction, and interference, are not modeled in this manner.

At surface boundaries, we normally model what happens with light by means of a reflectance function. These functions can be measured directly by means of *gonioreflectometers*, leading to a large amount of tabled data, which can be more compactly represented by various different functions. Nonetheless, these reflectance functions are empirical in nature, i.e., they abstract away the chemistry that happens when a photon is absorbed and re-emitted by an electron. Thus, reflectance functions are useful for modeling in computer graphics, but do not offer an explanation as to why certain wavelengths of light are absorbed and others are reflected. We can therefore not use reflectance functions to explain why the light reflected off a banana has a spectral composition that appears to us as yellow. For that, we would have to study molecular orbital theory, a topic beyond the scope of this book.

Finally, when light reaches the retina, it is transcoded into electrical signals that are propagated to the brain. A large part of the brain is devoted to processing visual signals, part of which gives rise to the sensation of color. Thus, even if we know the spectrum of light that is reflected off a banana, we do not know yet why humans associate the term "yellow" with it. Moreover, as we will find out in the remainder of this chapter, our perception of color is vastly more complicated than it would seem at first glance. It changes with illumination, varies between observers, and varies within an observer over time.

In other words, the spectrum of light coming off a banana is perceived in the context of an environment. To predict how an observer perceives a "banana spectrum" requires knowledge of the environment that contains the banana as well as the observer's environment. In many instances, these two environments are the same. However, when we are displaying a photograph of a banana on a monitor, then these two environments will be different. As human visual perception depends on the environment the observer is in, it may perceive the banana in the photograph differently from how an observer directly looking at the banana would perceive it. This has a significant impact on how we should deal with color and illustrates the complexities associated with color.

To emphasize the crucial role that human vision plays, we only have to look at the definition of color: "Color is the aspect of visual perception by which an observer may distinguish differences between two structure-free fields of view of the same size and shape, such as may be caused by differences in the spectral composition of the radiant energy concerned in the observation" (Wyszecki & Stiles, 2000). In essence, without a human observer there is no color.

Luckily, much of what we know about color can be quantified, so that we can carry out computations to correct for the idiosyncrasies of human vision and thereby display images that will appear to observers the way the designer of those images intended. This chapter contains the theory and mathematics required to do so.

21.1 Colorimetry

Colorimetry is the science of color measurement and description. Since color is ultimately a human response, color measurement should begin with human observation. The photodetectors in the human retina consist of rods and cones. The rods are highly sensitive and come into play in low light conditions. Under normal lighting conditions, the cones are operational, mediating human vision. There are three cone types and together they are primarily responsible for color vision.

Although it may be possible to directly record the electrical output of cones while some visual stimulus is being presented, such a procedure would be invasive, while at the same time ignoring the sometimes substantial differences between observers. Moreover, much of the measurement of color was developed well before such direct recording techniques were available.

The alternative is to measure color by means of measuring the human response to patches of color. This leads to color matching experiments, which will be described later in this section. Carrying out these experiments have resulted in several standardized observers, which can be thought of as statistical approximations of actual human observers. First, however, we need to describe some of the assumptions underlying the possibility of color matching, which are summarized by Grassmann's laws.

21.1.1 Grassmann's Laws

Given that humans have three different cone types, the experimental laws of color matching can be summed up as the trichromatic generalization (Wyszecki & Stiles, 2000), which states that any color stimulus can be matched completely with an additive mixture of three appropriately modulated color sources. This feature of color is often used in practice, for instance by televisions and monitors which reproduce many different colors by adding a mixture of red, green, and blue light for each pixel. It is also the reason that renderers can be built using only three values to describe each color.

The trichromatic generalization allows us to make color matches between any given stimulus and an additive mixture of three other color stimuli. Grassmann was the first to describe the algebraic rules to which color matching adheres. They are known as Grassmann's laws of additive color matching (Grassmann, 1853) and are given here.

- **Symmetry law.** If color stimulus A matches color stimulus B, then B matches A.

- **Transitive law.** If A matches B and B matches C, then A matches C.

- **Proportionality law.** If A matches B, then αA matches αB, where α is a positive scale factor.

- **Additivity law.** If A matches B, C matches D, and $A+C$ matches $B+D$, then it follows that $A + D$ matches $B + C$.

The additivity law forms the basis for color matching and colorimetry as a whole.

21.1.2 Cone Responses

Each cone type is sensitive to a range of wavelengths, spanning most of the full visible range. However, sensitivity to wavelengths is not evenly distributed, but contains a peak wavelength at which sensitivity is greatest. The location of this peak wavelength is different for each cone type. The three cone types are classified as S, M, and L cones, where the letters stand for short, medium, and long, indicating where in the visible spectrum the peak sensitivity is located.

The response of a given cone is then the magnitude of the electrical signal it outputs, as a function of the spectrum of wavelengths incident upon the cone. The cone response functions for each cone type as a function of wavelength λ are then given by $L(\lambda)$, $M(\lambda)$, and $S(\lambda)$. They are plotted in Figure 21.2.

The actual response to a stimulus with a given spectral composition $\Phi(\lambda)$ is then given for each cone type by

$$L = \int_\lambda \Phi(\lambda)\, L(\lambda)\, d\lambda,$$

$$M = \int_\lambda \Phi(\lambda)\, M(\lambda)\, d\lambda,$$

$$S = \int_\lambda \Phi(\lambda)\, S(\lambda)\, d\lambda.$$

This triple of integrated responses are known as tristimulus values.

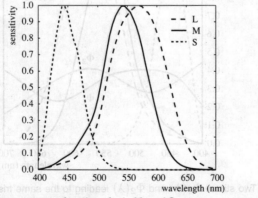

Figure 21.2. The cone response functions for L, M, and S cones.

21.1.3 Color Matching Experiments

Given that tristimulus values are created by integrating the product of two functions over the visible range, it is immediately clear that the human visual system does not act as a simple wavelength detector. Rather, our photo-receptors act as approximately linear integrators. As a result, it is possible to find two different spectral compositions, say $\Phi_1(\lambda)$ and $\Phi_2(\lambda)$, that after integration yield the same response (L, M, S). This phenomenon is known as *metamerism*, an example of which is shown in Figure 21.3.

Metamerism is the key feature of human vision that allows the construction of color reproduction devices, including the color figures in this book and anything reproduced on printers, televisions, and monitors.

Color matching experiments also rely on the principle of metamerism. Suppose we have three differently colored light sources, each with a dial to alter its intensity. We call these three light sources primaries. We should now be able to adjust the intensity of each in such a way that when mixed together additively, the resulting spectrum integrates to a tristimulus value that matches the perceived color of a fourth unknown light source. When we carry out such an experiment, we have essentially matched our primaries to an unknown color. The positions of our three dials are then a representation of the color of the fourth light source.

In such an experiment, we have used Grassmann's laws to add the three spectra of our primaries. We have also used metamerism, because the combined spectrum of our three primaries is almost certainly different from the spectrum of the

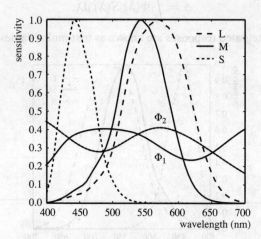

Figure 21.3. Two stimuli $\Phi_1(\lambda)$ and $\Phi_2(\lambda)$ leading to the same tristimulus values after integration.

fourth light source. However, the tristimulus values computed from these two spectra will be identical, having produced a color match.

Note that we do not actually have to know the cone response functions to carry out such an experiment. As long as we use the same observer under the same conditions, we are able to match colors and record the positions of our dials for each color. However, it is quite inconvenient to have to carry out such experiments every time we want to measure colors. For this reason, we do want to know the spectral cone response functions and average those for a set of different observers to eliminate inter-observer variability.

21.1.4 Standard Observers

If we perform a color matching experiment for a large range of colors, carried out by a set of different observers, it is possible to generate an average color matching dataset. If we specifically use monochromatic light sources against which to match our primaries, we can repeat this experiment for all visible wavelengths. The resulting tristimulus values are then called *spectral tristimulus values*, and can be plotted against wavelength λ, shown in Figure 21.4.

By using a well-defined set of primary light sources, the spectral tristimulus values lead to three color matching functions. The Commission Internationale d'Eclairage (CIE) has defined three such primaries to be monochromatic light sources of 435.8, 546.1, and 700 nm, respectively. With these three monochromatic light sources, all other visible wavelengths can be matched by adding differ-

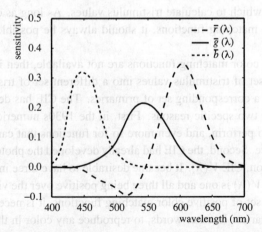

Figure 21.4. Spectral tristimulus values averaged over many observers. The primaries where monochromatic light sources with wavelengths of 435.8, 546.1, and 700 nm.

ent amounts of each. The amount of each required to match a given wavelength λ is encoded in color matching functions, given by $\bar{r}(\lambda)$, $\bar{g}(\lambda)$, and $\bar{b}(\lambda)$ and plotted in Figure 21.4. Tristimulus values associated with these color matching functions are termed R, G, and B.

Given that we are adding light, and light cannot be negative, you may have noticed an anomaly in Figure 21.4: to create a match for some wavelengths, it is necessary to subtract light. Although there is no such thing as negative light, we can use Grassmann's laws once more, and instead of subtracting light from the mixture of primaries, we can add the same amount of light to the color that is being matched.

The CIE $\bar{r}(\lambda)$, $\bar{g}(\lambda)$, and $\bar{b}(\lambda)$ color matching functions allow us to determine if a spectral distribution Φ_1 matches a second spectral distribution Φ_2 by simply comparing the resulting tristimulus values obtained by integrating with these color matching functions:

$$\int_\lambda \Phi_1(\lambda)\,\bar{r}(\lambda) = \int_\lambda \Phi_2(\lambda)\,\bar{r}(\lambda),$$

$$\int_\lambda \Phi_1(\lambda)\,\bar{g}(\lambda) = \int_\lambda \Phi_2(\lambda)\,\bar{g}(\lambda),$$

$$\int_\lambda \Phi_1(\lambda)\,\bar{b}(\lambda) = \int_\lambda \Phi_2(\lambda)\,\bar{b}(\lambda).$$

Of course, a color match is only guaranteed if all three tristimulus values match.

The importance of these color matching functions lies in the fact that we are now able to communicate and describe colors compactly by means of tristimulus values. For a given spectral function, the CIE color matching functions provide a precise way in which to calculate tristimulus values. As long as everybody uses the same color matching functions, it should always be possible to generate a match.

If the same color matching functions are not available, then it is possible to transform one set of tristimulus values into a different set of tristimulus values appropriate for a corresponding set of primaries. The CIE has defined one such a transform for two specific reasons. First, in the 1930s numerical integrations were difficult to perform, and even more so for functions that can be both positive and negative. Second, the CIE had already developed the photopic luminance response function, CIE $V(\lambda)$. It became desirable to have three integrating functions, of which $V(\lambda)$ is one and all three being positive over the visible range.

To create a set of positive color matching functions, it is necessary to define imaginary primaries. In other words, to reproduce any color in the visible spectrum, we need light sources that cannot be physically realized. The color matching functions that were settled upon by the CIE are named $\bar{x}(\lambda)$, $\bar{y}(\lambda)$, and $\bar{z}(\lambda)$

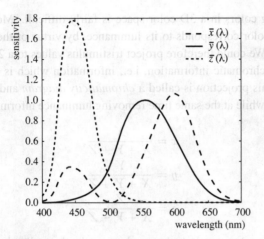

Figure 21.5. The CIE $\bar{x}(\lambda)$, $\bar{y}(\lambda)$, and $\bar{z}(\lambda)$ color matching functions.

and are shown in Figure 21.5. Note that $\bar{y}(\lambda)$ is equal to the photopic luminance response function $V(\lambda)$ and that each of these functions is indeed positive. They are known as the CIE 1931 standard observer.

The corresponding tristimulus values are termed X, Y, and Z, to avoid confusion with R, G, and B tristimulus values that are normally associated with realizable primaries. The conversion from (R, G, B) tristimulus values to (X, Y, Z) tristimulus values is defined by a simple 3×3 transform:

$$\begin{bmatrix} X \\ Y \\ Z \end{bmatrix} = \frac{1}{0.17697} \begin{bmatrix} 0.4900 & 0.3100 & 0.2000 \\ 0.17697 & 0.81240 & 0.01063 \\ 0.0000 & 0.0100 & 0.9900 \end{bmatrix} \cdot \begin{bmatrix} R \\ G \\ B \end{bmatrix}.$$

To calculate tristimulus values, we typically directly integrate the standard observer color matching functions with the spectrum of interest $\Phi(\lambda)$, rather than go through the CIE $\bar{r}(\lambda)$, $\bar{g}(\lambda)$, and $\bar{b}(\lambda)$ color matching functions first, followed by the above transformation. It allows us to calculate consistent color measurements and also determine when two colors match each other.

21.1.5 Chromaticity Coordinates

Every color can be represented by a set of three tristimulus values (X, Y, Z). We could define an orthogonal coordinate system with X, Y, and Z axes and plot each color in the resulting 3D space. This is called a *color space*. The spatial extent of the volume in which colors lie is then called the color gamut.

Visualizing colors in a 3D color space is fairly difficult. Moreover, the Y-value of any color corresponds to its luminance, by virtue of the fact that $\bar{y}(\lambda)$ equals $V(\lambda)$. We could therefore project tristimulus values to a 2D space which approximates chromatic information, i.e., information which is independent of luminance. This projection is called a *chromaticity diagram* and is obtained by normalization while at the same time removing luminance information:

$$x = \frac{X}{X+Y+Z},$$

$$y = \frac{Y}{X+Y+Z},$$

$$z = \frac{Z}{X+Y+Z}.$$

Given that $x + y + z$ equals 1, the z-value is redundant, allowing us to plot the x and y chromaticities against each other in a chromaticity diagram. Although x and y by themselves are not sufficient to fully describe a color, we can use these two chromaticity coordinates and one of the three tristimulus values, traditionally Y, to recover the other two tristimulus values:

$$X = \frac{x}{y} Y,$$

$$Z = \frac{1-x-y}{y} Y.$$

By plotting all monochromatic (spectral) colors in a chromaticity diagram, we obtain a horseshoe-shaped curve. The points on this curve are called *spectrum loci*. All other colors will generate points lying inside this curve. The spectrum locus for the 1931 standard observer is shown in Figure 21.6. The purple line

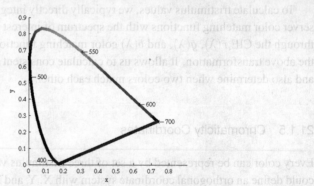

Figure 21.6.   The spectrum locus for the CIE 1931 standard observer.   (See also Plate XXVIII.)

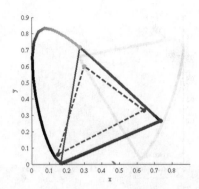

Figure 21.7. The chromaticity boundaries of the CIE RGB primaries at 435.8, 546.1, and 700 nm (solid) and a typical HDTV (dashed). (See also Plate XXIX.)

between either end of the horseshoe does not represent a monochromatic color, but rather a combination of short and long wavelength stimuli.

A (non-monochromatic) primary can be integrated over all visible wavelengths, leading to (X, Y, Z) tristimulus values, and subsequently to an (x, y) chromaticity coordinate, i.e., a point on a chromaticity diagram. Repeating this for two or more primaries yields a set of points on a chromaticity diagram that can be connected by straight lines. The volume spanned in this manner represents the range of colors that can be reproduced by the additive mixture of these primaries. Examples of 3-primary systems are shown in Figure 21.7.

Chromaticity diagrams provide insight into additive color mixtures. However, they should be used with care. First, the interior of the horseshoe should not be colored, as any color reproduction system will have its own primaries and can only reproduce some parts of the chromaticity diagram. Second, as the CIE color matching functions do not represent human cone sensitivities, the distance between any two points on a chromaticity diagram is not a good indicator for how differently these colors will be perceived.

A more uniform chromaticity diagram was developed to at least in part address the second of these problems. The CIE $u'v'$ chromaticity diagram provides a perceptually more uniform spacing and is therefore generally preferred over (x, y) chromaticity diagrams. It is computed from (X, Y, Z) tristimulus values by applying a different normalization,

$$u' = \frac{4X}{X + 15Y + 3Z},$$
$$v' = \frac{9Y}{X + 15Y + 3Z}.$$

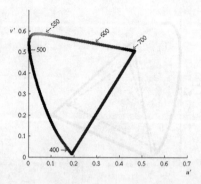

Figure 21.8. The CIE $u'v'$ chromaticity diagram. (See also Plate XXX.)

and can alternatively be computed directly from (x, y) chromaticity coordinates:

$$u' = \frac{4x}{-2x + 12y + 3},$$

$$v' = \frac{9y}{-2x + 12y + 3}.$$

A CIE $u'v'$ chromaticity diagram is shown in Figure 21.8.

21.2   Color Spaces

As explained above, each color can be represented by three numbers, for instance defined by (X, Y, Z) tristimulus values. However, its primaries are imaginary, meaning that it is not possible to construct a device that has three light sources (all positive) that can reproduce all colors in the visible spectrum.

For the same reason, image encoding and computations on images may not be practical. There is, for instance, a large number of possible XYZ values that do not correspond to any physical color. This would lead to inefficient use of available bits for storage and to a higher requirement for bit-depth to preserve visual integrity after image processing. Although it may be possible to build a capture device that has primaries that are close to the CIE XYZ color matching functions, the cost of hardware and image processing make this an unattractive option. It is not possible to build a display that corresponds to CIE XYZ. For these reasons, it is necessary to design other color spaces: physical realizability, efficient encoding, perceptual uniformity, and intuitive color specification.

The CIE XYZ color space is still actively used, mostly for the conversion between other color spaces. It can be seen as a device-independent color space.

Other color spaces can then be defined in terms of their relationship to CIE XYZ, which is often specified by a specific transform. For instance, linear and additive trichromatic display devices can be transformed to and from CIE XYZ by means of a simple 3×3 matrix. Some nonlinear additional transform may also be specified, for instance to minimize perceptual errors when data is stored with a limited bit-depth, or to enable display directly on devices that have a nonlinear relationship between input signal and the amount of light emitted.

21.2.1 Constructing a Matrix Transform

For a display device with three primaries, say red, green, and blue, we can measure the spectral composition of the emitted light by sending the color vectors $(1, 0, 0)$, $(0, 1, 0)$, and $(0, 0, 1)$. These vectors represent the three cases namely where one of the primaries is full on, and the other two are off. From the measured spectral output, we can then compute the corresponding chromaticity coordinates (x_R, y_R), (x_G, y_G), and (x_B, y_B).

The *white point* of a display is defined as the spectrum emitted when the color vector $(1, 1, 1)$ is sent to the display. Its corresponding chromaticity coordinate is (x_W, y_W). The three primaries and the white point characterize the display and are each required to construct a transformation matrix between the display's color space and CIE XYZ.

These four chromaticity coordinates can be extended to chromaticity triplets reconstructing the z-coordinate from $z = 1 - x - y$, leading to triplets (x_R, y_R, z_R), (x_G, y_G, z_G), (x_B, y_B, z_B), and (x_W, y_W, z_W). If we know the maximum luminance of the white point, we can compute its corresponding tristimulus value (X_W, Y_W, Z_W) and then solve the following set of equations for the luminance ratio scalars S_R, S_G, and S_B:

$$X_W = x_R\, S_R + x_G\, S_G + x_B\, S_B,$$
$$Y_W = y_R\, S_R + y_G\, S_G + y_B\, S_B,$$
$$Z_W = z_R\, S_R + z_G\, S_G + z_B\, S_B.$$

The conversion between RGB and XYZ is then given by

$$\begin{bmatrix} X \\ Y \\ Z \end{bmatrix} = \begin{bmatrix} x_R\, S_R & x_G\, S_G & x_B\, S_B \\ y_R\, S_R & y_G\, S_G & y_B\, S_B \\ z_R\, S_R & z_G\, S_G & z_B\, S_B \end{bmatrix} \begin{bmatrix} R \\ G \\ B \end{bmatrix}.$$

The luminance of any given color can be computed by evaluating the middle row of a matrix constructed in this manner:

$$Y = y_R\, S_R\, R + y_G\, S_G\, G + y_B\, S_B\, B.$$

	R	G	B	White
x	0.6400	0.3000	0.1500	0.3127
y	0.3300	0.6000	0.0600	0.3290

Figure 21.9. The (x, y) chromaticity coordinates for the primaries and white point specified by ITU-R BT.709. The sRGB standard also uses these primaries and white point.

To convert between XYZ and RGB of a given device, the above matrix can simply be inverted.

If an image is represented in an RGB color space for which the primaries and white point are unknown, then the next best thing is to assume that the image was encoded in a standard RGB color space. A reasonable choice is then to assume that the image was specified according to ITU-R BT.709, which is the specification used for encoding and broadcasting of HDTV. Its primaries and white point are specified in Table 21.9. Note that the same primaries and white point are used to define the well-known sRGB color space. The transformation between this RGB color space and CIE XYZ is and vice-versa given by

$$
\begin{bmatrix} X \\ Y \\ Z \end{bmatrix} = \begin{bmatrix} 0.4124 & 0.3576 & 0.1805 \\ 0.2126 & 0.7152 & 0.0722 \\ 0.0193 & 0.1192 & 0.9505 \end{bmatrix} \begin{bmatrix} R \\ G \\ B \end{bmatrix};
$$

$$
\begin{bmatrix} R \\ G \\ B \end{bmatrix} = \begin{bmatrix} 3.2405 & -1.5371 & -0.4985 \\ -0.9693 & 1.8706 & 0.0416 \\ 0.0556 & -0.2040 & 1.0572 \end{bmatrix} \begin{bmatrix} X \\ Y \\ Z \end{bmatrix}.
$$

By substituting the maximum RGB values of the device, we can compute the white point. For ITU-R BT.709, the maximum values are $(R_W, G_W, B_W) = (100, 100, 100)$, leading to a white point of $(X_W, Y_W, Z_W) = (95.05, 100.00, 108.90)$.

In addition to a linear transformation, the sRGB color space is characterized by a subsequent nonlinear transform. The nonlinear encoding is given by

$$
R_{\text{sRGB}} = \begin{cases} 1.055\, R^{1/2.4} - 0.055 & R > 0.0031308, \\ 12.92\, R & R \leq 0.0031308; \end{cases}
$$

$$
G_{\text{sRGB}} = \begin{cases} 1.055\, G^{1/2.4} - 0.055 & G > 0.0031308, \\ 12.92\, G & G \leq 0.0031308; \end{cases}
$$

$$
B_{\text{sRGB}} = \begin{cases} 1.055\, B^{1/2.4} - 0.055 & B > 0.0031308, \\ 12.92\, B & B \leq 0.0031308. \end{cases}
$$

This nonlinear encoding helps minimize perceptual errors due to quantization errors in digital applications.

21.2.2 Device-Dependent RGB Spaces

As each device typically has its own set of primaries and white point, we call the associated RGB color spaces device-dependent. It should be noted that even if all these devices operate in an RGB space, they may have very different primaries and white points. If we therefore have an image specified in some RGB space, it may appear very different to us, depending upon which device we display it.

This is clearly an undesirable situation, resulting from a lack of color management. However, if the image is specified in a known RGB color space, it can first be converted to XYZ, which is device independent, and then subsequently it can be converted to the RGB space of the device on which it will be displayed.

There are several other RGB color spaces that are well defined. They each consist of a linear matrix transform followed by a nonlinear transform, akin to the aforementioned sRGB color space. The nonlinear transform can be parameterized as follows:

$$R_{\text{nonlinear}} = \begin{cases} (1+f)\,R^{\gamma} - f & t < R \leq 1, \\ s\,R & 0 \leq R \leq t; \end{cases}$$

$$G_{\text{nonlinear}} = \begin{cases} (1+f)\,G^{\gamma} - f & t < G \leq 1, \\ s\,G & 0 \leq G \leq t; \end{cases}$$

$$B_{\text{nonlinear}} = \begin{cases} (1+f)\,B^{\gamma} - f & t < B \leq 1, \\ s\,B & 0 \leq B \leq t. \end{cases}$$

The parameters s, f, t and γ together with primaries and white point specify a class of RGB color spaces that are used in various industries. Several common transformations are listed in Table 21.10.

21.2.3 LMS Cone Space

The aforementioned cone signals can be expressed in terms of the CIE XYZ color space. The matrix transform to compute LMS signals from XYZ and vice-versa are given by

$$\begin{bmatrix} L \\ M \\ S \end{bmatrix} = \begin{bmatrix} 0.38971 & 0.68898 & -0.07868 \\ -0.22981 & 1.18340 & 0.04641 \\ 0.00000 & 0.00000 & 1.00000 \end{bmatrix} \begin{bmatrix} X \\ Y \\ Z \end{bmatrix};$$

$$\begin{bmatrix} X \\ Y \\ Z \end{bmatrix} = \begin{bmatrix} 1.91019 & -1.11214 & 0.20195 \\ 0.37095 & 0.62905 & 0.00000 \\ 0.00000 & 0.00000 & 1.00000 \end{bmatrix} \begin{bmatrix} L \\ M \\ S \end{bmatrix}.$$

Color space	XYZ to RGB matrix	RGB to XYZ matrix	Nonlinear transform
sRGB	$\begin{bmatrix} 3.2405 & -1.5371 & -0.4985 \\ -0.9693 & 1.8760 & 0.0416 \\ 0.0556 & -0.2040 & 1.0572 \end{bmatrix}$	$\begin{bmatrix} 0.4124 & 0.3576 & 0.1805 \\ 0.2126 & 0.7152 & 0.0722 \\ 0.0193 & 0.1192 & 0.9505 \end{bmatrix}$	$\gamma = 1/2.4 \approx 0.42$ $f = 0.055$ $s = 12.92$ $t = 0.0031308$
Adobe RGB (1998)	$\begin{bmatrix} 2.0414 & -0.5649 & -0.3447 \\ -0.9693 & 1.8760 & 0.0416 \\ 0.0134 & -0.1184 & 1.0154 \end{bmatrix}$	$\begin{bmatrix} 0.5767 & 0.1856 & 0.1882 \\ 0.2974 & 0.6273 & 0.0753 \\ 0.0270 & 0.0707 & 0.9911 \end{bmatrix}$	$\gamma = \frac{1}{2\frac{51}{256}} \approx \frac{1}{2.2}$ $f = $ N.A. $s = $ N.A. $t = $ N.A.
HDTV (HD-CIF)	$\begin{bmatrix} 3.2405 & -1.5371 & -0.4985 \\ -0.9693 & 1.8760 & 0.0416 \\ 0.0556 & -0.2040 & 1.0572 \end{bmatrix}$	$\begin{bmatrix} 0.4124 & 0.3576 & 0.1805 \\ 0.2126 & 0.7152 & 0.0722 \\ 0.0193 & 0.1192 & 0.9505 \end{bmatrix}$	$\gamma = 0.45$ $f = 0.099$ $s = 4.5$ $t = 0.018$
NTSC (1953)/ ITU-R BT.601-4	$\begin{bmatrix} 1.9100 & -0.5325 & -0.2882 \\ -0.9847 & 1.9992 & -0.0283 \\ 0.0583 & -0.1184 & 0.8976 \end{bmatrix}$	$\begin{bmatrix} 0.6069 & 0.1735 & 0.2003 \\ 0.2989 & 0.5866 & 0.1145 \\ 0.0000 & 0.0661 & 1.1162 \end{bmatrix}$	$\gamma = 0.45$ $f = 0.099$ $s = 4.5$ $t = 0.018$
PAL/SECAM	$\begin{bmatrix} 3.0629 & -1.3932 & -0.4758 \\ -0.9693 & 1.8760 & 0.0416 \\ 0.0679 & -0.2289 & 1.0694 \end{bmatrix}$	$\begin{bmatrix} 0.4306 & 0.3415 & 0.1783 \\ 0.2220 & 0.7066 & 0.0713 \\ 0.0202 & 0.1296 & 0.9391 \end{bmatrix}$	$\gamma = 0.45$ $f = 0.099$ $s = 4.5$ $t = 0.018$
SMPTE-C	$\begin{bmatrix} 3.5054 & -1.7395 & -0.5440 \\ -1.0691 & 1.9778 & 0.0352 \\ 0.0563 & -0.1970 & 1.0502 \end{bmatrix}$	$\begin{bmatrix} 0.3936 & 0.3652 & 0.1916 \\ 0.2124 & 0.7010 & 0.0865 \\ 0.0187 & 0.1119 & 0.9582 \end{bmatrix}$	$\gamma = 0.45$ $f = 0.099$ $s = 4.5$ $t = 0.018$
SMPTE-240M	$\begin{bmatrix} 2.042 & -0.565 & -0.345 \\ -0.894 & 1.815 & 0.032 \\ 0.064 & -0.129 & 0.912 \end{bmatrix}$	$\begin{bmatrix} 0.567 & 0.190 & 0.193 \\ 0.279 & 0.643 & 0.077 \\ 0.000 & 0.073 & 1.016 \end{bmatrix}$	$\gamma = 0.45$ $f = 0.1115$ $s = 4.0$ $t = 0.0228$
Wide Gamut	$\begin{bmatrix} 1.4625 & -0.1845 & -0.2734 \\ -0.5228 & 1.4479 & 0.0681 \\ 0.0346 & -0.0958 & 1.2875 \end{bmatrix}$	$\begin{bmatrix} 0.7164 & 0.1010 & 0.1468 \\ 0.2587 & 0.7247 & 0.0166 \\ 0.0000 & 0.0512 & 0.7740 \end{bmatrix}$	$\gamma = $ N.A. $f = $ N.A. $s = $ N.A. $t = $ N.A.

Figure 21.10. Transformations for standard RGB color spaces (after (Pascale, 2003)).

This transform is known as the Hunt-Pointer-Estevez transform (Hunt, 2004) and is used in chromatic adaptation transforms as well as in color appearance modeling.

21.2.4   CIE 1976 $L^*a^*b^*$

Color opponent spaces are characterized by a channel representing an achromatic channel (luminance), as well as two channels encoding color opponency. These are frequently red-green and yellow-blue channels. These color opponent channels thus encode two chromaticities along one axis, which can have both positive and negative values. For instance, a red-green channel encodes red for positive values and green for negative values. The value zero encodes a special case: neutral which is neither red or green. The yellow-blue channel works in much the same way.

As at least two colors are encoded on each of the two chromatic axes, it is not possible to encode a mixture of red and green. Neither is it possible to encode yellow and blue simultaneously. While this may seem a disadvantage, it is known that the human visual system computes similar attributes early in the visual pathway. As a result, humans are not able to perceive colors that are simultaneously red and green, or yellow and blue. We do not see anything resembling reddish-green, or yellowish-blue. We are, however, able to perceive mixtures of colors such as yellowish-red (orange) or greenish-blue, as these are encoded across the chromatic channels.

The most relevant color opponent system for computer graphics is the CIE 1976 $L^*a^*b^*$ color model. It is a perceptually more or less uniform color space, useful, among other things, for the computation of color differences. It is also known as CIELAB.

The input to CIELAB are the stimulus (X, Y, Z) tristimulus values as well as the tristimulus values of a diffuse white reflecting surface that is lit by a known illuminant, (X_n, Y_n, Z_n). CIELAB therefore goes beyond being an ordinary color space, as it takes into account a patch of color in the context of a known illumination. It can thus be seen as a rudimentary color appearance space.

The three channels defined in CIELAB are L^*, a^*, and b^*. The L^* channel encodes the lightness of the color, i.e., the perceived reflectance of a patch with tristimulus value (X, Y, Z). The a^* and b^* are chromatic opponent channels. The transform between XYZ and CIELAB is given by

$$\begin{bmatrix} L^* \\ a^* \\ b^* \end{bmatrix} = \begin{bmatrix} 0 & 116 & 0 & -16 \\ 500 & -500 & 0 & 0 \\ 0 & 200 & -200 & 0 \end{bmatrix} \begin{bmatrix} f(X/X_n) \\ f(Y/Y_n) \\ f(Z/Z_n) \\ 1 \end{bmatrix}.$$

The function f is defined as

$$f(r) = \begin{cases} \sqrt[3]{r} & \text{for } r > 0.008856, \\ 7.787\, r + \dfrac{16}{116} & \text{for } r \leq 0.008856. \end{cases}$$

As can be seen from this formulation, the chromatic channels do depend on the luminance Y. Although this is perceptually accurate, it means that we cannot plot the values of a^* and b^* in a chromaticity diagram. The lightness L^* is normalized between 0 and 100 for black and white. Although the a^* and b^* channels are not explicitly constrained, they typically in the range $[-128, 128]$.

As CIELAB is approximately perceptually linear, it is possible to take two colors, convert them to CIELAB, and then estimate the perceived color difference by computing the Euclidean distance between them. This leads to the following color difference formula:

$$\Delta E^*_{ab} = \left[(\Delta L^*)^2 + (\Delta a^*)^2 + (\Delta b^*)^2\right]^{1/2}.$$

The letter E stands for difference in sensation (in German, Empfindung) (Judd, 1932).

Finally, the inverse transform between CIELAB and XYZ is given by

$$X = X_n \begin{cases} \left(\dfrac{L^*}{116} + \dfrac{a^*}{500} + \dfrac{16}{116}\right)^3 & \text{if } L^* > 7.9996, \\ \dfrac{1}{7.787}\left(\dfrac{L^*}{116} + \dfrac{a^*}{500}\right) & \text{if } L^* \le 7.9996, \end{cases}$$

$$Y = Y_n \begin{cases} \left(\dfrac{L^*}{116} + \dfrac{16}{116}\right)^3 & \text{if } L^* > 7.9996, \\ \dfrac{1}{7.787}\dfrac{L^*}{116} & \text{if } L^* \le 7.9996, \end{cases}$$

$$Z = Z_n \begin{cases} \left(\dfrac{L^*}{116} - \dfrac{b^*}{200} + \dfrac{16}{116}\right)^3 & \text{if } L^* > 7.9996, \\ \dfrac{1}{7.787}\left(\dfrac{L^*}{116} - \dfrac{b^*}{200}\right) & \text{if } L^* \le 7.9996. \end{cases}$$

21.3 Chromatic Adaptation

The CIELAB color space just described takes as input both a tristimulus value of the stimulus and the tristimulus value of light reflected off a white diffuse patch. As such, it forms the beginnings of a system in which the viewing environment is taken into account.

The environment in which we observe objects and images has a large influence on how we perceive those objects. The range of viewing environments that we encounter in daily life is very large, from sunlight to starlight and from candlelight to fluorescent light. The lighting conditions not only constitute a very large range in the amount of light that is present, but also vary greatly in the color of the emitted light.

The human visual system accommodates these changes in the environment through a process called adaptation. Three different types of adaptation can be distinguished, namely light adaptation, dark adaptation, and chromatic adaptation. Light adaptation refers to the changes that occur when we move from a very dark to a very light environment. When this happens, at first we are dazzled by the light, but soon we adapt to the new situation and begin to distinguish objects in our environment. Dark adaptation refers to the opposite—when we go from a light environment to a dark environment. At first, we see very little, but after a given amount of time, details will start to emerge. The time needed to adapt to the dark is generally much longer than for light adaptation.

Chromatic adaptation refers to our ability to adapt, and largely ignore, variations in the color of the illumination. Chromatic adaptation is, in essence, the biological equivalent of the white balancing operation that is available on most modern cameras. The human visual system effectively normalizes the viewing conditions to present a visual experience that is fairly consistent. Thus, we exhibit a certain amount of color constancy: object reflectances appear relatively constant despite variations in illumination.

Although we are able to largely ignore changes in viewing environment, we are not able to do so completely. For instance, colors appear much more colorful on a sunny day than they do on a cloudy day. Although the appearances have changed, we do not assume that object reflectances themselves have actually changed their physical properties. We thus understand that the lighting conditions have influenced the overall color appearance.

Nonetheless, color constancy does apply to chromatic content. Chromatic adaptation allows white objects to appear white for a large number of lighting conditions, as shown in Figure 21.11.

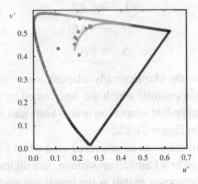

Figure 21.11. A series of light sources plotted in the CIE $u'v'$ chromaticity diagram. A white piece of paper illuminated by any of these light sources maintains a white color appearance. (See also Plate XXXI.)

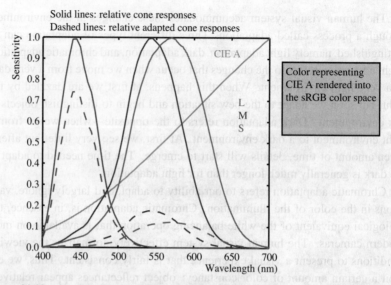

Solid lines: relative cone responses
Dashed lines: relative adapted cone responses

Figure 21.12. An example of von Kries–style independent photoreceptor gain control. The relative cone responses (solid line) and the relative adapted cone responses to CIE illuminant A (dashed) are shown. The separate patch of color represents CIE illuminant A rendered into the sRGB color space. (See also Plate XXXII.)

Computational models of chromatic adaptation tend to focus on the gain control mechanism in the cones. One of the simplest models assumes that each cone adapts independently to the energy that it absorbs. This means that different cone types adapt differently dependent on the spectrum of the light being absorbed. Such adaptation can then be modeled as an adaptive and independent rescaling of the cone signals:

$$L_a = \alpha\, L,$$
$$M_a = \beta\, M,$$
$$S_a = \gamma\, S,$$

where (L_a, M_a, S_a) are the chromatically adapted cone signals, and α, β, and γ are the independent gain controls which are determined by the viewing environment. This type of independent adaptation is also known as von-Kries adaptation. An example is shown in Figure 21.12.

The adapting illumination can be measured off a white surface in the scene. In the ideal case, this would be a Lambertian surface. In a digital image, the adapting illumination can also be approximated as the maximum tristimulus values of the scene. The light measured or computed in this manner is the adapting white, given by (L_w, M_w, S_w). Von Kries adaptation is then simply a scaling by the reciprocal of the adapting white, carried out in cone response space:

$$\begin{bmatrix} L_a \\ M_a \\ S_a \end{bmatrix} = \begin{bmatrix} \dfrac{1}{L_w} & 0 & 0 \\ 0 & \dfrac{1}{M_w} & 0 \\ 0 & 0 & \dfrac{1}{S_w} \end{bmatrix} \begin{bmatrix} L \\ M \\ S \end{bmatrix}.$$

In many cases, we are interested in what stimulus should be generated under one illumination to match a given color under a different illumination. For example, if we have a colored patch illuminated by daylight, we may ask ourselves what tristimulus values should be generated to create a matching color patch that will be illuminated by incandescent light.

We are thus interested in computing corresponding colors, which can be achieved by cascading two chromatic adaptation calculations. In essence, the above von Kries transform divides out the adapting illuminant—in our example, the daylight illumination. If we subsequently multiply in the incandescent illuminant, we have computed a corresponding color. If the two illuminants are given by $(L_{w,1}, M_{w,1}, S_{w,1})$ and $(L_{w,2}, M_{w,2}, S_{w,2})$, the corresponding color (L_c, M_c, S_c) is given by

$$\begin{bmatrix} L_c \\ M_c \\ S_c \end{bmatrix} = \begin{bmatrix} L_{w,2} & 0 & 0 \\ 0 & M_{w,2} & 0 \\ 0 & 0 & S_{w,2} \end{bmatrix} \begin{bmatrix} \dfrac{1}{L_{w,1}} & 0 & 0 \\ 0 & \dfrac{1}{M_{w,1}} & 0 \\ 0 & 0 & \dfrac{1}{S_{w,1}} \end{bmatrix} \begin{bmatrix} L \\ M \\ S \end{bmatrix}.$$

There are several more complicated and, therefore, more accurate chromatic adaptation transform in existence (Reinhard et al., 2008). However, the simple von Kries model remains remarkably effective in modeling chromatic adaptation and can thus be used to achieve white balancing in digital images.

The importance of chromatic adaptation in the context of rendering, is that we have moved one step closer to taking into account the viewing environment of the observer, without having to correct for it by adjusting the scene and rerendering our imagery. Instead, we can model and render our scenes, and then, as an image post-process, correct for the illumination of the viewing environment. To ensure that white balancing does not introduce artifacts, however, it is important to ensure that the image is rendered to a floating-point format. If rendered to traditional 8-bit image formats, the chromatic adaptation transform may amplify quantization errors.

21.4 Color Appearance

While colorimetry allows us to accurately specify and communicate color in a device-independent manner, and chromatic adaptation allows us to predict color matches across changes in illumination, these tools are still insufficient to describe what colors actually look like.

To predict the actual perception of an object, we need to know more information about the environment and take that information into account. The human visual system is constantly adapting to its environment, which means that the perception of color will be strongly influenced by such changes. Color appearance models take into account measurements of the stimulus itself, as well as the viewing environment. This means that the resulting description of color is independent of viewing condition.

The importance of color appearance modeling can be seen in the following example. Consider an image being displayed on an LCD screen. When making a print of the same image and viewing it in a different context, more often than not the image will look markedly different. Color appearance models can be used to predict the changes required to generate an accurate cross-media color reproduction (Fairchild, 2005).

Although color appearance modeling offers important tools for color reproduction, actual implementations tend to be relatively complicated and cumbersome in practical use. It can be anticipated that this situation may change over time. However, until then, we leave their description to more specialized text books (Fairchild, 2005).

Notes

Of all the books on color theory, Reinhard et al.'s work (Reinhard et al., 2008) is most directly geared towards engineering disciplines, including computer graphics, computer vision, and image processing. Other general introductions to color theory are given by Berns (Berns, 2000) and Stone (Stone, 2003). Wyszecki and Stiles have produced a comprehensive volume of data and formulae, forming an indispensable reference work (Wyszecki & Stiles, 2000). For color reproduction, we recommend Hunt's book (Hunt, 2004). Color appearance models are comprehensively described in Fairchild's book (Fairchild, 2005). For color issues related to video and HDTV Poynton's book is essential. (Poynton, 2003).

William B. Thompson

22

Visual Perception

The ultimate purpose of computer graphics is to produce images for viewing by people. Thus, the success of a computer graphics system depends on how well it conveys relevant information to a human observer. The intrinsic complexity of the physical world and the limitations of display devices make it impossible to present a viewer with the identical patterns of light that would occur when looking at a natural environment. When the goal of a computer graphics system is physical realism, the best we can hope for is that the system be *perceptually effective*: displayed images should "look" as intended. For applications such as technical illustration, it is often desirable to visually highlight relevant information and perceptual effectiveness becomes an explicit requirement.

Artists and illustrators have developed empirically a broad range of tools and techniques for effectively conveying visual information. One approach to improving the perceptual effectiveness of computer graphics is to utilize these methods in our automated systems. A second approach builds directly on knowledge of the human vision system by using perceptual effectiveness as an optimization criteria in the design of computer graphics systems. These two approaches are not completely distinct. Indeed, one of the first systematic examinations of visual perception is found in the notebooks of Leonardo da Vinci.

The remainder of this chapter provides a partial overview of what is known about visual perception in people. The emphasis is on aspects of human vision that are most relevant to computer graphics. The human visual system is extremely complex in both its operation and its architecture. A chapter such as this can at best provide a summary of key points, and it is important to avoid over generalizing from what is presented here. More in-depth treatments of visual perception can be found in Wandell (1995) and Palmer (1999); Gregory (1997) and Yantis (2000) provide additional useful information. A good computer vision reference such as Forsyth and Ponce (2002) is also helpful. It is important to note that despite over 150 years of intensive research, our knowledge of many aspects of vision is still very limited and imperfect.

22.1   Vision Science

Vision is generally agreed to be the most powerful of the senses in humans. Vision produces more useful information about the world than does hearing, touch, smell, or taste. This is a direct consequence of the physics of light (Figure 22.1). Illumination is pervasive, especially during the day but also at night due to moonlight, starlight, and artificial sources. Surfaces reflect a substantial portion of incident illumination and do so in ways that are idiosyncratic to particular materials and that are dependent on the shape of the surface. The fact that light (mostly) travels in straight lines through the air allows vision to acquire information from distant locations.

The study of vision has a long and rich history. Much of what we know about the eye traces back to the work of philosophers and physicists in the 1600s. Starting in the mid-1800s, there was an explosion of work by perceptual psychologists exploring the phenomenology of vision and proposing models of how vision might work. The mid-1900s saw the start of modern neuroscience, which investigates both the fine-scale workings of individual neurons and the large-scale architectural organization of the brain and nervous system. A substantial portion of neuroscience research has focused on vision. More recently, computer science has contributed to the understanding of visual perception by providing tools for precisely describing hypothesized models of visual computations and by allowing empirical examination of computer vision programs. The term *vision science* was coined to refer to the multidisciplinary study of visual perception involving perceptual psychology, neuroscience, and computational analysis.

Vision science views the purpose of vision as producing information about objects, locations, and events in the world from imaged patterns of light reaching the viewer. Psychologists use the term *distal stimulus* to refer to the physical world under observation and *proximal stimulus* to refer to the retinal image.[1] Us-

Light:

- travels far
- travels fast
- travels in straight lines
- interacts with stuff
- bounces off things
- is produced in nature
- has lots of energy

—Steven Shafer

Figure 22.1. The nature of light makes vision a powerful sense.

---

[1] In computer vision, the term *scene* is often used to refer to the external world, while the term *image* is used to refer to the projection of the scene onto a sensing plane.

ing this terminology, the function of vision is to generate a description of aspects of the distal stimulus given the proximal stimulus. Visual perception is said to be *veridical* when the description that is produced accurately reflects the real world. In practice, it makes little sense to think of these descriptions of objects, locations, and events in isolation. Rather, vision is better understood in the context of the motor and cognitive functions that it serves.

22.2   Visual Sensitivity

Vision systems create descriptions of the visual environment based on properties of the incident illumination. As a result, it is important to understand what properties of incident illumination the human vision system can actually detect. One critical observation about the human vision system is that it is primarily sensitive to *patterns* of light rather than being sensitive to the absolute magnitude of light energy. The eye does not operate as a photometer. Instead, it detects spatial, temporal, and spectral patterns in the light imaged on the retina and information about these patterns of light form the basis for all of visual perception.

There is a clear ecological utility to the vision system's sensitivity to variations in illumination over space and time. Being able to accurately sense changes in the environment is crucial to our survival.[2] A system which measures changes in light energy rather than the magnitude of the energy itself also makes engineering sense, since it makes it easier to detect patterns of light over large ranges in light intensity. It is a good thing for computer graphics that vision operates in this manner. Display devices are physically limited in their ability to project light with the power and dynamic range typical of natural scenes. Graphical displays would not be effective if they needed to produce the identical patterns of light as the corresponding physical world. Fortunately, all that is required is that displays be able to produce similar patterns of spatial and temporal change to the real world.

22.2.1   Brightness and Contrast

In bright light, the human visual system is capable of distinguishing gratings consisting of high contrast parallel light and dark bars as fine as 50–60 cycles/degree. (In this case, a "cycle" consists of an adjacent pair of light and dark bars.) For

---

[2]It is sometime said that the primary goals of vision are to support eating, avoiding being eaten, reproduction, and avoidance of catastrophe while moving. Thinking about vision as a goal-directed activity is often useful, but needs to be done so at a more detailed level.

Figure 22.2.   The contrast between stripes increases in a constant manner from top to bottom, yet the threshold of visibility varies with frequency.

comparison, the best currently available LCD computer monitor, at a normal viewing distance, can display patterns as fine as about 20 cycles/degree. The minimum contrast difference at an edge detectable by the human visual system in bright light is about 1% of the average luminance across the edge. In most 8-bit displays, differences of a single gray level are often noticeable over at least a portion of the range of intensities due to the nature of the mapping from gray levels to actual display luminance.

Characterizing the ability of the visual system to detect fine scale patterns (*visual acuity*) and to detect changes in brightness is considerably more complicated than for cameras and similar image acquisition devices. As shown in Figure 22.2, there is an interaction between contrast and acuity in human vision. In the figure, the scale of the pattern decreases from left to right while the contrast increases from top to bottom. If you view the figure at a normal viewing distance, it will be clear that the lowest contrast at which a pattern is visible is a function of the spatial frequency of the pattern.

There is a linear relationship between the intensity of light L reaching the eye from a particular surface point in the world, the intensity of light I illuminating that surface point, and the reflectivity R of the surface at the point being observed:

$$L = \alpha I \cdot R, \tag{22.1}$$

Figure 22.3. *Lightness constancy.* Cast a shadow over one of the patterns with your hand and notice that the apparent brightness of the two center squares remains nearly the same.

where α is dependent on the relationship between the surface geometry, the pattern of incident illumination, and the viewing direction. While the eye is only able to directly measure L, human vision is much better at estimating R than L. To see this, view Figure 22.3 in bright direct light. Use your hand to shadow one of the patterns, leaving the other directly illuminated. While the light reflected off of the two patterns will be significantly different, the apparent brightness of the two center squares will seem nearly the same. The term *lightness* is often used to describe the apparent brightness of a surface, as distinct from its actual luminance. In many situations, lightness is invariant to large changes in illumination, a phenomenon referred to as *lightness constancy*.

The mechanisms by which the human visual system achieves lightness constancy are not well understood. As shown in Figure 22.2, the vision system is relatively insensitive to slowly varying patterns of light, which may serve to discount the effects of slowly varying illumination. Apparent brightness is affected by the brightness of surrounding regions (Figure 22.4). This can aid lightness constancy when regions are illuminated dissimilarly. While this *simultaneous contrast* effect is often described as a modification of the perceived lightness of

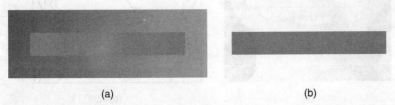

(a)   (b)

Figure 22.4. (a) Simultaneous contrast: the apparent brightness of the center bar is affected by the brightness of the surrounding area; (b) The same bar without a variable surround.

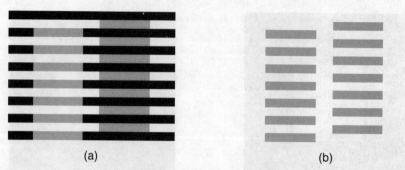

(a)   (b)

Figure 22.5. The Munker-White illusion shows the complexity of simultaneous contrast. In Figure 22.4, the central region looked lighter when the surrounding area was darker. In (a), the gray strips on the left look *lighter* than the gray strips on the right, even though they are nearly surrounded by regions of white; (b) shows the gray strips without the black lines.

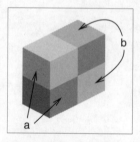

Figure 22.6. The perception of lightness is affected by the perception of 3D structure. The two surfaces marked (a) have the same brightness, as do the two surfaces marked (b) (after Adelson (1999)).

one region based on contrasting brightness in the surrounding region, it is actually much more complicated than that (Figures 22.5 and 22.6). For more on lightness perception, see (Gilchrist et al., 1999) and (Adelson, 1999).

While the visual system largely ignores slowly varying intensity patterns, it is extremely sensitive to *edges* consisting of lines of discontinuity in brightness. Edges in imaged light intensity often correspond to surface boundaries or other important features in the environment (Figure 22.7). The vision system can also detect localized differences in motion, stereo disparity, texture, and several other

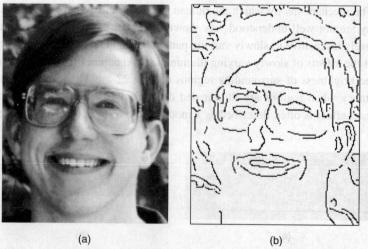

(a)   (b)

Figure 22.7. (a) Original gray scale image, (b) image *edges*, which are lines of high spatial variability in some direction.

Figure 22.8. The visual system sometimes sees "edges" even when there are no sharp discontinuities in brightness, as is the case at the right side of the central pattern in this image.

image properties. The vision system has very little ability, however, to detect spatial discontinuities in color when not accompanied by differences in one of these other properties.

Perception of edges seems to interact with perception of form. While edges give the visual system the information it needs to recognize shapes, slowly varying brightness can appear as a sharp edge if the resulting edge creates a more complete form (Figure 22.8). Figure 22.9 shows a *subjective contour*, an extreme form of this effect in which a closed contour is seen even though no such contour exists in the actual image. Finally, the vision system's sensitivity to edges also appears to be part of the mechanism involved in lightness perception. Note that the region enclosed by the subjective contour in Figure 22.9 appears a bit brighter than the surrounding area of the page. Figure 22.10 shows a different interaction between edges and lightness. In this case, a particular brightness profile at the edge has a dramatic effect on the apparent brightness of the surfaces to either side of the edge.

Figure 22.9. Sometimes, the visual system will "see" *subjective contours* without any associated change in brightness.

Figure 22.10. Perceived lightness depends more on local contrast at edges than on brightness across surfaces. Try covering the vertical edge in the middle of the figure with a pencil. This figure is an instance of the *Craik-O'Brien-Cornsweet illusion.*

As indicated above, people can detect differences in the brightness between two adjacent regions if the difference is at least 1% of the average brightness. This is an example of *Weber's law*, which states that there is a constant ratio between the *just noticeable differences* (jnd) in a stimulus and the magnitude of the stimulus:

$$\frac{\Delta I}{I} = k_1, \tag{22.2}$$

where I is the magnitude of the stimulus, ΔI is the magnitude of the just noticeable difference, and k_1 is a constant particular to the stimulus. Weber's law was postulated in 1846 and still remains a useful characterization of many perceptual effects. *Fechner's law*, proposed in 1860, generalized Weber's law in a way that allowed for the description of the strength of any sensory experience, not just jnd's:

$$S = k_2 \log(I), \tag{22.3}$$

where S is the perceptual strength of the sensory experience, I is the physical magnitude of the corresponding stimulus, and k_2 is a scaling constant specific to the stimulus. Current practice is to model the association between perceived and actual strength of a stimulus using a power function (*Stevens's law*):

$$S = k_3 I^b, \tag{22.4}$$

where S and I are as before, k_3 is another scaling constant, and b is an exponent specific to the stimulus. For a large number of perceptual quantities involving vision, $b < 1$. The CIE L*a*b* color space, described elsewhere, uses a modified Stevens's law representation to characterize perceptual differences between brightness values. Note that in the first two characterizations of the perceptual strength of a stimulus and in Steven's Law when $b < 1$, changes in the stimulus when it has a small average magnitude create larger perceptual effects than do the same physical change in the stimulus when it has a larger magnitude.

The "laws" describe above are not physical constraints on how perception operates. Rather, they are generalizations about how the perceptual system responds to particular physical stimuli. In the field of perceptual psychology, the quantitative study of the relationships between physical stimuli and their perceptual effects is called *psychophysics*. While psychophysical laws are empirically derived observations rather than mechanistic accounts, the fact that so many perceptual effects are well modeled by simple power functions is striking and may provide insights into the mechanisms involved.

22.2.2   Color

In 1666, Isaac Newton used prisms to show that apparently white sunlight could be decomposed into a *spectrum* of colors and that these colors could be recombined to produce light that appeared white. We now know that light energy is made up of a collection of photons, each with a particular wavelength. The *spectral distribution* of light is a measure of the average energy of the light at each wavelength. For natural illumination, the spectral distribution of light reflected off of surfaces varies significantly depending on the surface material. Characterizations of this spectral distribution can therefore provide visual information for the nature of surfaces in the environment.

Most people have a pervasive sense of color when they view the world. Color perception depends on the frequency distribution of light, with the visible spectrum for humans ranging from a wavelength of about 370 nm to a wavelength of about 730 nm (see Plate X). The manner in which the visual systems derives a sense of color from this spectral distribution was first systematically examined in 1801 and remained extremely controversial for 150 years. The problem is that the visual system responds to patterns of spectral distribution very differently than patterns of luminance distribution.

Even accounting for phenomena such as lightness constancy, distinctly different spatial distributions almost always look distinctly different. More importantly given that the purpose of the visual system is to produce descriptions of the distal stimulus given the proximal stimulus, perceived patterns of lightness correspond at least approximately to patterns of brightness over surfaces in the environment. The same is not true of color perception. Many quite different spectral distributions of light can produce a sense of any specific color. Correspondingly, the sense that a surface is a specific color provides little direct information about the spectral distribution of light coming from the surface. For example, a spectral

"The history of the investigation of colour vision is remarkable for its acrimony."

—Richard Gregory (1997)

distribution consisting of a combination of light at wavelengths of 700 nm and 540 nm, with appropriately chosen relative strengths, will look indistinguishable from light at the single wavelength of 580 nm. (Perceptually indistinguishable colors with different spectral compositions are referred to as *metamers*.) If we see the color "yellow," we have no way of knowing if it was generated by one or the other of these distributions or an infinite family of other spectral distributions. For this reason, in the context of vision the term *color* refers to a purely perceptual quality, not a physical property.

There are two classes of photoreceptors in the human retina. *Cones* are involved in color perception, while *rods* are sensitive to light energy across the visible range and do not provide information about color. There are three types of cones, each with a different spectral sensitivity (Figure 22.11). *S-cones* respond to short wavelengths in the blue range of the visible spectrum. *M-cones* respond to wavelengths in the middle (greenish) region of the visible spectrum. *L-cones* respond to somewhat longer wavelengths covering the green and red portions of the visible spectrum.

While it is common to describe the three types of cones as *red*, *green*, and *blue*, this is neither correct terminology nor does it accurately reflect the cone sensitivities shown in Figure 22.11. The *L-cones* and *M-cones* are broadly tuned, meaning that they respond to a wide range of frequencies. There is also substantial overlap between the sensitivity curves of the three cone types. Taken together, these two properties mean that it is not possible to reconstruct an approximation to the original spectral distribution given the responses of the three cone types. This is in contrast to spatial sampling in the retina (and in digital cameras), where

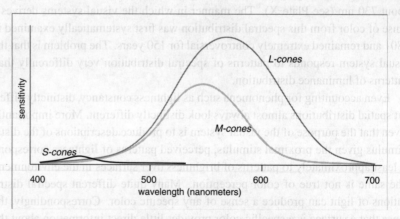

Figure 22.11. Spectral sensitivity of the *short, medium,* and *long* cones in the human retina.

the receptors are narrowly tuned in their spatial sensitivity in order to be able to detect fine detail in local contrast.

The fact that there are are only three types of color sensitive photoreceptors in the human retina greatly simplifies the task of displaying colors on computer monitors and in other graphical displays. Computer monitors display colors as a weighted combination of three fixed color distributions. Most often, the three colors are a distinct red, a distinct green, and a distinct blue. As a result, in computer graphics, color is often represented by a *red-green-blue* (RGB) triple, representing the intensities of red, green, and blue primaries needed to display a particular color. Three *basis colors* are sufficient to display most perceptible colors, since appropriately weighted combinations of three appropriately chosen colors can produce metamers for these perceptible colors.

There are at least two significant problems with the RGB color representation. The first is that different monitors have different spectral distributions for their red, green, and blue primaries. As a result, perceptually correct color rendition involves remapping RGB values for each monitor. This is of course only possible if the original RGB values satisfy some well defined standard, which is often not the case. See Chapter 21 for more information on this issue. The second problem is that RGB values do not define a particular color in a way that corresponds to subjective perception. When we see the color "yellow," we do not have the sense that it is made up of equal parts of red and green light. Rather, it looks like a single color, with additional properties involving brightness and the "amount" of color. Representing color as the output of the S-cones, M-cones, and L-cones is no help either, since we have no more phenomenological sense of color as characterized by these properties than we do as characterized by RGB display properties.

There are two different approaches to characterizing color in a way that more closely reflects human perception. The various CIE color spaces aim to to be "perceptually uniform" so that the magnitude of the difference in the represented values of two colors is proportional to the perceived difference in color (Wyszecki & Stiles, 2000). This turns out to be a difficult goal to accomplish, and there have been several modifications to the CIE model over the years. Furthermore, while one of the dimensions of the CIE color spaces corresponds to perceived brightness, the other two dimensions that specify chromaticity have no intuitive meaning.

The second approach to characterizing color in a more natural manner starts with the observation that there are three distinct and independent properties that dominate the subjective sense of color. *Lightness*, the apparent brightness of a surface, has already been discussed. *Saturation* refers to the purity or vividness of a color. Colors can range from totally unsaturated gray to partially saturated pastels to fully saturated "pure" colors. The third property, *hue*, corresponds most closely to the informal sense of the word "color" and is characterized in a manner similar to colors in the visible spectrum, ranging from dark violet to dark red. Plate XI shows a plot of the hue-saturation-lightness (HSV) color space. Since the relationship between brightness and lightness is both complex and not well understood, HSV color spaces almost always use brightness instead of attempting to estimate lightness. Unlike wavelengths in the spectrum, however, hue is usually represented in a manner that reflects the fact that the extremes of the visible spectrum are actually similar in appearance (Plate XII). Simple transformations exist between RGB and HSV representations of a particular color value. As a result, while the HSV color space is motivated by perceptual considerations, it contains no more information than does an RGB representation.

The hue-saturation-lightness approach to describing color is based on the spectral distribution at a single point and so only approximates the perceptual response to spectral distributions of light distributed over space. Color perception is subject to similar constancy and simultaneous contrast effects as is lightness/brightness, neither of which are captured in the RGB representation and as a result are not captured in the HSV representation. For an example of color constancy, look at a piece of white paper indoors under incandescent light and outdoors under direct sunlight. The paper will look "white" in both cases, even though incandescent light has a distinctly yellow hue and so the light reflected off of the paper will also have a yellow hue, while sunlight has a much more uniform color spectrum.

Another aspect of color perception not captured by either the CIE color spaces or HSV encoding is the fact that we see a small number of distinct colors when looking at a continuous spectrum of visible light (Plate X) or in a naturally occurring rainbow. For most people, the visible spectrum appears to be divided into four to six distinct colors: red, yellow, green, and blue, plus perhaps light blue and purple. Considering non-spectral colors as well, there are only eleven basic color terms commonly used in English: *red*, *green*, *blue*, *yellow*, *black*, *white*, *gray*, *orange*, *purple*, *brown*, and *pink*. The partitioning of the intrinsically continuous space of spectral distributions into a relatively small set of perceptual categories associated with well defined linguistic terms seems to be a basic property of perception, not just a cultural artifact (Berlin & Kay, 1969). The exact nature of the process, however, is not well understood.

22.2.3 Dynamic Range

Natural illumination varies in intensity over 6 orders of magnitude (Figure 22.12). The human vision system is able to operate over this full range of brightness levels. However, at any one point in time the visual system is only able to detect variations in light intensity over a much smaller range. As the average brightness to which the visual system is exposed changes over time, the range of discriminable brightnesses changes in a corresponding manner. This effect is most obvious if we move rapidly from a brightly lit outdoor area to a very dark room. At first, we are able to see little. After a while, however, details in the room start to become apparent. The *dark adaptation* that occurs involves a number physiological changes in the eye. It takes several minutes for significant dark adaptation to occur and 40 minutes or so for complete dark adaptation. If we then move back into the bright light, not only is vision difficult but it can actually be painful. *Light adaptation* is required before it is again possible to see clearly. Light adaptation occurs much more quickly than dark adaptation, typically requiring less than a minute.

direct sunlight	10^5
indoor lighting	10^2
moonlight	10^{-1}
starlight	10^{-3}

Figure 22.12. Approximate luminance level of a white surface under different types of illumination in candelas per meter squared (cd/m^2). (Wandell, 1995).

The two classes of photoreceptors in the human retina are sensitive to different ranges of brightness. The cones provide visual information over most of what we consider normal lighting conditions, ranging from bright sunlight to dim indoor lighting. The rods are only effective at very low light levels. *Photopic* vision involves bright light in which only the cones are effective. *Scotopic* vision involves dark light in which only the rods are effective. There is a range of intensities within which both cones and rods are sensitive to changes in light, which is referred to as *mesopic* conditions (see Chapter 23).

22.2.4   Field-of-View and Acuity

Each eye in the human visual system has a field-of-view of approximately 160° horizontal by 135° vertical. With binocular viewing, there is only partial overlap between the fields-of-view of the two eyes. This results in a wider overall field-of-view (approximately 200° horizontal by 135° vertical), with the region of overlap being approximately 120° horizontal by 135° vertical.

With normal or corrected-to-normal vision, we usually have the subjective experience of being able to see relatively fine detail wherever we look. This is an illusion, however. Only a small portion of the visual field of each eye is actually sensitive to fine detail. To see this, hold a piece of paper covered with normal-sized text at arms length, as shown in Figure 22.13. Cover one eye with the hand not holding the paper. While staring at your thumb and not moving your eye, note that the text immediately above your thumb is readable while the text to either side is not. High acuity vision is limited to a visual angle slightly larger than your thumb held at arm's length. We do not normally notice this because the eyes usually move frequently, allowing different regions of the visual field to be viewed at high resolution. The visual system then integrates this information over

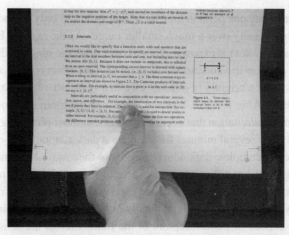

Figure 22.13. If you hold a page of text at arm's length and stare at your thumb, only the text near your thumb will be readable. *Photo by Peter Shirley.*

time to produce the subjective experience of the whole visual field being seen at high resolution.

There is not enough bandwidth in the human visual cortex to process the information that would result if there was a dense sampling of image intensity over the whole of the retina. The combination of variable density photoreceptor packing in the retina and a mechanism for rapid eye movements to point at areas of interest provides a way to simultaneously optimize acuity and field-of-view. Other animals have evolved different ways of balancing acuity and field-of-view that are not dependent on rapid eye movements. Some have only high acuity vision, but limited to a narrow field-of-view. Others have wide field-of-view vision, but limited ability to see detail.

The eye motions which focus areas of interest in the environment on the fovea are called *saccades*. Saccades occur very quickly. The time from a triggering stimulus to the completion of the eye movement is 150–200 ms. Most of this time is spent in the vision system planning the saccade. The actual motion takes 20 ms or so on average. The eyes are moving very quickly during a saccade, with the maximum rotational velocity often exceeding 500°/second. Between saccades, the eyes point towards an area of interest (*fixate*), taking 300 ms or so to acquire fine detail visual information. The mechanism by which multiple fixations are integrated to form an overall subjective sense of fine detail over a wide field of view is not well understood.

Figure 22.14 shows the variable packing density of cones and rods in the human retina. The cones, which are responsible for vision under normal lighting, are packed most closely at the *fovea* of the retina (Figure 22.14). When the eye

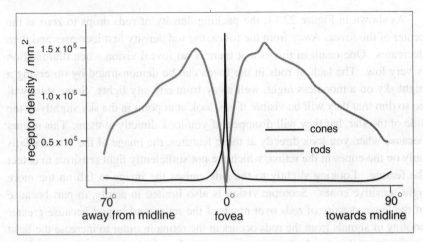

Figure 22.14. Density of rods and cone in the human retina (after Osterberg (1935)).

is fixated at a particular point in the environment, the image of that point falls on the fovea. The higher packing density of cones at the fovea results in a higher sampling frequency of the imaged light (see Chapter 9) and hence greater detail in the sampled pattern. Foveal vision encompasses about 1.7°, which is the same visual angle as the width of your thumb held at arm's length.

While a version of Figure 22.14 appears in most introductory texts on human visual perception, it provides only a partial explanation for the neurophysiological limitations on visual acuity. The output of individual rods and cones are pooled in various ways by neural interconnects in the eye, before the information is shipped along the optic nerve to the visual cortex.[3] This pooling filters the signal provided by the pattern of incident illumination in ways that have important impacts on the patterns of light that are detectable. In particular, the farther away from the fovea, the larger the area over which brightness is averaged. As a consequence, spatial acuity drops sharply away from the fovea. Most figures showing rod and cone packing density indicate the location of the retinal *blind spot*, where the nerve bundle carrying optical information from the eye to the brain passes through the retina, and there is no sensitivity to light. By and large, the only practical impact of the blind spot on real-world perception is its use as an illusion in introductory perception texts, since normal eye movements otherwise compensate for the temporary loss of information.

---

[3] All of the cells in the optic nerve and almost all cells in visual cortex have an associated retinal *receptive field*. Patterns of light hitting the retina outside of a cell's receptive field have no effect on the firing rate of that cell.

As shown in Figure 22.14, the packing density of rods drops to zero at the center of the fovea. Away from the fovea, the rod density first increases and then decreases. One result of this is that there is no foveal vision when illumination is very low. The lack of rods in the fovea can be demonstrated by observing a night sky on a moonless night, well away from any city lights. Some stars will be so dim that they will be visible if you look at at point in the sky slightly to the side of the star, but they will disappear if you look directly at them. This occurs because when you look directly at these features, the image of the features falls only on the cones in the retina, which are not sufficiently light sensitive to detect the feature. Looking slightly to the side causes the image to fall on the more light sensitive cones. Scotopic vision is also limited in acuity, in part because of the lower density of rods over much of the retina and in part because greater pooling of signals from the rods occurs in the retina in order to increase the light sensitivity of the visual information passed back to the brain.

22.2.5   Motion

When reading about visual perception and looking at static figures on a printed page, it is easy to forget that motion is pervasive in our visual experience. The patterns of light that fall on the retina are constantly changing due to eye and body motion and the movement of objects in the world. This section covers our ability to detect visual motion. Section 22.3.4 describes how visual motion can be used to determine geometric information about the environment. Section 22.4.3 deals with the use of motion to guide our movement through the environment.

The detectability of motion in a particular pattern of light falling on the retina is a complex function of speed, direction, pattern size, and contrast. The issue is further complicated because simultaneous contrast effects occur for motion perception in a manner similar to that observed in brightness perception. In the extreme case of a single small pattern moving against a contrasting, homogenous background, perceivable motion requires a rate of motion corresponding to $0.2°$–$0.3°$/second of visual angle. Motion of the same pattern moving against a textured pattern is detectable at about a tenth this speed.

With this sensitivity to retinal motion, combined with the frequency and velocity of saccadic eye movements, it is surprising that the world usually appears stable and stationary when we view it. The vision system accomplishes this in three ways. Contrast sensitivity is reduced during saccades, reducing the visual effects generated by these rapid changes in eye position. Between saccades, a variety of sophisticated and complex mechanisms adjust eye position to compensate for head and body motion and the motion of objects of interest in the world. Finally, the visual system exploits information about the position of the eyes to

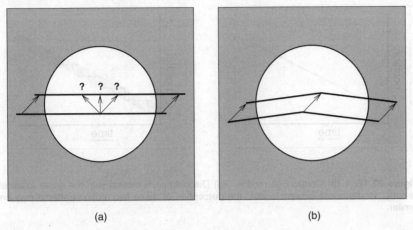

(a)   (b)

Figure 22.15.   The aperture problem: (a) If a straight line or edge moves in such a way that its end points are hidden, the visual information is not sufficient to determine the actual motion of the line. (b) 2D motion of a line is unambiguous if there are any corners or other distinctive markings on the line.

assemble a mosaic of small patches of high resolution imagery from multiple fixations into a single, stable whole.

The motion of straight lines and edges is ambiguous if no endpoints or corners are visible, a phenomenon referred to as the *aperture problem* (Figure 22.15). The aperture problem arises because the component of motion parallel to the line or edge does not produce any visual changes. The geometry of the real world is sufficiently complex that this rarely causes difficulties in practice, except for intentional illusions such as barber poles. The simplified geometry and texturing found in some computer graphics renderings, however, has the potential to introduce inaccuracies in perceived motion.

Real-time computer graphics, film, and video would not be possible without an important perceptual phenomena: discontinuous motion, in which a series of static images are visible for discrete intervals in time and then move by discrete intervals in space, can be nearly indistinguishable from continuous motion. The effect is called *apparent motion* to highlight that the appearance of continuous motion is an illusion.

Figure 22.16 illustrates the difference between continuous motion, which is typical of the real world, and apparent motion, which is generated by almost all dynamic image display devices. The motion plotted in Figure 22.16 (b) consists of an average motion comparable to that shown in Figure 22.16 (a), modulated by a high space-time frequency that accounts for the alternation between a stationary pattern and one that moves discontinuously to a new location. Apparent percep-

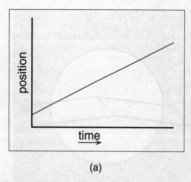
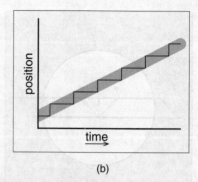

(a)   (b)

Figure 22.16. (a) Continuous motion. (b) Discontinuous motion with the same average velocity. Under some circumstances, the perception of these two motion patterns may be similar.

tion of continuous motion occurs because the visual system is insensitive to the high frequency component of the motion.

A compelling sense of apparent motion occurs when the rate at which individual images appear is above about 10 Hz, as long as the positional changes between successive images is not too great. This rate is not fast enough, however, to produce a satisfying sense of continuous motion for most image display devices. Almost all such devices introduce brightness variation as one image is switched to the next. In well lit conditions, the human visual system is sensitive to this varying brightness for rates of variations up to about 80 Hz. In lower light, detectability is present up to about 40 Hz. When the rate of alternating brightness is sufficiently high, *flicker fusion* occurs and the variation is no longer visible.

To produce a compelling sense of visual motion, an image display must therefore satisfy two separate constraints:

- images must be updated at a rate $\geq$ 10 Hz;
- any flicker introduced in the process of updating images must occur at a rate $\geq$ 60–80 Hz.

One solution is to require that the image update rate be greater than or equal to 60–80 Hz. In many situations, however, this is simply not possible. For computer graphics displays, the frame computation time is often substantially greater than 12–15 msec. Transmission bandwidth and limitations of older monitor technologies limit normal broadcast television to 25–30 images per second. (Some HDTV formats operate at 60 images/sec.) Movies update images at 24 frames/second due to exposure time requirements and the mechanical difficulties of physically moving film any faster than that.

Different display technologies solve this problem in different ways. Computer displays refresh the displayed image at ~70–80 Hz, regardless of how often the contents of the image change. The term *frame rate* is ambiguous for such displays, since two values are required to characterize this display: *refresh rate*, which indicates the rate at which the image is redisplayed and *frame update rate*, which indicates the rate at which new images are generated for display. Standard non-HDTV broadcast television uses a refresh rate of 60 Hz (NTSC, used in North America and some other locations) or 50 Hz (PAL, used in most of the rest of the world). The frame update rate is half the refresh rate. Instead of displaying each new image twice, the display is *interlaced* by dividing alternating horizontal image lines into even and odd *fields* and alternating the display of these even and odd fields. Flicker is avoided in movies by using a mechanical shutter to blink each frame of the film three times before moving to the next frame, producing a refresh rate of 72 Hz while maintaining the frame update rate of 24 Hz.

The use of apparent motion to simulate continuous motion occasionally produces undesirable artifacts. Best known of these is the *wagon wheel illusion* in which the spokes of a rotating wheel appear to revolve in the opposite direction from what would be expected given the translational motion of the wheel. The wagon wheel illusion is an example of temporal aliasing. Spokes, or other spatially periodic patterns on a rotating disk, produce a temporally periodic signal for viewing locations that are fixed with respect to the center of the wheel or disk. Fixed frame update rates have the effect of sampling this temporally periodic signal in time. If the temporal frequency of the sampled pattern is too high, under sampling results in an aliased, lower temporal frequency appearing when the image is displayed. Under some circumstances, this distortion of temporal frequency causes a spatial distortion in which the wheel appears to move backwards. Wagon wheel illusions are more likely to occur with movies than with video, since the temporal sampling rate is lower.

Problems can also occur when apparent motion imagery is converted from one medium to another. This is of particular concern when 24 Hz movies are transferred to video. Not only does a non-interlaced format need to be translated to an interlaced format, but there is no straightforward way to move from 24 frames per second to 50 or 60 fields per second. Some high-end display devices have the ability to partially compensate for the artifacts introduced when film is converted to video.

22.3 Spatial Vision

One of the critical operations performed by the visual system is the estimation of geometric properties of the visible environment, since these are central to determining information about objects, locations, and events. Vision has sometimes been described as *inverse optics*, to emphasize that one function of the visual system is to invert the image formation process in order to determine the geometry, materials, and lighting in the world that produced a particular pattern on light on the retina. The central problem for a vision system is that properties of the visible environment are confounded in the patterns of light imaged on the retina. Brightness is a function of both illumination and reflectance, and can depend on environmental properties across large regions of space due to the complexities of light transport. Image locations of a projected environmental location at best can be used to constrain the position of that location to a half-line. As a consequence, it is rarely possible to uniquely determine the nature of the world that produced a particular imaged pattern of light.

Determining *surface layout*—the location and orientation of visible surfaces in the environment—is thought to be a key step in human vision. Most discussions of how the vision system extracts information about surface layout from the patterns of light it receives divide the problem into a set of *visual cues*, with each cue describing a particular visual pattern which can be used to infer properties of surface layout along with the needed rules of inference. Since surface layout can rarely be determined accurately and unambiguously from vision alone, the process of inferring surface layout usually requires additional, non-visual information. This can come from other senses or assumptions about what is likely to occur in the real world.

Visual cues are typically categorized into four categories. *Ocularmotor cues* involve information about the position and focus of the eyes. *Disparity cues* involve information extracted from viewing the same surface point with two eyes, beyond that available just from the positioning of the eyes. *Motion cues* provide information about the world that arises from either the movement of the observer or the movement of objects. *Pictorial cues* result from the process of projecting 3D surface shapes onto a 2D pattern of light that falls on the retina. This section deals with the visual cues relevant to the extraction of geometric information about individual points on surfaces. More general extraction of location and shape information is covered in Section 22.4.

22.3.1 Frames of Reference and Measurement Scales

Descriptions of the location and orientation of points on a visible surface must be done within the context of a particular frame of references that specifies the origin, orientation, and scaling of the coordinate system used in representing the geometric information. The human vision system uses multiple frames of reference, partially because of the different sorts of information available from different visual cues and partly because of the different purposes to which the information is put (Klatzky, 1998). *Egocentric* representations are defined with respect to the viewer's body. They can be subdivided into coordinate systems fixed to the eyes, head, or body. *Allocentric* representations, also called *exocentric* representations, are defined with respect to something external to the viewer. Allocentric frames of reference can be local to some configuration of objects in the environment or can be globally defined in terms of distinctive locations, gravity, or geographic properties.

The distance from the viewer to a particular visible location in the environment, expressed in an egocentric representation, is often referred to as *depth* in the perception literature. Surface orientation can be represented in either egocentric or allocentric coordinates. In egocentric representations of orientation, the term *slant* is used to refer to the angle between the line of sight to the point and the surface normal at the point, while the term *tilt* refers to the orientation of the projection of the surface normal onto a plane perpendicular to the line of sight.

Distance and orientation can be expressed in a variety of *measurement scales*. *Absolute* descriptions are specified using a standard that is not part of the sensed information itself. These can be culturally defined standards (e.g, meters), or standards relative to the viewer's body (e.g., eye height, the width of one's shoulders). *Relative* descriptions relate one perceived geometric property to another (e.g., point a is twice as far away as point b). *Ordinal* descriptions are a special

Cue	a	r	o	Requirements for absolute depth
Accommodation	x	x	x	very limited range
Binocular convergence	x	x	x	limited range
Binocular disparity	-	x	x	limited range
Linear perspective, height in picture, horizon ratio	x	x	x	requires viewpoint height
Familiar size	x	x	x	
Relative size	-	x	x	
Aerial perspective	?	x	x	adaptation to local conditions
Absolute motion parallax	?	x	x	requires viewpoint velocity
Relative motion parallax	-	-	x	
Texture gradients	-	x	-	
Shading	-	x	-	
Occlusion	-	-	x	

Figure 22.17. Common visual cues for absolute (a), relative (r), and ordinal (o) depth.

case of relative measure in which the sign, but not the magnitude, of the relation is all that is represented. Figure 22.17 provides a list of the most commonly considered visual cues, along with a characterization of the sorts of information they can potentially provide.

22.3.2   Ocularmotor Cues

Ocularmotor information about depth results directly from the muscular control of the eyes. There are two distinct types of ocularmotor information. *Accommodation* is the process by which the eye optically focuses at a particular distance. *Convergence* (often referred to as *vergence*) is the process by which the two eyes are pointed towards the same point in three-dimensional space. Both accommodation and convergence have the potential to provide absolute information about depth.

Physiologically, focusing in the human eye is accomplished by distorting the shape of the lens at the front of the eye. The vision system can infer depth from the amount of this distortion. Accommodation is a relatively weak cue to distance and is ineffective beyond about 2 m. Most people have increasing difficultly in focusing over a range of distances as they get beyond about 45 years old. For them, accommodation becomes even less effective.

Those not familiar with the specifics of visual perception sometimes confuse depth estimation from accommodation with depth information arising out of the

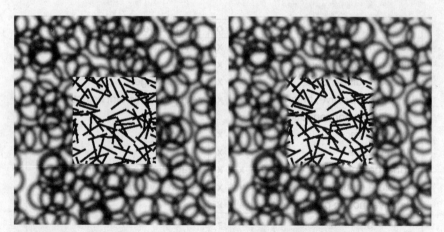

Figure 22.18. Does the central square appear in front of the pattern of circles or is it seen as appearing through a square hole in the pattern of circles? The only difference in the two images is the sharpness of the edge between the line and circle patterns (Marshall et al. (1999), used by permission).

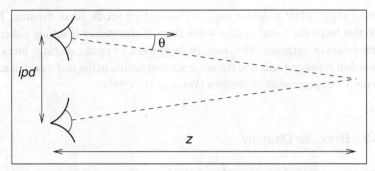

Figure 22.19. The *vergence* of the two eyes provides information about the distance to the point on which the eyes are fixated.

blur associated with limited depth-of-field in the eye. The accommodation depth cue provides information about the distance to that portion of the visual field that it is in focus. It does not depend on the degree to which other portions of the visual field are out of focus, other than that blur is used by the visual system to adjust focus. Depth-of-field does seem to provide a degree of ordinal depth information (Figure 22.18), though this effect has received only limited investigation.

If two eyes fixate on the same point in space, trigonometry can be used to determine the distance from the viewer to the viewed location (Figure 22.19). For the simplest case, in which the point of interest is directly in front of the viewer,

$$z = \frac{ipd/2}{\tan \theta},\tag{22.5}$$

where z is the distance to a point in the world, *ipd* is the *interpupillary distance* indicating the distance between the eyes, and θ is the *vergence angle* indicating the orientation of the eyes relative to straight ahead. For small θ, which is the case for the geometric configuration of human eyes, $\tan \theta \approx \theta$ when θ is expressed in radians. Thus, differences in vergence angle specify differences in depth by the following relationship:

$$\Delta\theta \approx \frac{ipd}{2} \cdot \frac{1}{\Delta z}.\tag{22.6}$$

As $\theta \to 0$ in uniform steps, Δz gets increasingly larger. This means that stereo vision is less sensitive to changes in depth as the overall depth increases. Convergence in fact only provides information on absolute depth for distances out to a few meters. Beyond that, changes in distance produce changes in vergence angle that are too small to be useful.

There is an interaction between accommodation and convergence in the human visual system: accommodation is used to help determine the appropriate vergence angle, while vergence angle is used to help set the focus distance. Normally, this helps the visual system when there is uncertainty is setting either accommodation or vergence. However, stereographic computer displays break the relationship between focus and convergence that occurs in the real world, leading to a number of perceptual difficulties (Wann et al., 1995).

22.3.3 Binocular Disparity

The vergence angle of the eyes when fixated on a common point in space is only one of the ways that the visual system is able to determine depth from binocular stereo. A second mechanism involves a comparison of the retinal images in the two eyes and does not require information about where the eyes are pointed. A simple example demonstrates the effect. Hold your arm straight out in front of you, with your thumb pointed up. Stare at your thumb and then close one eye. Now, simultaneously open the closed eye and close the open eye. Your thumb will appear to be more or less stationary, while the more distant surfaces seen behind your thumb will appear to move from side to side (Figure 22.20). The change in retinal position of points in the scene between the left and right eyes is called *disparity*.

The binocular disparity cue requires that the vision system be able to match the image of points in the world in one eye with the imaged locations of those points in the other eye, a process referred to as the *correspondence problem*. This is a relatively complicated process and is only partially understood. Once correspondences have been established, the relative positions on which particular

(left eye image)   (right eye image)

Figure 22.20. Binocular disparity. The view from the left and right eyes shows an offset for surface points at depths different from the point of fixation. *Images courtesy Peter Shirley.*

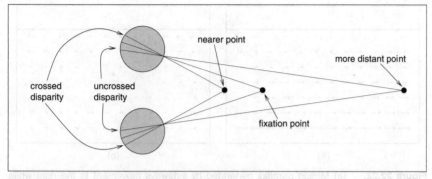

Figure 22.21. Near the line of sight, surface points nearer than the fixation point produce disparities in the opposite direction from those associated with surface points more distant than the fixation point.

points in the world project onto the left and right retinas indicate whether the points are closer than or farther away than the point of fixation. *Crossed disparity* occurs when the corresponding points are displaced outward relative to the fovea and indicates that the surface point is closer than the point of fixation. *Uncrossed disparity* occurs when the corresponding points are displaced inward relative to the fovea and indicates that the surface point is farther away than the point of fixation (Figure 22.21).[4] Binocular disparity is a relative depth cue, but it can provide information about absolute depth when scaled by convergence. Equation (22.5) applies to binocular disparity as well as binocular convergence. As with convergence, the sensitivity of binocular disparity to changes in depth decreases with depth.

22.3.4 Motion Cues

Relative motion between the eyes and visible surfaces will produce changes in the image of those surfaces on the retina. Three-dimensional relative motion between the eye and a surface point produces two-dimensional motion of the projection of the surface point on the retina. This retinal motion is given the name *optic flow*. Optic flow serves as the basis for several types of depth cues. In addition, optic flow can be used to determine information about how a person is moving in the world and whether or not a collision is imminent (Section 22.4.3).

If a person moves to the side while continuing to fixate on some surface point, then optic flow provides information about depth similar to stereo disparity. This

---

[4]Technically, crossed and uncrossed disparities indicate that the surface point generating the disparity is closer to or farther away from the *horopter*. The horopter is not a fixed distance away from the eyes but rather it is a curved surface passing through the point of fixation.

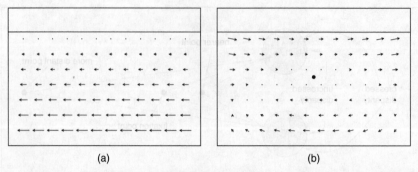

(a)   (b)

Figure 22.22. (a) Motion parallax generated by sideways movement to the right while looking at an extended ground plane. (b) The same motion, with eye tracking of the fixation point.

is referred to as *motion parallax*. For other surface points that project to retinal locations near the fixation point, zero optic flow indicates a depth equivalent to the fixation point; flow in the opposite direction to head translation indicates nearer points, equivalent to crossed disparity; and flow in the same direction as head translation indicates farther points, equivalent to uncrossed disparity (Figure 22.22). Motion parallax is a powerful cue to relative depth. In principle, motion parallax can provide absolute depth information if the visual system has access to information about the velocity of head motion. In practice, motion parallax appears at best to be a weak cue for absolute depth.

In addition to egocentric depth information due to motion parallax, visual motion can also provide information about the three-dimensional shape of objects moving relative to the viewer. In the perception literature, this is known as the *kinetic depth effect*. In computer vision, it is referred to as *structure-from-motion*. The kinetic depth effect presumes that one component of object motion is *rotation in depth*, meaning that there is a component of rotation around an axis perpendicular to the line of sight.

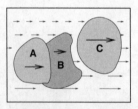

Figure 22.23. Discontinuities in optic flow signal surface boundaries. In many cases, the sign of the depth change (i.e., the ordinal depth) can be determined.

Optic flow can also provide information about the shape and location of surface boundaries, as shown in Figure 22.23. Spatial discontinuities in optic flow almost always either correspond to depth discontinuities or result from independently moving objects. Simple comparisons of the magnitude of optic flow are insufficient to determine the sign of depth changes, except in the special case of a viewer moving through an otherwise static world. Even when independently moving objects are present, however, the sign of the change in depth across surface boundaries can often be determined by other means. Motion often changes the portion of the more distant surface visible at surface boundaries. The appearance (*accretion*) or disappearance (*deletion*) of surface texture occurs because the nearer, occlud*ing* surface progressively uncovers or covers portions of the more

distant, occlud*ed* surface. Comparisons of the motion of surface texture to either
side of a boundary can also be used to infer ordinal depth, even in the absence
of accretion or deletion of the texture. Discontinuities in optic flow and accre-
tion/deletion of surface texture are referred to as *dynamic occlusion* cues and are
another powerful source of visual information about the spatial structure of the
environment.

The speed that a viewer is traveling relative to points in the world cannot be
determined from visual motion alone (see Section 22.4.3). Despite this limitation,
it is possible to use visual information to determine the time it will take to reach a
visible point in the world even when speed cannot be determined. When velocity
is constant, *time-to-contact* (often referred to as *time-to-collision*) is given by the
retinal size of an entity towards which the observer is moving, divided by the rate
at which that image size is increasing.[5] In the biological vision literature, this is
often called the *τ function* (Lee & Reddish, 1981). If distance information to the
structure in the world on which the time-to-collision estimate is based is available,
then this can be used to determine speed.

22.3.5 Pictorial Cues

An image can contain much information about the spatial structure of the world
from which it arose, even in the absence of binocular stereo or motion. As evidence for this, note that the world still appears three-dimensional even if we close
one eye, hold our head stationary, and nothing moves in the environment. (As
discussed in Section 22.5, the situation is more complicated in the case of photographs and other displayed images.) There are three classes of such *pictorial
depth cues*. The best known of these involve *linear perspective*. There are also
a number of *occlusion cues* that provide information about ordinal depth even in
the absence of perspective. Finally, *illumination cues* involving shading, shadows
and interreflections, and aerial perspective also provide visual information about
spatial layout.

The term *linear perspective* is often used to refer to properties of images involving object size in the image scaled by distance, the convergence of parallel
lines, the ground plane extending to a visible horizon, and the relationship between the distance to objects on the ground plane and the image location of those
objects relative to the horizon (Figure 22.24). More formally, linear perspective
cues are those visual cues which exploit the fact that under perspective projection,
the image location onto which points in the world are projected is scaled by $\frac{1}{z}$,

Figure 22.24. The
classical linear perspective
effects include object size
scaled by distance, the convergence of parallel lines,
the ground plane extending
to a visible horizon, and position on the ground plane
relative to the horizon. *Image courtesy Sam Pullara.*

---

[5]The terms time-to-collision and time-to-contact are misleading, since contact will only occur if
the viewer's trajectory actually passes through or near the entity under view.

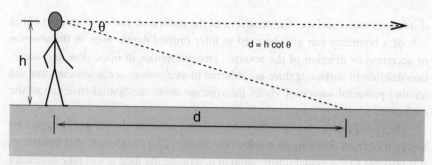

Figure 22.25. Absolute distance to locations on the ground plane can be determined based on declination angle from the horizon and eye height.

where z is the distance from the point of projection to the point in the environment. Direct consequences of this relationship are that points that are farther away are projected to points closer to the center of the image (convergence of parallel lines) and that the spacing between the image of points in the world decreases for more distant world points (object size in the image is scaled by distance).[6] The fact that the image of an infinite flat surface in the world ends at a finite horizon is explained by examining the perspective projection equation as $z \to \infty$.

With the exception of size-related effects described in Section 22.4.2, most pictorial depth cues involving linear perspective depend on objects of interest being in contact with a ground plane. In effect, these cues estimate not the distance to the objects but, instead, the distance to the contact point on the ground plane. Assuming observer and object are both on top of a horizontal ground plane, then locations on the ground plane lower in the view will be close. Figure 22.25 illustrates this effect quantitatively. For a viewpoint h above the ground and an *angle of declination* θ between the horizon and a point of interest on the ground, the point in question is a distance $d = h \cot \theta$ from the point at which the observer is standing. The angle of declination provides relative depth information for arbitrary fixed viewpoints and can provide absolute depth when scaling by eye height (h) is possible.

While the human visual system almost certainly makes use of angle of declination as a depth cue, the exact mechanisms used to acquire the needed information are not clear. The angle θ could be obtained relative to either gravity or the visible horizon. There is some evidence that both are used in human vision. Eye height h could be based on posture, visually determined by looking at the ground at one's feet, or learned by experience and presumed to be constant. While a

---

[6]The actual mathematics for analyzing the specifics of biological vision are different, since eyes are not well approximated by the planar projection formulation used in computer graphics and most other imaging applications.

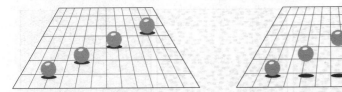

Figure 22.26. Shadows can indirectly function as a depth cue by associating the depth of an object with a location on the ground plane (after Kersten et al. (1997)).

number of researchers have investigated this issue, if and how these values are determined is not yet known with certainty.

Shadows provide a variety of types of information about three-dimensional spatial layout. *Attached shadows* indicate that an object is in contact with another surface, often consisting of the ground plane. *Detached shadows* indicate that an object is close to some surface, but not in contact with that surface. Shadows can serve as an indirect depth cue by causing an object to appear at the depth of the location of the shadow on the ground plane (Yonas et al., 1978). When utilizing this cue, the visual system seems to make the assumption that light is coming from directly above (Figure 22.26).

Vision provides information about surface orientation as well as distance. It is convenient to represent visually determined surface orientation in terms of *tilt*, defined as the orientation in the image of the projection of the surface normal, and *slant*, defined as the angle between the surface normal and the line of sight.

A visible surface horizon can be used to find the orientation of an (effectively infinite) surface relative to the viewer. Determining tilt is straightforward, since the tilt of the surface is the orientation of the visible horizon. Slant can be recovered as well, since the lines of sight from the eye point to the horizon define a plane parallel to the surface. In many situations, either the surface horizon is not visible or the surface is small enough that its far edge does not correspond to an actual horizon. In such cases, visible texture can still be used to estimate orientation.

In the context of perception, the term *texture* refers to visual patterns consisting of sub-patterns replicated over a surface. The sub-patterns and their distribution can be fixed and regular, as for a checkerboard, or consistent in a more statistical sense, as in the view of a grassy field.[7] When a textured surface is viewed from an oblique angle, the projected view of the texture is distorted relative to the actual markings on the surface. Two quite distinct types of distortions occur (Knill, 1998), both affected by the amount of slant. The position and size

---

[7]In computer graphics, the term *texture* has a different meaning, referring to any image that is applied to a surface as part of the rendering process.

(a)   (b)   (c)

Figure 22.27.   Texture cues for slant. (a) Near surface exhibiting compression and texture gradient; (b) distant surface exhibiting only compression; (c) variability in appearance of near surface with regular geometric variability.

of texture elements are subject to the linear perspective effects described above. This produces a *texture gradient* (Gibson, 1950) due to both element size and spacing decreasing with distance (Figure 22.27(a)). Both the image of individual texture elements and the distribution of elements are *foreshortened* under oblique viewing (Figure 22.27(b)). This produces a compression in the direction of tilt. For example, an obliquely viewed circle appears as an ellipse, with the ratio of the minor to major axes equal to the cosine of the slant. Note that foreshortening itself is not a result of linear perspective, though in practice both linear perspective and foreshortening provide information about slant.[8]

For texture gradients to serve as a cue to surface slant, the average size and spacing of texture elements must be constant over the textured surface. If spatial variability in size and spacing in the image is not due in its entirely to the projection process, then attempts to invert the effects of projection will produce incorrect inferences about surface orientation. Likewise, the foreshortening cue fails if the shape of texture elements is not isotropic, since then asymmetric texture element image shapes would occur in situations not associated with oblique viewing. These are examples of the assumptions often required in order for spatial visual cues to be effective. Such assumptions are reasonable to the degree that they reflect commonly occurring properties of the world.

Shading also provides information about surface shape (Figure 22.28). The brightness of viewed points on a surface depends on the surface reflectance and the orientation of the surface with respect to directional light sources and the observation point. When the relative position of an object, viewing direction, and illumination direction remain fixed, changes in brightness over a constant reflectance surface are indications of changes in the orientation of the surface of

---

[8]A third form of visual distortion occurs when surfaces with distinct 3D surface relief are viewed obliquely (Leung & Malik, 1997), as shown in Figure 22.27(c). Nothing is currently know about if or how this effect might be used by the human vision system to determine slant.

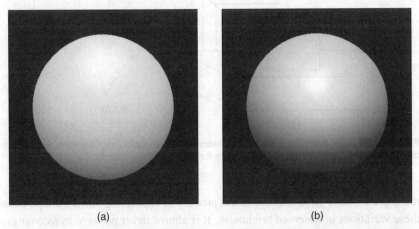

(a)   (b)

Figure 22.28. Shape-from-shading. The images in (a) and (b) appear to have different 3D shapes because of differences in the rate of change of brightness over their surfaces.

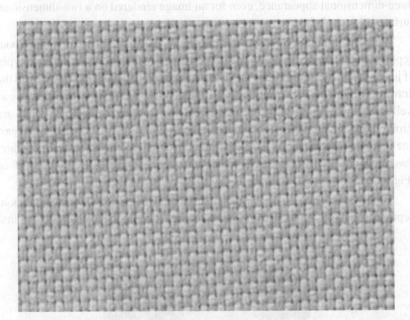

Figure 22.29. Shading can generate a strong perception of three-dimensional shape. In this figure, the effect is stronger if you view the image from several meters away using one eye. It becomes yet stronger if you place a piece of cardboard in front of the figure with a hole cut out slightly smaller than the picture (see Section 22.5). *Image courtesy Albert Yonas.* (See also Plate XIII.)

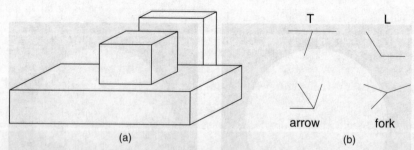

(a)   (b)

Figure 22.30.   (a) Junctions provide information about occlusion and the convexity or concavity of corners. (b) Common junction types for planar surface objects.

the object. *Shape-from-shading* is the process of recovering surface shape from these variations in observed brightness. It is almost never possible to recover the actual orientation of surfaces from shading alone, though shading can often be combined with other cues to provide an effective indication of surface shape. For surfaces with fine-scale geometric variability, shading can provide a compelling three-dimensional appearance, even for an image rendered on a two-dimensional surface (Figure 22.29).

There are a number of pictorial cues that yield ordinal information about depth, without directly indicating actual distance. In line drawings, different types of junctions provide constraints on the 3D geometry that could have generated the drawing (Figure 22.30). Many of these effects occur in more natural images as well. Most perceptually effective of the junction cues are *T-junctions*, which are strong indicators that the surface opposite the stem of the T is occluding at least one more distant surface. T-junctions often generate a sense of *amodal completion*, in which one surface is seen to continue behind a nearer, occluding surface (Figure 22.31).

Atmospheric effects cause visual changes that can provide information about depth, particularly outdoors over long distances. Leonardo da Vinci was the first

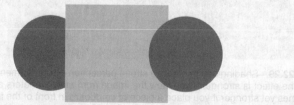

Figure 22.31.   T-junctions cause the left disk to appear to be continuing behind the rectangle, while the right disk appears in front of the rectangle which is seen to continue behind the disk.

to describe *aerial perspective* (also called *atmospheric perspective*), in which scattering reduces the contrast of distant portions of the scene and causes them to appear more bluish than if they were nearer (da Vinci, 1970) (see Plate XX). Aerial perspective is predominantly a relative depth cue, though there is some speculation that it may affect perception of absolute distance as well. While many people believe that more distant objects look blurrier due to atmospheric effects, atmospheric scattering actually causes little blur.

22.4   Objects, Locations, and Events

While there is fairly wide agreement among current vision scientists that the purpose of vision is to extract information about objects, locations, and events, there is little consensus on the key features of what information is extracted, how it is extracted, or how the information is used to perform tasks. Significant controversies exist about the nature of object recognition and the potential interactions between object recognition and other aspects of perception. Most of what we know about location involves low-level spatial vision, not issues associated with spatial relationships between complex objects or the visual processes required to navigate in complex environments. We know a fair amount about how people perceive their speed and heading as they move through the world, but have only a limited understanding of actual event perception. Visual attention involves aspects of the perception of objects, locations, and events. While there is much data about the phenomenology of visual attention for relatively simple and well controlled stimuli, we know much less about how visual attention serves high-level perceptual goals.

22.4.1   Object Recognition

Object recognition involves segregating an image into constituent parts corresponding to distinct physical entities and determining the identity of those entities. Figure 22.32 illustrates a few of the complexities associated with this process. We have little difficulty recognizing that the image on the left is some sort of vehicle, even though we have never before seen this particular view of a vehicle nor do most of us typically associate vehicles with this context. The image on the right is less easily recognizable until the page is turned upside down, indicating an orientational preference in human object recognition.

Object recognition is thought to involve two, fairly distinct steps. The first step organizes the visual field into *groupings* likely to correspond to objects and

(a)   (b)

Figure 22.32. The complexities of object recognition. (a) We recognize a vehicle-like object even though we have likely never seen this particular view of a vehicle before. (b) The image is hard to recognize based on a quick view. It becomes much easier to recognize if the book is turned upside down.

surfaces. These grouping processes are very powerful (see Figure 22.33), though there is little or no conscious awareness of the low-level image features that generate the grouping effect.[9] Grouping is based on the complex interaction of proximity, similarities in the brightness, color, shape, and orientation of primitive structures in the image, common motion, and a variety of more complex relationships.

The second step in object recognition is to interpret groupings as identified objects. A computational analysis suggests that there are a number of distinctly

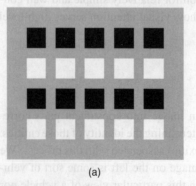 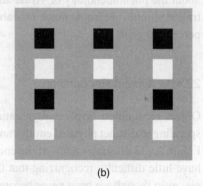

(a)   (b)

Figure 22.33. Images are perceptually organized into groupings based on a complex set of similarity and organizational criteria. (a) Similarity in brightness results in four horizontal groupings. (b) Proximity resulting in three vertical groupings.

---

[9]The most common form of visual camouflage involves adding visual textures that fool the perceptual grouping processes so that the view of the world cannot be organized in a way that separates out the object being camouflaged.

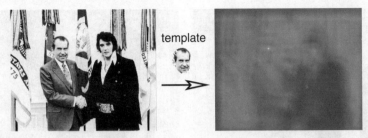

Figure 22.34. Template matching. The bright spot in the right image indicates the best match location to the template in the left image. *Image courtesy National Archives and Records Administration.*

different ways in which an object can be identified. The perceptual data is unclear as to which of these are actually used in human vision. Object recognition requires that the vision system have available to it descriptions of each class of object sufficient to discriminate each class from all others. Theories of object recognition differ in the nature of the information describing each class and the mechanisms used to match these descriptions to actual views of the world.

Three general types of descriptions are possible. *Templates* represent object classes in terms of prototypical views of objects in each class. Figure 22.34 shows a simple example. *Structural descriptions* represent object classes in terms of distinctive features of each class likely to be easily detected in views of the object, along with information about the geometric relationships between the features. Structural descriptions can either be represented in 2D or 3D. For 2D models of objects types, there must be a separate description for each distinctly different potential view of the object. For 3D models, two distinct forms of matching strategies are possible. In one, the three-dimensional structure of the viewed object is determined prior to classification using whatever spatial cues are available and then this 3D description of the view is matched to 3D prototypes of known objects. The other possibility is that some mechanism allows the determination of the orientation of the yet-to-be identified object under view. This orientation information is used to rotate and project potential 3D descriptions in a way that allows a 2D matching of the description and the viewed object. Finally, the last option for describing the properties of object classes involves *invariant features* which describe classes of objects in terms of more generic geometric properties, particularly those that are likely be be insensitive to different views of the object.

22.4.2 Size and Distance

In the absence of more definitive information about depth, objects which project onto a larger area of the retina are seen as closer compared with objects which

Figure 22.35. Left: perspective and familiar size cues are consistent. Right: perspective and familiar size cues are inconsistent. *Images courtesy Peter Shirley, Scott Kuhl, and J. Dylan Lacewell.*

project to a smaller retinal area, an effect called *relative size*. A more powerful cue involves *familiar size*, which can provide information for absolute distance to recognizable objects of known size. The strength of familiar size as a depth cue can be seen in illusions such as Figure 22.35, in which it is put in conflict with ground-plane, perspective-based depth cues. Familiar size is one part of the *size-distance* relationship, relating the physical size of an object, the optical size of the same object projected onto the retina, and the distance of the object from the eye (Figure 22.36).

When objects are sitting on top of a flat ground plane, additional sources for depth information become available, particularly when the horizon is either vis-

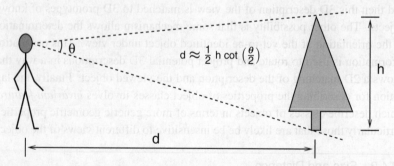

Figure 22.36. The *size-distance relationship* allows the distance to objects of known size to be determined based on the visual angle subtended by the object. Likewise, the size of an object at a know distance can be determined based on the visual angle subtended by the object.

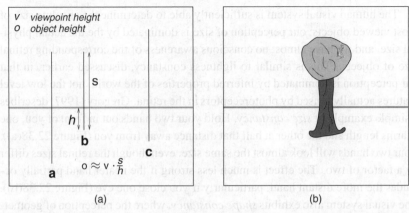

v viewpoint height
o object height

$$o \approx v \cdot \frac{s}{h}$$

(a)   (b)

Figure 22.37. (a) The *horizon ratio* can be used to determine depth by comparing the visible portion of an object below the horizon to the total vertical visible extent of the object. (b) A real-world example.

ible or can be derived from other perspective information. The angle of declination to the contact point on the ground is a relative depth cue and provides absolute egocentric distance when scaled by eye height, as previously shown in Figure 22.25. The *horizon ratio*, in which the total visible height of an object is compared with the visible extent of that portion of the object appearing below the horizon, can be used to determine the actual size of objects, even when the distance to the objects is not known (Figure 22.37). Underlying the horizon ratio is the fact that for a flat ground plane, the line of sight to the horizon intersects objects at a position that is exactly an eye height above the ground.

(a)   (b)

Figure 22.38. (a) Size constancy makes hands positioned at different distances from the eye appear to be nearly the same size for real-world viewing, even though the retinal sizes are quite different. (b) The effect is less strong when one hand is partially occluded by the other, particularly when one eye is closed. *Images courtesy Peter Shirley and Pat Moulis.*

The human visual system is sufficiently able to determine the absolute size of most viewed objects; our perception of size is dominated by the the actual physical size, and we have almost no conscious awareness of the corresponding retinal size of objects. This is similar to lightness constancy, discussed earlier, in that our perception is dominated by inferred properties of the world, not the low level features actually sensed by photoreceptors in the retina. Gregory (1997) describes a simple example of *size constancy*. Hold your two hands out in front of you, one at arms length and the other at half that distance away from you (Figure 22.38(a)). Your two hands will look almost the same size, even though the retinal sizes differ by a factor of two. The effect is much less strong if the nearer hand partially occludes the more distant hand, particularly if you close one eye (Figure 22.38(b)). The visual system also exhibits *shape constancy*, where the perception of geometric structure is close to actual object geometry than might be expected given the distortions of the retinal image due to perspective (Figure 22.39).

Figure 22.39. Shape constancy—the table looks rectangular even though its shape in the image is an irregular four sided polygon.

22.4.3   Events

Most aspects of event perception are beyond the scope of this chapter, since they involve complex non-visual cognitive processes. Three types of event perception are primarily visual, however, and are also of clear relevance to computer graphics. Vision is capable of providing information about how a person is moving in the world, the existence of independently moving objects in the world, and the potential for collisions either due to observer motion or due to objects moving towards the observer.

Vision can be used to determine rotation and the direction of translation relative to the environment. The simplest case involves movement towards a flat surface oriented perpendicularly to the line of sight. Presuming that there is sufficient surface texture to enable the recovery of optic flow, the flow field will form a symmetric pattern as shown in Figure 22.40(a). The location in the field of view of the *focus of expansion* of the flow field will have an associated line of sight corresponding to the direction of translation. While optic flow can be used to visually determine the direction of motion, it does not contain enough information to determine speed. To see this, consider the situation in which the world is made twice as large and the viewer moves twice as fast. The decrease in the magnitude of flow values due to the doubling of distances is exactly compensated for by the increase in the magnitude of flow values due to the doubling of velocity, resulting in an identical flow field.

Figure 22.40(b) shows the optic flow field resulting from the viewer (or more accurately, the viewer's eyes) rotating around the vertical axis. Unlike the situa-

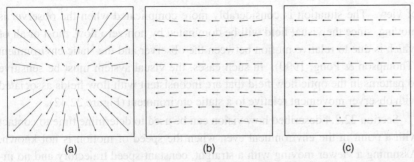

(a) (b) (c)

Figure 22.40. (a) Movement towards a flat, textured surface produces an expanding flow field, with the *focus of expansion* indicating the line of sight corresponding to the direction of motion. (b) The flow field resulting from rotation around the vertical axis while viewing a flat surface oriented perpendicularly to the line of sight. (c) The flow field resulting from translation parallel to a flat, textured surface.

tion with respect to translational motion, optic flow provides sufficient information to determine both the axis of rotation and the (angular) speed of rotation. The practical problem in exploiting this is that the flow resulting from pure rotational motion around an axis perpendicular to the line of sight is quite similar to the flow resulting from pure translation in the direction that is perpendicular to both the line of sight and this rotational axis, making it difficult to visually discriminate between the two very different types of motion (Figure 22.40(c)). Figure 22.41 shows the optical flow patterns generated by movement through a more realistic environment.

If a viewer is completely stationary, visual detection of moving objects is easy, since such objects will be associated with the only non-zero optic flow in the field

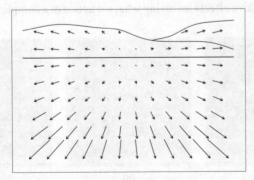

Figure 22.41. The optic flow generated by moving through an otherwise static environment provides information about both the motion relative to the environment and the distances to points in the environment. In this case, the direction of view is depressed from the horizon, but as indicated by the focus of expansion, the motion is parallel to the ground plane.

of view. The situation is considerably more complicated when the observer is moving, since the visual field will be dominated by non-zero flow, most or all of which is due to relative motion between the observer and the static environment (Thompson & Pong, 1990). In such cases, the visual system must be sensitive to patterns in the optic flow field that are inconsistent with flow fields associated with observer movement relative to a static environment (Figure 22.42).

Section 22.3.4 described how vision can be used to determine time to contact with a point in the environment even when the speed of motion is not known. Assuming a viewer moving with a straight, constant-speed trajectory and no independently moving objects in the world, contact will be made with whatever surface is in the direction of the line of sight corresponding to the focus of expansion at a time indicated by the τ relationship. An independently moving object complicate the matter of determining if a collision will in fact occur. Sailors use a method for detecting potential collisions that may also be employed in the human visual system: for non-accelerating straight-line motion, collisions will occur with objects that are visually expanding but otherwise remain visually stationary in the egocentric frame of reference.

One form of more complex event perception merits discussion here, since it is so important in interactive computer graphics. People are particularly sensitive to motion corresponding to human movement. Locomotion can be recognized when the only features visible are lights on the walker's joints (Johansson, 1973). Such *moving light displays* are often even sufficient to recognize properties such as the sex of the walker and the weight of the load that the walker may be carrying. In computer graphics renderings, viewers will notice even small inaccuracies in animated characters, particularly if they are intended to mimic human motion.

The term *visual attention* covers a range of phenomenon from where we point our eyes to cognitive effects involving what we notice in a complex scene and how

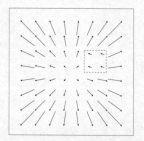

Figure 22.42. Visual detection of moving objects from a moving observation point requires recognizing patterns in the optic flow that cannot be associated with motion through a static environment.

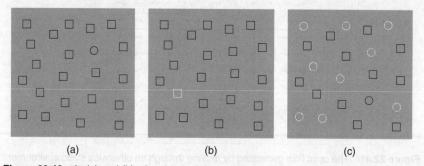

Figure 22.43. In (a) and (b), visual attention is quickly drawn to the item of different shape or color. In (c), sequential search appears to be necessary in order to find the one item that differs in both shape and color.

we interpret what we notice (Pashler, 1998). Figure 22.43 provides an example of how attentional processes affect vision, even for very simple images. In the left two panels, the one pattern differing in shape or color from the rest immediately "pops out" and is easily noticed. In the panel on the right, the one pattern differing in both shape and color is harder to find. The reason for this is that the visual system can do a parallel search for items distinguished by individual properties, but requires more cognitive, sequential search when looking for items that are indicated by the simultaneous presence of two distinguishing features. Graphically based human-computer interfaces should be (but often are not!) designed with an understanding of how to take advantage of visual attention processes in people so as to communicate important information quickly and effectively.

22.5 Picture Perception

So far, this chapter has dealt with the visual perception that occurs when the world is directly imaged by the human eye. When we view the results of computer graphics, of course, we are looking at rendered images and not the real world. This has important perceptual implications. In principle, it should be possible to generate computer graphics that appears indistinguishable from the real world, at least for monocular viewing without either object or observer motion. Imagine looking out at the world through a glass window. Now, consider coloring each point on the window to exactly match the color of the world originally seen at that point.[10] The light reaching the eye is unchanged by this operation, meaning that perception should be the same whether the painted glass is viewed or the real world is viewed through the window. The goal of computer graphics can be thought of as producing the colored window without actually having the equivalent real-world view available.

The problem for computer graphics and other visual arts is that we can't in practice match a view of the real world by coloring a flat surface. The brightness and dynamic range of light in the real world is impossible to recreate using any current display technology. Resolution of rendered images is also often less that the finest detail perceivable by human vision. Lightness and color constancy are much less apparent in pictures than in the real world, likely because the visual system attempts to compensate for variability in the brightness and color of the illumination based on the ambient illumination in the viewing environment rather than the illumination associated with the rendered image. This is why the real-

---

[10]This idea was first described by the painter Leon Battista Alberti in 1435 and is now known as *Alberti's Window*. It is closely related to the *camera obscura*.

istic appearance of color in photographs depends on film color balanced for the nature of the light source present when the photograph was taken and why realistic color in video requires a white-balancing step. While much is known about how limitations in resolution, brightness, and dynamic range affect the detectability of simple patterns, almost nothing is known about how these display properties affect spatial vision or object identification.

We have a better understanding of other aspects of this problem, which psychologists refer to as the perception of *pictorial space* (S. Rogers, 1995). One difference between viewing images and viewing the real world is that accommodation, binocular stereo, motion parallax, and perhaps other depth cues may indicate that the surface under view is much different that the distances in the world that it is intended to represent. The depths that are seen in such a situation tend to be somewhere between the depths indicated by the pictorial cues in the image and the distance to the image itself. When looking at a photograph or computer display, this often results in a sense of scale smaller than intended. On the other hand, seeing a movie in a big-screen theater produces a more compelling sense of spaciousness than does seeing the same movie on television, even if the distance to the TV is such that the visual angles are the same, since the movie screen is farther away.

Computer graphics rendered using perspective projection has a viewpoint, specified as a position and direction in model space, and a view frustum, which specifies the horizontal and vertical field of view and several other aspects of the viewing transform. If the rendered image is not viewed from the correct location, the visual angles to the borders of the image will not match the frustum used in creating the image. All visual angles within the image will be distorted as well, causing a distortion in all of the pictorial depth and orientation cues based on linear perspective. This effect occurs frequently in practice, when a viewer is positioned either too close or too far away from a photograph or display surface. If the viewer is too close, the perspective cues for depth will be compressed, and the cues for surface slant will indicate that the surface is closer to perpendicular to the line of sight than is actually the case. The situation is reversed if the viewer is too far from the photograph or screen. The situation is even more complicated if the line of sight does not go through the center of the viewing area, as is commonly the case in a wide variety of viewing situations.

The human visual system is able to partially compensate for perspective distortions arising from viewing an image at the wrong location, which is why we are able to sit in different seats at a movie theater and experience a similar sense of the depicted space. When controlling viewing position is particularly important, *viewing tubes* can be used. These are appropriately sized tubes, mounted in a fixed position relative to the display, and through which the viewer sees the display. The viewing tube constrains the observation point to the (hopefully) correct position. Viewing tubes are also quite effective at reducing the conflict in depth information between the pictorial cues in the image and the actual display surface. They eliminate both stereo and motion parallax, which if present would correspond to the display surface, not the rendered view. If they are small enough in diameter, they also reduce other cues to the location of the display surface by hiding the picture frame or edge of the display device. Exotic visually immersive display devices such as head-mounted displays (HMDs) go further in attempting to hide visual cues to the position of the display surface while adding binocular stereo and motion parallax consistent with the geometry of the world being rendered.

Erik Reinhard

23

Tone Reproduction

As discussed in Chapter 22, the human visual system adapts to a wide range of viewing conditions. Under normal viewing, we may discern a range of around 4 to 5 log units of illumination, i.e., the ratio between brightest and darkest areas where we can see detail may be as large as $100,000 : 1$. Through adaptation processes, we may adapt to an even larger range of illumination. We call images that are matched to the capabilities of the human visual system *high dynamic range*.

Visual simulations routinely produce images with a high dynamic range (Ward Larson & Shakespeare, 1998). Recent developments in image-capturing techniques allow multiple exposures to be aligned and recombined into a single high dynamic range image (Debevec & Malik, 1997). Multiple exposure techniques are also available for video. In addition, we expect future hardware to be able to photograph or film high dynamic range scenes directly. In general, we may think of each pixel as a triplet of three floating point numbers.

As it is becoming easier to create high dynamic range imagery, the need to display such data is rapidly increasing. Unfortunately, most current display devices, monitors and printers, are only capable of displaying around 2 log units of dynamic range. We consider such devices to be of low dynamic range. Most images in existence today are represented with a byte-per-pixel-per-color channel, which is matched to current display devices, rather than to the scenes they represent.

Typically, low dynamic range images are not able to represent scenes without loss of information. A common example is an indoor room with an out-

597

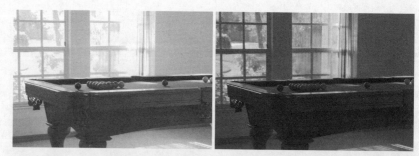

Figure 23.1. With conventional photography, some parts of the scene may be under- or over-exposed. To visualize the snooker table, the view through the window is burned out in the left image. On the other hand, the snooker table will be too dark if the outdoor part of this scene is properly exposed. Compare with Figure 23.2, which shows a high dynamic range image prepared for display using a tone reproduction algorithm.

door area visible through the window. Humans are easily able to see details of both the indoor part and the outside part. A conventional photograph typically does not capture this full range of information—the photographer has to choose whether the indoor or the outdoor part of the scene is properly exposed (see Figure 23.1). These decisions may be avoided by using high dynamic range imaging and preparing these images for display using techniques described in this chapter (see Figure 23.2).

There are two strategies available to display high dynamic range images. First, we may develop display devices which can directly accommodate a high dynamic range (Seetzen et al., 2003, 2004). Second, we may prepare high dynamic range images for display on low dynamic range display devices (Upstill, 1985). This is currently the more common approach and the topic of this chapter. Although we foresee that high dynamic range display devices will become widely used in the (near) future, the need to compress the dynamic range of an image may diminish, but will not disappear. In particular, printed media such as this book are by their very nature low dynamic range.

Figure 23.2. A high dynamic range image tonemapped for display using a recent tone reproduction operator (Reinhard & Devlin, 2005). In this image, both the indoor part and the view through the window are properly exposed.

Compressing the range of values of an image for the purpose of display on a low dynamic range display device is called tonemapping or tone reproduction.

Figure 23.3. Linear scaling of high dynamic range images to fit a given display device may cause significant detail to be lost (left and middle). The left image is linearly scaled. In the middle image high values are clamped. For comparison, the right image is tonemapped, allowing details in both bright and dark regions to be visible.

A simple compression function would be to normalize an image (see Figure 23.3 (left)). This constitutes a linear scaling which tends to be sufficient only if the dynamic range of the image is only marginally higher than the dynamic range of the display device. For images with a higher dynamic range, small intensity differences will be quantized to the same display value such that visible details are lost. In Figure 23.3 (middle) all pixel values larger than a user-specified maximum are set to this maximum (i.e., they are clamped). This makes the normalization less dependent on noisy outliers, but here we lose information in the bright areas of the image. For comparison, Figure 23.3 (right) is a tonemapped version showing detail in both the dark and the bright regions.

In general linear scaling will not be appropriate for tone reproduction. The key issue in tone reproduction is then to compress an image while at the same time preserving one or more attributes of the image. Different tone reproduction algorithms focus on different attributes such as contrast, visible detail, brightness or appearance.

Figure 23.4. Image used for demonstrating the goal of tone reproduction in Figure 23.5.

Ideally, displaying a tonemapped image on a low dynamic range display device would create the same visual response in the observer as the original scene. Given the limitations of display devices, this will not be achievable, although we could aim for approximating this goal as closely as possible.

As an example, we created the high dynamic range image shown in Figure 23.4. This image was then tonemapped and displayed on a display device. The display device itself was then placed in the scene such that it displays its own background (Figure 23.5). In the ideal case, the display should appear transpar-

Figure 23.5. After tonemapping the image in Figure 23.4 and displaying it on a monitor, the monitor is placed in the scene approximately at the location where the image was taken. Dependent on the quality of the tone reproduction operator, the result should appear as if the monitor is transparent.

ent. Dependent on the quality of the tone reproduction operator, as well as the nature of the scene being depicted, this goal may be more or less achievable.

23.1   Classification

Although it would be possible to classify tone reproduction operators by which attribute they aim to preserve, or for which task they were developed, we classify algorithms according to their general technique. This will enable us to show the differences and similarities between a significant number of different operators, and so, hopefully, contribute to the meaningful selection of specific operators for given tone reproduction tasks.

The main classification scheme we follow hinges upon the realization that tone reproduction operators are based on insights gained from various disciplines. In particular, several operators are based on knowledge of human visual perception.

The human visual system detects light using photoreceptors located in the retina. Light is converted to an electrical signal which is partially processed in the retina and then transmitted to the brain. Except for the first few layers of cells in the retina, the signal derived from detected light is transmitted using impulse trains. The information-carrying quantity is the frequency with which these electrical pulses occur.

The range of light that the human visual system can detect is much larger than the range of frequencies employed by the human brain to transmit information. Thus, the human visual system effortlessly solves the tone reproduction problem—a large range of luminances is transformed into a small range of frequencies of impulse trains. Emulating relevant aspects of the human visual system is therefore a worthwhile approach to tone reproduction; this approach is explained in more detail in Section 23.7.

A second class of operators is grounded in physics. Light interacts with surfaces and volumes before being absorbed by the photoreceptors. In computer graphics, light interaction is generally modelled by the rendering equation. For purely diffuse surfaces, this equation may be simplified to the product between light incident upon a surface (illuminance), and this surface's ability to reflect light (reflectance) (Oppenheim et al., 1968).

Since reflectance is a passive property of surfaces, for diffuse surfaces it is, by definition, low dynamic range—typically between 0.005 and 1 (Stockham, 1972). The reflectance of a surface cannot be larger than 1, since then it would reflect more light than was incident upon the surface. Illuminance, on the other hand, can produce arbitrarily large values and is limited only by the intensity and proximity of the light sources.

The dynamic range of an image is thus predominantly governed by the illuminance component. In the face of diffuse scenes, a viable approach to tone reproduction may therefore be to separate reflectance from illuminance, compress the illuminance component, and then recombine the image.

However, the assumption that all surfaces in a scene are diffuse is generally incorrect. Many high dynamic range images depict highlights and/or directly visible light sources (Figure 23.3). The luminance reflected by a specular surface may be almost as high as the light source it reflects.

Various tone reproduction operators currently used split the image into a high dynamic range base layer and a low dynamic range detail layer. These layers would represent illuminance and reflectance if the depicted scene were entirely diffuse. For scenes containing directly visible light sources or specular highlights, separation into base and detail layers still allows the design of effective tone reproduction operators, although no direct meaning can be attached to the separate layers. Such operators are discussed in Section 23.5.

23.2 Dynamic Range

Conventional images are stored with one byte per pixel for each of the red, green and blue components. The dynamic range afforded by such an encoding depends on the ratio between smallest and largest representable value, as well as the step size between successive values. Thus, for low dynamic range images, there are only 256 different values per color channel.

High dynamic range images encode a significantly larger set of possible values; the maximum representable value may be much larger and the step size between successive values may be much smaller. The file size of high dynamic

Figure 23.6. Dynamic range of 2.65 $\log_2$ units.

Figure 23.7. Dynamic range of 3.96 $\log_2$ units.

Figure 23.8. Dynamic range of 4.22 $\log_2$ units.

Figure 23.9. Dynamic range of 5.01 $\log_2$ units.

Figure 23.10. Dynamic range of 6.56 $\log_2$ units.

range images is therefore generally larger as well, although at least one standard (the OpenEXR high dynamic range file format (Kainz et al., 2003)) includes a very capable compression scheme.

A different approach to limit file sizes is to apply a tone reproduction operator to the high dynamic data. The result may then be encoded in JPEG format. In addition, the input image may be divided pixel-wise by the tonemapped image. The result of this division can then be subsampled and stored as a small amount of data in the header of the same JPEG image (G. Ward & Simmons, 2004). The file size of such sub-band encoded images is of the same order as conventional JPEG encoded images. Display programs can display the JPEG image directly or may reconstruct the high dynamic range image by multiplying the tonemapped image with the data stored in the header.

In general, the combination of smallest step size and ratio of the smallest and largest representable values determines the dynamic range that an image encoding scheme affords. For computer-generated imagery, an image is typically stored as a triplet of floating point values before it is written to file or displayed on screen, although more efficient encoding schemes are possible (Reinhard et al., 2005). Since most display devices are still fitted with eight-bit D/A converters, we may think of tone reproduction as the mapping of floating point numbers to bytes such that the result is displayable on a low dynamic range display device.

The dynamic range of individual images is generally smaller, and is determined by the smallest and largest luminances found in the scene. A simplistic approach to measure the dynamic range of an image may therefore compute the ratio between the largest and smallest pixel value of an image. Sensitivity to outliers may be reduced by ignoring a small percentage of the darkest and brightest pixels.

Alternatively, the same ratio may be expressed as a difference in the logarithmic domain. This measure is less sensitive to outliers. The images shown in the margin on this page are examples of images with different dynamic ranges. Note that the night scene in this case does not have a smaller dynamic range than the day scene. While all the values in the night scene are smaller, the ratio between largest and smallest values is not.

However, the recording device or rendering algorithm may introduce noise which will lower the useful dynamic range. Thus, a measurement of the dynamic range of an image should factor in noise. A better measure of dynamic range would therefore be a signal-to-noise ratio, expressed in decibels, as used in signal processing.

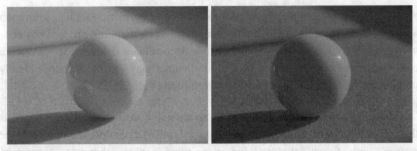

Figure 23.11. Per-channel gamma correction may desaturate the image. The left image was desaturated with a value of $s = 0.5$. The right image was not desaturated ($s = 1$). (See also Plate XIV)

23.3 Color

Tone reproduction operators normally compress luminance values, rather than work directly on the red, green, and blue components of a color image. After these luminance values have been compressed into display values $L_d(x, y)$, a color image may be reconstructed by keeping the ratios between color channels the same as they were before compression (using $s = 1$) (Schlick, 1994b):

$$I_{r,d}(x, y) = \left(\frac{I_r(x, y)}{L_v(x, y)} \right)^s L_d(x, y),$$

$$I_{g,d}(x, y) = \left(\frac{I_g(x, y)}{L_v(x, y)} \right)^s L_d(x, y),$$

$$I_{b,d}(x, y) = \left(\frac{I_b(x, y)}{L_v(x, y)} \right)^s L_d(x, y).$$

The results frequently appear over-saturated, because human color perception is non-linear with respect to overall luminance level. This means that if we view an image of a bright outdoor scene on a monitor in a dim environment, our eyes are adapted to the dim environment rather than the outdoor lighting. By keeping color ratios constant, we do not take this effect into account.

Alternatively, the saturation constant s may be chosen smaller than one. Such per-channel gamma correction may desaturate the results to an appropriate level, as shown in Figure 23.11 and Plate XIV (Fattal et al., 2002). A more comprehensive solution is to incorporate ideas from the field of color appearance modeling into tone reproduction operators (Pattanaik et al., 1998; Fairchild & Johnson, 2004; Reinhard & Devlin, 2005).

Finally, if an example image with a representative color scheme is already available, this color scheme may be applied to a new image.Such a mapping of colors between images may be used for subtle color correction such as saturation adjustment or for more creative color mappings. The mapping proceeds by converting both source and target images to a decorrelated color space. In such a color space, the pixel values in each color channel may be treated independently without introducing too many artifacts (Reinhard et al., 2001).

Mapping colors from one image to another in a decorrelated color space is then straightforward: compute the mean and standard deviation of all pixels in the source and target images for the three color channels separately. Then, shift and scale the target image so that in each color channel the mean and standard deviation of the target image is the same as the source image. The resulting image is then obtained by converting from the decorrelated color space to RGB and clamping negative pixels to zero. The dynamic range of the image may have changed as a result of applying this algorithm. It is therefore recommended to apply this algorithm on high dynamic range images and apply a conventional tone reproduction algorithm afterwards. A suitable decorrelated color space is the opponent space from Section 21.2.4.

Figure 23.12. Image used for demonstrating the color transfer technique. Results are shown in Figures 23.13 and 23.31. (See also Plates XV, XVI and XVIII.)

The result of applying such a color transform to the image in Figure 23.12 is shown in Figure 23.13.

Figure 23.13. The image on the left is used to adjust the colors of the image shown in Figure 23.12. The result is shown on the right. (See also Plate XVI.)

23.4   Image Formation

For now we assume that an image is formed as the result of light being diffusely reflected off of surfaces. Later in this chapter we relax this constraint to scenes directly depicting light sources and highlights. The luminance L_v of each pixel is then approximated by the following product:

$$L_v(x, y) = r(x, y) \, E_v(x, y).$$

Here, r denotes the reflectance of a surface, and E_v denotes the illuminance. The subscript v indicates that we are using photometrically weighted quantities. Alternatively, we may write this expression in the logarithmic domain (Oppenheim et al., 1968):

$$\begin{aligned}
D(x, y) &= \log(L_v(x, y)) \\
&= \log(r(x, y) \, E_v(x, y)) \\
&= \log(r(x, y)) + \log(E_v(x, y)).
\end{aligned}$$

Photographic transparencies record images by varying the density of the material. In traditional photography, this variation has a logarithmic relation with luminance. Thus, in analogy with common practice in photography, we will use the term *density representation* (D) for log luminance. When represented in the log domain, reflectance and illuminance become additive. This facilitates separation of these two components, despite the fact that isolating either reflectance or illuminance is an under-constrained problem. In practice, separation is possible only to a certain degree and depends on the composition of the image. Nonetheless, tone reproduction could be based on disentangling these two components of image formation, as shown in the following two sections.

23.5   Frequency-Based Operators

For typical diffuse scenes, the reflectance component tends to exhibit high spatial frequencies due to textured surfaces as well as the presence of surface edges. On the other hand, illuminance tends to be a slowly varying function over space.

Since reflectance is low dynamic range and illuminance is high dynamic range, we may try to separate the two components. The frequency-dependence of both reflectance and illuminance provides a solution. We may for instance compute the Fourier transform of an image and attenuate only the low frequencies. This compresses the illuminance component while leaving the reflectance component

Figure 23.14. Bilateral filtering removes small details but preserves sharp gradients (left). The associated detail layer is shown on the right.

largely unaffected—the very first digital tone reproduction operator known to us takes this approach (Oppenheim et al., 1968).

More recently, other operators have also followed this line of reasoning. In particular, bilateral and trilateral filters were used to separate an image into base and detail layers (Durand & Dorsey, 2002; Choudhury & Tumblin, 2003). Both filters are edge-preserving smoothing operators which may be used in a variety of different ways. Applying an edge-preserving smoothing operator to a density image results in a blurred image in which sharp edges remain present (Figure 23.14 (left)). We may view such an image as a base layer. If we then pixel-wise divide the high dynamic range image by the base layer, we obtain a detail layer which contains all the high frequency detail (Figure 23.14 (right)).

For diffuse scenes, base and detail layers are similar to representations of illuminance and reflectance. For images depicting highlights and light sources,

this parallel does not hold. However, separation of an image into base and detail layers is possible regardless of the image's content. By compressing the base layer before recombining into a compressed density image, a low dynamic range density image may be created (Figure 23.15). After exponentiation, a displayable image is obtained.

Figure 23.15. An image tonemapped using bilateral filtering. The base and detail layers shown in Figure 23.14 are recombined after compressing the base layer.

Edge-preserving smoothing operators may also be used to compute a local adaptation level for each pixel, which may be used in a spatially varying or local tone reproduction operator. We describe this use of bilateral and trilateral filters in Section 23.7.

Figure 23.16. The image on the left (tonemapped using gradient-domain compression) shows a scene with highlights. These highlights show up as large gradients on the right, where the magnitude of the gradients is mapped to a grayscale (black is a gradient of 0, white is the maximum gradient in the image).

23.6 Gradient-Domain Operators

The arguments made for the frequency-based operators in the preceding section also hold for the gradient field. Assuming that no light sources are directly visible, the reflectance component will be a constant function with sharp spikes in the gradient field. Similarly, the illuminance component will cause small gradients everywhere.

Humans are generally able to separate illuminance from reflectance in typical scenes. The perception of surface reflectance after discounting the illuminant is called *lightness*. To assess the lightness of an image depicting only diffuse surfaces, B. K. P. Horn was the first to separate reflectance and illuminance using a gradient field (Horn, 1974). He used simple thresholding to remove all small gradients and then integrated the image, which involves solving a Poisson equation using the Full Multigrid Method (Press et al., 1992).

The result is similar to an edge-preserving smoothing filter. This is according to expectation since Oppenheim's frequency-based operator works under the same assumptions of scene reflectivity and image formation. In particular, Horn's work was directly aimed at "mini-worlds of Mondrians," which are simplified versions of diffuse scenes which resemble the abstract paintings by the famous Dutch painter Piet Mondrian.

Horn's work cannot be employed directly as a tone reproduction operator, since most high dynamic range images depict light sources. However, a relatively small variation will turn this work into a suitable tone reproduction operator. If light sources or specular surfaces are depicted in the image, then large gradients will be associated with the edges of light sources and highlights. These cause the image to have a high dynamic range. An example is shown in Figure 23.16, where the highlights on the snooker balls cause sharp gradients.

Figure 23.17. An image tonemapped using gradient-domain compression.

We could therefore compress a high dynamic range image by attenuating large gradients, rather than thresholding the gradient field. This approach was taken by Fattal et al. who showed that high dynamic range imagery may be successfully compressed by integrating a compressed gradient field (Figure 23.17) (Fattal et al., 2002). Fattal's gradient-domain compression is not limited to diffuse scenes.

23.7 Spatial Operators

In the following sections, we discuss tone reproduction operators which apply compression directly on pixels without transformation to other domains. Often global and local operators are distinguished. Tone reproduction operators in the former class change each pixel's luminance values according to a compressive function which is the same for each pixel. The term global stems from the fact that many such functions need to be anchored to some values determined by analyzing the full image. In practice, most operators use the geometric average $\bar{L}_v$ to steer the compression:

$$\bar{L}_v = \exp\left(\frac{1}{N}\sum_{x,y}\log(\delta + L_v(x,y))\right). \tag{23.1}$$

In Equation (23.1), a small constant δ is introduced to prevent the average to become zero in the presence of black pixels. The geometric average is normally mapped to a predefined display value. The effect of mapping the geometric average to different display values is shown in Figure 23.18. Alternatively, sometimes the minimum or maximum image luminance is used. The main challenge faced in the design of a global operator lies in the choice of the compressive function.

On the other hand, local operators compress each pixel according to a specific compression function which is modulated by information derived from a selection of neighboring pixels, rather than the full image. The rationale is that a bright pixel in a bright neighborhood may be perceived differently than a bright pixel in a dim neighborhood. Design challenges in the development of a local operator involves choosing the compressive function, the size of the local neighborhood

Figure 23.18. Spatial tonemapping operator applied after mapping the geometric average to different display values (left: 0.12, right: 0.38).

for each pixel, and the manner in which local pixel values are used. In general, local operators achieve better compression than global operators (Figure 23.19), albeit at a higher computational cost.

Both global and local operators are often inspired by the human visual system. Most operators employ one of two distinct compressive functions, which is orthogonal to the distinction between local and global operators. Display values $L_d(x, y)$ are most commonly derived from image luminances $L_v(x, y)$ by the

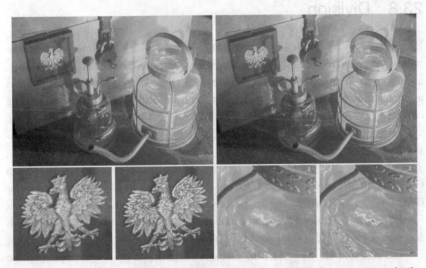

Figure 23.19. A global tone reproduction operator (left) and a local tone reproduction operator (right) (Reinhard et al., 2002) of each image. The local operator shows more detail; for example the metal badge on the right shows better contrast and the highlights are crisper.

following two functional forms:

$$L_d(x, y) = \frac{L_v(x, y)}{f(x, y)}, \tag{23.2}$$

$$L_d(x, y) = \frac{L_v(x, y)}{L_v(x, y) + f^n(x, y)}. \tag{23.3}$$

In these equations, $f(x, y)$ may either be a constant or a function which varies per pixel. In the former case, we have a global operator, whereas a spatially varying function $f(x, y)$ results in a local operator. The exponent n is usually a constant which is fixed for a particular operator.

Equation (23.2) divides each pixel's luminance by a value derived from either the full image or a local neighborhood. Equation (23.3) has an S-shaped curve on a log-linear plot and is called a sigmoid for that reason. This functional form fits data obtained from measuring the electrical response of photoreceptors to flashes of light in various species. In the following sections, we discuss both functional forms.

23.8   Division

Each pixel may be divided by a constant to bring the high dynamic range image within a displayable range. Such a division essentially constitutes linear scaling, as shown in Figure 23.3. While Figure 23.3 shows ad-hoc linear scaling, this approach may be refined by employing psychophysical data to derive the scaling constant $f(x, y) = k$ in Equation (23.2) (G. J. Ward, 1994; Ferwerda et al., 1996).

Alternatively, several approaches exist that compute a spatially varying divisor. In each of these cases, $f(x, y)$ is a blurred version of the image, i.e., $f(x, y) = L_v^{\text{blur}}(x, y)$. The blur is achieved by convolving the image with a Gaussian filter (Chiu et al., 1993; Rahman et al., 1996). In addition, the computation of $f(x, y)$ by blurring the image may be combined with a shift in white point for the purpose of color appearance modeling (Fairchild & Johnson, 2002; G. M. Johnson & Fairchild, 2003; Fairchild & Johnson, 2004).

The size and the weight of the Gaussian filter has a profound impact on the resulting displayable image. The Gaussian filter has the effect of selecting a weighted local average. Tone reproduction is then a matter of dividing each pixel by its associated weighted local average. If the size of the filter kernel is chosen too small, then haloing artifacts will occur (Figure 23.20 (left)). Haloing is a common problem with local operators and is particularly evident when tone mapping relies on division.

Figure 23.20.   Images tonemapped by dividing by Gaussian blurred versions. The size of the filter kernel is 64 pixels for the left image and 512 pixels for the right image. For division-based algorithms, halo artifacts are minimized by choosing large filter kernels.

In general, haloing artifacts may be minimized in this approach by making the filter kernel large (Figure 23.20 (right)). Reasonable results may be obtained by choosing a filter size of at least one quarter of the image. Sometimes even larger filter kernels are desirable to minimize artifacts. Note, that in the limit, the filter size becomes as large as the image itself. In that case the local operator becomes global, and the extra compression normally afforded by a local approach is lost.

The functional form whereby each pixel is divided by a Gaussian blurred pixel at the same spatial position thus requires an undesirable tradeoff between amount of compression and severity of artifacts.

23.9 Sigmoids

Equation (23.3) follows a different functional form from simple division, and, therefore, affords a different tradeoff between amount of compression, presence of artifacts, and speed of computation.

Sigmoids have several desirable properties. For very small luminance values, the mapping is approximately linear, so that contrast is preserved in dark areas of the image. The function has an asymptote at one, which means that the output mapping is always bounded between 0 and 1.

In Equation (23.3), the function $f(x, y)$ may be computed as a global constant or as a spatially varying function. Following common practice in electrophysiology, we call $f(x, y)$ the *semi-saturation* constant. Its value determines which values in the input image are optimally visible after tonemapping. In particular, if we assume that the exponent n equals 1, then luminance values equal to the semi-saturation constant will be mapped to 0.5. The effect of choosing different semi-saturation constants is shown in Figure 23.21.

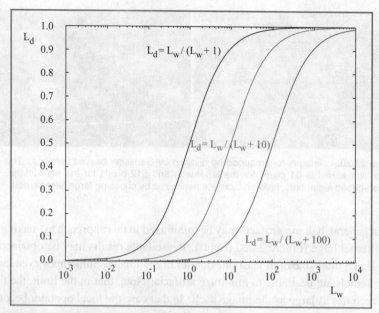

Figure 23.21. The choice of semi-saturation constant determines how input values are mapped to display values.

The function $f(x, y)$ may be computed in several different ways (Reinhard et al., 2005). In its simplest form, $f(x, y)$ is set to $\bar{L}_v/k$, so that the geometric average is mapped to user parameter k (Figure 23.22) (Reinhard et al., 2002). In this case, a good initial value for k is 0.18, although for particularly bright or dark scenes this value may be raised or lowered. Its value may be estimated from the image itself (Reinhard, 2003). The exponent n in Equation (23.3) may be set to 1.

In this approach, the semi-saturation constant is a function of the geometric average, and the operator is therefore global. A variation of this global opera-

Figure 23.22. A linearly scaled image (left) and an image tonemapped using sigmoidal compression (right).

Figure 23.23. Linear interpolation varies contrast in the tonemapped image. The parameter a is set to 0.0 in the left image, and to 1.0 in the right image.

tor computes the semi-saturation constant by linearly interpolating between the geometric average and each pixel's luminance:

$$f(x, y) = a\, L_v(x, y) + (1 - a)\, \bar{L}_v.$$

The interpolation is governed by user parameter a which has the effect of varying the amount of contrast in the displayable image (Figure 23.23) (Reinhard & Devlin, 2005). More contrast means less visible detail in the light and dark areas and vice versa. This interpolation may be viewed as a half-way house between a fully global and a fully local operator by interpolating between the two extremes without resorting to expensive blurring operations.

Although operators typically compress luminance values, this particular operator may be extended to include a simple form of chromatic adaptation. It thus presents an opportunity to adjust the level of saturation normally associated with tonemapping, as discussed at the beginning of this chapter.

Rather than compress the luminance channel only, sigmoidal compression is applied to each of the three color channels:

$$I_{r,d}(x, y) = \frac{I_r(x, y)}{I_r(x, y) + f^n(x, y)},$$

$$I_{g,d}(x, y) = \frac{I_g(x, y)}{I_g(x, y) + f^n(x, y)},$$

$$I_{b,d}(x, y) = \frac{I_b(x, y)}{I_b(x, y) + f^n(x, y)}.$$

The computation of $f(x, y)$ is also modified to bilinearly interpolate between the geometric average luminance and pixel luminance and between each independent color channel and the pixel's luminance value. We therefore compute the geometric average luminance value $\bar{L}_v$, as well as the geometric average of the red, green and blue channels ($\bar{I}_r$, $\bar{I}_g$, and $\bar{I}_b$). From these values, we compute $f(x, y)$

Figure 23.24. Linear interpolation for color correction. The parameter c is set to 0.0 in the left image, and to 1.0 in the right image. (See also Plate XVII.)

for each pixel and for each color channel independently. We show the equation for the red channel ($f_r(x, y)$):

$$G_r(x, y) = c\, I_r(x, y) + (1 - c)\, L_v(x, y),$$
$$\bar{G}_r(x, y) = c\, \bar{I}_r + (1 - c)\, \bar{L}_v,$$
$$f_r(x, y) = a\, G_r(x, y) + (1 - a)\, \bar{G}_r(x, y).$$

The interpolation parameter a steers the amount of contrast as before, and the new interpolation parameter c allows a simple form of color correction (Figure 23.24 and Plate XVII).

So far we have not discussed the value of the exponent n in Equation (23.3). Studies in electrophysiology report values between $n = 0.2$ and $n = 0.9$ (Hood et al., 1979). While the exponent may be user-specified, for a wide variety of images we may estimate a reasonable value from the geometric average luminance $\bar{L}_v$ and the minimum and maximum luminance in the image ($L_{\min}$ and $L_{\max}$) with the following empirical equation:

$$n = 0.3 + 0.7 \left(\frac{L_{\max} - \bar{L}_v}{L_{\max} - L_{\min}} \right)^{1.4}.$$

The several variants of sigmoidal compression shown so far are all global in nature. This has the advantage that they are fast to compute, and they are very suitable for medium to high dynamic range images. For very high dynamic range images, it may be necessary to resort to a local operator, since this may give some extra compression. A straightforward method to extend sigmoidal compression replaces the global semi-saturation constant by a spatially varying function, which may be computed in several different ways.

In other words, the function $f(x, y)$ is so far assumed to be constant, but may also be computed as a spatially localized average. Perhaps the simplest way to accomplish this is to once more use a Gaussian blurred image. Each pixel in a blurred image represents a locally averaged value which may be viewed as a suitable choice for the semi-saturation constant[1].

As with division-based operators discussed in the previous section, we have to consider haloing artifacts. However, when an image is divided by a Gaussian blurred version of itself, the size of the Gaussian filter kernel needs to be large in order to minimize halos. If sigmoids are used with a spatially variant semi-saturation constant, the Gaussian filter kernel needs to be made small in order to minimize artifacts. This is a significant improvement, since small amounts of Gaussian blur may be efficiently computed directly in the spatial domain. In other words, there is no need to resort to expensive Fourier transforms. In practice, filter kernels of only a few pixels width are sufficient to suppress significant artifacts while at the same time producing more local contrast in the tonemapped images.

One potential issue with Gaussian blur is that the filter blurs across sharp contrast edges in the same way that it blurs small details. In practice, if there is a large contrast gradient in the neighborhood of the pixel under consideration, this causes the Gaussian-blurred pixel to be significantly different from the pixel itself. This is the direct cause for halos. By using a very large filter kernel in a division-based approach, such large contrasts are averaged out.

Figure 23.25. Example image used to demonstrate the scale selection mechanism shown in Figure 23.26.

In sigmoidal compression schemes, a small Gaussian filter minimizes the chances of overlapping with a sharp contrast gradient. In that case, halos still occur, but their size is such that they usually go unnoticed and instead are perceived as enhancing contrast.

Another way to blur an image, while minimizing the negative effects of nearby large contrast steps, is to avoid blurring over such edges. A simple, but computationally expensive way, is to compute a stack of Gaussian-blurred images with different kernel sizes. For each pixel, we may choose the largest Gaussian that does not overlap with a significant gradient.

In a relatively uniform neighborhood, the value of a Gaussian-blurred pixel should be the same regardless of the filter kernel size. Thus, the difference between a pixel filtered with two different Gaussians should be approximately zero.

---

[1] Although $f(x, y)$ is now no longer a constant, we continue to refer to it as the semi-saturation constant.

Figure 23.26. Scale selection mechanism: the left image shows the scale selected for each pixel of the image shown in Figure 23.25; the darker the pixel, the smaller the scale. A total of eight different scales were used to compute this image. The right image shows the local average computed for each pixel on the basis of the neighborhood selection mechanism.

This difference will only change significantly if the wider filter kernel overlaps with a neighborhood containing a sharp contrast step, whereas the smaller filter kernel does not.

It is possible, therefore, to find the largest neighborhood around a pixel that does not contain sharp edges by examining differences of Gaussians at different kernel sizes. For the image shown in Figure 23.25, the scale selected for each pixel is shown in Figure 23.26 (left). Such a scale selection mechanism is employed by the photographic tone reproduction operator (Reinhard et al., 2002) as well as in Ashikhmin's operator (Ashikhmin, 2002).

Once the appropriate neighborhood for each pixel is known, the Gaussian blurred average L_{blur} for this neighborhood (shown on the right of Figure 23.26) may be used to steer the semi-saturation constant, such as for instance employed by the photographic tone reproduction operator:

$$L_d = \frac{L_w}{1. + L_{blur}}.$$

An alternative, and arguably better, approach is to employ edge-preserving smoothing operators, which are designed specifically for removing small details while keeping sharp contrasts in tact. Several such filters, such as the bilateral filter (Figure 23.27), trilateral filter, Susan filter, the LCIS algorithm and the mean shift algorithm are suitable, although some of them are expensive to compute (Durand & Dorsey, 2002; Choudhury & Tumblin, 2003; Pattanaik & Yee, 2002; Tumblin & Turk, 1999; Comaniciu & Meer, 2002).

23.10 Other Approaches

Although the previous sections together discuss most tone reproduction operators to date, there are one or two operators that do not directly fit into the above cate-

Figure 23.27.   Sigmoidal compression (left) and sigmoidal compression using bilateral filtering to compute the semi-saturation constant (right). Note the improved contrast in the sky in the right image.

gories. The simplest of these are variations of logarithmic compression, and the other is a histogram-based approach.

Dynamic range reduction may be accomplished by taking the logarithm, provided that this number is greater than 1. Any positive number may then be non-linearly scaled between 0 and 1 using the following equation:

$$L_d(x,y) = \frac{\log_b(1 + L_v(x,y))}{\log_b(1 + L_{\max})}$$

While the base b of the logarithm above is not specified, any choice of base will do. This freedom to choose the base of the logarithm may be used to vary the base with input luminance, and thus achieve an operator that is better matched to the image being compressed (Drago et al., 2003). This method uses Perlin and Hoffert's bias function which takes user parameter p (Perlin & Hoffert, 1989):

$$\mathrm{bias}_p(x) = x^{\log_{10}(p)/\log_{10}(1/2)}.$$

Figure 23.28.   Logarithmic compression using base 10 logarithms (left) and logarithmic compression with varying base (right).

Making the base b dependent on luminance and smoothly interpolating bases between 2 and 10, the logarithmic mapping above may be refined:

$$L_d(x,y) = \frac{\log_{10}(1 + L_v(x,y))}{\log_{10}(1 + L_{\max})} \cdot \frac{1}{\log_{10}\left(2 + 8\left(\left(\dfrac{L_v(x,y)}{L_{\max}}\right)^{\log_{10}(p)/\log_{10}(1/2)}\right)\right)}.$$

For user parameter p, an initial value of around 0.85 tends to yield plausible results (Figure 23.28 (right)).

Alternatively, tone reproduction may be based on histogram equalization. Traditional histogram equalization aims to give each luminance value equal probability of occurrence in the output image. Greg Ward refines this method in a manner that preserves contrast (Ward Larson et al., 1997).

First, a histogram is computed from the luminances in the high dynamic range image. From this histogram, a cumulative histogram is computed such that each bin contains the number of pixels that have a luminance value less than or equal to the luminance value that the bin represents. The cumulative histogram is a monotonically increasing function. Plotting the values in each bin against the luminance values represented by each bin therefore yields a function which may be viewed as a luminance mapping function. Scaling this function, such that the vertical axis spans the range of the display device, yields a tone reproduction operator. This technique is called histogram equalization.

Ward further refined this method by ensuring that the gradient of this function never exceeds 1. This means, that if the difference between neighboring values in the cumulative histogram is too large, this difference is clamped to 1. This avoids the problem that small changes in luminance in the input may yield large differences in the output image. In other words, by limiting the gradient of the cumulative histogram to 1, contrast is never exaggerated. The resulting algorithm is called histogram adjustment (see Figure 23.29).

Figure 23.29. A linearly scaled image (left) and a histogram adjusted image (right). *Image created with the kind permission of the Albin Polasek museum, Winter Park, Florida.*

23.11   Night Tonemapping

The tone reproduction operators discussed so far nearly all assume that the image represents a scene under *photopic* viewing conditions, i.e., as seen at normal light levels. For *scotopic* scenes, i.e., very dark scenes, the human visual system exhibits distinctly different behavior. In particular, perceived contrast is lower, visual acuity (i.e., the smallest detail that we can distinguish) is lower, and everything has a slightly blue appearance.

To allow such images to be viewed correctly on monitors placed in photopic lighting conditions, we may preprocess the image such that it appears as if we were adapted to a very dark viewing environment. Such preprocessing frequently takes the form of a reduction in brightness and contrast, desaturation of the image, blue shift, and a reduction in visual acuity (Thompson et al., 2002).

A typical approach starts by converting the image from RGB to XYZ. Then, scotopic luminance V may be computed for each pixel:

$$V = Y \left[1.33 \left(1 + \frac{Y+Z}{X} \right) - 1.68 \right].$$

This single channel image may then be scaled and multiplied by an empirically chosen bluish gray. An example is shown in Figure 23.30. If some pixels are in the photopic range, then the night image may be created by linearly blending the bluish gray image with the input image. The fraction to use for each pixel depends on V.

Loss of visual acuity may be modelled by low-pass filtering the night image, although this would give an incorrect sense of blurriness. A better approach is to apply a bilateral filter to retain sharp edges while blurring smaller details (Tomasi & Manduchi, 1998).

Figure 23.30. Simulated night scene using the image shown in Figure 23.12. (See also Plates XV and XIX.)

Finally, the color transfer technique outlined in Section 23.3 may also be used to transform a day-lit image into a night scene. The effectiveness of this approach depends on the availability of a suitable night image from which to transfer colors. As an example, the image in Figure 23.12 is transformed into a night image in Figure 23.31.

Figure 23.31. The image on the left is used to transform the image of Figure 23.12 into a night scene, shown here on the right. (See also Plate XVIII.)

23.12 Discussion

Since global illumination algorithms naturally produce high dynamic range images, direct display of the resulting images is not possible. Rather than resort to linear scaling or clamping, a tone reproduction operator should be used. Any tone reproduction operator is better than using no tone reproduction. Dependent on the requirements of the application, one of several operators may be suitable.

For instance, real-time rendering applications should probably resort to a simple sigmoidal compression, since these are fast enough to also run in real time. In addition, their visual quality is often good enough. The histogram adjustment technique (Ward Larson et al., 1997) may also be fast enough for real-time operation.

For scenes containing a very high dynamic range, better compression may be achieved with a local operator. However, the computational cost is frequently substantially higher, leaving these operators suitable only for non-interactive applications. Among the fastest of the local operators is the bilateral filter due to the optimizations afforded by this technique (Durand & Dorsey, 2002).

This filter is interesting as a tone reproduction operator by itself, or it may be used to compute a local adaptation level for use in a sigmoidal compression function. In either case, the filter respects sharp contrast changes and smoothes over smaller contrasts. This is an important feature that helps minimize halo artifacts which are a common problem with local operators.

An alternative approach to minimize halo artifacts is the scale selection mechanism used in the photographic tone reproduction operator (Reinhard et al., 2002), although this technique is slower to compute.

In summary, while a large number of tone reproduction operators is currently available, only a small number of fundamentally different approaches exist. Fourier-domain and gradient-domain operators are both rooted in knowledge of image formation. Spatial-domain operators are either spatially variant (local) or global in nature. These operators are usually based on insights gained from studying the human visual system (and the visual system of many other species).

24

Global Illumination

Many surfaces in the real world receive most or all of their incident light from other reflective surfaces. This is often called *indirect lighting* or *mutual illumination*. For example, the ceilings of most rooms receive little or no illumination directly from luminaires (light emitting objects). The direct and indirect components of illumination are shown in Figure 24.1.

Although accounting for the interreflection of light between surfaces is straightforward, it is potentially costly because all surfaces may reflect any given surface, resulting in as many as $O(N^2)$ interactions for N surfaces. Because the entire global database of objects may illuminate any given object, accounting for indirect illumination is often called the *global illumination* problem.

There is a rich and complex literature on solving the global illumination problem (e.g., (Appel, 1968; Goral et al., 1984; Cook et al., 1984; Immel et al., 1986;

Figure 24.1. In the left and middle images, the indirect and direct lighting, respectively, are separated out. On the right, the sum of both components is shown. Global illumination algorithms account for both the direct and the indirect lighting.

Kajiya, 1986; Malley, 1988)). In this chapter we discuss two algorithms as examples: particle tracing and path tracing. The first is useful for walkthrough applications such as maze games, and as a component of batch rendering. The second is useful for realistic batch rendering. Then we discuss separating out "direct" lighting where light takes exactly once bounce between luminaire and camera.

24.1   Particle Tracing for Lambertian Scenes

Recall the transport equation from Section 20.2:

$$L_s(\mathbf{k}_o) = \int_{\text{all } \mathbf{k}_i} \rho(\mathbf{k}_i, \mathbf{k}_o) L_f(\mathbf{k}_i) \cos \theta_i d\sigma_i.$$

The geometry for this equation is shown Figure 24.2. When the illuminated point is Lambertian, this equation reduces to:

$$L_s = \frac{R}{\pi} \int_{\text{all } \mathbf{k}_i} L_f(\mathbf{k}_i) \cos \theta_i d\sigma_i,$$

where R is the diffuse reflectance. One way to approximate the solution to this equation is to use finite element methods. First, we break the scene into N surfaces each with unknown surface radiance L_i, reflectance R_i, and emitted radiance E_i. This results in the set of N simultaneous linear equations

$$L_i = E_i + \frac{R_i}{\pi} \sum_{j=1}^{N} k_{ij} L_j,$$

where k_{ij} is a constant related to the original integral representation. We then solve this set of linear equations, and we can render N constant-colored polygons. This finite element approach is often called *radiosity*.

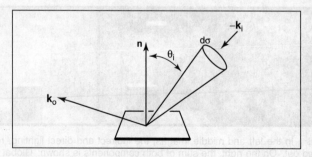

Figure 24.2. The geometry for the transport equation in its directional form.

An alternative method to radiosity is to use a statistical simulation approach by randomly following light "particles" from the luminaire though the environment. This is a type of *particle tracing*. There are many algorithms that use some form of particle tracing; we will discuss a form of particle tracing that deposits light in the textures on triangles. First, we review some basic radiometric relations. The radiance L of a Lambertian surface with area A is directly proportional to the incident power per unit area:

$$L = \frac{\Phi}{\pi A}, \tag{24.1}$$

where Φ is the outgoing power from the surface. Note that in this discussion, all radiometric quantities are either spectral or RGB depending on the implementation. If the surface has emitted power Φ_e, incident power Φ_i, and reflectance R, then this equation becomes

$$L = \frac{\Phi_e + R\Phi_i}{\pi A}.$$

If we are given a model with Φ_e and R specified for each triangle, we can proceed luminaire by luminaire, firing power in the form of particles from each luminaire. We associate a texture map with each triangle to store accumulated radiance, with all texels initialized to

$$L = \frac{\Phi_e}{\pi A}.$$

If a given triangle has area A and n_t texels, and it is hit by a particle carrying power ϕ, then the radiance of that texel is incremented by

$$\Delta L = \frac{n_t \phi}{\pi A}.$$

Once a particle hits a surface, we increment the radiance of the texel it hits, probabilistically decide whether to reflect the particle, and if we reflect it we choose a direction and adjust its power.

Note that we want the particle to terminate at some point. For each surface we can assign a reflection probability p to each surface interaction. A natural choice would be to let $p = R$ as it is with light in nature. The particle would then scatter around the environment not losing or gaining any energy until it is absorbed. This approach works well when the particles carry a single wavelength (Walter et al., 1997). However, when a spectrum or RGB triple is carried by the ray as is often implemented (Jensen, 2001), there is no single R and some compromise for the value of p should be chosen. The power ϕ' for reflected particles should be adjusted to account for the possible extinction of the particles:

$$\phi' = \frac{R\phi}{p}.$$

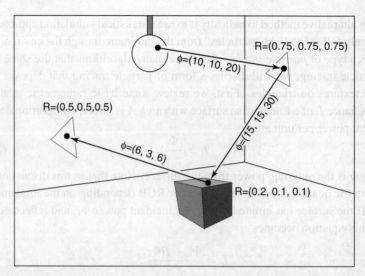

Figure 24.3. The path of a particle that survives with probability 0.5 and is absorbed at the last intersection. The RGB power is shown for each path segment.

Note that p can be set to any positive constant less than one, and that this constant can be different for each interaction. When $p > R$ for a given wavelength, the particle will gain power at that wavelength, and when $p < R$ it will lose power at that wavelength. The case where it gains power will not interfere with convergence because the particle will stop scattering and be terminated at some point as long as $p < 1$. For the remainder of this discussion we set $p = 0.5$. The path of a single particle in such a system is shown in Figure 24.3.

A key part to this algorithm is that we scatter the light with an appropriate distribution for Lambertian surfaces. As discussed in Section 14.4.1, we can find a vector with a cosine (Lambertian) distribution by transforming two canonical random numbers (ξ_1, ξ_2) as follows:

$$\mathbf{a} = \left(\cos\left(2\pi\xi_1\right)\sqrt{\xi_2}, \sin\left(2\pi\xi_1\right)\sqrt{\xi_2}, \sqrt{1 - \xi_2} \right). \qquad (24.2)$$

Note that this assumes the normal vector is parallel to the z-axis. For a triangle, we must establish an orthonormal basis with $\mathbf{w}$ parallel to the normal vector. We can accomplish this as follows:

$$\mathbf{w} = \frac{\mathbf{n}}{\|\mathbf{n}\|},$$

$$\mathbf{u} = \frac{\mathbf{p}_1 - \mathbf{p}_0}{\|\mathbf{p}_1 - \mathbf{p}_0\|},$$

$$\mathbf{v} = \mathbf{w} \times \mathbf{u},$$

where $\mathbf{p}_i$ are the vertices of the triangle. Then, by definition, our vector in the appropriate coordinates is

$$\mathbf{a} = \cos\left(2\pi\xi_1\right)\sqrt{\xi_2}\mathbf{u} + \sin\left(2\pi\xi_1\right)\sqrt{\xi_2}\mathbf{v} + \sqrt{1 - \xi_2}\mathbf{w}. \qquad (24.3)$$

In pseudocode our algorithm for $p = 0.5$ and one luminaire is:

```
for (Each of n particles) do
    RGB phi = Φ/n
    compute uniform random point a on luminaire
    compute random direction b with cosine density
    done = false
    while not done do
        if (ray a + tb hits at some point c ) then
            add nₜRϕ/(πA) to appropriate texel
            if (ξ₁ > 0.5) then
                ϕ = 2Rϕ
                a = c
                b = random direction with cosine density
            else
                done = true
```

Here ξ_i are canonical random numbers. Once this code has run, the texture maps store the radiance of each triangle and can be rendered directly for any viewpoint with no additional computation.

24.2 Path Tracing

While particle tracing is well suited to precomputation of the radiances of diffuse scenes, it is problematic for creating images of scenes with general BRDFs or scenes that contain many objects. The most straightforward way to create images of such scenes is to use *path tracing* (Kajiya, 1986). This is a probabilistic method that sends rays from the eye and traces them back to the light. Often path tracing is used only to compute the indirect lighting. Here we will present it in a way that captures all lighting, which can be inefficient. This is sometimes called *brute force* path tracing. In Section 24.3, more efficient techniques for direct lighting can be added.

In path tracing, we start with the full transport equation:

$$L_s(\mathbf{k}_o) = L_e(\mathbf{k}_o) + \int_{\text{all } \mathbf{k}_i} \rho(\mathbf{k}_i, \mathbf{k}_o)L_f(\mathbf{k}_i) \cos\theta_i d\sigma_i.$$

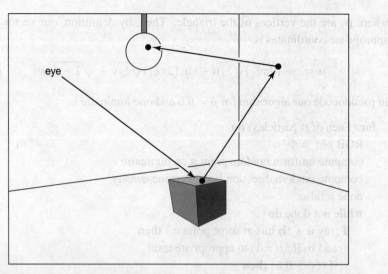

Figure 24.4. In path tracing, a ray is followed through a pixel from the eye and scattered through the scene until it hits a luminaire.

We use Monte Carlo integration to approximate the solution to this equation for each viewing ray. Recall from Section 14.3, that we can use random samples to approximate an integral:

$$\int_{x \in S} g(x)d\mu \approx \frac{1}{N} \sum_{i=1}^{N} \frac{g(x_i)}{p(x_i)},$$

where the x_i are random points with probability density function p. If we apply this directly to the transport equation with $N = 1$ we get

$$L_s(\mathbf{k}_o) \approx L_e(\mathbf{k}_o) + \frac{\rho(\mathbf{k}_i, \mathbf{k}_o)L_f(\mathbf{k}_i)\cos\theta_i d\sigma_i}{p(\mathbf{k}_i)}.$$

So if we have a way to select random directions $\mathbf{k}_i$ with a known density p, we can get an estimate. The catch is that $L_f(\mathbf{k}_i)$ is itself an unknown. Fortunately we can apply recursion and use a statistical estimate for $L_f(\mathbf{k}_i)$ by sending a ray in that direction to find the surface seen in that direction. We end when we hit a luminaire and L_e is non-zero (Figure 24.4). This method assumes lights have zero reflectance, or we would continue to recurse.

In the case of a Lambertian BRDF ($\rho = R/\pi$), we can use a cosine density function:

$$p(\mathbf{k}_i) = \frac{\cos\theta_i}{\pi}.$$

A direction with this density can be chosen according to Equation (24.3). This allows some cancellation of cosine terms in our estimate:

$$L_s(\mathbf{k}_o) \approx L_e(\mathbf{k}_o) + RL_f(\mathbf{k}_i).$$

In pseudocode such a path tracer for Lambertian surfaces would operate just like the ray tracers described in Chapter 4, but the *raycolor* function would be modified:

RGB raycolor(ray $\mathbf{a} + t\mathbf{b}$, int depth)
if (ray hits at some point $\mathbf{c}$) **then**
    RGB $c = L_e(-\mathbf{b})$
    if (depth < maxdepth) **then**
        compute random direction $\mathbf{d}$
        return $c + R$ raycolor($\mathbf{c} + s\mathbf{d}$, depth+1)
else
    return background color

This will result in a very noisy image unless either large luminaires or very large numbers of samples are used. Note the color of the luminaires must be well above one (sometimes thousands or tens of thousands) to make the surfaces have final colors near one, because only those rays that hit a luminaire by chance will make a contribution, and most rays will contribute only a color near zero. To generate the random direction $\mathbf{d}$, we use the same technique as we do in particle tracing (see Equation (24.2)).

In the general case we might want to use spectral colors or use a more general BRDF. In practice, we should have the material class contain member functions to compute a random direction as well as compute the p associated with that direction. This way materials can be added transparently to an implementation.

24.3 Accurate Direct Lighting

This section presents a more physically-based method of direct lighting than Chapter 10. These methods will be useful in making global illumination algorithms more efficient. The key idea is to send shadow rays to the luminaires as described in Chapter 4, but to do so with careful bookkeeping based on the transport equation from the previous chapter. The global illumination algorithms can be adjusted to make sure they compute the direct component exactly once. For example, in particle tracing, particles coming directly from the luminaire would not be logged, so the particles would only encode indirect lighting. This makes nice looking shadows much more efficiently than computing direct lighting in the context of global illumination.

24.3.1 Mathematical Framework

To calculate the direct light from one *luminaire* (light emitting object) onto a non-emitting surface, we solve a form of the transport equation from Section 20.2:

$$L_s(\mathbf{x}, \mathbf{k}_o) = \int_{\text{all } \mathbf{x}'} \frac{\rho(\mathbf{k}_i, \mathbf{k}_o) L_e(\mathbf{x}', -\mathbf{k}_i) v(\mathbf{x}, \mathbf{x}') \cos \theta_i \cos \theta'}{\|\mathbf{x} - \mathbf{x}'\|^2} dA' . \qquad (24.4)$$

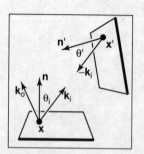

Figure 24.5. The direct lighting terms for Equation (24.4).

Recall that L_e is the emitted radiance of the source, v is a visibility function that is equal to 1 if $\mathbf{x}$ "sees" $\mathbf{x}'$ and zero otherwise, and the other variables are as illustrated in Figure 24.5.

If we are to sample Equation (24.4) using Monte Carlo integration, we need to pick a random point $\mathbf{x}'$ on the surface of the luminaire with density function p (so $\mathbf{x}' \sim p$). Just plugging into Equation (14.5) with one sample yields

$$L_s(\mathbf{x}, \mathbf{k}_o) \approx \frac{\rho(\mathbf{k}_i, \mathbf{k}_o) L_e(\mathbf{x}', -\mathbf{k}_i) v(\mathbf{x}, \mathbf{x}') \cos \theta_i \cos \theta'}{p(\mathbf{x}') \|\mathbf{x} - \mathbf{x}'\|^2} . \qquad (24.5)$$

If we pick a uniform random point on the luminaire, then $p = 1/A$, where A is the area of the luminaire. This gives

$$L_s(\mathbf{x}, \mathbf{k}_o) \approx \frac{\rho(\mathbf{k}_i, \mathbf{k}_o) L_e(\mathbf{x}', -\mathbf{k}_i) v(\mathbf{x}, \mathbf{x}') A \cos \theta_i \cos \theta'}{\|\mathbf{x} - \mathbf{x}'\|^2} . \qquad (24.6)$$

We can use Equation (24.6) to sample planar (e.g., rectangular) luminaires in a straightforward fashion. We simply pick a random point on each luminaire.

The code for one luminaire is:

```
color directLight( x, k_o, n)
pick random point x' with normal vector n' on light
d = x' - x
k_i = d/‖d‖
if (ray x + td has no hits for t < 1 - ε) then
    return ρ(k_i, k_o)L_e(x', -k_i)(n · d)(-n' · d)/‖d‖⁴
else
    return 0
```

The above code needs some extra tests such as clamping the cosines to zero if they are negative. Note that the term $\|\mathbf{d}\|^4$ comes from the distance squared term

Figure 24.6. Various soft shadows on a backlit sphere with a square and an area light source. Top: 1 sample. Bottom: 100 samples. Note that the shape of the light source is less important than its size in determining shadow appearance.

and the two cosines, e.g., $\mathbf{n} \cdot \mathbf{d} = \|\mathbf{d}\| \cos \theta$ because $\mathbf{d}$ is not necessarily a unit vector.

Several examples of soft shadows are shown in Figure 24.6.

24.3.2 Sampling a Spherical Luminaire

Though a sphere with center $\mathbf{c}$ and radius R can be sampled using Equation (24.6), this sampling will yield a very noisy image because many samples will be on the back of the sphere, and the $\cos \theta'$ term varies so much. Instead, we can use a more complex $p(\mathbf{x}')$ to reduce noise.

The first non-uniform density we might try is $p(\mathbf{x}') \propto \cos \theta'$. This turns out to be just as complicated as sampling with $p(\mathbf{x}') \propto \cos \theta' / \|\mathbf{x}' - \mathbf{x}\|^2$, so we instead discuss that here. We observe that sampling on the luminaire this way is the same as using a constant density function $q(\mathbf{k}_i) = \text{const}$ defined in the space of directions subtended by the luminaire as seen from $\mathbf{x}$. We now use a coordinate

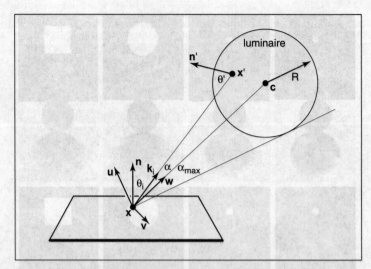

Figure 24.7. Geometry for direct lighting at point **x** from a spherical luminaire.

system defined with **x** at the origin, and a right-handed orthonormal basis with
w = (**c** − **x**)/‖**c** − **x**‖, and **v** = (**w** × **n**)/‖(**w** × **n**)‖ (see Figure 24.7). We
also define (α, ϕ) to be the azimuthal and polar angles with respect to the uvw
coordinate system.

The maximum α that includes the spherical luminaire is given by

$$\alpha_{\max} = \arcsin\left(\frac{R}{\|\mathbf{x} - \mathbf{c}\|}\right) = \arccos\sqrt{1 - \left(\frac{R}{\|\mathbf{x} - \mathbf{c}\|}\right)^2}.$$

Thus, a uniform density (with respect to solid angle) within the cone of directions
subtended by the sphere is just the reciprocal of the solid angle $2\pi(1 - \cos\alpha_{\max})$
subtended by the sphere:

$$q(\mathbf{k}_i) = \frac{1}{2\pi\left(1 - \sqrt{1 - \left(\frac{R}{\|\mathbf{x}-\mathbf{c}\|}\right)^2}\right)}.$$

And we get

$$\begin{bmatrix} \cos\alpha \\ \phi \end{bmatrix} = \begin{bmatrix} 1 - \xi_1 + \xi_1\sqrt{1 - \left(\frac{R}{\|\mathbf{x}-\mathbf{c}\|}\right)^2} \\ 2\pi\xi_2 \end{bmatrix}.$$

This gives us the direction $\mathbf{k}_i$. To find the actual point, we need to find the first
point on the sphere in that direction. The ray in that direction is just $(\mathbf{x} + t\mathbf{k}_i)$,

Figure 24.8. A sphere with $L_e = 1$ touching a sphere of reflectance 1. Where the two spheres touch, the reflective sphere should have $L(\mathbf{x}') = 1$. Left: 1 sample. Middle: 100 samples. Right: 100 samples, close-up.

where $\mathbf{k}_i$ is given by

$$
\mathbf{k}_i = \begin{bmatrix} u_x & v_x & w_x \\ u_y & v_y & w_y \\ u_z & v_z & w_z \end{bmatrix} \begin{bmatrix} \cos\phi\sin\alpha \\ \sin\phi\sin\alpha \\ \cos\alpha \end{bmatrix}.
$$

We must also calculate $p(\mathbf{x}')$, the probability density function with respect to the area measure (recall that the density function q is defined in solid angle space). Since we know that q is a valid probability density function using the ω measure, and we know that $d\Omega = dA(\mathbf{x}')\cos\theta'/\|\mathbf{x}' - \mathbf{x}\|^2$, we can relate any probability density function $q(\mathbf{k}_i)$ with its associated probability density function $p(\mathbf{x}')$:

$$
q(\mathbf{k}_i) = \frac{p(\mathbf{x}')\cos\theta'}{\|\mathbf{x}' - \mathbf{x}\|^2}. \tag{24.7}
$$

So we can solve for $p(\mathbf{x}')$:

$$
p(\mathbf{x}') = \frac{\cos\theta'}{2\pi\|\mathbf{x}' - \mathbf{x}\|^2 \left(1 - \sqrt{1 - \left(\frac{R}{\|\mathbf{x} - \mathbf{c}\|}\right)^2}\right)}.
$$

A good debugging case for this is shown in Figure 24.8.

24.3.3 Non-diffuse Luminaries

There is no reason the luminance of the luminaire cannot vary with both direction and position. For example, it can vary with position if the luminaire is a television. It can vary with direction for car headlights and other directional sources. Little in our analysis need change from the previous sections, except that $L_e(\mathbf{x}')$ must change to $L_e(\mathbf{x}', -\mathbf{k}_i)$. The simplest way to vary the intensity with direction is to use a Phong-like pattern with respect to the normal vector $\mathbf{n}'$. To avoid using an exponent in the term for the total light output, we can use the form

$$
L_e(\mathbf{x}', -\mathbf{k}_i) = \frac{(n+1)E(\mathbf{x}')}{2\pi}\cos^{(n-1)}\theta',
$$

where $E(\mathbf{x}')$ is the *radiant exitance* (power per unit area) at point $\mathbf{x}'$, and n is the Phong exponent. You get a diffuse light for $n = 1$. If the light is non-uniform across its area, e.g., as a television set is, then E will not be a constant.

Frequently Asked Questions

• My pixel values are no longer in some sensible zero-to-one range. What should I display?

You should use one of the *tone reproduction* techniques described in Chapter 23.

• What global illumination techniques are used in practice?

For batch rendering of complex scenes, path tracing with one level of reflection is often used. Path tracing is often augmented with a particle tracing prepro- cess as described in Jensen's book in the chapter notes. For walkthrough games, some form of world-space preprocess is often used, such as the particle tracing described in this chapter. For scenes with very complicated specular transport, an elegant but involved method, Metropolis Light Transport (Veach & Guibas, 1997) may be the best choice.

• How does the ambient component relate to global illumination?

For diffuse scenes, the radiance of a surface is proportional to the product of the irradiance at the surface and the reflectance of the surface. The ambient com- ponent is just an approximation to the irradiance scaled by the inverse of π. So although it is a crude approximation, there can be some methodology to guessing it (M. F. Cohen et al., 1988), and it is probably more accurate than doing nothing, i.e., using zero for the ambient term. Because the indirect irradiance can vary widely within a scene, using a different constant for each surface can be used for better results rather than using a global ambient term.

• Why do most algorithms compute direct lighting using traditional ray tracing?

Although global illumination algorithms automatically compute direct lighting, and it is in fact slightly more complicated to make them compute only indi- rect lighting, it is usually faster to compute direct lighting separately. There are three reasons for this. First, indirect lighting tends to be smooth compared to

Figure 24.9. A comparison between a rendering and a photo. *Image courtesy Sumant Pattanaik and the Cornell Program of Computer Graphics.* (See also Plate XXI.)

direct lighting (see Figure 24.1) so coarser representations can be used, e.g., low-resolution texture maps for particle tracing. The second reason is that light sources tend to be small, and it is rare to hit them by chance in a "from the eye" method such as path tracing, while direct shadow rays are efficient. The third reason is that direct lighting allows stratified sampling so it converges rapidly compared to unstratified sampling. The issue of stratification is the reason that shadow rays are used in Metropolis Light Transport despite the stability of its default technique for dealing with direct lighting as just one type of path to handle.

• How artificial is it to assume ideal diffuse and specular behavior?

For environments that have only matte and mirrored surfaces, the Lambertian/specular assumption works well. A comparison between a rendering using that assumption and a photograph is shown in Figure 24.9.

• How many shadow rays are needed per pixel?

Typically between 16 and 400. Using narrow penumbra, a large ambient term (or a large indirect component), and a masking texture (Ferwerda et al., 1997) can reduce the number needed.

• How do I sample something like a filament with a metal reflector where much of the light is reflected from the filament?

Typically the whole light is replaced by a simple source that approximates its aggregate behavior. For viewing rays, the complicated source is used. So a car headlight would look complex to the viewer, but the lighting code might see simple disk-shaped lights.

● Isn't something like the sky a luminaire?

Yes, and you can treat it as one. However, such large light sources may not be helped by direct lighting; the brute-force techniques are likely to work better.

Notes

Global illumination has its roots in the fields of heat transfer and illumination engineering as documented in *Radiosity: A Programmer's Perspective* (Ashdown, 1994). Other good books related to global illumination include *Radiosity and Global Illumination* (M. F. Cohen & Wallace, 1993), *Radiosity and Realistic Image Synthesis* (Sillion & Puech, 1994), *Principles of Digital Image Synthesis* (Glassner, 1995), *Realistic Image Synthesis Using Photon Mapping* (Jensen, 2001), *Advanced Global Illumination* (Dutré et al., 2002), and *Physically Based Rendering* (Pharr & Humphreys, 2004). The probabilistic methods discussed in this chapter are from *Monte Carlo Techniques for Direct Lighting Calculations* (Shirley et al., 1996).

Exercises

1. For a closed environment, where every surface is a diffuse reflector and emittor with reflectance R and emitted radiance E, what is the total radiance at each point? *Hint: for $R = 0.5$ and $E = 0.25$ the answer is 0.5.* This is an excellent debugging case.

2. Using the definitions from Chapter 20, verify Equation (24.1).

3. If we want to render a typically-sized room with textures at centimeter-square resolution, approximately how many particles should we send to get an average of about 1000 hits per texel?

4. Develop a method to take random samples with uniform density from a disk.

5. Develop a method to take random samples with uniform density from a triangle.

6. Develop a method to take uniform random samples on a "sky dome" (the inside of a hemisphere).

25

Reflection Models

As we discussed in Chapter 20, the reflective properties of a surface can be summarized using the BRDF (Nicodemus et al., 1977; Cook & Torrance, 1982). In this chapter, we discuss some of the most visually important aspects of material properties and a few fairly simple models that are useful in capturing these properties. There are many BRDF models in use in graphics, and the models presented here are meant to give just an idea of non-diffuse BRDFs.

25.1 Real-World Materials

Many real materials have a visible structure at normal viewing distances. For example, most carpets have easily visible pile that contributes to appearance. For our purposes, such structure is not part of the material property but is, instead, part of the geometric model. Structure whose details are invisible at normal viewing distances, but which do determine macroscopic material appearance, are part of the material property. For example, the fibers in paper have a complex appearance under magnification, but they are blurred together into an homogeneous appearance when viewed at arm's length. This distinction between microstructure that is folded into BRDF is somewhat arbitrary and depends on what one defines as "normal" viewing distance and visual acuity, but the distinction has proven quite useful in practice.

In this section we define some categories of materials. Later in the chapter, we present reflection models that target each type of material. In the notes at the end of the chapter some models that account for more exotic materials are also discussed.

25.1.1   Smooth Dielectrics and Metals

Dielectrics are clear materials that refract light; their basic properties were summarized in Chapter 4. Metals reflect and refract light much like dielectrics, but they absorb light very, very quickly. Thus, only very thin metal sheets are transparent at all, e.g., the thin gold plating on some glass objects. For a smooth material, there are only two important properties:

1. How much light is reflected at each incident angle and wavelength.

2. What fraction of light is absorbed as it travels through the material for a given distance and wavelength.

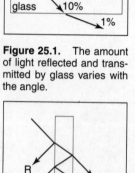

Figure 25.1. The amount of light reflected and transmitted by glass varies with the angle.

The amount of light transmitted is whatever is not reflected (a result of energy conservation). For a metal, in practice, we can assume all the light is immediately absorbed. For a dielectric, the fraction is determined by the constant used in Beer's Law as discussed in Chapter 4.

The amount of light reflected is determined by the *Fresnel equations* as discussed in Chapter 4. These equations are straightforward, but cumbersome. The main effect of the Fresnel Equations is to increase the reflectance as the incident angle increases, particularly near grazing angles. This effect works for transmitted light as well. These ideas are shown diagrammatically in Figure 25.1. Note that the light is repeatedly reflected and refracted as shown in Figure 25.2. Usually only one or two of the reflected images is easily visible.

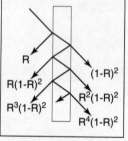

Figure 25.2. Light is repeatedly reflected and refracted by glass, with the fractions of energy shown.

25.1.2   Rough Surfaces

If a metal or dielectric is roughened to a small degree, but not so small that diffraction occurs, then we can think of it as a surface with *microfacets* (Cook & Torrance, 1982). Such surfaces behave specularly at a closer distance, but viewed at a further distance seem to spread the light out in a distribution. For a metal, an example of this rough surface might be brushed steel, or the "cloudy" side of most aluminum foil.

For dielectrics, such as a sheet of glass, scratches or other irregular surface features make the glass blur the reflected and transmitted images that we can normally see clearly. If the surface is heavily scratched, we call it *translucent* rather than transparent. This is a somewhat arbitrary distinction, but it is usually clear whether we would consider a glass translucent or transparent.

25.1.3 Diffuse Materials

A material is *diffuse* if it is matte, i.e., not shiny. Many surfaces we see are diffuse, such as most stones, paper, and unfinished wood. To a first approximation, diffuse surfaces can be approximated with a Lambertian (constant) BRDF. Real diffuse materials usually become somewhat specular for grazing angles. This is a subtle effect, but can be important for realism.

25.1.4 Translucent Materials

Many thin objects, such as leaves and paper, both transmit and reflect light diffusely. For all practical purposes no clear image is transmitted by these objects. These surfaces can add a hue shift to the transmitted light. For example, red paper is red because it filters out non-red light for light that penetrates a short distance into the paper, and then scatters back out. The paper also transmits light with a red hue because the same mechanisms apply, but the transmitted light makes it all the way through the paper. One implication of this property is that the transmitted coefficient should be the same in both directions.

25.1.5 Layered Materials

Many surfaces are composed of "layers" or are dielectrics with embedded particles that give the surface a diffuse property (Phong, 1975). The surface of such materials reflects specularly as shown in Figure 25.3, and thus obeys the Fresnel equations. The light that is transmitted is either absorbed or scattered back up to the dielectric surface where it may or may not be transmitted. That light that is transmitted, scattered, and then retransmitted in the opposite direction forms a diffuse "reflection" component.

Note that the diffuse component also is attenuated with the degree of the angle, because the Fresnel equations cause reflection back into the surface as the angle increases as shown in Figure 25.4. Thus instead of a constant diffuse BRDF, one that vanishes near the grazing angle is more appropriate.

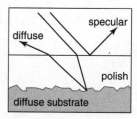

Figure 25.3. Light hitting a layered surface can be reflected specularly, or it can be transmitted and then scatter diffusely off the substrate.

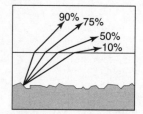

Figure 25.4. The light scattered by the substrate is less and less likely to make it out of the surface as the angle relative to the surface normal increases.

25.2 Implementing Reflection Models

A BRDF model, as described in Section 20.1.6, will produce a rendering which is more physically based than the rendering we get from point light sources and Phong-like models. Unfortunately, real BRDFs are typically quite complicated and cannot be deduced from first principles. Instead, they must either be measured and directly approximated from raw data, or they must be crudely approximated in an empirical fashion. The latter empirical strategy is what is usually done, and the development of such approximate models is still an area of research. This section discusses several desirable properties of such empirical models.

First, physical constraints imply two properties of a BRDF model. The first constraint is energy conservation:

$$\text{for all } \mathbf{k}_i, R(\mathbf{k}_i) = \int_{\text{all } \mathbf{k}_o} \rho(\mathbf{k}_i, \mathbf{k}_o) \cos \theta_o \, d\sigma_o \leq 1.$$

If you send a beam of light at a surface from any direction $\mathbf{k}_i$, then the total amount of light reflected over all directions will be at most the incident amount. The second physical property we expect all BRDFs to have is reciprocity:

$$\text{for all } \mathbf{k}_i, \mathbf{k}_o, \rho(\mathbf{k}_i, \mathbf{k}_o) = \rho(\mathbf{k}_o, \mathbf{k}_i).$$

Second, we want a clear separation between diffuse and specular components. The reason for this is that, although there is a mathematically-clean delta function formulation for ideal specular components, delta functions must be implemented as special cases in practice. Such special cases are only practical if the BRDF model clearly indicates what is specular and what is diffuse.

Third, we would like intuitive parameters. For example, one reason the Phong model has enjoyed such longevity is that its diffuse constant and exponent are both clearly related to the intuitive properties of the surface, namely surface color and highlight size.

Finally, we would like the BRDF function to be amenable to Monte Carlo sampling. Recall from Chapter 14 that an integral can be sampled by N random points $x_i \sim p$ where p is defined with the same measure as the integral:

$$\int f(x) d\mu \approx \frac{1}{N} \sum_{j=1}^{N} \frac{f(x_j)}{p(x_j)}.$$

Recall from Section 20.2 that the surface radiance in direction $\mathbf{k}_o$ is given by a transport equation:

$$L_s(\mathbf{k}_o) = \int_{\text{all } \mathbf{k}_i} \rho(\mathbf{k}_i, \mathbf{k}_o) L_f(\mathbf{k}_i) \cos \theta_i d\sigma_i.$$

If we sample directions with pdf $p(\mathbf{k}_i)$ as discussed in Chapter 24, then we can approximate the surface radiance with samples:

$$L_s(\mathbf{k}_o) \approx \frac{1}{N} \sum_{j=1}^{N} \frac{\rho(\mathbf{k}_j, \mathbf{k}_o) L_f(\mathbf{k}_j) \cos \theta_j}{p(\mathbf{k}_j)}.$$

This approximation will converge for any p that is non-zero where the integrand is non-zero. However, it will only converge well if the integrand is not very large relative to p. Ideally, $p(\mathbf{k})$ should be approximately shaped like the integrand $\rho(\mathbf{k}_j, \mathbf{k}_o) L_f(\mathbf{k}_j) \cos \theta_j$. In practice, L_f is complicated, and the best we can accomplish is to have $p(\mathbf{k})$ shaped somewhat like $\rho(\mathbf{k}, \mathbf{k}_o) L_f(\mathbf{k}) \cos \theta$.

For example, if the BRDF is Lambertian, then it is constant and the "ideal" $p(\mathbf{k})$ is proportional to $\cos \theta$. Because the integral of p must be one, we can deduce the leading constant:

$$\int_{\text{all } \mathbf{k} \text{ with } \theta < \pi/2} C \cos \theta \, d\sigma = 1.$$

This implies that $C = 1/\pi$, so we have

$$p(\mathbf{k}) = \frac{1}{\pi} \cos \theta.$$

An acceptably efficient implementation will result as long as p doesn't get too small when the integrand is non-zero. Thus, the constant pdf will also suffice:

$$p(\mathbf{k}) = \frac{1}{2\pi}.$$

This emphasizes that many pdfs may be acceptable for a given BRDF model.

25.3   Specular Reflection Models

For a metal, we typically specify the reflectance at normal incidence $R_0(\lambda)$. The reflectance should vary according to the Fresnel equations, and a good approximation is given by (Schlick, 1994a)

$$R(\theta, \lambda) = R_0(\lambda) + (1 - R_0(\lambda))(1 - \cos \theta)^5.$$

This approximation allows us to just set the normal reflectance of the metal either from data or by eye.

For a dielectric, the same formula works for reflectance. However, we can set $R_0(\lambda)$ in terms of the refractive index $n(\lambda)$:

$$R_0(\lambda) = \left(\frac{n(\lambda) - 1}{n(\lambda) + 1}\right)^2.$$

Typically, n does not vary with wavelength, but for applications where dispersion is important, n can vary. The refractive indices that are often useful include water ($n = 1.33$), glass ($n = 1.4$ to $n = 1.7$), and diamond ($n = 2.4$).

Figure 25.5. Renderings of polished tiles using coupled model. These images were produced using a Monte Carlo path tracer. The sampling distribution for the diffuse term is $\cos\theta/\pi$.

25.4   Smooth Layered Model

Reflection in matte/specular materials, such as plastics or polished woods, is governed by Fresnel equations at the surface and by scattering within the subsurface. An example of this reflection can be seen in the tiles in the renderings in Figure 25.5. Note that the blurring in the specular reflection is mostly vertical due to the compression of apparent bump spacing in the view direction. This effect causes the vertically-streaked reflections seen on lakes on windy days; it can either be modeled using explicit micro-geometry and a simple smooth-surface reflection model or by a more general model that accounts for this asymmetry.

We could use the traditional Lambertian-specular model for the tiles, which linearly mixes specular and Lambertian terms. In standard radiometric terms, this can be expressed as

$$\rho(\theta, \phi, \theta', \phi'\lambda) = \frac{R_d(\lambda)}{\pi} + R_s\rho_s(\theta, \phi, \theta', \phi'),$$

where $R_d(\lambda)$ is the hemispherical reflectance of the matte term, R_s is the specular reflectance, and ρ_s is the normalized specular BRDF (a weighted Dirac delta function on the sphere). This equation is a simplified version of the BRDF where R_s is independent of wavelength. The independence of wavelength causes a highlight that is the color of the luminaire, so a polished rather than a metal appearance will be achieved. Ward (G. J. Ward, 1992) suggests to set $R_d(\lambda) + R_s \leq 1$ in order to conserve energy. However, such models with constant R_s fail to show the increase in specularity for steep viewing angles. This is the key point: in the real world the relative proportions of matte and specular appearance change with the viewing angle.

One way to simulate the change in the matte appearance is to explicitly dampen $R_d(\lambda)$ as R_s increases (Shirley, 1991):

$$\rho(\theta, \phi, \theta', \phi', \lambda) = R_f(\theta)\rho_s(\theta, \phi, \theta', \phi') + \frac{R_d(\lambda)(1 - R_f(\theta))}{\pi},$$

where $R_f(\theta)$ is the Fresnel reflectance for a polish-air interface. The problem with this equation is that it is not reciprocal, as can been seen by exchanging θ and θ'; this changes the value of the matte damping factor because of the multiplication by $(1 - R_f(\theta))$. The specular term, a scaled Dirac delta function, is reciprocal, but this does not make up for the non-reciprocity of the matte term. Although this BRDF works well, its lack of reciprocity can cause some rendering methods to have ill-defined solutions.

We now present a model that produces the matte/specular tradeoff while remaining reciprocal and energy conserving. Because the key feature of the new model is that it couples the matte and specular scaling coefficients, it is called a *coupled* model (Shirley et al., 1997).

Surfaces which have a glossy appearance are often a clear dielectric, such as polyurethane or oil, with some subsurface structure. The specular (mirror-like) component of the reflection is caused by the smooth dielectric surface and is independent of the structure below this surface. The magnitude of this specular term is governed by the Fresnel equations.

The light that is not reflected specularly at the surface is transmitted through the surface. There, either it is absorbed by the subsurface, or it is reflected from a pigment or a subsurface and transmitted back through the surface of the polish. This transmitted light forms the matte component of reflection. Since the matte component can only consist of the light that is transmitted, it will naturally decrease in total magnitude for increasing angle.

To avoid choosing between physically plausible models and models with good qualitative behavior over a range of incident angles, note that the Fresnel equations that account for the specular term, $R_f(\theta)$, are derived directly from the physics of the dielectric-air interface. Therefore, the problem must lie in the matte term. We could use a full-blown simulation of subsurface scattering as implemented, but this technique is both costly and requires detailed knowledge of subsurface structure, which is usually neither known nor easily measurable. Instead, we can modify the matte term to be a simple approximation that captures the important qualitative angular behavior shown in Figure 25.4.

Let us assume that the matte term is not Lambertian, but instead is some other function that depends only on θ, θ' and λ: $\rho_m(\theta, \theta', \lambda)$. We discard behavior that depends on ϕ or ϕ' in the interest of simplicity. We try to keep the formulas reasonably simple because the physics of the matte term is complicated and sometimes requires unknown parameters. We expect the matte term to be close to constant, and roughly rotationally symmetric (He et al., 1992).

An obvious candidate for the matte component $\rho_m(\theta, \theta', \lambda)$ that will be reciprocal is the *separable* form $kR_m(\lambda)f(\theta)f(\theta')$ for some constant k and matte reflectance parameter $R_m(\lambda)$. We could merge k and $R_m(\lambda)$ into a single term, but we choose to keep them separated because this makes it more intuitive to set $R_m(\lambda)$—which must be between 0 and 1 for all wavelengths. Separable BRDFs have been shown to have several computational advantages, thus we use the separable model:

$$\rho(\theta, \phi, \theta', \phi', \lambda) = R_f(\theta)\rho_s(\theta, \phi, \theta', \phi') + kR_m(\lambda)f(\theta)f(\theta').$$

We know that the matte component can only contain energy not reflected in the surface (specular) component. This means that for $R_m(\lambda) = 1$, the incident and reflected energy are the same, which suggests the following constraint on the BRDF for each incident θ and λ:

$$R_f(\theta) + 2\pi k f(\theta) \int_0^{\frac{\pi}{2}} f(\theta') \cos\theta' \sin\theta' d\theta' = 1. \tag{25.1}$$

We can see that $f(\theta)$ must be proportional to $(1 - R_f(\theta))$. If we assume that matte components that absorb some energy have the same directional pattern as this ideal, we get a BRDF of the form

$$\rho(\theta, \phi, \theta', \phi', \lambda) = R_f(\theta)\rho_s(\theta, \phi, \theta', \phi') + kR_m(\lambda)[1 - R_f(\theta)][1 - R_f(\theta')].$$

We could now insert the full form of the Fresnel equations to get $R_f(\theta)$, and then use energy conservation to solve for constraints on k. Instead, we will use the approximation discussed in Section 25.1.1 We find that

$$f(\theta) \propto (1 - (1 - \cos\theta)^5).$$

Applying Equation (25.1) yields

$$k = \frac{21}{20\pi(1 - R_0)}. \tag{25.2}$$

The full coupled BRDF is then

$$\rho(\theta, \phi, \theta', \phi', \lambda) =$$
$$\left[R_0 + (1 - \cos\theta)^5(1 - R_0)\right]\rho_s(\theta, \phi, \theta', \phi') +$$
$$kR_m(\lambda)\left[1 - (1 - \cos\theta)^5\right]\left[1 - (1 - \cos\theta')^5\right]. \tag{25.3}$$

The results of running the coupled model is shown in Figure 25.5. Note that for the high viewpoint, the specular reflection is almost invisible, but it is clearly visible in the low-angle photograph image, where the matte behavior is less obvious.

For reasonable values of refractive indices, R_0 is limited to approximately the range 0.03 to 0.06 (the value $R_0 = 0.05$ was used for Figure 25.5). The value of R_s in a traditional Phong model is harder to choose, because it typically must be tuned for viewpoint in static images and tuned for a particular camera sequence for animations. Thus, the coupled model is easier to use in a "hands-off" mode.

25.5 Rough Layered Model

The previous model is fine if the surface is smooth. However, if the surface is not ideal, some spread is needed in the specular component. An extension of the coupled model to this case is presented here (Ashikhmin & Shirley, 2000). At a given point on a surface, the BRDF is a function of two directions, one in the direction towards the light and one in the direction towards the viewer. We would like to have a BRDF model that works for "common" surfaces, such as metal and plastic, and has the following characteristics:

1. **plausible.** As defined by Lewis (R. R. Lewis, 1994), this refers to the BRDF obeying energy conservation and reciprocity.

2. **anisotropy.** The material should model simple anisotropy, such as seen on brushed metals.

3. **intuitive parameters.** For material, such as plastics, there should be parameters R_d for the substrate and R_s for the normal specular reflectance as well as two roughness parameters n_u and n_v.

4. **Fresnel behavior.** Specularity should increase as the incident angle decreases.

5. **non-Lambertian diffuse term.** The material should allow for a diffuse term, but the component should be non-Lambertian to assure energy conservation in the presence of Fresnel behavior.

6. **Monte Carlo friendliness.** There should be some reasonable probability density function that allows straightforward Monte Carlo sample generation for the BRDF.

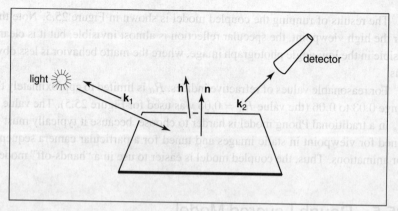

Figure 25.6. Geometry of reflection. Note that $\mathbf{k}_1$, $\mathbf{k}_2$, and $\mathbf{h}$ share a plane, which usually does not include $\mathbf{n}$.

A BRDF with these properties is a Fresnel-weighted Phong-style cosine lobe model that is anisotropic.

We again decompose the BRDF into a specular component and a diffuse component (Figure 25.6). Accordingly, we write our BRDF as the classical sum of two parts:

$$\rho(\mathbf{k}_1, \mathbf{k}_2) = \rho_s(\mathbf{k}_1, \mathbf{k}_2) + \rho_d(\mathbf{k}_1, \mathbf{k}_2), \qquad (25.4)$$

where the first term accounts for the specular reflection (this will be presented in the next section). While it is possible to use the Lambertian BRDF for the diffuse term $\rho_d(\mathbf{k}_1, \mathbf{k}_2)$ in our model, we will discuss a better solution in Section 25.5.2 and how to implement the model in Section 25.5.3. Readers who just want to implement the model should skip to that section.

25.5.1 Anisotropic Specular BRDF

To model the specular behavior, we use a Phong-style specular lobe but make this lobe anisotropic and incorporate Fresnel behavior while attempting to preserve the simplicity of the initial mode. This BRDF is

$$\rho(\mathbf{k}_1, \mathbf{k}_2) = \frac{\sqrt{(n_u + 1)(n_v + 1)}}{8\pi} \frac{(\mathbf{n} \cdot \mathbf{h})^{n_u \cos^2 \phi + n_v \sin^2 \phi}}{(\mathbf{h} \cdot \mathbf{k}_i) \max(\cos \theta_i, \cos \theta_o)} F(\mathbf{k}_i \cdot \mathbf{h}) . \quad (25.5)$$

Again we use Schlick's approximation to the Fresnel equation:

$$F(\mathbf{k}_i \cdot \mathbf{h}) = R_s + (1 - R_s)(1 - (\mathbf{k}_i \cdot \mathbf{h}))^5, \qquad (25.6)$$

where R_s is the material's reflectance for the normal incidence. Because $\mathbf{k}_i \cdot \mathbf{h} = \mathbf{k}_o \cdot \mathbf{h}$, this form is reciprocal. We have an empirical model whose terms are

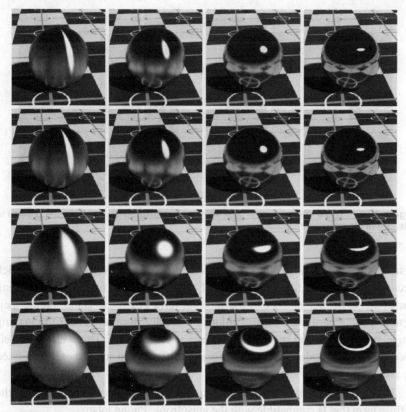

Figure 25.7. Metallic spheres for exponents 10, 100, 1000, 10000 increasing both left-to-right and top-to-bottom.

chosen to enforce energy conservation and reciprocity. A full rationalization for the terms is given in the paper by Ashikhmin, listed in the chapter notes.

The specular BRDF of Equation (25.5) is useful for representing metallic surfaces where the diffuse component of reflection is very small. Figure 25.7 shows a set of metal spheres on a texture-mapped Lambertian plane. As the values of parameters n_u and n_v change, the appearance of the spheres shift from rough metal to almost perfect mirror, and from highly anisotropic to the more familiar Phong-like behavior.

25.5.2 Diffuse Term for the Anisotropic Phong Model

It is possible to use a Lambertian BRDF together with the anisotropic specular term; this is done for most models, but it does not necessarily conserve energy. A

Figure 25.8. Three views for $n_u = n_v = 400$ and a diffuse substrate. Note the change in intensity of the specular reflection.

better approach is a simple angle-dependent form of the diffuse component which accounts for the fact that the amount of energy available for diffuse scattering varies due to the dependence of the specular term's total reflectance on the incident angle. In particular, diffuse color of a surface disappears near the grazing angle, because the total specular reflectance is close to one. This well-known effect cannot be reproduced with a Lambertian diffuse term and is therefore missed by most reflection models.

Following a similar approach to the coupled model, we can find a form of the diffuse term that is compatible with the anisotropic Phong lobe:

$$\rho_d(\mathbf{k}_1, \mathbf{k}_2) = \frac{28R_d}{23\pi}(1 - R_s)\left(1 - \left(1 - \frac{\cos\theta_i}{2}\right)^5\right)\left(1 - \left(1 - \frac{\cos\theta_o}{2}\right)^5\right).$$

(25.7)

Here R_d is the diffuse reflectance for normal incidence, and R_s is the Phong lobe coefficient. An example using this model is shown in Figure 25.8.

25.5.3 Implementing the Model

Recall that the BRDF is a combination of diffuse and specular components:

$$\rho(\mathbf{k}_1, \mathbf{k}_2) = \rho_s(\mathbf{k}_1, \mathbf{k}_2) + \rho_d(\mathbf{k}_1, \mathbf{k}_2).$$

(25.8)

The diffuse component is given in Equation (25.7); the specular component is given in Equation (25.5). It is not necessary to call trigonometric functions to compute the exponent, so the specular BRDF can be written:

$$\rho(\mathbf{k}_1, \mathbf{k}_2) = \frac{\sqrt{(n_u + 1)(n_v + 1)}}{8\pi} (\mathbf{n} \cdot \mathbf{h})^{\frac{(n_u(\mathbf{h} \cdot \mathbf{u})^2 + n_v(\mathbf{h} \cdot \mathbf{v})^2)/(1-(\mathbf{hn})^2)}{(\mathbf{h} \cdot \mathbf{k}_i)\max(\cos\theta_i, \cos\theta_o)}} F(\mathbf{k}_i \cdot \mathbf{h}).$$

$$(25.9)$$

In a Monte Carlo setting, we are interested in the following problem: given $\mathbf{k}_1$, generate samples of $\mathbf{k}_2$ with a distribution whose shape is similar to the cosine-weighted BRDF. Note that greatly undersampling a large value of the integrand is a serious error, while greatly oversampling a small value is acceptable in practice. The reader can verify that the densities suggested below have this property.

A suitable way to construct a pdf for sampling is to consider the distribution of half vectors that would give rise to our BRDF. Such a function is

$$p_h(\mathbf{h}) = \frac{\sqrt{(n_u + 1)(n_v + 1)}}{2\pi} (\mathbf{nh})^{n_u \cos^2\phi + n_v \sin^2\phi}, \qquad (25.10)$$

where the constants are chosen to ensure it is a valid pdf.

We can just use the probability density function $p_h(\mathbf{h})$ of Equation (25.10) to generate a random $\mathbf{h}$. However, to evaluate the rendering equation, we need both a reflected vector $\mathbf{k}_o$ and a probability density function $p(\mathbf{k}_o)$. It is important to note that if you generate $\mathbf{h}$ according to $p_h(\mathbf{h})$ and then transform to the resulting $\mathbf{k}_o$:

$$\mathbf{k}_o = -\mathbf{k}_i + 2(\mathbf{k}_i \cdot \mathbf{h})\mathbf{h}, \qquad (25.11)$$

the density of the resulting $\mathbf{k}_o$ is **not** $p_h(\mathbf{k}_o)$. This is because of the difference in measures in $\mathbf{h}$ and $\mathbf{k}_o$. So the actual density $p(\mathbf{k}_o)$ is

$$p(\mathbf{k}_o) = \frac{p_h(\mathbf{h})}{4(\mathbf{k}_i \mathbf{h})}. \qquad (25.12)$$

Note that in an implementation where the BRDF is known to be this model, the estimate of the rendering equation is quite simple as many terms cancel out.

It is possible to generate an $\mathbf{h}$ vector whose corresponding vector $\mathbf{k}_o$ will point inside the surface, i.e., $\cos\theta_o < 0$. The weight of such a sample should be set to zero. This situation corresponds to the specular lobe going below the horizon and is the main source of energy loss in the model. Clearly, this problem becomes progressively less severe as n_u, n_v become larger.

The only thing left now is to describe how to generate $\mathbf{h}$ vectors with the pdf of Equation (25.10). We will start by generating $\mathbf{h}$ with its spherical angles in the range $(\theta, \phi) \in [0, \frac{\pi}{2}] \times [0, \frac{\pi}{2}]$. Note that this is only the first quadrant of the hemisphere. Given two random numbers (ξ_1, ξ_2) uniformly distributed in $[0, 1]$, we can choose

$$\phi = \arctan\left(\sqrt{\frac{n_u + 1}{n_v + 1}} \tan\left(\frac{\pi \xi_1}{2}\right)\right), \qquad (25.13)$$

and then use this value of ϕ to obtain θ according to

$$\cos\theta = (1 - \xi_2)^{1/(n_u \cos^2\phi + n_v \sin^2\phi + 1)}. \tag{25.14}$$

To sample the entire hemisphere, we use the standard manipulation where ξ_1 is mapped to one of four possible functions depending on whether it is in $[0, 0.25)$, $[0.25, 0.5)$, $[0.5, 0.75)$, or $[0.75, 1.0)$. For example for $\xi_1 \in [0.25, 0.5)$, find $\phi(1 - 4(0.5 - \xi_1))$ via Equation (25.13), and then "flip" it about the $\phi = \pi/2$ axis. This ensures full coverage and stratification.

For the diffuse term, use a simpler approach and generate samples according to a cosine distribution. This is sufficiently close to the complete diffuse BRDF to substantially reduce variance of the Monte Carlo estimation.

Frequently Asked Questions

• My images look too smooth, even with a complex BRDF. What am I doing wrong?

BRDFs only capture subpixel detail that is too small to be resolved by the eye. Most real surfaces also have some small variations, such as the wrinkles in skin, that can be seen. If you want true realism, some sort of texture or displacement map is needed.

• How do I integrate the BRDF with texture mapping?

Texture mapping can be used to control any parameter on a surface. So any kinds of colors or control parameters used by a BRDF should be programmable.

• I have very pretty code except for my material class. What am I doing wrong?

You are probably doing nothing wrong. Material classes tend to be the ugly thing in everybody's programs. If you find a nice way to deal with it, please let me know! My own code uses a shader architecture (Hanrahan & Lawson, 1990) which makes the material include much of the rendering algorithm.

Notes

There are many BRDF models described in the literature, and only a few of them have been described here. Others include (Cook & Torrance, 1982; He et al.,

1992; G. J. Ward, 1992; Oren & Nayar, 1994; Schlick, 1994a; Lafortune et al., 1997; Stam, 1999; Ashikhmin et al., 2000; Ershov et al., 2001; Matusik et al., 2003; Lawrence et al., 2004; Stark et al., 2005). The desired characteristics of BRDF models is discussed in *Making Shaders More Physically Plausible* (R. R. Lewis, 1994).

Exercises

1. Suppose that instead of the Lambertian BRDF we used a BRDF of the form $C \cos^a \theta_i$. What must C be to conserve energy?

2. The BRDF in Exercise 1 is not reciprocal. Can you modify it to be reciprocal?

3. Something like a highway sign is a *retroreflector*. This means that the BRDF is large when $\mathbf{k}_i$ and $\mathbf{k}_o$ are near each other. Make a model inspired by the Phong model that captures retroreflection behavior while being reciprocal and conserving energy.

Naty Hoffman

26

Computer Graphics in Games

Of all the applications of computer graphics, computer and video games attract perhaps the most attention. The graphics methods selected for a given game have a profound effect, not only on the game engine code, but also on the art asset creation, and even sometimes on the *gameplay*, or core game mechanics.

Although game graphics rely on the material in all of the preceding chapters, two chapters are particularly germane. Games need to make highly efficient use of graphics hardware, so an understanding of the material in Chapter 18 is important. Of course, games are interactive applications, and, as such, many of the principles detailed in Chapter 19 apply.

In this chapter, I will detail the specific considerations that apply to graphics in game development, from the platforms on which games run to the game production process.

26.1   Platforms

Here, I use the term *platform* to refer to a specific combination of hardware, operating system, and API (application programming interface) for which a game is designed. Games run on a large variety of platforms, ranging from virtual machines used for browser-based games to dedicated game consoles using specialized hardware and APIs.

In the past, it was common for games to be designed for a single platform. The increasing cost of game development has made this rare; *multiplatform* game development is now the norm. The incremental increase in development cost to support multiple platforms is more than repaid by a potential doubling or tripling of the customer base.

Some platforms are quite loosely defined. For example, when developing a game for the Windows PC platform, the developer must account for a very large variety of possible hardware configurations. Games are even expected to run (and run well) on PC configurations that did not exist when the game was developed! This is only possible due to the abstractions afforded by the APIs defining the Windows platform.

One way in which developers account for wide variance in graphics performance is by *scaling*—adjusting graphics quality in response to system capabilities. This can ensure reasonable performance on low-end systems, while still achieving competitive visuals on high-performance systems. This adjustment is sometimes done automatically by profiling the system performance, but more often this control is left in the hands of the user, who can best judge his personal preferences for quality versus speed. Display resolution is easiest to adjust, followed by antialiasing quality. It is also fairly common to offer several quality levels for visual effects such as shadows and motion blur, including the option of turning the effect off entirely.

Differences in graphics performance can be so large that some machines may not run the game at a playable frame rate, even with the lowest quality settings; for this reason PC game developers publish minimum and recommended machine specifications for each game.

As platforms, game consoles are strictly defined. When developing a game for, e.g., Nintendo's Wii console, the developer knows exactly what hardware the game will run on. If the platform's hardware implementation is changed (often done to reduce manufacturing costs), the console manufacturer must ensure that the new implementation behaves *exactly* like the previous one, including timing and performance. This is not to say that the console developer's task is easy; console APIs tend to be much less abstract and closer to the underlying hardware. This gives console development its own set of difficulties. In some sense, multiplatform development (which commonly includes at least two different console platforms and often Windows as well) is the hardest of all, since the multiplatform game developer has neither the assurance of a fixed platform or the convenience of a single high-level API.

Browser-based *virtual machines* such as Adobe Flash are an interesting class of game platforms. Although such virtual machines run on a wide class of hardware from personal computers to mobile phones, the high degree of abstraction provided by the virtual machine results in a stable and unified development platform. The relative ease of development for these platforms and the huge pool of potential customers makes them increasingly attractive to game developers. However, these platforms are defined by the lowest common denominator of the supported hardware, and virtual machines have lower performance than native code on any given platform. For these reasons, such platforms are best suited to games with modest graphics requirements.

Platforms can also be characterized by their openness to development, which is a business or legal distinction rather than a technical one. For example, Windows is open in the sense that development tools are widely available, and there are no gatekeepers controlling access to the marketplace of Windows games. Apple's iPhone is a somewhat more restricted platform in that all applications need to pass a certification process and certain classes of applications are banned outright. Consoles are the most restrictive game platforms, where access to the development tools is tightly controlled. This is opening up somewhat with the introduction of online console game marketplaces, which tend to be more open. A particularly interesting example is Microsoft's Xbox LIVE Community Games service, where the development tools are freely available and the "gatekeeping" is performed primarily by peer review. Games distributed through this service must use a virtual machine platform provided by Microsoft for security reasons.

The game platform determines many elements of the game experience. For example, PC gamers use keyboard and mouse, while console gamers use specialized game controllers. Many console games support multiple players on the same console, either sharing a screen or providing a window for each player. Due to the difficulty of sharing keyboard and mouse, this type of play is not found on PC. A handheld game system will have a different control scheme than a touch-screen phone, etc.

Although game platforms vary widely, some common trends can be discerned. Most platforms have multiple processing cores, divided between general-purpose (CPU) and graphics-specific (GPU). Performance gains over time are due mostly to increases in core count; gains in individual core performance are modest. As GPU cores grow in generality, the lines between GPU and CPU cores are increasingly blurred. Storage capacity tends to increase at a slower rate than processing power, and communication bandwidth (between cores as well as between each core and storage) grows at a slower pace still.

26.2 Limited Resources

One of the primary challenges of game graphics is the need to manage multiple pools of limited resources. Each platform imposes its own constraints on hardware resources such as processing time, storage, and memory bandwidth. At a higher level, development resources also need to be managed; there is a fixed-size team of programmers, artists and game designers with limited time to complete the game, hopefully without working *too* much overtime! This needs to be taken into account when deciding which graphics techniques to adopt.

26.2.1 Processing Time

Early game developers only had to worry about budgeting a single processor. Current game platforms contain multiple CPU and GPU cores. These processors need to be carefully synchronized to avoid deadlocks or excessive stalls.

Since the time consumed by a single rendering command is highly variable, graphics processors are decoupled from the rest of the system via a *command buffer*. This buffer acts as a queue; commands are deposited on one end and the GPU reads rendering commands from the other. Increasing the size of this buffer decreases the chances of GPU starvation. It is fairly common for games to buffer an entire frame's worth of rendering commands before sending them to the GPU; this guarantees that GPU starvation does not occur. However, this approach requires reserving enough storage space for two full frame's worth of commands (the GPU works on one, while the CPU deposits commands in the other). It also increases the latency between the user's input and the display, which can be problematic for fast-paced games.

Processing budgets are determined by the *frame rate*, which is the frequency at which the frame buffer is refreshed with new renderings of the scene. On fixed platforms (such as consoles), the frame rate experienced by the user is essentially the same one seen by the game developer, so fairly strict frame–rate limits can be imposed. Most games target a frame rate of 30 frames per second (fps); in games where response latency is especially important, the target is often 60 fps. On highly variable platforms (such as PCs), the frame-rate budgets are (by necessity) defined more loosely.

The required frame rate gives the graphics programmer a fixed budget per frame to work with. In the case of a 30 fps target, the CPU cores have 33 milliseconds to gather inputs, process the game logic, perform any physical simulations, traverse the scene description, and send the rendering commands to the graphics hardware. In parallel, other tasks such as audio and network processing must be handled, with their own required response times. While this is happening, the GPU is typically executing the graphics commands submitted during the previous frame.

In most cases, CPU cores are a *homogeneous* resource; all cores are the same, and any of them are equally well suited to a given workload (there are some exceptions, such as the Cell processor used in Sony's PLAYSTATION 3 console).

In contrast, GPUs contain a *heterogeneous* mix of resources, each specialized to a certain set of tasks. Some of these resources consist of fixed-function hardware (for triangle rasterization, alpha blending, and texture sampling), and some are programmable cores. On older GPUs, programmable cores were further differentiated into vertex and pixel processing cores; newer GPU designs have *unified shader cores* which can execute any of the programmable shader types.

Such heterogeneous resources are budgeted separately. Typically, at any point, only one resource type will be the bottleneck, and the others will have excess capacity. On the one hand, this is good, since this capacity can be leveraged to improve visual quality without decreasing performance. On the other hand, it makes it harder to improve performance, since decreasing usage of any of the non-bottleneck resources will have no effect. Even decreasing usage of the bottleneck resource may only improve performance slightly, depending on the degree of utilization of the "next bottleneck."

26.2.2 Storage

Game platforms, like any modern computing system, possess multi-stage *storage hierarchies*, with smaller, faster memory types at the top and larger, slower storage at the bottom. This arrangement is borne of engineering necessity, although it does complicate life for the developer. Most platforms include optical disc storage, which is extremely slow and is used mostly for delivery. On platforms such as Windows, a lengthy installation process is performed once to move all data from the optical disc onto the hard drive, which is significantly faster. The optical disc is never used again (except as an anti-piracy measure). On console platforms, this is less common, although it does sometimes happen when a hard drive is guaranteed to be present, as on Sony's PLAYSTATION 3 console. More often, the hard drive (if present) is only used as a cache for the optical disc.

The next step up the memory hierarchy is RAM, which on many platforms is divided into general system RAM and VRAM (video RAM) which benefits from a high-speed interface to the graphics hardware. A game level may be too large to fit in RAM, in which case the game developer needs to manage moving the data in and out of RAM as needed. On platforms such as Windows, virtual memory is often used for this. On console platforms, custom data streaming and caching systems are typically employed.

Finally, both the CPU and GPU boast various kinds of on-chip memory and caches. These are extremely small and fast and are usually managed by the graphics API.

Graphics resources take up a lot of memory, so they are a primary focus of storage budgets in game development. Textures are usually the greatest memory consumers, followed by geometry (vertex data), and finally other types of graphics data such as animations. Not all memory can be used for graphics—audio also takes up a fair bit, and game logic may use sizeable data structures. As in the case of processing time, budgeting tends to be somewhat looser on Windows, where the exact amount of memory present on the user's system is unknown and virtual memory covers a multitude of sins. In contrast, memory budgeting on console platforms is quite strict—often the lead programmer keeps track of memory on a spreadsheet and a programmer requiring more memory for their system needs to beg, borrow, or steal it from someone else.

The various levels of the memory hierarchy differ not only in size, but also in access speed. This has two separate dimensions: *latency* and *bandwidth*.

Latency is the time that elapses between a storage access request and its final fulfillment. This varies from a few clock cycles (for on-chip cache) to millions of clock cycles (for data residing on optical disc). Latency is usually an issue for read access (although write latency can also be an issue if the result needs to be read back from memory soon after). In some cases, the read request is *blocking*, which means that the processor core that submitted the read can do nothing else until the request is fulfilled. In other cases, the read is *non-blocking*; the processing core can submit the read request, do other types of processing, and then use the results of the read after it has arrived. Texture accesses by the GPU are an example of non-blocking reads; an important aspect of GPU design is to find ways to "hide" texture read latency by performing unrelated computations while the texture read is being fulfilled.

For this latency hiding to work, there must be a sufficient amount of computation relative to texture accesses. This is an important consideration for the shader writer; the optimal mix of computation vs. texture access keeps changing (in favor of more computation) as memory fails to keep up with increases in processing power.

Bandwidth refers to the maximum rate of transfer to and from storage. It is typically measured in gigabytes per second.

26.2.3 Development Resources

Besides hardware resources, such as processing power and storage space, the game graphics programmer also has to contend with a different kind of limited resource—the time of his team-mates! When selecting graphics techniques, the engineering resources needed to implement each technique must be taken into account, as well as any tools necessary to compute the input data (in many cases, tools can take significantly more time than implementing the technique itself). Perhaps most importantly, the impact on artist productivity must be taken into account. Most graphics techniques use assets created by game artists, who comprise by far the largest part of most modern game teams. The graphics programmer must foster the artist's productivity and creativity, which will ultimately determine the visual quality of the game.

26.3 Optimization Techniques

Making wise use of these limited resources is the primary challenge of the game graphics programmer. To this end, various optimization techniques are commonly employed.

In many games, pixel shader processing is a primary bottleneck. Most GPUs contain hierarchical depth-culling hardware which can avoid executing pixel shaders on occluded surfaces. To make good use of this hardware, opaque objects can be rendered back-to-front. Alternatively, optimal depth-culling usage can be achieved by performing a *depth pre-pass*, i.e., rendering all the opaque objects into the depth buffer (without any color output or pixel shaders) before rendering the scene normally. This does incur some overhead (due to the need to render every object twice), but in many cases the performance gain is worth it.

The fastest way to render an object is to not render it at all; thus any method of discerning early on that an object is occluded can be useful. This saves not only pixel processing but also vertex processing and even CPU time that would be spent submitting the object to the graphics API. View frustum culling (see Section 8.4.1) is universally employed, but in many games it is not sufficient. High-level occlusion culling algorithms are often used, utilizing data structures such as PVS (potentially visible sets) or BSP (binary spatial partitioning) trees to quickly narrow down the pool of potentially visible objects.

Even if an object is visible, it may be at such a distance that most of its detail can be removed without apparent effect. LOD (level-of-detail) algorithms render different representations of an object based on distance (or other factors, such as screen coverage or importance). This can save significant processing, vertex processing in particular. Examples can be seen in Figure 26.1.

In many cases, processing can be performed before the game even starts. The results of such *preprocessing* can be stored and used each frame, thus speeding

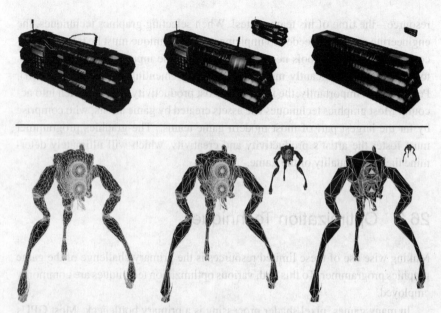

Figure 26.1. Two examples of game objects at a varying level of detail. The small inset images show the relative sizes at which the simplified models might be used. *Upper row of images courtesy Crytek; lower row courtesy Valve Corp.*

up the game. This is most commonly employed for lighting, where global illumination algorithms are utilized to compute lighting throughout the scene and store it in lightmaps and other data structures for later use.

26.4 Game Types

Since game requirements vary widely, the selection of graphics techniques is driven by the exact type of game being developed.

The allocation of processing time depends strongly on the frame rate. Currently, most console games tend to target 30 frames per second, since this enables much higher graphics quality. However, certain game types with fast gameplay require very low latency, and such games typically render at 60 frames per second. This includes music games such as *Guitar Hero* and first-person shooters such as *Call of Duty*.

The frame rate determines the available time to render the scene. The composition of the scene itself also varies widely from game to game. Most games have a division between *background geometry* (scenery, mostly static) and *foreground geometry* (characters and dynamic objects). These are handled differently by the rendering engine. For example, background geometry will often have lightmaps containing precomputed lighting, which is not feasible for foreground objects. Precomputed lighting is typically applied to foreground objects via some type of volumetric representation which can take account of the changing position of each object over time.

Some games have relatively enclosed environments, where the camera remains largely in place. The purest examples are fighting games such as the *Street Fighter* series, but this is also true to some extent for games such as *Devil May Cry* and *God of War*. These games have cameras that are not under direct player control, and the game play tends to move from one enclosed environment to another, spending a significant amount of playing time in each. This allows the game developer to lavish large amounts of resources (processing, storage, and artist time) on each room or enclosed environment, resulting in very high levels of graphics fidelity.

Other games have extremely large worlds, where the player can move about freely. This is most true for "sandbox games" such as the *Grand Theft Auto* series and online role-playing games such as *World of Warcraft*. Such games pose great challenges to the graphics developer, since resource allocation is very difficult when during each frame the player can see a large extent of the world. Further complicating things, the player can freely go to some formerly distant part of the world and observe it from up close. Such games typically have changing time of day, which makes precomputation of lighting difficult at best, if not impossible.

Most games, such as first-person shooters, are somewhere between the two extremes. The player can see a fair amount of scenery each frame, but movement through the game world is somewhat constrained. Many games also have a fixed time of day for each game level, for ease of lighting precomputation.

The number of foreground objects rendered also varies widely between game types. Real-time strategy games such as the *Command and Conquer* series often have many dozens, if not hundreds, of units visible on screen. Other types of games have more limited quantities of visible characters, with fighting games at the opposite extreme, where only two characters are visible, each rendered with extremely high detail. A distinction must be drawn between the number of characters visible at any time (which affects budgeting of processing time) and the number of *unique* characters which can potentially be visible at short notice (which affects storage budgets).

The type or *genre* of game also determines audience expectations of the graphics. For example, first-person shooters have historically had very high levels of graphics fidelity, and this expectation drives the graphics design when developing

Figure 26.2. *Crysis* exemplifies the realistic and detailed graphics expected of first-person shooters. *Image courtesy Crytek.* (See also Plate XXXIII.)

Figure 26.3. An example of highly stylized, non-photorealistic rendering from the game *Okami. Image courtesy Capcom Entertainment, Inc.* (See also Plate XXXIV.)

new games in that genre; see Figure 26.2. On the other hand, puzzle games have typically had relatively simplistic graphics, so most game developers will not invest large amounts of programming or art resources into developing photorealistic graphics for such games.

Although most games aim for a photorealistic look, a few do attempt more stylized rendering. One interesting example of this is *Okami*, which can be seen in Figure 26.3.

The management of development resources also differs by game type. Most games have a closed development cycle of one to two years, which ends after the game ships. Recently it has become common to have downloadable content (DLC), which can be purchased after the game ships, so some development resources need to be reserved for that. Persistent-world online games have a never-ending development process where new content is continually being generated, at least as long as the game is economically viable (which may be a period of decades).

The creative exploitation of the specific requirements and restrictions of a particular game is the hallmark of a skilled game graphics programmer. A good example is the game *LittleBigPlanet*, which has a "two-and-a-half-dimensional" game world comprising a small number of two-dimensional layers, as well as a

Figure 26.4. The *LittleBigPlanet* developers took care to choose techniques that fit the game's constraints, combining them in unusual ways to achieve stunning results. *LittleBigPlanet* © 2007 Sony Computer Entertainment Europe. Developed by Media Molecule. *LittleBigPlanet is a trademark of Sony Computer Entertainment Europe.* (See also Plate XXXV.)

non-interactive background. The graphics quality of this game is excellent, driven by the use of unusual rendering techniques specialized to this type of environment; see Figure 26.4.

26.5   The Game Production Process

The game production process starts with the basic game design or concept. In some cases (such as sequels), the basic gameplay and visual design is clear, and only incremental changes are made. In the case of a new game type, extensive prototyping is needed to determine gameplay and design. Most cases sit somewhere in the middle, where there are some new gameplay elements and the visual design is somewhat open. After this step there may be a *greenlight* stage where some early demo or concept is shown to the game publisher to get approval (and funding!) for the game.

The next step is typically *pre-production*. While other teams are working on finishing up the last game, a small core team works on making any needed changes to the game engine and production tool chain, as well as working out the rough details of any new gameplay elements. This core team is working under a strict deadline. After the existing game ships and the rest of the team comes back from a well-deserved vacation, the entire tool chain and engine must be ready for them. If the core team misses this deadline, several dozen developers may be left idle—an extremely expensive proposition!

Full production is the next step, with the entire team creating art assets, designing levels, tweaking gameplay, and implementing further changes to the game engine. In a perfect world, everything done during this process would be used in the final game, but in reality there is an iterative nature to game development which will result in some work being thrown out and redone. The goal is to minimize this with careful planning and prototyping.

When the game is functionally complete, the final stage begins. The term *alpha release* usually refers to the version which marks the start of extensive internal testing, *beta release* to the one which marks the start of extensive external testing, and *gold release* to the final release submitted to the console manufacturer, but different companies have slightly varying definitions of these terms. In any case, testing, or *quality assurance* (QA) is an important part of this phase, and it involves testers at the game development studio, at the publisher, at the console manufacturer, and possibly external QA contractors as well. These various rounds of testing result in bug reports which are submitted back to the game developers and worked on until the next release.

After the game ships, most of the developers go on vacation for a while, but a small team may have to stay to work on patches or downloadable content. In the meantime, a small core team has been working on pre-production for the next game ...

Art asset creation is an aspect of game production that is particularly relevant to graphics development, so I will go into it in some detail.

26.5.1 Asset Creation

While the exact process of art asset creation varies from game to game, the outline I give here is fairly representative. In the past, a single artist would create an entire asset from start to finish, but this process is now much more specialized, involving people with different skill sets working on each asset at various times. Some of these stages have clear dependencies (for example, a character cannot be animated until it is rigged and cannot be rigged before it is modeled). Most game developers have well-defined approval processes, where the art director or a lead artist signs off on each stage before the asset is sent on to the next. Ideally an asset proceeds through each stage exactly once, but in practice changes may be made that require resubmission.

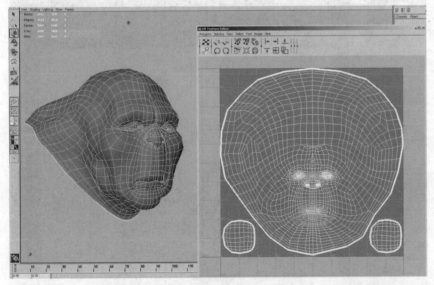

Figure 26.5. A mesh being modeled in Maya, with associated texture parameterization. *Image courtesy Keith Bruns.*

Initial Modeling

Typically the art asset creation process starts by modeling the object geometry. This step is performed in a general-purpose modeling package such as Maya, MAX or Softimage. The modeled geometry will be passed directly to the game engine, so it is important to minimize vertex count while preserving good silhouettes. Character meshes must also be constructed so as to be amenable to animation.

In this stage, a two-dimensional surface parameterization for textures is usually created. It is important that this parameterization be highly continuous, since discontinuities require vertex duplication and may cause filtering artifacts. An example of a mesh with its associated texture parameterization is shown in Figure 26.5.

Texturing

In the past texturing was a straightforward process of painting a color texture, typically in Photoshop. Now specialized detail modeling packages such as ZBrush or Mudbox are commonly used to sculpt fine surface detail. Figures 26.6 and 26.7 show an example of this process.

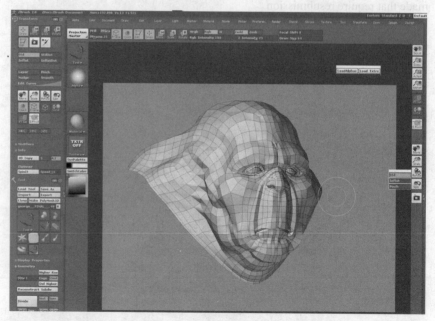

Figure 26.6. The mesh from Figure 26.5 has been brought into ZBrush for detail modeling. *Image courtesy Keith Bruns.*

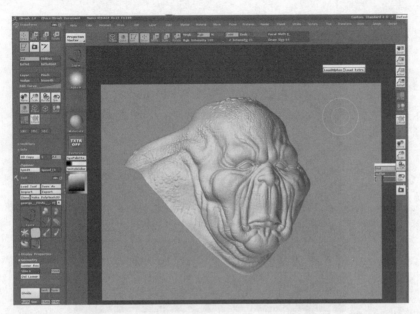

Figure 26.7. The mesh from Figure 26.6, with fine detail added to it in ZBrush. *Image courtesy Keith Bruns.*

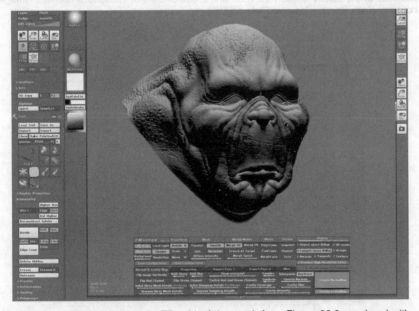

Figure 26.8. A visualization (in ZBrush) of the mesh from Figure 26.6, rendered with a normal map derived from the detailed mesh in Figure 26.7. The bottom of the figure shows the interface for ZBrush's "Zmapper" tool, which was used to derive the normal map. *Image courtesy Keith Bruns.*

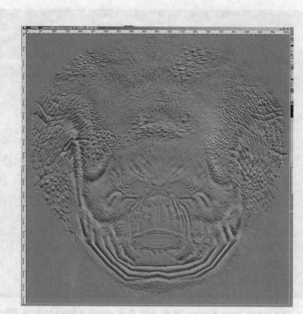

Figure 26.9. The normal map used in Figure 26.8. In this image, the red, green and blue channels of the texture contain the X, Y, and Z coordinates of the surface normals. *Image courtesy Keith Bruns.* (See also Plate XXXVI.)

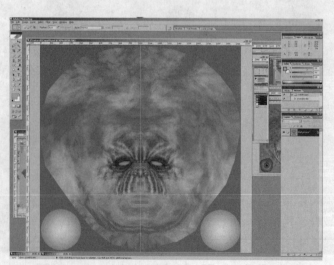

Figure 26.10. An early version of a diffuse color texture for the mesh from Figure 26.8, shown in Photoshop. *Image courtesy Keith Bruns.* (See also Plate XXXVII.)

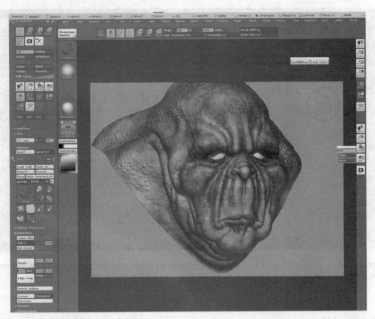

Figure 26.11. A rendering (in ZBrush) of the mesh with normal map and early diffuse color texture (from Figure 26.10) applied. *Image courtesy Keith Bruns.* (See also Plate XXXVIII.)

Figure 26.12. Final version of the color texture from Figure 26.10. *Image courtesy Keith Bruns.* (See also Plate XXXIX.)

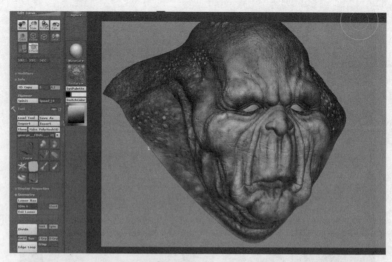

Figure 26.13.   Rendering of the mesh with normal map and final color texture (from Figure 26.12) applied. *Image courtesy Keith Bruns.* (See also Plate XL.)

If this additional detail were to be represented with actual geometry, millions of triangles would be needed. Instead, the detail is commonly "baked" into a normal map which is applied onto the original, coarse mesh, as shown in Figures 26.8 and 26.9.

Besides normal maps, multiple textures containing surface properties such as diffuse color, specular color, and smoothness (specular power) are also created. These are either painted directly on the surface in the detail modeling application, or in a two-dimensional application such as Photoshop. All of these texture maps use the surface parameterization defined in the initial modeling phase. When the texture is painted in a two-dimensional painting application, the artist must frequently switch between the painting application and some other application which can show a three-dimensional rendering of the object with the texture applied. This iterative process is illustrated in Figures 26.10, 26.11, 26.12, and 26.13.

Shading

Shaders are typically applied in the same application used for initial modeling. In this process, a shader (from the set of shaders defined for that game) is applied to the mesh. The various textures resulting from the detail modeling stage are applied as inputs to this shader, using the surface parameterization defined during initial modeling. Various other shader inputs are set via visual experimentation ("tweaking"); see Figure 26.14.

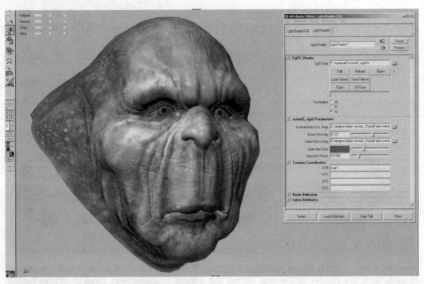

Figure 26.14. Shader configuration in Maya. The interface on the right is used to select the shader, assign textures to shader inputs, and set the values of non-texture shader inputs (such as the "Specular Color" and "Specular Power" sliders). The rendering on the left is updated dynamically while these properties are modified, enabling immediate visual feedback. *Image courtesy Keith Bruns.* (See also Plate XLI.)

Lighting

In the case of background scenery, lighting artists will typically start their work after modeling, texturing, and shading has been completed. Light sources are placed and their effect computed in a pre-processing step. The results of this process are stored in lightmaps for later use by the rendering engine.

Animation

Character meshes undergo several additional steps related to animation. The primary method used to animate game characters is *skinning*. This requires a *rig*, consisting of a hierarchy of transform nodes that is attached to the character, a process known as *rigging*. The area of effect of each transform node is painted onto a subset of mesh vertices. Finally, animators create animations that move, rotate, and scale these transform nodes, "dragging" the mesh behind them.

A typical game character will have many dozens of animations, corresponding to different modes of motion (walking, running, turning) as well as different actions such as attacks. In the case of a main character, the number of animations can be in the hundreds. Transitions between different animations also need to be defined.

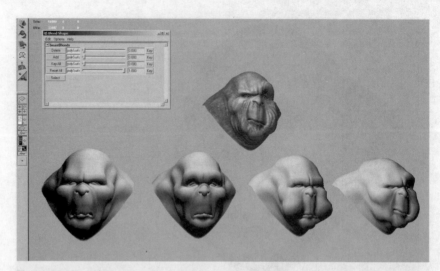

Figure 26.15. Morph target interface in Maya. The bottom row shows four different morph targets, and the model at the top shows the effects of combining several morph targets together. The interface at the upper left is used to control the degree to which each morph target is applied. *Image courtesy Keith Bruns.*

For facial animation, another technique, called *morph targets* is sometimes employed. In this technique, the mesh vertices are directly manipulated to deform the mesh. Different copies of the deformed mesh are stored (e.g., for different facial expressions) and combined by the game engine at runtime. The creation of morph targets is shown in Figure 26.15.

Notes

There is a huge amount of information on real-time rendering and game programming available, both in books and online. Here are some resources I can recommend from personal familiarity:

Game Developer Magazine is a good source of information on game development, as are slides from the talks given at the annual *Game Developers Conference* (GDC) and Microsoft's *Gamefest* conference. The *GPU Gems* and *ShaderX* book series also contain good information—all of the former and the first two of the latter are also available online.

Eric Lengyel's *Mathematics for 3D Game Programming & Computer Graphics*, now in its second edition, is a good reference for the various types of math used in graphics and games. A specific area of game programming that is closely related to graphics is collision detection, for which Christer Ericson's *Real-Time Collision Detection* is the definitive resource.

Since its first edition in 1999, Eric Haines and Tomas Akenine-Möller's *Real-Time Rendering* has endeavored to cover this fast-growing field in a thorough manner. As a longtime fan of this book, I was glad to have the opportunity to be a coauthor on the third edition, which came out in mid-2008.

Reading is not enough—make sure you play a variety of games regularly to get a good idea of the requirements of various game types, as well as the current state of the art.

Exercises

1. Examine the visuals of two dissimilar games. What differences can you deduce in the graphics requirements of these two games? Analyze the effect on rendering time, storage budgets, etc.

Tamara Munzner

27

Visualization

A major application area of computer graphics is *visualization*, where computer-generated images are used to help people understand both spatial and non-spatial data. Visualization is used when the goal is to augment human capabilities in situations where the problem is not sufficiently well defined for a computer to handle algorithmically. If a totally automatic solution can completely replace human judgement, then visualization is not typically required. Visualization can be used to generate new hypotheses when exploring a completely unfamiliar dataset, to confirm existing hypotheses in a partially understood dataset, or to present information about a known dataset to another audience.

Visualization allows people to offload cognition to the perceptual system, using carefully designed images as a form of *external memory*. The human visual system is a very high-bandwidth channel to the brain, with a significant amount of processing occurring in parallel and at the pre-conscious level. We can thus use external images as a substitute for keeping track of things inside our own heads. For an example, let us consider the task of understanding the relationships between a subset of the topics in the splendid book *Gödel, Escher, Bach: The Eternal Golden Braid* (Hofstadter, 1979); see Figure 27.1.

When we see the dataset as a text list, at the low level we must read words and compare them to memories of previously read words. It is hard to keep track of just these dozen topics using cognition and memory alone, let alone the hundreds of topics in the full book. The higher-level problem of identifying neighborhoods, for instance finding all the topics two hops away from the target topic Paradoxes, is very difficult.

Infinity - Lewis Carroll	Epimenides - Self-ref
Infinity - Zeno	Epimenides - Tarski
Infinity - Paradoxes	Tarski - Epimenides
Infinity - Halting problem	Halting problem - Decision procedures
Zeno - Lewis Carroll	Halting problem - Turing
Paradoxes - Lewis Carroll	Lewis Carroll - Wordplay
Paradoxes - Epimenides	Tarski - Truth vs. provability
Paradoxes - Self-ref	Tarski - Undecidability

Figure 27.1. Keeping track of relationships between topics is difficult using a text list.

Figure 27.2 shows an external visual representation of the same dataset as a node-link graph, where each topic is a node and the linkage between two topics is shown directly with a line. Following the lines by moving our eyes around the image is a fast low-level operation with minimal cognitive load, so higher-level neighborhood finding becomes possible. The placement of the nodes and the routing of the links between them was created automatically by the dot graph drawing program (Gansner et al., 1993).

We call the mapping of dataset attributes to a visual representation a *visual encoding*. One of the central problems in visualization is choosing appropriate encodings from the enormous space of possibile visual representations, taking into account the characteristics of the human perceptual system, the dataset in question, and the task at hand.

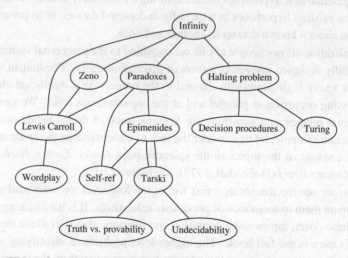

Figure 27.2. Substituting perception for cognition and memory allows us to understand relationships between book topics quickly.

27.1 Background

27.1.1 History

People have a long history of conveying meaning through static images, dating back to the oldest known cave paintings from over thirty thousand years ago. We continue to visually communicate today in ways ranging from rough sketches on the back of a napkin to the slick graphic design of advertisements. For thousands of years, cartographers have studied the problem of making maps that represent some aspect of the world around us. The first visual representations of abstract, nonspatial datasets were created in the 18th century by William Playfair (Friendly, 2008).

Although we have had the power to create moving images for over one hundred and fifty years, creating dynamic images interactively is a more recent development only made possible by the widespread availability of fast computer graphics hardware and algorithms in the past few decades. Static visualizations of tiny datasets can be created by hand, but computer graphics enables interactive visualization of large datasets.

27.1.2 Resource Limitations

When designing a visualization system, we must consider three different kinds of limitations: computational capacity, human perceptual and cognitive capacity, and display capacity.

As with any application of computer graphics, computer time and memory are limited resources and we often have hard constraints. If the visualization system needs to deliver interactive response, then it must use algorithms that can run in a fraction of a second rather than minutes or hours.

On the human side, memory and attention must be considered as finite resources. Human memory is notoriously limited, both for long-term recall and for shorter-term working memory. Later in this chapter, we discuss some of the power and limitations of the low-level visual attention mechanisms that carry out massively parallel processing of the visual field. We store surprisingly little information internally in visual working memory, leaving us vulnerable to *change blindness*, the phenomenon where even very large changes are not noticed if we are attending to something else in our view (Simons, 2000). Moreover, vigilance is also a highly limited resource; our ability to perform visual search tasks degrades quickly, with far worse results after several hours than in the first few minutes (Ware, 2000).

Display capacity is a third kind of limitation to consider. Visualization designers often "run out of pixels," where the resolution of the screen is not large enough to show all desired information simultaneously. The *information density* of a particular frame is a measure of the amount of information encoded versus the amount of unused space. There is a tradeoff between the benefits of showing as much as possible at once, to minimize the need for navigation and exploration, and the costs of showing too much at once, where the user is overwhelmed by visual clutter.

27.2 Data Types

Many aspects of a visualization design are driven by the type of the data that we need to look at. For example, is it a table of numbers, or a set of relations between items, or inherently spatial data such as a location on the Earth's surface or a collection of documents?

We start by considering a table of data. We call the rows *items* of data and the columns are *dimensions*, also known as *attributes*. For example, the rows might represent people, and the columns might be names, age, height, shirt size, and favorite fruit.

We distinguish between three types of dimensions: quantitative, ordered, and categorical. *Quantitative* data, such as age or height, is numerical and we can do arithmetic on it. For example, the quantity of 68 inches minus 42 inches is 26 inches. With *ordered* data, such as shirt size, we cannot do full-fledged arithmetic, but there is a well-defined ordering. For example, Large minus Medium is not a meaningful concept, but we know that Medium falls between Small and Large. *Categorical* data, such as favorite fruit or names, does not have an implicit ordering. We can only distinguish whether two things are the same (apples) or different (apples vs. bananas).

Relational data, or *graphs*, are another data type where *nodes* are connected by *links*. One specific kind of graph is a *tree*, which is typically used for hierarchical data. Both nodes and edges can have associated attributes. The word *graph* is unfortunately overloaded in visualization. The node-link graphs we discuss here, following the terminology of graph drawing and graph theory, could also be called *networks*. In the field of statistical graphics, graph is often used for *chart*, as in the line charts for time-series data shown in Figure 27.10.

Some data is inherently spatial, such as geographic location or a field of measurements at positions in three-dimensional space as in the MRI or CT scans used by doctors to see the internal structure of a person's body. The information associated with each point in space may be an unordered set of scalar quantities, or indexed vectors, or tensors. In contrast, non-spatial data can be visually encoded using spatial position, but that encoding is chosen by the designer rather than given implicitly in the semantics of the dataset itself. This choice is the one of the most central and difficult problems of visualization design.

27.2.1 Dimension and Item Count

The number of data dimensions that need to be visually encoded is one of the most fundamental aspects of the visualization design problem. Techniques that work for a low-dimensional dataset with a few columns will often fail for very high-dimensional datasets with dozens or hundreds of columns. A data dimension may have hierarchical structure, for example with a time series dataset where there are interesting patterns at multiple temporal scales.

The number of data items is also important: a visualization that performs well for a few hundred items often does not scale to millions of items. In some cases the difficulty is purely algorithmic, where a computation would take too long; in others it is an even deeper perceptual problem that even an instantaneous algorithm could not solve, where visual clutter makes the representation unusable by a person. The range of possible values within a dimension may also be relevant.

27.2.2 Data Transformation and Derived Dimensions

Data is often transformed from one type to another as part of a visualization pipeline for solving the domain problem. For example, an original data dimension might be made up of quantitative data: floating point numbers that represent temperature. For some tasks, like finding anomalies in local weather patterns, the raw data might be used directly. For another task, like deciding whether water is an appropriate temperature for a shower, the data might be transformed into an ordered dimension: hot, warm, or cold. In this transformation, most of the detail is aggregated away. In a third example, when making toast, an even more lossy transformation into a categorical dimension might suffice: burned or not burned.

The principle of transforming data into *derived dimensions*, rather than simply visually encoding the data in its original form, is a powerful idea. In Figure 27.10, the original data was an ordered collection of time-series curves. The transformation was to cluster the data, reducing the amount of information to visually encode to a few highly meaningful curves.

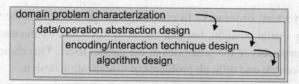
domain problem characterization
data/operation abstraction design
encoding/interaction technique design
algorithm design

Figure 27.3. Four nested layers of validation for visualization.

27.3 Human-Centered Design Process

The visualization design process can be split into a cascading set of layers, as shown in Figure 27.3. These layers all depend on each other; the output of the level above is input into the level below.

27.3.1 Task Characterization

A given dataset has many possible visual encodings. Choosing which visual encoding to use can be guided by the specific needs of some intended user. Different questions, or *tasks*, require very different visual encodings. For example, consider the domain of software engineering. The task of understanding the coverage of a test suite is well supported by the Tarantula interface shown in Figure 27.11. However, the task of understanding the modular decomposition of the software while refactoring the code might be better served by showing its hierarchical structure more directly as a node-link graph.

Understanding the requirements of some target audience is a tricky problem. In a human-centered design approach, the visualization designer works with a group of target users over time (C. Lewis & Rieman, 1993). In most cases, users know they need to somehow view their data but cannot directly articulate their needs as clear-cut tasks in terms of operations on data types. The iterative design process includes gathering information from the target users about their problems through interviews and observation of them at work, creating prototypes, and observing how users interact with those prototypes to see how well the proposed solution actually works. The software engineering methodology of requirements analysis can also be useful (Kovitz, 1999).

27.3.2 Abstraction

After the specific domain problem has been identified in the first layer, the next layer requires abstracting it into a more generic representation as operations on the data types discussed in the previous section. Problems from very different domains can map to the same visualization abstraction. These generic operations include sorting, filtering, characterizing trends and distributions, finding anomalies and outliers, and finding correlation (Amar et al., 2005). They also include operations that are specific to a particular data type, for example following a path for relational data in the form of graphs or trees.

This abstraction step often involves data transformations from the original raw data into derived dimensions. These derived dimensions are often of a different type than the original data: a graph may be converted into a tree, tabular data may be converted into a graph by using a threshold to decide whether a link should exist based on the field values, and so on.

27.3.3 Technique and Algorithm Design

Once an abstraction has been chosen, the next layer is to design appropriate visual encoding and interaction techniques. Section 27.4 covers the principles of visual encoding, and we discuss interaction principles in Sections 27.5. We present techniques that take these principles into account in Sections 27.6 and 27.7.

A detailed discussion of visualization algorithms is unfortunately beyond the scope of this chapter.

27.3.4 Validation

Each of the four layers has different validation requirements.

The first layer is designed to determine whether the problem is correctly characterized: is there really a target audience performing particular tasks that would benefit from the proposed tool? An immediate way to test assumptions and conjectures is to observe or interview members of the target audience, to ensure that the visualization designer fully understands their tasks. A measurement that cannot be done until a tool has been built and deployed is to monitor its adoption rate within that community, although of course many other factors in addition to utility affect adoption.

The next layer is used to determine whether the abstraction from the domain problem into operations on specific data types actually solves the desired problem. After a prototype or finished tool has been deployed, a field study can be carried out to observe whether and how it is used by its intended audience. Also, images produced by the system can be analyzed both qualitatively and quantitatively.

The purpose of the third layer is to verify that the visual encoding and interaction techniques chosen by the designer effectively communicate the chosen abstraction to the users. An immediate test is to justify that individual design choices do not violate known perceptual and cognitive principles. Such a justification is necessary but not sufficient, since visualization design involves many tradeoffs between interacting choices. After a system is built, it can be tested through formal laboratory studies where many people are asked to do assigned tasks so that measurements of the time required for them to complete the tasks and their error rates can be statistically analyzed.

A fourth layer is employed to verify that the algorithm designed to carry out the encoding and interaction choices is faster or takes less memory than previous algorithms. An immediate test is to analyze the computational complexity of the proposed algorithm. After implementation, the actual time performance and memory usage of the system can be directly measured.

27.4   Visual Encoding Principles

We can describe visual encodings as graphical elements, called *marks*, that convey information through visual channels. A zero-dimensional mark is a point, a one-dimensional mark is a line, a two-dimensional mark is an area, and a three-dimensional mark is a volume. Many *visual channels* can encode information, including spatial position, color, size, shape, orientation, and direction of motion. Multiple visual channels can be used to simultaneously encode different

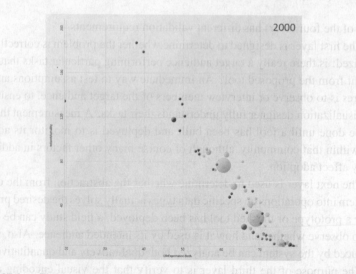

Figure 27.4.   The four visual channels of horizontal and vertical spatial position, color, and size are used to encode information in this scatterplot chart *Image courtesy George Robertson* (Robertson et al., 2008), © IEEE 2008.

data dimensions; for example, Figure 27.4 shows the use of horizontal and vertical spatial position, color, and size to display four data dimensions. More than one channel can be used to redundantly code the same dimension, for a design that displays less information but shows it more clearly.

27.4.1 Visual Channel Characteristics

Important characteristics of visual channels are distinguishability, separability, and popout.

Channels are not all equally distinguishable. Many psychophysical experiments have been carried out to measure the ability of people to make precise distinctions about information encoded by the different visual channels. Our abilities depend on whether the data type is quantitative, ordered, or categorical. Figure 27.5 shows the rankings of visual channels for the three data types. Figure 27.6 shows some of the default mappings for visual channels in the Tableau/Polaris system, which take into account the data type.

Spatial position is the most accurate visual channel for all three types of data, and it dominates our perception of a visual encoding. Thus, the two most important data dimensions are often mapped to horizontal and vertical spatial positions.

However, the other channels differ strongly between types. The channels of length and angle are highly discriminable for quantitative data but poor for ordered and categorical, while in contrast hue is very accurate for categorical data but mediocre for quantitative data.

We must always consider whether there is a good match between the dynamic

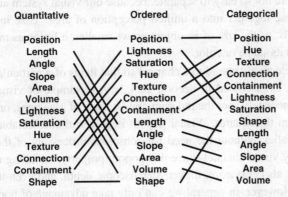

Figure 27.5. Our ability to perceive information encoded by a visual channel depends on the type of data used, from most accurate at the top to least at the bottom. *Redrawn and adapted from (Mackinlay, 1986).*

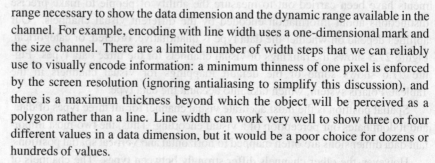

Figure 27.6. The Tableau/Polaris system default mappings for four visual channels according to data type. *Image courtesy Chris Stolte* (Stolte et al., 2008), © 2008 IEEE. (See also Plate XLII.)

range necessary to show the data dimension and the dynamic range available in the channel. For example, encoding with line width uses a one-dimensional mark and the size channel. There are a limited number of width steps that we can reliably use to visually encode information: a minimum thinness of one pixel is enforced by the screen resolution (ignoring antialiasing to simplify this discussion), and there is a maximum thickness beyond which the object will be perceived as a polygon rather than a line. Line width can work very well to show three or four different values in a data dimension, but it would be a poor choice for dozens or hundreds of values.

Some visual channels are *integral*, fused together at a pre-conscious level, so they are not good choices for visually encoding different data dimensions. Others are *separable*, without interactions between them during visual processing, and are safe to use for encoding multiple dimensions. Figure 27.7 shows two channel pairs. Color and position are highly separable. We can see that horizontal size and vertical size are not so easy to separate, because our visual system automatically integrates these together into a unified perception of area. Size interacts with many channels: as the size of an object grows smaller, it becomes more difficult to distinguish its shape or color.

We can selectively attend to a channel so that items of a particular type "pop out" visually, as discussed in Section 22.4.3. An example of visual popout is when we immediately spot the red item amidst a sea of blue ones, or distinguish the circle from the squares. Visual popout is powerful and scalable because it occurs in parallel, without the need for conscious processing of the items one by one. Many visual channels have this popout property, including not only the list above but also curvature, flicker, stereoscopic depth, and even the direction of lighting. However, in general we can only take advantage of popout for one channel at a time. For example, a white circle does not pop out from a group of circles and squares that can be white or black, as shown in Figure 22.43. When we

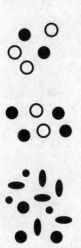

Figure 27.7. Color and location are separable channels well suited to encode different data dimensions, but the horizontal size and and vertical size channels are automatically fused into an integrated perception of area. *Redrawn after (Ware, 2000).*

need to search across more than one channel simultaneously, the length of time it takes to find the target object depends linearly on the number of objects in the scene.

27.4.2 Color

Color can be a very powerful channel, but many people do not understand its properties and use it improperly. As discussed in Section 22.2.2, we can consider color in terms of three separate visual channels: hue, saturation, and lightness. Region size strongly affects our ability to sense color. Color in small regions is relatively difficult to perceive, and designers should use bright, highly saturated colors to ensure that the color coding is distinguishable. The inverse situation is true when colored regions are large, as in backgrounds, where low saturation pastel colors should be used to avoid blinding the viewer.

Hue is a very strong cue for encoding categorical data. However, the available dynamic range is very limited. People can reliably distinguish only around a dozen hues when the colored regions are small and scattered around the display. A good guideline for color coding is to keep the number of categories less than 8, keeping in mind that the background and the neutral object color also count in the total.

For ordered data, lightness and saturation are effective because they have an implicit perceptual ordering. People can reliably order by lightness, always placing gray in between black and white. With saturation, people reliably place the less saturated pink between fully saturated red and zero-saturation white. However, hue is not as as good a channel for ordered data because it does not have an implicit perceptual ordering. When asked to create an ordering of red, blue, green, and yellow, people do not all give the same answer. People can and do learn conventions, such as green-yellow-red for traffic lights, or the order of colors in the rainbow, but these constructions are at a higher level than pure perception. Ordered data is typically shown with a discrete set of color values.

Quantitative data is shown with a *colormap*, a range of color values that can be continuous or discrete. A very unfortunate default in many software packages is the rainbow colormap, as shown in Figure 27.8. The standard rainbow scale suffers from three problems. First, hue is used to indicate order. A better choice would be to use lightness because it has an implicit perceptual ordering. Even more importantly, the human eye responds most strongly to luminance. Second, the scale is not perceptually linear: equal steps in the continuous range are not perceived as equal steps by our eyes. Figure 27.8 shows an example, where the rainbow colormap obfuscates the data. While the range from -2000 to -1000

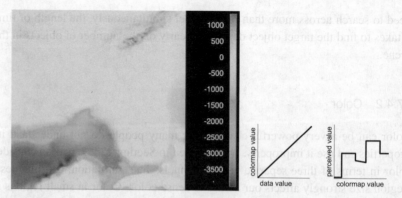

Figure 27.8. The standard rainbow colormap has two defects: it uses hue to denote ordering, and it is not perceptually isolinear. *Image courtesy Bernice Rogowitz.* (See also Plate XLIV.

has three distinct colors, cyan, green, and yellow, a range of the same size from −1000 to 0 simply looks yellow throughout. The graphs on the right show that the perceived value is strongly tied to the luminance, which is not even monotonically increasing in this scale.

In contrast, Figure 27.9 shows the same data with a more appropriate colormap, where the lightness increases monotonically. Hue is used to create a semantically meaningful categorization: the viewer can discuss structure in the dataset, such as the dark blue sea, the cyan continental shelf, the green lowlands, and the white mountains.

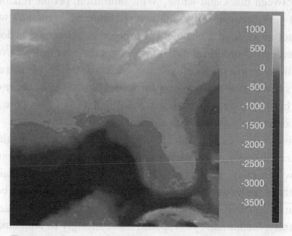

Figure 27.9. The structure of the same dataset is far more clear with a colormap where monotonically increasing lightness is used to show ordering and hue is used instead for segmenting into categorical regions. *Image courtesy Bernice Rogowitz.* (See also Plate XLIV.)

In both the discrete and continuous cases, colormaps should take into account whether the data is sequential or diverging. The ColorBrewer application (www. colorbrewer.org) is an excellent resource for colormap construction (Brewer, 1999).

Another important issue when encoding with color is that a significant fraction of the population, roughly 10% of men, is red-green color deficient. If a coding using red and green is chosen because of conventions in the target domain, redundantly coding lightness or saturation in addition to hue is wise. Tools such as the web site http://www.vischeck.com should be used to check whether a color scheme is distinguishable to people with color deficient vision.

27.4.3 2D vs. 3D Spatial Layouts

The question of whether to use two or three channels for spatial position has been extensively studied. When computer-based visualization began in the late 1980s, and interactive 3D graphics was a new capability, there was a lot of enthusiasm for 3D representations. As the field matured, researchers began to understand the costs of 3D approaches when used for abstract datasets (Ware, 2001).

Occlusion, where some parts of the dataset are hidden behind others, is a major problem with 3D. Although hidden surface removal algorithms such as Z-buffers and BSP trees allow fast computation of a correct 2D image, people must still synthesize many of these images into an internal mental map. When people look at realistic scenes made from familiar objects, usually they can quickly understand what they see. However, when they see an unfamiliar dataset, where a chosen visual encoding maps abstract dimensions into spatial positions, understanding the details of its 3D structure can be challenging even when they can use interactive navigation controls to change their 3D viewpoint. The reason is once again the limited capacity of human working memory (Plumlee & Ware, 2006).

Another problem with 3D is *perspective distortion*. Although real-world objects do indeed appear smaller when they are further from our eyes, foreshortening makes direct comparison of object heights difficult (Tory et al., 2006). Once again, although we can often judge the heights of familiar objects in the real world based on past experience, we cannot necessarily do so with completely abstract data that has a visual encoding where the height conveys meaning. For example, it is more difficult to judge bar heights in a 3D bar chart than in multiple horizontally aligned 2D bar charts.

Another problem with unconstrained 3D representations is that text at arbitrary orientations in 3D space is far more difficult to read than text aligned in the 2D image plane (Grossman et al., 2007).

Figure 27.10 illustrates how carefully chosen 2D views of an abstract dataset can avoid the problems with occlusion and perspective distortion inherent in 3D

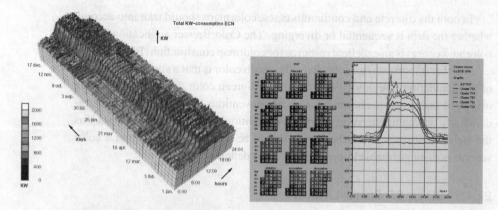

Figure 27.10. Left: A 3D representation of this time series dataset introduces the problems of occlusion and perspective distortion. Right: The linked 2D views of derived aggregate curves and the calendar allow direct comparison and show more fine-grained patterns. *Image courtesy Jarke van Wijk* (van Wijk & van Selow, 1999), © 1999 IEEE. (See also Plate XLV.)

views. The top view shows a 3D representation created directly from the original time-series data, where each cross-section is a 2D time-series curve showing power consumption for one day, with one curve for each day of the year along the extruded third axis. Although this representation is straightforward to create, we can only see large-scale patterns such as the higher consumption during working hours and the seasonal variation between winter and summer. To create the 2D linked views at the bottom, the curves were hierarchically clustered, and only aggregate curves representing the top clusters are drawn superimposed in the same 2D frame. Direct comparison between the curve heights at all times of the day is easy because there is no perspective distortion or occlusion. The same color coding is used in the calendar view, which is very effective for understanding temporal patterns.

In contrast, if a dataset consists of inherently 3D spatial data, such as showing fluid flow over an airplane wing or a medical imaging dataset from an MRI scan, then the costs of a 3D view are outweighed by its benefits in helping the user construct a useful mental model of the dataset structure.

27.4.4 Text Labels

Text in the form of labels and legends is a very important factor in creating visualizations that are useful rather than simply pretty. Axes and tick marks should be labelled. Legends should indicate the meaning of colors, whether used as discrete patches or in continuous color ramps. Individual items in a dataset typically have meaningful text labels associated with them. In many cases showing all labels at all times would result in too much visual clutter, so labels can be shown for a subset of the items using label positioning algorithms that show labels at a desired density while avoiding overlap (Luboschik et al., 2008). A straightforward way to choose the best label to represent a group of items is to use a greedy algorithm based on some measure of label importance, but synthesizing a new label based on the characteristics of the group remains a difficult problem. A more interaction-centric approach is to only show labels for individual items based on an interactive indication from the user.

27.5 Interaction Principles

Several principles of interaction are important when designing a visualization. Low-latency visual feedback allows users to explore more fluidly, for example by showing more detail when the cursor simply hovers over an object rather than requiring the user to explicitly click. Selecting items is a fundamental operation when interacting with large datasets, as is visually indicating the selected set with highlighting. Color coding is a common form of highlighting, but other channels can also be used.

Many forms of interaction can be considered in terms of what aspect of the display they change. Navigation can be considered a change of viewport. Sorting is a change to the spatial ordering; that is, changing how data is mapped to the spatial position visual channel. The entire visual encoding can also be changed.

27.5.1 Overview First, Zoom and Filter, Details on Demand

The influential mantra "Overview first, zoom and filter, details on demand" (Shneiderman, 1996) elucidates the role of interaction and navigation in visualization design. Overviews help the user notice regions where further investigation might be productive, whether through spatial navigation or through filtering. As we discuss below, details can be presented in many ways: with popups from clicking or cursor hovering, in a separate window, and by changing the layout on the fly to make room to show additional information.

27.5.2 Interactivity Costs

Interactivity has both power and cost. The benefit of interaction is that people can explore a larger information space than can be understood in a single static image.

However, a cost to interaction is that it requires human time and attention. If the user must exhaustively check every possibility, use of the visualization system may degenerate into human-powered search. Automatically detecting features of interest to explicitly bring to the user's attention via the visual encoding is a useful goal for the visualization designer. However, if the task at hand could be completely solved by automatic means, there would be no need for a visualization in the first place. Thus, there is always a tradeoff between finding automatable aspects and relying on the human in the loop to detect patterns.

27.5.3 Animation

Animation shows change using time. We distinguish animation, where successive frames can only be played, paused, or stopped, from true interactive control. There is considerable evidence that animated transitions can be more effective than jump cuts, by helping people track changes in object positions or camera viewpoints (Heer & Robertson, 2007). Although animation can be very effective for narrative and storytelling, it is often used ineffectively in a visualization context (Tversky et al., 2002). It might seem obvious to show data that changes over time by using animation, a visual modality that changes over time. However, people have difficulty in making specific comparisons between individual frames that are not contiguous when they see an animation consisting of many frames. The very limited capacity of human visual memory means that we are much worse at comparing memories of things that we have seen in the past than at comparing things that are in our current field of view. For tasks requiring comparison between up to several dozen frames, side-by-side comparison is often more effective than animation. Moreover, if the number of objects that change between frames is large, people will have a hard time tracking everything that occurs (Robertson et al., 2008). Narrative animations are carefully designed to avoid having too many actions occurring simultaneously, whereas a dataset being visualized has no such constraint. For the special case of just two frames with a limited amount of change, the very simple animation of flipping back and forth between the two can be a useful way to identify the differences between them.

27.6   Composite and Adjacent Views

A very fundamental visual encoding choice is whether to have a single composite *view* showing everything in the same frame or window, or to have multiple views adjacent to each other.

27.6.1 Single Drawing

When there are only one or two data dimensions to encode, then horizontal and vertical spatial position are the obvious visual channel to use, because we perceive them most accurately and position has the strongest influence on our internal mental model of the dataset. The traditional statistical graphics displays of line charts, bar charts, and scatterplots all use spatial ordering of marks to encode information. These displays can be augmented with additional visual channels, such as color and size and shape, as in the scatterplot shown in Figure 27.4.

The simplest possible mark is a single pixel. In *pixel-oriented* displays, the goal is to provide an overview of as many items as possible. These approaches use the spatial position and color channels at a high information density, but preclude the use of the size and shape channels. Figure 27.11 shows the Tarantula software visualization tool (Jones et al., 2002), where most of the screen is devoted to an overview of source code using one-pixel high lines (Eick et al., 1992). The color and brightness of each line shows whether it passed, failed, or had mixed results when executing a suite of test cases.

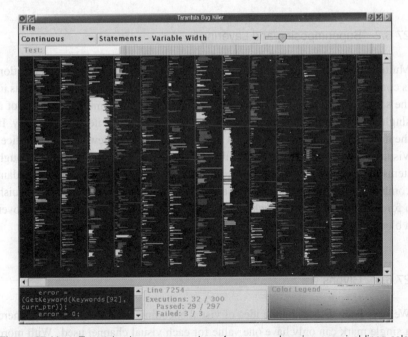

Figure 27.11.   Tarantula shows an overview of source code using one-pixel lines color coded by execution status of a software test suite. *Image courtesy John Stasko* (Jones et al., 2002). (See also Plate XLVI.)

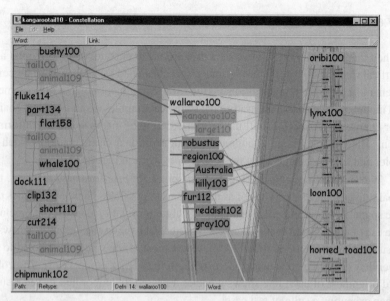

Figure 27.12.   Visual layering with size, saturation, and brightness in the Constellation system (Munzner, 2000). (See also Plate XLVII.)

27.6.2   Superimposing and Layering

Multiple items can be superimposed in the same frame when their spatial position is compatible. Several lines can be shown in the same line chart, and many dots in the same scatterplot, when the axes are shared across all items. One benefit of a single shared view is that comparing the position of different items is very easy. If the number of items in the dataset is limited, then a single view will often suffice. Visual layering can extend the usefulness of a single view when there are enough items that visual clutter becomes a concern. Figure 27.12 shows how a redundant combination of the size, saturation, and brightness channels serves to distinguish a foreground layer from a background layer when the user moves the cursor over a block of words.

27.6.3   Glyphs

We have been discussing the idea of visual encoding using simple marks, where a single mark can only have one value for each visual channel used. With more complex marks, which we will call *glyphs*, there is internal structure where sub-regions have different visual channel encodings.

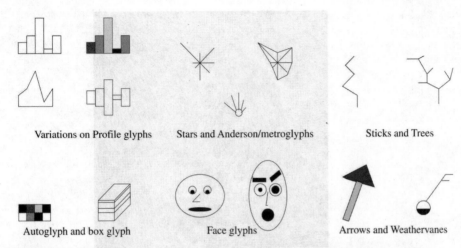

Figure 27.13. Complex marks, which we call *glyphs*, have subsections that visually encode different data dimensions. *Image courtesy Matt Ward* (M. O. Ward, 2002).

Designing appropriate glyphs has the same challenges as designing visual encodings. Figure 27.13 shows a variety of glyphs, including the notorious faces originally proposed by Chernoff. The danger of using faces to show abstract data dimensions is that our perceptual and emotional response to different facial fea-

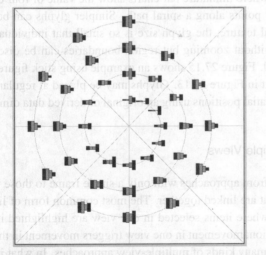

Figure 27.14. Complex glyphs require significant display area so that the encoded information can be read. *Image courtesy Matt Ward, created with the SpiralGlyphics software* (M. O. Ward, 2002). (See also Plate XLIII.)

Figure 27.15. A dense array of simple glyphs. *Image courtesy Georges Grinstein* (S. Smith et al., 1991), © 1991 IEEE.

tures is highly nonlinear in a way that is not fully understood, but the variability is greater than between the visual channels that we have discussed so far. We are probably far more attuned to features that indicate emotional state such as eyebrow orientation than other features such as nose size or face shape.

Complex glyphs require significant display area for each glyph, as shown in Figure 27.14 where miniature bar charts show the value of four different dimensions at many points along a spiral path. Simpler glyphs can be used to create a global visual texture, the glyph size is so small that individual values cannot be read out without zooming but region boundaries can be discerned from the overview level. Figure 27.15 shows an example using stick figures of the kind in the upper right in Figure 27.13. Glyphs may be placed at regular intervals, or in data-driven spatial positions using an original or derived data dimension.

27.6.4   Multiple Views

We now turn from approaches with only a single frame to those which use multiple views that are linked together. The most common form of linkage is linked highlighting, where items selected in one view are highlighted in all others. In linked navigation, movement in one view triggers movement in the others.

There are many kinds of multiple-view approaches. In what is usually called simply the *multiple-view* approach, the same data is shown in several views, each of which has a different visual encoding that shows certain aspects of the dataset most clearly. The power of linked highlighting across multiple visual encodings is that items that fall in a contiguous region in one view are often distributed very differently in the other views. In the *small-multiples* approach, each view has the same visual encoding for different datasets, usually with shared axes between frames so that comparison of spatial position between them is meaningful. Side-by-side comparison with small multiples is an alternative to the visual clutter of superimposing all the data in the same view, and to the human memory limitations of remembering previously seen frames in an animation that changes over time.

The *overview-and-detail* approach is to have the same data and the same visual encoding in two views, where the only difference between them is the level of zooming. In most cases, the overview uses much less display space than the detail view. The combination of overview and detail views is common outside of visualization in many tools ranging from mapping software to photo editing. With a *detail-on-demand* approach, another view shows more information about some selected item, either as a popup window near the cursor or in a permanent window in another part of the display.

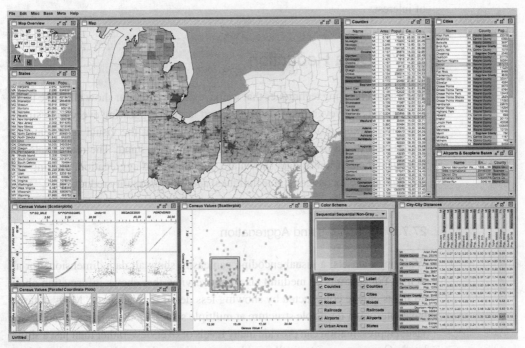

Figure 27.16. The Improvise toolkit was used to create this multiple-view visualization. *Image courtesy Chris Weaver.* (See also Plate XLVIII.)

Determining the most appropriate spatial position of the views themselves with respect to each other can be as significant a problem as determining the spatial position of marks within a single view. In some systems, the location of the views is arbitrary and left up to the window system or the user. Aligning the views allows precise comparison between them, either vertically, horizontally, or with an array for both directions. Just as items can be sorted within a view, views can be sorted within a display, typically with respect to a derived variable measuring some aspect of the entire view as opposed to an individual item within it.

Figure 27.16 shows a visualization of census data that uses many views. In addition to geographic information, the demographic information for each county includes population, density, gender, median age, percent change since 1990, and proportions of major ethnic groups. The visual encodings used include geographic, scatterplot, parallel coordinate, tabular, and matrix views. The same color encoding is used across all the views, with a legend in the bottom middle. The scatterplot matrix shows linked highlighting across all views, where the blue items are close together in some views and scattered in others. The map in the upper-left corner is an overview for the large detail map in the center. The tabular views allow direct sorting by and selection within a dimension of interest.

27.7   Data Reduction

The visual encoding techniques that we have discussed so far show all of the items in a dataset. However, many datasets are so large that showing everything simultaneously would result in so much visual clutter that the visual representation would be difficult or impossible for a viewer to understand. The main strategies to reduce the amount of data shown are overviews and aggregation, filtering and navigation, the focus+context techniques, and dimensionality reduction.

27.7.1   Overviews and Aggregation

With tiny datasets, a visual encoding can easily show all data dimensions for all items. For datasets of medium size, an overview that shows information about all items can be constructed by showing less detail for each item. Many datasets have internal or derivable structure at multiple scales. In these cases, a multiscale visual representation can provide many levels of overview, rather than just a single level. Overviews are typically used as a starting point to give users clues about where to drill down to inspect in more detail.

For larger datasets, creating an overview requires some kind of visual summarization. One approach to data reduction is to use an *aggregate* representation where a single visual mark in the overview explicitly represents many items.

The challenge of aggregation is to avoid eliminating the interesting signals in the dataset in the process of summarization. In the cartographic literature, the problem of creating maps at different scales while retaining the important distinguishing characteristics has been extensively studied under the name of *cartographic generalization* (Slocum et al., 2008).

27.7.2 Filtering and Navigation

Another approach to data reduction is to *filter* the data, showing only a subset of the items. Filtering is often carried out by directly selecting ranges of interest in one or more of the data dimensions.

Navigation is a specific kind of filtering based on spatial position, where changing the viewpoint changes the visible set of items. Both geometric and non-geometric zooming are used in visualization. With geometric zooming, the camera position in 2D or 3D space can be changed with standard computer graphics controls. In a realistic scene, items should be drawn at a size that depends on their distance from the camera, and only their apparent size changes based on that distance. However, in a visual encoding of an abstract space, nongeometric zooming can be useful. In *semantic zooming*, the visual appearance of an object changes dramatically based on the number of pixels available to draw it. For instance, an abstract visual representation of a text file could change from a tiny color-coded box with no label to a medium-sized box containing only the filename as a text label to a large rectangle containing a multi-line summary of the file contents. In realistic scenes, objects that are sufficiently far away from the camera are not visible in the images, for example, after they subtend less than one pixel of screen area. With *guaranteed visibility*, one of the original or derived data dimensions is used as a measure of importance, and objects of sufficient importance must have some kind of representation visible in the image plane at all times.

27.7.3 Focus+Context

Focus+context techniques are another approach to data reduction. A subset of the dataset items are interactively chosen by the user to be the focus and are drawn in detail. The visual encoding also includes information about some or all of the rest of the dataset shown for context, integrated into the same view that shows the focus items. Many of these techniques use carefully chosen distortion to combine magnified focus regions and minified context regions into a unified view.

One common interaction metaphor is a moveable fisheye lens. Hyperbolic geometry provides an elegant mathematical framework for a single radial lens that affects all objects in the view. Another interaction metaphor is to use multiple lenses of different shapes and magnification levels that affect only local regions. Stretch and squish navigation uses the interaction metaphor of a rubber sheet where stretching one region squishes the rest, as shown in Figure 27.17. The borders of the sheet stay fixed so that all items are within the viewport, although many items may be compressed to subpixel size. The fisheye metaphor is not limited to a geometric lens used after spatial layout; it can be used directly on structured data, such as a hierarchical document where some sections are collapsed while others are left expanded.

These distortion-based approaches are another example of non-literal navigation in the same spirit as nongeometric zooming. When navigating within a large and unfamiliar dataset with realistic camera motion, users can become disoriented at high zoom levels when they can see only a small local region. These approaches are designed to provide more contextual information than a single

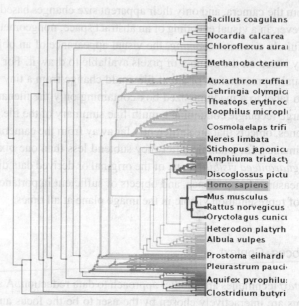

Figure 27.17. The TreeJuxtaposer system features stretch and squish navigation and guaranteed visibility of regions marked with colors (Munzner et al., 2003). (See also Plate XLIX).

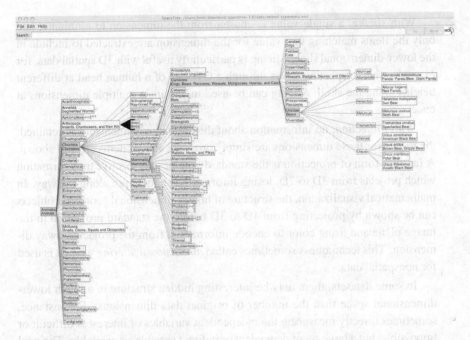

Figure 27.18. The SpaceTree system shows the path between the root and the interactively chosen focus node to provide context (Grosjean et al., 2002).

undistorted view, in hopes that people can stay oriented if landmarks remain recognizeable. However, these kinds of distortion can still be confusing or difficult to follow for users. The costs and benefits of distortion, as opposed to multiple views or a single realistic view, are not yet fully understood. Standard 3D perspective is a particularly familiar kind of distortion and was explicitly used as a form of focus+context in early visualization work. However, as the costs of 3D spatial layout discussed in Section 27.4 became more understood, this approach became less popular.

Other approaches to providing context around focus items do not require distortion. For instance, the SpaceTree system shown in Figure 27.18 elides most nodes in the tree, showing the path between the interactively chosen focus node and the root of the tree for context.

27.7.4   Dimensionality Reduction

The data reduction approaches covered so far reduce the number of items to draw. When there are many data dimensions, *dimensionality reduction* can also be effective.

With *slicing*, a single value is chosen from the dimension to eliminate, and only the items matching that value for the dimension are extracted to include in the lower-dimensional slice. Slicing is particularly useful with 3D spatial data, for example when inspecting slices through a CT scan of a human head at different heights along the skull. Slicing can be used to eliminate multiple dimensions at once.

With *projection*, no information about the eliminated dimensions is retained; the values for those dimensions are simply dropped, and all items are still shown. A familiar form of projection is the standard graphics perspective transformation which projects from 3D to 2D, losing information about depth along the way. In mathematical visualization, the structure of higher-dimensional geometric objects can be shown by projecting from 4D to 3D before the standard projection to the image plane and using color to encode information from the projected-away dimension. This technique is sometimes called *dimensional filtering* when it is used for nonspatial data.

In some datasets, there may be interesting hidden structure in a much lower-dimensional space than the number of original data dimensions. For instance, sometimes directly measuring the independent variables of interest is difficult or impossible, but a large set of dependent or indirect variables is available. The goal is to find a small set of dimensions that faithfully represent most of the structure or variance in the dataset. These dimensions may be the original ones, or synthesized new ones that are linear or nonlinear combinations of the originals. Principal component analysis is a fast, widely used linear method. Many nonlinear approaches have been proposed, including multidimensional scaling (MDS). These methods are usually used to determine whether there are large-scale clusters in the dataset;

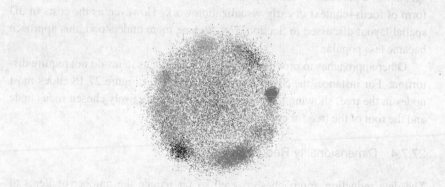

Figure 27.19. Dimensionality reduction with the Glimmer multidimensional scaling approach shows clusters in a document dataset (Ingram et al., 2009), © 2009 IEEE. (See also Plate L.)

the fine-grained structure in the lower-dimensional plots is usually not reliable because information is lost in the reduction. Figure 27.19 shows document collection in a single scatterplot. When the true dimensionality of the dataset is far higher than two, a matrix of scatterplots showing pairs of synthetic dimensions may be necessary.

27.8 Examples

We conclude this chapter with several examples of visualizing specific types of data using the techniques discussed above.

27.8.1 Tables

Tabular data is extremely common, as all spreadsheet users know. The goal in visualization is to encode this information through easily perceivable visual channels rather than forcing people to read through it as numbers and text. Figure 27.20 shows the Table Lens, a focus+context approach where quantitative

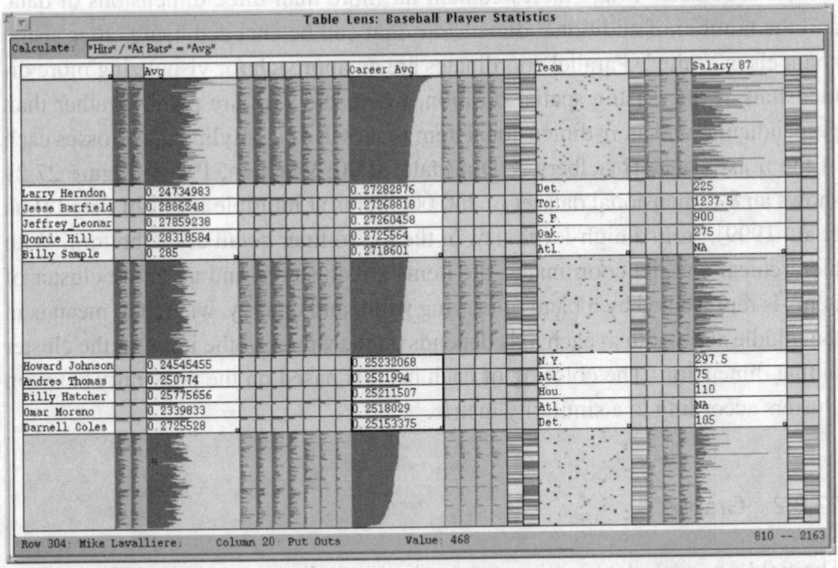

Figure 27.20. The Table Lens provides focus+context interaction with tabular data, immediately reorderable by the values in each dimension column. *Image courtesy Stuart Card* (Rao & Card, 1994), © 1994 ACM, Inc. Included here by permission.

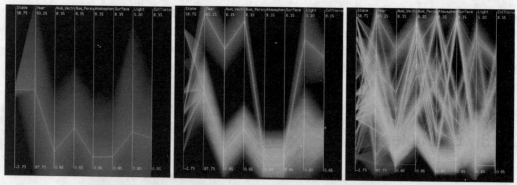

Figure 27.21. Hierarchical parallel coordinates show high-dimensional data at multiple levels of detail. *Image courtesy Matt Ward* (Fua et al., 1999), © 1999 IEEE. (See also Plate LI).

values are encoded as the length of one-pixel high lines in the context regions, and shown as numbers in the focus regions. Each dimension of the dataset is shown as a column, and the rows of items can be resorted according to the values in that column with a single click in its header.

The traditional Cartesian approach of a scatterplot, where items are plotted as dots with respect to perpendicular axes, is only usable for two and three dimensions of data. Many tables contain far more than three dimensions of data, and the number of additional dimensions that can be encoded using other visual channels is limited. Parallel coordinates are an approach for visualizing more dimensions at once using spatial position, where the axes are parallel rather than perpendicular and an n-dimensional item is shown as a polyline that crosses each of the n axes once (Inselberg & Dimsdale, 1990; Wegman, 1990). Figure 27.21 shows an 8-dimensional dataset of 230,000 items at multiple levels of detail (Fua et al., 1999), from a high-level view at the top to finer detail at the bottom. With hierarchical parallel coordinates, the items are clustered and an entire cluster of items is represented by a band of varying width and opacity, where the mean is in the middle and width at each axis depends on the values of the items in the cluster in that dimension. The coloring of each band is based on the proximity between clusters according to a similarity metric.

27.8.2 Graphs

The field of graph drawing is concerned with finding a spatial position for the nodes in a graph in 2D or 3D space and routing the edges between these nodes (Di Battista et al., 1999). In many cases the edge-routing problem is simplified by using only straight edges, or by only allowing right-angle bends for the class of *orthogonal* layouts, but some approaches handle true curves. If the graph has directed edges, a layered approach can be used to show hierarchical structure through the horizontal or vertical spatial ordering of nodes, as shown in Figure 27.2.

A suite of aesthetic criteria operationalize human judgements about readable graphs as metrics that can be computed on a proposed layout (Ware et al., 2002). Figure 27.22 shows some examples. Some metrics should be minimized, such as the number of edge crossings, the total area of the layout, and the number of right-angle bends or curves. Others should be maximized, such as the angular resolution or symmetry. The problem is difficult because most of these criteria are individually NP-hard, and moreover they are mutually incompatible (Brandenburg, 1988).

Many approaches to node-link graph drawing use force-directed placement, motivated by the intuitive physical metaphor of spring forces at the edges drawing together repelling particles at the nodes. Although naive approaches have high time complexity and are prone to being caught in local minima, much work has gone into developing more sophisticated algorithms such as GEM (Frick et al., 1994) or IPSep-CoLa (Dwyer et al., 2006). Figure 27.23 shows an interactive system using the *r*-PolyLog energy model, where a focus+context view of the clustered graph is created with both geometric and semantic fisheye (van Ham & van Wijk, 2004).

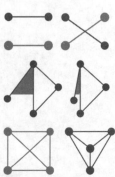

Figure 27.22. Graph layout aesthetic criteria. Top: Edge crossings should be minimized. Middle: Angular resolution should be maximized. Bottom: Symmetry is maximized on the left, whereas crossings are minimized on the right, showing the conflict between the individually NP-hard criteria.

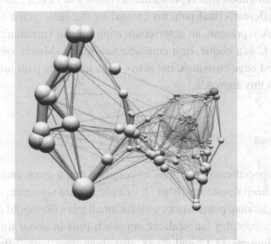

Figure 27.23. Force-directed placement showing a clustered graph with both geometric and semantic fisheye. *Image courtesy Jarke van Wijk* (van Ham & van Wijk, 2004), © 2004 IEEE.

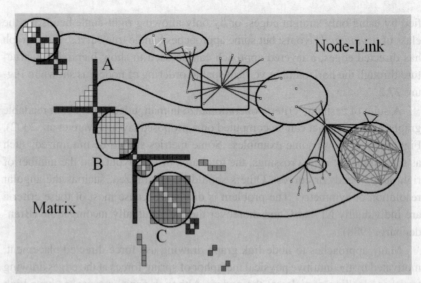

Figure 27.24.   Graphs can be shown with either matrix or node-link views. *Image courtesy Jean-Daniel Fekete* (Henry & Fekete, 2006), © 2006 IEEE.

Graphs can also be visually encoded by showing the adjacency matrix, where all vertices are placed along each axis and the cell between two vertices is colored if there is an edge between them. The MatrixExplorer system uses linked multiple views to help social science researchers visually analyze social networks with both matrix and node-link representations (Henry & Fekete, 2006). Figure 27.24 shows the different visual patterns created by the same graph structure in these two views: A represents an actor connecting several communities; B is a community; and C is a clique, or a complete sub-graph. Matrix views do not suffer from cluttered edge crossings, but many tasks including path following are more difficult with this approach.

27.8.3   Trees

Trees are a special case of graphs so common that a great deal of visualization research has been devoted to them. A straightforward algorithm to lay out trees in the two-dimensional plane works well for small trees (Reingold & Tilford, 1981), while a more complex but scalable approach runs in linear time (Buchheim et al., 2002). Figures 27.17 and 27.18 also show trees with different approaches to spatial layout, but all four of these methods visually encode the relationship between parent and child nodes by drawing a link connecting them.

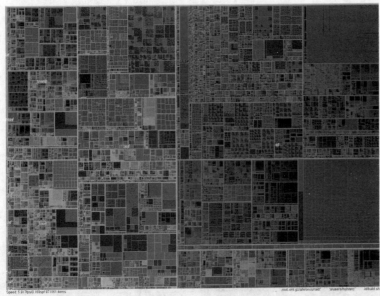

Figure 27.25. Treemap showing a filesystem of nearly one million files. *Image courtesy Jean-Daniel Fekete* (Fekete & Plaisant, 2002), © 2002 IEEE. (See also Plate LII.)

Treemaps use containment rather than connection to show the hierarchical relationship between parent and child nodes in a tree (B. Johnson & Shneiderman, 1991). That is, treemaps show child nodes nested within the outlines of the parent node. Figure 27.25 shows a hierarchical filesystem of nearly one million files, where file size is encoded by rectangle size and file type is encoded by color (Fekete & Plaisant, 2002). The size of nodes at the leaves of the tree can encode an additional data dimension, but the size of nodes in the interior does not show the value of that dimension; it is dictated by the cumulative size of their descendants. Although tasks such as understanding the topological structure of the tree or tracing paths through it are more difficult with treemaps than with node-link approaches, tasks that involve understanding an attribute tied to leaf nodes are well supported. Treemaps are space-filling representations that are usually more compact than node-link approaches.

27.8.4 Geographic

Many kinds of analysis such as epidemiology require understanding both geographic and nonspatial data. Figure 27.26 shows a tool for the visual analysis of a cancer demographics dataset that combines many of the ideas described in

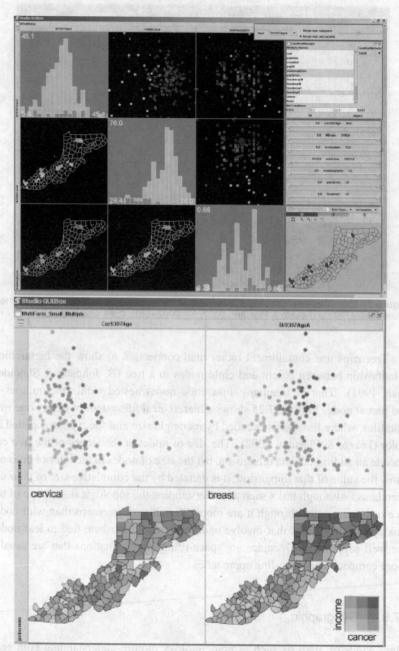

Figure 27.26.   Two matrices of linked small multiples showing cancer demographic data (MacEachren et al., 2003), © 2003 IEEE. (See also Plate LIII).

this chapter (MacEachren et al., 2003). The top matrix of linked views features small multiples of three types of visual encodings: geographic maps showing Appalachian counties at the lower left, histograms across the diagonal of the matrix, and scatterplots on the upper right. The bottom 2×2 matrix, linking scatterplots with maps, includes the color legend for both. The discrete bivariate sequential colormap has lightness increasing sequentially for each of two complementary hues and is effective for color-deficient people.

27.8.5 Spatial Fields

Most nongeographic spatial data is modeled as a field, where there are one or more values associated with each point in 2D or 3D space. Scalar fields, for example CT or MRI medical imaging scans, are usually visualized by finding isosurfaces or using direct volume rendering. Vector fields, for example flows in water or air, are often visualized using arrows, streamlines (McLouglin et al., 2009), and *line integral convolution* (LIC) (Laramee et al., 2004). Tensor fields, such as those describing the anisotropic diffusion of molecules through the human brain, are particularly challenging to display (Kindlmann et al., 2000). In the next chapter, spatial fields are discussed in detail.

Frequently Asked Questions

• What conferences and journals are good places to look for further information about visualization?

The IEEE VisWeek conference comprises three subconferences: InfoVis (Information Visualization), Vis (Visualization), and VAST (Visual Analytics Science and Technology). There is also a European EuroVis conference and an Asian PacificVis venue. Relevant journals include IEEE TVCG (Transactions on Visualization and Computer Graphics) and Palgrave Information Visualization.

• What software and toolkits are available for visualization?

The most popular toolkit for spatial data is `vtk`, a C/C++ codebase available at www.vtk.org. For abstract data, the Java-based `prefuse` (http://www.prefuse.org) and Processing (processing.org) toolkits are becoming widely used. The ManyEyes site from IBM Research (www.many-eyes.com) allows people to upload their own data, create interactive visualizations in a variety of formats, and carry on conversations about visual data analysis.

28

Spatial-Field Visualization

The topic of visualization was introduced in the previous chapter, together with visual encodings appropriate for a wide range of types of data. For many visualization applications, the main challenge lies in finding the appropriate spatial mapping of the data, but in other cases the data comes with a natural mapping. For instance, a photograph is a set of measured data that has an obvious visualization: simply display it on the screen. However, other ways of displaying the data may be useful as well, depending on what the user is trying to learn from it. An X-ray radiograph used to diagnose a broken bone is another example of a 2D image that is normally displayed directly.

An X-ray is a 2D *scalar field*: a dataset that describes a function $\mathbb{R}^2 \to \mathbb{R}$, in this case representing a projection of the density of a patient's body onto a plane. Other kinds of medical images, such as computed tomagraphy (CT) images or magnetic resonance images (MRIs), are 2D scalar fields that describe *slices* through a patient's body rather than projections. If many closely-spaced slices are measured, then the resulting dataset is a *3D scalar field*, or *volume dataset*, representing a function $\mathbb{R}^3 \to \mathbb{R}$. This type of data can be displayed one slice at a time, but it also invites perspective or orthographic views that can provide additional insight into 3D shape.

The importance of scalar fields has led to a number of special techniques and algorithms, particularly for rendering 3D views of volume data. As with other kinds of visualization, the primary goal is to map the relevant features of the data into visual features that play to the strengths of the human visual system.

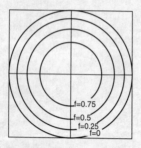

Figure 28.1. A contour plot for four levels of the function 1 - x² - y².

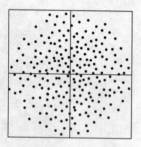

Figure 28.2. A random density plot for four levels of the function 1 - x² - y².

Figure 28.3. A grayscale density plot of the function 1 - x² - y².

28.1 2D Scalar Fields

For simplicity, assume that our 2D scalar data is defined as

$$f(x, y) = \begin{cases} 1 - x^2 - y^2, & \text{if } x^2 + y^2 < 1, \\ 0 & \text{otherwise,} \end{cases} \quad (28.1)$$

over the square $(x, y) \in [-1, 1]^2$. In practice, we often have a sampled representation on a rectilinear grid that we interpolate to get a continuous field. We will ignore that issue in 2D for simplicity.

One way to visualize a 2D field is to draw lines at a finite set of values $f(x, y) = f_i$ (shown for the function in Equation 28.1 in Figure 28.1). This is done on many topographic maps to indicate elevation. Isocontours are excellent at communicating slope, but are hard to read "globally" to understand large trends and extrema in the data.

Another common way to visualize 2D data is to use small pseudorandom dots whose density is proportional to the value of the function. This is shown for our test function in Figure 28.2. Such random density plots are useful for display on black-and-white media, but are otherwise usually not a good choice for visualization. Random density plots look smoother and smoother as more and smaller dots are used maintaining overall density. As the dot size shrinks below human visual acuity, the image looks smooth. This results in a grayscale continuous tone plot of the function. It is hard for humans to read such plots, because our ability to detect absolute intensity levels is poor. For this reason, color or thresholding is often used. This is shown in grayscale in Figure 28.3. Formally, we can specify such a mapping with just a function g that maps scalar values to colors:

$$g : \mathbb{R} \mapsto [0, 1]^3.$$

Here $[0, 1]^3$ refers to the RGB cube. A common strategy is to specify a set of colors to which specific values map and linearly interpolate colors between them. A set of colors that increases in intensity and cycles in hue is often used. Such a set of colors for the domain $[0, 1]$ is

$$g(0.00) = (0.0, 0.0, 0.0)$$
$$g(0.25) = (0.0, 0.0, 1.0)$$
$$g(0.50) = (1.0, 0.0, 0.0)$$
$$g(0.75) = (1.0, 1.0, 0.0)$$
$$g(1.00) = (1.0, 1.0, 1.0)$$

These plots are often called *pseudocolor* displays. We can also display the function as a height plot as shown in Figure 28.4. This type of plot is good for showing the shape of a function. Note that this plot makes it more obvious that the function is spherical.

Often, more than one of these methods are used together in a single image, such as a colored or contoured height plot. Another hybrid technique that is often used is to shade the height plot and view it orthogonally from above. This is a *shaded relief map*, often used for geographical applications.

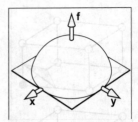

Figure 28.4. A height plot of the function.

28.2 3D Scalar Fields

In 3D we can use some of the same techniques as in 2D. We can make a contour plot, where each contour is a 3D surface called an *isosurface*. We can also generalize a random density plot to 3D by scattering particles in 3D. If we take the limit, as we did in 2D to get a pseudocolor display, then we get *direct volume rendering*. These two methods are covered here. It is not clear how to generalize height plots, because we have run out of dimensions.

28.2.1 Isosurfaces

Given a 3D scalar field $f(x, y, z)$ we can create an isosurface for $f(x, y, z) = f_0$. In practice, we will have f defined in a 3D rectilinear table that we interpolate for intermediate values. An example image is shown in Figure 28.5

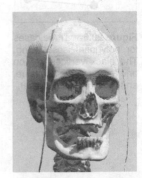

Figure 28.5. An isosurface from the NIH/NIM Visible Female data set.

There are two basic approaches to creating images of isosurfaces. The first is to explicitly create a polygonal representation of the isosurface and then render that representation using standard rendering techniques. The second is to use ray tracing to create an image by direct intersection calculation. In ray tracing, no explicit surface is computed. The explicit approach is better when we have small datasets, or we need the isosurface itself rather than just an image of it. The ray tracing approach is better for large datasets where we just need the image of the isosurface.

Creating Polygonal Isosurfaces

The basic idea of creating polygonal isosurfaces treats every rectilinear cell as a separate problem (Wyvill et al., 1986; W. E. Lorensen & Cline, 1987). Given an

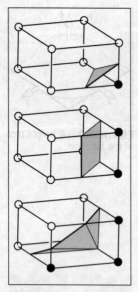

Figure 28.6. Three cases for polygonal isosurfacing. The black vertices are on one side of the isovalue, and the white on the other.

isovalue f_0, there is a surface in the cell if the minimum and maximum of the eight vertex values surround f_0. What surfaces occur depend on the arrangement of values above and below f_0. This is shown for three cases in Figure 28.6.

There are a total of $2^8 = 256$ cases for vertices above and below the isovalue. We can just enumerate all the cases in a table, and do a look-up. We can also take advantage of some symmetries to reduce the table size. For example, if we reverse above/below vertices, we can halve the table size. If we are willing to do flips and rotations, we can reduce the table to size 16, where only 15 of the cases have polygons.

Ray Tracing

Although the above algorithm, usually called *marching cubes* is elegant and simple, some care must be taken to ensure accurate results (Nielson, 2003).

The algorithm for intersecting a ray with an isosurface has three phases: traversing a ray through cells which do not contain an isosurface, analytically computing the isosurface when intersecting a voxel containing the isosurface, shading the resulting intersection point (Lin & Ching, 1996; Parker, Parker, et al., 1999). This process is repeated for each pixel on the screen.

To find an intersection, the ray $\mathbf{a} + t\mathbf{b}$ traverses cells in the volume checking each cell to see if its data range bounds an isovalue. If it does, an analytic computation is performed to solve for the ray parameter t at the intersection with the isosurface:

$$\rho(x_a + tx_b, y_a + ty_b, z_a + tz_b) - \rho_{\text{iso}} = 0.$$

When approximating ρ with a trilinear interpolation between discrete grid points, this equation will expand to a cubic polynomial in t. This cubic can then be solved in closed form to find the intersections of the ray with the isosurface in that cell. Only the roots of the polynomial which are contained in the cell are examined. There may be multiple roots corresponding to multiple intersection points. In this case, the smallest t (closest to the eye) is used. There may also be no roots of the polynomial, in which case the ray misses the isosurface in the cell.

A rectilinear volume is composed of a three-dimensional array of point samples that are aligned to the Cartesian axes and are equally spaced in a given dimension. A single cell from such a volume is shown in Figure 28.7. Other cells can be generated by exchanging indices (i, j, k) for the zeros and ones in the figure.

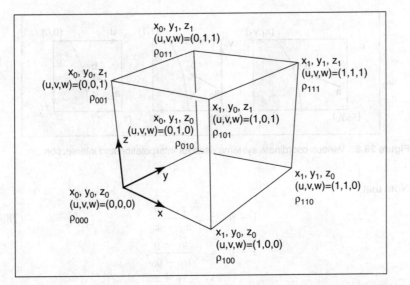

Figure 28.7. The geometry for a cell. A "nice" uvw coordinate system is used to make interpolation math cleaner.

The density at a point within the cell is found using *trilinear* interpolation:

$$
\begin{aligned}
\rho(u, v, w) \quad = \quad & (1-u)(1-v)(1-w)\rho_{000} && (28.2)\\
+ \; & (1-u)(1-v)(w)\rho_{001}\\
+ \; & (1-u)(v)(1-w)\rho_{010}\\
+ \; & (u)(1-v)(1-w)\rho_{100}\\
+ \; & (u)(1-v)(w)\rho_{101}\\
+ \; & (1-u)(v)(w)\rho_{011}\\
+ \; & (u)(v)(1-w)\rho_{110}\\
+ \; & (u)(v)(w)\rho_{111},
\end{aligned}
$$

where

$$
u = \frac{x - x_0}{x_1 - x_0}, \qquad (28.3)
$$

$$
v = \frac{y - y_0}{y_1 - y_0},
$$

$$
w = \frac{z - z_0}{z_1 - z_0}.
$$

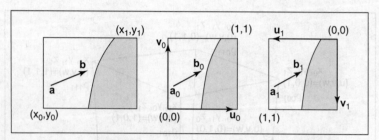

Figure 28.8. Various coordinate systems used for interpolation and intersection.

Note that

$$1 - u = \frac{x_1 - x}{x_1 - x_0}, \tag{28.4}$$

$$1 - v = \frac{y_1 - y}{y_1 - y_0},$$

$$1 - w = \frac{z_1 - z}{z_1 - z_0}.$$

If we redefine $u_0 = 1 - u$ and $u_1 = u$, and use similar definitions for v_0, v_1, w_0, w_1, then we get (Figure 28.8)

$$\rho = \sum_{i,j,k=0,1} u_i v_j w_k \rho_{ijk}.$$

It is interesting that the true trilinear isosurface can be fairly complex. The case where two opposite corners of the cube are on opposite sides of the isovalue from the other six vertices is shown in Figure 28.9. This is quite different from the two triangles given by polygonal isosurfacing for that case. One advantage of direct intersection with the trilinear surface is that ambiguous cases do not arise.

For a given point (x, y, z) in the cell, the surface normal is given by the gradient with respect to (x, y, z):

$$\mathbf{N} = \vec{\nabla}\rho = \left(\frac{\partial \rho}{\partial x}, \frac{\partial \rho}{\partial y}, \frac{\partial \rho}{\partial z} \right).$$

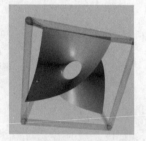

Figure 28.9. A true tri-linear isosurface generated using direct ray tracing.

Thus, the normal vector of $(N_x, N_Y, N_z) = \vec{\nabla}\rho$ is

$$N_x = \sum_{i,j,k=0,1} \frac{(-1)^{i+1} v_j w_k}{x_1 - x_0} \rho_{ijk},$$

$$N_y = \sum_{i,j,k=0,1} \frac{(-1)^{j+1} u_i w_k}{y_1 - y_0} \rho_{ijk},$$

$$N_z = \sum_{i,j,k=0,1} \frac{(-1)^{k+1} u_i v_j}{z_1 - z_0} \rho_{ijk}.$$

Given a ray $\mathbf{p} = \mathbf{a} + t\mathbf{b}$, the intersection with the isosurface occurs when $\rho(\mathbf{p}) = \rho_{\text{iso}}$. We can convert this ray into coordinates defined by (u_0, v_0, w_0): $\mathbf{p}_0 = \mathbf{a}_0 + t\mathbf{b}_0$ and a second ray defined by $\mathbf{p}_1 = \mathbf{a}_1 + t\mathbf{b}_1$. Here the rays are in the two coordinate systems (Figure 28.8):

$$\mathbf{a}_0 = (u_0^a, v_0^a, w_0^a) = \left(\frac{x_1 - x_a}{x_1 - x_0}, \frac{y_1 - y_a}{y_1 - y_0}, \frac{z_1 - z_a}{z_1 - z_0} \right),$$

and

$$\mathbf{b}_0 = (u_0^b, v_0^b, w_0^b) = \left(\frac{x_b}{x_1 - x_0}, \frac{y_b}{y_1 - y_0}, \frac{z_b}{z_1 - z_0} \right).$$

These equations are different because $\mathbf{a}_0$ is a location and $\mathbf{b}_0$ is a direction. The equations are similar for $\mathbf{a}_1$ and $\mathbf{b}_1$:

$$\mathbf{a}_1 = (u_1^a, v_1^a, w_1^a) = \left(\frac{x_a - x_0}{x_1 - x_0}, \frac{y_a - y_0}{y_1 - y_0}, \frac{z_a - z_0}{z_1 - z_0} \right),$$

and

$$\mathbf{b}_1 = (u_1^b, v_1^b, w_1^b) = \left(\frac{-x_b}{x_1 - x_0}, \frac{-y_b}{y_1 - y_0}, \frac{-z_b}{z_1 - z_0} \right).$$

Note that t is the same for all three rays; it can be found by traversing the cells and doing a brute-force algebraic solution for t. The intersection with the isosurface $\rho(\mathbf{p}) = \rho_{\text{iso}}$ occurs when

$$\rho_{\text{iso}} = \sum_{i,j,k=0,1} \left(u_i^a + t u_i^b \right) \left(v_j^a + t v_j^b \right) \left(w_k^a + t w_k^b \right) \rho_{ijk}.$$

This can be simplified to a cubic polynomial in t:

$$At^3 + Bt^2 + Ct + D = 0,$$

where

$$A = \sum_{i,j,k=0,1} u_i^b v_j^b w_k^b \rho_{ijk},$$

$$B = \sum_{i,j,k=0,1} \left(u_i^a v_j^b w_k^b + u_i^b v_j^a w_k^b + u_i^b v_j^b w_k^a \right) \rho_{ijk},$$

$$C = \sum_{i,j,k=0,1} \left(u_i^b v_j^a w_k^a + u_i^a v_j^b w_k^a + u_i^a v_j^a w_k^b \right) \rho_{ijk},$$

$$D = -\rho_{\text{iso}} + \sum_{i,j,k=0,1} u_i^a v_j^a w_k^a \rho_{ijk}.$$

The solution to a cubic polynomial is discussed in *Cubic and Quartic Roots* (Schwarze, 1990). His code is available on the web in several *Graphics Gems* archive sites. Two modifications are needed to use it: linear solutions (his code assumes A is non-zero), and the EQN_EPS parameter is set to 1.0e-30, which provided for maximum stability for large coefficients.

28.2.2 Direct Volume Rendering

Another way to create a picture of a 3D scalar field is to do a 3D random density plot using small opaque spheres. To avoid complications, the spheres can be made a constant color and, in effect, they are light emitters with no reflectance. Such a random density plot can be implemented directly using ray tracing and small spheres, or with 3D points using a traditional graphics API. As in 2D, we can take the limit as the sphere size goes to zero. This yields a 3D analog of the pseudocolor display and is usually called *direct volume rendering* (Levoy, 1988; Drebin et al., 1988; Sabella, 1988; Upson & Keeler, 1988).

There are two parameters that affect the appearance of a volume rendering: sphere color, and sphere density. These are controlled by a user-specified *transfer function*:

$$\text{color} = c(\rho),$$
$$\text{number density} = d(\rho).$$

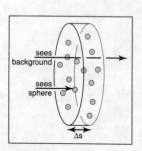

Figure 28.10. A thin slab filled with opaque spheres.

Here the *number density* is the number of spheres per unit volume. If we assume that the spheres have a small cross-sectional area a, and we consider a region along the line of sight that is of a small thickness Δs such that no spheres appear to overlap (Figure 28.10), then the color is

$$L(s + \Delta s) = (1 - F)L(s) + Fc,$$

where F is the fraction of the disk that is covered by spheres as seen from the viewing direction. Because the disk is very thin, we can ignore spheres visually overlapping, so this fraction is just the total cross-sectional area of the spheres divided by the area A of the disk:

$$F = \frac{daA\,\Delta s}{A} = da\Delta s,$$

which yields

$$L(s + \Delta s) = (1 - da\,\Delta s)L(s) + da\Delta sc.$$

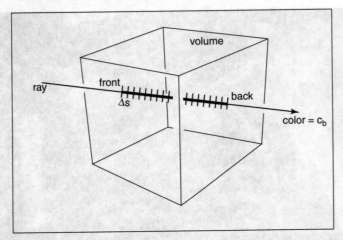

Figure 28.11. For direct volume rendering, we can take constant size steps along the ray and numerically integrate.

We can rearrange terms to give something like a definition of the derivative:

$$\frac{L(s + \Delta s) - L(s)}{\Delta s} = -daL(s) + dac.$$

If we take the limit $\Delta s \to 0$, we get a differential equation:

$$\frac{dL}{ds} = -daL(s) + dac.$$

For constant d and c this equation has the solution

$$L(s) = L(0)e^{-das} + c\left(1 - e^{-das}\right).$$

This would allow us to analytically compute color for constant density/color regions. However, in practice both d and c vary along the ray, and there is no analytic solution to the differential equation. So, in practice, we use a numerical technique. A simple way to proceed is to start at the back of the ray and incrementally step along the ray as shown in Figure 28.11.

We can apply the original equation for each Δs slice:

$$L(s + \Delta s) = (1 - d(x, y, z)a\,\Delta s)L(s) + d(x, y, z)a\,\Delta s c(x, y, z).$$

In pseudocode, we initialize the color to the background color c_b and then traverse the volume from back to front:

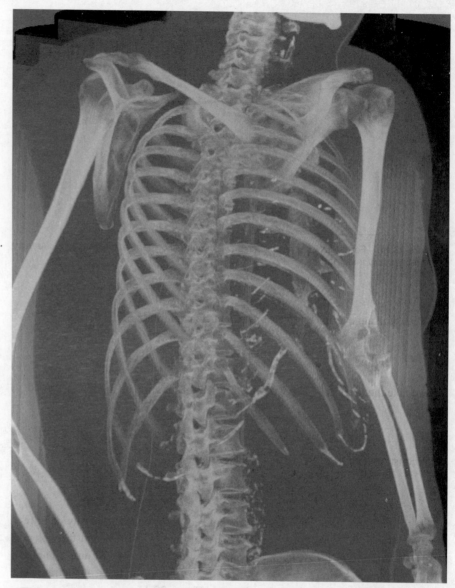

Figure 28.12. A maximum-intensity projection of the NIH/NIM Visible Female dataset. Each pixel contains a grayscale value that corresponds to the maximum density encountered along that ray. *Image courtesy Steve Parker.*

find volume entry and exit points **a** and **b**

$L = c_b$

$\Delta s = $ distance(**a**, **b**)

p = **b**

for $i = 1$ to N **do**

$\quad$**p** = **p** $- \Delta s(\mathbf{b} - \mathbf{a})$

$\quad L = L + (1 - d(\mathbf{p})a\Delta s L + d(\mathbf{p})a\,\Delta s c(\mathbf{p}))$

The step size Δs will determine the quality of the integration. To reduce the number of variables, we can use a new density function $g(\mathbf{p}) = d(\mathbf{p})a$.

In some applications direct volume rendering is used to render something similar to surfaces. In these cases the transfer function on density is "on" or "off" and the gradient of the number density is used to get a surface normal for shading. This can produce images of pseudosurfaces that are less sensitive to noise than traditional isosurfacing.

Another way to do volume rendering is *maximum-intensity projection*. Here, we set each pixel to the maximum density value encountered along a ray. This turns the ray integration into a search along the ray which is more efficient. Figure 28.12 shows an image generated using maximum-intensity projection.

Frequently Asked Questions

• What is the best transfer function for direct volume rendering?

The answer depends highly on the application and the characteristics of the data. Some empirical tests have been run and can be found in (Pfister et al., 2001). Various optical models used in direct volume rendering are described in (Max, 1995).

• What do I do to visualize vector or tensor data?

Vector data is often visualized using streamlines, arrows, and *line-integral convolution* (LIC). Such techniques are surveyed in (Interrante & Grosch, 1997). Tensor data is more problematic. Even simple diffusion tensor data is hard to visualize effectively because you just run out of display dimensions for mapping of data dimensions. See (Kindlmann et al., 2000).

• How do I interactively view a volume by changing isovalues?

One way is to use ray tracing on a parallel machine. The other is to use polygonal isosurfacing with a preprocess that helps search for cells containing an isosurface.

That search can be implemented using the data structure in (Livnat et al., 1996).

• My volume data is unstructured tetrahedra. How do I do isosurfacing or direct volume rendering?

Isosurfacing can still be done in a polygonal fashion, but there are fewer cases to preprocess. Ray tracing can also be used for isosurfacing or direct volume rendering, but the traversal algorithm must progress through the unstructured data either using neighbor pointers (Garrity, 1990) or by adding cells to an efficiency structure (Parker, Parker, et al., 1999).

• What is "splatting" for direct volume rendering?

Splatting refers to projecting semitransparent voxels onto the screen using some sort of painters' algorithm (Laur & Hanrahan, 1991).

Exercises

1. If we have a tetrahedral data element with densities at each of the four vertices, how many "cases" are there for polygonal isosurfaces?

2. Suppose we have n^3 data elements in a volume. If the densities in the volume are "well behaved," approximately how many cells will contain an isosurface for a particular isovalue?

3. Should we add shadowing to direct volume rendering? Why or why not?

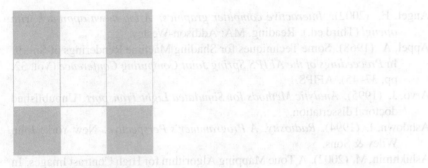

References

Adelson, E. H. (1999). Lightness Perception and Lightness Illusions. In M. S. Gazzaniga (Ed.), *The New Cognitive Neurosciences* (Second ed., pp. 339–351). Cambridge, MA: MIT Press.

Adzhiev, V., Cartwright, R., Fausett, E., Ossipov, A., Pasko, A., & Savchenko, V. (1999, Sep). Hyperfun Project: A Framework for Collaborative Multi-dimensional F-rep Modeling. In *Implicit Surfaces '99* (p. 59-69). Aire-la-ville, Switzerland: Eurographics Association.

Akenine-Möller, T., Haines, E., & Hoffman, N. (2008). *Real-Time Rendering* (Third ed.). Wellesley, MA: A K Peters.

Akkouche, S., & Galin, E. (2001). Adaptive Implicit Surface Polygonization Using Marching Triangles. *Computer Graphics Forum*, 20(2), 67–80.

Akleman, E., & Chen, J. (1999). Generalized Distance Functions. In *Proceedings of the International Conference on Shape Modeling and Applications* (pp. 72–79). Washington, DC: IEEE Computer Society.

Amanatides, J., & Woo, A. (1987). A Fast Voxel Traversal Algorithm for Ray Tracing. In *Proceedings of Eurographics* (pp. 1–10). Amsterdam: Elsevier Science Publishers.

Amar, R., Eagan, J., & Stasko, J. (2005). Low-Level Components of Analytic Activity in Information Visualization. In *Proc. IEEE Symposium on Information Visualization (InfoVis)* (pp. 111–117). Washington, DC: IEEE Computer Society.

American National Standard Institute. (1986). *Nomenclature and Definitions for Illumination Engineering*. ANSI Report (New York). (ANSI/IES RP-16-1986).

Angel, E. (2002). *Interactive computer graphics: A top-down approach with opengl* (Third ed.). Reading, MA: Addison-Wesley.

Appel, A. (1968). Some Techniques for Shading Machine Renderings of Solids. In *Proceedings of the AFIPS Spring Joint Computing Conference* (Vol. 32, pp. 37–45). AFIPS.

Arvo, J. (1995). *Analytic Methods for Simulated Light Transport*. Unpublished doctoral dissertation.

Ashdown, I. (1994). *Radiosity: A Programmer's Perspective*. New York: John Wiley & Sons.

Ashikhmin, M. (2002). A Tone Mapping Algorithm for High Contrast Images. In *EGRW '02: Proceedings of the 13th Eurographics Workshop on Rendering* (pp. 145–155). Aire-la-Ville, Switzerland: Eurographics Association.

Ashikhmin, M., Premože, S., & Shirley, P. (2000). A Microfacet-Based BRDF Generator. In *Proceedings of SIGGRAPH* (pp. 65–74). Reading, MA: Addison-Wesley Longman.

Ashikhmin, M., & Shirley, P. (2000). An Anisotropic Phong BRDF Model. *journal of graphics tools*, 5(2), 25–32.

Baerentzen, J., & Christensen, N. (2002, May). Volume Sculpting Using the Level-Set Method. In *SMI '02: Proceedings of Shape Modeling International 2002 (SMI '02)* (p. 175-182). Washington, DC: IEEE Computer Society.

Barr, A. H. (1984). Global and Local Deformations of Solid Primitives. *Proc. SIGGRAPH '84 Computer Graphics*, 18(3), 21-30.

Bartels, R. H., Beatty, J. C., & Barsky, B. A. (1987). *An Introduction to Splines for Use in Computer Graphics and Geometric Modeling*. San Francisco, CA: Morgan Kaufmann.

Barthe, L., Dodgson, N. A., Sabin, M. A., Wyvill, B., & Gaildrat, V. (2003). Two-dimensional Potential Fields for Advanced Implicit Modeling Operators. *Computer Graphics Forum*, 22(1), 23–33.

Barthe, L., Mora, B., Dodgson, N. A., & Sabin, M. A. (2002). Interactive Implicit Modelling based on C1 Reconstruction of Regular Grids. *International Journal of Shape Modeling*, 8(2), 99-117.

Baumgart, B. (1974, October). *Geometric Modeling for Computer Vision* (Tech. Rep. No. AIM-249). Palo Alto, CA: Stanford University AI Laboratory.

Beck, K., & Andres, C. (2004). *Extreme Programming Explained: Embrace Change* (Second ed.). Reading, MA: Addison-Wesley.

Berlin, B., & Kay, P. (1969). *Basic Color Terms: Their Universality and Evolution*. Berkeley, CA: University of California Press.

Berns, R. S. (2000). *Billmeyer and saltzman's principles of color technology* (3rd ed.). New York: John Wiley and Sons.

Blinn, J. (1982). A Generalization of Algebraic Surface Drawing. *ACM Transactions on Graphics*, 1(3), 235–258.

Blinn, J. (1996). *Jim Blinn's Corner*. San Francisco, CA: Morgan Kaufmann.

Blinn, J. F. (1976). Texture and Reflection in Computer Generated Images. *Communications of the ACM*, *19*(10), 542-547.

Blinn, J. F. (1978). Simulation of Wrinkled Surfaces. *Proc. SIGGRAPH '78 Computer Graphics*, *12*(3), 286–292.

Bloomenthal, J. (1988). Polygonization of Implicit Surfaces. *Computer Aided Geometric Design*, *4*(5), 341-355.

Bloomenthal, J. (1990). Calculation of Reference Frames Along a Space Curve. In A. Glassner (Ed.), *Graphics Gems* (pp. 567–571). Boston: Academic Press.

Bloomenthal, J. (1995). *Skeletal Design of Natural Forms*. Unpublished doctoral dissertation, University of Calgary, Canada.

Bloomenthal, J. (1997). Bulge Elimination in Convolution Surfaces. *Computer Graphics Forum*, *16*(1), 31–41.

Bloomenthal, J., & Shoemake, K. (1991). Convolution Surfaces. *Proc. SIGGRAPGH '91, Computer Graphics*, *25*(4), 251–257.

Brandenburg, F. J. (1988). Nice Drawing of Graphs are Computationally Hard. In P. Gorney & M. J. Tauber (Eds.), *Visualization in Human-Computer Interaction* (pp. 1–15). Berlin: Springer-Verlag.

Bresenham, J. E. (1965). Algorithm for Computer Control of a Digital Plotter. *IBM Systems Journal*, *4*(1), 25–30.

Brewer, C. A. (1999). Color Use Guidelines for Data Representation. In *Proc. Section on Statistical Graphics* (pp. 55–60). Alexandria, VA: American Statistical Association.

Buchheim, C., Jünger, M., & Leipert, S. (2002). Improving Walker's Algorithm to Run in Linear Time. In *GD '02: Revised Papers from the 10th International Symposium on Graph Drawing* (pp. 344–353). London: Springer-Verlag.

Buck, I., Foley, T., Horn, D., Sugerman, J., Fatahalian, K., Houston, M., et al. (n.d.). Brook for GPUs: Stream Computing on Graphics Hardware. *ACM Transactions on Graphics (TOG) (Proc. SIGGRAPH 2004*.

Buschmann, F., Meunier, R., Rohnert, H., Sommerlad, P., & Stal, M. (1996). *Pattern-Oriented Software Architecture* (Vols. 1, A System of Patterns). New York: John Wiley & Sons.

Campagna, S., Kobbelt, L., & Seidel, H.-P. (1998). Directed Edges—A Scalable Representation for Triangle Meshes. *journal of graphics tools*, *3*(4), 1–12.

Carr, J. C., Beatson, R. K., Cherrie, J. B., Mitchell, T. J., Fright, W. R., McCallum, B. C., et al. (2001). Reconstruction and representation of 3d objects with radial basis functions. In *Siggraph '01: Proceedings of the 28th annual conference on computer graphics and interactive techniques* (pp. 67–76). New York: ACM.

Carr, N. A., Hall, J. D., & Hart, J. C. (2002). The Ray Engine. In *HWWS '02: Proceedings of the ACM SIGGRAPH/EUROGRAPHICS Conference on Graphics Hardware* (pp. 37–46). Aire-la-Ville, Switzerland: Eurographics Association.

Catmull, E. (1975). Computer Display of Curved Surfaces. In *IEEE Conference on Computer Graphics, Pattern Recognition and Data Structures* (pp. 11–17). Los Alamitos, CA: IEEE Press.

Chiu, K., Herf, M., Shirley, P., Swamy, S., Wang, C., & Zimmerman, K. (1993). Spatially Nonuniform Scaling Functions for High Contrast Images. In *Proceedings of Graphics Interface '93* (pp. 245–253). Wellesley, MA: A K Peters & Canadian Human-Computer Communications Society.

Choudhury, P., & Tumblin, J. (2003). The Trilateral Filter for High Contrast Images and Meshes. In *EGRW '03: Proceedings of the 14th Eurographics Workshop on Rendering* (pp. 186–196). Aire-la-Ville, Switzerland: Eurographics Association.

Cleary, J., Wyvill, B., Birtwistle, G., & Vatti, R. (1983). A Parallel Ray Tracing Computer. In *Proceedings of the Association of Simula Users Conference* (pp. 77–80).

Cohen, E., Riesenfeld, R. F., & Elber, G. (2001). *Geometric Modeling with Splines: An Introduction*. Wellesley, MA: A K Peters.

Cohen, M. F., Chen, S. E., Wallace, J. R., & Greenberg, D. P. (1988). A Progressive Refinement Approach to Fast Radiosity Image Generation. In *SIGGRAPH '88: Proceedings of the 15th Annual Conference on Computer Graphics and Interactive Techniques* (pp. 75–84). New York: ACM Press.

Cohen, M. F., & Wallace, J. R. (1993). *Radiosity and Realistic Image Synthesis*. Cambridge, MA: Academic Press, Inc.

Comaniciu, D., & Meer, P. (2002). Mean Shift: A Robust Approach Toward Feature Space Analysis. *IEEE Transactions on Pattern Analysis and Machine Intelligence, 24*(5), 603–619.

Cook, R. L. (1984). Shade Trees. *Proc. SIGGRAPH '84, Computer Graphics, 18*(3), 223–231.

Cook, R. L., Carpenter, L., & Catmull, E. (1987). The Reyes Image Rendering Architecture. *Proc. SIGGRAPH '87 Computer Graphics, 21*(4), 95–102.

Cook, R. L., Porter, T., & Carpenter, L. (1984). Distributed Ray Tracing. *Proc. SIGGRAPH '84, Computer Graphics, 18*(3), 137–145.

Cook, R. L., & Torrance, K. E. (1982). A Reflectance Model for Computer Graphics. *ACM Transactions on Graphics, 1*(1), 7–24.

Coombe, G., Harris, M. J., & Lastra, A. (2004). Radiosity on Graphics Hardware. In *GI '04: Proceedings of the 2004 Conference on Graphics Interface* (pp. 161–168). Wellesley, MA: A K Peters & Canadian Human-Computer Communications Society.

Crow, F. C. (1978). The Use of Grayscale for Improved Raster Display of Vectors and Characters. In *SIGGRAPH '78: Proceedings of the 5th Annual Conference on Computer Graphics and Interactive Techniques* (pp. 1–5). New York: ACM Press.

Crowe, M. J. (1994). *A History of Vector Analysis.* Mineola, NY: Dover.

Curless, B., & Levoy, M. (1996). A Volumetric Method for Building Complex Models from Range Images. In *SIGGRAPH '96: Proceedings of the 23rd Annual Conference on Computer Graphics and Interactive Techniques* (pp. 303–312). Reading, MA: Addison-Wesley.

da Vinci, L. (1970). *The Notebooks of Leonardo da Vinci* (Vol. 1). Mineola, NY: Dover Press.

Dachsbacher, C., Vogelgsang, C., & Stamminger, M. (2003). Sequential Point Trees. *ACM Transactions on Graphics, (Proc. SIGGRAPH 03), 22*(3), 657–662.

Debevec, P. E., & Malik, J. (1997). Recovering High Dynamic Range Radiance Maps from Photographs. In *SIGGRAPH '97: Proceedings of the 24th Annual Conference on Computer Graphics and Interactive Techniques* (pp. 369–378). Reading, MA: Addison-Wesley.

De Boor, C. (1978). *A Practical Guide to Splines.* Berlin: Springer-Verlag.

De Boor, C. (2001). *A Practical Guide to Splines.* Berlin: Springer-Verlag.

deGroot, E., & Wyvill, B. (2005). Rayskip: Faster Ray Tracing of Implicit Surface Animations. In *GRAPHITE '05: Proceedings of the 3rd International Conference on Computer Graphics and Interactive Techniques in Australasia and South East Asia* (pp. 31–36). New York: ACM Press.

DeRose, T. (1989). *A Coordinate-Free Approach to Geometric Programming* (Tech. Rep. No. 89-09-16). Seattle, WA: University of Washington.

Di Battista, G., Eades, P., Tamassia, R., & Tollis, I. G. (1999). *Graph Drawing: Algorithms for the Visualization of Graphs.* Englewood Cliffs, NJ: Prentice Hall.

Dinh, H., Slabaugh, G., & Turk, G. (2001). Reconstructing Surfaces Using Anisotropic Basis Functions. In *International Conference on Computer Vision (ICCV) 2001* (pp. 606–613). Washington, DC: IEEE.

Dobkin, D. P., & Mitchell, D. P. (1993). Random-Edge Discrepancy of Supersampling Patterns. In *Proceedings of Graphics Interface* (pp. 62–69). Wellesley, MA: A K Peters & Canadian Human-Computer Communications Society.

Dooley, D., & Cohen, M. F. (1990). Automatic Illustration of 3D Geometric Models: Lines. In *SI3D '90: Proceedings of the 1990 Symposium on Interactive 3D Graphics* (pp. 77–82). New York: ACM Press.

Doran, C., & Lasenby, A. (2003). *Geometric Algebra for Physicists.* Cambridge, UK: Cambridge University Press.

Drago, F., Myszkowski, K., Annen, T., & Chiba, N. (2003). Adaptive Logarithmic Mapping for Displaying High Contrast Scenes. *Computer Graphics Forum, 22*(3), 419–426.

Drebin, R. A., Carpenter, L., & Hanrahan, P. (1988). Volume Rendering. *Proc. SIGGRAPH '88, Computer Graphics, 22*(4), 64–75.

Duchon, J. (1977). Constructive Theory of Functions of Several Variables. In (pp. 85–100). Berlin: Springer-Verlag.

Durand, F., & Dorsey, J. (2002). Fast Bilateral Filtering for the Display of High-Dynamic-Range Images. *ACM Transactions on Graphics*, *21*(3), 257–266.

Dutré, P., Bala, K., & Bekaert, P. (2002). *Advanced Global Illumination*. Wellesley, MA: A K Peters.

Dwyer, T., Koren, Y., & Marriott, K. (2006). IPSep-CoLa: An Incremental Procedure for Separation Constraint Layout of Graphs. *IEEE Trans. Visualization and Computer Graphics (Proc. InfoVis 06)*, *12*(5), 821–828.

Eberly, D. (2000). *3D Game Engine Design: A Practical Approach to Real-Time Computer Graphics*. San Francisco, CA: Morgan Kaufmann.

Eberly, D. (2004). *3D Game Engine Architecture: Engineering Real-Time Applications with Wild Magic*. San Francisco, CA: Morgan Kaufmann.

Eckman, P., & Friesen, W. V. (1978). *Facial Action Coding System*. Palo Alto, CA: Consulting Psychologists Press.

Eick, S. G., Steffen, J. L., & Sumner, E. E., Jr. (1992). Seesoft-A Tool for Visualizing Line Oriented Software Statistics. *IEEE Trans. Software Eng.*, *18*(11), 957–968.

Ershov, S., Kolchin, K., & Myszkowski, K. (2001). Rendering Pearlescent Appearance Based on Paint-Composition Modelling. *Computer Graphics Forum*, *20*(3), 227–238.

Fairchild, M. D. (2005). *Color Appearance Models* (Second ed.). New York: John Wiley & Sons.

Fairchild, M. D., & Johnson, G. M. (2002). Meet iCAM: An Image Color Appearance Model. In *IS&T/SID 10th Color Imaging Conference* (pp. 33–38). Springfield, VA: Society for Imaging Science & Technology.

Fairchild, M. D., & Johnson, G. M. (2004). The iCAM Framework for Image Appearance, Image Differences, and Image Quality. *Journal of Electronic Imaging*, *13*, 126–138.

Farin, G. (2002). *Curves and Surfaces for CAGD: A Practical Guide*. San Francisco, CA: Morgan Kaufmann.

Farin, G., & Hansford, D. (2004). *Practical Linear Algebra: A Geometry Toolbox*. Wellesley, MA: A K Peters.

Farin, G., Hoschek, J., & Kim, M.-S. (Eds.). (2002). *Handbook of Computer Aided Geometric Design*. Amsterdam: Elsevier.

Fattal, R., Lischinski, D., & Werman, M. (2002). Gradient Domain High Dynamic Range Compression. *ACM Transactions on Graphics*, *21*(3), 249–256.

Fekete, J.-D., & Plaisant, C. (2002). Interactive Information Visualization of a Million Items. In *Proc. IEEE Symposium on Information Visualization (InfoVis 02)* (pp. 117–124). Washington, DC: IEEE Computer Scoiety.

Fernando, R. (Ed.). (2004). *GPU Gems: Programming Techniques, Tips, and Tricks for Real-Time Graphics*. Reading, MA: Addison-Wesley.

Fernando, R., & Killgard, M. J. (2003). *The Cg Tutorial: The Definitive Guide to Programmable Real-Time Graphics*. Reading, MA: Addison-Wesley.

Ferwerda, J. A., Pattanaik, S., Shirley, P., & Greenberg, D. P. (1996). A Model of Visual Adaptation for Realistic Image Synthesis. In *SIGGRAPH '96: Proceedings of the 23rd Annual Conference on Computer Graphics and Interactive Techniques* (pp. 249–258). New York: ACM Press.

Ferwerda, J. A., Shirley, P., Pattanaik, S. N., & Greenberg, D. P. (1997). A Model of Visual Masking for Computer Graphics. In *SIGGRAPH '97: Proceedings of the 24th Annual Conference on Computer Graphics and Interactive Techniques* (pp. 143–152). Reading, MA: Addison-Wesley.

Foley, J. D., Van Dam, A., Feiner, S. K., & Hughes, J. F. (1990). *Computer Graphics: Principles and Practice* (Second ed.). Reading, MA: Addison-Wesley.

Forsyth, D. A., & Ponce, J. (2002). *Computer Vision: A Modern Approach*. Englewoods Cliffs, NJ: Prentice Hall.

Francis S. Hill, J. (2000). *Computer Graphics Using OpenGL* (Second ed.). Englewood Cliffs, NJ: Prentice Hall.

Frick, A., Ludwig, A., & Mehldau, H. (1994). A Fast Adaptive Layout Algorithm for Undirected Graphs. In *GD '94: Proceedings of the DIMACS International Workshop on Graph Drawing* (pp. 388–403). London: Springer-Verlag.

Friendly, M. (2008). A Brief History of Data Visualization. In *Handbook of Data Visualization* (pp. 15–56). (Web document, http://www.math.yorku.ca/SCS/Gallery/milestone/.)

Frisken, S., Perry, R., Rockwood, A., & Jones, T. (2000). Adaptively Sampled Distance Fields. In *Siggraph '00: Proceedings of the 27th Annual Conference on Computer Graphics and Interactive Techniques* (p. 249-254). New York: ACM Press/Addison-Wesley Publishing Co.

Fua, Y.-H., Ward, M. O., & Rundensteiner, E. A. (1999). Hierarchical Parallel Coordinates for Exploration of Large Datasets. In *Proc. IEEE Visualization Conference (Vis '99)* (pp. 43–50). Washington, DC: IEEE COmputer Society.

Fujimoto, A., Tanaka, T., & Iwata, K. (1986). ARTSccelerated Ray-Tracing System. *IEEE Computer Graphics & Applications*, 6(4), 16–26.

Galin, E., & Akkouche, S. (1999). Incremental Polygonization of Implicit Surfaces. *Graphical Models*, 62(1), 19–39.

Gamma, E., Helm, R., Johnson, R., & Vlissides, J. (1995). *Design Patterns—Elements of Reusable Object-Oriented Software*. Reading, MA: Addison-Wesley.

Gansner, E. R., Koutsofios, E., North, S. C., & Vo, K.-P. (1993, March). A Technique for Drawing Directed Graphs. *IEEE Transactions on Software Engineering*, 19(3), 214–229.

Garrity, M. P. (1990). Raytracing Irregular Volume Data. In *VVS '90: Proceedings of the 1990 Workshop on Volume Visualization* (pp. 35–40). New York: ACM Press.

Gascuel, M.-P. (1993, Aug). An Implicit Formulation for Precise Contact Modeling Between Flexible Solids. In *SIGGRAPH '93: Proceedings of the 20th Annual Conference on Computer Graphics and Interactive Techniques* (p. 313-320). New York: ACM Press.

Gibson, J. J. (1950). *The Perception of the Visual World*. Cambridge, MA: Riverside Press.

Gilchrist, A. L., Kossyfidis, C., Bonato, F., Agostini, T., Cataliotti, J., Li, X., et al. (1999). An Anchoring Theory of Lightness Perception. *Psychological Review*, *106*(4), 795–834.

Glassner, A. (1984). Space Subdivision for Fast Ray Tracing. *IEEE Computer Graphics & Applications*, *4*(10), 15–22.

Glassner, A. (1988). Spacetime Ray Tracing for Animation. *IEEE Computer Graphics & Applications*, *8*(2), 60–70.

Glassner, A. (Ed.). (1989). *An Introduction to Ray Tracing*. London: Academic Press.

Glassner, A. (1995). *Principles of Digital Image Synthesis*. San Francisco, CA: Morgan Kaufmann.

Goldberg, A., & Robson, D. (1989). *Smalltalk-80: The Language*. Reading, MA: Addison-Wesley.

Goldman, R. (1985). Illicit Expressions in Vector Algebra. *ACM Transactions on Graphics*, *4*(3), 223–243.

Goldsmith, J., & Salmon, J. (1987). Automatic Creation of Object Hierarchies for Ray Tracing. *IEEE Computer Graphics & Applications*, *7*(5), 14–20.

Gooch, A., Gooch, B., Shirley, P., & Cohen, E. (1998). A Non-Photorealistic Lighting Model for Automatic Technical Illustration. In *SIGGRAPH '98: Proceedings of the 25th Annual Conference on Computer Graphics and Interactive Techniques* (pp. 447–452). New York: ACM Press.

Goral, C. M., Torrance, K. E., Greenberg, D. P., & Battaile, B. (1984). Modeling the Interaction of Light between Diffuse Surfaces. *Proc. SIGGRAPH '84, Computer Graphics*, *18*(3), 213–222.

Gouraud, H. (1971). Continuous Shading of Curved Surfaces. *Communications of the ACM*, *18*(6), 623-629.

Grassmann, H. (1853). Zur Theorie der Farbenmischung. *Annalen der Physik und Chemie*, *89*, 69–84.

Gregory, R. L. (1997). *Eye and Brain: The Psychology of Seeing* (Fifth ed.). Princeton, NJ: Princeton University Press.

Grosjean, J., Plaisant, C., & Bederson, B. (2002). SpaceTree: Supporting Exploration in Large Node Link Tree, Design Evolution and Empirical Evaluation. In *Proc. IEEE Symposium on Information Visualization (InfoVis)* (pp. 57–64). Washington, DC: IEEE Computer Society.

Grossman, T., Wigdor, D., & Balakrishnan, R. (2007). Exploring and Reducing the Effects of Orientation on Text Readability in Volumetric Displays. In *Proc. ACM Conf. Human Factors in Computing Systems (CHI)* (pp. 483–492). New York: ACM Press.

Hammersley, J., & Handscomb, D. (1964). *Monte-Carlo Methods*. London: Methuen.

Hanrahan, P., & Lawson, J. (1990). A Language for Shading and Lighting Calculations. In *SIGGRAPH '90: Proceedings of the 17th Annual Conference on Computer Graphics and Interactive Techniques* (pp. 289–298). New York: ACM Press.

Hanson, A. J. (2005). *Visualizing Quaternions*. San Francisco, CA: Morgan Kaufmann.

Harris, M. J. (2004). Fast Fluid Dynamics Simulation on the GPU. In *GPU Gems: Programming Techniques, Tips, and Tricks for Real-Time Graphics* (chap. 38). Reading, MA: Addison-Wesley.

Harris, M. J., Baxter, W. V., Scheuermann, T., & Lastra, A. (2003). Simulation of Cloud Dynamics on Graphics Hardware. In *HWWS '03: Proceedings of the ACM SIGGRAPH/EUROGRAPHICS Conference on Graphics Hardware* (pp. 92–101). Aire-la-Ville, Switzerland: Eurographics Association.

Hart, J. C., & Baker, B. (1996, Oct). Implicit Modeling of Tree Surfaces. In *Proceedings of Implicit Surfaces '96* (p. 143-152). Aire-la-Ville, Switzerland: Eurographics Association.

Hartmann, E. (1998). A Marching Method for the Triangulation of Surfaces. *The Visual Computer, 14*(3), 95–108.

Hausner, M. (1998). *A Vector Space Approach to Geometry*. Mineola, NY: Dover.

Havran, V. (2000). *Heuristic Ray Shooting Algorithms*. Unpublished doctoral dissertation, Czech Technical University in Prague.

He, X. D., Heynen, P. O., Phillips, R. L., Torrance, K. E., Salesin, D. H., & Greenberg, D. P. (1992). A Fast and Accurate Light Reflection Model. *Proc. SIGGRAPH '92, Computer Graphics, 26*(2), 253–254.

Hearn, D., & Baker, M. P. (1986). *Computer Graphics*. Englewood Cliffs, N.J.: Prentice Hall.

Heer, J., & Robertson, G. (2007). Animated Transitions in Statistical Data Graphics. *IEEE Trans. on Visualization and Computer Graphics (Proc. InfoVis07), 13*(6), 1240–1247.

Heidrich, W., & Seidel, H.-P. (1998). Ray-Tracing Procedural Displacement Shaders. In *Proceedings of Graphics Interface* (pp. 8–16). Wellesley, MA: A K Peters & Canadian Human-Computer Communications Society.

Henry, N., & Fekete, J.-D. (2006). MatrixExplorer: a Dual-Representation System to Explore Social Networks. *IEEE Trans. Visualization and Computer Graphics (Proc. InfoVis 06), 12*(5), 677–684.

Hoffmann, B. (1975). *About Vectors*. Mineola, NY: Dover.

Hofstadter, D. (1979). *Gödel, Escher, Bach: an Eternal Golden Braid*. New York: Basic Books.

Hood, D. C., Finkelstein, M. A., & Buckingham, E. (1979). Psychophysical Tests of Models of the Response Function. *Vision Research*, *19*, 401–406.

Hoppe, H. (1994). *Surface Reconstruction from Unorganized Points*. Unpublished doctoral dissertation, University of Washington.

Hoppe, H. (1999). Optimization of Mesh Locality for Transparent Vertex Caching. In *SIGGRAPH '99: Proceedings of the 26th Annual Conference on Computer Graphics and Interactive Techniques* (pp. 269–276). Reading, MA: Addison-Wesley.

Horn, B. K. P. (1974). Determining Lightness from an Image. *CVGIP*, *3*, 277–299.

Hughes, J. F., & Möller, T. (1999). Building an Orthonormal Basis from a Unit Vector. *journal of graphics tools*, *4*(4), 33–35.

Hunt, R. W. G. (2004). *The Reproduction of Color* (6th ed.). Chichester, UK: John Wiley and Sons.

IEEE Standards Association. (1985). *IEEE Standard for Binary Floating-Point Arithmetic* (Tech. Rep.). New York: IEEE Report. (ANSI/IEEE Std 754-1985)

Igarashi, T., Matsuoka, S., & Tanaka, H. (1999). Teddy: A Sketching Interface for 3D Freeform Design. In *Siggraph '99: Proceedings of the 26th Annual Conference on Computer Graphics and Interactive Techniques* (pp. 409–416). New York: ACM Press/Addison-Wesley Publishing Co.

Immel, D. S., Cohen, M. F., & Greenberg, D. P. (1986). A Radiosity Method for Non-Diffuse Environments. *Proc. SIGGRAPH '86, Computer Graphics*, *20*(4), 133–142.

Ingram, S., Munzner, T., & Olano, M. (2009). Glimmer: Multilevel MDS on the GPU. *IEEE Trans. Visualization and Computer Graphics*, *15*(2), 249–261.

Inselberg, A., & Dimsdale, B. (1990). Parallel Coordinates: A Tool for Visualizing Multi-Dimensional Geometry. In *Vis '90: Proceedings of the 1st Conference on Visualization '90*. Los Alamitos, CA: IEEE Computer Society Press.

Interrante, V., & Grosch, C. (1997). Strategies for Effectively Visualizing 3D Flow with Volume LIC. In *VIS '97: Proceedings of the 8th Conference on Visualization '97* (pp. 421–ff.). Los Alamitos, CA: IEEE Computer Society Press.

Jansen, F. W. (1986). Data Structures for Ray Tracing. In *Proceedings of a Workshop Eurographics Seminars on Data Structures for Raster Graphics* (pp. 57–73). New York: Springer-Verlag.

Jensen, H. W. (2001). *Realistic Image Synthesis Using Photon Mapping*. Wellesley, MA: A K Peters.

Jensen, H. W., Marschner, S. R., Levoy, M., & Hanrahan, P. (2001). A Practical Model for Subsurface Light Transport. In *Siggraph '01: Proceedings of the*

28th Annual Conference on Computer Graphics and Interactive Techniques (pp. 511–518). New York: ACM Press.

Johansson, G. (1973). Visual Perception of Biological Motion and a Model for Its Analysis. *Perception & Psychophysics, 14*, 201–211.

Johnson, B., & Shneiderman, B. (1991). Treemaps: A Space-filling Approach to the Visualization of Hierarchical Information. In *VIS '91: Proceedings of the 2nd Conference on Visualization '91* (pp. 284–291). Los Alamitos, CA: IEEE Computer Society Press.

Johnson, G. M., & Fairchild, M. D. (2003). Rendering HDR Images. In *IS&T/SID 11th Color Imaging Conference* (pp. 36–41). Springfield, VA: Society for Imaging Science & Technology.

Jones, J. A., Harrold, M. J., & Stasko, J. (2002). Visualization of Test Information to Assist Fault Localization. In *ICSE '02: Proceedings of the 24th International Conference on Software Engineering* (pp. 467–477). New York: ACM Press.

Judd, D. B. (1932). Chromaticity Sensibility to Stimulus Differences. *Journal of the Optical Society of America, 22*, 72–108.

Kainz, F., Bogart, R., & Hess, D. (2003). The OpenEXR Image File Format. In *SIGGRAPH Technical Sketches*. New York: ACM Press. (see also: http://www.openexr.com/)

Kajiya, J. T. (1986). The Rendering Equation. *Proc SIGGRAPH '86 Computer Graphics, 20*(4), 143–150.

Kalos, M., & Whitlock, P. (1986). *Monte Carlo Methods, Basics*. New York: Wiley-Interscience.

Kalra, D., & Barr, A. (1989, July). Guaranteed Ray Intersections with Implicit Functions. *Computer Graphics (Proc. SIGGRAPH 89), 23*(3), 297-306.

Kay, D. S., & Greenberg, D. (1979). Transparency for Computer Synthesized Images. *Proc. SIGGRAPH '79 Computer Graphics, 13*(2), 158–164.

Kernighan, B. W., & Pike, R. (1999). *The Practice of Programming*. Reading, MA: Addison-Wesley.

Kersten, D., Mamassian, P., & Knill, D. C. (1997). Moving Cast Shadows Induce Apparent Motion in Depth. *Perception, 26*(2), 171–192.

Kindlmann, G., Weinstein, D., & Hart, D. (2000). Strategies for Direct Volume Rendering of Diffusion Tensor Fields. *IEEE Transactions on Visualization and Computer Graphics, 6*(2), 124–138.

Kirk, D., & Arvo, J. (1988). The Ray Tracing Kernel. In *Proceedings of Ausgraph*. Melbourne, Australia: Australian Computer Graphics Association.

Klatzky, R. L. (1998). Allocentric and Egocentric Spatial Representations: Definitions, Distinctions, and Interconnections. In C. Freksa, C. Habel, & K. F. Wender (Eds.), *Spatial Cognition—An Interdiciplinary Approach to Representation and Processing of Spatial Knowledge* (Vol. 5, pp. 1–17). Berlin: Springer-Verlag.

Knill, D. C. (1998). Surface Orientation From Texture: Ideal Observers, Generic Observers and the Information Content of Texture Cues. *Vision Research*, *38*, 1655–1682.

Kollig, T., & Keller, A. (2002). Efficient Multidimensional Sampling. *Computer Graphics Forum*, *21*(3), 557–564.

Kovitz, B. L. (1999). *Practical Sofware Requirements: A Manual of Content & Style*. New York: Manning.

Lacroute, P., & Levoy, M. (1994). Fast Volume Rendering Using a Shear-Warp Factorization of the Viewing Transformation. In *Proceedings of SIGGRAPH 94* (pp. 451–458). New York: ACM Press.

Lafortune, E. P. F., Foo, S.-C., Torrance, K. E., & Greenberg, D. P. (1997). Non-Linear Approximation of Reflectance Functions. In *Proceedings of SIGGRAPH '97* (pp. 117–126). Reading, MA: Addison-Wesley.

Laramee, R. S., Hauser, H., Doleisch, H., Vrolijk, B., Post, F. H., & Weiskopf, D. (2004). The State of the Art in Flow Visualization: Dense and Texture-Based Techniques. *Computer Graphics Forum*, *23*(2), 203–221.

Lasseter, J. (1987). Principles of Traditional Animation Applied to 3D Computer Animation. *Proc. SIGGRAPH '87, Computer Graphics*, *21*(4), 35–44.

Lastra, A., Molnar, S., Olano, M., & Wang, Y. (1995). Real-Time Programmable Shading. In *SI3D '95: Proceedings of the 1995 Symposium on Interactive 3D Graphics* (pp. 59–66). New York: ACM Press.

Laur, D., & Hanrahan, P. (1991). Hierarchical Splatting: A Progressive Refinement Algorithm for Volume Rendering. *Computer Graphics*, *25*(4), 285–288. (SIGGRAPH '91)

Lawrence, J., Rusinkiewicz, S., & Ramamoorthi, R. (2004). Efficient BRDF Importance Sampling Using a Factored Representation. *ACM Transactions on Graphics (Proc. SIGGRAPH '04)*, *23*(3), 496–505.

Lee, D. N., & Reddish, P. (1981). Plummeting Gannets: A Paradigm of Ecological Optics. *Nature*, *293*, 293–294.

Lefohn, A., Kniss, J., & Owens, J. (2005). Implementing Efficient Parallel Data Structures on GPUs. In *GPU Gems 2: Programming Techniques for High-Performance Graphics and General Purpose Computation* (chap. 33). Reading, MA: Addison-Wesley.

Lefohn, A. E., Kniss, J. M., Hansen, C. D., & Whitaker, R. T. (2003). Interactive Deformation and Visualization of Level Set Surfaces Using Graphics Hardware. In *IEEE Visualization* (pp. 75–82). Los Alamitos, CA: IEEE Press.

Leung, T., & Malik, J. (1997). On Perpendicular Texture: Why Do We See More Flowers in the Distance? In *Proc. IEEE Conference on Computer Vision and Pattern Recognition* (pp. 807–813). Los Alamitos, CA: IEEE Press.

Levoy, M. (1988). Display of Surfaces from Volume Data. *IEEE Computer Graphics & Applications*, *8*(3), 29–37.

Levoy, M. (1990). Efficient Ray Tracing of Volume Data. *ACM Transactions on Graphics, 9*(3), 245–261.

Lewis, C., & Rieman, J. (1993). *Task-Centered User Interface Design: A Practical Introduction.* http://hcibib.org/tcuid/.

Lewis, R. R. (1994). Making Shaders More Physically Plausible. *Computer Graphics Forum, 13*(2), 109–120.

Lin, C.-C., & Ching, Y.-T. (1996). An Efficient Volume-Rendering Algorithm with an Analytic Approach. *The Visual Computer, 12*(10), 515–526.

Livnat, Y., Shen, H.-W., & Johnson, C. R. (1996). A Near Optimal Isosurface Extraction Algorithm Using the Span Space. *IEEE Transactions on Visualization and Computer Graphics, 2*(1), 73–84.

Loop, C. (2000). *Managing Adjacency in Triangular Meshes* (Tech. Rep. No. MSR-TR-2000-24). Bellingham, WA: Microsoft Research.

Lorensen, W., & Cline, H. (1987). Marching Cubes: A High Resolution 3D Surface Construction Algorithm. *Computer Graphics (Proc. SIGGRAPH 87), 21*(4), 163-169.

Lorensen, W. E., & Cline, H. E. (1987). Marching Cubes: A High Resolution 3D Surface Construction Algorithm. *Proc. SIGGRAPH '87, Computer Graphics, 21*(4), 163–169.

Luboschik, M., Schumann, H., & Cords, H. (2008). Particle-Based Labeling: Fast Point-Feature Labeling without Obscuring Other Visual Features. *IEEE Trans. on Visualization and Computer Graphics (Proc. InfoVis08), 14*(6), 1237–1244.

MacEachren, A., Dai, X., Hardisty, F., Guo, D., & Lengerich, G. (2003). Exploring High-D Spaces with Multiform Matrices and Small Multiples. In *Proc. ieee symposium on information visualization (infovis)* (pp. 31–38). Washington, DC: IEEE Computer Society Press.

Mackinlay, J. (1986). Automating the Design of Graphical Presentations of Relational Information. *ACM Trans. on Graphics (TOG), 5*(2), 110–141.

Malley, T. (1988). *A Shading Method for Computer Generated Images.* Unpublished master's thesis, Computer Science Department, University of Utah.

Marschner, S. R., & Lobb, R. J. (1994, Oct). An Evaluation of Reconstruction Filters for Volume Rendering. In *VIS '94: Proceedings of the Conference on Visualization '94* (p. 100-107). Washington, DC: IEEE Computer Society Press.

Marshall, J. A., Burbeck, C. A., Arely, D., Rolland, J. P., & Martin, K. E. (1999). Occlusion Edge Blur: A Cue to Relative Visual Depth. *Journal of the Optical Society of America A, 13*, 681–688.

Matusik, W., Pfister, H., Brand, M., & McMillan, L. (2003). A Data-Driven Reflectance Model. *ACM Transactions on Graphics (Proc. SIGGRAPH '03), 22*(3), 759–769.

Max, N. (1995). Optical Models for Direct Volume Rendering. *IEEE Transactions on Visualization and Computer Graphics, 1*(2), 99–108.

McCool, M., Toit, S. D., Popa, T., Chan, B., & Moule, K. (2004). Shader Algebra. *ACM Transactions on Graphics (Proc.SIGGRAPH '04)*, *23*(3), 787–795.

McLouglin, T., Laramee, R. S., Peikert, R., Post, F. H., & Chen, M. (2009). Over Two Decades of Integration-Based Geometric Flow Visualization. In *Proc. Eurographics 2009, State of the Art Reports*. Aire-la-Ville, Switzerland: Eurographics Association.

Meyers, S. (1995). *More Effective C++: 35 New Ways to Improve Your Programs and Designs*. Reading, MA: Addison-Wesley.

Meyers, S. (1997). *Effective C++: 50 Specific Ways to Improve Your Programs and Designs* (Second ed.). Reading, MA: Addison-Wesley.

Mitchell, D. P. (1990, May). Robust Ray Intersection with Interval Arithmetic. In *Graphics interface '90* (p. 68-74). Wellesley, MA: Canadian Human-Computer Communications Society & A K Peters.

Mitchell, D. P. (1996). Consequences of Stratified Sampling in Graphics. In *SIGGRAPH '96: Proceedings of the 23rd Annual Conference on Computer Graphics and Interactive Techniques* (pp. 277–280). New York: ACM Press.

Mitchell, D. P., & Netravali, A. N. (1988). Reconstruction Filters in Computer Graphics. *Computer Graphics*, *22*(4), 221–228.

Molnar, S., Eyles, J., & Poulton, J. (1992). Pixelflow: High-Speed Rendering Using Image Composition. *Computer Graphics*, *26*(2), 231–240. (SIGGRAPH '92)

Morse, B., Yoo, T., Rheingans, P., Chen, D., & Subramanian, K. (2001). Interpolating Implicit Surfaces from Scattered Surface Data Using Compactly Supported Radial Basis Functions. In *Proceedings of shape modeling international* (p. 89-98). Washington, DC: IEEE COmputer Society.

Mortenson, M. (1985). *Geometric Modeling*. New York: John Wiley & Sons.

Munkres, J. (2000). *Topology* (Second ed.). Englewood Cliffs, NJ: Prentice Hall.

Munzner, T. (2000). *Interactive Visualization of Large Graphs and Networks*. Unpublished doctoral dissertation, Stanford University Department of Computer Science.

Munzner, T., Guimbretière, F., Tasiran, S., Zhang, L., & Zhou, Y. (2003). TreeJuxtaposer: Scalable Tree Comparison Using Focus+Context with Guaranteed Visibility. *ACM Transactions on Graphics (Proc. SIGGRAPH '03)*, *22*(3), 453–462.

Museth, K., Breen, D., Whitaker, R., & Barr, A. (2002). Level Set Surface Editing Operators. *ACM Transactions on Graphics*, *21*(3), 330-338.

Muuss, M. J. (1995). Towards Real-Time Ray-Tracing of Combinatorial Solid Geometric Models. In *Proceedings of BRL-CAD Symposium*.

Nicodemus, F. E., Richmond, J. C., Hsia, J. J., Ginsberg, I., & Limperis, T. (1977). *Geometrical Considerations and Nomenclatture for Reflectance* (Tech. Rep. No. 160). Washington, D.C.: National Bureau of Standards.

Nielson, G. M. (2003). On Marching Cubes. *IEEE Transactions on Visualization and Computer Graphics*, *9*(3), 283–297.

Nishimura, H., Hirai, A., Kawai, T., Kawata, T., Shirikawa, I., & Omura, K. (1985). Object Modeling by Distribution Function and a Method of Image Generation. In *J. Electronics Comm. Conf. '85* (Vol. J69-D, pp. 718–725).

Ohtake, Y., Belyaev, A., & Pasko, A. (2003). Dynamic Mesh Optimization for Polygonized Implicit Surfaces with Sharp Features. *The Visual Computer*, *19*(2), 115–126.

Olano, M., & Lastra, A. (1998). A Shading Language on Graphics Hardware: The Pixelflow Shading System. In *SIGGRAPH '98: Proceedings of the 25th Annual Conference on Computer Graphics and Interactive Techniques* (pp. 159–168). New York: ACM Press.

Oppenheim, A. V., Schafer, R., & Stockham, T. (1968). Nonlinear Filtering of Multiplied and Convolved Signals. *Proceedings of the IEEE*, *56*(8), 1264–1291.

Oren, M., & Nayar, S. K. (1994). Generalization of Lambert's Reflectance Model. In *SIGGRAPH '94: Proceedings of the 21st Annual Conference on Computer Graphics and Interactive Techniques* (pp. 239–246). New York: ACM Press.

Osher, S., & Sethian, J. A. (1988). Fronts Propagating with Curvature-Dependent Speed: Algorithms Based on Hamilton–Jacobi Formulations. *Journal of Computational Physics*, *79*(1), 12-49.

Osterberg, G. (1935). Topography of the Layer of Rods and Cones in the Human Retina. *Acta Ophthalmologica*, *6*(1), 11–97. (Supplement)

Overveld, K. van, & Wyvill, B. (2004). Shrinkwrap: An Efficient Adaptive Algorithm for Triangulating an Iso-Surface . *The Visual Computer*, *20*(6), 362-369.

Paeth, A. W. (1990). A Fast Algorithm for General Raster Rotation. In *Graphics Gems* (pp. 179–195). Boston, MA: Academic Press.

Palmer, S. E. (1999). *Vision Science—Photons to Phenomenology*. Cambridge, MA: MIT Press.

Parker, S., Martin, W., Sloan, P., Shirley, P., Smits, B., & Hansen, C. (1999). Interactive Ray Tracing. In *ACM Symposium on Interactive 3D Graphics* (pp. 119–126). New York: ACM Press.

Parker, S., Parker, M., Livnat, Y., Sloan, P.-P., Hansen, C., & Shirley, P. (1999). Interactive Ray Tracing for Volume Visualization. *IEEE Transactions on Visualization and Computer Graphics*, *5*(3).

Pascale, D. (2003). *A review of RGB color spaces* (Tech. Rep.). The BabelColor Company. (www.babelcolor.com)

Pashler, H. E. (1998). *The Psychology of Attention*. Cambridge, MA: MIT Press.

Pasko, A., Adzhiev, V., Sourin, A., & Savchenko, V. (1995). Function representation in geometric modeling: concepts, implementation and applications. *The Visual Computer*, *11*(8), 419–428.

Pasko, G., Pasko, A., Ikeda, M., & Kunii, T. (2002, May). Bounded Blending Operations. In *Proceedings of the International Conference on Shape Modeling and Applications (SMI 2002)* (p. 95-103). Washington, DC: IEEE Computer Society.

Pattanaik, S. N., Ferwerda, J. A., Fairchild, M. D., & Greenberg, D. P. (1998). A Multiscale Model of Adaptation and Spatial Vision for Realistic Image Display. In *SIGGRAPH '98: Proceedings of the 25th Annual Conference on Computer Graphics and Interactive Techniques* (pp. 287–298). New York: ACM Press.

Pattanaik, S. N., & Yee, H. (2002). Adaptive Gain Control for High Dynamic Range Image Display. In *SCCG '02: Proceedings of the 18th Spring Conference on Computer Graphics* (pp. 83–87). New York: ACM Press.

Patterson, J., Hoggar, S., & Logie, J. (1991). Inverse Displacement Mapping. *Computer Graphics Forum, 10*(2), 129–139.

Peachey, D. R. (1985). Solid Texturing of Complex Surfaces. *Proc. SIGGRAPH '85, Computer Graphics, 19*(3), 279–286.

Peercy, M. S., Olano, M., Airey, J., & Ungar, P. J. (2000). Interactive Multi-Pass Programmable Shading. In *SIGGRAPH '00: Proceedings of the 27th Annual Conference on Computer Graphics and Interactive Techniques* (pp. 425–432). Reading, MA: Addison-Wesley.

Penna, M., & Patterson, R. (1986). *Projective Geometry and Its Applications to Computer Graphics*. Englewood Cliffs, NJ: Prentice Hall.

Perlin, K. (1985). An Image Synthesizer. *Computer Graphics, 19*(3), 287–296. (SIGGRAPH '85)

Perlin, K., & Hoffert, E. M. (1989). Hypertexture. *Computer Graphics, 23*(3), 253–262. (SIGGRAPH '89)

Pfister, H., Lorensen, B., Bajaj, C., Kindlmann, G., Schroeder, W., Avila, L. S., et al. (2001). The Transfer Function Bake-Off. *IEEE Computer Graphics & Applications, 21*(3), 16–22.

Pharr, M., & Fernando, R. (Eds.). (2005). *GPU Gems 2: Programming Techniques for High-Performance Graphics and General Purpose Computation*. Reading, MA: Addison-Wesley.

Pharr, M., & Hanrahan, P. (1996). Geometry Caching for Ray-Tracing Displacement Maps. In *Proceedings of the Eurographics Workshop on Rendering Techniques '96* (pp. 31–40). London, UK: Springer-Verlag.

Pharr, M., & Humphreys, G. (2004). *Physically Based Rendering*. San Francisco, CA: Morgan Kaufmann.

Pharr, M., Kolb, C., Gershbein, R., & Hanrahan, P. (1997). Rendering Complex Scenes with Memory-Coherent Ray Tracing. In *SIGGRAPH '97: Proceedings of the 24th Annual Conference on Computer Graphics and Interactive Techniques* (pp. 101–108). Reading, MA: Addison-Wesley.

Phong, B.-T. (1975). Illumination for Computer Generated Images. *Communications of the ACM, 18*(6), 311–317.

Pineda, J. (1988). A Parallel Algorithm for Polygon Rasterization. *Proc. SIG-GRAPH '88, Computer Graphics*, 22(4), 17–20.

Pitteway, M. L. V. (1967). Algorithm for Drawing Ellipses or Hyperbolae with a Digital Plotter. *Computer Journal*, 10(3), 282–289.

Pixar. (2000). *The RenderMan Interface Specification.* Emeryville, CA.

Plauger, P. J. (1991). *The Standard C Library.* Englewood Cliffs, NJ: Prentice Hall.

Plumlee, M., & Ware, C. (2006). Zooming Versus Multiple Window Interfaces: Cognitive Costs of Visual Comparisons. *Proc. ACM Trans. on Computer-Human Interaction (ToCHI)*, 13(2), 179–209.

Porter, T., & Duff, T. (1984). Compositing Digital Images. In *SIGGRAPH '84: Proceedings of the 11th Annual Conference on Computer Graphics and Interactive Techniques* (pp. 253–259). New York: ACM Press.

Poynton, C. (2003). *Digital Video and HDTV: Algorithms and Interfaces.* San Francisco: Morgan Kaufmann Publishers.

Press, W. H., Teukolsky, S. A., Vetterling, W. T., & Flannery, B. P. (1992). *Numerical Recipes in C: The Art of Scientific Computing* (Second ed.). Cambridge, UK: Cambridge University Press.

Prosise, J. (1999). *Programming Windows with MFC* (Second ed.). Bellingham, WA: Microsoft Press.

Proudfoot, K., Mark, W. R., Tzvetkov, S., & Hanrahan, P. (2001). A Real-Time Procedural Shading System for Programmable Graphics Hardware. In *SIGGRAPH '01: Proceedings of the 28th Annual Conference on Computer Graphics and Interactive Techniques* (pp. 159–170). New York: ACM Press.

Purcell, T. J., Buck, I., Mark, W. R., & Hanrahan, P. (2002). Ray Tracing on Programmable Graphics Hardware. *ACM Transactions on Graphics (Proc. SIGGRAPH '02)*, 21(3), 703–712.

Rahman, Z., Jobson, D. J., & Woodell, G. A. (1996). A Multiscale Retinex for Color Rendition and Dynamic Range Compression. In *SPIE Proceedings: Applications of Digital Image Processing XIX* (Vol. 2847). Bellingham, WA: SPIE.

Rao, R., & Card, S. K. (1994). The Table Lens: Merging Graphical and Symbolic Representations in an Interactive Focus+Context Visualization for Tabular Information. In *Proc. ACM Human Factors in Computing Systems (CHI)* (pp. 318–322). New York: ACM Press.

Reeves, W. T. (1983). Particle Systems—A Technique for Modeling a Class of Fuzzy Objects. *ACM Transactions on Graphics*, 2(2), 91–108.

Reingold, E. M., & Tilford, J. S. (1981). Tidier Drawings of Trees. *IEEE Trans. Software Engineering*, 7(2), 223–228.

Reinhard, E. (2003). Parameter Estimation for Photographic Tone Reproduction. *journal of graphics tools*, 7(1), 45–51.

Reinhard, E., Ashikhmin, M., Gooch, B., & Shirley, P. (2001). Color Transfer Between Images. *IEEE Computer Graphics and Applications*, *21*, 34–41.

Reinhard, E., & Devlin, K. (2005). Dynamic Range Reduction Inspired by Photoreceptor Physiology. *IEEE Transactions on Visualization and Computer Graphics*, *11*(1), 13–24.

Reinhard, E., Khan, E. A., Akyüz, A. O., & Johnson, G. M. (2008). *Color Imaging: Fundamentals and Applications*. Wellesley: A K Peters.

Reinhard, E., Stark, M., Shirley, P., & Ferwerda, J. (2002). Photographic Tone Reproduction for Digital Images. *ACM Transactions on Graphics (Proc. SIGGRAPH '02)*, *21*(3), 267–276.

Reinhard, E., Ward, G., Debevec, P., & Pattanaik, S. (2005). *High Dynamic Range Imaging*. San Francisco: Morgan Kaufmann.

Requicha, A. A. G. (1980). Representations for Rigid Solids: Theory, Mthods and Systems. *Computing Surveys*, *12*(4), 437–464.

Reuter, P. (2003). *Reconstruction and Rendering of Implicit Surfaces from Large Unorganized Point Sets*. Unpublished doctoral dissertation, LABRI - Universite Bordeaux.

Reynolds, C. W. (1987). Flocks, Herds and Schools: A Distributed Behavioral Model. *Proc. SIGGRAPH '87, Computer Graphics*, *21*(4), 25–34.

Ricci, A. (1973, May). Constructive Geometry for Computer Graphics. *Computer Journal*, *16*(2), 157-160.

Riesenfeld, R. F. (1981, January). Homogeneous Coordinates and Projective Planes in Computer Graphics. *IEEE Computer Graphics & Applications*, *1*(1), 50–55.

Roberts, L. (1965, May). *Homogenous Matrix Representation and Manipulation of N-Dimensional Constructs* (Tech. Rep. No. MS-1505). Lexington, MA: MIT Lincoln Laboratory.

Robertson, G., Fernandez, R., Fisher, D., Lee, B., & Stasko, J. (2008). Effectiveness of Animation in Trend Visualization. *IEEE Trans. on Visualization and Computer Graphics (Proc. InfoVis08)*, *14*(6), 1325–1332.

Rogers, D. F. (1985). *Procedural Elements for Computer Graphics*. New York: McGraw Hill.

Rogers, D. F. (1989). *Mathematical Elements for Computer Graphics*. New York: McGraw Hill.

Rogers, D. F. (2000). *An Introduction to NURBS: With Historical Perspective*. San Francisco, CA: Morgan Kaufmann.

Rogers, S. (1995). Perceiving Pictorial Space. In W. Epstein & S. Rogers (Eds.), *Perception of Space and Motion* (Vol. 5, pp. 119–163). San Diego: Academic Press.

Rost, R. J. (2004). *OpenGL Shading Language*. Reading, MA: Addison Wesley.

Roth, S. (1982). Ray Casting for Modelling Solids. *Computer Graphics and Image Processing*, *18*(2), 109–144.

Rubin, S. M., & Whitted, T. (1980). A 3-Dimensional Representation for Fast Rendering of Complex Scenes. *Proc. SIGGRAPH '80, Computer Graphics*, *14*(3), 110–116.

Rusinkiewicz, S., & Levoy, M. (2000). QSplat: A Multiresolution Point Rendering System for Large Meshes. In *SIGGRAPH '00: Proceedings of the 27th Annual Conference on Computer Graphics and Interactive Techniques* (pp. 343–352). Reading, MA: Addison-Wesley.

Rvachev, V. L. (1963). On the analytic description of some geometric objects. *Reports of the Ukrainian Acadamey of Sciences*, *153*, 765-767.

Sabella, P. (1988). A Rendering Algorithm for Visualizing 3D Scalar Fields. *Proc. SIGGRAPH '88, Computer Graphics*, *22*(4), 51–58.

Saito, T., & Takahashi, T. (1990). Comprehensible Rendering of 3-D Shapes. *Proc. SIGGRAPH '90, Computer Graphics*, *24*(4), 197–206.

Salomon, D. (1999). *Computer Graphics and Geometric Modeling*. New York: Springer-Verlag.

Savchenko, V., Pasko, A., Okunev, O., & Kunii, T. (1995). Function Representation of Solids Reconstructed from Scattered Surface Points and Contours. *Computer Graphics Forum*, *14*(4), 181-188.

Savchenko, V. V., Pasko, A. A., Sourin, A. I., & Kunii, T. L. (1998). Volume Modelling: Representations and Advanced Operations. In *CGI '98: Proceedings of the Computer Graphics International 1* (p. 4-13). Washington, DC: IEEE COmputer Society.

Sbert, M. (1997). *The Use of Global Random Directions to Compute Radiosity. Global Monte Carlo Techniques*. PhD. thesis, Universitat Politènica de Catalunya.

Schlick, C. (1994a). An Inexpensive BRDF Model for Physically-Based Rendering. *Computer Graphics Forum*, *13*(3), 233–246.

Schlick, C. (1994b). Quantization Techniques for the Visualization of High Dynamic Range Pictures. In P. Shirley, G. Sakas, & S. Müller (Eds.), *Photorealistic Rendering Techniques* (pp. 7–20). Berlin: Springer-Verlag.

Schmidt, R., Grimm, C., & Wyvill, B. (2006, July). Interactive Decal Compositing with Discrete Exponential Maps. *ACM Transactions on Graphics*, *25*(3), 605–613.

Schmidt, R., Wyvill, B., & Galin, E. (2005). Interactive Implicit Modeling with Hierarchical Spatial Caching. In *SMI '05: Proceedings of the International Conference on Shape Modeling and Applications 2005* (pp. 104–113). Washington, DC: IEEE Computer Society. (Accepted for publication).

Schmidt, R., Wyvill, B., Sousa, M. C., & Jorge, J. A. (2005). Shapeshop: Sketch-Based Solid Modeling with BlobTrees. In *Proceedings of the 2nd Eurographics Workshop on Sketch-Based Interfaces and Modeling*. Aire-la-ville, Switzerland: Eurographics Association.

Schwarze, J. (1990). Cubic and Quartic Roots. In *Graphics Gems* (pp. 404–407). San Diego, CA: Academic Press Professional, Inc.

Sederberg, T. W., & Parry, S. R. (1986). Free-Form Deformation of Solid Geometric Models. *Proc. SIGGRAPH '86, Computer Graphics, 20*(4), 151–160.

Seetzen, H., Heidrich, W., Stuerzlinger, W., Ward, G., Whitehead, L., Trentacoste, M., et al. (2004). High Dynamic Range Display Systems. *ACM Transactions on Graphics (Proc. SIGGRAPH '04), 23*(3), 760–768.

Seetzen, H., Whitehead, L. A., & Ward, G. (2003). A High Dynamic Range Display Using Low and High Resolution Modulators. In *The Society for Information Display International Symposium*. San Jose, CA: Society for Information Display.

Segal, M., Korobkin, C., Widenfelt, R. van, Foran, J., & Haeberli, P. (1992). Fast Shadows and Lighting Effects Using Texture Mapping. *Proc. SIGGRAPH '92, Computer Graphics, 26*(2), 249–252.

Shannon, C. E., & Weaver, W. (1964). *The Mathematical Theory of Communication*. Urbana, IL: University of Illinois Press.

Shapiro, V. (1988). *Theory of R-Functions and Applications: A Primer* (Tech. Rep. No. CPA88-3). Ithaca, NY: Cornell University.

Shapiro, V. (1994). Real Functions for Representation of Rigid Solids. *Computer Aided Geometric Design, 11*, 153–175.

Shene, C.-K. (2003). *CS 3621 Introduction to Computing with Geometry Notes*. Available from World Wide Web. (http://www.cs.mtu.edu/~shene/COURSES/cs3621/NOTES/notes.html)

Sherstyuk, A. (1999). Interactive Shape Design with Convolution Surfaces. In *SMI '99: Proceedings of the International Conference on Shape Modeling and Applications* (p. 56-65). Washington, DC: IEEE Computer Society.

Shirley, P. (1991). *Physically Based Lighting Calculations for Computer Graphics*. Unpublished doctoral dissertation, University of Illinois, Urbana-Champaign.

Shirley, P., Smits, B., Hu, H., & Lafortune, E. (1997). A Practitioners' Assessment of Light Reflection Models. In *PG '97: Proceedings of the 5th Pacific Conference on Computer Graphics and Applications* (pp. 40–49). Los Alamitos, CA: IEEE Computer Society.

Shirley, P., Wang, C., & Zimmerman, K. (1996). Monte Carlo Techniques for Direct Lighting Calculations. *ACM Transactions on Graphics, 15*(1), 1–36.

Shneiderman, B. (1996). The Eyes Have It: A Task by Data Type Taxonomy for Information Visualizations. In *Proc. IEEE Visual Languages* (pp. 336–343). Washington, DC: IEEE Computer Society.

Shreiner, D. (Ed.). (2004). *OpenGL Reference Manual: The Official Reference Document to OpenGL, Version 1.4* (Fourth ed.). Reading, MA: Addison-Wesley.

Shreiner, D., Neider, J., Woo, M., & Davis, T. (2004). *OpenGL Programming Guide* (Fourth ed.). Reading, MA: Addison-Wesley.

Sillion, F. X., & Puech, C. (1994). *Radiosity and Global Illumination*. San Francisco, California: Morgan Kaufmann Publishers, Inc.

Simons, D. J. (2000). Current Approaches to Change Blindness. *Visual Cognition*, 7(1/2/3), 1–15.

Slocum, T. A., McMaster, R. B., Kessler, F. C., & Howard, H. H. (2008). *Thematic Cartography and Geovisualization* (3rd ed.). Englewood Cliffs, NJ: Prentice Hall.

Smith, A. R. (1995). *A Pixel is Not a Little Square!* (Technical Memo No. 6). Bellingham, WA: Microsoft Research.

Smith, S., Grinstein, G., & Bergeron, R. D. (1991). Interactive Data Exploration with a Supercomputer. In *VIS '91: Proceedings of the 2nd Conference on Visualization '91* (pp. 248–254). Los Alamitos, CA: IEEE Computer Society Press.

Smits, B. E., Shirley, P., & Stark, M. M. (2000). Direct Ray Tracing of Displacement Mapped Triangles. In *Proceedings of the Eurographics Workshop on Rendering Techniques 2000* (pp. 307–318). London, UK: Springer-Verlag.

Snyder, J. M., & Barr, A. H. (1987). Ray Tracing Complex Models Containing Surface Tessellations. *Proc. SIGGRAPH '87, Computer Graphics*, 21(4), 119–128.

Sobel, I., Stone, J., & Messer, R. (1975). *The Monte Carlo Method*. Chicago, IL: University of Chicago Press.

Solomon, H. (1978). *Geometric Probability*. Philadelphia, PA: SIAM Press.

Stam, J. (1999). Diffraction Shaders. In *SIGGRAPH '99: Proceedings of the 26th Annual Conference On Computer Graphics And Interactive Techniques* (pp. 101–110). Reading, MA: Addison-Wesley.

Stark, M. M., Arvo, J., & Smits, B. (2005). Barycentric Parameterizations for Isotropic BRDFs. *IEEE Transactions on Visualization and Computer Graphics*, 11(2), 126–138.

Stockham, T. (1972). Image Processing in the Context of a Visual Model. *Proceedings of the IEEE*, 60(7), 828–842.

Stolte, C., Tang, D., & Hanrahan, P. (2008). Polaris: A System for Query, Analysis, and Visualization of Multidimensional Databases. *Commun. ACM*, 51(11), 75–84.

Stone, M. C. (2003). *A Field Guide to Digital Color*. Natick, MA: A K Peters.

Strang, G. (1988). *Linear Algebra and Its Applications* (Third ed.). Florence, KY: Brooks Cole.

Sutherland, I. E., Sproull, R. F., & Schumacker, R. A. (1974). A Characterization of Ten Hidden-Surface Algorithms. *ACM Computing Surveys*, 6(1), 1–55.

Thompson, W. B., & Pong, T. C. (1990). Detecting Moving Objects. *International Journal of Computer Vision*, 4(1), 39–57.

Thompson, W. B., Shirley, P., & Ferwerda, J. (2002). A Spatial Post-Processing Algorithm for Images of Night Scenes. *journal of graphics tools*, *7*(1), 1–12.

Tomasi, C., & Manduchi, R. (1998). Bilateral Filtering for Gray and Color Images. In *Proc. IEEE International Conference on Computer Vision* (pp. 836–846). Washington, DC: IEEE.

Tory, M., Kirkpatrick, A. E., Atkins, M. S., & Möller, T. (2006). Visualization task performance with 2D, 3D, and combination displays. *IEEE Trans. Visualization and Computer Graphics (TVCG)*, *12*(1), 2–13.

Tumblin, J., & Turk, G. (1999). LCIS: A boundary Hierarchy for Detail-Preserving Contrast Reduction. In A. Rockwood (Ed.), *SIGGRAPH '99: Proceedings of the 26th Annual Conference on Computer Graphics and Interactive Techniques* (pp. 83–90). Reading, MA: Addison Wesley Longman.

Turk, G., & Levoy, M. (1994). Zippered Polygon Meshes from Range Images. In *SIGGRAPH '94: Proceedings of the 21st Annual Conference on Computer Graphics and Interactive Techniques* (pp. 311–318). New York: ACM Press.

Turk, G., & O'Brien, J. (1999). Shape Transformation Using Variational Implicit Functions. In *SIGGRAPH '99: Proceedings of the 26th Annual Conference on Computer Graphics and Interactive Techniques* (pp. 335–342). New York: ACM Press/Addison-Wesley Publishing Co.

Turk, G., & O'Brien, J. F. (2002). Modelling with Implicit Surfaces that Interpolate. *ACM Transactions on Graphics*, *21*(4), 855–873.

Turkowski, K. (1990). Properties of Surface-Normal Transformations. In *Graphics Gems* (pp. 539–547). Boston: Academic Press.

Tversky, B., Morrison, J., & Betrancourt, M. (2002). Animation: Can It Facilitate? *International Journal of Human Computer Studies*, *57*(4), 247–262.

Upson, C., & Keeler, M. (1988). V-Buffer: Visible Volume Rendering. *Proc. SIGGRAPH '88, Computer Graphics*, *22*(4), 59–64.

Upstill, S. (1985). *The Realistic Presentation of Synthetic Images: Image Processing in Computer Graphics*. Unpublished doctoral dissertation, University of California at Berkeley.

van Aken, J., & Novak, M. (1985). Curve-Drawing Algorithms for Raster Displays. *ACM Transactions on Graphics*, *4*(2), 147–169.

van Ham, F., & van Wijk, J. J. (2004). Interactive Visualization of Small World Graphs. In *INFOVIS '04: Proceedings of the IEEE Symposium on Information Visualization* (pp. 199–206). Washington, DC: IEEE Computer Society Press.

van Wijk, J. J., & van Selow, E. R. (1999). Cluster and Calendar-Based Visualization of Time Series Data. In *INFOVIS '99: Proceedings of the 1999 IEEE Symposium on Information Visualization* (pp. 4–9). Washington, DC: IEEE Computer Society Press.

Veach, E., & Guibas, L. J. (1997). Metropolis Light Transport. In *SIGGRAPH '97: Proceedings of the 24th Annual Conference on Computer Graphics and Interactive Techniques* (pp. 65–76). Reading, MA: Addison-Wesley.

Wald, I., Slusallek, P., Benthin, C., & Wagner, M. (2001). Interactive Distributed Ray Tracing of Highly Complex Models. In *Proceedings of the 12th Eurographics Workshop on Rendering Techniques* (pp. 277–288). London, UK: Springer-Verlag.

Walter, B., Hubbard, P. M., Shirley, P., & Greenberg, D. F. (1997). Global Illumination Using Local Linear Density Estimation. *ACM Transactions on Graphics*, *16*(3), 217–259.

Wandell, B. A. (1995). *Foundations of Vision*. Sunderland, MA: Sinauer Associates.

Wann, J. P., Rushton, S., & Mon-Williams, M. (1995). Natural Problems for Stereoscopic Depth Perception in Virtual Environments. *Vision Research*, *35*(19), 2731–2736.

Ward, G., & Simmons, M. (2004). Subband Encoding of High Dynamic Range Imagery. In *First ACM Symposium on Applied Perception in Graphics and Visualization (APGV)* (pp. 83–90). NY: ACM Press.

Ward, G. J. (1992). Measuring and Modeling Anisotropic Reflection. *Proc. SIGGRAPH '92, Computer Graphics*, *26*(2), 265–272.

Ward, G. J. (1994). The RADIANCE Lighting Simulation and Rendering System. In A. Glassner (Ed.), *SIGGRAPH '94: Proceedings of the 21st Annual Conference on Computer Graphics and Interactive Techniques* (pp. 459–472). New York: ACM Press.

Ward, M. O. (2002, December). A taxonomy of glyph placement strategies for multidimensional data visualization. *Information Visualization Journal*, *1*(3-4), 194–210.

Ward Larson, G., Rushmeier, H., & Piatko, C. (1997). A Visibility Matching Tone Reproduction Operator for High Dynamic Range Scenes. *IEEE Transactions on Visualization and Computer Graphics*, *3*(4), 291–306.

Ward Larson, G., & Shakespeare, R. A. (1998). *Rendering with Radiance*. San Francisco, CA: Morgan Kaufmann Publishers.

Ware, C. (2000). *Information Visualization: Perception for Design*. Boston, MA: Morgan Kaufmann/Academic Press.

Ware, C. (2001). Designing With a 2 1/2 D Attitude. *Information Design Journal*, *10*(3), 255–262.

Ware, C., Purchase, H., Colpys, L., & McGill, M. (2002). Cognitive Measures of Graph Aesthetics. *Information Visualization*, *1*(2), 103–110.

Warn, D. R. (1983). Lighting Controls for Synthetic Images. *Proc. SIGGRAPH '83, Computer Graphics*, *17*(3), 13–21.

Watt, A. (1991). *Advanced Animation and Rendering Techniques*. Reading, MA: Addison-Wesley.

Watt, A. (1993). *3D Computer Graphics*. Reading, MA: Addison-Wesley.

Wegman, E. J. (1990, Sep). Hyperdimensional Data Analysis Using Parallel Coordinates. *Journ. American Statistical Association*, *85*(411), 664–675.

Wei, L.-Y., & Levoy, M. (2000). Fast Texture Synthesis Using Tree-Structured Vector Quantization. In *SIGGRAPH '00: Proceedings of the 27th Annual Conference on Computer Graphics and Interactive Techniques* (pp. 479–488). New York: ACM Press/Addison-Wesley Publishing Co.

Whitted, T. (1980). An Improved Illumination Model for Shaded Display. *Communications of the ACM*, *23*(6), 343–349.

Williams, A., Barrus, S., Morley, R. K., & Shirley, P. (2005). An Efficient and Robust Ray-Box Intersection Algorithm. *journal of graphics tools*, *10*(1), 49–54.

Williams, L. (1978). Casting Curved Shadows on Curved Surfaces. *Proc. SIGGRAPH '78, Computer Graphics*, *12*(3), 270–274.

Williams, L. (1983). Pyramidal Parametrics. *Proc. SIGGRAPH '83, Computer Graphics*, *17*(3), 1–11.

Williams, L. (1991). Shading in Two Dimensions. In *Proceedings of Graphics Interface* (pp. 143–151). Wellesley, MA: A K Peters & Canadian Human-Computer Communications Society.

Wyszecki, G., & Stiles, W. (2000). *Color Science: Concepts and Methods, Quantitative Data and Formulae* (Second ed.). New York: Wiley.

Wyvill, B., Galin, E., & Guy, A. (1999). Extending the CSG Tree: Warping, Blending and Boolean Operations in an Implicit Surface Modeling System. *Computer Graphics Forum*, *18*(2), 149-158.

Wyvill, B., McPheeters, C., & Wyvill, G. (1986). Data Structures for Soft Objects. *The Visual Computer*, *2*(4), 227-234.

Yantis, S. (Ed.). (2000). *Visual Perception: Essential Readings*. London, UK: Taylor & Francis Group.

Yessios, C. I. (1979). Computer Drafting of Stones, Wood, Plant and Ground Materials. *Proc. SIGGRAPH '79, Computer Graphics*, *13*(2), 190–198.

Yonas, A., Goldsmith, L. T., & Hallstrom, J. L. (1978). The Development of Sensitivity to Information from Cast Shadows in Pictures. *Perception*, *7*, 333–342.

Index

3D scalar field, 709

A/D converter, 187
access
    blocking, 658
    non-blocking, 658
adaptation, 549
    chromatic, 548
adjoint matrix, 101
aerial perspective, 585
affine transformation, 130
aliased, 180
aliasing, 186, 188, 189, 212,
      213, 226–228, 231
alpha channel, 66
alpha mask, 66
alpha release, 664
ambient shading, 235
amodal completion, 584
analog-to-digital converter, 187
angle, 18
    cosine, 19
    sine, 19
animation, 2
anti-umbra, 311
antialiasing, 212, 213
aperture problem, 569
API. *See* application program
      interface

apparent motion, 569
application program interface,
      1, 4
arc length, 343
arc-length parameterized curve,
      40
array
    padded, 298
    tiling, 298
artifacts, 61
artistic shading, 239
associativity, 194, 197
attribute variables, 457
average, 319

B-spline
    control points, 373
    curve, 372, 373
    filter, 204, 213
    function
      Fourier transform,
        224
    interpolation, 380
    non-uniform, 378
    NURBS, 382
    repeated knots, 380
    uniform cubic, 377
    uniform quadratic, 375
backface elimination, 182

background geometry, 660
backlight, 55
banding, 62
bandwidth
    memory, 658
barycentric coordinates, 44–46,
      166, 338
basic execution model, 456
basis, 22
    function, 348
    matrix, 351
    vectors, 22
Bernstein basis polynomials,
      367
beta release, 664
Bézier curves, 365
bidirectional reflectance
      distribution
      function, 524, 637
    Lambertian, 525
bijection, 15
binary images, 56
binary space partitioning tree,
      289, 316
    ray tracing, 287
blending function, 348, 354
blocking access, 658
blurring, 210
boundaries, 263

745